MAY
AT 10

PRAISE FOR *CAMERON AT 10*

"Explosive ... Authoritative yet uncompromisingly tough ... A gripping and at times astonishing account of the people who rule us."
MAIL ON SUNDAY

"These pages are a masterclass in so-called 'tick-tock' narrative – a minute-by-minute account, studded with detailed recollections and observations ... A formidable achievement ... Magisterial ... If I were Mr Corbyn, I'd get busy reading." MATTHEW D'ANCONA, *EVENING STANDARD*

"A substantial piece of work – a blow-by-blow account, impeccably researched and carefully documented, of the highs and lows of the first Cameron administration. The authors appear to have enjoyed almost total access. Their judgements are on the whole balanced and the narrative compelling."
CHRIS MULLIN, *THE OBSERVER*

"A monumental first draft of history."
JOHN RENTOUL, *THE INDEPENDENT*

"While Lord Ashcroft may have started a brief craze for pig jokes ... the more interesting (and damaging) disclosures come in the other new book about him, *Cameron at 10* by Anthony Seldon and Peter Snowdon."
FRASER NELSON, *SUNDAY TELEGRAPH*

"Rigorously researched, giving an insight into the inner workings of Cameron's No. 10 and the coalition that we have not seen before ... While Ashcroft and Oakeshott's *Call Me Dave* should by no means be dismissed, ultimately the offering from Seldon and Snowdon feels a far more substantial look at an intriguing political leader."
INDEPENDENT ON SUNDAY

"An immensely thorough work ... It contains a more damaging passage than any in their rival's unauthorised work."
DOMINIC LAWSON, *SUNDAY TIMES*

"Where Seldon excels is in his understanding of political relationships. Seldon and Snowdon are adept at convincing friends and colleagues to talk candidly." *THE TIMES*

"Seldon and Snowdon are particularly strong on foreign policy ... *Cameron at 10* is an invaluable resource." *DAILY TELEGRAPH*

"Measured and thoughtful ... *Cameron at 10* is a fascinating book."
JAMES BLOODWORTH, DAILY BEAST

MAY AT 10

ANTHONY SELDON
WITH RAYMOND NEWELL

Biteback Publishing

First published in Great Britain in 2019 by
Biteback Publishing Ltd
Westminster Tower
3 Albert Embankment
London SE1 7SP

ISBN 978-1-78590-517-9

10 9 8 7 6 5 4 3 2 1

A CIP catalogue record for this book is available from the British Library.

Set in Adobe Garamond Pro

Printed and bound in Great Britain by
CPI Group (UK) Ltd, Croydon CR0 4YY

FSC
www.fsc.org

MIX
Paper from
responsible sources
FSC® C020471

To Jeremy Heywood, Lord Heywood of Whitehall (1961–2018),
and to the civil service he led, the finest in the world.

Profits from this book will be donated to the Heywood Foundation.

CONTENTS

Boris Johnson thought he should have been Prime Minister in 2016 instead of May. Whether in her Cabinet or outside, he constantly probed away at her. Here, he observes her during the 2017 general election campaign.

INTRODUCTION

The result of the EU referendum on 23 June 2016 meant that Theresa May, who succeeded David Cameron as Prime Minister three weeks later, had only one overriding task as premier: to take Britain out of the European Union.

THE VERDICT OF HISTORY

On the face of it, the judgement of history on her premiership looks bleak. She failed in that primary objective, and to realise many of the hopes she aroused of addressing Britain's 'burning injustices' and creating a country that works for everyone, which she spoke about with such passion on her first day in No. 10. She bequeathed to her successor the responsibility for delivering Brexit, a harder task with the country much more divided, alongside many other issues that she was unable to resolve, including social care. She failed, too, to strengthen the two institutions she said she cared about most deeply. The Union was palpably weaker when she left office than when she arrived, for all her initial success strengthening Scotland's support for remaining within the UK. The Conservative Party, too, was by 2019 more divided, as was politics overall, than at any point since Britain became a democracy a hundred years earlier. She did not defend effectively enough key institutions, including the civil service, the judiciary, Cabinet conventions or even universities when they came under attack. Her fixation with immigration and specifically deterring overseas students, smartly reversed by her successor, damaged Britain's overseas relations, notably with India. Britain's standing in the world was lower in 2019 than it had been in 2016. In September 2018, she was humiliatingly ridiculed by her fellow EU leaders at a summit in Salzburg, while the US President, a guest of Britain, showed her blatant contempt in July 2018 and again on his state visit in June 2019. But to dismiss Theresa May as a hapless Prime Minister, as contemporary commentators did, is too facile. The reality is rather different.

Theresa May had many admirable qualities: a tireless work ethic, courage, frugality, physical and mental endurance, a hawk-eye for detail, a profound sense of duty and an unselfconscious integrity among them. She led the country in her final months with an almost superhuman determination to secure a withdrawal agreement with the European Union and then steer it through Parliament, despite being attacked by many, not least in her own party. She deserved more praise for her November 2018 deal than contemporaries granted her, though had she put the case for the agreement earlier and handled her colleagues with greater ability, it would have stood a better chance of getting through. Failure to do so has hurt the nation greatly. As she realised late in the day, securing agreement at home was much more problematic than with the EU. She inspired loyalty in those who worked most closely with her and who knew her best, at a time when the uniquely long and existential tensions might have blown many other Downing Street teams wide apart. More than many Prime Ministers, she learnt and improved on the job. After her nadir, the 2017 general election, she became an increasingly confident and competent leader at home and abroad, more adept both at dealing with leaders overseas, not least a uniquely tricky US President, and at implementing her agenda at home.

Her skill abroad was best revealed in her marshalling of the international response in the aftermath of the Russian poisonings in Salisbury, and after the chemical weapons attacks in Syria, in the spring of 2018. At home, she oversaw a stable if underdynamic economy where the numbers of those in work reached a record high. She fought the Treasury to introduce a pivotal long-term plan for the NHS in 2018. Mostly away from public gaze, and in the face of party opposition, she became a late advocate of environmental reform at home and internationally. The vulnerable and those on the margins of society aroused her genuine concern, and, despite some lapses, she brought significant improvement to the lives of those affected by mental illness, gender and racial discrimination and domestic violence. She did more for women than the only other female Prime Minister, Margaret Thatcher. Contemporaries saw May's last two months as a flurry of activity in search of a personal legacy: they are better seen as the culmination of work to which she had been devoting herself since at least July 2016, and before. Had it not been for Brexit, she might well have become a reasonably good, if unspectacular, Prime Minister.

Her qualities, impressive though they were, were not, however, the ones most needed by a British Prime Minister in the months and years following the June 2016 referendum. May was a miniaturist, a details person, when what was needed was a leader with strategic clarity, charisma and intellectual confidence. She came to office knowing little about economics, which prevented her from understanding better the complexities involved and the difficulties on customs arrangements, finance and trade. Greater economic confidence would have allowed her to challenge better her orthodox Chancellor, Philip Hammond, who repeatedly blocked her.

She understood little about government, including the powers and limitations of her office, how to make Cabinet government and the civil service work for her, and how to advocate and persuade. These skills were not optional extras for the task in hand. Her six years at the Home Office were not a good preparation for her, most especially because she imported wholesale her same inward-looking philosophy into Downing Street.

More serious than either deficiency, she knew precious little about British and European history or about how the EU worked. The seismic tensions between the direct democracy of the EU referendum and parliamentary democracy in Westminster were never fully comprehended by her, so she never successfully reconciled them. Nor did she understand the significance of the murder of the Labour MP Jo Cox by a white supremacist during the referendum campaign (the first time an MP had been assassinated in over twenty-five years), which laid bare the deep societal tensions and dangers that Brexit brought to the surface. Nor did she take on board that the official and unofficial Leave campaigns in the referendum were not advocating a hard Brexit but instead a smooth transition to a close relationship with the EU post-Brexit.

She sailed into the negotiations not understanding clearly enough the historical context of the EU and European integration, nor the Good Friday Agreement and Irish border, nor what she sought from Brexit, nor how to achieve her ends. She came to power with a wide degree of support and goodwill from across the nation, including from the 48 per cent who voted Remain, many of whom accepted that Brexit had to happen. The EU regarded her as a serious and meticulous politician with whom they could do business. The biggest single indictment of Theresa May is that she blew all that goodwill and respect, and within twelve months had become a figure of contempt across the political spectrum. We will never know if she might have got a more consensual Brexit through in 2016–17. The point is, she never tried.

Successful Prime Ministers see themselves as figures in a historical process, taking over the country at one point and leaving it at another. They have a vision for their premiership. In contrast, May's point of reference was not the nation's history and the needs and possibilities of the hour, but her own personal history and experience of life. That's a very different thing. Her lodestar was not the UK as a whole but Maidenhead, middle class, conservative, white and inward-looking. There was no composure or reflective quality about her premiership, no fundamental taking stock of the predicament Britain found itself in and how best she could take the country to a better place.

The inflection point of her premiership was the general election in June 2017, which changed everything, and which is reflected in the structure of this book. Part One, 'The Making of the Premiership', sees May carrying all before her, riding high in the polls, at the peak of her power, in control of Cabinet, the party and agenda, but not in control of her office nor the Brexit process. Her two prodigiously talented and dominant aides, Nick Timothy and Fiona Hill, who had worked with her in the Home Office and moulded her for No. 10, were all-powerful as her joint chiefs of staff, and provided the strategic clarity she was unwilling to provide – or incapable of providing – herself.

The general election saw the emperor's clothes fall away. Timothy and Hill emboldened her to call it, but so did her two most powerful Cabinet ministers: Brexit Secretary David Davis, who wanted it to obtain a larger Commons majority to barrel through a harder Brexit, and Chancellor Philip Hammond, who wanted to avoid any post-Brexit economic dip damaging Conservative prospects for a general election held in 2020. The campaign revealed her as indecisive, defensive and petulant, pushed around by campaign manager Lynton Crosby, failing to provide any clear lead on messaging or substance, and incapable of projecting out to the nation any strong personal authority or vision. She alone was responsible for the decision to call the general election, and for the chaotic way it was fought, not Timothy and Hill, whom she elected to blame for it. She equally had been responsible for the way they conducted themselves when in No. 10. The buck stops with the PM. If lieutenants at No. 10 overstep the mark, the PM is responsible. She had still to learn this truth. If her premiership was a learning arc, this was ground zero. Like a Shakespearian tragic hero, she learnt – but too little and too late.

Part Two, 'The Unravelling of the Premiership', sees a different Theresa May emerge, struggling at first to find her voice in a political ecosystem so vastly different. Cabinet, from her Chancellor down, knew they were unsackable, and they barely concealed their contempt for her, as did her increasingly rebellious MPs on both sides of the Brexit divide. Her personal authority in tatters, her two strategists sacked, her majority gone, she was at the mercy of her own MPs and her new partners in the Commons, the DUP, while the EU saw a diminished PM whom it had even less reason to heed.

Yet she bonded with her new chief of staff, Gavin Barwell, and his deputy, JoJo Penn, in this second period, and slowly crafted a new style as leader, as all around her was falling apart, in her quest to find a path for Britain's exit from the EU. The Grenfell Tower fire just after the general election was seen as further evidence of her weakness; after initially listening to advice to stay away, she began to trust her own instincts and met the families affected. It was the beginning of the emergence of May as her own person. Her final year saw her at her best. She departed No. 10, unlike David Cameron, a more respected figure than before, though her best was never enough to overcome her earlier shortcomings.

EUROPE

The key question historians will ask about May's premiership is whether the difficulty of securing an agreement with the EU that could pass Parliament was so overwhelming that no one could have achieved it, or whether she failed to achieve Brexit because of the way she conducted affairs.

The challenge for May was greater, and the stakes higher, than for any Prime Minister domestically for 100 years. The years to come will see several official inquiries into what went wrong in these critical years. Leadership of the very highest quality was required to steer Britain safely through.

The difficulties were legion. No country had ever left the EU, and

the Article 50 process, which Britain had played a lead part in drafting, intentionally made it extremely difficult for any country to depart
on favourable terms, stacking the cards heavily in favour of the EU.
Unless Britain was prepared to crash out with no deal, it had to secure
the willing backing of the EU. The diminishing landing area between
any deal that the EU would agree to and what the hard Brexit wing of
her party would support was so small by the end of her premiership as
to be almost non-existent.

She faced a Labour leader in Jeremy Corbyn who was set against any
deal or cooperation, and whose sole objective was to prise her out of
No. 10 and substitute himself. If you throw into the mix the problem of
the Northern Irish border and the solution to it that became the backstop, you have the perfect storm. May went to great lengths to avoid
a Northern Ireland-only backstop and accommodate the DUP's demands, only for them to betray the confidence-and-supply agreement
signed in 2017 and vote against the withdrawal agreement. The DUP
was prepared to risk, for its own short-term party advantage rather than
the interests of Northern Ireland (which voted 56 per cent Remain), a
no deal or a Corbyn government, rather than accept a UK-wide backstop which would guarantee no divergence between Northern Ireland
and the rest of the UK. It is a decision they may come to regret. May
didn't understand until too late that the EU would never compromise
its founding principles and the integrity of the single market. By its
own lights, the EU considers it made compromises to help get Britain over the line. Many Brexiteers aroused impossible expectations by
claiming Brexit would be straightforward if only approached in the
right way, and when this proved illusory they preferred to label the EU
the culprit, shifting any blame from themselves.

Those who argued for a harder Brexit believed by the end of May's
premiership that her mistakes were a series of 'if onlys'. If only she had
insisted on a harder form of Brexit from the very beginning, preparing
with warlike precision for no deal; if only she had shown Thatcher-like

strength consistently to Brussels; if only she had held some of the conversations in London, as well as in Belfast, Edinburgh and Cardiff, rather than supinely travelling to the EU all the time; if only she had insisted that the sequencing of the talks, the timetable and the content were fully a matter for British participation; if only she had shown more backbone, she could have won through. Johnson would have been like this, they argued, had he become PM in 2016 rather than in 2019. But these 'what ifs' reveal a lack of comprehension of the legal processes and what might have been achievable under Article 50, which expressly ruled out much of what Brexiteers sought and limited the scope for UK manoeuvrability. May was continuously battling against unreasonable expectations – inadequately challenged, and even fanned, by herself.

The errors she made in pursuing Brexit were considerable. We can divide them into the two halves of her premiership. The seeds of failure lie in the period between her arrival at No. 10 and her calling the general election nine months later. In her two party conference speeches in October 2016, and at Lancaster House in January 2017, she outlined a hard Brexit vision which she came to realise would never pass through the House of Commons with the small majority she then had; hence her decision to call the general election. Worse, she repeatedly denied that a hard Brexit was her intent, insisting that she had not ruled out membership of the customs union and single market when to all intents and purposes she had. Her Brexit declarations were a slate of amateur contradictions: she wanted 'frictionless trade' but to be free from the EU institutions which enable it; she called for 'no return to the borders of the past' in Ireland without recognising the EU's decisive role in removing such borders and the sacrifices in regulatory autonomy necessary to achieve that; she insisted that 'no deal is better than a bad deal' without understanding what no deal meant and the measures necessary to realise such a Brexit without causing serious harm. Not even her 2017 manifesto would escape such contradictions: it outlined a 'deep and special partnership' with the EU which was neither deep nor special.

These contradictions might not have been included had May been prepared to listen more widely from the outset. Had she consulted former Prime Ministers, constitutional experts and historians, retired diplomats and other officials who had worked all their lives with the EU, and had she not cut out the Treasury, the FCO and the Northern Ireland Office, she would have understood better the challenges before her in taking Britain out of the EU. But she was never intellectually confident enough nor willing to seek out such advice, repeatedly showing a blithe disregard for listening to the armies of experts who understood the EU in favour of a tight troupe of trusties. Only in January 2019 did she at last pick up the phone to her four predecessors as Prime Minister to seek their counsel on Brexit. She realised then what a support they might have been, as it might have been for her to have had a figure like Willie Whitelaw to Thatcher, above ambition and with the wisdom of experience, guiding her at such a crucial time. Wisdom was not much in evidence in her premiership, any more than it had been under Cameron, whose premiership also suffered from a lack of broad advice and reflection. The figure who came closest to supplying it for her was her remarkable husband Philip, who played the part as perfectly as any PM's spouse in history.

She did not build a coalition of support for her Brexit, consulting neither her Chancellor nor her senior Cabinet colleagues, nor the Cabinet Secretary, about what she would be saying at the party conference. Having said 'no deal is better than a bad deal', she did not prepare seriously for such an eventuality, nor was she candid about the risks to the country, nor the difficulties of negotiating the future trade deal with the EU, if Britain left unilaterally without a deal. She used inflammatory language – 'citizens of nowhere' – which antagonised her own Remain MPs as well as the EU. She offered no vision of the future relationship between Britain and the EU, because she *had* no clear vision, seeing Brexit as a problem to be solved rather than a historic opportunity to reimagine Britain's future in a new world.

She did not understand how difficult Brexit would be, nor, from the very moment she came to office, did she give Brexit the urgency it required. Like Tony Blair in his first period in office, she frittered time away, content to blame her predecessor for stopping the civil service from planning for Brexit rather than leading the hard graft from the front from her first days and weeks. May's attitude to time, including the two-year negotiating period stipulated by Article 50, put the UK at a serious disadvantage. To activate Article 50 on 29 March 2017 before a clear vision for the future relationship had been devised and negotiating goals clearly defined was foolish, and the EU knew it. Brexit required difficult long-term choices and military-style week-by-week planning, but not till her final months did May impart that strong and consistent sense of direction.

Her initial Brexit stance was all but doomed the moment that the results of the general election were known on 9 June 2017. The one remaining chance she had for achieving Brexit might have proved politically fatal for her, but a Prime Minister with a more statesmanlike understanding of history would have attempted it. It would have been to reach out to other parties in the House of Commons, as indeed she did in April and May 2019 after her deal had been defeated three times, by which time MPs' willingness to compromise had all but evaporated. She refused to face up to the harsh truth in June 2017 that her plan would likely not pass through Parliament, burying her head in the sand to survive the squalls at all costs.

Mistakes from this point forward mattered, because a deal could still have passed. In December 2017, to the incredulity of the EU, she went to Brussels to finalise the first phase of Brexit in the joint report, without first guaranteeing that her partners in the House of Commons, the DUP, were willing to support it. She was too ready to embrace what became known as the backstop – to signal that progress was being made – and she failed to understand that she was assenting to what would become a major stumbling block in the key parliamentary votes over a year later. Her failure to plan Brexit properly from Day 1 had resulted in one of her many fudges: the joint report coupled with her red lines gave the irreconcilable position of Britain leaving the single market and customs union but with no hard border between Northern Ireland and the Republic, and no border down the Irish Sea. This makeshift solution would inevitably unravel: the only question was when. Yet rather than opening up her Brexit strategy, she continued with her first-term policy of secrecy, believing with her ever-closer team that only by playing her cards close to her chest and using time to bounce her Cabinet would they have any hope of success.

After December 2017, the chances of winning the support of her hardline Brexit MPs in the European Research Group (ERG) were perilously thin. They had banked her promises of a hard Brexit in her first term and were either unwilling or unable to accept that the parliamentary logic after the general election suggested a softer Brexit was now on the cards. Worse, she entertained and gave credence to their suggestions that technology would be able to solve the Irish border problem, allowing talk of 'max fac' and 'technological solutions', neither of which would wash with the EU. Such proposals became a Brexiteer panacea through sheer repetition, not least by Brexiteer Cabinet ministers. Had their proposals been challenged more openly by a Prime Minister with a sharper vision and a stronger voice, one who enforced collective Cabinet responsibility on the dominating issue of her day, fewer Conservative MPs might have been willing to break the whip to vote against her deal. Instead, when backbenchers saw the proposal that if after two years the 'alternative arrangements' for the Irish border did not work or the UK did not have a future trading relationship with the EU obviating the need for a border, the UK would remain in a customs union, they judged it a compromise too far. The ERG sensed the freedom of a no-deal Brexit in their nostrils, and despite her efforts, up to and including falling on her sword for the deal, there was nothing May could do to turn their heads.

Her remark to George Osborne during his sacking in 2016 that he should 'get to know the party better' can now only be reflected on with bitter irony. She walked into key Cabinet meetings at Chequers on 6 July 2018 without having cleared her Brexit proposals with her senior colleagues, resulting in the resignations of her Brexit and Foreign Secretaries. The outgoing Brexit Secretary who did not believe in her proposals was replaced by another even more sceptical and less biddable. At Cabinet in Downing Street on 14 November, May repeated her mistake by again not bringing key ministers behind her in advance. She then appointed an Attorney General who would not give her the verdict she desperately needed, delivering his legal advice damningly to Parliament and sinking her hopes of passing a Brexit deal before the 29 March deadline. Repeated concessions were made to MPs who would still not support the withdrawal agreement. If she had followed the advice she gave Osborne, her premiership would not have ended as it did.

The lack of understanding was not just of her MPs. Too late in the day, she realised that only a softer form of Brexit, involving some form of customs union, was necessary for Northern Ireland. For her to have a Damascus moment in Belfast just one month before the UK was due to leave, that she could not countenance no deal, was astonishing. The ERG were unimpressed by her change of heart, and without gaining the support of at least two out of the three potentially biddable factions – the ERG, the DUP and fringe Labour MPs – her deal would never pass. She ended up advocating a soft Brexit and abandoning her tribalism to reach out to other parties too late, negating her initial strategy in 2016 and still not securing Britain's exit. Her resilience and courage in her final months were in many ways deeply admirable. But Prime Ministers need brain and emotional intelligence, not just brawn.

A more inclusive or a more consistently tough approach may well have stumbled and eventually led to failure, whether in Brussels or in Westminster. But they would have provided more consistency, clearer expectations and a discernible narrative to Brexit from No. 10. To fail in such a way would have been understandable. But May demanded a bespoke arrangement with the EU, only to discover that she didn't know whether that was really possible. The many difficulties she faced when she became PM cannot be an excuse for the unforced errors she made through ignorance, intransigence and ineptitude.

A HISTORIC PREMIERSHIP

May's 1,106 days in office (the twenty-third shortest to date of the fifty-five since 1721) were remarkable in historical terms. Outside of re-shuffles, it saw thirty-five ministerial resignations – the highest annual rate in modern history. It witnessed the first and the fourth biggest government defeats in parliamentary history. The defeat on 15 January 2019 on the first meaningful vote by 230 (432 to 202) far outstrips the previous historic landmark, the losses of 166 and 161 votes suffered by the minority Labour government under Prime Minister Ramsay MacDonald in 1924. The fourth biggest defeat would come less than two months later, the government losing by 149 votes (391 to 242) on 12 March on the second meaningful vote. Following the 2017 general election, there were twenty-eight government defeats, the second highest number (after the 1976–79 Callaghan government) since 1945. The May government suffered five defeats on a single day on 3 April 2019, the most in history. The 2017–19 parliamentary session was the longest in modern history.

The May 2019 European elections saw the Conservatives' worst performance in a national election in the party's history since the 1830s, coming fifth with just 9.1 per cent of the vote. The volatility of her three years in office can be seen by the rise of the Brexit Party, which didn't exist when she came to power, but which was the largest party in the European elections just before she left. Under May, conventions of collective responsibility and Cabinet government were stretched to breaking point. Ill-discipline and leaking never recovered from the suspension of collective responsibility by Cameron during the referendum campaign. On 13 March 2019, three Cabinet ministers openly defied a three-line whip in a vote but were not dismissed by May. Cabinet ministers challenged not just the authority and objectivity of the Prime Minister over Cabinet but also that of the Cabinet Secretary and Cabinet Office.

Speaker of the House of Commons John Bercow broke several conventions, including allowing a vote in January 2019 on an amendment (from Dominic Grieve MP) to a government business motion; allowing backbench MPs to use Standing Orders for emergency debates to take control of the order paper and initiate legislation; and citing a precedent dating back to 1604 to prevent the government from putting the same question to the House (a third meaningful vote on the withdrawal agreement and political declaration) more than once.

The Prime Minister regularly referred to the historic nature of the task of bringing about Brexit, as on 15 January 2019 when she called it 'the most important vote in our political lives'. There was no constitutional crisis under May, but rather, from the Chequers Cabinet in July 2018 to May 2019 when she announced her retirement, a prolonged and troubling political crisis for which she cannot escape responsibility.

THE WRITING OF *MAY AT 10*

This is the sixth book in my series about modern Prime Ministers. It is not the history of the government and its policies, nor of the wider political landscape, but of the Prime Minister and 10 Downing Street: the view from the PM's study.

The book is over 200,000 words and based on 175 interviews, a lower number than for previous books, and concentrated more on figures very close to the Prime Minister. The unattributed interview quotations throughout come from these individuals. The identity of the source, and the context of the quotation, can be confirmed in time against the fully typed interview records in the Bodleian Library, Oxford, alongside the many millions of words of interviews for my earlier PM and other books.

Most of the key figures in May's premiership talked to me, some many times over. All history relies on the evidence available to the author. Historical figures who leave behind large archives, including copious letters, diaries and memoirs, will always figure larger than those who did not. It is the craft of the historian to compensate for this disparity as best they can. Others will judge how well I succeeded in being fair to all sides in a particularly polarised premiership.

The most difficult challenges specifically for a contemporary historian are that we do not know how events turn out. Would *Cameron at 10* have been written differently if we knew how the referendum would play out? Certainly. The vote turned a potentially highly successful premiership upside down. This book goes to press before it is known whether subsequent Brexit efforts have been successful. If they have, May's own struggle will be judged differently by history.

The second challenge is that such a book, the first draft of history, lacks the benefit of documents, though some were made available to me. It lacks the benefit, too, of books. With the exception of those by the incomparable Tim Shipman, few have been written. I trod through mostly virgin snow. Some 90 per cent of *May at 10* relies upon the primary source, interviews, quoted liberally throughout the book (albeit not attributed to the most important source, officials, for obvious reasons). We tried to clear all quotations with their source and the book was read over by several who were in or close by Downing Street, invaluable for factual accuracy and sparking fresh memories.

For the previous two books in the series, I had co-authors: Guy Lodge on *Brown at 10*, and Peter Snowdon on *Cameron at 10*. For this volume I relied on a researcher, Raymond Newell, who had just completed his undergraduate study at my university, and a particularly brilliant one he was too. I acknowledge my debt of gratitude to him and others at the end of the book.

Will the judgements on May differ greatly in the deluge of literature to come? Time will tell, but I believe the judgements in the earlier five books have stood the test of time. My first such book saw Major as a good PM, an unpopular view at the time, but now more accepted. Above all, I hope this book is, in part at least, worthy of the late figure who helped me in all those earlier PM books, Jeremy Heywood, to whom it is dedicated. It could equally have been dedicated to the much-maligned officials who strove to do their best for their political masters, who served under him. Heywood respected May as a deeply committed and serious politician: to dismiss her and her premiership as a complete failure is neither fair nor historically accurate.

Anthony Seldon
September 2019

PART ONE

THE MAKING OF THE PREMIERSHIP

Theresa May had been Britain's longest serving Home Secretary in sixty years.
For her first year at No. 10, her mindset remained that of Home Secretary.

CHAPTER 1

MADE IN THE HOME OFFICE

The nation was still in a state of disbelief on 13 July 2016. Few had anticipated that Remain would lose the referendum just three weeks earlier. Even fewer predicted that Theresa May would become the next Prime Minister, replacing David Cameron, who announced his resignation the morning after the result. But here she was, standing proud, tall and confident as she delivered her first speech as Prime Minister outside No. 10.

> David Cameron has led a one-nation government, and it is in that spirit that I also plan to lead ... The full title of my party is the Conservative and Unionist Party, and that word 'Unionist' is very important to me ... We believe in a Union not just between the nations of the United Kingdom but between all of our citizens, every one of us, whoever we are and wherever we're from.
>
> That means fighting against the burning injustice that, if you're born poor, you will die on average nine years earlier than others. If you're black, you're treated more harshly by the criminal justice system than if you're white. If you're a white, working-class boy, you're less likely than anybody else in Britain to go to university. If you're at a state school, you're less likely to reach the top professions than if you're educated privately. If you're a woman, you will earn

less than a man. If you suffer from mental health problems, there's not enough help to hand. If you're young, you'll find it harder than ever before to own your own home.

But the mission to make Britain a country that works for everyone means more than fighting these injustices. If you are from an ordinary working-class family, life is much harder than many people in Westminster realise. You have a job, but you don't always have job security. You have your own home, but you worry about paying a mortgage. You can just about manage but you worry about the cost of living and getting your kids into a good school…

I know you're working around the clock, I know you're doing your best, and I know that sometimes life can be a struggle. The government I lead will be driven not by the interests of the privileged few, but by yours.

As we leave the European Union, we will forge a bold new positive role for ourselves in the world, and we will make Britain a country that works not for a privileged few but for every one of us.

Theresa May made her statement just after seeing Her Majesty the Queen, having accepted her invitation to form a new government as Prime Minister. Her words rank among the more powerful of the opening gambits of her fifty-three predecessors who accepted the job from the monarch. Less dramatic, maybe, than when the Duke of Wellington rode into Downing Street on his horse Copenhagen when he became Prime Minister in January 1828. Less immediately arresting, too, than Margaret Thatcher's words outside 10 Downing Street on 4 May 1979, when Britain's first woman Prime Minister said:

I would just like to remember some words of St Francis of Assisi which I think are really just particularly apt at the moment. 'Where there is discord, may we bring harmony. Where there is error, may we bring truth. Where there is doubt, may we bring faith. And where there is despair, may we bring hope.'

But no other Prime Minister had given such a confident assertion of the direction in which they were going to lead the country. No other Prime Minister had provided so many hostages to fortune. It spoke volumes of her ambition and confidence.

May's speech was widely and favourably commented upon. The normally sceptical *Guardian* said, 'She delivered one of the boldest statements of intent a Conservative prime minister may ever have made. If she envisaged this as a way of introducing herself to the voters who will never have paid much attention to her in the past, she will have made an impact.'[1]

The speech became the rallying cry for action in her first year as Prime Minister, chiming with the spirit of a nation that wanted strong leadership. 'The doorstep speech was the guiding document for us in the Policy Unit,' says John Godfrey, her first head of policy. 'It was framed and put up all around the building, including in the waiting room at No. 10. In the Policy Unit, we constantly referred to it.'[2] She spoke of her passion for the Union and made a powerful commitment to preserve the United Kingdom – the 'precious bond' that holds the nations together. The large numbers across the country who had little previous idea of who she was sat up and paid attention. She was promising a new direction for the nation. The speech ushered in a honeymoon period for May that was to last for almost a year, one of the longest for any incoming Prime Minister. The perfect start, one might have thought. But few foresaw that the speech provided three clues to how May would struggle to find success in office.

First, there was nothing of any substance about how she was to approach Brexit, the dominant concern of her premiership, in a way that would bring her divided party together behind her, bring the country together and guarantee Britain's future prosperity, security and stability. She offered no hint as to how she might unify a nation that had split itself, just three short weeks before, 52 to 48 per cent in favour of leaving the EU, with feelings of betrayal still raw. Would she deliver Brexit as a national or as a tribal leader? Would she interpret the referendum result as a mandate for a complete withdrawal from Europe, or for retaining some continuities? Her lack of clarity in the speech suggested a lack of clarity in her own mind about where she was heading and how she was going to get there.

Second, as she had been elected unopposed, she had no personal mandate for the direction of travel and aspirations she outlined. Her leadership election speech in Birmingham the week before had outlined some radical ideas, including an industrial strategy, a bigger role for regional cities, a tough line on tax evasion, an economy and society that worked for everybody and a greater stake for those who felt dispossessed in areas left behind. But what was her legitimacy for enacting these ideas? And what was the status of the party's winning manifesto from 2015? She had emerged by default as the victor in the Conservative Party contest for leader, and hence Prime Minister. On what authority, many of her MPs asked, quietly at first, then more noisily, was she leading the country in a different, and far more centrist, version of Conservatism?

Third, and perhaps most tellingly, the words were not her own. They were penned by Nick Timothy, who, along with Fiona Hill, was the co-architect of her bid to become Prime Minister. A gifted word-smith, Timothy had written the bulk of the speech in fifteen minutes in the Home Secretary's room in the House of Commons while Hill was spending time secreted away with May, preparing her for the speech.[3] May looked at the draft and requested just a few changes on tax policy, to keep open the option of reducing the top rate. He sought to encapsulate her thinking – which he had also helped forge – on social injustice and helping those 'just about managing'. She delivered it exactly as Timothy wrote it.[4]

THE MAKING OF THERESA MAY

Theresa May was born on 1 October 1956, the very day that fifteen nations whose ships used the Suez Canal, including Britain, France and (West) Germany, formed the Suez Canal Users' Association. May was only four weeks old when British and French forces invaded Egypt. Comparisons are inevitably drawn between the conduct of the Suez crisis presided over by May's Conservative predecessor as Prime Minister Anthony Eden and the Brexit crisis she presided over. Not since Eden, many believe, has there been such an unsuccessful Prime Minister.

May's distinctive character and style as Prime Minister were shaped by a number of critical events earlier in her life. Her father, Hubert Brasier, an Anglo-Catholic vicar, and her mother, Zaidee, had no other children. In a rare comment on being an only child, she later said, 'You don't feel the same need to be in a big group … You're given more of a sense of … relying on yourself a bit more.'[5] With no siblings at home, and with a mother and father often out on church business, she was thrown onto her own resources, spending long hours alone. She later recalled that her father 'couldn't always be there necessarily when you wanted him to be'.[6] At the age of twelve she began her lifelong 'love affair' with the Conservative Party, 'the relationship that has meant more to her than any bar that with her parents and husband'.[7] Many years later, on one of her first trips abroad as Prime Minister to the G20 summit in Hangzhou, China, she turned to Fiona Hill in the car and said, to Hill's surprise, 'You're like the sister I never had.' Hill took her to mean that, because she'd never had any siblings, especially a sister, she'd never had anyone in whom she could confide or with whom she could have fun.[8] As a government minister much later in life, she would find little reason to reach out to others, to enquire how they were, or to share her own feelings with them.

Her education made little obvious impact on her. She was bright and successful but did not shine academically and showed little evidence of being intellectually excited by what she learnt in the class-room or activities in which she participated outside. For two years, she attended St Juliana's, a Catholic convent school, before moving to Holton Park, a girls' grammar, which became a mixed comprehensive, Wheatley Park, during her time as a pupil. She has said and done little since she gave up formal education to suggest that it set her alight, and she has displayed little obvious interest in reading books, attending lectures, the theatre or concerts or going to art galleries. She won a place as a commoner at St Hugh's College, Oxford, in October 1974 to read geography. Conservative politics was her principal extracurricular excitement. She met her future husband, Philip, at a disco organised by the Oxford University Conservative Association: 'He was good looking and there was an immediate attraction ... We were jointly interested in politics.' They began to meet up at the Conservative events, 'so we had some common interests to start off with', she later recalled.[9] She revelled in his company, and found even less need for other friendships. She graduated with a second-class degree in 1977 (the classification was not then split into 2:1s and 2:2s).

Philip, just under a year younger, had become President of the Oxford Union in his final year at university. He proposed to her in the spring of 1979, and they were married by her father on 6 September 1980, at her local childhood church of St Mary's. The Mays settled in Wimbledon. Her life revolved around work at the Bank of England, at which she made steady if unspectacular progress, and serving as a Conservative councillor in the south London district of Merton. Philip, whose career at Oxford had been the more glittering, decided to forsake his own ambitions in politics for the sake of hers. They had no children. Many couples who are without children are immensely curious about and engaged with the children of family and friends. 'You look at families all the time,' she later said, 'and you see that there is something there that you don't have.'[10] We can never know how different May might have been had she had siblings or children of her own. It seems to have made her more inward and dependent upon Philip, and him on her. As an adult, she developed neither an empathetic persona nor any obvious curiosity about the lives of others.

In October 1981, just a year after her marriage, her father was driving his Morris Marina to Evensong in a nearby church when he was hit by an oncoming Range Rover. He suffered severe injuries and died a few hours later in hospital. Several months later, her mother also died, succumbing to the multiple sclerosis she had contracted shortly before May went to university. To have lost both parents in such a short space of time at the age of only twenty-five, and with no close family to share the grief, and no children in whom to sublimate her emotions, was an incredibly cruel blow. The loss of her parents affected her greatly. She could not bear to tell her friends, many of whom discovered only much later.[11] The loss drew her still closer to Philip, the undoubted cornerstone of her life. 'Crucially, I had huge support in my husband,' she later said, 'and that was very important for me. He was a real rock for me. He has been all the time we've been married, but particularly then, of course, being faced with the loss of both parents within a relatively short space of time.'[12]

Besides her husband, two other rocks in her life have been the church – she attends St Andrew's Church, Sonning, every week in the constituency when she can, where the Conservative-inclined vicar, Reverend Jamie Taylor, is a great source of solace to her – and her constituency of Maidenhead, which she first won as an MP in 1997, the year the Conservatives entered opposition after eighteen years in power. She has no close friends in national politics, and the friendships she does have revolve around her constituency association and her church. Church bolsters her sense of duty and mission to be of service, while the constituency gives her life a sense of profound purpose. Its importance could be seen at her fiftieth birthday party in 2006: constituents, rather than school, university, banking or political friends, made up the bulk of her guests.[13] When she first became Prime Minister, officials 'were struck by her enthusiasm to get back to Maidenhead as much as possible – she'd do a lot of her thinking there'.[14] Political advisor Chris Wilkins notes, 'What she liked best was going to Maidenhead. You had to convince her very hard that she should do something else if it got in the way of that.'[15] Everyday activities, going to Waitrose, picking up her dry cleaning or visiting her personal trainer kept her grounded. She was rarely happier than when she was knocking on doors in the constituency and taking part in old-style political campaigning. When she's not doing that, she's happiest at home with Philip, curled up on the settee with him watching boxsets on television over a glass of wine. Cooking is her favourite pastime, along with watching programmes like *The Great British Bake Off* on television, with cricket, a shared interest with her father, a distant second.

She climbed dutifully up the ministerial ladder, beginning when William Hague appointed her shadow Secretary of State for Education in June 1999, where she held a traditionalist view and drew on experience from her time in charge of education as a local councillor for Merton. May rose to political prominence as chair of the Conservative Party, a position she held from July 2002 to November 2003, when she famously delivered her 'nasty party' speech. Then leader Iain Duncan Smith is purported to have agreed with what she said, but, under the surface, he was fuming, and it created even more distance in their relationship. She was closer to his successor, Michael Howard, who appointed her shadow Environment Secretary in November 2003. Later, David Cameron appointed her shadow Leader of the Commons, which gave her a broader vision across policy, and she remained in post from 2005 to 2009. However, she made her biggest impact as Home Secretary between May 2010 and July 2016, and it was at the Home Office that she encountered the two biggest influences on her political career: Nick Timothy and Fiona Hill.

May was diagnosed with Type 2 diabetes in 2013, following a blood test after a recent bout of weight loss. When the tablets she was prescribed failed to work, further tests revealed that she had Type 1 diabetes, which is more unusual to develop later in life. She was prescribed insulin injections, initially two a day, subsequently increased to four a day, adding extra pressures to her job. 'I go to a lot of functions where I'm eating and I speak at dinners, so that brings an added complication … I have to make sure that I have tested and know where I am, and adjust as necessary,' she explained. Following her diagnosis, she wrote to schools in her Maidenhead constituency, ensuring they understood the support required by students with Type 1 diabetes, and she is seen as an ambassador by the diabetic community for showing that people can lead a very busy and successful life despite having the condition.[16]

WHAT DOES THERESA MAY BELIEVE?

May's core beliefs have shaped her politics, but it is easy to lose sight of what they are because her speeches have almost invariably been written for her by aides and officials. More instinctive than intellectual, she owes her beliefs not to philosophers or to a reading of literature and history, despite the fact that at Oxford she was president of the Edmund Burke Society (Philip May succeeded her the following year). She is at heart pragmatic: her beliefs in life have been forged by her experience of it.

She was fired up in part by injustice and was instinctively supportive of the underdog, a position owing much to her lived Christianity, to which she rarely refers. She presented herself often as anti-status quo and anti-privilege, a supporter of working people against the middle and upper classes, an advocate for those from ethnic minorities and those who attended state rather than private schools. She championed the rights of women in the workplace when she was shadow Minister for Women and Equality from 2007 to 2010. She scorned the public school entitlement of her Conservative contemporaries, epitomised by David Cameron (Eton) and George Osborne (St Paul's School), both of whom attended the elitist and macho Bullingdon Club at Oxford. She once slammed her hand on the oval table in her room in No. 10 when someone suggested that Cameron and Osborne were the party's 'modernisers'. 'I'm the original moderniser,' she shouted.[17] She was passionate about changing the perception of the Conservative Party from the party of the privileged, like Cameron and Osborne, to the party of the aspirational and those from modest backgrounds, like former leader Margaret Thatcher. She would occasionally blurt out, 'Because I'm not a bloke and don't go around talking to journalists and being clever, people forget what I did. I am the authentic moderniser. I am the person who gave the nasty party speech.'

The post she enjoyed most before Home Secretary was chair of the Conservative Party. But how far was she herself responsible for her most memorable sound bite: 'You know what people call us? The nasty party'? She was close at this time to other modernisers, notably Michael Gove and Nick Boles, friendships that were not to blossom. Mark MacGregor, the feisty chief executive at Conservative Central Office and a fervent moderniser, had been agitating for a full-blooded assault, but it needed May to deliver the message. Some credit MacGregor with responsibility for prodding her into making such an uncharacteristically outspoken statement about how the new party needed to change and modernise. Although her political advisor Chris Wilkins wrote the speech, she insisted on including those words.[18] It captured a truth about the party, and the arrogance and sense of entitlement of many of its big beasts, though as Prime Minister she found it hard to prevail against public school bullies. What she really loved as party chair was the side of the job that defeated many others: travelling the country visiting associations, attending dinners and going door-to-door campaigning.

May's world view was shaped, however, less by the conversations she had in constituencies around Britain than by her intensive preoccupation with one: her own, Maidenhead. Without political friends in Westminster or beyond, her social life revolved around friendships within Maidenhead, and her views on a range of issues were significantly a reflection of the views she heard from them – inevitably middle class, provincial and conservative.

She believed very strongly in belonging and a sense of identity at both family and national level, with a fondness for communities and traditional values. She was suspicious of the merits of immigration, and deeply sceptical about the benefit of students from abroad studying at British universities. This brought her into conflict with the intelligentsia (not that it worried her), as did her support for grammar schools (ditto). She approved of the latter for providing opportunities for working-class children, and argued for them in her first senior position in the shadow Cabinet, as shadow Secretary of State for Education. A deep believer in the British nation and in the importance of the Union, as seen in her first doorstep speech and frequent trips to Scotland, Wales and Northern Ireland, she became fixated as Prime Minister by the need to hold the Union together.

Comparisons with Thatcher, whose beliefs were often different from her own, were inevitable but always made her feel uncomfortable. On economics, she harked back to pre-Thatcher days, with her scepticism about markets and her belief that intervention and stewardship are often required to get the best out of markets in the interests of all. Despite her time at the Bank of England, economics and finance were never subjects on which May felt confident or which she prioritised, placing national security and social values way above them.

One cannot comprehend May's beliefs without considering Philip, her closest (indeed, only) true friend and her most influential counsellor before and after she entered Downing Street. Long before she was elected to Parliament in 1997, they were on a joint mission. Philip has been utterly devoted to her every step of the way, playing the role of her constant supporter faultlessly, helping her manage her ascent, her time at the summit and her descent. Their political views chime, though he is more instinctively pro-European than she is, and even more naturally cautious.

THE WAXING OF TIMOTHY AND HILL

May needed others to turn her instincts into words if she was to ever rise above her contemporaries. Two figures rivalled, and for a time even exceeded, the influence of Philip: Nick Timothy and Fiona Hill. Timothy grew up in a working-class family in Birmingham, his father a factory worker who became head of sales at a local steel and wire company, his mother a school secretary. Prodigiously bright, he attended an all-boys' grammar school in Birmingham and went on to Sheffield University, where he gained a first-class degree in politics. He first encountered May in 2002 when he went to work at the Conservative Research Department (CRD). They formed a close bond, sharing a similar social background and a common belief in social injustice and building a fairer society. He went back to work for her for a year in 2007 before returning to the CRD and was a natural choice as her special advisor when, in 2010, Cameron appointed her Home Secretary.

Hill grew up in a similarly modest background, in Greenock, outside Glasgow, went to university in Paisley (now the University of the West of Scotland), and worked her way up as a journalist, first on the *Scottish Daily Record* and then on *The Scotsman*, writing on a range of subjects from football to news, until she landed a job at Sky News. While there, she married Tim Cunningham, a TV executive, whose name she took, before returning to using the name Hill after they separated. A committed Conservative and Unionist, she joined the press office of the Conservative Party in 2006. Hill, seven years Timothy's senior, became inseparable from him, forging one of closest and most influential alliances in modern British politics. Very few others acquired their precious status, so great was May's distrust of people. For any outsider, it was exceedingly hard to gain her full confidence. Once gained, her trust was absolute, and she rarely questioned their judgement or way of operating. 'Back then, I used to find it very hard to say where I ended and Theresa began,' observes Nick Timothy,[19] words that echoed precisely those of former No. 10 policy chief Andrew Adonis on his relationship with Tony Blair.[20] Timothy and Hill were the perfect match for May, complementing her in those areas where she was not strong. Timothy was the ideas man, the strategic thinker and the wordsmith; Hill was the tactical thinker who challenged the status quo and expanded the options available to May, taking no prisoners in doing so, and ensuring that her boss was always presented in the best possible light. She was fiercely determined and single-minded, with a sixth sense for how stories would play in the media.

Timothy, just weeks beyond his thirtieth birthday, moved into May's Home Office inner sanctum in May 2010, acquiring considerable power. He quickly realised that the team was incomplete. May had appointed Annabel 'Bee' Roycroft as her second special advisor, who'd replaced Timothy as special advisor when he had left her at the end of 2007. Timothy told May she needed an advisor with national-level media experience, who would help shape May's whole agenda and presentation. He convinced May that Hill was the right person for the job. 'We'd overlapped when I was in the Conservative Research Department,' says Timothy. 'I'd seen what she was like to work with in the run-up to the 2010 general election. She was brilliant, having the tenacity to drive issues through the system, spotting dangers and eliminating them early on.'[21] Roycroft was relegated within the team, and though May offered her civil service roles as a policy advisor and speechwriter, she turned them down. Hill was pleased to be at the centre of the action working with two people she admired, May and Timothy. Hill reportedly told friends later, 'I should have reflected more on the way May dumped Bee for me after they'd been so close. There's something very clinical and cold about her.' Timothy and Hill took just weeks to establish their Home Office style with May. 'The chemistry between us really worked,' says Hill. 'We would talk early in the morning, we would talk throughout the day between meetings, and we would talk again in the evening. We became extremely close, not just on work, but helping each other through difficulties too.'[22]

May was no rookie: since entering the House thirteen years before, she'd held six shadow Cabinet posts, handled efficiently if not with distinction. How did two young special advisors wield so much influence over her when in post? The answer is that she valued them because they made her a stronger and more plausible figure in one of the biggest and most challenging jobs in government, Home Secretary, much bigger than any other she'd held before. Her strengths were not in devising policy, taking decisive action or leading a department. Nor were they in presenting herself in public and projecting a strong image. Suddenly, she was surrounded by an army of Home Office officials and legions of external figures – the police, intelligence officers, the immigration service and others – whom she found it almost impossible to read and understand.

Timothy and Hill gave her confidence and certainty and ordered her life. They translated her inchoate principles and tendencies into firm policy, adding significant input of their own. Representation of workers on boards, corporate responsibility and grammar schools came more from Timothy, as did social and racial equality. Hill's specialisms were domestic violence, counter-terrorism, organised crime and modern slavery. These ideas positioned May more in the centre of politics, whereas the traditional Home Secretary job – 'chasing extremists around the world and banging on about immigration', as Timothy describes it – made her come across as right-wing.[23] Quicker, brighter, subtler, and better at handling people, they outshone all her ministerial and official team for influence on her. They avoided exposing her weaknesses, and instead drew on her strengths: her ability to digest detailed policy briefs, a relentless work ethic and her sense of fairness. She came across as most authentically her own person when she saw injustice from a distant establishment, as when she set up the criminal inquiry in 2012 into the 1989 Hillsborough stadium football tragedy. 'She felt very keenly a sense of responsibility to those families who had lost loved ones,' recalls Will Tanner, a close and trusted advisor of May's. 'Lots of people tried to deter her from setting up the inquiry.'[24]

May's record in other areas as Home Secretary showed rather less compassion and came under fire for itself being 'nasty'. Immigration was a topic she felt very strongly about, believing that too many immigrants had entered the country under Tony Blair and Gordon Brown, and she had no qualms about – indeed, she showed satisfaction in – trying to fulfil the aim in the 2010 manifesto to reduce annual net migration to the tens of thousands. Though the goal was never met, she placed severe restrictions on non-EU migrants and created a 'hostile environment' for illegal immigration, which she defined as 'deport first and hear appeals later'. Employers and landlords were required to carry out onerous identity checks. 'In the UK illegally? Go home or face arrest' declared advertising vans, which were withdrawn after a public outcry shortly after their introduction in 2013. 'If one aim has defined May's political career it is her desire to dramatically reduce immigration to the UK,' said the *New Statesman*.[25]

Her strong stance and her lack of obvious empathy for migrants and their children made her vulnerable to criticism. The decision to destroy the landing cards of Windrush-generation Caribbean-born British citizens was not May's personal choice, having been taken by the UK Border Agency under Labour in 2009. But the effects of her regime and hostile environment policy contributed to the deportation of legal citizens, and without landing cards they often lacked proof of legal status – a matter which would come back to haunt her as Prime Minister.

May's vision on immigration reflected that of her Conservative constituents in Maidenhead. So too did her view on universities, which she thought had become too elitist and needed rebalancing towards technical and vocational education. Rarely has Britain had a Prime Minister less supportive of higher education. Her antipathy crystallised around student visas, where she bought wholesale the belief that there were too many bogus and staying-on students in the UK (despite evidence to the contrary), and she was almost alone in her team in persisting in wanting to count overseas students in the total immigration numbers. 'She thought many overseas students were not high-end graduates,' Nick Timothy says. 'The majority are not at red-brick universities. Control of numbers was her big thing and her view of student visas was reinforced by her view that universities were becoming commoditised.'[26]

Police reform was another area which chimed with her deep instincts. She thought the police had got away with manipulating the government in the past and needed standing up to, and she was fierce in the way she handled them. She was booed offstage by angry officers at the Police Federation annual conference in 2012 when she told them they should 'stop pretending' they were being 'picked on' by the government. She cut their spending by 20 per cent as part of the austerity programme, with officer numbers falling by 19,000 by the end of her Home Office tenure, and she stood up for black communities who disproportionately experienced stop-and-search.[27] Again, her stance backfired when soaring knife crime and the terrorist attacks during the 2017 general election campaign were blamed on her cuts.

May thus cut a strong figure as Home Secretary, to the surprise – and, increasingly, the concern – of Cameron and Osborne, as the coalition government's senior woman in a job historically seen as one of the more difficult in Cabinet. Inevitably, people began to ask whether she might one day become Prime Minister herself. She had indeed harboured such thoughts and ambitions of her own, but she did not share them more widely, aware of the widespread scepticism, stemming from her lack of soulmates or even companions in politics, and lack of firm opinions on major political issues. Chris Wilkins was one of several to see her ambition at the time:

I had no sense when she was Conservative Party chair that she wanted to become party leader, nor later on; but you could never tell with her. I do not know what was underneath her thinking or what was truly on her mind. But though I worked closely with her,

I hardly knew her at all, though I knew her better than many in politics did.[28]

Wilkins's own conviction was that she didn't have what it took to be Prime Minister. On the day she was appointed to the Home Office, he exchanged messages with political allies, and together they concluded that she was not up to even being Home Secretary. But when he found out that Timothy was going to work for her, he thought that she would cope.[29] She certainly didn't have the ability in his eyes, nor that of many contemporaries, to rise any higher than Home Secretary.

Timothy, however, believes that she flirted with the idea of having a pop at the time of the 2005 leadership election, when Michael Howard stood down: 'She asked me about the leadership election, and only later did I realise that she was asking my opinion on whether or not she should stand.'[30] Timothy's advice was to use the opportunity to campaign on the causes she believed in, such as bringing more women into politics. She accepted the counsel and backed Cameron in the leadership election. As early as her first autumn as Home Secretary, Timothy and Hill discussed whether she had it in her to go to No. 10. The former's view was that she didn't, but Hill was more optimistic and thought she was open to advice. She'd listen to Philip, as always her closest influence, who would be the decisive factor. So her two chiefs of staff, Timothy and Hill, organised a dinner with both of them in September 2010 at the Skylon restaurant near the Royal Festival Hall. JoJo Penn, who had joined the Home Office as a policy advisor, was another present.[31] Penn was a protégé of Timothy, who had been impressed by her work at the Conservative Research Department.[32]

As the five sat down at a table looking out over the River Thames, May was still uncertain about the reason, if any, for their dining together. Timothy was uncomfortable about asking the question himself, so Hill launched in. 'Would you like to be Prime Minister?' 'Yes,' was her immediate reaction. The one word had been spoken, the pact agreed. The rest of the meal was spent discussing other matters. For the next two years, they were all careful not to say or do anything to destabilise her relationship with Cameron or to make it appear that she was anxious to advance her own agenda: 'She was very clear she would never be involved in undermining the Prime Minister. She never wanted to appear – or be – disloyal. It stopped us doing proper planning behind the scenes,' says Timothy.[33] But from late 2012 May became increasingly restless to put her own mark on the party, egged on strongly by her team. On 9 March 2013, she gave a speech about the case for leaving the European Convention on Human Rights which, though poorly delivered, put down a marker that here was a Cabinet minister with strong views of her own. Three months later, on 12 June 2013, she gave another landmark speech to the Reform think tank's annual dinner. Far from exceptional in content, it was a not uncritical defence of government policy that ranged beyond her brief as Home Secretary. It confirmed her pulling power and revealed to Timothy and Hill the influence she had if she carried on making public speeches.

An early challenge looked possible with the Scottish referendum, held in September 2014. Together with the highly political Stephen Parkinson, who had now joined the team, the chiefs thought she was in with a chance if Scotland voted to leave and Cameron fell (as he himself thought a serious risk). Indeed, Cameron had planned to resign the morning of the referendum result if the result had gone against him.[34] But Scotland voted 55 to 45 per cent to remain in the Union, and her moment silently passed.

But not their ambition, which was only stirred further by Cameron's newly revealed fragility. Less than two weeks after the Scottish referendum came her most confident party conference speech, on 30 September, written by Timothy while in the United States. A powerful statement about the risks of extremism and the need for strong counter-terrorism measures, her speech was preceded by a headline-grabbing gambit. She was introduced by a black student from Brixton called Alexander Paul (once mentored by Timothy), who told the conference of the psychological effects of the police's use of stop-and-search powers without reasonable grounds. 'I too am a law-abiding citizen with no criminal past,' he said, 'yet I have been stopped and searched not once or twice, but over twenty times between the ages of thirteen and eighteen.' His highlighting of the treatment experienced by many young black people made a powerful statement of intent about May and the kind of Britain she wanted to see. *The Sun* described her as 'Maggie May'[35] above an article that began, 'Steely-eyed Theresa May positioned herself as the Tories' "new Iron Lady"'.[36] Comparisons to Margaret Thatcher were becoming more frequent.

In November 2014, three events coincided in one week that seriously agitated her rivals as Cameron's successor, above all Osborne. She appeared on both BBC Radio 4's *Desert Island Discs* and, broadcast on the same day, the BBC's *Andrew Marr Show*, again interpreted as a bid to raise her profile, even though her team protested that she did so at the instigation of No. 10. Equally, they said (totally fairly), they had had no foreknowledge of the timing of *Desert Island Discs*. Three days later, on 26 November, she introduced in Parliament new counter-terrorism powers. It culminated in newspaper headlines saying, 'This is Theresa May's week'. The *Sunday Telegraph* speculated on whether it was 'the first stage of a campaign to bolster her image ahead of a bid for the Conservative Party leadership'[37] and the *Daily Mail* spoke of 'Theresa's three-day media blitz',[38] while commentator James Kirkup asked, 'Has Theresa May just declared war on Downing Street?'[39]

Timothy and Hill were so alarmed about adverse publicity that even members of her team were cut out from knowing about her designs on No. 10. One advisor who joined the team after the election in 2015 says, 'There was some knowledge when I joined the team that her leadership bid was an ambition. But she was very gnomic about it and would never acknowledge it to anybody.' Will Tanner, who joined the Home Office as an official in 2013 and moved into May's office in 2014, had the same experience: 'It was not at all clear to me when I was at the Home Office that she wanted to be Prime Minister. I had heard that there had been a dinner [at the Skylon restaurant] but it was not openly discussed.'[40]

Despite their attempts at secrecy, her ambition inflamed other rivals to the Cameron crown, especially those in pole position. 'Halfway through the coalition government, suddenly Osborne realised May was no longer compliant and was a potential rival for his next job,' says Hill.[41] Her team had picked up that Osborne had only wanted her appointed to the Home Office so that she would be the lightning rod for its cuts that would fall heavily on police, with the subsequent rise in crime giving a pretext for then moving her on, replacing her with a younger and more amenable Home Secretary as the deficit narrowed and the austerity drive ended. Osborne in truth never took her that seriously and was baffled, as were others in Cabinet, when she emerged as a credible successor to Cameron.

Everything about May and Osborne grated on each other – philosophically, culturally and socially. Fifteen years his elder, she viewed him as a 'boy's boy', upper not middle class, urban not shire, and cosmopolitan not nationalistic. Their first skirmishes were over immigration and student visas. Their teams echoed and reinforced the antipathy between their bosses, seeing slights even where none were intended. Osborne (with a compliant Cameron) relentlessly promoted his own supporters, helping them into safe seats in Parliament and thereafter helping them up the ministerial ladder. Today, Osborne downplays the tension:

Theresa May had the view that I, David Cameron and Her Majesty's Treasury were doing her down at the Home Office. But it was not true. As Chancellor of the Exchequer, I regarded her as one of my equals. It had been my idea to make her Home Secretary in 2010. If I'd have become Prime Minister myself, I'd have made her Defence or Foreign Secretary. I thought at the Home Office she was her own person. I hadn't minded when we'd clashed over some things. I thought she was a big figure, and robust debates over big policy decisions are what can and should happen in government.[42]

The friction with Osborne was manageable so long as May and Cameron remained on good terms. She took great pains to ensure she had a good relationship with the Prime Minister. Nick Timothy explains:

> On many issues, David and Theresa were on the same page, including immigration and counter-terrorism. The main priority of the coalition government was the economy, and they were pretty much in the same place on that. The main fault line of the coalition government was on civil liberties, which was bang on her territory.[43]

When things became tricky, she and Cameron would get together and patch things up, despite her increasing suspicion that Osborne was whispering in his ear. Tensions cranked up following the appointment of Craig Oliver as director of communications, after Andy Coulson left over the phone-hacking scandal in 2011. Oliver rapidly became a hate figure to May's team, and while relations were better with the emollient chief of staff Ed Llewellyn, they were more fractious with Kate Fall, his deputy.[44] 'Craig Oliver was always paranoid that we were trying to launch a coup. I thought that he had built his relationship with David in part on imagining dragons and then slaying them,' Timothy says.[45] To Oliver, the way that May, Timothy and Hill 'unilaterally declared independence' at the Home Office was the cause of the problem. 'It was a constant battle to get them to engage properly on anything,' he says. Oliver became the front figure of the increasing battle between No. 10 and the Home Office from 2013, 'because no one else seemed willing to take her on'.[46] From 2014, relations began to fray with other big beasts in Cabinet too. Whereas Timothy and Hill had had a good relationship with Gove, May's once positive relationship with him had soured, and he was one of her few Cabinet colleagues whom she actively disliked. Tension with Mayor of London Boris Johnson was growing too. By the final year of the coalition government, relations with both were becoming distinctly uncomfortable, and they were about to get even uglier.

Cameron and Osborne had moved Gove from Education Secretary to Chief Whip in July 2014, believing he had become a liability with teachers. With a general election looming less than a year away, they wanted to tackle unwelcome political noise elsewhere, and they turned their sights on Hill and Timothy. Hill was caught up in a bitter and increasingly public struggle with Gove, who believed that the Home Office was not doing enough to stand up to Islamism. May took the MI5 and police line, that the danger was not Islam per se but the mixing of Islamism with violent thinking. Tensions flared up explosively one night in June 2014, after Gove had briefed journalists that the Home Office was to blame for an Islamist takeover of schools in Birmingham. Hill reacted furiously, placing documents in the public domain suggesting that the Education Department had been negligent when Gove had been in charge.[47] Cabinet Secretary Jeremy Heywood was asked by Cameron to investigate the spat. Timothy and Stephen Parkinson wrote a joint letter to Heywood saying that all three were equally guilty and the leak was not just from Hill, reasoning that Cameron would not demand all three of them be sacked. But No. 10 wouldn't buy it, and May ultimately agreed that Hill would have to go, after Cameron threatened that she herself might have to resign if she clung on to her advisor.[48] May was free to fight another day, but one of her lieutenants had been sacrificed to spare her, and not for the last time.

Hill's departure did not bring peace between the Home Office and No. 10. Downing Street wanted further scalps, May's team suspecting Oliver was behind the offensive. Hill herself became an associate director for the Centre for Social Justice think tank, working to combat modern slavery, but she grieved deeply her lost job and felt a deep bitterness towards May. She had her first rocky period, too, with Timothy, and mourned no longer being in the team. Timothy wanted to be known as the sole chief of staff, leading to tensions within the remaining team, and making him even more of a target for No. 10. The agent provocateur was the chair of the party, Grant Shapps, whom May's team suspected of trying to prove his loyalty to Osborne, the likely next leader, by setting himself up as the disposer of Osborne's enemies. In December 2014, seven months after Hill's departure, Timothy and Parkinson found themselves summarily dropped from the list of Conservative candidates, allegedly for refusing to campaign in the Rochester by-election the previous month. May's attempts to hold on to Timothy came to nothing. He was out in the cold.[49] What antagonised Timothy in particular was that the West Midlands seat of Aldridge-Brownhills, which he craved, had been quietly contacted to stop him being selected for it. He was convinced that Osborne was ultimately responsible, with Oliver his fellow assassin and Shapps merely the willing executioner.[50] Timothy's treatment would encourage him to temporarily leave front-line politics, but the bitterness he and Hill felt went very deep and simmered dangerously. He recalls:

> I had had enough. We didn't think a leadership election was going to come up any time soon, and I needed a break. Things had gone badly wrong with No. 10. Craig Oliver had poisoned No. 10 against us and made me feel they would try to get rid of us. Fi had been sacked and I had been thrown off the candidates list. I wanted to do something else.[51]

Any hopes in the No. 10 or Osborne camps that May might have been weakened with Hill and Timothy gone from the Home Office were soon disabused. Cameron's surprise announcement during the 2015 general election campaign that he would not be fighting again sent an early leadership contest right back up the agenda. The slender majority of twelve that Cameron won in the general election on 7 May 2015, against the predictions of many, was not a disappointment to Hill and Timothy. It suggested that the end of Cameron's premiership would only come sooner, in spite of the rigidities imposed by the Fixed-Term Parliaments Act. Nor were they too frustrated that Cameron had kept May at the Home Office in his post-election reshuffle, though Timothy had believed they might move her on to Defence or the Foreign Office and had contemplated staying on if they did.[52] A change to a fresh post might have revealed her weaknesses. But, as one Cameron advisor comments, 'Cameron was reluctant to move her: he took the view she was workmanlike, hadn't screwed up, was a woman, and he'd leave her.'

2015–16 AND REAPPOINTMENT

In the autumn of 2015, Theresa and Philip May convened a dinner at the Corinthia Hotel by the Embankment and Whitehall, to which they invited Hill, Timothy and Will Tanner, who more than anyone stepped up after Timothy's and Hill's departures. Initially a civil servant focusing on police reform, Tanner broadened his interest to include counter-terrorism and immigration when he succeeded Parkinson as special advisor in the autumn of 2015. He shared a close personal and ideological bond with May.[53] The EU referendum, due to be held on 23 June 2016, was the dominant issue of discussion that evening. The consensus view was that it would divide the Conservative Party again, after a period of comparative calm over Europe under Cameron, and would provide fresh opportunities for a May candidacy. 'Do you actually want to do this?' Hill asked her bluntly again, as she had at the Skylon dinner. May again replied in one word: 'Yes.' There was no need to discuss her answer. Everyone was clear that they should forge ahead on their course, and May herself did not need to know what preparations were being made.

Osborne was now very obviously the front-runner to succeed

Cameron. May knew that her best chance was to concentrate on doing the best possible job as Home Secretary, ensure no more spats by pugnacious special advisors fighting on her behalf, and avoid a screw-up that could end her prospects. May herself was absolutely adamant: in public, as in private, she wasn't prepared to do any active campaigning until the moment Cameron announced that he was standing down.[54] But behind the scenes Timothy (now working at the free school champion the New Schools Network) and Hill had the green light from her to prepare for the candidacy they had spent five years anticipating, though they were still far from confident of victory. Neither foresaw how quickly events would unfold.

THE REFERENDUM CAMPAIGN: 2015–16

After the 2015 general election, May reverted to her stoic self, forging ahead with her personal projects on counter-terrorism, security and immigration, while keeping her head very firmly under the parapet. It took her time to adjust to her new team: she never found change easy. Tanner shared a close ideological outlook with May on many issues, as did Alex Dawson (half-brother to one of Cameron's team in No. 10, Gabby Bertin), who had joined from the Conservative Research Department as a second special advisor to replace Timothy. Other members of her new team who were to play prominent roles subsequently in No. 10 were JoJo Penn, who had returned from studying in the US, and Liz Sanderson.

Shortly after Easter 2016, Timothy and Hill made a secret visit to May in her home in Maidenhead to glean where she thought MPs stood on her in the event of an early leadership election. The task was not helped by May's ignorance of, and lack of a relationship with, many Tory MPs. 'We were not at all advanced,' agrees a senior member of her campaign staff. 'In contrast, Boris had been planning it for a while. He was disorganised by nature, whereas we were dis-organised by design and timidity.' Despite Timothy and Hill being no longer physically present, relations with No. 10 remained edgy. As 23 June approached, No. 10 became increasingly anxious about how she would declare in the referendum. Pressure from Cameron, as well as from Llewellyn and Oliver, intensified as the weeks passed. Although Cameron had said in public that he didn't want anyone to declare until after his February 2016 re-negotiation with the EU, May felt constant pressure behind the scenes, from No. 10 to declare for Remain on the one side and from Timothy to declare for Leave from the other. She kept her intentions from her team, who thought her main concern was that not enough had been done to satisfy people's concerns on immigration and taking back control of the borders; this worried her more than anything about the EU.

According to Tanner, meanwhile,

her main preoccupation was ensuring people, especially the most vulnerable, did not suffer economically. She feared an economic downturn. She cared too about sovereignty, but from the point of view of security rather than trade. She saw the EU as inflexible and ideological, as against the UK, which she saw as pragmatic. My sense was she only decided to come out for Remain about two weeks before she declared her allegiance in public.[55]

Hill, who was always more pro-EU than Timothy, and could normally read May's mind better than most, was in the dark, too, on how she would declare:

We were all very Eurosceptic at the Home Office, as so much of what we wanted to do was hampered by the EU. We were against the EU courts in particular. I always assumed she would come out for Brexit. I was genuinely surprised that she came out for Remain.

It was partly out of loyalty to David Cameron, but she also had a personal feeling in favour of the EU, but she then was always ambivalent.[56]

Pressure from the Cameron camp almost tipped her into Leave, especially when a deeply frustrated Osborne put the boot into her during the campaign, with stories that she'd be sacked appearing in *The Sun* newspaper. With the atmosphere becoming very nasty, Team May blamed Osborne and his team for the threats.

Timothy remained the most single-mindedly pro-Brexit among her supporters, although he was not physically with her in the Home Office. It was to him that she turned to write her speech during the referendum campaign which, although pro-Remain, suggested significant ambivalence and made her the most pro-Brexit of all those in Cabinet who came out for Remain. The speech countered 'those that say the sky will fall in' if Britain was to leave the EU, and referred expressly to her scepticism regarding the value to Britain of the European Court of Human Rights, advancing the case for leaving it instead of the EU. But it was what she said about Turkey not joining the EU that was the most striking. May told Timothy directly, 'I don't want to say that Turkey should not join.' She believed their support against terrorism and the migrant crisis to be vitally important and was reluctant to strain the relationship. But he wrote back a terse reply explaining why she should say it, and why he believed it was important that Turkey was not a member of the EU. Timothy prevailed, indicatively, and her speech was unequivocal about the case for Turkey not gaining membership status.

Like all May's team, Timothy expected Cameron to carry the day, and took himself off to Sicily to get away from it.

None of us expected Brexit. And none of us expected David to announce he was going immediately after the result. I went to Sicily because I hadn't anticipated that result. I couldn't stand the campaign and I was away in a remote mountain village when the referendum result came through. My phone kept on vibrating through the night, which woke me. I went down to breakfast and heard Cameron's resignation speech. It was all very strange. I vividly remember a German couple who said very sternly, 'Some questions should never be asked.'[57]

Timothy immediately called May, who was so distraught that she was in tears about the result. He and Hill saw her cry only half a dozen times in their entire career together, and then it was mainly from frustration. But now there was sadness too. 'The ones who voted for Brexit will be the ones who suffer the most,' she told him, thinking of those in the left-behind areas. Here in a nutshell, Timothy now believes, was the core of her entire belief on Brexit. 'Ultimately, she saw Brexit as a damage-limitation exercise for those she thought would lose out, rather than what it could and should have been: a positive opportunity for a new start for Britain.' The one silver lining she saw that she relayed to him down the telephone line was the greater opportunity it would now give to control immigration. Timothy remembers being impatient with her on the phone, but he had no doubts about her intention: she was going for the leadership.[58]

THE LEADERSHIP CAMPAIGN: 24 JUNE–11 JULY 2016

An hour-long conference call took place between Hill, Timothy, Penn and Damian Green, May's long-standing friend from university and political colleague, to plan the next steps. On the call also were the first MPs to come onside: George Hollingbery (May's parliamentary private secretary) and two whips, Simon Kirby and Kris Hopkins. Time was short, they acknowledged together, with the election teams of other candidates far ahead of them.

Cameron delivered his resignation speech outside No. 10 at 8.15 a.m.

on 24 June, saying that he was leaving to ensure the country would have a 'strong, determined and committed leadership' to take Britain through Brexit. May watched it and called Hill to tell her she was ready to run, and ready for the campaign that she would need to fight. They met in person at 1 p.m. All traces of her tears at the result had disappeared in the few hours since she had spoken to Timothy. She hugged Hill and was, for her, highly animated and excited at the prospect of becoming Prime Minister.[59] Tanner's twenty-eighth birthday fell on that day. The party planned for that evening was immediately cancelled as he swung into action, calling Dawson and Penn and convening a meeting in May's rooms in the Home Office.[60] The race was on.

Hill talked May through the strategy later that day and spoke again to Timothy as he was making hurried plans for his return from Sicily. A skeleton staff came together in her house in Wimbledon to start planning. Johnson's team called to ask if May was willing to do a deal with Boris. 'Bog off,' was the reply.[61] With Osborne dead in the water with the referendum loss, they considered Johnson their principal rival, followed by Sajid Javid and Jeremy Hunt. Indeed, much of the early support for May came specifically from the 'Stop Boris' MPs.[62] Andrea Leadsom emerged a few days later, while Liam Fox's star was already fading, to their surprise, as they had expected him to do better. But Gove was a nagging worry too. They knew that Gove wouldn't support May. But what was he up to? None of them knew.

Timothy was back in action by Saturday, and he and Hill began directing operations jointly. One who joined the team that weekend comments, 'Nick and Fi totally ran the show. Everyone was very much working for them.' Here was the moment that they had awaited for years, and they had a deep certainty and conviction about what needed to be done. As Timothy puts it:

Theresa trusted us. She would really only comment on the odd phrase or a particular point of strategy. But she had confidence in us to get the rhetoric and her voice right. Her leadership campaign was very focused. Fi and I did what we always did for her: we gave her the strategy, organisation and policy content.[63]

They counted upon a team of loyal lieutenants. Tanner joined forces with Penn, working on lists of MPs in May's room in the Home Office on the Saturday, and from Sunday in her office in the House of Commons.[64] Lizzie Loudon, another to join at this time, had been up in Scotland and had been neglecting to pick up calls from the Gove and Johnson teams. Once back in London, she went to see Hill, who had been impressed by her knowledge on Brexit (she'd spent a year as media advisor to Iain Duncan Smith and had worked on the Vote Leave campaign). She had good contacts across the media, including with *New Statesman* editor Jason Cowley and *Guardian* journalists Patrick Wintour and Nick Watt.[65] On Sunday evening, Gavin Williamson, who had been Cameron's parliamentary private secretary and knew the parliamentary party inside out, came on board: they considered this a real coup. Indeed it was. No one, including Timothy and especially May herself, had much knowledge of MPs across the party. Williamson knew the MPs inside out. Sunday also saw George Osborne formally retire from the fray, recognising that he was too tarred by the referendum to have a realistic chance of success. May's team gave a vengeful cheer.

By the end of the weekend, Johnson looked as if he might walk away with it. Headlines in the *Daily Telegraph* on Monday morning suggested he had 100 names behind him. It made May's team work even more frantically on Monday, going through all their lists and making pleading calls. By late evening, it seemed to be paying off, and they were pleased to see the *Daily Telegraph* suggesting that Johnson was losing support. Williamson had instituted 8 a.m. meetings in the Commons with MPs from Tuesday. They followed inner-team meetings, which provided stability and purpose, and leveraged to the full his deep links across the party.[66] Promising support came from MPs like Alan Duncan and Justine Greening, who had backed Remain, and Chris Grayling, who had been prominent in the Leave campaign. Nicky Morgan's prospects burned for a time, with backing from the liberal wing of the party and supporters transferring from Osborne. But when she ran out of road, she switched her allegiance to Johnson on the grounds that he was the candidate at the time most likely to unify the party. Gove's alliance with Johnson, brokered on the Saturday after the referendum, with Gove receiving the post of Chancellor of the Exchequer in return for his support, equally burned bright for a time. A formidable pairing of the two big beasts, both with Brexit credentials and the ability to draw votes from across the party, it too soon fell apart. Gove began to realise, with Johnson's failure to confirm Andrea Leadsom's support, that he was not backing the right man. Nominations were to close at noon on 30 June, one week after the referendum. That morning, Morgan's special advisor Luke Tryl was in her office in the Education Department when she phoned in high excitement: 'You will never guess what has happened: Michael is standing.'[67] She immediately threw in her lot behind him and became his proposer, while at the same time Johnson lost two other leading women, Liz Truss and Amber Rudd. May's team were as shocked as anyone by Gove's decision. 'It had not been clear to us to begin with what Michael was going to do,' says Timothy. 'If he was going to run or position himself for a job. There has always been a split between the Michael who wants to lead and the part of him who is not quite sure if it is right.'[68]

Positioning themselves on the EU was one of the earliest challenges for May's team. They met with some officials for a briefing about the preparations for Brexit, only to be told, 'No work has been done, Home Secretary.' Immediately after the referendum, Olly Robbins, May's Second Permanent Secretary at the Home Office, had been brought in by Heywood to be the lead figure in planning Brexit, based in the Cabinet Office. Timothy came up with the idea of creating a fresh Brexit Department to ensure that, if May was to emerge as the victor, they would have at least one department untainted by the Whitehall pro-EU mindset, to be given added legitimacy by appointing a Brexiteer to lead it.

May rapidly had to establish her own identity and policy platform. Timothy and Hill decided that the most suitable venue to launch her campaign was the Royal United Services Institute (RUSI), the world's oldest security think tank, where she had announced her counter-terrorism and extremism policy in November 2014. On the morning of the speech, 30 June, the closing day for nominations, her team found out at 7 a.m. that the landscape was about to change rapidly. Social media was alive with talk about Johnson, Gove, Nick Boles and Andrea Leadsom. When the team arrived at RUSI, they saw Sam Coates of *The Times* make a face at them to indicate something big was up: they quickly concluded that it was to do with their principal rival's campaign, but they did not know what.

Again, May's speech was written by Timothy, and she made few alterations. She was visibly nervous as she stepped up onto the podium. It was to be one of only two speeches that she made during the leadership contest. Although both speeches were overshadowed by events off-stage, they still revealed much about her thinking. She announced 'three clear reasons for my candidacy'. First, the country needed 'strong, proven leadership' to lead it through the uncertainty and to negotiate the best possible terms for leaving the European Union. Second, to 'unite the party and the country', with her powerful commitment to uniting all the nations of the United Kingdom. Third, to offer a 'bold, new, positive vision for the future of our country', one which would ensure a future 'that works not for a privileged few but for every one of us'. Then she said she wanted to clarify a few matters. First and most importantly, 'Brexit means Brexit', a phrase coined by Timothy which was to come back to haunt her: 'There must be no attempts to remain inside the EU, no attempts to rejoin it through the backdoor, and no second referendum.' Next came other words that she, Timothy and Hill would for ever regret: 'There should be no general election until 2020.' Distinguishing herself from Cameron and Osborne on fiscal policy, 'We should no longer seek to reach a Budget surplus by the end of the parliament' – more delay than new direction. On the mechanisms of Brexit, she announced her intention to create a new department responsible for conducting Britain's negotiation with the EU to be led by a senior Secretary of State who themselves campaigned for Britain to leave the EU. As Prime Minister, she was to fall short on many of these promises.

The speech was never cleverer than in the words written to describe herself, which made her social weaknesses appear as virtues: 'I know I'm not a showy politician. I don't tour the television studios. I don't gossip about people over lunch. I don't go drinking in Parliament's bars. I don't often wear my heart on my sleeve. I just get on with the job in front of me.'

She finished by talking about her successes as Home Secretary, judged to include: taking on the Police Federation; exposing police corruption, from Stephen Lawrence to Hillsborough; and deporting Abu Qatada. Whisked straight back to the Home Office in her official car, she went smartly up to her office and put on the television, where she saw the announcement that Johnson had withdrawn following Gove's bid, recognising that his cause was lost. It rapidly became the news story of the day, eclipsing May's speech and preventing it receiving the full attention and scrutiny that it merited.

Nominations duly closed at noon. May and Gove were the favourites, with Crabb, Fox and Leadsom the other three candidates. Leadsom had been in two minds whether to run: Gove's standing, coupled with Johnson's inability to issue a statement or written promise of a No. 11 job, spurred her into action.[69] It was a remarkably depleted list.

No Osborne, no Johnson, no Hunt. Deep within Whitehall, senior Permanent Secretaries met with Jeremy Heywood. They, like most others, were underwhelmed by the quality and lack of experience. They concluded that May was the best choice, not because she voted Remain but because she was methodical and serious and wasn't wild or unproven at leading the country at such a pivotal moment. May's team now focused their attention on Gove, the candidate they feared, who launched his campaign and policy platform the following day, 1 July: 'We all thought to ourselves, "There's no way that you came up with all that policy in twelve hours,"' says Timothy.[70] With just three days before the first Tory leadership ballot, the May team went into overdrive, working from their new offices in Westminster. As the pendulum swung towards May, they received a surge of calls from MPs pledging their support. She made it clear that she would make no deals, a calculated risk meaning that some MPs, like Priti Patel, who had previously been toying with standing herself, didn't come over openly to support her until late in the day. But that was May's style.

On Tuesday 5 July, the first Tory leadership ballot saw May emerge clearly in the lead with 165 votes (50.2 per cent), Leadsom second on sixty-six, followed by Gove on forty-eight, Crabb on thirty-four and Fox on sixteen. Fox was duly eliminated while Crabb withdrew later that day. Two days later, on 7 July, came the ballot to whittle the remaining candidates down to just two, who would then go before the Conservative Party members in the country to decide. May received 199 votes, a majority, but according to Nick Timothy, 'The big thing in her mind was she didn't get 200, which disappointed her.'[71] Gove, to the surprise of many, came third and was eliminated, MPs still furious at him for stabbing Johnson in the back. He reflects on the defeat: 'After the referendum, the parliamentary Conservative Party was in a state of mild shock. Theresa seemed the safe choice, especially after the bust-up I had with Boris, though I think the evidence is she'd have won even had we stood.'[72] According to the rules, there would now follow two months of national campaigning before the Conservative membership had their say on the final two in September. Hill had a hunch that 'this isn't going to run the full course to the autumn'.[73]

The early signs were that Leadsom was going to be a much more formidable competitor than Johnson or Gove, not least with the money of Vote Leave backer Arron Banks behind her and the benefits of access to Leave.EU's database. But, behind her calm exterior, Leadsom was appraising whether she really wanted to go ahead with it now that the reality had dawned, and she had already been hurt by what her team considered a deeply unpleasant campaign against her orchestrated by Grayling. It was so offensive that she had a meeting, unknown to anybody at the time, with 1922 Committee chair Graham Brady to discuss the mechanism if she decided to withdraw.[74] On Saturday 9 July, an interview with her appeared in *The Times*, by journalist Rachel Sylvester. *The Times* had been asking for an interview for some days, and the Leadsom team had agreed to it only late in the day. Rather than it taking place in London, as Sylvester had expected, at the last minute Leadsom's team asked for it to be conducted in Milton Keynes, close to her South Northamptonshire constituency. Sylvester found it an 'almost surreal' experience talking to her in a coffee shop while the fire alarm went off and babies cried all around. She found Leadsom very agitated when she turned up, clearly overwrought and distracted. She asked Leadsom about her references to being a mother in the EU referendum debates, to which she replied:

> Yes ... I am sure Theresa will be really sad she doesn't have children so I don't want this to be 'Andrea has children, Theresa hasn't' because I think that would be really horrible, but genuinely, I feel that being a mum means you have a very real stake in the future of our country, a tangible stake. She possibly has nieces, nephews, lots of people, but I have children who are going to have children who will directly be a part of what happens next.[75]

Tim Loughton, Leadsom's campaign manager, believes she was drawn into a deliberate trap by *The Times*.[76] Sylvester denies this flatly, but reflects, 'I don't think her comments on May's childlessness were a mistake – she meant to humanise herself and differentiate herself from her rival. I remember thinking it was really mean.' Sylvester didn't immediately realise, though, that there was a story in it, let alone the massive one it became.[77] Sylvester is adamant that *The Times* did not give her any instructions to stitch up Leadsom: indeed, there was nothing in the way the interview was conducted to suggest that was Sylvester's personal intention. But the May camp had no doubt that *The Times*, who did not like Leadsom, wrote it up deliberately in a way to cause trouble. Sam Coates texted one of May's team to say, 'You can thank me now or you can thank me later.' One of May's team comments, 'They knew exactly what they were doing with the way they published the interview: it was very calculating.' A storm ensued on publication, with Leadsom accused of punching below the belt. Hill gave firm instructions that there was to be 'no comment at all' on the furore following the interview, so they were not seen to be digging the knife in but letting the story run its natural course.[78]

On Monday 11 July, May travelled up to Birmingham accompanied by Philip, Lizzie Loudon and another aide, Rupert Oldham-Reid, leaving Timothy and Hill in London, for the second of a planned series of speeches laying out her platform. As May was reading her notes in the green room fifteen minutes before she went on the stage, her team received a message that Leadsom was anxious to speak to her. May messaged Hill back in London to ask whether she should take the call. 'I said that on balance she should. But she didn't call me back to tell me what she had said.' May asked for Liam Fox, who was with her to introduce her to speak, to leave the room so that she could talk to Leadsom alone. 'I'm pulling out,' Leadsom told a passive May. 'But I appreciate you not saying anything till I have told my staff and made my announcement public.' May thanked her politely. 'I think things are going to change a bit,' she said to Philip, who then embraced her and gave her a kiss. 'Don't tell the campaign team yet,' Philip said to her. 'We should honour her wishes.' She then went up onto the stage and kept her mind focused on her text, giving no indication about what she had just learnt.[79] Hill recalls, 'I watched her give her speech and heard her voice wavering at one point, so I thought that something might have happened.'[80] The team back in London, though, were in the dark as they watched her speak.

Her Birmingham speech was intended to broaden out her platform to embrace the economy and saw her pivot decisively leftwards. Her drafting team had broadened, too, to include John Godfrey, soon to be her head of policy in No. 10, as well as Tanner and Penn. The principal author, though, remained Nick Timothy, who remembers, 'I wanted it to take the policy agenda forward, moving into areas such as corporate behaviour, tax evasion, workers on boards, energy prices, job security and industrial strategy. We were crafting the agenda for what was looking increasingly likely to be her premiership.'[81]

The choice of Birmingham, Timothy's hometown, was symbolic. The heart of industrial Britain for 200 years, it had faced major structural decline. May began strongly:

> We need to reform the economy to allow more people to share in the country's prosperity. We need to put people back in control of their lives. We need to give more people more opportunity. And we need to get tough on irresponsible behaviour in big business ... So if I'm Prime Minister ... we're going to have not just consumers represented on company boards but employees as well.

In an unashamed attack on the excesses of crony capitalism, she went for the 'irrational, unhealthy and growing gap between what ... companies pay their workers and what they pay their bosses'. She advocated binding shareholder votes on corporate pay, greater transparency on top-end pay, and reform of competition law so markets worked better for all. Individual and corporate tax avoidance and evasion were other targets. 'It is not anti-business to say that big business needs to change.'

In her closing passages, Timothy wrote words that showed quite how radical a leader he planned May to be. 'This is a different kind of Conservatism, I know,' she said. 'It marks a break with the past.' Here was a Conservatism that believed in communities, not just markets; in society, not just individualism; in an active role for the state, rather than seeing the state as the enemy; and which wanted to return to the Burkean One Nation tradition of conservatism uniting all, not just the successful and well-off.

From Robert Peel to Lady Thatcher, from Joseph Chamberlain to Winston Churchill, throughout history it has been the Conservative Party's role to rise to the occasion and to take on the vested interests before us, to break up power when it is concentrated among the few, to lead on behalf of the people.

The words could only have come from Timothy. May's view of the Conservative Party was one based on her own experiences within it, not its history. Then, with a peroration about the need to come together 'as a party and as a country', she quit the stage.

As soon as she left, the cocoon of the British state closed in around the Prime Minister-elect, and security whisked her and Philip back to London in an official car. Her team were desperate to ask her what Leadsom had said. As soon as she was safely in the car, she phoned Hill. 'I've won,' she said, exploding with elation as she spoke.[82] Timothy and Hill had worked tirelessly to hear these words for six years. They knew now they would have to move at pace. May was driven to the campaign office, where she made a short speech over drinks to the twenty or so team members present, thanking them for their hard work. They were still in a state of shock, expecting the leadership contest to have gone on until September. 'Everyone was slightly delirious,' recalls Loudon. 'We'd been anticipating a difficult, multi-week campaign, which we thought we could win, though nothing was certain. Suddenly, we discovered it was all over.'[83]

The team's phones immediately lit up with calls from former backers of Leadsom wanting to speak to them, desperately hoping for jobs and favour. While the team went off to a pub on Horseferry Road near the Home Office to celebrate, May and Philip went to her nearby flat with Timothy and Hill. While there, Heywood called from the Cabinet Office: 'I have made room for you in the building: you need to get to work on your Cabinet.' Her two lieutenants shot off to it, working until 11 p.m. on 11 July before returning at 4 a.m. the next morning. The Cameron team asked for time to allow him to take one final Prime Minister's Questions in the House, as Blair had done nine years before. All day on 12 July, Timothy, Hill and May worked tightly together finalising the Cabinet and the team they were to take with them to Downing Street. On Wednesday 13 July, May was summoned to Buckingham Palace for the Queen to invite her to become Prime Minister. Moments earlier, on the street outside No. 10, Cameron's final words were to wish her well, saying she would provide what the country needed: 'strong and stable leadership'.

The Home Secretary, the longest-serving in recent history, suddenly found herself Prime Minister. But being Home Secretary is poor preparation for No. 10. Prime Ministers need to be wide-ranging, strong communicators and creative. The Home Office is a bunker. And the longer an incumbent is there, the more its tendrils choke its political boss. If the Home Secretary has an introverted personality, the effect, as No. 10 was about to find out, could be even more pronounced.

Theresa May's chiefs of staff Nick Timothy and Fiona Hill, whom she imported into No. 10 from the Home Office, shaped every aspect of her first ten months as Prime Minister.

CHAPTER 2

FORTRESS NO. 10

Tuesday 12 July 2016 was the single most important day in May's premiership. The truncated leadership campaign gave her little time to prepare herself, to think through what she wanted to achieve, or how to achieve it. Ted Heath, in contrast, had five years to prepare as Leader of the Opposition for No. 10, Thatcher four, Blair three and Cameron five. In recent history, Gordon Brown hadn't been Leader of the Opposition, but he'd spent ten years preparing for the premiership as Chancellor. Only John Major in November 1990 found himself hurtled through the black door with no time at all to prepare. Brown and Major, like May, had similarly beleaguered and difficult premierships, never entirely on the front foot.

The unseemly rush placed even more raw power in the hands of Timothy and Hill, the two people who had made her Prime Minister. They rank among the most influential Prime Minister's advisors in modern British history, even if they were at the top for less than a year. It took this one day, 12 July, for all their preparations over the previous six years to be scrunched together. Decisions were taken on her agenda, the style that her premiership would adopt, the team within No. 10 who were to shape her, who were to be the ministers in her government and, as significantly, who was to be shown the door.

THE MAY AGENDA

May had shown at the Home Office that she was a politician with a strong instinct for helping the vulnerable. We see it in her support for the Hillsborough families whose loved ones had perished in the tragedy at Sheffield in April 1989; in her standing up for the powerless against the police and other parts of the establishment; in her support for black people in stop and search; and in her desire to help those who suffered from prejudice, whether racial minorities or those with mental health problems. But her skills did not extend to strategic thinking or policy formation, nor to persuasion: she was not good at winning others over to her views. All Prime Ministers depend heavily upon those around them. Not since Anthony Eden, whose experience was in foreign policy alone, was a Prime Minister so totally dependent on their team. The circumstances she suddenly found herself in on 12 July added greatly to her dependency. As Nick Timothy puts it:

> Our biggest disadvantage was that the leadership campaign didn't run its course, which meant that we were unable to develop her programme. We knew what the main challenges and problems were but didn't have the opportunity or the time to work them through into properly formed policies or expose them to public scrutiny.[1]

The sudden cessation of the leadership election meant that May, her character and grasp of ideas were not fully exposed to scrutiny. Had she had a deep well of reading of political philosophy or history upon which to draw, she might have been better placed for the catapult into No. 10. But she travelled ideologically and historically light. The two speeches in her leadership campaign, at RUSI and in Birmingham, were high on rhetoric and ambition but short on detail. Many of the ideas were a radical departure for a Conservative leader, with roots in the domestic policies of Joseph Chamberlain, the Liberal Unionist leader whose party merged with the Conservatives in 1912, forming the Conservative and Unionist Party. It had similarities to the thinking of Conservative Prime Ministers Benjamin Disraeli, Stanley Baldwin and Harold Macmillan. It begged the question: how far were these ideas those of May herself, and how far those of Timothy? Will Tanner puts it thus:

> We didn't have enough time to work up our agenda ideas in the head-to-head with Andrea Leadsom. There wasn't the time to set out and gain legitimacy for the more radical parts of it. It meant we were reactive from early on and didn't have a coherent enough agenda from which the Whitehall departments could lead, even though we were trying to drive policy hard from No. 10. The departments would come back at No. 10 and say, 'She doesn't really believe all this stuff, does she?' Yet she did.[2]

The May agenda, such as it was, consisted of four broad elements. On detailed policy for leaving the European Union, and on Britain's future relationship with it, the cupboard was almost bare when she arrived at No. 10. Cameron and Osborne had given a very clear directive to the civil service: no contingency planning for a Leave vote was to take place during the referendum campaign. So Whitehall was waiting to be told what to do. The decision was announced during the leadership competition to create the Department for Exiting the European Union (DExEU), but not the strategy on Brexit that the department was to adopt. May had strong instincts on the EU and how Brexit might take place. But her policy for Brexit was an open book when she became Prime Minister, on which others, particularly Timothy, would write the words.

Economic and industrial reform, her second theme, was almost entirely based on Timothy's thinking. It included putting workers on boards, making changes to corporate governance, intervening in the market to reduce fluctuations and short-termism, and introducing moves to reduce regional disparities. Less-publicised policy goals of

Timothy's included rethinking investment in human capital, expanding infrastructure spending and making energy costs more affordable. Overall, the programme most resembled the policies of Tony Blair, more than those of any Conservative Prime Minister since Thatcher. The agenda needed considerable preparation and pitch-rolling if it was to gain traction, due to the demands it placed on Whitehall and its lack of underlying popularity with Conservative MPs.

Her third theme, 'a country that worked for everyone', resonated deeply with May and was the policy area where her own instincts chimed most closely with those of Timothy. They shared a distaste for the arrogance of governing elites, which had led to an 'us and them' split, with a forgotten lower-middle-class group. Many living across the country, especially in deprived areas, felt they had been ignored and were experiencing stagnating incomes, a rising cost of living, extremism and increases in immigration, with local communities suffering from an unsympathetic government economic policy driven by Cameron's austerity agenda in the wake of the global financial crisis of 2007–08. Government, whether from Brussels or London, seemed very remote. The civil service and media jumped on May's phrase 'just about managing' (the so-called JAMs), but many felt it was never precisely defined. According to one source, Whitehall could be frustrated with Timothy's lack of clarity on detail:

> Officials in No. 10 thought, 'How can we help define JAMs for you?' But Nick didn't seem to want to define it. He wanted it to be all things to all people. It only became clear later that he wanted to leave it undefined so that it could have broad appeal at an early general election.

This strand of thinking had most in common with that of Major, who was similarly hampered by his own lack of time to work his inchoate thoughts into a policy agenda before being overtaken by parliamentary division and a thinning majority.[3]

Like Major also, May had many socially conscious beliefs based on justice and fair treatment. She wanted to see action on mental health and on modern slavery, and extending to building more grammar schools, as a way of giving the educational advantages that were enjoyed by those who could purchase a private education to all with the academic ability to gain from one.

The fourth theme was that May believed passionately in the Union, in its preservation and security, and in the Conservative Party, to which she had given her life's work. The last thing she wanted to see was either the Conservative Party or the Union damaged or disintegrating.

With a full campaign or a long period in opposition as leader, these four sets of ideas might have been worked up into policies with legitimacy, proper funding and a broad basis of support. But she had none of these. We shall see how this worked out in practice, as Cabinet ministers and their Whitehall departments struggled to implement changes and work to brief, while her close team felt ever-mounting frustration at the inertia across Whitehall. May's own inability, or unwillingness, to drive the policy hard against resistance ended up frustrating even her own team. The need to secure a mandate for the agenda was to be a core reason in calling the early general election in 2017, an action that she had expressly ruled out in the leadership campaign and afterwards. It played its part, too, in the controversial Conservative manifesto in that election, leading to the disastrous result for the Tories and thus the problems of her ensuing two years. The seeds of not just her first year in power but the entire May premiership were thus sown.

THE MAY STYLE

When she first became Prime Minister, some insiders, including senior officials, saw evidence of a new, more inclusive style. One source points to examples such as 'her No. 10 doorstep speech; reaching out in some of the Cabinet appointments; her early trip to Scotland when she was photographed with Nicola Sturgeon, two female leaders; her passion for all parts of the Union'. But soon the May style, in part because of lack of preparation, came to be defined by what she was against rather than what she was for. It emerged as a self-consciously puritanical, minimalist and unflashy style, and proud of it. It had a ring of the 'quiet man' description of himself by her fellow Christian Iain Duncan Smith at the October 2003 party conference. May had a distaste for the granting of honours and favours, and, for all her own love of clothes, she was horrified to learn that Samantha Cameron had a clothing allowance from the Conservative Party, quickly putting an end to it. Though she enjoyed the status of the office, she didn't want to be hosting flashy receptions and wanted to minimise her personal exposure to the media. She presented herself as hard-working Theresa, 'plain Theresa', the woman from an ordinary British background who understood the concerns of ordinary British people. She was going to be on your side.

So she positioned her premiership as a reaction to Cameron and Osborne's reign, though the opening words of her Downing Street speech gave no indication of the distaste that she and some of her team had for them:

> In David Cameron, I follow in the footsteps of a great, modern Prime Minister. Under David's leadership, the government stabilised the economy, reduced the Budget deficit and helped more people into work than ever before. But David's true legacy is not about the economy but about social justice ... David Cameron has led a one-nation government, and it is in that spirit that I also plan to lead.

The words, sincerely delivered by May, cloaked a deep negativity still disguised by Timothy and Hill towards a select few of the Cameron team, above all Oliver and Osborne, as well as the visceral dislike they shared with May of the upper-class, male, privileged world of Cameron and Osborne, with their public school entitlement. According to Chris Wilkins, 'Theresa May genuinely thought that Cameron and Osborne had not done time in the party, as she herself had done and worked her way up, and that they didn't understand modernisation. She thought they were superficial, and emblematic of the social class with a very different outlook to hers.'[4]

Lizzie Loudon remembers the mood: 'Everything became "Year Zero" when Theresa May took over. She felt the Osborne team had blocked her repeatedly at the Home Office. She had a deep contempt for him and the David Cameron chummy public school style. Any mention of Osborne's phrases, like "financial security", were banned.'[5]

The new team demanded that it be called a 'new government', not a continuation government. They interpreted Brexit as a vote for change. A senior official in No. 10 recalls:

> They wanted to ensure that 'Day 1' was the day that she took over. They had very little time for what happened before she became Prime Minister. No Twitter was one feature of her new style, another deliberate reaction. Her disdain for the entire David Cameron team at No. 10 was obvious to us all. Civil servants who had worked for Cameron were treated with suspicion. For the initial period, they really didn't want civil servants in the room at her key daily meetings.

Not since the Blair team arrived in May 1997 had an incoming administration held such suspicion of the civil service. Indeed, we have to go back to the arrival of the Harold Wilson team at No. 10 in October 1964 to find such a social clash with the civil service and revulsion at an outgoing administration. By any standards, it was extraordinarily naive and counterproductive.

To many Conservative MPs, the distancing of Cameron and Osborne seemed in poor taste as well as bad politics. Supporters of

Osborne were particularly angry. One insider recalls, 'What really infuriated Conservative MPs was the trashing of Osborne and everything that he had achieved. They hated the trashing of his financial record.'

The initial few months saw May's team indulge in some score-settling for slights, both real and imagined, over the previous six years. Oliver was the target of the most egregious example of their animosity. May had been awarded the 2016 'Politician of the Year' by *The Spectator* and had to deliver a speech at their annual awards dinner on 2 November. She and her team debated whether she should go, deciding only at the last minute that she would. Jokes were suddenly required. They knocked around various ideas, including several that were particularly poisonous. Osborne and Johnson were the principal subjects, but it was Oliver who received the full force of the ire. May delivered these words in front of the crowded room and television cameras:

> I am particularly pleased to see Craig Oliver … sorry, 'Sir' Craig, is here tonight … In his book … Craig says that when he heard the result of the referendum, he walked out of the office, he walked into Whitehall and he started retching violently. I have to say, I think we all know that feeling. Most of us experienced it too when we saw his name on the resignation honours list.

It displayed an extraordinary lack of judgement for a Prime Minister and showed how much she had yet to learn about the office. Oliver says:

> It was a surreal experience. Part of me was mortified, part fascinated at what I was witnessing – the Prime Minister demeaning herself and scoring points in a hard hat and a high-vis jacket. I gritted my teeth and grinned. At the end, many people told me they thought she appeared vindictive and petty. It was the worst of a steady campaign to make our lives difficult.[6]

Oliver thought that the jibe came from Hill; in fact, the author was Chris Wilkins, who says that he had not intended her to use it and was shocked when he saw on the news that she had.[7]

Timothy came to regret the approach that they adopted towards Cameron and the team:

> Looking back, we drew too much on the contrast between DC and Theresa and pissed off a lot of people. Sometimes there was un-authorised briefing coming out of the building which disparaged David's record. The media jumped on it and hyped it up. Those briefings shouldn't have happened, and we shouldn't have drawn the contrast: we should have emphasised we were building on what they had achieved, as we did in the Downing Street speech.[8]

Both behind the scenes and in the open, Cameron proved to be a loyal former Prime Minister to his successor. Unlike Heath and Thatcher, he did not show disdain, whatever he may have felt. He was on the phone when she wanted to talk to him, and he came in to speak to her. He'd send occasional texts to her or to her team to say he was seeing a foreign leader and could he do anything to help? On her side, she agreed to Cameron's chief of staff, Ed Llewellyn, becoming British Ambassador in Paris. She accepted, too, his honours list, which aroused widespread criticism for the peerages to several of his team, among other gongs, recognising that it was his prerogative. In private, Timothy and Hill were irritated and thought it poor.

THE NO. 10 TEAM

Margaret Thatcher was the last commanding Prime Minister to run No. 10 without a chief of staff. No Prime Minister since has found it possible to govern without one. Managing the multi-dimensional aspects of their job and driving their command across Whitehall and the country requires a political loyalist by their side. Blair brought in former Foreign Office diplomat Jonathan Powell to be his chief of staff and appointed former journalist Alastair Campbell to the role of press secretary and then director of communications and strategy. Both had powers over civil servants, to the alarm of senior mandarins.

Gordon Brown stumbled in his team organisation as Prime Minister until he brought Heywood back into No. 10 as Permanent Secretary. David Cameron chose to retain the chief of staff title, bringing with him his old friend who had done the same job in opposition, Ed Llewellyn, with Kate Fall and Oliver Downden to be his deputy chiefs of staff.

May had not given detailed thought to how she was to run Downing Street. No more a student of government than she was of history, she had remarkably little understanding of how No. 10 operated. Not having spent time as Leader of the Opposition, learning about policy and process across the whole of Whitehall, was a disadvantage, and nor could she do as Blair and Cameron had done and import a significantly sized Leader of the Opposition team into Downing Street. So, when she suddenly found herself Prime Minister in waiting on 12 July, she had to think very quickly. Hill had discussed in vague terms with Timothy the idea of appointing a civil servant as chief of staff in the Heywood mould, leaving them to act behind the scenes as chief advisors, removing some pressure and taking the spotlight off them.[9] They alighted on the idea of appointing Simon King, who had been a private secretary for Home Affairs in No. 10 to Brown and Cameron before becoming director of strategy at the Home Office. But he had moved to the private sector and was unavailable. History might have been very different had he been in a position to accept the job.[10] No other candidates came to mind who could command the trust of No. 10 and had an existing relationship with Timothy and Hill. They were out of time. The cupboard was bare. Timothy and Hill discussed their dilemma with Heywood on 12 July. 'Why don't you two guys do it together?' he suggested. In the absence of a better alternative, they fell in with his idea. Hill was adamant she was not going to be a mere communications director, while Timothy was never convinced the joint chiefs plan would work. They often talked about how to divide up responsibilities between them in No. 10 but never landed on a resolution. Thus was taken, on the hoof, one of the biggest decisions of May's premiership. As joint chiefs of staff (or 'the chiefs', as they came to be known), Timothy and Hill had no clear job description. The creators of the May premiership now found themselves jointly in the driving seat as its scriptwriters, with prodigious power potentially at their disposal.

They were two of the most controversial, driven and brilliant figures to have served at the heart of Downing Street in recent times. But they were young and inexperienced. To achieve the best out of them, and to mitigate their downsides in No. 10 – over-zealousness, secrecy and belligerence – they needed a powerful figure above them to shape them and, when necessary, put them in their place. No one did.

Timothy and Hill were acutely aware of May's weaknesses as Home Secretary. They understood how these weaknesses would be harshly illuminated on the much bigger stage of No. 10, and they over-compensated for them. For the model to work, the Prime Minister needed to direct the chiefs of staff and delineate clear responsibilities and boundaries between them. May was incapable and unwilling to do so. Instead, the chiefs of staff found themselves directing the Prime Minister. It was never going to work. They set out to manage her at No. 10 as they had done at the Home Office, reading all the submissions that went into her box, commenting on them and directing what she might say in writing, in Cabinet, in key announcements and in her speeches. While Timothy concentrated on developing her domestic agenda and Europe policy, Hill focused on strategy, presentation and troubleshooting. No. 10 has no rule book on how to make it work optimally. Every incoming Prime Minister makes it up. Officials are often too wary to advise them, while historians are not asked. Trying to run May's premiership as she set out to do so was never going to work.

Hill, like Timothy, was given freedom by May to write her own job description. She wrote an almost impossibly broad role for herself. She knew better than anyone how far short May fell of the presentational attributes that a modern Prime Minister needs, not least following such natural performers as Cameron and Blair. She spoke at length to May about how to step up mentally from Home Secretary to Prime Minister, how to conduct herself in public, and how to dress, telling her, 'You need to get a wardrobe that looks more prime ministerial than you looked as Home Secretary.'[11] The additional physical scrutiny a female Prime Minister faces from the media, though archaic and discriminatory, was, she explained, a fact of life. May refused voice coaching, speech and media training.

Hill did not limit her brief to presentation and communication. She pushed hard to get her priorities through the system, including domestic violence and modern slavery. The former eventually made it into a Bill, while the latter encountered resistance from the Home Office, where modern slavery was regarded as a distraction from their prime focus, counter-terrorism. Scotland was another Hill passion, and her views chimed with May's own pro-Union instincts. As someone who had grown up in Glasgow and cut her teeth on Scottish newspapers, Hill made it a priority to outwit the call for a second referendum from SNP leader Nicola Sturgeon, aided in this task by Minister for the Cabinet Office Ben Gummer. National security policy continued to captivate Hill, and she invested considerable energy into saving the Ministry of Defence budget, while throwing herself into a range of other causes, from working to improve prisons, to trying to orientate parts of the NHS towards exports. But much of her time was taken up with day-to-day management of No. 10, and although she tried to steer well clear of the press and communications, she failed to do so, with unhappy results, not least for those staff charged with this work.[12] Right up to her dismissal on the day after the 2017 general election, she remained May's closest female confidante. She had the clearest sense of anyone in No. 10 of what actions were necessary to make progress at home and in Europe, not least in leading the charge, from as early as October 2016, for an early general election as essential for May's agenda.[13]

Seven years younger than Hill, Timothy was only thirty-six when he became the most powerful figure in No. 10's policy-making. He had already known May for fourteen years, well over a third of his life. Timothy says, 'She had left a lot of the policy and communications to us in the Home Office, and probably relied on us if I'm totally honest to strategise for her as well. That continued in No. 10.'[14] Contemporaries differ about exactly how much of the May agenda came from her own head and how much from Timothy's. One member of the Policy Unit who worked with May and Timothy says, 'Every single thing Theresa May uttered of any significance came out of Nick Timothy's head. I never saw her say anything that wasn't from him. As soon as he went after the 2017 general election, she stopped saying anything fresh.' Tanner, deputy head of policy until the general election of 2017, takes a different view: 'It does a massive disservice to Theresa May to say Nick Timothy was the puppetmaster. What he did was to understand her world view and to translate it into policy. Nick Timothy was above all a translator.'[15]

One senior official they inherited from Cameron says of Timothy and Hill, 'They made her into Prime Minister. I don't think she would have gone on to be Prime Minister without them. They were both brilliant in many ways. Nick was one of the finest political strategists I have ever met, up there with Rupert Harrison [chief of staff to George Osborne].'

Whether two such capable people might have performed better and more harmoniously in and outside Downing Street if they had worked under a more assertive Prime Minister remains an open question. Insiders speculated why she did not intervene to alter their modus operandi and put them back in their box after concerns regarding their untrammelled power and style emerged as early as September 2016, only two months into her premiership. Some question whether she did in fact notice. Others wonder whether she cared, given that she owed her political life to them, knowing she was not yet strong enough to succeed without them, and she lacked the ability to command her Cabinet without them on the attack. Nick Timothy sums up the structural shortcomings:

> I think the problem was we appointed a Cabinet team that was pretty variable, and [we] didn't have the political authority or buy-in to get them to deliver. We probably were a bit too combative, which is fine in a department like the Home Office when you're trying to keep it going, but it's very different in No. 10.

Prime responsibility for failing to keep them in check falls on May. But why did senior officials, notably Cabinet Secretary Heywood and Principal Private Secretary Simon Case, not do more to intervene, given May's failure to do so? It appears they were wary of taking Hill and Timothy on. It was Heywood, after all, who had sealed Hill's fate when she was ejected from the Home Office in 2014. No. 10 officials were eager to prove their loyalty to the new May team. As one puts it:

> We were very aware of the intense resentment May, Timothy and Hill had towards No. 10 from the Home Office, and the suspicion that they had for the civil service machine. When they themselves moved into Downing Street, we thought it necessary and expedient to build a good working relationship with them.

Heywood was worried about his own survival for the first few weeks, knowing how closely associated he was in the minds of its chiefs with the Cameron premiership and its slights on her. He needed to make his number with them. So he was vexed about the bad blood they caused but was unsure what could be done to improve matters. Some think he was at fault for condoning the harassment of staff in No. 10, and equally that he went too far to appease Timothy on Brexit in 2016–17. Perhaps this was 'a stain', as one official put it, on Heywood's final period in office, but his approach, born of experience, had always been to pick his battles.

Timothy and Hill's relationship with some Cabinet ministers became intensely hostile. Their frustration with the lack of progress across departments led to barbed and cold relationships and escalating briefing wars with their teams. Within No. 10 itself, the relationships grew tense. Comparisons were made with the fractious No. 10 of Gordon Brown, another Prime Minister who found it hard to adjust from his former department to No. 10.[16] A series of May's wider team, including Case himself, his deputy Will Macfarlane, the Prime Minister's official spokesperson Helen Bower, director of communications Katie Perrior and press secretary Lizzie Loudon, all suffered at their hands. As the months passed, Timothy and Hill fell out more frequently with each other, their instructions confusing staff in No. 10 because they could be contradictory. An atmosphere of hesitance and worry arose in which staff were afraid of making mistakes or saying the wrong thing. The confusion spread across Whitehall. 'It's very difficult for Whitehall to run well when they can't have a clear sight of what the PM is really thinking,' comments one special advisor. Neither of the chiefs was strong at team building or adept at getting the best out of people. The internal drama and havoc surrounding the pair have been recounted at length by Tim Shipman in his magisterial *Fall Out*.[17] But we should be wary of making Timothy and Hill convenient scapegoats, as many became eager to do after the 2017 general election.

We should balance merited criticism with recognition that, having made her into a Prime Minister, they were in office during the most successful period of her premiership, when she was in an extended honeymoon period, and laid the foundations for her future agenda. A senior official who knew them well summed it up: 'They made her a better Prime Minister, if not always a better human being.' Since leaving No. 10, both chiefs of staff have reflected on their ten months in charge. Hill says:

> Looking back at it all and re-thinking it, we had too much power, too much authority. We were never elected. The reason we did is that she is not a policy person, and she let us. Her strengths were taking decisions presented to her: she was not good at working out what she wanted to do, either domestically or in foreign policy. We both had far more power than constitutionally we should have done. At no point did I feel, with the exception of Jeremy [Heywood], that anyone else was trying to shape what we were doing.[18]

Timothy reflects back in a different light:

> The joint chief of staff plan never worked. The model we had at the Home Office was of a joint and interoperable relationship across communications and across all policy. That was never going to work in Downing Street. Everything there is much quicker. You are pulled in many more directions. In No. 10, there is simply too much to do, and to be done at speed. All paper for her went through us: but that's how paper-based government works. So, yes, we controlled what she saw – but she wanted our advice. We were doing what she wanted us to do.[19]

MAY'S NO. 10 TEAM: RINGS OF INFLUENCE

No. 10 operates as a court, not at all unlike the Tudor and Stuart courts that swirled around the monarch just 100 yards to the east in the now all but demolished Whitehall Palace. Power in No. 10 was much more concentrated in May's first period as Prime Minister until the June 2017 general election than in the two years after, though all of No. 10 is becoming prone to the 'iron law of oligarchy'. We can best understand the influence that different figures had in her court by a series of concentric circles, recognising that, depending on the issue, some figures were more important than others. Nothing in No. 10 ever remains static; some wax in influence while others wane, though the core usually remains consistent.

In the inner circle were just four figures. There was May herself, of course, along with Timothy and Hill, who were akin to family, somewhere between the children she never bore and the siblings she never had. As in royal courts, May trusted very few and, like the monarch, when she gave her trust, she gave it uncritically. The final figure in the inner circle was her husband Philip, the best friend in her life: indeed, the only true friend in her life. Deeply proud of all that she'd achieved, he would play the part of consort with consummate skill, tirelessly supporting, encouraging and affirming her. But unlike some consorts, such as Denis Thatcher and Cherie Blair, he was without known opinions on many subjects. He did have views, however; though a Remainer, he was first and foremost a Conservative Party loyalist, accepting of the referendum result but fearful of a possible party split. In the first year, his views were particularly pronounced on one issue: whether to call an early general election. His concern, as ever, was to protect his beloved wife from unnecessary risk.

Six figures were in the next ring. The first, Jeremy Heywood, Cabinet Secretary since 2011 and the pre-eminent civil servant of his day, was a settled figure in the secondary circle of influence from the autumn. The very few officials May did trust had first to prove their loyalty and competence to her, as had Home Office Permanent Secretary Mark Sedwill and Director General of MI5 Andrew Parker. 'The civil servants she liked best were those who were older, experienced and male, and who she knew. She was particularly suspicious of women,' comments one official. Another observes:

To those of us who had worked for Cameron in No. 10, it felt like it was another political party coming in. The May team wanted to tear the official machine up and start all over again. It was the transition from Major to Blair in May 1997 all over again. They arrived looking as though they were a completely fresh party in the midst of enemies, with a deep distrust of any official who had advised her predecessor, but without a convincing story of why she herself wanted to be Prime Minister.

Heywood was something special, a civil servant with sublime technical, political and interpersonal skills. He had taken a break from the civil service between 2003 and 2007 to work at the investment bank Morgan Stanley before returning to bring focus to Brown's premiership.

Permanent Secretary in charge of domestic policy from June 2007, he was upgraded to Permanent Secretary of 10 Downing Street six months later. He knew he could not lead on all aspects of government policy personally and declared his priority areas, none more important than infrastructure, where he saw himself thinking thirty years ahead for the country. (Short term-focusing ministers rarely do this.) With May, he recognised she would be dominated by Brexit, and he would need to help find a 'Brexit-proof' agenda and legacy beyond the EU, hence his support for the 'three Hs' – Hinkley Point, HS2 and Heathrow's third runway. Education and STEM (science, technology, engineering and mathematics) were equally areas he invested time in, pushing for money to boost teacher supply, science and technology, and facilitating the inquiry to be headed by Philip Augar into the funding of further and higher education. This was announced in the 2017 manifesto, as was the government's social care policy, a running sore that had long needed addressing.

Clean energy and security of supply was another long-term issue facing the country that captivated Heywood. His enthusiasm for

Hinkley Point came from his desire to see diversity of supply, as was his staunch backing for fracking. The psychology of human behaviour intrigued him, and he was an enthusiastic backer of the government's Behavioural Insights Team, or, colloquially, the 'nudge unit'. He talked regularly to its head, David Halpern, but failed to persuade the chiefs of the merits of exploring nudge thinking across Whitehall and beyond – at least not to the extent he wished.

Heywood devoted considerable time to his job as head of the civil service, focusing on three areas: diversity, digitisation and commercialisation.[20] He was a hyperactive leader, and his Permanent Secretaries and No. 10 officials would receive regular emails challenging their thinking or recommending they read a novel, article or lecture, sent at all hours of the day and night, even at the weekend. Never an easy taskmaster, he would stress-test new proposals remorselessly with officials: but once convinced of their merits, he would be a tireless advocate for the policy with the Prime Minister.

Heywood was above all a Treasury person, with unrivalled knowledge of economics, trade and finance. A bigger figure than any Treasury mandarin, he was peerless across Whitehall. He ensured that, much to the Treasury's distaste after the Cameron days, when Osborne was left a largely free hand in Budgets and Autumn Statements, May's No. 10 should be active partners in key decisions. When Heywood spoke, everyone, even Treasury officials, took note. He had lacunae though, including foreign policy, and his knowledge of the workings of the EU was not profound, though it did not deflect him from his determination to deliver on the PM's Brexit policy, unsure of its clarity at times though he was.

Delivering for the Prime Minister of the day was his key feature, ensuring that they always had the advice of the official machine at their disposal. May, like the chiefs, recognised his value. Within weeks, they were going to say to him, 'We want the system to do this.' He then told them candidly if it could deliver for them. Heywood had made Brown a much more effective Prime Minister.[21] He had made the coalition work for Cameron and Nick Clegg. As long as he was by her side, there was a sense that May was going to be all right.

Heywood's signature skill of providing 'thinking round corners' solutions on the single most important item for the Prime Minister proved at first to be almost his undoing. To May and her team, he was 'Cameron's man', his agent and deliverer. 'Early on, a lot of people told us we had to get rid of him,' Timothy says. 'They were saying, "He's the master of the dark arts." But we said categorically, "No!"'[22] One senior Whitehall official adds, 'He had a dreadful relationship with the incoming Prime Minister. He worked flat out to build one. There was a sword of Damocles over him. He was suspended by a very thin thread. They wielded the sword and it could have cut the thread at any moment.'

Heywood was just fifty-four in July 2016 and could have earned vastly more money in a private sector eager to acquire him. But he saw it as his duty to stay in post and, as head of the civil service, guide the country through Brexit and beyond. So he ignored the rebuffs, and said, 'I kept sending them in material until they started listening.' One No. 10 official recalls how Heywood would 'just turn up at her 8.30 meeting in her study and insist he be included, and eventually was. But it took several months for him to be fully established.' Timothy rebuts this view: 'He was invited, and never excluded. We worked closely with him from the start. Even before Theresa went in, Fi and I worked from his office with him. I always felt my relationship with him was a good one.'

Wilkins observed how Heywood worked his magic: 'Jeremy very quickly changed the attitudes of people around her from suspicion to realising that he was indispensable. Quickly and adeptly, he got on board with her programme. He made them realise that he was wanting to help them achieve, not frustrate, their agenda.'[23] Hill knew better than anyone that Heywood, while delivering for Cameron, was a player with his dark side. But she was the first to grasp that this unconventional civil servant could work as effectively for them as he had done for Cameron, Brown, Blair and Major. Even while May was still Home Secretary, Hill had arranged quite frequent dates for May and Heywood to have dinner, via a friend in Heywood's private office. She was pivotal in ensuring that Heywood quickly gained May's trust. 'From early on, we didn't do anything without speaking to Jeremy. I can't recall a single decision we didn't run past him. She soon had a very respectful relationship with him,' she says.[24] Hill and Timothy worked with him to secure better settlements with the Ministry of Justice and the Ministry of Defence, on a trade deal with the Trump administration, developing the social care policy, industrial strategy and housing, and landing a succession of new appointments May wanted or needed.[25] John Godfrey, May's head of policy, speaks for May:

> Heywood was simply the best person in that building and had the most steadying influence. He would think ahead to every last detail. When we arrived, he helped us to work out how to do what we wanted to do. He knew everything about the machinery of government and would help us identify three or four things and then latch on to them.[26]

Heywood was diagnosed with cancer in June 2017, but witness after witness confirms that there was no slowing of his pace. Questions remain, though, on why he did not get a better grip on the dysfunctional No. 10 and its relations with sore Cabinet ministers, and whether his determination to prove himself to the new team prevented them doing more to challenge May's approach to Brexit.

Chris Wilkins and JoJo Penn were in the same ring of influence. Wilkins describes his role thus:

My job was to frame the government narrative, run all opinion research, help to write the speeches to drive the narrative forward, to oversee the grid, and to work closely on implementation, communication and policy. The conventional wisdom was that Nick and Fi helped create the persona of 'Theresa May the politician' [and] Nick, Fi and I created that of 'Theresa May the Prime Minister'. There's something in that.[27]

Another young, state-educated moderniser, Wilkins brought intellectual clarity and strategic acumen to the team, as well as his quality in speechwriting. A staunch advocate of an early general election, he found himself sidelined during the campaign and departed soon after.[28] Penn, meanwhile, was the only member of her close political team to survive the post-general election purge. Appointed deputy chief of staff when May arrived in No. 10, she continued to hold the title after the general election. 'I've pretty well done the same job all the way through despite the change of chiefs,' she said prior to May's resignation. 'My key job is to help advise and support the Prime Minister to allow her to do her job. I'm regularly in attendance at meetings with her, offer policy advice and try to coordinate the best possible opinion for her, working closely with the communications and speechwriting teams.'[29] Penn, steady, trusted and forever loyal, was the one No. 10 figure apart from Philip to remain throughout May's entire premiership. Joining her in the second circle of influence was Gavin Williamson, an inspired choice as Chief Whip, who used his vast knowledge of Conservative MPs to keep the party together in her honeymoon first ten months and became an increasingly influential and prominent voice in May's morning meetings at No. 10. The job suited Williamson's skills and character to perfection. Known as the 'smiling assassin', he was much better suited to it than to being a Cabinet minister, which ended in tears when he was dismissed as Defence Secretary in May 2019.

Two figures joined this outer-inner ring after May became Prime Minister. The first, James Slack, had been approached to become the Prime Minister's official spokesman (PMOS) as early as autumn 2016, when he was working for the *Daily Mail* as a close confidant to editor-in-chief Paul Dacre. Timothy and Hill had known Slack since Home Office days and had liked, rated and trusted him. Heywood, who had suffered gratuitously offensive stories in the *Daily Mail*, to which he was unable as an official to respond, was not enthusiastic. He didn't believe Slack would possess the qualities of trust and integrity needed for this sensitive, high-profile position. However, he also wanted to bring Antonia Romeo, an energetic protégé, back from the UN Consul General job in New York to be Permanent Secretary at the Department for International Trade (DIT).[30] A trade-off, Slack for Romeo, was duly negotiated. The PMOS is a Whitehall position, so a civil service commissioner oversaw the appointment process, out of which Slack emerged 'head and shoulders' above his competitors. Weeks of negotiation followed before he joined on 10 February 2017, replacing Helen Bower, who went on to a distinguished career as director of communications at the Foreign Office. Within weeks, Slack was embedded at the heart of May's team, widely liked and respected by all.

Ben Gummer didn't enter Parliament until 2010 but had already come to prominence as junior minister at the Department for Health after the 2015 general election. Heywood thought he would make an excellent choice as Minister for the Cabinet Office. May had little idea what the Cabinet Office did, still less the precise responsibilities of the minister in charge of it. Timothy confesses:

It was an appointment we weren't certain about, as we hadn't decided who should be Minister for the Cabinet Office and didn't know Ben very well. But Jeremy told us, 'The civil service think he's wonderful,' and the whips also told us, 'He's very good.' We knew he was very bright so took a punt. He was a great minister and he slotted in really well.[31]

Gummer himself recalls, 'My appointment was a huge surprise. I'd told her I was an Osborne supporter in the leadership campaign, and I wasn't expecting a post. My job was a merger of the policy work Francis Maude and the delivery work Oliver Letwin had done under Cameron.'[32] Like many in this ring, he was still under forty and fiercely passionate about the May policy cause. He had a meteoric rise after July 2016, handling his vast portfolio – including oversight of the civil service, the constitution, cyber security, implementation of policy, and Scotland – with unusual skill. In a Cabinet where May lacked friends and allies, he rapidly became the golden boy. Journalist Andrew Gimson wrote of Gummer in March 2017 that he had become 'the most important Minister whose role you've never heard of … Gummer enjoys the confidence of May and her advisers, who describe him as "first-class".'[33] Before long, he was being spoken of as 'the Deputy Prime Minister'. By early 2017, it was hard to find many areas of domestic policy in which Gummer was not involved. When Timothy had to find a co-author to write the Conservative manifesto before the general election in 2017, he turned to Gummer, fatefully, for this seminal task of envisioning the next five years.

Mark Sedwill was the final figure to join this circle when, in mid-April 2017, he moved across from Permanent Secretary at the Home Office to become National Security Advisor, replacing Mark Lyall Grant, who had held the post since September 2015. Lyall Grant had many of the properties that May admired in officials – older, experienced and male. He equally had many of the characteristics she loathed – Etonian, Foreign Office, a Cameron loyalist and, she thought, condescending. May wanted to replace him with someone she liked and rated, viewing him as a diplomat in a security position, the world she knew best. Lyall Grant was a consistently poor performer on civil service annual appraisals, and Heywood supported May's reasoning. He attempted to remove him in the first week of May's premiership, but Hill persuaded Heywood that Lyall Grant should serve out the remaining six months until his retirement, a decision she would later regret.[34]

The middle circle contained a range of figures, several of whom grew in importance during the ten months preceding the general election. Will Tanner joined No. 10 as deputy chief of policy. His creative mind and performance in the Home Office saw him become May's most influential policy advisor besides Timothy till the general election, after which he resigned to co-found the right-of-centre think tank Onward. 'I was involved in both the economic and social sides, managing the output and ensuring that policy development was operationally effective,'[35] he says. Olly Robbins, appointed Permanent Secretary of the new DExEU Department, was the dominant voice below Timothy's on Brexit. Another Home Office import, he had been Second Permanent Secretary to Sedwill since September 2015, where his responsibilities included immigration, borders and free movement (until Heywood plucked him into the Cabinet Office the day after the referendum). Briefly Principal Private Secretary to the Prime Minister at the time of the transition from Tony Blair to Gordon Brown, he was another Heywood protégé who possessed some of his boss's gifts for making himself indispensable to new teams. Robbins did not enjoy an easy relationship, though, with the DExEU Secretary of State, David Davis, and aroused the ire of some Brexiteers. But generally he worked well in the first ten months with Timothy, who says:

Olly was the kind of person Theresa May liked working with. He fitted her mould. The risk was, as she didn't trust politicians, she placed too much trust in officials. In the endless meetings in the PM's office on Brexit, Olly Robbins was present, but no David Davis. Olly and I worked well together on Brexit. Back then he was definitely responsive to the political directions he was given by the PM, directly and through me.[36]

Further out was another circle of influence, containing figures who were powerful operators on narrower fields. Will Macfarlane, a Treasury civil servant and Deputy Principal Private Secretary to the Prime Minister, oversaw the intensely fraught relationship between May and Hammond, working closely with Heywood to restore it to some functionality. Simon Case, Macfarlane's boss, though never enjoying a comfortable relationship with May, Timothy and Hill, kept No. 10 functioning and communications flowing at a difficult time in its history. Within the private office, and below Case and Macfarlane, Jonny Hall became an increasingly influential Foreign Affairs private secretary, albeit not the commanding figure of some of his predecessors before the National Security Advisor post was created in 2010. Lizzie Loudon, Alex Dawson, political secretary Stephen Parkinson and government relations director Chris Brannigan were talented and dedicated aides, whose fortunes and influence rose and fell over the first ten months.

Finally, an outer ring consisted of figures like policy chief John Godfrey and legal advisor Harry Carter. It contained, too, a number of those who fell out with May's team, including Katie Perrior, Helen Bower, Mark Lyall Grant and Ivan Rogers, the UK's Permanent Representative to the EU until January 2017 and a leading sceptic on the line taken by May on Brexit. Perrior was involved in the leadership campaign, but her appointment to the major position of director of communications at No. 10 was not a best fit with her talents. She was never intended to be a permanent team member. One official comments, 'Had it continued as expected until a September denouement, Hill and Timothy would have discovered that her strengths were not those which the job demanded.' Another working on the campaign expresses surprise: 'It was not clear that she was directing comms during the campaign. Fi was doing that and Lizzie [Loudon] was doing much more than Katie was. I had imagined that Fi was going to be director of comms and Lizzie press sec.' Perrior became increasingly disgruntled and was a vocal critic of the two chiefs after she resigned in April 2017.

MAY'S TIMETABLE

No. 10 is a fluid place, surprisingly so considering its work. To compound the absence of a written constitution listing a Prime Minister's powers, the lack of any job description for a Prime Minister or for the staff they bring in with them is the absence of any agreed plan for how best the Prime Minister and their team can optimise their effectiveness and time. Every new Prime Minister and team bursts into No. 10 supercharged on adrenalin, with only a very subjective and slim understanding of how to make it work. Needless pain and time are squandered while they learn. Some never do. Cameron rapidly fell into the routine of convening in his office an 8.30 morning meeting and one to take stock at 4 p.m. With no time to prepare, May simply adopted the Cameron plan. As Penn says, 'The PM, though, soon dropped the afternoon meeting as it was not practical bringing everyone together – though occasionally we would have an informal stock-take amongst ourselves.'[37] Timothy adds, 'The purpose of the 8.30 meeting changed too. It was more about Theresa's own day and less about handling the politics and media of the day's events.'

May was always anxious to get away from No. 10 on Thursday evening to be in her constituency on Friday, even if she was going to Chequers at the weekend. Prime Ministers' parliamentary constituencies are often ignored as they focus on bigger affairs, but, for May, Maidenhead was of primary importance, socially, politically and emotionally. She liked Chequers too – not all Prime Ministers do – and went there as often as she could, enjoying being looked after by the staff, which freed up her time to relax and work.[38] On Mondays, the 8.30 a.m. meeting would often be held as late as 10.30 a.m. so she could come up from Maidenhead or Chequers for it.

She quickly decided she did not want to work in the Cabinet Room, as some Prime Ministers do, but from the office at its east end, first selected by Blair after 1997, which became known as his den. Brown worked from No. 12, but Cameron also used this room for six years. May was at pains to make the room more businesslike, stripping out the settees and establishing a glass oval table in the middle, around which the team sat. The 8.30 morning meeting was preceded in her first year by a presentation and communications meeting held in the Cabinet Room at 8 a.m., chaired by Timothy or Hill initially, but subsequently by Penn after they grew tired of it. May herself then chaired the 8.30 a.m. meeting, which would often last half an hour. Case and Macfarlane would circulate an agenda before the start of the meeting, covering the media, parliamentary day and other business. The regular cast list was substantial: Timothy and Hill, Heywood, Wilkins, Perrior, Penn, Brannigan, Parkinson, Dawson, Tanner, Macfarlane, Case himself and Slack (after he joined in 2017). Several parliamentarians had standing invitations too: Gummer, Williamson and Leader of the House of Lords Natalie Evans. Cabinet meetings were held from 9.30 to 11 on Tuesday mornings. May would prepare meticulously for them and took great pains to conduct them in a businesslike way, respectful of the views of her colleagues. Heywood sat alertly by her side, never intervening on substance but pointing out if he spotted a minister wanting to speak.

In contrast to Cameron, May liked to receive written submissions, and she would take immense trouble over the papers in her Prime Minister's box, which she would work through meticulously – laboriously, indeed – every evening. At first, she went off to Maidenhead with just one box on Thursday evening for the weekend, but soon her workload mounted, not the least with Brexit, so more boxes were sent off to her over the weekend. Cameron had a much more instinctive trust of advice he was given by his officials, so his box notes were often brief. May wanted more information given to her. It meant more paperwork and, with Timothy and Hill expecting to comment on all submissions to her, a much slower decision-making process.

In No. 10, proximity to the Prime Minister denotes power. Off the anteroom to the Cabinet Room, at the end of the long corridor from the front door into Downing Street, lie two rooms. In the room nearest the Cabinet Room itself, the chiefs had their base, and held their confidential meetings there. It was nicknamed by Timothy and Hill 'the bollocking room', because, when Cameron was still Prime Minister, that was where they were called in from the Home Office to receive dressings-down. Wilkins sat in the second of the two rooms which were off from the left of the anteroom. May's study was through the double doors to the right at the end of the Cabinet Room. Beyond that lay the long oblong room used by her staff. The table immediately to the left was where the chiefs used to work, facing each other. Opposite them sat the Principal and Deputy Principal Private Secretaries, and behind them sat Penn and the duty clerks.

For thirty minutes on 13 July 2016, No. 10 was in suspended animation while it clapped Cameron as the outgoing Prime Minister, before clapping in Theresa May as the new boss. 'From the very first second, the very vast difference was clear,' recalls Ed Whiting, deputy PPS. 'In their personality, approach, energy levels, intellectual curiosity, methods of problem-solving, the contrast could not have been starker. May was very methodical. She wanted everything orderly and ordered. She wanted to know what was happening next.'[39] The easy-going 'chumocracy' of Cameron's day was over. No. 10 is always a reflection of the personality of the Prime Minister. With May, it was more anxious and formal. It was smokier, too. Hill, Penn, Godfrey and Tanner were among the regular smokers. There was a regular procession down the stairs and out into the garden till May asked them to stop smoking outside.[40] There was also more drinking – if not at receptions then after work. No. 10 had become a more high-stakes, if less healthy, place.

APPOINTING HER CABINET TEAM

Prime Ministers are often surprised at how little executive power they have: they are critically dependent on the capability and loyalty of their Cabinet ministers, above all in the great departments of the Treasury, the Foreign Office, Home Office and Defence as well as, in the past twenty-five years, the delivery departments of Education, Health and Welfare. Yet over the course of her first year May had become disappointed, with very few of her Cabinet measuring up to the expectation that she and the chiefs had of them. Within just months, even before the general election in 2017, they had become the least loyal and cohesive Cabinet in modern British political history, with a complete breakdown in collective Cabinet responsibility and the highest resignation rate since 1945 after the election.

It began so promisingly. Tuesday 12 July was crunch day, with key decisions on Cabinet taken by May and the chiefs, and with significant input from Heywood, as well as Williamson, whom she elevated from her campaign manager to Chief Whip. In the brief time they had to construct the Cabinet, they had two major principles in mind: repaying loyalty and the mantra 'Brexit abroad, social reform at home'.[41]

Reducing the overall size of Cabinet was another major objective, as was marking a return to Cabinet government and Cabinet committees, after the overly casual style of Cameron and Blair, with his renowned 'sofa government'. They aimed to make the government more socially meritocratic, with only a fifth of her ministerial appointments having attended private schools (as opposed to half under Cameron), though she failed to live up to her ambition to appoint more women.[42] May announced that she would set up four new committees to help her achieve her primary objectives, including one on Brexit. She was to chair all of them – one sees Heywood's influence here, but also how deeply May's Home Office mindset ran; it was in part modelled on what she knew and liked about the National Security Council. But she was to fall a long way short of restoring either Cabinet government or the classic model of Cabinet committees, which had not existed properly since the days of Thatcher.[43] Before the autumn of 2016, the key decisions were back to being taken in No. 10, and with the exception of the National Security Council, which played to her strengths, the much-vaunted restoration of Cabinet committees chaired by her came to little.

To deliver on Brexit, and to help Britain prepare for the new post-Brexit world, she appointed four figures, all prominent Brexiteers. David Davis, who had been planning to back Boris before coming over to her camp, needed a senior job as one of the party's biggest beasts, a credible challenger for the party leadership in 2001 and 2005 and a prominent Brexiteer. He had a close relationship with Hill dating back fifteen years to when he was party chairman. They thought he had the bluster and personality, as well as the credibility with the right of the party, to drive Brexit through, so chose him as DExEU Secretary.[44]

Liam Fox was appointed to run the newly created Department for International Trade. Another high-profile MP, in 2011 he had been removed from the post of Defence Secretary after then Cabinet Secretary Gus O'Donnell deemed he had breached the ministerial code. Priti Patel became International Development Secretary. The biggest surprise of the reshuffle was the fourth Brexiteer, Boris Johnson, going to the Foreign Office. Labour MP Kevin Brennan caught some of the popular reaction when he said that making Johnson Foreign Secretary was 'the strangest move since Caligula appointed his horse a senator'.[45]

It was May's own decision to give him the Foreign Office, feeling that he had been badly treated by Gove in the leadership contest, seeing him as a potential asset, and wanting to give him a chance to show that he could be a thoughtful and effective Cabinet minister. 'He was deeply surprised in his brief interview in the Cabinet Room when May said, "I've decided to give you a really big job,"' Hill says, recalling Johnson's eyes watering.[46] Timothy remembers the conversation in the Cabinet Room:

> She told Boris, 'I want you to be my Foreign Secretary.' He was blown away, gobsmacked, and said, 'This is a great honour,' and how much he wanted the job. He then added, 'I feel, having played a part in making Brexit happen, a real responsibility in making sure that it works out.' I remember wondering if he was entirely sure whether it would work out. The PM then started talking about creating DExEU and DIT. He sounded suspicious but didn't challenge her. She then said, 'You and I have a patchy history, but I know there are two Borises. A deadly serious, intellectual, capable and very effective person; and a playing-around Boris. I want this to be your opportunity to show you can be the former.' I remember thinking at the time if that was a bit supercilious and wondered if she had been wise to say it. But anyway, he took it on the chin.[47]

Some later speculated that she set him up for a fall, knowing that he would disappoint as Foreign Secretary. 'That was not in her mind in appointing him,' both Timothy and Hill assert. But senior officials in the Foreign Office had a different take: 'It was a mistake to appoint a known enemy to Foreign Secretary. She never trusted him and he knew she never trusted him. For the relationship between Prime Minister and Foreign Secretary to work, there has to be trust. There was such hostility. It was awful.'

To balance the four Brexiteers, they put in social reformers to the domestic departments, drawn from the centre-left of the party with strong Remain credentials. Hence she appointed Justine Greening to a beefed-up Education Department, with increased responsibilities for higher education and apprenticeships. Amber Rudd was slotted into May's old department, the Home Office, while Damian Green went to the Department for Work and Pensions. Despite rumours that he was to be moved, they quickly decided to leave Jeremy Hunt at Health, a post he had held steadily since September 2012. Another steady performer, Michael Fallon, Defence Secretary since July 2014, was also left in post. Andrea Leadsom, her challenger for the leadership, was promoted from Energy to the Department for Environment, Food and Rural Affairs (DEFRA).

May's personal imprint was very much felt on the last major appointment of the reshuffle: Philip Hammond as Chancellor. She'd had a fairly good working relationship with him under Cameron, and she wanted someone on whom she could utterly depend, who would be serious and respected, not least with market concerns just three weeks after the referendum. She had signalled during the leadership campaign that Osborne's fiscal policy would be eased; she wanted someone who would be in line with her working agenda, and she thought it was Hammond. Despite May's work at the Bank of England, her understanding of economics and finance was limited, another reason she needed somebody completely solid. 'She's fiscally conservative, but, like all PMs, she likes spending money. She was pro-small business but sceptical about big business. She thought fiscal discipline was good and inflation was bad, so she was really quite conventional,' comments Hammond.[48]

She didn't have to appoint Hammond. She could have appointed Rudd to the Treasury, though part of the reason she put Rudd in the Home Office was to ensure her successor wouldn't be too liberal on immigration. May saw herself in Rudd – somebody who would have to try to control immigration while enacting social reforms. One team member laments, 'She was wrong – Amber didn't try to control immigration, and despite being adamant she wanted Hammond, believing they got on and had similar views, the opposite was the case. It's been very surprising how little May knew her colleagues, and has been one of the biggest weaknesses of her premiership.'

She could even have left Osborne in post as Chancellor, but she considered him unappointable as the creator of 'Project Fear' in the referendum campaign. Hill later regarded the callous sacking of Osborne as 'the biggest mistake we made; we never even debated it'.[49] The chiefs had no illusions about Osborne, knowing that he had been remorselessly plotting against her, as indeed they had been plotting against him. During the referendum campaign in particular, they suspected Osborne had been gunning for May, including threatening to sack her. But they had thought he had done pretty well overall as Chancellor. Hill thinks on reflection May could have told him, 'I know you want to be Prime Minister, and I'll work with you to make it happen when I give up.'[50] Timothy debated whether they should offer Osborne the post of Defence Secretary: 'It would have been difficult for him given the Conservative Party's commitments to the armed forces, but equally it would have been bad for her too if he had turned it down. On balance, we decided not to do it.'[51]

But the manner in which she told Osborne about his departure, and his perception of May's team as trashing his economic record, led to an even deeper enmity that rebounded against her in the months and years to come. So too did the reshuffle, a virtual cleanout of Osborne's closest allies, with Sajid Javid moved sideways and down from Business to Housing, Communities and Local Government, Matt Hancock becoming a junior minister, and Oliver Letwin dismissed. Osborne had been Cameron's right-hand man for eleven years, five in opposition and six in government. He had been more than Chancellor of the Exchequer: in many ways, he had operated as joint Prime Minister.[52] He had for several years been promoting allies and colleagues to test their suitability for his future government. How she handled Osborne as heir presumptive would be a litmus test for her.

Osborne has a clear recollection of his meeting with her on Wednesday 13 July:

She came back from Buckingham Palace in the early evening. I was up in my flat above No. 10 where I had been told to wait for her to call. Very shortly after her return, I was summoned down. It was just me and her, nobody else. 'Congratulations, Prime Minister,' I said, thinking I must have been one of the first to say that. 'It still feels very strange,' she replied, before continuing swiftly, 'Look, there is no space for you in the administration.' I could take that, but then she went on to say, 'I hope you understand if I give you some advice as an "older sister". You need to get to know the Conservative Party better.' Our meeting finished very soon after that. I couldn't wait to get out of the room. I was told to leave by the back door. It was all quite shocking. Downing Street was where I lived with my wife and children. Dismissing me was a perfectly reasonable call for a Prime Minister wanting to have a new Chancellor. But she could have handled it so much better. They gave no thought to how they should conduct the interview. Nor to how I might react. They could have told me in advance and allowed me to walk out with David Cameron so I could have coupled my resignation with his. She could have said, 'You've done so much for the party. I'm sorry that there's no space for you, but I'm grateful for your six years as Chancellor.' If you were getting rid of a supply teacher, you might have said at least that to them. They could then have briefed how valuable I had been. Instead they briefed that I got it wrong on Brexit and needed to learn. I was told just to clear out. It was like an out-of-body experience. I couldn't believe I was on the wrong end of such an amateur way of doing business.[53]

The rage Osborne felt towards May rebounded against him. Had he shown more sangfroid, and not resigned his seat in high dudgeon, he would have been in pole position to have succeeded her, perhaps as early as straight after the general election.

Gove was the other principal Cameron Cabinet minister not given a job. But May considered he had been a 'double betrayer', by supporting Vote Leave and by stabbing Johnson in the back. She didn't want him to be in permanent exile, though. One aide summarises the situation: 'Gove listened to her implicit message and went off quietly to the back benches; Osborne concluded there was no way back and decided to declare war.' Osborne says he would have stayed in the House of Commons rather than resigning his Tatton seat in May 2017 if 'there had been any indication at all she had wanted me'.[54] After he took on the editorship of the *London Evening Standard* in May 2017, he took revenge on her in the paper's columns. He was famously reported to have said to more than one person that he wouldn't rest 'until she is chopped up in bags in my freezer'.[55]

May's team had agonised over Gove. Timothy saw the advantage of giving him a post, but Hill was clear that 'there could be no job for him, because of his standing in the party. Perhaps in the future, but not now.'[56] Heywood was tight-lipped. The establishment, including Whitehall and Buckingham Palace, had concerns about Gove's judgement and ability to retain confidential information. Some blamed him for a story in *The Sun* in which the Queen was reported to have said that the EU was heading 'in the wrong direction', which led to a headline in the paper during the referendum campaign: 'Queen Backs Brexit'. Gove played the game, and a year later was back in Cabinet as Environment Secretary.[57]

Nicky Morgan was another to be shown the door. While Education Secretary, she had a series of clashes with May, including over the latter's plan to have parents confirm their right to be in the country if their children attended a school, which Morgan said she found abhorrent. A convinced Osbornite, she made no secret of her leadership preferences.[58] To May's surprise, Morgan told her team that she would back her, but instead she backed Johnson and then Gove. The antipathy was mutual. Neither May nor Timothy rated her work or philosophy as Education Secretary. Disposing of her was an easy decision.[59]

May had intended to reappoint Stephen Crabb as her Work and Pensions Secretary. But when he was unable to provide the assurances over his personal life that she had demanded after *The Times* broke the story that he was embroiled in a sexting scandal, she put Damian Green into the slot. She had originally planned to make Green Culture Secretary, so this provided a hole for the Home Office junior minister Karen Bradley to fill. James Brokenshire, another Home Office loyalist, was rewarded with Northern Ireland Secretary. Others, like Dominic Raab, were victims of the sheer speed of the appointments operation. Because of his family, Raab said he didn't want a job with foreign travel. But the message that came back to her team was that he did want a foreign job. When offered one at DIT, he turned it down.

'Ruthless' was how the appointments process was described by former Conservative Foreign Secretary Malcolm Rifkind.[60] It certainly stunned many in her party who expected her to build incrementally on the Cameron legacy. It was widely seen as a 'radical reboot'.[61] Timothy denies this was their intention: 'The reshuffle was knowingly radical but it looked bloody; we didn't mean it to be so.'[62]

One official observes:

I remember thinking how odd and different to Cameron she was in her appointments, because when she finished talking about what her sheet had given to her to say, she had absolutely nothing further to offer. She wasn't able to extemporise or respond to the feelings of the minute. George Osborne, Michael Gove and Nicky Morgan were all in various states of disappointment, without hope or clear direction as to what they could do to return to the top of the party.

May enjoyed the power she now had but found the meetings stressful, and once the Cabinet appointments were over on Saturday, she heaved a sigh of relief. Tellingly, she didn't know many of her fellow MPs at all well, so was content to leave the appointment of Ministers of State to Williamson and Heywood, both of whom had seen potential candidates perform close up under Cameron. According to one watching the process, Williamson had a very clear view of what he wanted from the party for it to work for the Prime Minister. 'By the time he got down to Parliamentary Secretaries,' Williamson says, 'Heywood was no longer directly involved, and I appointed most of them because she didn't know their names!'[63] 'When I was appointed Chief Whip, there was really an astonishing ignorance of Conservative MPs in No. 10!'

As Cabinet ministers assembled in No. 10 for their first full Cabinet meeting on Tuesday 19 July, they had confidence in their new leader. They sensed they were about to make history. Her premiership had begun.

MAY'S PREMIERSHIP: THE FIRST THREE MONTHS

Arriving back in No. 10 after seeing the Queen in Buckingham Palace, May was applauded into the building through the long corridor behind the door by many of the same staff who had clapped out Cameron shortly beforehand. His political team had left quietly through the Cabinet Office into Whitehall, many in tears. But the timing had been mishandled, and they bumped into May's political team arriving. There were words of congratulations and a few awkward hugs. 'The tension would have been much higher had Craig Oliver been there,' says one.

Now in the Cabinet Room, May was at last at peace, with Philip by her side and Timothy and Hill, Heywood, Case and Penn also present. May's premiership began with an awkward silence. The two civil servants looked at their feet, waiting for her to say something. At last, Timothy could stand it no longer, and burst out with a comment to Penn, who had been planning to join Uber after her recent return from Harvard: 'I bet you're glad you didn't take the job.' Looking back, he says, 'It was a random thing to say, but someone had to break the silence.'[64]

Many Prime Ministers – Wilson, Heath, Thatcher, Blair and Cameron come to mind – begin their time at No. 10 with a riot of furious activity, as if they don't have a second to waste. Not so with May. Officials were surprised that 'the pace was really quite slow'. Timothy and Hill were beavering away, but on Brexit in particular there was no obvious fresh direction from on high. 'I can't recall any major drive,' said one official, an assertion Timothy adamantly disagrees with – a reflection of officials being sidelined by the new team. Upstairs in the Policy Unit, Godfrey and Tanner busied themselves on planning the domestic agenda: mental health, social inclusion, employment and education.[65] 'We were very clear that whilst Brexit was going to be very important, it should only be part of the whole story of her premiership,' says Godfrey.[66] Timothy, meanwhile, was like a whirling dervish. Having taken his holiday in Sicily during the referendum campaign, he remained in No. 10 working seven-day weeks throughout the rest of July and August.[67] Increasingly concerned and agitated that others did not share his urgency, his attention focused on May herself.

> I was finding the PM a bit frustrating because she wasn't engaging with the agenda that much. I kept thinking that there was work to be done for the party conference speech, but I was pushing against a brick wall. Chris Wilkins and I spent a lot of time trying to develop the thinking for conference.[68]

May was enjoying being Prime Minister, spending much of her first two weeks travelling, including trips to Scotland, Wales and Northern

Ireland, as well as Berlin to visit Angela Merkel, and Paris to see François Hollande. May's team quickly discovered they lacked a figure like the legendary Liz Sugg, who had planned all of Cameron's trips with military efficiency. Sarah Bartholomew, who had worked on the Olympics in 2012, rose to fill the vacuum and became one of the first officials to gain the trust of her team. May was enchanted by the trappings of office, especially her audiences with the Queen, whom she had always revered.

The early trips to Scotland, Wales and Northern Ireland were deliberate. A Unionist to her fingertips, she wanted to make a point about restating the case for the United Kingdom immediately after the referendum. The chiefs were strong supporters: 'Fi was brilliant at remembering to prod her to talk about all four nations, especially Scotland, at each and every opportunity,' says Tanner. 'Much work was done to highlight the failures of the devolved governments where it was seen they had not delivered.'[69] On Northern Ireland, she frequently sat in on meetings about the border and restoring devolved government, but happily delegated much of the task of bringing the Northern Irish parties back to the table to the ever-loyal Brokenshire.

In the second week of August, she and Philip left for a ten-day break to Switzerland. The Alps had been a regular holiday destination during their three and a half decades of their marriage, with Lucerne and Zermatt particular favourites: 'The views are spectacular, the air is clear and you can get some peace and quiet,' she said.[70] Hill worked to ensure that her holiday was kept light of boxes: 'We did a lot of looking after her, and wanted her to have a proper break to return refreshed.'[71]

May's first major international event would be the G20 summit at Hangzhou on 4–5 September. Her main public task was to reassure her fellow G20 leaders that the UK would be a 'dependable partner' and was 'open for business', especially given discouraging remarks from President Obama, who had said that the US would prioritise trade with the EU and Pacific nations.[72] It provided May's first opportunity to meet Chinese President Xi Jinping, President Obama himself and President Putin.

The British Prime Minister is a prominent leader on the world stage, especially with Brexit looming, and May was short on experience here too. Hill spoke to her about the importance of forging personal relationships, never her strong suit, and, to make matters more difficult, May made it clear to her that she couldn't see the need or purpose of doing so. It was too far outside her comfort zone. Hill worked particularly hard pushing May to form a personal relationship with Russian leader Vladimir Putin, coaching her in the importance of bilateral relationships if she was to make the impact that she needed to internationally. Hill thought that Putin had been very deferential to her, and on the way to Hangzhou Airport, she said to May in the back of her official car, 'I think you should try and start a new kind of relationship with Putin. It might yield benefits, including in Syria. I think you should go to Moscow.' May would have none of it: 'There is absolutely no way I want a relationship with that man,' she said adamantly. End of conversation.

Two weeks later, she spoke at the annual UN General Assembly in New York. Friends of Antonia Romeo, the British Consul General, say that at the dinner in the British Consulate afterwards, with a large group of chief executives, what struck Romeo was the way that May let the chief executives talk over her, without showing that she minded at all. Romeo reportedly thought it a clever move.

FORGING NEW RELATIONSHIPS: PARLIAMENT, THE PARTY AND THE PRESS

May had to learn the job of being Prime Minister in many fresh areas. As we have seen, the task was rendered more difficult because, unlike Blair and Cameron, she hadn't had experience as Leader of the

Opposition. She was quite extraordinarily apprehensive as she prepared in No. 10 for her first PMQs on 20 July, one week after taking office. Few Prime Ministers acquitted themselves so impressively on their first outing. When the PMQs team – a mixture of special advisors and officials – met together that morning, they were fairly certain that Corbyn would try to go for her on her Downing Street doorstep speech. One of the team, official Ed de Minckwitz, came up with the line that won her the day. After Corbyn asked her to expand on what she had said about 'unscrupulous bosses', she replied:

> I suspect there are many members on the opposition benches who might be familiar with an unscrupulous boss; a boss who doesn't listen to his workers; a boss who requires some of his workers to double their workload; and maybe even a boss who exploits the rules to further his own career.

She then leant forward from the dispatch box and delivered the punchline, in a style eerily reminiscent of Thatcher: 'Remind him of anybody?' When her team saw her afterwards, she couldn't believe she had managed to pull it off so successfully. Her knees were still knocking together as she prepared for her imminent departure that afternoon to see Merkel in Berlin.

May wanted to treat the House of Commons with conspicuous respect, in contrast to how she felt Cameron behaved. It went down particularly well with Speaker John Bercow, who had a famously poor relationship with her predecessor. May reassured Bercow in private early on that she would be respectful of Parliament, and he was impressed that she was committed to taking the House seriously. You can see this in the evident warmth of his greeting to her at his first Prime Minister's Questions on 20 July. Her relationship with Bercow did not nosedive until well after the 2017 general election, when it did so spectacularly. Parliament brought out May's best personal qualities:

remembering her brief, having a firm grip on detail and visibly treating others with respect. But despite taking the Commons much more seriously than Blair, Brown or Cameron, she never truly mastered it with the easy confidence some Prime Ministers had, and while Corbyn rarely created serious difficulties for her, she never really nailed him, as a defter Prime Minister would have done.

May has loved the Conservative Party all her life and spent thousands of hours at association events and dinners. She was at her most relaxed with her Maidenhead constituency faithful. But she wasn't comfortable spending time with Conservative MPs. Gavin Williamson tried in vain, telling her:

'While you're riding high, build capital.' I wanted her to go to the House of Commons Tea Rooms after PMQs and chat to people, but she wouldn't do that. She preferred a Pret A Manger salad in her room in the House of Commons. She never got it: she was never interested in talking to MPs or inviting them to parties at No. 10 or Chequers.[73]

May was never confident or happy talking to journalists and didn't see the point in giving them her time. Her team's initial approach to the media was to try to control the flow of information to a handful of friendly journalists, as she had done at the Home Office, including James Slack at the *Daily Mail*, Tim Shipman at the *Sunday Times*, Francis Elliott at *The Times* and Tom Newton Dunn of *The Sun*. It took time for them to understand that she could not control information at No. 10 in the same way as at the Home Office. To the frustration of the professional communications team she had at her disposal, May didn't want to step up to the very different world of dealing with the media as Prime Minister, as opposed to Home Secretary.

'She was no good at charming editors or journalists,' says one observer. 'Her attitude was "Why should we bother trying to win them over?" She didn't read newspapers and was not particularly eager to know what they were saying: indeed, it is curious how lacking in curiosity she was.' It is hard to think of a Prime Minister since Clement Attlee who was less concerned to impress the press, or who took so little interest in journalists. Even Churchill, especially in his peacetime premiership, was obsessed by newspapers and his relationship with their owners.[74]

May was at her least comfortable with newspaper editors. Tony Gallagher of *The Sun* decided early on that he didn't rate her, but his paper kept supporting her. John Witherow of *The Times* took exception to some of her policy approaches, including putting workers on boards and the return of grammar schools, and regarded her as lightweight. Neither did he like her backing of the third runway at Heathrow, nor Hinkley Point, No. 10 aides believed. Chris Evans, editor of the *Daily Telegraph*, had lunch with her in the early autumn, but the conversation was difficult and laboured: 'She'd answer his questions and then run out of things to say.' With none was there any rapport, fun conversation or small talk.

Newspaper profiles were seen as a way of compensating. A notable early interview was with Tim Shipman of the *Sunday Times* in October 2016. He had checked with No. 10 if they were happy for him to ask how she felt about her parents no longer being alive to see her become Prime Minister. Fine, they responded. The aide prepping her said she fell totally silent when the question was put to her, so they suggested how they felt in a similar situation after their father passed away before being able to see them in No. 10. May didn't react. So the aide was surprised when May in her interview repeated to Shipman verbatim, 'I wish my parents could see it ... They would be extremely proud of me. I hope they would be.'

It proved to be one of the most revealing interviews of her premiership, helped by the trust that she and her team had built up with Shipman over the years. On her brand of Conservatism, she said,

'I'm always a bit suspicious of "isms". I do want a government that works for everybody, not a privileged few. That's my driving force.' No references were offered to any political influences or to being stimulated by any particular political tradition or philosophy. Hers was a Conservatism born from her experience of life. What about her political heroes? She mentioned none. She refused even to be drawn on Margaret Thatcher: 'I haven't had a role model in my political career.' Well, what had influenced her most in her life? Another significant admission: 'I don't analyse things in that sense,' she replied. Moving on to the present, he coaxed out of her more disarmingly honest answers. Why had she not done more in her first eleven weeks to make progress on Brexit? She didn't want to verbalise her thoughts but referred him to her speech she was to deliver that day at the party conference, in which she was to say, 'Today marks the first stage of the UK becoming a sovereign and independent country.' What about calling a general election before 2020? There was no apprehension that this would be such a defining question of her premiership. She replied, 'I think an early general election would introduce a note of instability for people … This isn't about political games, it's about what is right for the country.'

The interview turned to softer territory. She steered clear of claiming a cultural or intellectual hinterland: 'Philip and I both enjoy walking, and I love cooking.' She had not found time to read since she'd returned from Switzerland in August, but she liked Donna Leon crime thrillers set in Venice, and *The Razor's Edge* by Somerset Maugham (whose principal figure, a veteran of the First World War, abandons his wealthy friends and lifestyle to seek spiritual enlightenment in India). A curious choice, but suggestive perhaps of her own rejection of upper-class privilege, and her own beliefs, which she was at pains to avoid talking about. Christianity was the great unexplored theme, a faith she shared totally with husband Philip. She never spoke about it, even to practising Christians close to her, not even to Hill (a Roman

Catholic), though Gummer, whose grandfather was also a clergyman, thought that sense of duty 'was the reason she got up in the morning'.[75] An official who knew her as well as anyone said her faith was 'utterly defining, but she never wanted to be defined by it'. She relied on her Christian faith for the strength to keep going through adversity.

Never before or since had May given so much away in a public profile, all the more remarkable because she has been one of the shyest and most introverted of Britain's fifty-four Prime Ministers. As a footnote, Shipman copied in his article the message he had received from the newspaper's transcription service: 'Theresa May is a very nice woman and the transcriber thoroughly enjoyed listening to her,' adding his observation: 'No one has sent such a message to me about a politician before.'[76]

Jason Cowley, editor of the *New Statesman*, was another to press for an early interview. He had become intrigued by her new vision for Conservativism, with an active role for the state, a rejection of the unbridled free market, and a vision of a just society. In her readiness to interpret the electorate's rejection of the EU as part of the 'mass disaffection', he saw echoes of the thinking of *New Statesman* luminary John Gray.[77] Was this a sea change in politics, he wondered? *The Guardian*'s Rafael Behr was another to believe that May's agenda could pose a credible challenge to Corbyn's Labour Party. It did not take long for them to realise that the mind behind the thinking was not May's but Timothy's, and their interest soon waned.

When May first became Prime Minister, Corbyn telephoned her and they swapped pleasantries for three or four minutes. The look on her face, aides thought, told them she thought, 'He is really weird.' She had no respect for him, nor any time. The relationship between a Prime Minister and Leader of the Opposition is often strained, but theirs was a total non-relationship. But the Labour MP who made her 'see red' was Yvette Cooper, her sparring partner at the Home Office when Cooper had been shadow Home Secretary. Cooper wanted to be included more in national security matters after Cameron's departure, but May thought that she couldn't trust her. Cooper brought out the worst in May. Not that Labour preoccupied her thoughts much at all. 'When it came to Parliament', Timothy recalls, 'we were much less focused on Labour than on our rebel Tories, even in that first ten months until the general election.'[78] The thorns among Tory MPs were not at that time Brexiteers, but the twelve to fifteen ardent Remain MPs.

TEST CASE: HER FIRST BIG INVESTMENT DECISIONS

The first big decisions of her premiership concerned the 'three Hs': HS2, Heathrow's third runway and Hinkley Point, the £18 billion nuclear power station in Somerset, the first to be built for twenty years, jointly financed by the French and Chinese governments. She continued her backing for HS2 as Prime Minister: 'She was utterly convinced it was right and never seriously considered cancelling it,' says a member of her team. It already had considerable commitment from government, but, as another official says, 'The view was that as we were so heavily invested on HS2, it was too late for us to change course despite some commercial concerns.' On Heathrow, Howard Davies's commission had finally reported in July 2015 in favour of a third runway. 'May was utterly determined to go ahead with it: she felt it had gone on long enough,' says an official. 'She didn't want to dig it up again,' says another. 'For her, it was about management of colleagues, [Zac] Goldsmith and [Boris] Johnson.'

It was Hinkley Point that proved the battleground. May's private office wrote a note in her box in her first week, saying the deal was effectively 70–80 per cent complete, and her final decision was needed for sign-off. The note explained that the government would not have to pay anything for the plant, only for the energy, albeit at a high price.

She ticked the note. Civil servants were familiar enough with Timothy's stance towards the Chinese, not least because of a blog he had written when at the New Schools Network on the ConservativeHome website entitled 'The Government is selling our national security to China'.[79] Officials nevertheless believed that, as she had signed it off in her box, Hinkley would get the go-ahead. Done and dusted, they said.

Heywood, Case and a senior official from the Department for Business, Energy and Industrial Strategy (BEIS) then heard in late July that the Prime Minister wanted to see them urgently in her office. Timothy in particular was deeply concerned about energy policy and the financing, and rebelled at what he saw as her being rushed into a decision. Timothy says, 'The more we looked at it, and the more meetings we had on it, the more the Prime Minister began to feel the wool was being pulled over her eyes. She felt that she was being bounced into the decision, and she reacted against it.'[80] What then followed in her office has been described by a civil servant as 'an incredibly unpleasant meeting. The Prime Minister, Nick and Fi piled into us with real ferocity.' There was 'cold fury' from the Prime Minister, with 'four-letter words' spoken. May made Heywood feel he had been unpatriotic for supposedly encouraging the French to pressure her into agreeing to the plan. She then left to talk to the media, who had been invited in for a summer party. The chiefs tried to soothe Heywood, but questioning his integrity, as he felt she had done, was explosive. The officials retreated afterwards to Heywood's study in the Cabinet Office, where he was still reeling. 'I was never treated in this way by Gordon. I was never treated in this way by Tony,' he said, still in shock.

The episode revealed May out of her depth, caught in the middle of powerful forces. On the one side, a Whitehall heavily invested in the decision, as well as two major international partners. On the other, the chiefs. She called François Hollande that week to warn him about the concerns of her new government. The French President pressed her to forge ahead, as did the Chinese. But she nevertheless decided to put a pause on the deal. She did not want her first major public decision, barely a fortnight into the job, to be in support of a policy that had been driven by Osborne and Cameron, and which meant partnering on a sensitive area of energy security with China. Her instinctive wariness, fully endorsed by Timothy, carried the day.[81] The Chinese government, taken aback by the decision and perturbed by the apparent loss of the convivial relationship they had enjoyed with Cameron's No. 10, was uncertain what it might portend.

In mid-September, the government changed its mind on Hinkley. It announced that, after imposing 'significant new safeguards' to protect national security, the nuclear power deal with the French and Chinese would go ahead after all. The BBC's Laura Kuenssberg reported having been advised that 'you can hardly tell the difference between' the initial deal and the one they approved, and that the National Security Council had itself concluded there were not threats from China with the original deal.[82] Those who opposed Hinkley felt she backed down. What officials learnt was that if Timothy and/or Hill was not on board, there was no guarantee May would continue along her original course. Her relationship with Heywood stabilised soon after, but Hinkley Point was the low point. May and her team picked a fight deliberately, officials felt. May apologised to Heywood later that day – while he resolved to avoid any future stand-up row with her.

THE SCHOOLS SPEECH: SEPTEMBER

The rest of July and August passed more peacefully, with Timothy still itching to press ahead with their domestic agenda. May had had time during her leadership campaign to give only two speeches: it had been Timothy's intention that her next speech should address social disadvantage and education. So when she suddenly found herself propelled into No. 10, his first thought was for her to give the speech before the summer holidays. They decided against it on the grounds that 'that's when rows take off. So it was scheduled for early September.'[83] Wilkins drafted it, drawing on her interest in meritocracy and social mobility. They sought to extend opportunities beyond just academies and free schools to a new wave of grammar schools across the country, wanting to see them start up in deprived areas and not confined to mainly middle-class areas in the home counties. To Timothy, building more grammar schools was not a right-wing policy, but the opposite: it was about giving greater opportunities to all. One member of the team close to him believes that 'Nick Timothy had a chip on his shoulder about posh people like the Camerons sending their children to private schools that people like him could not afford. He pressed the case for grammar schools very hard, and personally ensured that it was her first policy speech as Prime Minister.'

Nick Timothy puts his case for the policy differently:

Our analysis was that free schools and academies were and are great. But you have to understand that they are merely an opportunity – they give freedoms to school leaders and to communities to do something different. But they only work where there is the human and social capital to make the most of that opportunity. We wanted to get new people and organisations into the school system to provide that capital – and we identified selective schools, universities, independent schools and faith schools, because there were rules getting in the way of new Catholic schools.[84]

Shortly after May's arrival, Timothy called Rachel Wolf, the sole Cameron survivor in the Policy Unit, to join him for a cup of tea. 'I want to expand the number of grammar schools,' he told her. 'I want to put together a plan on how it might happen which can go into the Prime Minister's box to read.'[85] Foreshadowing the skirmishes that were to dominate the following few months, Timothy fell out badly on this point with the Education Secretary, Justine Greening. May's team had been uncertain about whether to give Greening the position, but given her support for May's candidacy and reputable status within the party, they felt they had to do so. What they admired most was her genuine commitment to social mobility: 'We thought she had a good backstory and talked a good game on social inclusion,' says one of May's team. They were convinced that May had made it plain on her appointment that grammar schools would be part of the policy programme. Greening was equally adamant that she had signed up to no such understanding.

Timothy met Greening in late July. 'He was extremely clear and explained exactly what he wanted to see,' says one witness. 'She came straight back at him saying she didn't like the grammar school plan, making her own view very clear. It was obvious to me that Justine Greening was not the person in charge of education policy.' May's team disagree with this account of events, saying that Greening, throughout her tenure, assured May that she was delivering the policy, while briefing the press that she was against it. Greening was the first Cabinet minister to fall out with May's No. 10, with briefings and counter-briefings to the press intensifying from the first month. 'Greening was sour and unconstructive. She briefed the media constantly. She was utterly opposed to the policy of selection and faith schools. But she never said she opposed them to our faces,' says one of May's team. Greening and the DfE were convinced the policy was not May's but Timothy's, and she hinted as much in one meeting with the Prime Minister. An incandescent May responded vigorously, 'Nick Timothy is not the Prime Minister; I am. This is my policy.' May indeed had spoken about grammar schools in her maiden speech in the House of Commons on 2 June 1997, and she had a strong personal commitment to them. Valuable support for them came too from Graham Brady, chairman of the 1922 Committee, who spoke out in support of grammar schools in July 2016, a week after May's appointment as Prime Minister.[86]

May's personal support didn't smooth the path for such a controversial policy. Grumbles were soon heard within No. 10, too, as some aides and officials thought that too much political time and capital was being expended on a policy with which the educational establishment and much of the commentariat had no sympathy. The DfE, drawing on educational research which was highly sceptical of the efficacy of grammar schools, was against the policy from Day 1. Dissent spread from the DfE across Whitehall to the Treasury, who later put blocks in the way of more free schools. Timothy blamed Greening and her officials, especially Permanent Secretary Jonathan Slater, for opposition to the reforms. Tensions came to a head when, three days before May was due to give her September education speech, Slater turned up ('uninvited') to a meeting at No. 10 and 'deliberately' (they claimed) revealed critical comments on selection to spying cameras. Spread across the news was an extract documenting Greening's 'clear position' that grammar schools 'should be presented … as an option, and only to be pursued once we have worked with the existing grammars to show how they can be expanded and reformed in ways which avoid disadvantaging those who don't get in'.[87]

May delivered her long-anticipated education speech on 9 September at the august venue of the British Academy in London. The government's priorities, she said, were 'those of ordinary working-class people'. Its ambition was for Britain to be 'the world's great meritocracy – a country where everyone has a fair chance to go as far as their talent and their hard work will allow'. She produced a wish list to make this ambition a reality. First, she wanted 'our universities to do more to help us to improve the quality of schools'. Second, 'to remove the obstacles that stop more good faith schools from opening'. Third, 'to encourage some of our biggest independent schools to bring their knowledge, expertise and resources to bear to help improve the quality and capacity of schools for those who cannot afford to pay'. Fourth, 'to relax the restrictions that stop selective schools from expanding'. Finally, 'to focus on the new grammars of the future … [as] just one element of a truly diverse system which … can give every child the support they need to go as far as their talents can take them'. Mindful of the scepticism towards expanding grammar schools, Timothy toned down the advocacy, recommending them only as one of several solutions. But, as Tom Swarbrick from the No. 10 press office recalls,

> We were taken aback by the response of the media to her speech. It was almost universally: 'So, you're bringing back grammar schools?' It was not as we hoped, which was for them to say, 'You're offering people greater choice? That's good.' It hadn't been pitch-rolled in the media long enough, so journalists conveyed an impression almost as if we were going backwards rather than forwards, and that it was playing into the fear that Brexit was a return to the 1950s.[88]

Brexit, the subject that was to dominate her tenure in No. 10, kept breaking into every facet of her work as Prime Minister. She wanted her legacy to be defined by more than that. But first she had to deal with Brexit to clear her path for the important domestic reform she wanted her premiership to be all about.

May surprised many in the EU, in her party and in her own Cabinet by opting for such a hard Brexit line in her party conference and Lancaster House speeches. Here, May arrives at the Council of the European Union in Brussels.

CHAPTER 3

A HARD COURSE TO BREXIT, 2016–17

'**I**'m going for Remain,' May announced to a startled group of her closest aides at dinner at Westminster's Corinthia Hotel in the late spring of 2016, just weeks before the referendum.[1] There is an irony that May, exactly like Cameron before her, never wanted Britain's relationship with the EU to be their dominant issue, but both had their premierships utterly overshadowed by it, May far more so than Cameron. To understand how May lost control of the process, this chapter looks at the seven key Brexit decisions she took before the general election in June 2017.

MAY DECIDES TO BACK REMAIN

On 23 January 2013, in a speech at the Bloomberg offices in the City of London, Cameron had promised that if the Conservatives won a majority at the 2015 general election, the government would negotiate more favourable arrangements for Britain remaining in the EU before holding a referendum on whether Britain should stay in or leave. It was the most fateful and historic decision of Cameron's premiership, and he believes it was inevitable (though nothing in history is) under pressure from the prolonged and rising anti-EU feeling within his party and the country.[2] In the European parliamentary elections in May 2014, UKIP secured more votes and seats than any other single party, the first time both the Conservatives and Labour had been beaten in a nationwide poll since 1906. With the 2015 general election in the bag, Cameron repeated his promise, confirmed in the Conservatives' manifesto pledge, to hold an in/out referendum on Britain's membership of the EU before the end of 2017. Once he concluded his underachieving renegotiation with the EU in February 2016, he announced that the referendum would be held on 23 June, earlier than many expected.

No. 10 then brought May, along with Boris Johnson and Michael Gove, under 'massive' pressure to declare that she would support Remain. But she held her counsel, even from Timothy and Hill (neither one still working with her at the Home Office). Timothy recalls, 'I remember thinking she was leaving it late, really late. Everyone was starting to think that she would back Leave. I spoke to her on the phone and said she really needed to decide and make her position public before it got out of hand.'[3]

Hill organised the dinner at the Corinthia Hotel precisely to force the decision on how May should position herself during the campaign. Hill was very clear that May would be much better placed as a contender to succeed Cameron if she were to vote for Brexit. As Hill recalls:

> Her statement out of the blue that she was going to support Remain was a body blow to Nick and me. Our calculations showed it would hurt her. I was taken aback and told her directly that I didn't think it would help her cause. When I got back to my home after the dinner, I told Charles [Farr, Hill's partner at the time], 'Fuck me, she's going to go Remain.' He was phlegmatic, but I said, 'It will make everything much harder.'[4]

Hill was right: it did make life much harder for May. Had she identified herself as a Leaver during the referendum campaign, she would have found the task of holding the party together in office very different.

She would have been able to steer her own course more easily, without the constant threat from Brexiteers in Cabinet, from her backbenchers and the many vocal Brexiteers in the press, needing to see that she was sound on Brexit. Coming out for Remain was her first important decision on Brexit. And while her husband Philip was a firm Remainer, she seems to have taken the decision entirely on her own.

So what exactly did Theresa May think about the EU and, more particularly, leaving it? Those who worked with her most closely over her three years at No. 10 agree that she came to the job with very little understanding of the EU, including the single market and the customs union. One official says, 'I spent as much time talking to her as anyone, and I cannot tell you at the end of all those conversations what she actually thinks.'

What May did understand and had mastered was her experience of the EU as Home Secretary from 2010. Will Tanner, who worked for her there, believes the reason that she came out for Remain was her fear about economic downturn, adding, 'She was never ideological, always deeply pragmatic, and her main preoccupation was ensuring that people would not suffer economically. She did care about sovereignty, but from the point of view not of trade but [of] security. I was surprised she went for Remain. I didn't think she would.'[5]

One advisor believes May's motive went beyond just loyalty to Cameron, though that weighed with her: 'She had a personal feeling about the EU, hence her tears when she heard the result of the referendum.' So she placed her sense of national interest above her own personal career interest, as urged on her by advisors, and in contrast to Johnson.

May's formative experience at the Home Office was negotiating Protocol 36 of the Lisbon Treaty, which concerned the controversial European Arrest Warrant (EAW). Against the odds she had triumphed in getting her way against her fellow European Interior Ministers, the UK receiving opt-out concessions from the EU on police and criminal justice measures. Once in No. 10, her frequent refrain was: 'They told me it was impossible to get Protocol 36 through, but it wasn't. We did it, and we will again.'[6] Another May refrain was: 'I'm sick of people saying to me that we can't go for an ambitious new Brexit model designed around the UK's interests and needs. Britain is the fifth largest economy in the world.' Peter Storr, another she brought in from the Home Office to No. 10, says, 'The comment reflected her own view. You could always tell whether her words reflected her own thinking or somebody else's, because of the passion with which she would speak them.'[7]

May's Home Office experience of the EU had played to her strengths, which were all about process, not policy formation. As Prime Minister, she went on to conduct negotiations with the EU much as she had conducted them with her opposite numbers in the EU as Home Secretary, failing to appreciate that negotiating with the EU on British withdrawal was immeasurably more complex. An official who worked with her closely says:

In common with most Cabinet ministers, she understood little of the detail of the EU. What she did know and understand was how to get things done in the EU as Home Secretary. It taught her to go carefully and slowly in the EU and engage in the detail. It taught her to focus on the outcome she wanted and to work backwards on how to get there. She learnt that you achieve what you want in Brussels not by shouting at people, or grandstanding or walking out, but by grinding away at the detail.

It irritated May when advisors pointed out to her that she could no longer cherry-pick as Prime Minister as she had done in the Justice and Home Affairs Council. 'We have to get away from the binary thinking of the past,' she would say. She developed a habit early on in No. 10 of taking her reading glasses off in her hand, putting her head downwards and telling embarrassed colleagues in meetings, 'Look, I did negotiations as Home Secretary. I did negotiations in the Bank of England. I know how to negotiate.'

During the referendum campaign, Timothy had the delicate task of ensuring that she gave a nuanced rather than an unequivocal Remain message in her first public announcement. Of the two chiefs, Timothy was the ideological Eurosceptic, while Hill was a reluctant Remainer. No fan of the European Commission, Hill was antagonised by the hurdles that May had been forced to jump through as Home Secretary, but she would have preferred not to have left the EU at this point.[8]

Timothy wrote May's first speech of the referendum campaign for 25 April, into which he poured all his pent-up beef against the EU. Delivered at the Institute of Mechanical Engineers in London, the prime focus was the European Convention on Human Rights (ECHR), which had delayed her drive to extradite the extremist Abu Hamza for several years, and which almost stopped the deportation of Abu Qatada altogether. She said:

> The ECHR can bind the hands of Parliament, adds nothing to our prosperity, makes us less secure by preventing the deportation of dangerous foreign nationals – and does nothing to change the attitudes of governments like Russia's when it comes to human rights ... So regardless of the EU referendum, my view is this: if we want to reform human rights laws in this country, it isn't the EU we should leave, but the ECHR and the jurisdiction of its court.

The speech was widely and correctly interpreted as her reaching out to Eurosceptics, while offering a direct challenge to Cameron and No. 10. It also threw down the gauntlet to Michael Gove, then Justice Secretary, who had put forward his own proposals for a British Bill of Rights, based on Britain staying within the convention. But it was a memorable passage towards the end that truly staked her out as an independent voice on the EU: 'I do not want to stand here and insult people's intelligence by claiming that everything about the EU is perfect, that membership of the EU is wholly good, nor do I believe those that say the sky will fall in if we vote to leave.'

The speech laid down two very clear markers: May was not going to listen to advice on how to do Brexit, the most important decision by any PM since 1945, from any other than her very close circle. Second, although undeniably a Remainer, with all the woe that would bring her, she was neither an ideological nor an emotional Remainer. The die had been cast.

CREATING TWO NEW DEPARTMENTS: KEEPING CONTROL IN NO. 10

The moment Timothy and Hill heard the referendum result, in the early morning of 24 June, they knew they were in a race against time. How might May, if victorious in the leadership race, best deliver Brexit? On one point the two were completely clear. Whitehall, they believed, was imbued with 'pro-EU' sentiment, and they would have to design a new institutional apparatus if Brexit was to be delivered in the right way and at the right time. The optics were important too. She would be most vulnerable, they correctly anticipated, from hard Brexiteers, who would always claim her heart wasn't in it.

They had a particular antipathy, shared by May, towards the two departments that had traditionally overseen relations with the EU: the Foreign and Commonwealth Office (FCO) and the Treasury. As one senior official puts it:

At the Home Office, they had felt badly treated by the political bosses of both the Treasury and the FCO, as well as by the institutions they ran. May was right in feeling marginalised by them. Frankly, they had made their bed because of how they treated her, and now they had to lay in it.

She had a different relationship with both institutions. For the Treasury she had a respect, like Blair, if not any affection (some Prime Ministers, such as Wilson after 1964 or Thatcher from the very beginning of her premiership, didn't even have respect). For the FCO, however, she felt almost disdain, partly socially based because of what she saw as the patronising upper-class style of some senior diplomats, but also philosophical, believing they were uncritical supporters of the Brussels establishment.

That was how May's team conceived of two entirely new Whitehall departments – a significant constitutional innovation – to drive through the central plank of her premiership. Accordingly, on 14 July 2016, her second day in office, the two new departments were officially created. The Department for Exiting the European Union brought together the European Directorate within the FCO, the Europe Unit within the Cabinet Office, and the United Kingdom's Permanent Representative to the EU (UKREP), from the FCO. The Department for International Trade was given the express task of striking and extending trade agreements between the UK and non-EU states in preparation for the moment that Britain left (EU law forbade the UK negotiating trade deals with third-party countries until it had actually exited the bloc). The department took on former responsibilities for trade and investment from the FCO, as well as from the Department for Business.

The creation of DIT, in May's second crucial decision on Brexit, sent powerful shockwaves across Whitehall and still more across the EU, where it proved particularly controversial. Given that its purpose was to coordinate and develop an independent trade policy for the UK, including free trade agreements beyond the EU, it signalled a full-blooded Brexit was coming. In Whitehall, Ivan Rogers was vocal among those who thought setting up DIT was premature:

> The very act of setting up DIT sent a powerful statement to Brussels, who asked, 'What's the point in doing this unless the UK is going to be going for an autonomous trade policy?' The signal it gave was that the UK was closing down its options before talks had even begun.[9]

May didn't see it that way. In part, it was because she had yet to understand the full implications of leaving the customs union, or to learn the tortured difficulties of establishing 'an independent trade policy'. Neither did she accept or comprehend that appointing two senior Secretaries of State with vested interests in a hard Brexit outcome to these two key departments might be narrowing down her options. She was the pilot flying the airship Britain into the clouds without any fixed idea of her destination. Optics certainly loomed large. One Europe advisor speculates whether DIT had been established mostly for presentational purposes, to appeal to the Brexiteers in the party who had preached the benefits of new trade deals:

> In the crucial day or two when it was set up, there was no one around who knew enough to point out that it was against EU law for any member state to negotiate a bilateral trade deal with another or a third country with which the EU itself had a deal.

Another adds that, had May listened, they 'wouldn't have advocated for a separate DIT, as it needed to be a part of the Foreign Office as in other countries'.

May confirmed to Jeremy Heywood her intentions about the two new departments when they met on 11 July, the day Leadsom withdrew from the race. He was not happy, especially about DExEU: 'Jeremy was sceptical about machinery of government changes being the solution to anything,' says one official. But he felt unable to resist May's push for them – he was told it was a commitment which could not be changed – and so he kept his reservations to himself. As one of her team recalls, 'I specifically remember asking him what he thought, and he was enthusiastic. I was impressed by how he said, "I never said there were no benefits to Brexit. Now we've made the decision we must maximise the benefits and minimise the risks." He seemed very pro-DIT.'

Heywood had other worries too. To the suspicion with which May,

Timothy and Hill regarded the civil service in general was added their scepticism about whether Whitehall would deliver impartially and enthusiastically on Brexit. Were May and her team right to be sceptical? Heywood was aware that the Whitehall cupboard was largely bare on contingency planning for Brexit, but, as he asserted when asked, this had been expressly banned by Cameron and Osborne during the referendum campaign, the government's official position being that Britain should remain within the EU. Worrying Heywood further was the very evident sense of 'collective grieving' across much of Whitehall at the result of the referendum, as one official describes: 'Most senior mandarins had spent their entire career working with the EU, and were convinced that, on balance, it was beneficial to Britain, and that extricating Britain would be an enormous, perhaps impossible, task, and also extremely unpredictable.'

'It's an open question whether the civil service should have looked more at itself,' says another senior official.

> But Jeremy felt very upset when people said the civil service were not impartial and hadn't done their homework. He had chaired a regular meeting in his room in the Cabinet Office for several weeks, bringing in key figures from the Treasury, No. 10 and the Home Office to plan for the enactment of the measures, for example on free movement, that Cameron had negotiated in February 2016 at the EU Council.

When the leadership contest was declared, mandarins thought that they would then have more time than they did, says Ivan Rogers. 'When senior civil servants met during the leadership competition, we thought we had another eight weeks to get our thinking together. Suddenly it was truncated and we had no time to set up any apparatus.'[10]

So Whitehall's lack of preparedness for a Leave vote gnawed away at Heywood even before the result was known. Two nights before the referendum, on 21 June, he called in Olly Robbins, Second Permanent Secretary at the Cabinet Office, to a highly confidential meeting, telling him, 'Although the indications still look as if the referendum will be won by Remain, I want to have somebody lined up of Permanent Secretary rank to put in front of the PM as Brexit supremo should the referendum be won by Leave, so I can say, "This is the plan."' Heywood told the dumbfounded Robbins that the new post would revolve around two issues, finance and immigration, both of which Robbins knew inside out, having worked at the Treasury since he joined the civil service in 1996, as Principal Private Secretary at No. 10 in 2006, in a variety of national security jobs, and finally as Second Permanent Secretary at the Home Office, with responsibility for immigration, free movement and borders. 'Thanks, but I'm enjoying the Home Office,' he told Heywood definitively. Other names were batted around, including Michael Ellam and Jon Cunliffe, both of whom had considerable EU and financial experience. Far more, indeed, than Robbins.

Robbins thought little more of it until the morning of 24 June, when he received another urgent summons to the Cabinet Office to see Heywood. 'Well, what do you think?' said a tired but imperious Heywood. Robbins told him he was still unwilling. 'I'm sorry to say this, Olly, but there are some jobs that a Cabinet Secretary needs his officials to do, and I need you to do this, now.' Robbins, knowing how bitterly divided the country was, and how his job would place him under a spotlight that officials normally don't experience, said, 'All right, but I don't want my family dragged in.' Heywood reassured him: 'Don't worry, you'll be on the same side as the people who might go for you: you'll be delivering their Brexit.' Like most, Heywood failed to foresee how bitter Brexit would prove.

Cameron had been expecting to deliver a celebratory speech at seven o'clock on the morning of 24 June as the markets opened, declaring his pleasure and confidence in the result. Instead, now in deep shock at the result, he delivered a very different message at 8.15 a.m.: his resignation to the nation. He nevertheless found time to assent readily to Heywood's suggestion of Robbins to head the Cabinet Office's Brexit team.

May, still just a contender to succeed, had yet to be asked. Robbins was a senior official in her department, and she was not happy with his relocation. But Oliver Letwin, whom Cameron had immediately appointed his Europe advisor the day of the referendum result, helped persuade May to accept the loss of Robbins.[11]

> May was not at all happy and took a few days to agree, eventually won over by the argument that, if she was to emerge as the winner in the leadership race, she would have alongside her someone doing the top Europe job with whom she had worked and in whom she had confidence.[12]

Her consent gained, Heywood worked quickly to establish the Europe Unit 'Mark 1', placed within the Cabinet Office, and the forerunner of DExEU.

On 13 July, with David Davis formally appointed to DExEU by the new Prime Minister, Robbins went into the building to take part in the classic civil service ritual of the Permanent Secretary greeting his newly appointed Cabinet minister and walking with them to their department. Except that in this case, DExEU had yet to have a physical location. So he walked Davis round the corner in Whitehall and straight back into the Cabinet Office, where they talked late into the night.

The consternation across Whitehall from the creation of DExEU and DIT was felt most strongly at the Treasury and the FCO, who deeply resented being sidelined on the key issue of the day, their expertise scorned. Some of the anger was directed at Heywood personally. Had he been so eager to prove himself to the heavily suspicious May team, they asked, that he allowed himself to be swept along with decisions against his better judgement? Some thought he had colluded with his new masters, over-eager to please. His defenders reply, 'Come on, he's a civil servant. His job is to deliver for his political masters.'

No sooner had they created their brace of new departments than

May and her chiefs became concerned about maintaining control over the Secretaries of State she appointed to run them, David Davis and Liam Fox. Might DExEU and DIT become separate empires, every bit as unwieldy and independent-minded as the Whitehall departments they had emerged from? One No. 10 official comments, 'It was typical of Nick and Fi that they were never happy delegating away power, which is precisely what they'd done by creating DexEU and DIT. Whereas they had to do that for political reasons, they moved smartly to build up compensating capacity very close to them.'

So, in August, they did what they often did and went fishing back in the Home Office pond, which is where they landed Peter Storr. As May's chief negotiator on Protocol 36 in 2012–14, Storr had earned their trust and respect. He had just the skills they sought. As he recalls, 'I think she had been impressed with what we had achieved in the negotiations, so three or so weeks after she became Prime Minister she invited me to set up a new outfit, the Europe Unit, nominally attached to the Policy Unit in No. 10 itself.'[13]

To beef up Storr's new unit, Timothy and Hill brought in long-time Conservative EU specialist Denzil Davidson, a special advisor to William Hague and Philip Hammond as Foreign Secretary from 2010 to 2016. Davidson was a Remainer, but they chose him all the same, justifying the choice, as Davidson says, 'because I was a Conservative, because I knew my stuff, and because they knew I was trustworthy'.[14]

This gave more capacity and authority on Brexit at the heart of No. 10, but before even the end of August they realised that they needed still more heavyweight firepower. A vacant position was open to them, that of the Prime Minister's advisor for Europe, held since 2013 by Tom Scholar, until he left in the summer of 2016 to become Permanent Secretary at the Treasury. Finding a suitable replacement was proving difficult. Robbins's name came up, but the FCO were extremely unhappy, one official claiming, 'He doesn't understand the intricacies of the EU, hasn't worked substantially in different fields, and his style is too closed, to the exclusion of others.' The FCO argued instead for Julian King, nominated by Cameron in one of his final decisions, to succeed Jonathan Hill as the European Commissioner in Brussels. Simon McDonald, FCO Permanent Secretary, had a rare argument about it with Heywood, who remained set on Robbins. Even though Robbins had only one month earlier been appointed Permanent Secretary at DexEU, Heywood nevertheless asserted that he could combine it with being Scholar's successor as PM's advisor on the EU, widely known as the 'Sherpa'.

Timothy was open-minded about Robbins becoming May's Sherpa, Hill more of a sceptic, but neither considered overturning the appointment. Both could see the benefit, and he had worked with May previously. Robbins had found late July and August an unsettling period at DExEU. May and Timothy had regularly sought his advice, asking him for a whole range of papers for the PM. At the end of August, as it became clear he was already carrying out the role in practice, he was formally given the 'Sherpa' title. Few foresaw that having the same figure being both DExEU Permanent Secretary and the Prime Minister's own senior figure on the EU was likely to create difficulties.

The appointment unleashed fresh waves of anger against Heywood from those in the FCO who felt that the keys to Brexit would be handed to an official less than qualified to drive it. One fellow official says:

> Heywood had very many qualities. But a weakness – or was it for a civil servant? – was an over-eagerness to please his political masters. Olly knew even less about the intricacies of the EU than Jeremy himself. Jeremy told May's chiefs that he would produce clean skins who had no backstory on the EU. And so he did.

Ivan Rogers was particularly outraged that his old department, the Treasury, was being marginalised in the Brexit discussions: 'Jeremy cut the Treasury completely out of Brexit negotiations. But its head [Tom

Scholar] had done the job and knew about it, and many Treasury officials worked on the EU. To have excluded them from Brexit was insane.'[15]

May's great play about the restoration of Cabinet government after Cameron included the establishment of the European Union Exit and Trade Committee, which she was to chair. Every Cabinet minister who'd campaigned for Leave – Johnson, Davis, Fox, Grayling, Patel and Leadsom – was appointed to it, as well as five Remain supporters: Hammond, Rudd, Green, Greg Clark and party chairman Patrick McLoughlin. The balancing was very deliberate, very May. The committee met weekly, considered weighty papers, had lengthy discussions and held some gravitas in the system. But it was not where power lay.

May had absolutely no intention of letting her Cabinet ministers loose on subjects she herself was finding it hard to grasp. Instead, she wanted the key discussions and decisions on Brexit to be taken in No. 10 – specifically, in her own room. No politicians welcome. The key figures invited to these Europe strategy meetings were officials: Robbins, Rogers (Tim Barrow, from January 2017), Principal Private Secretary Simon Case (Peter Hill from April 2017), Peter Storr, Denzil Davidson, EU lead in the private office Catherine Page, Timothy, Hill, Penn and, as always, Heywood. May could not have been more brazen: 'I don't want DD or Boris there,' she said. Davis repeatedly asked if he could attend, but his requests were always refused. The chiefs liked him personally and thought he was adept at handling Tory MPs in the House, but May herself thought he was prone to leaking and was not in command of the detail, nor sufficiently cerebral.

No. 10's Europe strategy meetings were usually held on Wednesday afternoons, often only for an hour, almost always to consider a paper by Robbins decided upon at the meeting the week before. Usually his paper would arrive with attendees, to their irritation, only the night before the meeting. 'Managing the DExEU department and the "Sherpa" role was a difficult challenge for Robbins,' says a colleague in his defence. This proved particularly irritating for Ivan Rogers, who had to travel in from Brussels the night before or early in the morning of the meeting if he wanted to see the paper in advance, Robbins refusing to provide a digital copy for security reasons. Chris Wilkins joined the list of attendees soon after it was established: 'I quickly discovered that the one meeting of the week that really mattered on the EU was held on the Wednesday afternoon, called the Europe strategy meeting.'[16] Timothy had invited him to come, in favour of more input from special advisors. Like a university tutorial, Robbins would spend the first ten minutes reading out his paper. 'All significant deals on the EU in the first nine months, and I believe since, were taken in her Europe strategy meeting,' says a top No. 10 official.

As the months ground on, the truth dawned on May's ministers that the Cabinet Committee on Brexit, and indeed full Cabinet, was not where the key decisions on Brexit were being taken. Resentments grew. Ivan Rogers took a scathing view:

> She wanted the Europe strategy meeting in her room so she could listen to her senior officials without her Cabinet ministers. I don't blame her for this. It's what Blair did. You listen to the experts, understand it, get your head clear, and then you go and talk to your Cabinet colleagues about it. She's a secretive person, and she wanted confidential meetings with her core team where she could understand issues including the single market, the customs union and the European Court of Justice, which she really didn't understand.[17]

In Cabinet, Johnson, Davis, Fox and Hammond would ask increasingly probing questions about the evolution of Brexit policy. What was it? Where was it being decided? When would they be able to discuss it? May would respond by regaling them with long lists of facts. They were not satisfied with this, nor with her telling them, 'Of course the EU will compromise in the end.' Frustrations were mounting.

She refused to cede power from her Europe strategy meetings to the Cabinet committee. As the weeks went on, she still struggled to master the intricacies of the EU and leaving it. One official in attendance commented, 'May was painstaking in trying to grapple with the complexity of the detail. She would always read through the paper with great diligence, unless an unexpected event took her attention away.' But she lacked a clear sense of where she wanted to go, and was unable to keep the peace among increasingly fractious colleagues, or give a clear direction to those who attended.

'The meetings would almost invariably involve a disagreement between Timothy and Robbins and break up without a clear resolution. Decisions were often then taken by Timothy and May away from the group, when they would talk either one on one or over the phone.'

Timothy denies that most of the key decisions were taken outside the meetings. But he quickly emerged as the greatest single influence on May's Brexit thinking, and was the most consistent voice on all the seven major decisions she took in her first ten months in office. Timothy had one great advantage over Rogers and Robbins: after fifteen years with her, he knew May's mind inside out. He saw her day in, day out. And he knew the Conservative Party. He had the Brexiteers banging ever more loudly on his door, but contrary to those who say his mind was closed, he tried to range widely in his contacts, talking at length to former diplomats, notably Christopher Meyer, former British Ambassador to the United States. He tried hard, too, to work with Rogers and Robbins and understand their approach. So what exactly did this most formative of influences on the Prime Minister think about how to make Brexit a reality? His mind was very clear: 'I always thought we were heading towards a third-country, free-trade arrangement that would be deeper and broader than a conventional FTA, but it would be an FTA nonetheless. I thought it would be deeper than Canada, but not a customs union and certainly not anything like the Norway arrangement.'[18]

From early on, May's own thinking became indistinguishable from Timothy's. He says he tried to verbalise the thoughts she had, but he also channelled her thinking because his approach was far more decisive than hers. As he says of her:

> From very early on, if ministers or officials began to talk about retaining bits of the EU in certain ways, she would be very cross. She would plonk her elbow on the table and place her reading glasses in her hand, wave them up and down and say, 'You're thinking about it the wrong way. We're leaving the EU. It will be a new relationship altogether. It has to be different. I want an altogether new relationship, with the United Kingdom outside of the EU's institutions and legal framework.'[19]

When Timothy now reflects, he does not accept that he was the all-powerful figure on her Brexit thinking up to the 2017 general election. All he was trying to do, he asserts, was to help a far from clear, far from articulate and far from knowledgeable Prime Minister to clarify her mind and achieve a workable Brexit:

> When I was there in No. 10 for the first year, she trusted me totally. Fi said to me I gave her the confidence to propose something positive on Brexit, but she was not confident. She did not know who else to trust. Fiona was always wary of the influence on her of Olly Robbins and told her, 'You've got to choose between DD and Robbins.' She chose Robbins. I think one of her weaknesses is that she finds it hard to trust politicians, while she thinks that the advisors and officials are hers.[20]

So whatever policy May would come up with, and despite the creation of DExEU and DIT, her Brexit plan would be made in No. 10, in her own study. She cut out the Treasury, she cut out the Foreign Office, she cut out her Cabinet ministers, she did not seek counsel from parliamentarians or academics, nor from former officials like David Hannay, John Kerr (a key figure in drawing up Article 50), Stephen Wall, Nigel Sheinwald or John Grant, all of whom had been British Permanent

Representatives to the EU. These officials constituted an informal think tank of deep experience and knowledge of how the EU worked and thought. But either she didn't think it was important or valuable to talk to them, or she thought their advice would be tainted. Her plan for Britain leaving the EU, the biggest domestic decision Britain had taken for fifty years, was going to be made by her, unsure though she was of what she wanted or how to deliver Brexit, as moulded by Timothy.

MAY'S FIRST PLAN: A BESPOKE DEAL FOR BRITAIN

Brexit always had to be a negotiation. Britain believes in the rule of law and had signed a series of treaties with the European Union. Walking out unilaterally from the EU was never a serious option, certainly not if Britain wanted to continue to trade with EU countries or be taken seriously in the international community. So what the EU thought about Brexit mattered. And they were not at all happy about the referendum result on 23 June. Jean-Claude Juncker, President of the European Commission since 2014, was unusual in predicting that the country would vote Leave. Most EU leaders thought, or wanted to think, that Remain would win. Nevertheless, Brussels was far more advanced in its contingency planning for a Leave vote than Whitehall.[21] Their great fear was that the result on 23 June, from a country so economically powerful and dominant in the EU since it joined in 1973, could set in train a domino reaction that could spell the end of the entire European project. They worried about the encouragement Britain's vote might give, with populism on the rise and a series of nationalist parties riding high in the polls, all of whom were to differing extents anti-EU.

On 29 June, less than a week after Britain's vote, the heads of the other twenty-seven member states met in Brussels for the EU Council in a state of some anxiety, alongside a deflated and pained

Cameron, representing Britain for the final time. The statement the EU leaders released was unequivocal. They were not going to push the boat out to ease Britain's departure:

> We, the Heads of State or Government of 27 Member States, as well as Presidents of the European Council and the European Commission, deeply regret the outcome of the referendum in the UK but we respect the will expressed by a majority of the British people. Until the UK leaves the EU, EU law continues to apply to and within the UK, both when it comes to rights and obligations.

EU leaders reckoned that the strategy Britain would adopt under any successor to Cameron would be to try to pick apart the solidarity of EU member countries one by one. Not on their watch, they said. So they determined to deliver a unified and very strong corporate message to the new British leader, which was that there would be 'no negotiations without notification', i.e. they were not prepared even to discuss the terms of Britain's departure, and they would do so as a group, until Britain had given formal notification that it was going to leave. It would have to do this by invoking Article 50, which stated that 'any Member State may decide to withdraw from the Union in accordance with its own constitutional requirements'. No member state had ever in its history withdrawn from the European Union. The stakes were sky-high for all. In those first weeks after the referendum result, most EU leaders, however naively, believed (and hoped) that the incoming Prime Minister would come back to them, seeking a more satisfactory renegotiation for Britain than Cameron had managed to achieve in February.

Rogers was the man whose task it was to represent Britain's position:

> I told the EU very clearly, 'We're not going to come back with even bigger demands than Cameron did. It simply won't happen. We're

definitely leaving the EU. We have a new Prime Minister in Theresa May. Don't freeze her out.' But they really didn't want to get to know her. They were extraordinarily nervous about what Britain might do and what the vote might portend for the future of the EU.[22]

All Prime Ministers draw heavily on their own experience when they arrive in No. 10. They have nowhere else to go. All the same, Downing Street officials were surprised by quite how formative the Home Office experience had been on their new Prime Minister. 'Her initial view was that she would handle Brexit specifically as she had done on the EU's Justice and Home Affairs Council, which tends to be quite pragmatic and open to deals,' says one. Rogers, who had worked closely with her at the Home Office, tried to suggest that it was not a useful precedent: 'I found her serious, reliable and operational. But equally she thought that everything as Prime Minister would be like negotiating Protocol 36.'[23] Storr was one of many who tried to explain at length that negotiating Brexit would be different, and she couldn't dictate what she wanted:

> My own view, having spent years working with the EU and Commission, is that they would adopt an approach above all to protect the integrity of the EU, even if it inflicted damage on some of their members, including Germany. Guided by the treaties and precedent, they would look at third-party options for Britain, and we should thus be examining variations on the Norway, Swiss and Canada models to see what we could achieve. This was not her view. She would regularly and forcefully make the point to officials and others that she was fed up with being guided towards third-country options, that we were the fifth largest economy in the world. She would say, 'I'm sick of people saying to me that we have to go for such options. We will go for a bespoke, ambitious model designed around British interests and British needs.'[24]

Rogers and Case argued the same point repeatedly with her: 'You can't pick and mix on the customs union and single market, but she kept coming back with, "We have to get away from the binary thinking of the past."' Wilkins was another who saw the circular argument play out: 'She was clear from the beginning that she wanted a bespoke deal for Europe that no other country had. She was very forceful about it.'[25] But she didn't know precisely what she meant by a 'bespoke British deal'.

As the EU leaders predicted, she began by trying to pick them off one by one. She embarked upon a series of visits to European capitals, beginning with Merkel in Berlin on 20 July before moving on to see Hollande in Paris on 21 July, just a week after the terrorist attack in Nice. Further trips were made to the Netherlands, Denmark, Spain and Italy, and she saw other EU leaders as they came through London. So why did she not see that her bespoke plan would not work? Before she left on the trips, she was told very clearly by officials that

> leaders like Merkel and Hollande will put their commitment to the European project above their narrow national interest, and certainly above their bilateral relationship with Britain. The unity of the EU will be their prize. Officials explained that her fellow EU leaders would not be prioritising Brexit above other pressing issues, including migration, Eurozone worries and counter-terrorism. They told her that she would do well if she managed to get Brexit into the top five issues for them to concentrate upon.

'The strategy was very clearly to deal with individual countries, and to fight against the monolithic EU response at the June council,' recalls one No. 10 official involved in the negotiations. Guy Verhofstadt, who led for the European Parliament on Brexit, says, 'We never thought Mrs May was wily enough to pick off EU countries one by one. She never fully understood our desire to work together, but it wasn't a big worry for us.'[26]

Besides her goal of securing a bespoke deal with the EU, and to take any third-party plan off the shelf, she had two further strategies: to negotiate with the EU Council far more than the Commission, which was considered much more legalistic and inflexible; and for any discussions on Britain's future relationship with the EU to run *in parallel* with withdrawal agreement talks. This final point drew on the experience of the Cameron team that, if Britain left the EU before agreeing on terms, it would do so outside the tent and be treated as an outsider. It was therefore much better when making the transition out of the EU to know what the future relationship would be before leaving. David Davis understood this point very clearly, famously foreshadowing timetabling as the coming 'row of the summer' in 2017.

So what came of May's plan? While many leaders were initially sceptical, and she was not strong at charming or persuading them, neither was their response totally negative or dismissive. It gave her some grounds for thinking that Brussels might be flexible in offering Britain a bespoke Brexit deal. But within weeks it became clear that the strategy wasn't working, and the EU27 would remain united. There had been insufficient progress with her approach before currents of protest surged in the run-up to the party conference in early October. Conservative members, as well as the EU, the Cabinet and the Labour Party, put pressure on her to trigger Article 50 and begin formal negotiations. What she was to say at the party conference spelled the end of her July and August strategy. Leverage to secure her aims was thus lost. Lost too was leverage that might have been provided by additional time to prepare for no deal.

Indeed, there was no serious preparation for no deal before the triggering of Article 50. Questions are rightly asked, and not just by Brexiteers, about why preparation for no deal was not dramatically escalated across Whitehall. 'The biggest mistake May made was not preparing for no deal from the start. If she had done so, it would have sent a message to the EU and been her biggest bargaining tool. I don't know why she didn't do it,' says Cameron's first policy chief, James

O'Shaughnessy.[27] For a Prime Minister whose rhetoric relied in part on being able to leave without a deal if the EU's offer was sufficiently poor, it was an odd omission. 'I never heard Theresa May talk to me about no deal. Never,' says Michel Barnier.[28] Martin Selmayr, Juncker's chief of staff and believed to be the most powerful man in the EU, says, 'On our side, we never saw no deal under May as a credible threat. It would have meant walking away from forty-five years of marriage, not settling anything, just an outright war.'[29]

May and her team are certainly guilty of believing that Brexit was going to be much simpler, quicker and easier than it proved. They did not factor in fully the complexities of negotiating with the EU, nor the tough trade-offs that May would have to make for the Union with Northern Ireland if she wanted to pursue her bespoke arrangement. Almost all of Whitehall failed to spot how problematic Northern Ireland's unique position would be. Francis Campbell, born in County Down, was a rare exception among diplomats in highlighting the issues early on.

Claims by Brexiteers during the referendum campaign, and for many years before and after, helped set expectations that could never, in all reality, be fulfilled. Michael Gove said that 'getting out of the EU can be quick and easy – the UK holds most of the cards' (9 April); John Redwood (a fellow of All Souls, Oxford) that leaving the EU 'can be quick and easy' (17 July); David Davis that 'there will be no downside to Brexit, only a considerable upside' (10 October). Such comments by senior politicians played their part in contributing to a belief that the hard part, winning the referendum against a prejudiced British establishment, was over, and that implementing the decision would in contrast be relatively straightforward and painless. Many on both sides failed to appreciate how difficult Brexit would prove. No. 10 would regularly complain that 'it never ceases to amaze us that Davis, Johnson, Grayling and Fox et al. constantly underestimate the sheer complexity of what we were trying to do'. Civil servants equally did not convey to politicians or to the country the complexity of the process, and when they did, they were not heard. May was no different, and she held an ungrounded and dangerously deluded confidence that a deal was near. 'They're dealmakers,' she would say to officials, 'you just have to know how to handle them.'

How else might they have played it? She could have made a speech early on to acknowledge the massive significance of leaving the EU, and the ramifications for the UK's economy, its place in the world and its cohesion. She could have said that even though the vote had gone closely in favour of Brexit, the country was deeply divided on whether Britain should leave the EU, while the precise manner of leaving was not specified by the Brexit vote. She could have lowered expectations by saying that leaving the EU would be very difficult and lengthy. She could have sprung to the defence of those, including officials, who were attacked. She came to No. 10 with enormous goodwill and a collective determination to get Brexit done. George Osborne takes this view:

> From the outset, she should have played the unity card. She was from Remain but delivering Brexit. There was great empathy and support for her across the party. People wanted her to succeed. But instead of being the unity candidate she threw her lot in with the hard Brexiteers and drew hard red lines. She should have said in her first speech that she was there to represent the 52 per cent who voted for Brexit – and the 48 per cent who didn't – and she knew she couldn't satisfy either side completely. But she would come up with a settlement that both sides could live with. Sadly, she had little experience of reading the Tory Party or working with the EU. It was a disaster.[30]

Timothy above all was not in favour of her reaching out across to the other side, but it was May's responsibility for taking his advice. His view was diametrically opposed to Osborne's in substance, too. Osborne favoured a deal that included single market and customs union membership, such as Norway, one that some Brexiteers, including even Nigel Farage, had suggested as a possibility during the campaign. 'What else is the EU, if not a single market and customs union?' Timothy would respond.

One of the tasks of the Prime Minister is to educate the country in political realities, and May singly failed to do that. Any knowledge of history would have told her these were not ordinary decisions. But she knew no history. She arrived at No. 10 declaring that she was not going to ask more questions, but to get to work on delivering the answer. Political leaders have never-to-recur framing moments in their early weeks, when they can set the expectations and parameters of their entire premiership. Yet political realities of compromise and trade-offs were not seriously addressed. It was one of the worst failures of imagination and opportunity by any Prime Minister since 1945.

No single figure in Whitehall did more to warn May of the complexity of Brexit than Ivan Rogers. He had been signalling the dangers and risks of achieving a successful solution long before the referendum. When I interviewed him in Brussels in February 2015 when writing my book on Cameron, he struck me as like an Old Testament prophet. He called after me as I was walking away: 'None of them have any idea how difficult leaving the EU will prove.' Still more, he reminded me of the cleric played by Jack Hawkins in the film *Zulu*, who said to the soldiers left behind in Rorke's Drift as he was taken away in a cart: 'You're all going to die. Don't you realise? Can't you see? You're all going to die.' Rogers was not to last the course, progressively marginalised, written off for being too much of an Eeyore character, too relentlessly gloomy. True to script, he now blames himself for being insufficiently pessimistic.[31]

The British establishment has not been more collectively guilty of failure of anticipation since appeasement in the late 1930s. Given the profound splits in the country, in Parliament and in the Conservative Party, given the complete lack of clarity about what the referendum result denoted, and the belief that Brexit would be easy, it is hardly surprising that it ended in a car crash. May herself, who had a moment of real opportunity, was the principal culprit for a failure of foresight, a repeated occurrence not just at the onset but throughout her premiership.

Not until April 2019, after her plan was repeatedly defeated, did she contemplate 'reaching out' to a Labour Party and to a leader she despised, whom she thought extreme and unprincipled. But she had no thought when she first became Prime Minister of reaching out even across her own party, let alone Parliament or to the nation. As one of her closest officials acknowledges:

> With hindsight, it would have been better if she'd spoken to other politicians and been more candid about what the realistic chances were, and the difficulties, and involved Parliament earlier. It was an error and, if you asked her about it when, much later, she attempted to pass the withdrawal agreement, I think she would agree with that analysis.

Timothy puts the counter-argument:

> Theresa was a moderniser, but reaching out just wasn't her. It was not in her nature. Even if it had been, I'm not certain it would have worked at the time. Her determination was to lead and set a clear direction on Brexit. The Leave side were happy with her at this time, although some Remainers were not. I can't remember anybody saying, 'Let's take the parliamentary party off on an away-day and talk it all through.' I don't think that could have worked either – it would have been a bunfight.[32]

So there was no attempt to bring the nation together in 2016, or in 2017, even after the general election. Hers was going to be a tribal, not a national, Brexit solution. There was no telling the public that Brexit might involve 'blood, sweat and tears', no speech to set out the parameters and framing of Brexit. May was going to do it her own way. Even if she was unclear what her way was. As Selmayr says,

'The British government had no concept at any time, at the referendum and all the way through, about what was their vision of Brexit.'[33] She could have acted on what she herself said at the end: that Brexit requires politicians to 'find consensus in Parliament ... Such a consensus can only be reached if those on all sides of the debate are willing to compromise.'[34] May failed to take heed of the words of Sir Nicholas Winton that she cited in her valedictory speech as PM: 'Never forget that compromise is not a dirty word. Life depends on compromise.'

ANNUAL PARTY CONFERENCE SPEECH, OCTOBER 2016: POINT OF NO RETURN

May's next Brexit decision appeared to come out of a blue sky. To some it was a bold act of political theatre and decisive leadership; to others, naked short-termism and gallery-playing to the longer-term detriment of achieving a good deal. So what happened?

Divisions had been growing within May's Europe strategy group, as within Cabinet, after her initial plan of working bilaterally with EU leaders ran into the sand. The search was on for a fresh strategy. DExEU and DIT were making heavy work of understanding the mindset of the EU Commission and Council. Whereas the EU had for many months been studying British politicians, their social media, podcasts, lectures, speeches and articles, Whitehall had not been reciprocating. The result was that it misread and underestimated key Commission players, not least Martin Selmayr himself. Driven strongly by Heywood, the top British civil servants were on a ferocious learning curve to catch up, to learn more about the intricacies of the EU and how Brexit might best occur.

Rogers began with May's full confidence. During the leadership election, she called him to see her in early July to talk through how she should position herself against Andrea Leadsom during the leadership campaign. No special advisors were present as they talked over the mechanism of Article 50 and how best she might bring about Brexit. 'You have to stay on with me. You're our only expert,' she confided in him. She liked his unflashy, logical mind and valued his inputs into their Justice and Home Affairs Council discussions at the Home Office. Timothy had found Rogers clever during their encounters in the Home Office, though was sceptical about him after his association with Cameron's negotiation of February 2016. Rogers soon grated with many in May's team with his all-knowing and pessimistic manner, his focus being on problems, they said, rather than solutions.[35]

In Storr, Rogers had a keen advocate, who worked hard to remind May's team that Rogers was from the Treasury, not from the FCO, and his unrivalled grasp of the brief was invaluable to them. But Rogers's modus operandi eventually ground May down. She didn't enjoy wading through his long emails over the weekend listing a host of problems. 'The nub was that Ivan couldn't resist speaking up,' says one official. Cameron's nickname for Rogers had been 'Tin Hat', because he felt they all needed to don protective cover to withstand his intensity.[36] It was a mild adage compared to what he was later to be called by a different No. 10 team.

Within Cabinet, the unity so apparent in the first few weeks of May's premiership was unravelling by early autumn. The leading Brexiteers, Davis, Johnson and Fox, along with Grayling, Leadsom and Patel, argued that the referendum result dictated leaving both the single market and the customs union. Fox was champing at the bit: for his department, DIT, to make any sense, Britain had to leave both institutions and avoid close EU alignment to allow him the freedom to negotiate trade agreements with other countries, his whole ministerial *raison d'être*. Hammond soon emerged as the leader of the soft Brexit side, adamantly opposed to any of the harder forms of Brexit, in particular no deal. It was quite a departure from his Eurosceptical tone as Foreign Secretary, when he declared in March 2015 that the EU needed reshaping because it had 'gone off the rails'.[37] But as Chancellor from

July 2016, he worried increasingly that the risks of leaving the customs union would be 'large and unpredictable', whereas the benefits of any trade deals that Britain might achieve would be 'unpredictable and almost bound to be smaller'. He worried too about the impact on financial services and the City, and the sheer cost of leaving. Discussions became heated among Cabinet ministers, particularly with Greg Clark, the Business Secretary, emerging as Hammond's main ally. The Cabinet Committee on Brexit, rather than full Cabinet, became the focus for long and acrimonious debate. To officials, 'It often felt like "Boris management". All eyes were on how grumpy he would be that day, and how to handle him. It made the deliberations very difficult to manage.'

May had three party conferences as Prime Minister: one disastrous; one defiant; and one, her first, which was to prove agenda-changing. When she became Prime Minister, she was faced with an immediate wall of pressure to trigger Article 50 so she could start negotiating. It would come to a head at the party conference. Pressure came from many quarters. The EU itself pressed her, following up its June Council verdict that there would be 'no negotiation without notification'. Brexiteers, above all Davis and Fox, put considerable pressure on her to trigger, while backbench pressure began to build in earnest from early 2017. The Labour Party too campaigned for her to get on with it, with Corbyn himself calling for the triggering of Article 50 the day after the referendum. The Cabinet committee was overwhelmingly in favour of her triggering quickly. Timothy and Hill were in favour. But her officials were not: Heywood, Robbins, Casey, Storr and Rogers counselled her against bowing to the pressure. Rogers, never afraid of a scrap, took the argument to Davis, Johnson and Fox in the weeks running up to the party conference. Their response was: 'You really don't understand, Ivan: we'll be able to get trade deals before the Article 50 process is over. We need to make hay before the end of the process.' Rogers hit back at them over and over again, as did other officials, telling them, 'It's not that easy. It can't be done.' Rather than heeding the advice of those who knew and understood, Brexiteers preferred to listen to senior Conservative Eurosceptics, including John Redwood, IDS, Bill Cash and Bernard Jenkin, with their mantra of 'getting out of the EU can be quick and easy' as 'the UK holds most of the cards in the negotiation'. Former Cabinet colleague Peter Lilley said later that, had it only been done properly, a deal could have been completed in 'just ten minutes'.[38] The evidence for their assertions was not probed.

Against such a fevered clamour, May and her chiefs decided she would give two party conference speeches: on Sunday 2 October she would speak about Brexit, while on Wednesday 5 October she would talk about the rest of her agenda. Their motive was to avoid Brexit dominating the entire party conference. The task of writing the speech was again given to Timothy, with some input from the No. 10 Europe team. The former sketched out the first draft at his desk in the oblong room in No. 10 just outside May's office. He describes the process thus:

> I had a conversation with her before I started, to ask her what she wanted to get out of the speech. We had discussions on whether she should put more meat into it, talking about free movement and immigration from the EU, but we decided against … The conceptual thinking had all taken place in the various meetings and had been agreed: all I needed to do was set it out in a speech. We knew it was for the party audience, but for the country too. What she was saying was: Britain is definitely leaving, we'll be leaving in good time. And we will honour the referendum result, which means that Britain will regain control of its borders, its laws and money, and we will be negotiating a new relationship with the EU. That's what Brexit means.[39]

The speech was not shared widely before conference. Cabinet ministers say they had little chance to read it, much less to debate it. Here was a Prime Minister who had made much of her restoration of Cabinet government three months before deliberately locking out her

Chancellor and senior ministers from the most important domestic policy announcement in decades. As Timothy says, 'The PM didn't want us to share the speech much with others.'[40] Officials, too, were out of the loop. Rogers got wind of what she was planning when he was in Bratislava on 16 September for an 'EU jolly'. Olly Robbins phoned his mobile to tell him, 'They want to announce that we will invoke Article 50 by no later than the end of March 2017.' Rogers uttered an expletive. 'I don't think it is wise, do you?' Indeed, Rogers didn't. 'It is utterly foolish, deeply unwise, it will hugely damage negotiating terms for Britain.'[41] Were they too late to stop it? Rogers was incandescent that she was planning to make such sweeping statements before she had even attended her first EU Council meeting, to be held two weeks later, on 20–21 October in Brussels: 'Why the fuck is the Prime Minister saying this on the eve of her first Council meeting?' They spoke to Heywood, who swore that he had not seen what she was going to be saying. When he had, he was no more comfortable than them. An official close to the Cabinet Secretary comments, 'Heywood thought that it was massive epoch-making decisions by speech turned into a style of government.' Heywood, Robbins and Rogers wrangled with her right up until twelve hours before she was due to speak. Defeated, they speculated whether she was driven to give the Sunday speech through fear that she'd be challenged for the leadership by a Brexiteer if she didn't come out strongly at the party conference.

Even Peter Storr, the official whom May and the two chiefs most trusted, had failed to convince her:

Denzil Davidson and I wrote in persuasive terms not to trigger Article 50 and not to mention a leaving date in the speech. The more I looked at it, the more complex I thought this was going to be, and it would not give us time for any breakdowns in negotiations. I had also reached the view that Whitehall as a whole needed more than another two years to prepare for leaving the EU. But we were up against the political need for them to say something at the party conference: they had an audience to feed.[42]

Political expediency was not their only motive. Timothy and May wanted the strong statement because they believed that by announcing they were triggering Article 50 they would show the EU they were in the driving seat. 'They used speeches to drive agreement across Cabinet and the government. They consciously used the device to describe what the policy was going to be,' recalls Wilkins.[43] They wanted Brexit 'done and dusted', for May's premiership to be economically and socially transformative for Britain: 'They didn't want Europe to define her, which it might have done, so they had the idea to start off with Brexit on Sunday and get it out of the way,' says Tanner.[44]

She opened the speech by saying:

The Conservative Party is united in our determination to deliver [Brexit]. Because even now, some politicians ... say that the referendum isn't valid, that we need to have a second vote ... But come on. The referendum result was clear. It was legitimate. It was the biggest vote for change this country has ever known. Brexit means Brexit – and we're going to make a success of it ... We will invoke Article 50 no later than the end of March next year ... This historic Bill – which will be included in the next Queen's Speech – will mean that the 1972 Act, the legislation that gives direct effect to all EU law in Britain, will no longer apply from the date upon which we formally leave the European Union. And its effect will be clear. Our laws will be made not in Brussels but in Westminster ... I want to [talk about] our vision for the future relationship we will have with the European Union ... There is no such thing as a choice between 'soft Brexit' and 'hard Brexit'. This line of argument – in which 'soft Brexit' amounts to some form of continued EU membership and 'hard Brexit' is a conscious decision to reject trade with Europe – is simply a false dichotomy ... We have voted to leave the European Union and become a fully independent, sovereign country ... [We will not therefore] establish a relationship anything like the one we have had for the last forty years or more. So it is not going to be a 'Norway model'. It's not going to be a 'Switzerland model'. It is going to be an agreement between an independent, sovereign United Kingdom and the European Union.

The speech went down predictably with the Brexit-supporting press and the Eurosceptic wing of the Conservative Party. Widespread jubilation was evident among Brexiteers in Parliament and across the country. Their day of freedom had edged much closer. Conservative MPs who were pro-Remain were mostly resigned to it, if not happy. A minority who had been arguing for a second referendum felt rebuffed by her refusal even to countenance one. Timothy met David Davis for breakfast on the Monday morning. 'It's funny how everyone has reacted to the speech,' the DExEU Secretary said, 'because basically it was a statement of the bleeding obvious.' 'That's how we all viewed what was said in that speech, Theresa May included,'[45] Timothy responded. The Cabinet bit their tongues about not being consulted or being able to comment in advance, with only the Brexit subcommittee seeing a late advance copy of the speech.

Officials openly disparaged her over the speech: 'She never revealed to us until the last minute what her hand was,' says one. 'Total playing to the gallery. She didn't show it to us till thirty-six hours before.' Consternation ran notably high in the Treasury and the Foreign Office. 'It's true that Merkel and many others in Europe were pressurising them to trigger Article 50, but that didn't mean that we had to accept their timetable. It was the most utterly foolish mistake, and we got absolutely nothing from it,' says a senior diplomat. Another comments on the decision:

I genuinely don't think Theresa May realised what she was doing, triggering Article 50. She thought that she could trigger Article 50 and that would put great pressure on the EU to make concessions, and that the pressure would be on them rather than on the UK. She thought that Article 50 would be fine as long as she kept saying no deal was better than a bad deal, and that it was possible to achieve that.

Rogers is predictably blunt in his response:

> Champagne corks were popping in Brussels and EU capitals when they heard her comments. It was precisely what they wanted her to say. They thought it was wonderful, because it removed all her leverage over them. The French told me, 'We can't believe you have gone now on the Article 50 route without knowing how it will work out.'[46]

An official at No. 10 agrees: 'By triggering it, we lost our leverage over running talks on Britain's future relationship in parallel with withdrawal agreements. We lost out over the rules of the game.'

Critics pointed the finger of blame not at May, the Prime Minister who delivered the words, but at Timothy for writing the speech and failing to consult colleagues. He counters the charge: 'People now criticise the decision to trigger it when we did. But if we waited much longer, even more people would have said that it was unacceptably long since the referendum. She was criticised for triggering it without a plan, but she had a plan. She just abandoned it later.'[47]

Timothy is adamant that the decisions were shared by ministers and officials. He takes Rogers head-on:

> Ivan would be morose and negative in meetings, but I don't ever recall him saying, 'We shouldn't trigger it with the timetable proposed.' People forget how hard we tried initially to talk to the EU capitals, but they wouldn't talk until we did trigger. Ivan's advice was that the bilateral attempts had failed, what else was there to do?[48]

May's next speech, on Wednesday 5 October, intended to be about her wider agenda, was, despite their best efforts, 'entirely overshadowed by Europe', says Wilkins.[49] A prime reason was that she suggested an even harder Brexit than on Sunday. Again, her comments were not shared widely in advance, either with Cabinet colleagues or with officials. She told conference:

> [We must] stop quibbling, respect what the British people told us on 23 June, and take Britain out of the European Union. Because it took that typically British quiet resolve for people to go out and vote as they did: to defy the establishment, to ignore the threats, to make their voice heard. So let us have that same resolve now. And let's be clear about what is going to happen. Article 50 – triggered no later than the end of March. A Great Repeal Bill to get rid of the European Communities Act – introduced in the next parliamentary session. Our laws made not in Brussels but in Westminster. Our judges sitting not in Luxembourg but in courts across the land. The authority of EU law in this country ended for ever … It is, of course, too early to say exactly what agreement we will reach with the EU. It's going to be a tough negotiation, it will require some give and take. And while there will always be pressure to give a running commentary, it will not be in our national interest to do so … But let's state one thing loud and clear: we are not leaving the European Union only to give up control of immigration all over again. And we are not leaving only to return to the jurisdiction of the European Court of Justice. That's not going to happen. We are leaving to become, once more, a fully sovereign and independent country – and the deal is going to have to work for Britain.

Timothy had wanted to make much of her introducing Britain's 'Great Repeal Bill', with conscious echoes of the Great Reform Act of 1832 which set the country decisively on the path to becoming a representative democracy. Not that he persuaded her to include everything he wanted her to say in his bid to unify British democracy and sovereignty. She pulled back from saying explicitly that Britain would leave the single market and customs union. On the evening of the speech, she had to refute that she had decided Britain would leave the single market, claiming, 'All options are on the table.' But her words were widely taken in Britain and in Europe to signify that she intended to leave both institutions (though it was to be another three months before she would say that in public). There were no such equivocations over Britain leaving the jurisdiction of the European Court of Justice (ECJ), a topic on which both Timothy and May felt extremely strongly. FCO officials claim that she hadn't understood the difference between the ECJ and the ECHR, with which she had previously dealt, and that she had failed to understand the economic role of the ECJ. Officials closer to her in No. 10 held a less cynical view, arguing that 'she did understand the ECJ as it affected issues like free movement and counter-terrorism work, but not its full sweep or how deeply connected it was to the EU construct'. On free movement, May was unquestionably direct. Britain was to take complete control of immigration. Free movement was to end. Period.

Pro-Leave MPs and the press were delirious with excitement again after her Wednesday speech, though those inside No. 10 at the time deny that she had been egged on by them, or by her conversations with right-wing MPs.[50] Remainers and 'soft' Brexiteers had been roundly defeated. And before conference ended, indeed, they were battered by two further events. On Tuesday 4 October, Home Secretary Amber Rudd announced that the Home Office would be looking to tighten the residence labour market test that companies have to pass before recruiting workers from abroad. Foreign workers, she said in her speech, should not be able to 'take jobs that British people should do'. Later that day, the Home Office compounded an emerging reaction to her words when they said companies might be required to publish the proportion of foreign staff they employed. The Home Office under Rudd had followed No. 10's line on immigration and on Europe. 'These proposals had been on a list of possible initiatives for some time. No. 10 said, "Let's do it," so we did,' says a Home Office civil servant. Fearing a barrage of hostility, her staff advised May to close it down immediately, and she agreed to release a statement that Wilkins had drafted the day after the conference ended.[51] But when Hill heard what he had done, she demanded to know: 'Where did this come from? It is a great story. We don't want to close it down.' She persuaded May to let the story stand. It did so for a week until, on 12 October, May was accused in the House of Commons of using 'xenophobic language' and appeasing the 'nationalist wing' of the Conservative Party. At PMQs that day, May insisted there had never been any plan to 'name and shame' companies but that the government was merely undertaking a consultation exercise.[52] 'Rudd's speech had a terrible reaction in Europe,' says a Brussels insider. 'It was regarded as deeply offensive. She had a terrible time when she went to the Council of Ministers meeting. It was appalling. It did Britain enormous damage.'

The other conference issue that fanned the flames were comments about Scotland that May made in her Sunday speech, when she said that no 'divisive nationalists' would hold up the process of Britain exiting the EU. Still more controversial were comments in her closing speech, when she said that too many of the British establishment, in particular rich business elites, behaved as though they had 'more in common with international elites than with the people down the road', adding, 'If you believe you're a citizen of the world, you're a citizen of nowhere.'[53] Not that she or Timothy were remotely aware of it, but to the EU the phrase 'citizen of nowhere' had echoes of what Hitler had said to denigrate the Jews as a 'small, rootless, international clique … at home both nowhere and everywhere'.[54] 'It struck Juncker himself, as well as people in Brussels and across European capitals, especially in Germany, as deeply offensive,' says Rogers. 'It symbolised to them that the internationalist agenda of Cameron and Osborne was over. Here was a completely different era.'[55]

May's team were extremely content with the way both her speeches had landed. They felt they had taken on the establishment and the nay-sayers head-on and had won the day. They now had a timetable for Brexit in the public domain and were working purposefully towards the details of a plan, which they would unveil in more detail early in the New Year. They became increasingly irritated by officials who continued to claim that her words had 'dramatically restricted our chance of succeeding in negotiations, and dramatically reduced our flexibility', and on the future relationship had 'slammed the door shut' on most models, including Norway and Switzerland. Anger focused increasingly on Rogers himself, especially when it was reported to No. 10 that he had been going round telling everybody who'd listen, 'This is fucking madness.'[56] It was a million miles from Davis's 'bleeding obvious'.

The EU would still need to agree to any Brexit deal. The party conference had done more than tell the EU that Britain would not be opting for a distant third-country relationship. It had unleashed fresh waves of concern among European capitals and in the EU's diplomatic community in London that the way May was handling Brexit would help fuel a populist backlash against the European project and that it 'could unleash a concatenation of events that might spell the end of the EU'.[57] Brussels was not happy, but no one near May seemed that worried about it, while Tin Hat himself was blamed for pointing it out.

A showdown with Rogers was inevitable before long. Before the European Council met on 20–21 October, Rogers wrote May a ten-page brief, as he had done for Cameron, to flag up the issues and the angles she might take. One paragraph covered the shock in the EU at her party conference speeches, specifically Juncker's reaction. The EU Commission's head honcho had told British officials he'd read her speeches three times and concluded that Britain wanted to go much further away from the EU than he had ever anticipated, with her words on the ECJ, free movement and the financial settlement causing him particular 'surprise'. He concluded that the most Britain could now expect from the EU would be a free trade arrangement analogous to Canada, and that it could only be negotiated after Britain left in March 2019. Worse, Rogers's note reported Juncker saying it would take 'two to three years' to negotiate with the EU, and a further two to three years to ratify, so it might not come into action 'until the mid-2020s'. Rogers dated the minute 14 October.

The words about the very lengthy transitional arrangement went down especially badly with May and her team. Rogers received no official response but encountered a 'very frosty' reaction when he met them in Brussels six days later.[58] May herself was unusually apprehensive when she flew into Brussels on Thursday 20 October. This was her first EU Council, and the photographers were everywhere, hoping to catch the moments when she greeted her fellow EU leaders for the first time, knowing their burning resentment at her pronouncements before she had had her first formal meeting with them. Unlike at her previous Justice and Home Affairs Council meetings, May would be on her own as PM without aides in the room (only Juncker as Commission President and Tusk as Council President were permitted staff). Aides were not even allowed to come in with notes during the meeting, but her team would be allowed to listen in a separate room and could text her, as they did with Cameron, so she should keep her phone by her side. She slowly relaxed, and by the end of the second day, she was pleasantly surprised by how the meetings had gone and how cordial her opposite numbers were. Genuine sadness was expressed by EU leaders at Britain's decision. 'The brutal truth', said Donald Tusk, 'is that Brexit will be a loss for all of us. There will be no cakes on the table. For anyone. There will be only salt and vinegar.'

REFINING HER POSITION: LANCASTER HOUSE, JANUARY 2017

May now had no time to waste in pushing ahead with her thinking on Brexit. In December, Timothy carved out time to write a speech she would deliver at Lancaster House in central London on 17 January. The clock was ticking in London as in Brussels: Brexiteer dissent at the lack of progress was growing again, and the first critical articles about her were beginning to appear in the press. None made more impact than the *Economist* leader in January, entitled 'Theresa Maybe', suggesting that her prolonged honeymoon might be coming to an end.[59] The chiefs wanted her to give a very clear statement about her intent, from which policy would be drawn and communicated to the EU. Hill says, 'We had two aims: to clarify our direction of travel to Parliament and the country, and to tell the EU unequivocally that we were going to leave the single market.' Significantly, she adds, 'I don't think that May ever thought about it deeply.'[60]

Deep within the engine room of No. 10, and among Cabinet, tensions were rising as Christmas approached. Divisions within the Cabinet Committee on Brexit over the customs union had reached breaking point: Hammond continued to hold out for Britain's continued membership, but he was losing ground against Cabinet colleagues. Forever trying to find a solution for his political bosses, Heywood came up with a plan in the autumn of 2016 that would allow Britain to have a sovereign trade policy while also remaining in the customs union. The plan became known as the Facilitated Customs Arrangement, though it wouldn't gain that name or be circulated widely until after the general election of 2017. 'It's ridiculous: it will never work,' Rogers told him. 'May won't take no for an answer,' Heywood replied. 'There's no point in making them believe they can have the best of both worlds,' retorted Rogers. 'They believe they can. They don't accept that they can't,' the Cabinet Secretary responded. 'Well, I won't put my name to something that won't work,' Rogers said.[61] Heywood and Rogers had worked together closely as Treasury officials since the early 1990s. But now they were on opposing sides. It was rapidly becoming a personal as well as a professional breach, and it made Rogers question whether he could continue.

The catalyst for his departure was a voicemail on his mobile on the eve of the December EU Council from the BBC's Laura Kuenssberg: 'I'm afraid to tell you that the BBC will be leading on a memo you wrote before the October Council,' it said. Rogers recognised the approaching storm at once. 'Post-Brexit trade deal could take up to ten years and still fail, warns UK's EU ambassador' was the predictable and fatal headline in the *Daily Telegraph* following the BBC reports.[62]

'They've stabbed you in the back,' one of Rogers's colleagues told him. Rogers believed that Hill had leaked the memo to Kuenssberg. 'I had had a clear-the-air session with Fi in October, but it didn't seem to have done much good,' Rogers comments now.[63] Hill's and Timothy's beef was that Rogers was merely reporting gloomy predictions from EU leaders rather than suggesting robust ways through the thicket. The damage was done. There was no way back. 'I'm resigning, but I'll keep it quiet,' Rogers told his wife after the Council. He decided he would quit on 3 January, the first day back in the office after the holiday, but before May's Lancaster House speech, so no one could claim he was leaving in high dudgeon over it. The mandarins closed around and though none knew he was resigning, they thought moving him on would be prudent. Heywood had decided to relocate him to the ambassadorship in Berlin, an important role in Brexit given the centrality of Merkel to any future negotiation, but Rogers resigned before he could be told of the offer. Olly Robbins had been worrying about Rogers's state of mind for some time, and arranged to have a drink with him before Christmas. He found him in a better frame of mind but had no idea that Rogers had already decided to leave. Heywood was flying back from Cuba from a family holiday on 3 January when his office received notice of Rogers's intention to resign. Realising it was a fait accompli, as soon as the plane landed, he set to work on finding a replacement.

A senior advisor in May's camp was unrepentant when they heard:

He jumped. We didn't push him. His briefing before the October EU Council had put the PM in a very awkward position. He would turn up and rarely say anything constructive. But we let him quit with the narrative about talking truth to power, and we set about getting somebody who would act as a civil servant should do.

Top of the list Heywood produced was Tim Barrow, British Ambassador to Russia for over four years and ripe for a move. He slotted in seamlessly as Rogers's successor as Permanent Representative to the EU on 4 January, his appointment further evidence to May of Heywood's ability to magic up solutions. 'Tim Barrow was a much better fit, frankly, for us than Ivan Rogers ever was. He saw himself as someone who worked alongside Olly Robbins and the team rather than as somebody who was independent,' says Wilkins.[64] Barrow certainly lowered blood pressures all round and was subtle and practical. His approach was to make the deal, rather than challenge the orthodoxy, which suited May's team but may not have always been in the best interest of achieving the optimal outcome.

The decks were cleared for May to speak at Lancaster House. Timothy outlines his thinking:

It was her big speech that would set out the broad strategy. And it worked quite well. It took the party with her. It was well received at home. But more importantly the reaction in Europe was – so we were told – pretty good. They respected the fact that she said we would not cherry-pick and that rights and obligations must be held in balance. And that meant that if we didn't want the rules of the single market we couldn't be members of the single market. The tone was constructive but there was also a bit of steel. It basically said we want a positive relationship but it also warned them against punishing us.[65]

By the New Year, Timothy had produced an early cut of the text and shared it with the team. Wilkins worked to improve it, with some additions from Hill, framing it more with a global dimension, while Storr and Davidson inserted some optimistic language about the future relationships with the EU, reflecting the conversations they'd had with EU ambassadors in London.

Timothy and Hill were anxious about how May would perform as she stepped up onto the podium for what they believed was the most important speech on Britain's position in the world that a Prime Minister had given for many years. But she quickly got into her stride and delivered the speech confidently:

A little over six months ago, the British people voted for change … They voted to leave the European Union and embrace the world … I want us to be a truly global Britain – the best friend and neighbour to our European partners, but a country that reaches beyond the borders of Europe too … I know many fear that [Britain's decision to leave] might herald the beginning of a greater unravelling of the EU. But let me be clear: I do not want that to happen. It would not be in the best interests of Britain. It remains overwhelmingly and compellingly in Britain's national interest that the EU should succeed … We are leaving the European Union, but we are not leaving Europe … What I am proposing cannot mean membership of the single market … I know my emphasis on striking trade agreements with countries outside Europe has led to questions about whether Britain seeks to remain a member of the EU's customs union. And it is true that full customs union prevents us from negotiating our own comprehensive trade deals … Whether that means we must reach a completely new customs agreement, become an associate member of the customs union in some way, or remain a signatory to some elements of it, I hold no preconceived position. I have an open mind on how we do it ... I want us to have reached an agreement about our future partnership by the time the two-year Article 50 process has concluded. From that point onwards, we believe a phased process of implementation ... will be in our mutual self-interest ... We will seek to avoid a disruptive cliff edge ... But I must be clear. Britain wants to remain a good friend and neighbour to Europe. Yet I know there are some voices calling for a punitive deal that punishes Britain and discourages other countries from taking the same path. That would be an act of calamitous self-harm to the countries of Europe.

May's vision was presented in the form of a twelve-point plan for Britain, which included the fateful words that 'no deal for Britain is better than a bad deal for Britain'. 'The words were written by Nick, who believed them, but I don't think that she ever did. To her, it was just a tactic,' says Hill. 'I suspect she thought it was OK to say because she had made the calculation that we would never end up with the threat of no deal.'[66] It was a more collegiate speech than at the party conference, with inputs far earlier in the process from Robbins, from her officials at No. 10, and from Barrow, only ten days into his job. It was greeted euphorically by Brexiteers in the press and in Parliament. Nigel Farage described the speech on LBC Radio as 'brilliant'. May's aim, always present if often unstated, of holding the Conservative Party together, had been accomplished, at least for the time being, at the price of appeasing her right wing. The Brexit wing indeed applauded her; the Remainers were subdued and divided. For now, they were biding their time. They had no leaders. Cameron was keeping his powder dry. Osborne was shortly to declare that he would be standing down as an MP. Hammond was coming round to her view: 'I wasn't at all happy with her party conference speech, but I moved towards her with Lancaster House and tried to accept her position. I liked what she said about building a close and special relationship.'[67] Besides, he lacked the instinct for a fight. Secretly, Timothy was not unhappy that the leading Remainer in Cabinet was someone he regarded as so politically inept.

By the end of her fifth decisive intervention on Brexit, May had established some clarity: she wanted Britain to pursue an independent trade policy while maintaining 'frictionless trade' with the EU27, end membership of the single market, end free movement, take back control of British laws and remove oversight of the European Court of Justice, and ensure no return to the hard border in Ireland 'of the past'. But her speeches, above all Lancaster House, left many ambiguities, including the precise regulatory relationship, the post-Brexit customs union relationship and the future of Northern Ireland. She showed no understanding, because she didn't understand, that it was the EU's customs union and the single market which made possible the dismantling of the hard border.

While the EU expressed some pleasure at her positive comments, it thought that the speech overall was a mass of fudge and contradiction. Her wish for Britain to get its own way on free movement and financial arrangements was inconsistent with her claim that it wanted to maintain close trade and close security relationships and preserve the status quo in Northern Ireland. One of May's team remembers hearing from a German politician in the Commission that the speech was 'extremely logical'.[68] High praise indeed. But others heard a different tone in Brussels. One recalls being told, '"We don't think it adds up. From her party conference speech, we took away that she wanted no real relationship, but from Lancaster House, she is saying that she wants to leave, but she also wants trade, security and Northern Ireland." To EU ears, it was confusing.'

ARTICLE 50: 29 MARCH 2017

During the referendum campaign, Cameron had stated very clearly that if the electorate voted to leave, they would rightly expect the invoking of Article 50 'to start straight away'.[69] Shortly after becoming PM, May said that she wouldn't invoke Article 50 in the course of 2016. The government soon faced challenges from several quarters arguing in the High Court that only Parliament, not the Prime Minister, could invoke Article 50. Gina Miller, a Remain-voting fund manager, a principal proponent, argued that, as the referendum had been advisory rather than legally binding, it required Parliament's approval to trigger it. The government's case was that Cameron had made it very well known that he would respect the result of the referendum, and therefore the Prime Minister could use the Royal Prerogative to trigger Article 50.

No. 10 was not too concerned about the challenge because the legal advice it received in autumn 2016 was that Miller would not be successful in the High Court, due to pass verdict on 3 November. When it decided for Miller rather than the government, Brexiteers were furious. Most famously, and worryingly, the *Daily Mail* produced a front page with photographs of the three High Court judges under the headline 'Enemies of the People'.[70] The subheading was: 'Fury over "out of touch judges" who defied 17.4m Brexit voters and could trigger constitutional crisis'. The article was written by political editor James Slack (already in conversation with Timothy and Hill about joining No. 10), though the headline was wholly the paper's. May did not speak out clearly in defence of the independence of the judiciary – a significant omission.

May had been devising her response to Miller with Davis, who since the New Year had become close to May and the chiefs. They decided that if Miller was successful, it would need a Bill to go through Parliament. The path was paved by a government amendment to a Labour opposition day motion on 7 December 2016, which called on the government to invoke Article 50 by 31 March. The European Union (Notification of Withdrawal) Bill 2017 was duly introduced into the House of Commons on 26 January 2017,[71] passing through on the third reading on 8 February by 494 votes to 122. The House of Lords made a number of amendments, including very significantly that there should be a 'meaningful vote' by the House of Commons, which passed through the Upper House on 7 March by 366 votes to 268. A further amendment unilaterally declared the protection of EU nationals in the UK. The Bill returned to the Commons, where both amendments were defeated, and was then sent back to the Lords. It passed through both Houses unamended, gaining Royal Assent on 16 March.

The letter triggering Article 50 now had to be composed. Robbins wrote the first draft and Timothy came back with his own version several days later. They then held a 'weirdly academic' series of discussions in Timothy's room in No. 10, both managing to work collegially on the process. They were aware that it had to be 'completely water-tight'. The main point of difference between them was on the meaning of the phrase 'deep and special relationship'. Timothy says that in his own mind he was thinking about security and an FTA-style relationship on trade, whereas Robbins envisaged a much broader and more meaningful sense of the word 'relationship'.[72] One No. 10 official comments that the letter 'was a funny mixture of some warm words and threats. Guy Verhofstadt in particular thought it landed badly and was a threat, but other aspects of the letter were seeking partnership.'

The Article 50 letter was taken by Eurostar to Brussels, where Tim Barrow was to submit it personally to Donald Tusk in his capacity as President of the EU Council in front of the world's cameras on the specified deadline day, 29 March 2017. The letter included the words:

Earlier this month, the United Kingdom Parliament confirmed the result of the referendum by voting with clear and convincing majorities in both of its Houses for the European Union (Notification of Withdrawal) Bill. The Bill was passed by Parliament on 13 March … Today, therefore, I am writing to give effect to the democratic decision of the people of the United Kingdom. I hereby notify the European Council … of the United Kingdom's intention to withdraw from the European Union.

There could be no going back. The EU knew time was now on their side. Barnier kept repeating his catchphrase, 'the clock is ticking'. In private, he, like other senior EU leaders, thought May was deluded. She had no idea how difficult the negotiation was going to prove. The EU began to relax on another score too, as Verhofstadt says: 'Fear in the EU that Britain's referendum result would encourage other countries to leave was very real – but in the months following, we saw exactly the opposite of the populist reaction against the EU that Mr Farage talked about.'[73]

TRIGGERING THE 2017 GENERAL ELECTION

On the evening of 15 March 2017, Timothy accompanied Hill into the garden of No. 10 for one of her regular cigarettes. They were exhausted by the effort of getting Article 50 through Parliament, and by the sustained opposition from a small minority of Tory MPs. The government majority of only twelve weighed on their minds. As Hill recalls:

We were looking down the barrel of multiple fraught votes for Brexit to happen. Nick and I realised we just didn't have the arithmetic: our political capital had been used up in this parliament. We asked ourselves: how could we possibly get something through like Brexit that's far bigger than Article 50 with the same numbers we have now? It was one of those moments when Nick and I just had the same thought at the same time. And out it came: 'How on earth can we get something far bigger and beastlier through? We just don't have the numbers. We're going to have to have a general election.'[74]

On 18 April, the Prime Minister announced that a general election would be held on 8 June. Her seventh and final decision, inspired by parliamentary arithmetic, and with Davis and Hammond stiffening her resolve, had a critical impact on the outcome of Brexit. May went into the election campaign still with little idea about the details of a future relationship with the EU. A week after announcing the election, she invited to dinner at No. 10 Jean-Claude Juncker, Martin Selmayr, and Michel Barnier, on Wednesday 27 April. The calling of the election had gone down well in Brussels: Selmayr, a bellwether for EU opinion, called Robbins to say he thought it was 'an excellent strategic decision, and a very good thing for Brexit, because it would make a proper transition period possible, which would not have been the case had it been necessary to hurry the transition period through before a general election in 2020' (i.e. five years after Cameron had called the 2015 general election). But the mood darkened considerably soon after, resulting in a cessation of negotiations during the period of the election campaign. Dinner at No. 10 was not a success. The EU team were surprised by Davis 'bragging' that he was an independent operator, challenging openly and regularly what May said, and leaving the EU team embarrassed and uncomfortable. British officials found it hard to coordinate the mixed messages May and Davis were giving to the Europeans: 'The only way to get them to say anything consistent was to have a race to the top in terms of each outdoing the other in their ambition for what was achievable,' says one present. Selmayr's recollection is:

> I remember the dinner in Downing Street before the general election because I was blamed for it, and when you are blamed for something you remember it. It was a particularly harsh and bad memory. We had long debates on whether or not to go to London. I had to disrupt my holiday to go there. We in the end decided to go because you have to be open in a negotiation. What we heard there was no context or clarity, which shocked us. David Davis did most of the talking, saying that Brexit would be a success and a walk in the park, that it could be done on a couple of pages and that would be it. It was an

underestimation of the complexity of untangling forty-five years of membership. What shocked us most was mention of the Protocol 36 negotiations, when Theresa May was Home Secretary, when the whole Commission worked for two years to achieve something that Britain only opted out of but then decided to opt into certain other instruments. So when Protocol 36 was mentioned, this set all alarm bells ringing. On the return from London, we were depressed in the plane – Juncker said that the negotiation was never going to work and that if Barnier wanted to do another job, that would be fine. It wouldn't only be a difficult negotiation but might be an impossible one because the other side doesn't know what the negotiation is about even six or seven months after they had started the process.[75]

An account of the dinner was then leaked, the British believed by Selmayr, to the *Frankfurter Allgemeine Zeitung*. The paper claimed that Juncker had launched a scathing attack on May, warning her that Brexit 'cannot be a success', and that he left Downing Street 'ten times more sceptical' about the prospects of success than when he arrived. The report said that Juncker had called Merkel the following day and described May as 'deluding herself' and 'living in another galaxy', while Merkel accused Britain of suffering from 'Brexit delusions'. Juncker is said to have estimated the chance of the Brexit negotiations succeeding at under 50 per cent.[76] May and her team felt betrayed and very angry. They claimed her aim had been to try to get to know Juncker better, to talk through some issues, and to understand how progress could be made after the general election.[77]

Selmayr gives a different account of how the story came to light:

Juncker asked me the next morning, as I always did, to call all my colleagues in the other twenty-seven states and debrief them. When I called my German colleague, he told me that Juncker and Merkel had already spoken last night. He called her from his mobile and had given a live account of what happened because it had shocked him so much. This made the rounds and Merkel even said in a speech in the Bundestag that they live in another galaxy. Juncker repeated this in the press conference himself after the European Council. What was in the German media on Sunday was common knowledge among the twenty-seven leaders. So to blame one person was wrong![78]

One reason some in No. 10 believed Juncker, Selmayr and Barnier were so hostile was because they were disconcerted that the figures they regarded as the biggest influences on May – Timothy and Hill – were not present. They had resigned from their official roles as chiefs of staff to work on the general election campaign. The Europeans wanted to talk to the real power brokers. It revealed how out-of-touch, on the eve of the general election, the British were in understanding the minds of their EU partners.

Timothy and May had pushed May to trigger the general election in the belief that it would make the passage of May's Brexit vision not only possible but also achievable. The way the general election was to be conducted, and the result, ensured that neither would happen under her leadership.

Theresa May rode high in the polls and impressed overseas leaders in her first ten months. Here, she holds hands with newly elected US President Donald Trump at the White House on 27 January 2017.

CHAPTER 4

BUILDING HER BRAND

May knew that her premiership would be dominated by Brexit. But she wanted it to be about much more. She had her own vision of Conservatism and the fairer, more One-Nation Britain she wanted to see, one whose leader could stand proud and hold influence on the world stage. Just because it was articulated for her largely by Nick Timothy, it didn't mean that she didn't believe it passionately herself. Two further aims were equally dear to her: to hold the party together and to strengthen the Union after the referendum. The annual party conference in early October 2016 had been her first real opportunity to present her shop window to the public, which she elected to do in two distinctive speeches, one on leaving the EU, the other about her domestic agenda. She was about to find that realising her vision was more difficult than giving speeches about it, as departmental clashes stalled reform, visits abroad became more difficult with the election of Donald Trump, and personal relationships in Downing Street deteriorated.

A 'NEW CONSERVATISM': MAY'S PARTY CONFERENCE SPEECH, 5 OCTOBER

Timothy and Wilkins had approached May's second party conference speech, to be given on Wednesday 5 October, as an opportunity to fill in details of her domestic policy agenda and introduce the new Prime Minister, still largely unknown to most Conservative delegates, as a leader with strong and cogent views. They wanted to show the many who still hankered after Cameron and Osborne that the woman they had dismissed as 'submarine May' could command the party with her authenticity and honesty. Her Conservative Party would be more broadly based, socially and regionally, winning over the Labour voters disillusioned with years of drift under Ed Miliband that strategists at CCHQ said were there to be coaxed to the Tories in the wake of Brexit.

Hill, who had done so much to craft May as a leader, wanted her to make a splash when she walked onto the stage in Birmingham. Hence her idea of the PM's entrance being accompanied by the Rolling Stones classic 'Start Me Up'. May had never heard of the song till then, so Hill lent her the CD: 'She got into it and really quite liked it,' she recalls.¹ Indeed, it planted the germ of an idea for her even more showy entrance onto the stage at the party conference two years later. Her walk-on music deliberately envisaged a new era, with a brave new Conservative agenda reminiscent of Stanley Baldwin and Harold Macmillan, as articulated in the latter's book *The Middle Way*. Much was made of the speech being delivered in Birmingham, the hometown of both Timothy and his political hero, Joseph Chamberlain, who in the early twentieth century helped make the city a worldwide symbol of successful municipal government, with education, housing and social services. From Baldwin in the 1920s till Thatcher succeeded Edward Heath in 1975, the Conservative Party had advocated an active role for government. But then it moved in a more individualistic direction, extolling self-interest and the unbridled free market. This was the philosophy May tackled head-on in her Birmingham speech. She even had praise for Labour's most successful Prime Minister, Clement Attlee – a bold step. The speech located May's vision for the party firmly in the tradition of Conservatism that reached back all the way to Benjamin Disraeli.

'It's time to remember the good that government can do,' May announced from the stage. She criticised untrammelled free markets, the sacred cow of the Thatcherite tradition: 'Where markets are dysfunctional, we should be prepared to intervene. Where companies are exploiting the failures of the market in which they operate, where consumer choice is inhibited by deliberately complex pricing structures, we must set the market right.' The City of London was next in her sights, and she criticised the Bank of England's quantitative easing for 'some bad side effects', though she regarded the policy as ultimately necessary medicine for a sick economy. Companies were warned that adjustments needed to be made after the financial crisis had left large parts of Britain behind. Warming to her theme, she said, 'People with assets have got richer. People without them have suffered. People with mortgages have found their debts cheaper. People with savings have found themselves poorer. A change has got to come. And we are going to deliver it.'

Not since Heath attacked British businessman Tiny Rowland and the 'unacceptable face of capitalism'[2] in 1973 had the excesses of capitalism been so castigated by a Conservative Prime Minister. May made thinly veiled threats to bosses such as Mike Ashley of Sports Direct and Philip Green, whose Arcadia Group included BHS, and to corporations like Amazon and Google. That afternoon, Macfarlane found himself fielding perplexed phone calls from the Treasury and the Bank of England, May's old employer. Energy companies who were charging expensive tariffs also came in for criticism: 'It's just not right that two thirds of energy customers are stuck on the most expensive tariffs.' Nor was it right, she said, 'that the housing market continues to fail working people'. Business leaders and tax avoiders, too, came under the cosh: they 'don't understand what the very word "citizenship" means', and would be cracked down on. Further opprobrium was heaped on unaccountable wealthy elites and exploitative bosses, tax-dodging multinationals, and tech giants who refused to cooperate in the fight against crime: 'I am putting you on warning,' the Prime Minister said. 'This can't go on any more.'

Theresa May was presenting herself as champion of the dispossessed, the powerless and ordinary citizens across the country oppressed by a powerful elite. Theirs was the voice, she said, that had spoken in the referendum: 'Millions of our fellow citizens stood up and said they were not prepared to be ignored anymore.' Brexit would give them a 'once-in-a-generation chance to change the direction of our nation for good'.

The speech was a world apart from anything Cameron had delivered, or Osborne might have given had he been at the podium that day instead of May. In her search to build a Conservative Party for the early twenty-first century, she was doing more than reaching out to Labour voters disillusioned with Corbyn, who had been in office for just over a year, and to UKIP supporters and beyond. She was making a direct appeal to working-class voters whose 'dreams have been sacrificed in the service of others'. You are the people, she was saying, who have suffered most from the impact of low-skilled immigration, a constant May theme, and I am seeking your support. She was still a largely unknown figure. Did the party and the country know her better after this appeal? The speech, which at her own insistence avoided mawkish details about her personal life, barely succeeded in that mission. There was still a disconnect between the person at the podium and the words that came out of her mouth. She was still a largely unknown Prime Minister, the adage used to describe a predecessor as Conservative Prime Minister, Andrew Bonar Law. But people were prepared to forgive her for her lack of charisma, or even personality, at least for the time being.

May's speech deserved more widespread comment than it received. But it was overshadowed by her words about Europe in her previous conference speech three days earlier and by the ongoing furore around the Home Office announcement on foreign workers. Wilkins, who had co-written the speech with Timothy, says, 'We wanted to make it all about the country coming together, about the Conservative Party having a big heart and social conscience. But the broad theme was altogether lost because of noise about Europe and companies keeping lists of immigrants.'[3]

The May agenda, nevertheless, had been clearly laid out with clarity and ambition. Attention now pivoted to whether she had the leadership skill and Cabinet ministers able (and willing) to convert the fine words into policy. Had she the majority in the House of Commons to pass the legislation to enact the ideas? As *The Guardian* put it, 'Words are the easy bit. Policies and actions will define whether the change which Mrs May promised is a real possibility or not.'[4]

MAY: LEADER ON THE WORLD STAGE

In the first few weeks of the May premiership, there were echoes of the exuberance and optimism that marked the first months of Blair's premiership after May 1997. 'The sense was that, if we can get this right, Theresa May has a real chance to be the most grown-up figure in the West. By the end of the year Trump would be in the White House, Merkel on her long way out, and Macron raw and faltering,' says one of her team.[5] Fiona Hill had stellar ambitions for her boss: 'I wanted to position her as a very serious player on the world stage. If she was to be a world leader, she needed to have good bilateral relations, so I pressed her to take leading positions with India, the US, the Gulf and the Japanese leaders,' she says.[6] It would be May, rather than Boris Johnson at the Foreign Office, who would drive British foreign policy in this new era of our national history.

Johnson's power as Foreign Secretary was constrained from the outset. The creation of DExEU stripped out his responsibility for the single most important foreign policy objective of the government, exiting the EU, while the creation of DIT took trade policy firmly away from the FCO. Whatever May said to him on the day of his appointment, she showed little commitment in taking his contribution seriously once her government began its work. From now on, foreign affairs would be made in No. 10. Even DExEU and DIT quickly found out they were subordinate to Downing Street. Civil service appointments reflected this power structure. Jonny Hall, an official from DfID, replaced FCO thoroughbred Nigel Casey as the new Foreign Affairs private secretary in No. 10, a pivotal role, and Catherine Page, who did not have an FCO background either, was made responsible for the EU.

An early turf war with Johnson on British policy towards Israel was driven by Timothy. As Home Secretary, May had established strong links with the Jewish community in Britain, who supported her tough line on extremism. Matters came to a head in December, after Trump's election but before his inauguration, when Obama's outgoing Secretary of State, John Kerry, encouraged the UN to slap Israel down before the pro-Israel Trump arrived. Timothy urged May to say that Britain would no longer tolerate the habitual singling out of Israel for denigration by the UN's Human Rights Committee. He phoned Johnson to gain his support: 'Great, great, let's go for it,' the ebullient Foreign Secretary replied. But Johnson promptly changed his tone, the chiefs suspected after listening to his officials at the FCO. 'Of course, I'm as keen to be helpful to our supporters in north London as you are,' Johnson told one of May's staff, who surmised that self-interest rather than principle was Johnson's guiding star. May prevailed on the line to be taken at the UN, and Johnson accepted her judgement. But it marked the institutional differences between May's No. 10 and the Foreign Office that were to add strain to the personal relationship between the two principals.

Johnson would make periodic remarks that would irritate No. 10 and further aggravate the relationship. One came on 15 November, when he said that the UK would 'probably' leave the customs union, and another on 8 December, when he said that Saudi Arabia was 'a puppeteer' in the Middle East. When his attempts at levity backfired, as when he joked that Italy would have to offer tariff-free trade to sell its prosecco to the UK,[7] No. 10 failed to see the funny side. May finally lost patience with him in April 2017 over a leak to *The Sun* concerning her refusal to back air strikes in Syria, which overstepped security lines. But it was Johnson's constant neediness which, according to Hill, damaged their relationship most: 'He'd always be wanting to have meetings with her and she'd say, "No, sorry, I'm too busy."'[8] He wanted to be a close confidant on the evolution of Brexit policy, but she never wanted his input, another irritant between them. In Cabinet, she would be particularly cutting to him for not understanding the detail. A regular phrase Cabinet ministers heard was: 'No, Boris, it's not that simple.' His colleagues winced.

President Putin and Theresa May might have made an odd couple, but Hill identified the Russian leader as an early candidate for special attention. After May flatly refused to play ball with the idea, Hill searched around for other world leaders beyond the EU with whom May could form a close relationship. She alighted on President Xi of China. Given Timothy's known antipathy to China, and the fallout from the Hinkley Point decision, this also went nowhere, despite frantic efforts from Liu Xiaoming, the long-serving Chinese Ambassador in London, to build bridges.

India moved up the Rolodex, and she visited the country in November 2016 at the head of the big trade delegation. Much was made before the visit of India being especially chosen for the first bilateral visit by the new British Prime Minister outside Europe. India is the third largest investor in the UK, and the UK is the largest G20 investor in India. The omens looked good. Considerable work went into the preparation, and she took with her a high-powered delegation including university and business leaders. At the outset, she met Indian Prime Minister Narendra Modi to discuss Anglo-Indian relations and prospects for enhancing trade. Deals were signed worth £1 billion, laying the groundwork for a stated 1,300 new jobs in the UK – but this was paltry stuff.[9] She didn't hit it off with Modi: 'They were not remotely like-minded personalities,' says one who observed them together on the trip. Indeed, from Modi down, Indians' response to her was at best lukewarm. *The Hindu* newspaper described it as 'a lacklustre visit'. It was a far cry from Johnson's prediction that overseas countries outside the EU would 'jump at the chance' of trade deals with Britain.

Lack of personal chemistry alone does not explain the flop. May's attitude to overseas students does. With unhappy timing, a Home Office announcement three days before the trip placed new restrictions on overseas students, including two-tier visa rules and a crackdown on work visas. It came against a background of deep resentment in India towards her for introducing restrictive immigration policies when Home Secretary, which had led directly to a 50 per cent drop in Indian students enrolling in British universities.[10]

The trip revealed May at her worst on the foreign stage. Her lack of confidence and human touch militated against her befriending Modi and other senior Indians. Lord Bilimoria, a senior figure in the Anglo-Indian community, had been on similar prime ministerial trips to India with Blair and Brown, and twice with Cameron. This was the least successful of all of them, he judged, and Anglo-Indian relationships plunged to their worst point since before Major had opened up the bilateral relationship in the early 1990s. Bilimoria reflects:

It went wrong from the beginning, when she spoke in public alongside Modi. In her opening comments, she failed to make any mention of education or universities. He was too polite to make his displeasure obvious. In a private meeting, against heavy advice, she then mentioned the issue of the repatriation of 'overstaying' Indians in the UK, which caused grave offence, and she failed to take action on an issue that would have gone down very well, bringing

Indian business and tourist visitor visa fees into line with rules applying to Chinese visitors – four times lower. The whole visit was an avoidable disaster. Her hostility to international students, and to understanding the concerns of Indians, was obvious to all. Unlike all other Prime Ministers I have travelled with, she did not even take time to engage with the delegation accompanying her from the UK. Relations plummeted as a result.[11]

Her trip to the Gulf, four weeks later in early December, was far more successful. The high point was a speech to the Gulf Cooperation Council (GCC) of the six Gulf states, the first time a woman had addressed the council, with the Kings of Saudi Arabia and Bahrain listening to her, alongside the leaders of Qatar, the UAE, Kuwait and Oman. Hill, who had not gone to India, invested much in the Gulf visit. 'I wanted her to seek out trading partners with sovereign wealth funds. It was a trip she really enjoyed. She was warm with the leaders and her words landed really well.'[12] May announced plans for a £3 billion defence investment by Britain in the region, saying she was glad that Britain could rely on its 'oldest and most dependable friends' as she guided the country towards Brexit. She had been urged to raise the Gulf's attitude to women's rights. She avoided doing this head-on so as not to cause offence, but pressed the leaders to pursue 'essential' social and economic reforms, telling them that they had to build 'economies that work for everyone'. Could the Gulf's first female GCC speaker, and a champion of women's rights, have done more? Probably. But delivering hard messages, unless she was very sure of her ground, was not in her nature. Why did May succeed in the Gulf when she had failed utterly in India? It came back again to her Home Office background: when faced with a security-laden world such as the Gulf, she was comfortable, as she was with Arabs. In more complex and interpersonal diplomatic situations, such as India, she struggled. Which May would she display when she travelled to Washington?

An uncomfortable curtain warmer came with May's trip to the World Economic Forum at Davos on 19 January 2017, two days after her Lancaster House speech. She told the rich and powerful gathered in the Swiss resort that while 'some of our European partners feel that we have turned our back on them', the UK's decision to leave the EU was 'no rejection of our friends in Europe'. This clearly conflicted message did not land well with an audience still smarting from her 'citizens of nowhere' comment. Her speech received far less notice than the one by billionaire George Soros, who said, 'The people in the UK are in denial,' adding that he thought it 'unlikely' May, with her 'very divided Cabinet [and] very small majority', would remain in power.[13]

She was not in a good mood when she was taken by helicopter off the mountain to the airport, still less so when she saw that the Prime Minister's usual RAF BAe 146 plane was not on the tarmac to take her home, but rather a workaday model. 'Where's my plane?' an irate May demanded of the RAF officer charged with taking her home. 'I'm very sorry, Ma'am, but the Chancellor has taken your plane.' Whether it was because Hammond was the culprit or because Davos was not going to plan, she exploded. 'She went absolutely crazy,' says one witness. 'Her whole body contorted in anger and indignation.' Those with her were stunned. They had never seen her behave in this way, which was described as almost 'child-like'. The stress of Davos, the opposite of her natural milieu, had got to her, as had the pressured and unpredictable demands of the Prime Minister's life.

MAY AND TRUMP: NOVEMBER 2016–JANUARY 2017

In the summer and autumn of 2016, all eyes in Europe were on the United States as it approached the end of its presidential election campaign. The British Embassy in Washington, presided over by Ambassador Kim Darroch, a former National Security Advisor, was confident of a Hillary Clinton victory. That was good enough for May's team. Two women leading two of the world's most powerful countries sounded good to them. Three if you included Merkel. Neither of the chiefs concealed their personal dislike for Trump, and had written disobliging tweets before entering Downing Street, Hill describing Trump as a 'chump' in late 2015 and Timothy saying that he didn't want any 'reaching out' to Trump after he had all but secured the Republican nomination in May 2016. May had not established a good rapport with the outgoing Obama. When they had met at the Hangzhou G20 summit in early September, they had fallen out over policy towards Iran. May, following briefing from her FCO officials, urged the outgoing President to stand up to Tehran.[14]

The British Embassy's strong links with Clinton and the Democrats were not matched with Trump and his fluctuating entourage, largely because his world revolved around New York, not Washington: 'Trump is a New York guy: all his movers and shakers were there. He wasn't a Washington person at all,' says one official. After Trump's surprise victory on Tuesday 8 November, relations with the President-elect and his team thus needed a rapid turbo charge.

Darroch had been told by Trump's transition team that the British Prime Minister would be 'the first on the call list of the new President'. But in the shambles, including the sacking of the transition team, the priority list was lost. Darroch managed eventually to speak to Trump's personal assistant on 9 November at 6 p.m. Eastern Standard Time and was told, 'I have the President-elect standing next to me, put the Prime Minister on.' The ambassador had to explain that he was in Washington while the PM was in London. He put a hurried call through to No. 10, but, in another almost comic error, he was told that the Prime Minister had gone to bed (it was 11 p.m. in London) and couldn't speak to Donald Trump. By the time the conversation eventually took place, on 10 November, May was the ninth foreign leader he called. To the intense irritation of No. 10, the press interpreted this as a slight to May and to Britain. 'Donald Trump's snub to Theresa May is a huge embarrassment' was the *Daily Telegraph*'s headline.[15]

Anger focused on Darroch personally, who had already been under the spotlight because of suggestions that he be replaced in Britain's most prestigious overseas posting by the UKIP leader, Nigel Farage. This improbable saga began in July 2016 when Farage visited the Republican Convention in Cleveland and met some of Trump's aides, meeting Trump himself the following month at a fundraiser in Jackson, Mississippi. Trump took a shine to the ebullient Englishman and asked Farage to speak at the rally, introducing him as 'Mr Brexit'. Farage became the first British politician to speak with Trump in person after his election, at Trump Tower on 12 November. They hit it off so well that Trump sent a tweet suggesting that Britain should name Farage as the next British Ambassador: 'We assumed he thought ambassadors changed as in the US with an incoming administration,' says an embassy source.

No. 10 and the FCO very quickly, if politely, closed the story down. 'It was never remotely a possibility. We were emphatic to the incoming administration that it would never happen,' says Timothy.[16] The chiefs, who themselves were tightly controlling access to the Trump team, flew across to the US in December to meet Reince Priebus, Trump's newly selected chief of staff. 'Don't countenance for a moment that we might make Farage British Ambassador,' Hill told him. 'When I say the Prime Minister is serious about not having him, she is serious.'[17] In a telling moment, Priebus asked the chiefs, 'So tell me, what does Mrs May stand for? What is she about?' They looked at each other. A long pause. 'She's about delivering for people,' Timothy eventually said.

A series of conversations with business leaders had been arranged by Antonia Romeo, the British Consul General in New York, who knew the Trump team well. 'It was quickly apparent to British diplomats in New York and Washington that Timothy and Hill were calling the shots on the evolving policy towards the Trump administration, not the FCO,' says a source. Anthony Scaramucci, a member of Trump's new transition team and fleetingly White House director of communications the following year, concluded after a two-and-a-half-hour meeting with them that they had very different economic philosophies. 'Why is May so anti-business?' he asked British diplomats afterwards. Trump's team told Timothy and Hill that Gary Cohn, the president of Goldman Sachs, whom they had appointed Trump's chief economic advisor, would be dealing directly with Jeremy Heywood over an Anglo-American trade deal. The chiefs had their eyes opened during their visit. Their advice back to May was: 'Trump is not a conventional politician, and the development of a personal relationship with him will be critical.'[18] One diplomat comments that May's team were correct in their evaluation of Trump as a wholly different proposition, even if Whitehall at large was slow to catch on: 'I don't think Whitehall understood the change quickly. We were always playing catch-up with Donald Trump. We thought it was about old-fashioned diplomacy, but it was about business with Trump. It was all about business, it's all the art of the deal.'

Quite how unconventional Trump was, May's team would soon see. But first, the British establishment was working overtime to get May to see Trump in person ahead of any other foreign leader. Darroch tried a succession of phone calls to those close to the President-elect, eventually getting hold of his son-in-law, Jared Kushner, who invited him to Trump Tower. Kushner had earlier been in contact with other British diplomats by text to say that the UK was 'an important relationship for the US and to DJT'. It sounded promising. Darroch rushed to New York, then up the lift in Trump Tower, to discover all Kushner wanted to discuss with him was Israeli–Palestinian politics. So Darroch then called the mobile of Steve Bannon, chief strategist to Trump, who said, 'Come and see me at my house in DC tomorrow.'

Darroch, after three hours waiting, eventually saw Bannon, and they hatched the idea of May seeing Trump in the White House: 'Yeah, yeah, fantastic,' Bannon said.

May had already received an invitation by post to speak at the Republican Party's 'retreat' in Philadelphia just after Trump's inauguration on 20 January. The team thought this was a good opportunity 'to build bridges, cement a relationship with the Trump team and keep in touch with the emerging Trump project', says Wilkins.[19] Discussion had ensued over whether Trump and May should have their first meeting in Philadelphia or delay it till they met in Washington: the latter was decided, so some deft choreography was required to ensure that the two principals avoided bumping into each other at the retreat.[20] May was in good spirits when she flew to Philadelphia. Timothy seized on the speech she was to deliver as an opportunity for her to give a head-on repudiation of what had become known as the 'doctrine of the international community' first uttered by Tony Blair in April 1999, and which provided the justification for 'liberal interventionism' in Afghanistan and Iraq. May had been sceptical about such invasions, including Libya in 2011 and Cameron's plan to intervene with Obama in Syria, after chemical weapons had been used by the Assad regime, in August 2013. Timothy built on her inherent caution and scepticism about great-power invasions of other countries and wove it into a coherent philosophical speech, which again put down clear blue water between her and Cameron. 'It's what she felt,' says Timothy. 'All I did was verbalise it for her.'[21] Indicatively, the Foreign Office, which might have expected close involvement in such an agenda-setting speech, was, to its indignation, left out of the loop.

The speech was partly written as a direct warning to Trump to tone down some of the belligerent rhetoric of the campaign when he arrived in office. Britain and the US must never again intervene in other sovereign countries' affairs with the aim 'to remake the world in our own image', May told senior Republican figures in Philadelphia.

There must be no 'return to the failed policies of the past' that saw Britain and the US bogged down in conflicts in the Middle East. But she was not saying that Britain and the US should fail to honour their global obligations in tackling challenges as they emerged, not least the fight against ISIS. 'Nor can we afford to stand idly by when the threat is real and when it is in our interests to intervene. We must be strong, smart and hard-headed. And we must demonstrate the resolve necessary to stand up for our interests.'

An express warning came to Trump on Iran. The West had to push back against Tehran's 'malign influence in the Middle East', but equally, the Iran nuclear deal should be 'very carefully and rigorously policed', she said, rather than unpicked, as Trump had suggested.

It was a remarkably bold speech for May, a new Prime Minister still green in international matters, the strongest she was to give on foreign policy, and the one and only time she openly lectured Trump on how to exercise US influence on the world stage. It set out a strong intent for British foreign policy: to work with the Trump administration, but also to be clear where Britain differed. She spoke of a new era in the special relationship between the US and the UK, which she said was all the more needed in the world because of the rise of 'new enemies of the West and our values'. The rising challenge from China, as well as India, further underlined the need for both countries to work together. Britain would not be retreating from the world after Brexit, she said; quite the opposite. Under her premiership, Britain would take on an 'even more internationalist role' around the world. To address anxieties in the EU that May was about to form an exclusive relationship with Trump, which might be specifically anti-EU, she made a feature of praising European values in the speech, which landed well back in the EU.

The Republicans loved it, and they gave her a series of standing ovations, confirming that, in their new right-of-centre leader, Britain too had found an authority figure as forthright as their own bold new champion. The mood was captured by two Republicans overheard chatting as they were walking away, saying, 'Well, Maggie has been reborn, hasn't she?'

The next stage of May's journey was the short flight down to Washington. If Timothy was in charge of scripting May's utterances during the trip, Hill commanded the way the trip was presented and its messaging. May's team assembled at the British Embassy in the elegant Edwin Lutyens-designed residence in Massachusetts Avenue, two miles from the White House. At the last minute, as the convoy was leaving for Pennsylvania Avenue, they received a message from Buckingham Palace with their agreement that May could offer the President a state visit to Britain, which he craved. Diplomats didn't believe that it was necessary for May to offer it on their first meeting, but Hill pressed for it, the Palace agreed, and they decided to make it the top item at the press conference later that day. May's team were aware of the symbolism and the lift it could provide to a Britain preparing for Brexit. The chiefs had high hopes that a relationship between May and Trump might flower.

Breaking all White House protocols, Trump came to the door of the White House to greet her, and after a few moments together ('getting to know each other'), he escorted his British guests to the Oval Office. The agreed procedure was that both principals would have four staff with them: for May, Timothy and Hill as well as Darroch and Mark Sedwill, soon to become National Security Advisor; for Trump, Michael Flynn (his chosen National Security Advisor), Priebus and Bannon, none of whom were to last, as well as Kushner. Several features struck the British, including the lack of chemistry (hardly a surprise) between the two leaders: 'She's not his person at all, or vice versa,' says one. No one on the US side made any record of what was said. Trump's verbal domination and the style of discourse took them aback: 'He did all the talking. There was no working through an agenda. He just shot the breeze: very unusual.'

May's principal objective was to secure a pledge from Trump that the US would not pull out of NATO, fortified by the considerable apprehensions in Europe that Putin was considering invading the Baltic states. Trump provided her with the reassurances she sought, adding as a flourish, 'And you can tell people that.' She promptly did precisely that, drawing him in to fully commit himself to NATO in their press conference that followed. Discussion included Brexit, which Trump described as 'really good for the UK', and the state visit. Trump was thrilled to be told the news and it was clear to all that he was very happy to accept.

Then they moved out to the press conference. Trump opened by praising the special relationship, 'one of the great forces in history for justice and for peace', and reminding the world's media that his mother was born near Stornoway on the Isle of Lewis, which he described as 'serious Scotland'. In her own opening comments, May said for the first time in public that she was able to convey the hope of Her Majesty the Queen that the President and First Lady would pay a state visit to the UK later in 2017 (though in fact it wouldn't take place until June 2019). On NATO, she said, with uncharacteristic chutzpah, 'Mr President, I think you confirmed that you were 100 per cent behind NATO.' As she said those words, she looked across at him meaningfully standing at the podium to her left. To a question about the fascination that people had about how they would get on personally, Trump replied, 'I can often tell how I get along with someone very early, and I believe we're going to have a fantastic relationship.'[22]

Lunch followed, with a wider team joining from both sides. Trump's opening gambit was about the press conference: 'So, Theresa, who do you think won that?', meant in part as a joke, but also a search for validation, the British team thought.[23] Her FCO briefing suggested she should talk up his election victory, knowing that would put him in a good frame of mind. Throughout the meal, the President was relentlessly undiplomatic, launching into topic after topic for a couple of minutes, saying after each, 'What do you think of that, Theresa?'

Clearly probing her personally, he also sought to discover where the British government stood on a range of positions that would be important to him. An early line of questioning was on abortion and reducing fixed time limits. May was staunch in her reply: Britain had its abortion policy 'about right'. Trump was then 'extremely rude' about the EU, and recounted how he had been unable to develop an Italian island because of EU restrictions imposed upon him. The British team were surprised by how candid he was about Merkel, saying he thought she'd lose the election to be held in September 2017. He spoke about Islamic extremism and 'no-go areas in Britain'. Again, May interjected to correct him. He talked at length about his team and the Cabinet he was pulling together. Then he returned to how much he loved Britain, his mother adoring the Queen, and how 'you guys will always be the first through the door'.[24] Finally, on handling Brexit, he gave May three pieces of advice: 'Always ask for more than you want, always be prepared to litigate, and conclude what you want early on so you can go back and forward.'[25] She offered no response to this unsolicited Brexit guidance, which she was the recipient of again and again towards the end of her premiership.

May was in high spirits when she arrived back at the residence. 'That was quite something, wasn't it?' she said, to which her team replied, 'Perfect, a triumph, we're very, very happy.' Only then did she tell them about some comments that Trump had made when they were on their own, walking from the Oval Office to the press conference: 'By the way, he did hold my hand when we were leaving the Oval Office.' 'What?!' the team exclaimed. 'Did it get onto any of the cameras?' 'It must have done,' she replied. 'That wasn't the image we needed. We wanted to keep a distance from the President,' said one of the team. She told them that she had the impression that he didn't want to walk up on the ramp to the East Room for the press conference on his own with his fear of germs from the handrail, so she 'lent him her hand'. Several of May's team recall her laughing and relaxing with the team at the British residence in Washington as the high point of her entire premiership. Wilkins recalls:

> We all thought she was brilliant on that trip, at her very best, strong and refusing to be overawed. We never saw her better. Self-confidence was key: she'd been having a very good January, with Lancaster House and then the Philadelphia speech. She channelled the positive energy to help her perform well. Dragging the commitment to NATO out of the President was sheer quality. At lunch afterwards, she continually parried Trump's provocative comments, without alienating him.[26]

Some shine was taken off the trip by a disastrous visit to Turkey immediately afterwards: she flew overnight to Ankara direct from Washington. Her exhausted team had no prior warning of an Executive Order restricting US immigration from seven predominantly Muslim countries, and they were totally wrong-footed. The move exposed May to criticism for her own tight policy on immigration, as well as her unwillingness to criticise her new best friend. Outrage exploded in Britain and across the world. A frantic weekend of phone calls from the embassy to the White House followed while British diplomats tried to gain exemptions for dual-national Muslims living in the UK, until the Executive Order was thrown out as unconstitutional. 'Total chaos: it showed these guys around the President know absolutely nothing about government,' says an official.

The January trip to Trump showed May at her very best on the international stage: it made her staff wonder what she might have achieved if only she could have been always this effective. Those whose business it is to watch Prime Ministers in action internationally rated her as 'not bad' as a Prime Minister on the foreign stage. But 'to be really good as a Prime Minister, you need to be able to respond in the moment and think on your feet, and to be able to build personal relationships, because most foreign policy is about human relationships'. The US trip showed what she could achieve. Hill felt disappointed that May hadn't risen to the aspiration she had set her of becoming a major player on the world stage, as Cameron undoubtedly would have done had he stayed on: 'It was probably a step too far for her. Her mind was on Brexit, and she felt she had to sort that out, and was more comfortable doing that than working with international leaders who she barely knew.'[27]

Hill was puzzled by another facet too: 'I didn't see her ever feeling the need to form a personal opinion on any foreign leader, or to engage with them on a purely personal level.'[28] The leader closest in personality to her was Angela Merkel. It took time for a personal bond to form between them, but, by the end, it was her closest – indeed, only – serious overseas relationship. Merkel shared with her the perception that there was a need for 'angry white men' to 'humiliate female leaders', and what one had to do was 'soak it up' because it was the natural order of things in their world. Once one accepted it, she said, there can be the basis of a new relationship. 'The only leader I've seen who I believe Theresa May could talk to was Angela Merkel. They forged a real connection,' says one diplomat. Again, one is left wondering what might have been had May approached her relationship with Merkel in a more robust way earlier: indeed, with other world leaders too, all of whom would have welcomed it.

NO. 10–TREASURY RELATIONS AND THE 2016 AUTUMN STATEMENT

For the May premiership to deliver on her domestic agenda, and on her Brexit strategy, May needed a Chancellor with whom she could work closely. A strong working relationship with the Foreign Secretary, in contrast, hasn't been a requirement for the Prime Minister since the 1990s. But instead of a collaborative Chancellor, May had Philip Hammond. Jeremy Heywood, who had closely observed the relations between eight different Chancellors of the Exchequer and Prime Ministers, thought the relationship between May and Hammond deteriorated more quickly than any other he had known. Another official echoes the sentiment: 'It took only days for the May–Hammond relationship to sour, quicker than any in living memory.'

It is very rare for a Prime Minister to flourish if they have a bad relationship with their Chancellor. Thatcher's relationship deteriorated towards the end with Nigel Lawson, as had Major's in the latter stages with Norman Lamont. Blair had an increasingly dysfunctional relationship with Brown, to the detriment of his policy, while Brown himself never trusted Darling. None of these relationships were as poor as May's with Hammond during the first year, after which it improved markedly. The only wholly good Prime Minister–Chancellor relationship in the forty years since Thatcher came to power has been between John Major and Kenneth Clarke. A Chancellor needs to be their own person, but also in sympathy with what the Prime Minister is trying to do. The relationship goes wrong when they are too distant; equally, it is compromised when they are too close, a common criticism of Cameron's relationship with Osborne.

May appointed Hammond as Chancellor but very quickly came to regret it; Timothy even more so; less so Hill, who had worked with Hammond in 2006–08. Both May and Hammond shoulder responsibility for the distance between No. 10 and No. 11 during her premiership. The Chancellor traditionally has his House of Commons office next door to the Prime Minister's, indicating the importance of their relationship. After his appointment, Hammond chose to remain in the Foreign Secretary's room he had had under Cameron, around the corner. He told party chairman Patrick McLoughlin that 'it's not worth my while moving. If you think you can have a drink with Theresa and chew the cud, you can forget it.'[29] May's team speculated that he harboured a grudge against her dating back to the time that they both competed to become MP for Maidenhead, and he never forgot he lost out against her.

From the moment she became Prime Minister, they felt he showed her little admiration or respect.[30] Both principals indeed arrived in their new roles somewhat damaged. May had felt patronised and manipulated for six years by Osborne and by the Treasury, as indeed she often was. Osborne had wanted her as Home Secretary in part because she wouldn't oppose the cuts, and he cut her no slack. Hammond, who had secured the safe seat of Runnymede and Weybridge and entered Parliament in May 1997, at the same election as May, also felt periodically thwarted and marginalised by Cameron's team in No. 10. He had spent six years climbing the ministerial ladder in government since 2010, watching Cameron and Osborne work together almost as dual Prime Ministers, and had imagined that, when appointed Chancellor by May, he would adopt the same central role over domestic policy as Osborne, and as Brown before him. Osborne, indeed, had encouraged him to think that way, and spoke about how, during his tenure, the Treasury, not No. 10, had a free hand on Budgets and Autumn Statements.

May had no intention of replicating a Cameron–Osborne relationship now she had the keys to No. 10. 'Philip wanted to be number two in the government. But she wouldn't have it, and he knew it,' comments one official. She wasn't prepared to share the premiership with anybody, and most certainly not with Hammond, for whom she had no warmth at all. Hill had tried early on to arrange breakfasts and dinners between May and Hammond periodically, including their partners, but it did no good.[31] After Hammond's appointment, Hill met one of Cameron's No. 10 team, who asked 'why on earth' May had appointed Hammond, whom Cameron thought 'a nightmare', and had planned to shift from Foreign Secretary at the next reshuffle.

Hammond's relationship with Timothy was core to the poor relationship. Never good, it deteriorated very rapidly. Timothy says:

> He wanted to be treated like a partner at the top of the government, but she's not like that. She found him aggressive and disrespectful, and [he] gave us the impression that he resented the fact that she was Prime Minister, that he could do the job better. The truth is that he was not good at dealing with Theresa, and she wasn't good at dealing with him. They disagreed on huge areas of policy.[32]

Hammond puts the blame for the strained relationship more squarely on the chiefs than any policy disagreements with May:

> They were pure poison. It was simply the way that they were; they were a toxic mix in No 10. I knew Fi well, she'd been my press officer when I'd been an opposition spokesman. The relationship worked well when I was the boss but, once she was in power, she was quite intolerable. Nick hated me and made my life difficult wherever he could. The two of them were always leaking to the media that I was going to resign.[33]

As relationships between the Chancellor and the No. 10 chief of staff went, Hammond and Timothy's most resembled that between Gordon Brown and Jonathan Powell. But this was worse. Hammond knew how little May knew about economics and finance, as did Brown with Blair, and he exploited rather than accommodated himself to it.[34] She, meanwhile, absolutely hated his attempts to explain economic realities to her: 'Theresa, that's not how it works,' he would tell her regularly in their meetings.[35] Unlike Blair, she had never been Leader of the Opposition, so had never had to reply to the Budget, which would have given her a broader understanding of the economy, the work of the Chancellor, and the functioning of the Treasury. Instead, she had seen the Treasury only through the (very distorted) eyes of the Home Office. As Will Tanner puts it:

> She had run the Home Office in a command-and-control manner. She had learnt there to be mistrustful of the Treasury. Very early on, strategically, she and the chiefs took the decision that No. 10 would be the powerhouse. We would tell other departments what we wanted from them, then expect them to get on and do it. It meant a difficult relationship with the Treasury. She knew there would be resistance, so she and Nick decided to work policy up in No. 10 and then to tell departments what they were to do.[36]

Their initial fight came in the first few days over Hinkley Point. Before long, officials noticed that both figures were 'awful, awful at communicating with each other'. The tension was not soothed by Timothy, who was antagonised by Hammond's obvious scepticism about his role and his lack of enthusiasm for the entire May agenda on economic, industrial and social policy – even before they got on to Brexit. Briefing against Hammond started early on. 'The chiefs didn't treat him with respect, and he is a man with an ego,' says one insider.

May's team heard reports that Osborne and Hammond were lunching and dining regularly together, and they maintained a keen watch for signs of the former Chancellor exerting a malign influence over his successor. Will Macfarlane, the Deputy Principal Private Secretary at No. 10, was charged with the responsibility of improving the relationship between No. 10 and the Treasury as the tempo of meetings built up towards the Autumn Statement in 2016. He spoke regularly to Heywood about it, as well as to Hammond's Principal Private Secretaries, successively Conrad Smewing then Stuart Glassborow. After six years of harmony between the Treasury and No. 10, it was new territory for all. By early autumn 2016, it was apparent to Heywood that the relationship wasn't improving, so he talked to Tom Scholar, Permanent Secretary at the Treasury, to ask for his advice on what could be done. But Scholar said the Treasury was as baffled by it as him, and they saw no easy solution.

May had outlined a remarkably ambitious domestic agenda in her speech on 13 July and at her keynote party conference speech on 5 October. Ministers needed money to translate her words into active policy. But Hammond didn't want to provide money, and that lay at the core of the problem, above all with Timothy. A Treasury official speaks bluntly of the relations early that autumn:

> The Chancellor wasn't on the same page remotely as Nick Timothy on policy. He wanted to focus on the big questions of Brexit, where they also differed diametrically. If asked whether the government could have a domestic agenda and a Brexit agenda, he would always say, 'Prioritise the former.' He'd say, 'The economy is holding up, despite the Brexit uncertainty, but what we need to do is to get to the other side of Brexit.' He wasn't remotely interested in Nick Timothy, or the agenda that he was trying to push through.

The clash between Hammond and Timothy became very personal and very unpleasant. Timothy repeatedly railed against Hammond's obtuseness and lack of respect for the Prime Minister's agenda. Word came back to No. 10 that Hammond would be openly contemptuous in meetings at the Treasury of 'Nick Timothy's wacky ideas'. Underlying tensions exploded at a meeting in early November in the Prime Minister's office. 'We need to see fiscal changes that work for ordinary families,' Timothy told Hammond, staring at him very aggressively. 'No, you don't need to do anything. You just need to tell people that's what you want to do. That is enough,' Hammond retorted, to Timothy's fury.

Timothy became increasingly frustrated with May herself, whom he thought insufficiently assertive against Hammond. He watched on looking pained as Hammond ran rings around her. As an official recalls, 'The Chancellor knew the Prime Minister wasn't strong on figures and he would talk her into submission. There were long, long meetings in No. 10 leading up to the Autumn Statement. If there were ten items on the agenda, we rarely got beyond item number three. It was interminable.'[37]

Another Treasury official says, 'It was absolutely ghastly. The worst relationship I've ever seen in government. Nothing that we did to improve it worked, because the blood was so terrible. It hit rock bottom with the Autumn Statement in November 2016.' Another Treasury official said to Hill when she met him for a drink to discuss the impasse: 'Will this ever end? It's impossible to do business like this.'[38]

The Autumn Statement was fast upon them, and agreement had to be reached. One of the fights was over to national insurance contributions, which Hammond wanted to raise for Class 4, the self-employed. 'This is dangerous, Philip. Do you have backbench support?' May asked him. 'Yes, I have, I've been talking to them,' he replied. This disagreement dragged out over several meetings, with May blocking him several times, until eventually she relented and gave it her agreement on the basis that she had at least tried to make him rethink it.[39] Other disagreements were less soluble.

As the Autumn Statement approached, Heywood started chairing meetings with officials and special advisors from No. 10 and the Treasury, so he could arbitrate and pave the way for May's own meetings with Hammond. One official comments:

Jeremy was obviously very significant in that he gave No. 10 an economic heft, placing himself squarely in the middle of the Autumn Statement (and Budget) processes. It meant that the Treasury had to engage with No. 10 over it because Jeremy had inserted himself. Jeremy got on well with the Chancellor, but always saw his role as facilitating the Prime Minister, albeit one in Theresa May who didn't always say what she wanted. What he did was to translate her so the Chancellor understood what it was she wanted.

The Autumn Statement contained some progressive measures to support those 'just about managing', including on universal credit and a ban on upfront fees charged by letting agents. But, overall, the Treasury had won, and the Autumn Statement was a rebuff to May and Timothy's agenda. As *The Guardian* said, 'The autumn statement will have disappointed those who expected May's "Jam"-focused government to be quite different from Cameron's ... Today was her first big chance to strike out in a new direction but ... what was striking was the continuity.'[40]

Hammond had won the first round, but there would be bloody fights up ahead. The relationship between the Prime Minister and Chancellor was about to become even uglier.

IDEAS INTO POLICY

May became Prime Minister in July 2016 awash with ideas. But she had not won her own general election, lacked a personal mandate, and her own manifesto. She had appointed John Godfrey as head of her Policy Unit, Will Tanner as his deputy, and some highly capable staff below them. Within days of their appointments, they were hard at work in their upstairs offices overlooking Downing Street, trying to work up budgeted policy proposals. Coming to power between general elections poses peculiar problems, and May, at Heywood's prompting, recognised the need to bring order to her policy ideas. Hence, Ben Gummer, Minister for the Cabinet Office, was given the task of assessing the 2015 manifesto commitments – all 554 of them – to see which might be achievable. He set to work at once.

At the heart of the new reappraisal of priorities was May's analysis that the referendum result was only in part about the EU, including immigration; it was equally about the sense that, for many people across the country, government wasn't working for them. As Gummer puts it:

We believed the referendum provided an injunction that went beyond Brexit, in both style and substance. In substance, to govern for the whole nation, with special regard for those most ignored, many of whom had displayed their anger in the referendum ballot box. In style, it meant restoring a sense of integrity to politics, to promise only what we could deliver, and to deliver what we had promised. In the first instance, that involved a root-and-branch reformulation of the 2015 manifesto, realigning it with what the Prime Minister wanted to do and being realistic about what could and could not be delivered, especially given the fact that the all-consuming nature of Brexit made doing anything else in government extremely difficult.[41]

By August, Gummer had completed his task, and he presented it to Cabinet in September. His work envisaged three separate streams of activity for the government to focus on: industrial strategy, burning injustices (which included race, gender and poverty) and racial diversity. Cabinet demurred in places but was broadly supportive.

Director of strategy Chris Wilkins was then given the task of forging an overall narrative for the government to last the three and a half years until the general election expected in 2020, which became known as the 'Plan for Britain'. Picking up the baton from Gummer, he began work in earnest with a small team, conducting research and focus groups weekly. By the end of November, Wilkins had acquired a vast body of work, which in December and January he shaped into the plan that became public for the first time in May's Lancaster House speech.[42] His research showed clearly that 'the dominant concern people had was that life wasn't fair … So fairness became the dominant value to which we worked.'[43] As he said in a speech in July 2017:

> This agenda – with its focus on the broadest possible interpretation of Brexit, on ordinary working people – or at times specifically the so-called 'just about managing' – and critically, on a vision for the kind of country we wanted Britain to be, was brought together in the Lancaster House speech … where we first talked, quite deliberately, about our 'Plan for Britain' rather than just a Plan for Brexit.[44]

The Plan for Britain, having been put to Cabinet, was officially launched on 16 March and formed the centrepiece of May's speech to the Welsh spring conference the following day. Wilkins says:

> The six months we spent on the plan was about trying to provide a unifying vision for Britain post-Brexit. It was never a policy statement, but a strategic framework for others to operationalise. It was notably progressive on economics, on lifting the public sector pay cap, worker representations on boards, the industrial strategy, the shared prosperity fund and rebalancing the economy away from the south-east. The scope was very ambitious.[45]

While Wilkins was beavering away, Timothy was itching for policy progress. But as every new avenue opened up, Hammond stood in the road blocking their progress, refusing to commit the money needed. Free schools, which Timothy saw as a core part of May's education policy, saw one such 'No entrance' sign from Hammond. With progress on grammar schools being held up by Greening, free schools seemed propitious territory. But Hammond said he didn't believe they represented value for money. Instead, he wanted to see existing schools expanded, rather than new ones created. As Tanner recalls:

Philip was very obstructive to Theresa and Nick, even on areas [where] you would expect him to have been supportive, such as the expansion of free schools. We had a massive disagreement after he gave an outright 'no' to a new wave of free schools. It took a massive amount of work to get that over the line.[46]

In the end, compromise came when Hammond agreed to expand free schools as long as No. 10 agreed to reappraise capital projections. Hammond told Timothy, 'If I agree to free schools, I want DfE to look at existing surplus capacity and ensure it meets genuine needs,' recalls one official.

Disagreement over education policy also came from No. 10's push for funding to enable the overhaul of technical education, to be known as T-levels. Officials from No. 10 and the Treasury sat through multiple meetings working through the detail. A Treasury official recalls:

On the Friday evening before the announcement, they still hadn't agreed it, but No. 10 wanted to brief out to the Sunday papers. We didn't have a name for the new policy but out of the blue sky we came up with 'T-levels'. So that was what they became known as.

Education was a core component of May's industrial strategy to boost support for further education, technical and vocational qualifications and apprenticeships as viable forms of post-18 education to be ranked alongside university. The running was made by Greg Clark and BEIS, with regular No. 10 prodding. The Policy Unit's Neil O'Brien, previously special advisor to Osborne at the Treasury, rapidly showed his loyalty and worth to his new bosses. Part of his skill was knowing how to keep the Treasury onside. They visualised broadening out Osborne's 'Northern Powerhouse' initiative beyond Manchester to include other northern industrial cities such as Leeds, Liverpool and Sheffield. Much was made of the focus on 'city deals' and 'sector deals', including life sciences.

Progress was much swifter here than on the more contentious areas of corporate governance reform, which Hammond blocked at every point. Consultations with industrial leaders about spreading board representation to workers were discouraging: messages came back that it would encourage trade unions and damage the quality of corporate leadership. The policy was amended to a milder form in which non-exec board members were encouraged to be responsible for employees in their care. May was supportive of the broad thrust, and the encouragement to small- and medium-sized enterprises, though details of much of the agenda escaped her. She told one advisor that she thought Cameron and Osborne had been too close to big business. But it was unusual for Britain to have a Prime Minister who had spent so little time with captains of industry. She was somewhat in awe of the City and top entrepreneurs: she had not mixed with many top staff when she had been at the Bank of England, but she always listened closely to her husband Philip on City and financial matters.

Housing was an area that she understood, and she wanted action to boost affordable housing. Considerable pressure had accumulated across the political spectrum to boost housing numbers, supported by Sajid Javid as Secretary of State for Housing, Communities and Local Government, and Gavin Barwell as Minister for Housing and Planning. Both were crusaders for deregulation. At the party conference in October 2016, Javid said, 'Far too many young people cannot get a foot on the housing ladder … Let's be honest with ourselves, there is still a long way to go.' Tackling the housing shortfall was, he said, 'a moral duty',[47] his words roundly applauded by delegates. On 7 February 2017, he published a White Paper, 'Fixing our Broken Housing Market', setting out the government's intention to reform the housing market and boost supply. But the thrust was slowed by Hammond, who argued that the housing market should prevail: there was nothing wrong, he claimed, in the way that house builders operated and built new homes. While No. 10 constantly pressed for local government to release land for new homes, Hammond's retort was that it didn't represent 'good value for money'.

The impasse might have been unblocked had the Prime Minister weighed in. But May dragged her heels, even though she understood the need intellectually. At one meeting in her office, she flicked through a document the Policy Unit had prepared, spying that her constituency of Maidenhead was earmarked for 850 new homes. She swooped. 'You cannot be serious,' she said. May's personal focus group was her conversations in her constituency. It made her wary of homes going up in the south-east: hostility from middle-class residents made her uneasy. She didn't want to court unpopularity and expend political capital on more social housing for rent, owned by local authorities and housing associations. As with immigration, May was socially conservative and didn't want the way that people lived their lives to be disrupted. Javid found her 'Nimbyist approach' parochial and disappointing. This was not a sentiment unique to Javid – even members of May's own team believed her to be too timid on housing.

Javid's relationship with May and her team was one of the worst of any Cabinet minister during her first year in Downing Street, and they soon suspected him of being disloyal. The No. 10 political team was asked to prepare a record of stories where he might have been briefing against the PM. 'It was never explained to us what use would be made of it,' says one political aide. A particularly vicious spat occurred with Hill over rough sleeping: Javid favoured trying to criminalise it, to which Hill responded that he was a 'moron'. Conflict between Javid's special advisors and No. 10, to which Hill and Timothy were no strangers, added fuel to the flames. By early 2017, Javid was seething about the way he felt treated by them.

May's aversion to risk and lack of radicalism were equally evident in proposed reforms to health and social care. The Policy Unit thought that the NHS was ripe for reform, and that the internal markets introduced by Health Secretary Andrew Lansley under Cameron hadn't worked. May, even more than most PMs, was hyper-sensitive to the possibility of a winter crisis and she listened very attentively to what NHS chief executive Simon Stevens said. But she didn't favour significant change or any restructuring. She knew that the NHS was labyrinthine and that previous attempts to reform it had backfired. She didn't understand what had gone wrong or how to put it right. 'Don't touch it,' she thought to herself. But she did want to see increased funding for the NHS, though it didn't come till after the general election.

Mental health, however, was an area where she was prepared to push the boat out to take risks. She had been struck at the Home Office by the large numbers being detained in police cells with some form of mental health condition. She fought an eighteen-month battle from 2012 with Health Secretary Jeremy Hunt, which culminated in victory for her, largely because No. 10 decided in 2014 that it wanted to jump on the mental health bandwagon. So soil was fertile for her as PM. As Tanner says, 'It felt like mental health was a strong area that we could build on when she came into No. 10.'[48] In autumn 2016, Tanner worked hard on a groundbreaking speech for her, written after consulting widely with charities and academics including leading psychiatrist Simon Wessely. May delivered the speech, entitled 'The Shared Society', on 9 January 2017 at the Charity Commission. 'The burning injustice of mental health and inadequate treatment ... demands a new approach from government and society as a whole,' she said. It was one of the best-conceived speeches of her premiership, outlining a programme of action that had all been carefully planned, and with the Treasury giving more money than had been anticipated.

Leadership by May, even before Prince William and Prince Harry became seriously involved in mental health, gave the cause a decisive push. Her empathy for those who suffer could be deep, if patchy. She might not have allowed herself to be affected by the plight of migrant families, but mental health anguish touched a raw nerve in her. It is indicative that one of the charities of which she was patron, and in which she took a keen interest, was DrugFAM. Set up by one of her constituents, Elizabeth Burton-Phillips, who lost one of her twin sons to drugs, it seeks to help families who have an addict in their midst.[49] Domestic violence touched her deeply too, and she was eager to support the push to translate the agenda into legislation, driven by Hill.

MARCH 2017 BUDGET

Confidence was running high in No. 10 in early February, with Lancaster House and the US visit successfully over, and with the Conservatives doing well in the polls, helped by Corbyn's leadership of Labour. May's team, deeply frustrated by the lack of progress on domestic policy so far, saw the March Budget as the chance to kick-start her domestic agenda. But while Heywood and Macfarlane did everything to get the Treasury onside, again, the Chancellor was not for turning. He would not agree to throwing away money on what he considered half-baked schemes. No, Hammond had his eyes on a much bigger prize, a way of steering the country through Brexit to a financially strong future. As Wilkins recalls:

> Preparing for the Budget in March 2017 was agonising. No. 10 concluded early on that Hammond was again being tricky. It was hard to lead, with strongly competing agendas from No. 10 and the Treasury. We met in her room, initially weekly, then twice weekly, then more often. It was a power game. Hammond would try to wrest control of the meeting away from her and insist that we use

his scorecard, with his agenda items on top. Nick wanted his items on top. Nick was very concerned about the JAMs, and that they wouldn't get enough in the Budget. They had furious rows. The conversations kept coming back to what Nick wanted to do to try to provide the financial space to help, and Hammond resisting. It was not pleasant.[50]

Hammond went into the Budget round of talks still smarting from the rows over the Autumn Statement. But, below the surface, he remained steely: the Budget was his domain. Heywood and Macfarlane worked hard on the Treasury to try to find the money Timothy and May wanted to allow more spending. Tanner recalls the atmosphere in the build-up to the Budget: 'In No. 10 we thought that Philip Hammond was more interested in completing the agenda he inherited from George Osborne rather than helping us establish the agenda for an imaginative new government. He was very Tory, always very conscious of backbench Tory opinion.'[51]

Much angst had been caused in the Autumn Statement discussions because both principals arrived at meetings with different sets of figures. So Heywood and Macfarlane worked hard to ensure that May and Hammond had the same evaluations, figures and briefings before their meetings. This footwork mitigated only some of the difficulties. As Tanner recalls:

The March 2017 Budget was the Prime Minister's great opportunity to substantiate the JAMs agenda. Neither Hammond nor the Treasury liked the fact that she and No. 10 were trying to muscle in on their own plans. They argued over everything. Hammond picked apart No. 10's policies, including subsidised bus travel in support of those on low incomes. But the Treasury had their own ideas. The Budget could have been a high point for the May premiership. But it ended up going not nearly as far as she wanted. It was framed in a very orthodox way.[52]

No single Budget debate was more acrimonious than that over national insurance. Hammond was fixed on addressing its multi-billion-pound shortfall, which was due to expand further as more turned to self-employment. He returned again to the idea – first suggested during the Autumn Statement – of raising Class 4 national insurance contibutions. Different tax treatments for different forms of employment was unfair and unsustainable, he reasoned. May was unconvinced: the political impact of a tax hike, regardless of the policy arguments, could be significant. Hammond believed it was essential, especially, he observed, given the new spending required by the chiefs' plans on social care, the NHS and more. The pair clashed at a number of meetings. Hammond told No. 10 they were panicking. 'It'll be fine,' he said. 'Look at the polls, we're way ahead.' Hammond ploughed on, finalising the Budget package with the Office for Budget Responsibility.[53]

What Hammond and his team had ignored, however, was that Cameron's 2015 manifesto pledged a five-year tax lock – on income tax, VAT *and* national insurance contributions. Hammond thus delivered his speech on Wednesday 8 March entirely unaware of the turmoil that his words were about to stir. He had wanted a self-consciously low-key and balanced Budget, with none of the Brown/Osborne giveaways and gimmicks. He wanted to achieve favourable headlines by virtue of his pragmatism and raise new revenues to replace what he – or, as he saw it, No. 10 – was spending. The national insurance change proved popular at first, winning some support from the centre-left because the money raised was destined for health and social care. But when, after the post-Budget lobby briefing by Hammond's special advisor, it emerged that the policy contravened the 2015 manifesto, a storm was quickly whipped up. No. 10 came under immense pressure to reverse the policy. As May left for the European Council in Brussels on

10 March, she debated with her team what to do, ultimately resolving that she had to stick by her Chancellor. But Hammond's team, fearful that the Chancellor was about to be stitched up by May and Timothy, pre-emptively briefed the press. May was defending her Chancellor at the European Council when BBC *Newsnight* saw the counter-briefing from Hammond's team. Much of this appeared in the papers on Sunday 12 March, including Hammond's private words about May and Timothy, that they were 'economically illiterate'.[54] May hated being patronised, and exploded when she found out about the headlines and briefings. Yet again, No. 10 suspected that Osborne had been goading Hammond behind the scenes.

By early the following week, anger from Conservative MPs made No. 10 recognise that a U-turn on national insurance had become unavoidable. A meeting was convened to discuss what to do, at which Chief Whip Gavin Williamson and Leader of the House of Lords Natalie Evans told the Prime Minister they didn't believe there were the votes to get the Budget passed without a retreat. On the morning of Wednesday 15 March, May summoned Hammond to see her, telling him curtly that she had advised him against the policy and that now he was to reverse it. In a tense meeting, he accepted her instructions. Reports filtered back to her that Hammond subsequently met Osborne in his office in the Commons before making a statement to the House in which he admitted that the rise in national insurance contribution breached the 'wider understanding of the spirit' of the Tory manifesto. 'This is chaos. It is shocking and humiliating that the Chancellor has been forced to come here to reverse a key Budget decision announced less than a week ago,' responded Labour shadow Chancellor John McDonnell. Hammond's card was marked.

It embarrassed May, and her team began openly to acknowledge that they had appointed the wrong Chancellor in their haste the previous July. They knew that if she was to make progress on her domestic agenda, and increasingly on her Brexit agenda too, a new Chancellor would have to be appointed. But when? An early general election returning an increased majority could provide an opportunity, even if Hammond's removal was not a prime factor in their thinking.

Timothy made one final attempt after the Budget to change fiscal policy, asking for a memo from Douglas McNeill, the economics specialist they had brought into the Policy Unit. No. 10 argued for a 'balanced approach', allowing for greater government spending in line with the 'Plan for Britain', while still keeping debt levels on a downward trajectory. But the initiative went nowhere. Timothy by this point felt the domestic agenda was being hampered more by Theresa May herself than by any of her colleagues. Like Steve Hilton, Cameron's highly charged policy director from 2010 to 2013, he too began to suspect that his Prime Minister did not have the stomach for fiscal changes and radical reform. It had now been nine months since May had come to power, with little domestic achievement to show for it. Many factors were pointing towards one conclusion: with a majority of twelve, the absence of her own personal mandate, and Cabinet ministers in the key departments not committed to the cause, the chiefs began to realise the whole May project would go nowhere unless something dramatic happened to change the weather.

MAY'S ROADBLOCKS TO REFORM

May encountered many unforeseen difficulties translating her potent agenda into policy in her first nine months, including her lack of authority with no personal mandate, an unsympathetic Chancellor, the constant distraction of Brexit, and the slim parliamentary majority. We conclude this chapter by looking at some further factors, several exacerbated by May herself.

Prime Ministers can only be effective if they work through their

Cabinet ministers. The latter are the figures who can deliver the government's agenda via their departments, not the Prime Minister. She had neither won a general election nor been really tested in a leadership election, having won the contest, some ministers felt, by default. She would need an excellent working relationship with Cabinet, individually and collectively, if she was to compensate. Prime Ministers earn authority and respect from ministers in part on how effectively they conduct themselves in Cabinet, just as respect from MPs is earned by their conduct in the House. One official in attendance at Cabinet comments:

> She didn't enjoy chairing Cabinet. Nor did she enjoy the company of Cabinet colleagues. I began to think she thought Cabinet was a waste of her time. Her initial ambition was of a 'return to Cabinet government', similar to Gordon Brown when he became Prime Minister. But it was not true. She had neither the time, nor patience, nor inclination to discuss important matters in Cabinet and Cabinet committees. She chaired the Brexit Cabinet Committee, but the key issues rarely made it to the Committee, antagonising both Brexiteers and Remainers. She was much better at chairing the NSC, because she knew about it and was comfortable with security. Someone said she was a good poker player. But I don't think that's true, because she wasn't that subtle and didn't think deeply enough. On most prime ministerial issues, other than those she had dealt with at the Home Office, she didn't have a view at all. She had neither political friends nor any idea that they were important to a Prime Minister.

Another official shares a similar sentiment: 'She was the least collegiate Prime Minister I ever worked with, worse even than Gordon Brown because she was not as bright and lacked his intelligence and vision. She was very insular and couldn't communicate. She shared one trait with Brown, though: neither trusted people, and both were very tribal.'

Prime Ministers need to be able to persuade, charm and cajole their Cabinet. Raw power gets the Prime Minister nowhere if they're lacking in life and personality. But May proved no better at winning over Cabinet than she did MPs, the media or foreign leaders. Timothy agrees that she was partly the author of her own problems: 'She never trusted Cabinet and wasn't good at building personal relations.'[55]

Timothy believes that the problem ultimately lay less in her style than in the calibre of Cabinet ministers and their loyalty to her:

Many Cabinet ministers were opposed to her agenda from the very outset. To be honest, very few Cabinet ministers got what we were on about. Some who disliked her did so because of the line she was pursuing on Brexit, while others thought her policy was too left-wing (e.g. Philip Hammond) or too right-wing (e.g. Justine Greening).[56]

This contention is unproven. Her Cabinet were even less loyal to her after Timothy and Hill left. But they could have performed much more capably than they were allowed to, had they been better led and encouraged from the centre. Some responsibility for poor Cabinet relations rests with Timothy and Hill, as one advisor notes:

Nick and Fi made it clear they had no time personally for Cabinet, and often chose not to sit in on it, a very odd decision for chiefs of staff. They would make it clear they found Cabinet boring, and they would be very tribal with ministers assembling in the ante-room before meetings.

There were very few favourites. Ben Gummer and Damian Green were, as were David Davis and Greg Clark for a time. James Brokenshire and Karen Bradley, though more junior, were the most regularly in favour, as was Gavin Williamson as Chief Whip. May had serviceable relations in the first ten months with several, including Michael Fallon, Liam Fox, Andrea Leadsom and Amber Rudd. Relations were worst with Hammond, Javid, Johnson and Greening, and the hand of the chiefs played a part in all four.

Not getting the best out of Cabinet was compounded by a second structural problem: May found it hard to achieve the best from No. 10. The most effective Prime Ministers since Lloyd George through Attlee to Thatcher and Blair always brought their Downing Street officials onside, and were revered by them. Much smaller than other Whitehall departments, No. 10 is staffed by the cream of Whitehall, brilliant people who work tirelessly for the Prime Minister. But they have to be well-led. One No. 10 official says:

> From the beginning we noticed how suspicious she and her team were of the civil service. It made it much harder on a day-to-day basis. May's team operated so differently to the Cameron team. Her chiefs were tough, and we could understand that. But then at the heart of the operation was a complete introvert who did not assert herself.

The chiefs became the scapegoats for all that went wrong not only in the general election but in the first months of May's premiership, too. They certainly cannot escape blame. They channelled far too much work to May through themselves, causing blockages, delays and confusion. They never fully embraced how different Downing Street was to the Home Office, and how consistency, collegiality and clarity are required for a Prime Minister to succeed, as opposed to capriciousness (from Hill in particular), tribalism (from both) and personal ideological agendas (mostly from Timothy). Both could be vindictive, inside and outside the building. They might have thought some staff did not perform as well as they wished, but that does not excuse their unpleasantness to some that led to a culture of fear in the building. Hill in particular found the transition difficult, exacerbated greatly by her partner, chair of the Joint Intelligence Committee Charles Farr, being diagnosed with cancer in October 2016 and beginning chemotherapy in November (hence her missing May's India trip). Never the easiest of men, Farr became what has been described as unpleasant and unkind towards her. The sad situation understandably took its toll on both of them, and Hill was rarely at her best from that point on, becoming more difficult and fraught with some colleagues. In moments, she could still be dazzling in her strategic vision and political instincts. But she was struggling, and May did not appear to notice.

They were not institutional bullies. One senior official close to Heywood says, 'The chiefs were challenging, abrasive and high-maintenance, but they were not the devil incarnate. Courts of Prime Ministers attract such people, need such people!'

Heywood kept a close eye on the treatment of officials in No. 10. Bar the slighting of one, who was prevented from going on the Washington trip, complaints were not made to him. The chiefs' nastiness to some staff, aides as well as officials, was born of frustration, in-experience and being overwhelmed. They both now accept they did not always conduct themselves optimally. Neither are bad human beings – but the history of No. 10 is full of good people resorting to poor behaviour under its unique pressures and in the adrenalin-rich atmosphere.

May was the figure who needed to stamp her authority on Downing Street. But she showed from early on that she was incapable of asserting herself. No. 10 abhors a vacuum, and if the Prime Minister's personality doesn't fill it, then the personality of others will. Neither she nor her chiefs were adept at managing the No. 10 or ministerial teams, even though they hired some good people. The team who had worked so hard to bring her into No. 10 and make her premiership a success found they were marginalised, not invited into her study, nor up to the flat, nor to Chequers for convivial occasions. Not even

Timothy and Hill received invitations to go to Chequers with her outside of work. When she let her hair down with her inner circle, a different Theresa May could be seen, notably on trips abroad, relaxing in ambassadors' residences. She'd have a couple of glasses of whisky, her favourite drink, and tease (if repetitively) Timothy about his beard.[57] But she relaxed and brought those outside her immediate inner circle into her confidence all too infrequently.

May had gained the title of Prime Minister, but she had yet to learn how to act like one. All Prime Ministers learn on the job; there's no other place to learn. She'd been in power less than a year. The question now was: would she grow into her job, as all who became great Prime Ministers do?

May agreed that the general election campaign should focus on her but failed to provide the leadership, policy clarity and communication skills that were required.

CHAPTER 5

THE PIVOT: THE 2017 GENERAL ELECTION

'There should be no general election until 2020,' Theresa May announced emphatically on 30 June 2016, just one week after the referendum. Then, just after she became Prime Minister, she reiterated, 'I'm not going to be calling a snap election.' On 4 September, she told the nation she had been very clear that the full period until 2020 was needed to 'deal with the issues that the country is facing'. She returned to the theme of political stability when, on 1 October, the day before the party conference opened, she ruled out the possibility of a general election before 2020 because of the risk of 'instability' it posed. On 7 March 2017, No. 10, acting with the Prime Minister's authority, said of an early general election, 'It's not going to happen. It's not something she plans to do or wishes to do.' On 20 March, a Downing Street spokesman said categorically, 'There is not going to be a general election.'[1]

Historians and contemporaries do not always agree. But they will on one point about May at No. 10: the general election was the pivot of her entire premiership. Before the election, she enjoyed an extended honeymoon lasting ten months. After it, she endured two years of the most sustained attack on any Prime Minister in modern British history. This chapter will argue that she was right to call the general election when she did, if in error to have repeatedly ruled it out. But she was wrong to have elected to fight the general election in the way it was fought.

It marked the lowest point of her premiership: a total lack of leadership, vision and communication, and a blaming of others for the failure. Not for almost a hundred years had the Conservatives fought such a dysfunctional campaign, in the opinion of the historian of the party Stuart Ball. 'The only election campaign that comes close to being as poor was December 1923,' he writes.[2] Baldwin's tariff election was equally a snap election, called by a Prime Minister who had recently assumed office and who wanted to unite a divided party over a major and controversial change to Britain's trading relationship abroad. Both ended up diminished figures with hung parliaments.

DECISION TO CALL AN EARLY GENERAL ELECTION

Thus, May's mistake was not the calling of the general election in June 2017, but to have ruled it out at first, and then dithered in her timing and strategy when she did decide to go for it. To anybody with a glimmer of understanding of politics, it should have been obvious that a majority of twelve would never be sufficient for her to get her unorthodox domestic policy through Parliament, let alone a highly divisive and partisan Brexit deal. Her fear of losing the office she craved so deeply, so soon into her premiership, froze her with fear and prevented her thinking clearly.

Her team had first mentioned the possibility of her calling an early general election during the leadership campaign. When Timothy crafted her launch speeches, he was keen to rule out emphatic denials on the subject. She didn't agree.[3] She saw the logic but was petrified. 'At no point when Nick and I raised the subject with her did she reject it in a way that suggested she hadn't thought about it,' says Hill.[4] After failing to convince her during the leadership campaign, Timothy dropped the issue. Hill pursued it through the remainder of 2016. When the idea was again proposed to her early in the New Year, she again batted it away.

With the cause receding, two by-elections were held on 23 February. May had been particularly nervous about them, with vivid memories of the Richmond Park by-election on 1 December 2016, when Zac Goldsmith's resignation had paved the way for the Liberal Democrats to reclaim the seat. Party chairman Patrick McLoughlin says, 'The PM called me all the time during the Copeland and Stoke campaigns to check we were doing enough.'[5] The Copeland by-election had been triggered by the resignation of Jamie Reed, a vocal critic of Jeremy Corbyn. No one foresaw the extraordinary 8.5 per cent swing to the Conservatives, with local resident Trudy Harrison winning a narrow majority of just over 2,000, marking the first time the Labour Party had failed to take the seat since 1935, and the first gain for a governing party in a by-election since the Conservatives won Mitcham and Morden during the Falklands War in 1982. The same day, the Conservatives had managed to increase their share of the vote at the Stoke-on-Trent Central by-election, another optimistic outcome. Cabinet ministers texted the chiefs to say, 'The results make a general election a much better option: imagine the majority we'll get.'[6] None in Cabinet were more enthusiastic than David Davis and Philip Hammond; Davis believed it was vital for Brexit, Hammond for the success of his economic policy. One of Hammond's worries was that a 2020 general election would be held at the height of any post-Brexit disturbance to the economy, so holding one now could thus buy the party time.[7] But according to Timothy, despite the results, 'she still wasn't there yet'.

The tipping point was the passage of the European Union (Notification of Withdrawal) Act 2017. The first reading was on 26 January, after the Supreme Court upheld the Gina Miller case that Parliament's approval was required before triggering Article 50. Davis introduced the Bill, which had a tortuous time in both the Commons and the Lords. Throughout February, prolonged battles took place, grinding down the government – and, with it, May's political capital. The Bill eventually passed both Houses of Parliament unamended on Monday 13 March, to receive Royal Assent on 16 March.

It was on that Monday evening that Timothy and Hill decided, in the No. 10 garden, that they had to convince May about an early general election. Timothy says, 'We thought that, with a majority of twelve, we would find it very hard to get our legislation through on Brexit. It was clear that Labour was going to take a hostile position and oppose whatever line we took. But we were worried about our own hardline Remainers too.'[8]

To James Slack, who joined No. 10 as the Prime Minister's official spokesman in February, 'It had become obvious that they would not be able to deliver their style of Brexit without a bigger majority.'[9] For May, 'the penny finally dropped', according to her team, when she made the statement in the House on 29 March 2017 to say, 'A few minutes ago in Brussels, the UK's Permanent Representative to the EU handed a letter to the President of the European Council on my behalf … The Article 50 process is now underway.'[10] The mood in the chamber was 'weird', they recall: she was 'really quite shocked by it'.[11] Thus, 29 March was the date when May became intellectually convinced that an early general election was needed. But the obstacles to making it happen successfully were still considerable.

A week before the by-elections, on 16 February, a stock-taking conference had been convened at Chequers to review the lessons from the 2015 general election and to put planning in place for 2020, the presumed date for the next general election. Lynton Crosby, the Australian pollster who had been decisive in winning the 2015 contest for the Conservatives, had received a call from party chairman Patrick McLoughlin asking him to come along and give a presentation on a paid retainer from CCHQ. McLoughlin, the primary figure in convening the away-day, was only dimly aware that the chiefs had another agenda: to explore how ready the party might be for an early general election. 'Thinking ahead to 2020 and reviewing 2015 were the stated aims, but it was being used by the PM, Nick and Fi to test out what a 2017 general election might look like,' confirms one advisor. With Stephen Gilbert, the long-serving election supremo at CCHQ, Crosby presented a paper on how the Conservatives had won in 2015, oblivious to the chiefs' ulterior motive of establishing the basis for a snap election campaign. That part of the strategy day was uncontroversial. Chris Wilkins then presented a paper in which he argued, as director of strategy at No. 10, that in any future general election the Conservatives should position themselves as the 'change' party, appealing to new voters more resolutely than ever. 'Not so much Middle England as Working-Class England,' he said, giving a presentational polish to Timothy's philosophy.[12] In a harbinger of the ugly divisions that were to emerge during the general election campaign, Crosby made it clear that he believed that such thinking was 'total nonsense. It wasn't the strategy needed to secure the next election.'[13] Gilbert spoke to McLoughlin a week later and said, 'I'm not so sure what the thinking was for the Chequers meeting, but was it really because they want to start planning for an early general election?'

The battles over the passage of Article 50 were now joined by other factors pushing May towards an early general election. In March, she faced a backbench revolt on school spending cuts that underlined the narrowness of her majority. Speculation and pressure had been building in the press for an early poll. Significantly, former Conservative leader William Hague had written an article in the *Daily Telegraph* on 6 March arguing that, were she to hold one, it would allow her to put her Brexit plans to the people. No. 10 were quick to shut down speculation after the article, but it made its impression on thinking.[14] Polling was also making a significant impact on the PM. In November 2016, the party's lead over Labour had been just 5.3 per cent, but by the late spring it had risen to over 14 per cent.[15] May had begun to feel differently about herself in the New Year too: she started to believe in herself more after the US trip to address the UN General Assembly.

Another factor began to weigh with her now. She hated being reminded that she was only in power because of the general election victory won by her predecessor. She increasingly wanted her own victory and her own mandate. She began to think her time had come: 'She always felt a degree of impostor syndrome,' says Hill, 'feeling that she wasn't elected by the public. It really meant something to her.'[16]

Hammond's Budget on 8 March had been another factor pointing in the same direction, as Wilkins recalls:

> It made us realise that we were hamstrung by Cameron's manifesto, with all the fuss over national insurance. It was the spur to many discussions in the weeks following it. I talked to Nick, Nick talked to Fi, we all spoke to JoJo, and then all four of us started speaking. All four of us independently reached the same conclusion at about the same time.[17]

On Wednesday 15 March, the four of them trooped up to May's flat above Downing Street. The Article 50 Bill had been passed two days before: 'There was a feeling of calm in No. 10 that at last Article 50 was over, that we'd come to the end of something. But we were now beginning two years of negotiations. May knew what the meeting was about.' Philip sat by her side, listening intently. Wilkins remembers that she brought out some wine and crisps, and was struck that after eight months as the Prime Minister's political advisor and then director of strategy, this was his first experience of May's largesse. He recalls, 'It was the only time I was invited up to her flat.'[18] Hill launched in: 'You know how hard this is going to be, don't you?' 'Yes, I do,' May replied. 'You know how thin our majority is?' 'Yes, I do.' 'Have you seen the polling?' 'Yes, I have.' One immediate problem did concern May, however. 'We've got the Fixed Term Parliament Act in place: how do we get around that?' she asked. 'We've already thought about that and spoken to Harry Carter [the government's legal advisor],' replied Hill. 'We think it's doable.' May laughed as if to say, 'I knew you would have done something like this.' May then raised a volley of questions: 'How can we take London? How can we deal with the unpredictable?'[19] She then asked the killer question: 'How would it look if I called a general election: won't people say I'd changed my mind?' Their response was that it depended on how any announcement was framed. She asked, 'If I do this, won't everyone expect me to get a massive majority?' A pause. They said, 'The key thing is that it will be *your* majority for *your* agenda.'

May concluded the meeting by asking Timothy to talk in strict secrecy to Gilbert about it; she had great respect for his views.[20] Timothy promptly phoned to invite Gilbert to his home in London's Vauxhall on Sunday. When Gilbert pitched up, he found Hill there too. One present recalls the discussions:

> 'We're thinking of calling an early general election. Very confidential. What do you think?' 'It's worth thinking about, certainly,' I replied. 'A significant majority is certainly possible but we need to do some research.' Nick and Fi were clear they wanted to go for it and wanted a bigger majority so they could pass Brexit through Parliament. They told me that the PM had more or less decided to go for it but she needed to know what I thought. So I went away and said I'd look it over. They gave me a small list of people I could talk to: apart from both of them, it was Chris Wilkins, Alex Dawson and JoJo, but nobody else.

With speculation mounting, and the waiting media outside No. 10 scrutinising every visitor, Gilbert had to make a stealthy entry via the Cabinet Office to see May in the week beginning Monday 20 March. Easter recess was only ten days away, and the clock was ticking. Gilbert was struck by seeing Philip present alongside May in No. 10. He opened by saying he thought that it was on balance worth the risk: 'There are strong arguments for doing it, but if you decide you definitely aren't, comprehensively rule it out now, otherwise you'll run into trouble,' he counselled. He reminded her about the very bad experience Gordon Brown had soon after he became Prime Minister in autumn 2007, when he allowed speculation to grow and grow, with a very damaging impact on his premiership.

'What state is the party machine in?' she asked him directly. Gilbert had left CCHQ after the 2015 general election, but he told her that he had been speaking discreetly to various key people who were still there. He thought it was in pretty good order, he told her, although he could not be sure. There were three things, though, that she had to bear in mind if she was going to call an election soon: Crosby had to run it, because there was nobody else with the experience; the campaign would have to be focused on her herself, because polling showed that she was considerably more popular than the Conservative Party; and research would have to be conducted into the grounds that she would give for calling the general election, given her repeated statements to the contrary. According to one colleague, Gilbert said to May, 'I think you should do it. But you'll need Lynton to do the research and lead it for you.'

One advisor was struck by how anxious she was: 'What I remember most clearly when we met was her hand shaking on her folder, and how very, very anxious she looked. I didn't like what I saw. I thought, but I didn't say, "You don't have to do this if you don't want to."' The chiefs had reached the same conclusion about needing Crosby. 'I don't feel qualified to run it,' Timothy said after it was suggested that the No. 10 team could run it themselves. Gilbert was not eager to lead the campaign either. Since leaving CCHQ, he had become a working member of the House of Lords and developed a career as a consultant. He'd had enough of leading campaigns. But Hill was keen on Crosby and they had kept in touch over the years. If they were going to go for it early, it was Crosby, or nobody. May was not convinced. 'Why Lynton and nobody else?' she enquired of Hill.[21] Vital days were lost while she dithered over phoning him. Hill could wait no longer and sent Crosby a text on Signal, the cross-platform encrypted message system, asking him to do the research into how they could justify the election. His polling came back quickly and showed that May had a strong lead personally, that she was believed to have handled Brexit well so far, but that the only workable basis for calling an early general election was to get a stronger majority to secure the best deal out of the EU. Gilbert concurred: the campaign had to be about Europe, and if it appeared that she was fighting to gain a bigger majority for Conservative policies, it would go wrong.

May remained sceptical about Crosby. Her team kept telling her about his benefits: 'These are the guys that won the 2015 election campaign for Cameron.' She replied, 'Yes, but I remember the 2005 Michael Howard campaign, and I remember Zac Goldsmith's 2016 mayoral campaign.'[22] The former was criticised for its focus on immigration, deemed by some to be 'provocative and racist',[23] while the latter was widely seen as divisive and nasty.[24] Wilkins thinks that 'the speed and secrecy of the decision of calling the early election meant that we went to Lynton without a great deal of forethought',[25] while Hill notes, 'It started off on the wrong foot. She was always in two minds about using Lynton and calling the election. Lynton was always in two minds. The personalities and the chemistry were all wrong.'[26]

Crosby was in Fiji celebrating his wife's sixtieth birthday when he noticed a missed call on his phone. He didn't recognise the number. Once he dialled, he found May on the other end: 'I want Stephen [Gilbert] to speak with you,' she said. 'We think we'll need you for a job.' Crosby suspected she was toying with the thought of an election. The next day he spoke to Gilbert, who told him that there was a mood she should go for an election, suggesting that Crosby could run it. Crosby replied that he wasn't in a position to run the campaign but would be willing to help. He recalls the details of the conversation:

I asked if they had done any research as to what the likely outcome would be and how people would view it, and they said they hadn't. I made the point to Stephen that she had already ruled it out: 'Didn't she say that there wouldn't be an early election? Just because the polls say we're in front doesn't mean we will be, if you don't have a proper reason for an election you can't risk it.'

She shared some of his concerns: expectations of an easy victory were so high that protest voting and a low turnout were likely; calling an election that she'd previously ruled out risked accusations of hypocrisy; and the electorate saw no need to call a general election if she wanted it to get her domestic policy through.[27] But he agreed to play a leading – if unspecified – personal role, and for his company, Crosby Textor Group (in partnership with his polling colleague Mark Textor, or 'Tex'), to be officially appointed for £4 million. An extra £500,000 was to be spent on Jim Messina's consulting firm, the Messina Group, in an election that cost the Conservatives £18.5 million, according to the Electoral Commission (compared to Labour's £11 million).[28] The fee offered to Crosby was a powerful stimulus. Insiders say he later exaggerated his initial concerns to distance himself from the campaign and the eventual result.

Darren Mott had succeeded Gilbert as director of organisation, and from the week beginning 27 March, he tried to instil some organisation and order at CCHQ. Meetings began to be held with him, Gilbert and Alan Mabbutt, the party's director general, as well as May's team – not at CCHQ itself, because of the need for secrecy, but at the nearby St Ermin's Hotel in Westminster.[29] But there was no escaping the fact that CCHQ and the party in the country were ill-prepared for a general election so soon, despite telling May they were ready. It was all so rushed, as Dennis Kavanagh and Philip Cowley point out in their definitive account of the election, noting that in 2015, Crosby had been in charge of preparations for eighteen months before the campaign began. Now they had at most three months.[30]

The 8.30 a.m. meeting in May's room was cancelled on 27 March – unusually, because they almost always went ahead unless May was away. Chief Whip Gavin Williamson received a call to say that the

PM herself wanted to see him at 10.30 a.m. When he arrived at her office, just May, Timothy, Hill and Penn were present. 'This is extremely confidential,' May told him, 'but I'm thinking about calling a general election. What are your views?' Williamson replied that, while he hated general elections on the whole, he thought she'd never be stronger in terms of the polls. 'I'm off on holiday soon but I'll think about it when I'm away,' she told him. Something about the way she said it made him think her mind was already made up.[31]

Williamson's particular worry was that Labour, because of the Fixed Term Parliaments Act and the consequent need to secure their agreement to call a general election, might respond by calling a vote of no confidence in the government, which Conservative MPs would then have to support if they were to gain a majority. If they did so, it would make the government look self-serving and chaotic. The element of surprise was therefore key, because it would give Labour less time to think it through. 'I woke up every day in the recess worrying Labour might trigger the no-confidence vote because there was so much speculation about "would she go to the country?",' Williamson says. But the headlines during the recess were deflected by international news, including tensions over North Korea's missile testing.[32]

Theresa and Philip May left for their five-day walking holiday in Snowdonia, North Wales, on Thursday 6 April. The story to insiders was that she was using the time to think over the election issue. Philip had been the biggest block to her deciding earlier. Her team knew that winning him round was the key to her agreeing. But in fact she had made her mind up long before they departed, and Philip had reluctantly conceded. Hill recalls:

> Philip became involved quite late on. We had to convince him as well as her. We debated it intensely for two weeks in late March. Sometimes what we said to her would be relayed to Philip by her, and she'd come back with his objections. Sometimes he'd be in the room with us. We

talked about it in the flat in Downing Street. We talked about it in her house in Sonning. We had many meetings at this critical period.[33]

Civil servants in No. 10 knew that something was up because of all the secret meetings that May and her team were having, to which they weren't invited. 'The Prime Minister always had a deep respect for keeping the civil service apolitical, so she was keen not to involve us,' recalls one. Heywood thought the election was a good idea. Often when he saw Timothy and Hill in the morning he would say, 'You guys need an election.' Later, after they persuaded her to go for it, he told them, 'Brilliant, well done.'[34] Not all No. 10 officials thought the same way: 'I thought calling it was a bit of a sham,' says one. 'I didn't see any evidence that a small majority would hinder the delivery of Brexit.'

MAY TELLS THE WORLD

On Monday 10 April, May returned with Philip to London. A day later, McLoughlin was in his office in the House of Commons when his mobile rang. 'Patrick, where are you?' asked the Prime Minister. She wanted to see him urgently the next day, Wednesday 12 April. He recalls:

> I arrived twenty minutes early for the three o'clock meeting and was shown into a little room. She got straight down to business. 'What do you think about an early general election?' she said. I said I was somewhat shocked, that we're not ready, but if she had made up her mind, CCHQ would just get on with it. I told her about what Margaret Thatcher had said to the 1922 Committee in 1987, that the decision to call a general election is the toughest decision a Prime Minister can ever take. 'Tell me about it,' she told me, letting out a huge sigh.[35]

Having the party chair onside was critical, and May was relieved by his words. A larger group from the party then descended on her home in Sonning to talk in detail about how they would plan the election. May was evidently tense, and when Timothy let slip that Ben Gummer had been told, she flared up in anger. Timothy tried to reassure her that Gummer could be trusted and had to be told because he would be working on the manifesto. She was far from soothed. Others in Sonning shared anxiety about the mechanics of going early. When McLoughlin returned to London, he told Williamson how worried he was, how a variety of policies, not least on education and cost of living, were in the wrong place, and how unprepared the party organisation was, so soon after 2015, as no one had been gearing up because of the repeated denials.[36]

The tight circle in No. 10 of those who knew about the early election was a marker of who was in and who was out. One source recalls Timothy asking them, 'How do you feel about a general election?' They replied, 'I think it will be tough, but doable.' Some were not told at all, including Perrior, who stepped down after the announcement. Others, including Stephen Parkinson, John Godfrey and Chris Brannigan, were told by Timothy only on the morning of the Cabinet meeting on 18 April. Lizzie Loudon had been on holiday in France with Will Tanner, whom she was to marry in June 2019, when she heard through No. 10 circles that May was going to be making a statement:

> Will said it must be a war or something major. Neither of us thought that she possibly was calling an early general election because she had ruled it out so often. Failure to consult us, or tell us in advance, was a real kick in the teeth. It destroyed any desire for me to work with them again.[37]

On Sunday 16 April, a final pre-announcement planning meeting took place, 'the atmosphere not unlike field commanders on the eve of launching a major battle', remembers one No. 10 source. It was decided that

Cabinet would be told on Tuesday 18 April. May herself informed the big beasts, Hammond, Johnson, Fox and Rudd. Davis, Gummer and McLoughlin already knew.[38] Middle-rank Cabinet ministers, including Lidington, Grayling, Brokenshire and Bradley, were informed by Chief Whip Williamson in turn before morning Cabinet. 'I don't care what you think, but the Prime Minister is going to announce in Cabinet that she's calling a general election, and I need you to support the decision enthusiastically,' he told them. Not that he needed to say it: everyone he spoke to was enthusiastic, some thinking it positively inspired.[39]

May opened the Cabinet meeting that morning saying, 'I'd like to explain a decision I've come to recently. I've come to the conclusion that to deliver Brexit and to embark on negotiations, it is necessary to call a general election. So I've decided to call it on 8 June.' Justine Greening, one of those who had not been told, went pale and was visibly shocked. May stated her reasons for calling the election, before calling on McLoughlin to speak first, as party chair. He told Cabinet that CCHQ was ready and that 'the assessment of the position the Prime Minister finds herself in means it would be very difficult to get Brexit through with our current majority. We've got a good team at CCHQ.'[40] Cabinet ministers then spoke, all, to a man and woman, supporting the decision. 'No one, no one said it was a bad idea. Everyone said it was the right thing to do,' says McLoughlin.[41] Johnson looked the most disconcerted of all, and had reportedly told May beforehand that she should not do it.[42] Whatever he may have said to her, it is indisputable that, at the meeting itself, he spoke up positively in favour of the early election, though colleagues sensed with some reluctance. This they put down to his recognition that his own leadership ambitions would take a decisive hit, were May indeed to win the expected large majority. Hill later reported that Johnson's facial expression showed his colleagues that 'he knew he was fucked'.[43] Timothy remembers, 'I think that she would have told me if Boris had expressed any reluctance when she had her bilateral with him.'[44]

After the meeting, Cabinet ministers watched her make the announcement on a screen wheeled into the Cabinet Room, while reading a copy of the messaging they were handed out to relay in interviews. They fell silent as May launched into her speech on the doorstep outside No. 10:

> I have just chaired a meeting of the Cabinet where we agreed that the government should call a general election, to be held on 8 June … Last summer, after the country voted to leave the European Union, Britain needed certainty, stability and strong leadership, and since I became Prime Minister the government has delivered precisely that … If we do not hold a general election now, their political game-playing [by Labour, the Liberal Democrats, the SNP and the House of Lords] will continue and the negotiations with the European Union will reach the most difficult stage in the run-up to the next scheduled election … It was with reluctance that I decided the country needs this election, but it is with strong conviction that I say it is necessary to secure the strong and stable leadership the country needs to see us through Brexit and beyond.

May delivered the speech with confidence, as she always did with a set script. She stressed that she had 'only recently and reluctantly' reached her decision. Both words were self-evidently true.

This was a general election for May to lose. The first three weeks after the announcement saw confidence high. Evidence that May was on course for a landslide victory came on Thursday 4 May, exactly five weeks before general election day, in the local government elections. While the Conservatives gained 563 seats and took control of eleven councils, Labour lost 382 seats and lost seven councils in the worst local election for an opposition party since the 1980s. Election specialist John Curtice said, 'Labour is in deep trouble.'[45] Particularly pleasing for the Conservatives was Andy Street, former managing director of John Lewis, winning the mayoral election in the West Midlands, into which they had invested huge resources.[46] May stood at the apex of her career, the surprising Prime Minister who was, after less than a year, on track for a convincing majority in the region of 60–100. Total vindication of her brave if protracted decision was likely, giving her the margin she needed for Brexit, for her domestic agenda, and for holding both the party and the Union together. Had she won a handsome majority, she would have immediately repealed the Fixed Term Parliaments Act, putting her in charge of her own destiny. A premiership as long as Thatcher's or Blair's was not impossible; a May decade. So, what went wrong?

SIX REASONS THE DECISION BACKFIRED

REASON 1: DIVIDED LEADERSHIP

Successful general election campaigns depend upon a united strategic command. Yet not since 1923 had the Conservatives fought such a divided campaign.

Secrecy and rush hampered the clarity of strategic command from the outset. The media were told that Stephen Gilbert would be the manager (despite his initial protestations), working with 'consultants' Crosby, Textor and Messina. A picture quickly emerged, though, of two teams working not side by side but separately: 'the Australians' (Crosby and Textor) and 'the chiefs' (Timothy and Hill), with Gilbert and Mabbutt trying forlornly to link them together. Crosby may have wanted to convey the impression that he was playing a subdued role in the campaign, second fiddle to Textor and the chiefs.[47] But to Hill and Timothy, 'Lynton took full control from the outset. Everyone knew from the beginning that he was running it.'[48]

The chiefs and the party officials argued with him from the start that they wanted it to be a traditional general election campaign, with the major Secretaries of State closely involved, with daily press conferences and a focus on policy announcements. 'No fucking way' was the response from Crosby. (Crosby regularly used such language, though he was more restrained in front of May.) For all her reservations about Crosby, May nevertheless backed him to the hilt. Timothy and Hill, the two lodestars of her premiership, were relegated to subordinate positions. Whether they would have fared any better had they been listened to is a moot point. Had Crosby been on full power, as he had been in the 2015 general election, the outcome might have been very different. But in 2017 he was clearly a less committed, less optimistic and less energetic figure.

The atmosphere in CCHQ, which had started so positively, began to deteriorate soon after the local election highpoint. Timothy was locked away on the top floor in the building writing the manifesto with Ben Gummer, while Hill, following the departures of Perrior and Loudon, picked up the director of communications task:

> I was not at all happy doing it. It was a really bad time. Mark Textor was telling everyone what the messages of each day would be. The PM was barely present in CCHQ. She travelled round the country looking surly and miserable. Soon into the campaign, especially after a cyber attack and two terror attacks, I started having serious reservations. There was no leadership. The campaign was dull. It was going nowhere. It was utterly, utterly draining.[49]

The agreed strategy for the first week of the campaign was that the decision to call the early election should be justified. Crosby and Textor would hear none of it. They made it clear to staff at CCHQ that the campaign would be focusing on May as leader, because the focus groups had shown what a huge asset she was: 'We are framing this election as a choice between her and Jeremy Corbyn.' Period. Textor told staff, as Dennis Kavanagh and Philip Cowley put it, that 'no right-of-centre party across the world had ever had an electoral asset as strong as May; no left-of-centre party, by contrast, had ever had an electoral liability like Corbyn'.[50]

Crosby and Textor's strategy may have made sound professional sense. But it was not May's sense, and nor did it play to her strengths. It was not the reason that she called the general election, and it was about to play straight into her weaknesses. Only days into the campaign and its leaders had run headlong into a very major philosophical difference about how to fight it.

REASON 2: DIVISIONS OVER THE MANIFESTO

The manifesto was written by two deep-thinking idealists, with those best equipped to communicate it not involved in its formation, while the head of the campaign thought the entire document 'bullshit' and 'worse than useless'. Crosby held to the tenet that manifestos do not win general elections but they can lose them. In contrast, Labour's manifesto, which received far less scrutiny, gave their campaign a turbo boost.

Gummer, the star among Cabinet ministers in the eyes of May and her team, was lauded for his policy brain, his judgement and his very personable manner. In mid-March, Timothy had sent him a text asking to see him. 'What do you think of an early general election?' Timothy asked ('in the Nick way, that meant it was going to happen anyway'), but the real purpose of the meeting was to ask if Gummer was prepared to write the manifesto. He would, but he insisted on conditions: that the manifesto should include the environment and foreign aid, and that he could tell his wife Sarah about the general election, given that it would mean working throughout the Easter weekend rather than spending time with her and family.[51]

Gummer and Timothy chimed on their visions for the future of the country. In a series of walks around St James's Park, they talked with huge animation about how, given that May was on track for a landslide, they would use the manifesto to steer government policy in a totally fresh direction and reshape the country as a result. As Gummer says:

I accepted the responsibility with enormous trepidation. This was a manifesto for a post-Brexit Britain, that should attempt to address some of the underlying issues that caused the referendum result, and so took on an importance that extended beyond the normal five-year term. I felt I had to handle the writing with great care with Brexit coming, and Labour destroying itself. We had to make a pitch to being a national unity government, with a Conservative Prime Minister wanting to reach out way beyond the party. Brexit was a cry of pain by a large number of people who felt they had missed out. I felt we had to write a manifesto that would be honest and direct with them.[52]

Timothy had a similarly expansive vision of the transformative potential of the manifesto: 'The campaign basically had two different strategies at the same time. There was the Downing Street team strategy, based on what we had been doing before the campaign, and the Lynton strategy, which was very different and based on a single message, not policy or values.'[53] Both wanted to trade on May's profile as an honest person, standing apart from the political establishment, to help build a more responsible and fairer society. Their inspirations were different: Gummer was, like Hill, a practising Catholic, while Timothy's inspiration was secular, a vision of a benign government, inspired by his heroes not from the Bible but from recent British history. Further inputs to the manifesto came from the Policy Unit, notably Godfrey and Tanner. The former says:

Nick's vision was that the time had come for a more communitarian vision for the Conservative Party. Many parts of the country were being taken for granted by Labour, and Corbyn was leaving them behind. He wanted a manifesto to win over many who had never voted Conservative before. I thought it was vital the party didn't lose sight of what he was saying, because, sooner or later, it will have to reckon with what he was talking about, especially with real wages not increasing for twenty-five years.[54]

Tanner was inspired by their work: 'We felt we were defining a new vision for the Prime Minister, trying to reposition Conservatism back to a more historical tradition, more Burkean and less liberal, more Unionist and less England, more classless and less establishment, and trying to get the Conservative Party into a more electable place.'[55] They shared a cogent vision which, had the election gone the way they expected, could have seen the Conservative Party launch itself in a bold new direction not seen for forty years, when Thatcher had taken it to a very different place.

In the rush, no agreement had been reached about how long the manifesto should be. Cameron's 2015 manifesto, 'A Strong Leadership', had been considered too verbose, with too many hostages to fortune. Crosby and Textor argued for a very short manifesto. Others said that given the party had called the election, a fuller mandate was needed, laying out bold policies to take the country through and beyond Brexit until 2022, adding credibility to the party's case with the electorate.[56] May herself favoured a long manifesto, saying, 'I want to be honest with the public about all the things that are wrong in the country, and I want to show that I'm the person that can fix things for them.'[57] The much vaunted doorstep message by May on her first day, 'a country that works for everybody', had made surprisingly little impression on the public. Better communication of her message was required. Wilkins's 'Plan for Britain', six months in the writing, provided some structure for the manifesto writers, but they needed more, so short submissions were requested from Secretaries of State across Whitehall. Several responded, like Greening, Hunt and Javid, with short essays. The Policy Unit pitched in too, with a flood of ideas on topics including industrial strategy, corporate governance, mental health and technical education.

When Gummer and Timothy had honed the text, they sent the

relevant sections back to the Secretaries of State for their agreement. Most were content. Michael Fallon came back saying, 'Thank you, this is a big improvement on 2015 when I was just called in and expected to agree.' Two Cabinet ministers, Hunt and Javid, didn't see all of their own departmental coverage. The CCHQ aide in charge of the print-out for health overlooked sending the social care section to Hunt so he never saw it, though it was a policy that he had helped to develop, and he was briefed verbally. While the omission with Hunt was a cock-up, not sending the passage on social care to Javid was conspiracy. The team's reason was that they feared he might leak it. No Cabinet ministers had sight of the overall document except Hammond, who viewed it only days before publication. The final wording on fiscal policy, industrial strategy and investment was agreed between him and Gummer rather than with Timothy, because relations with the latter were so toxic.[58] May was kept abreast of the work, though she had little to add. Indeed, she seemed oddly detached from it. Crosby and Textor saw all the key planks in the manifesto at regular intervals and were able to test them. Their polling did not suggest the problems that lay ahead, though it did reveal that the social care policy was little understood by the public. The one main change Crosby demanded was to the wording of the free vote on fox hunting, a policy which would prove damaging on the doorstep but was viewed as important in attracting donor backing and activists on the ground for a Conservative Party thin on local campaign support.

The manifesto team converged on May's home at Sonning on Sunday 14 May, just four days before it was published. Gummer told May he thought that there were five 'hand grenades', as he called them, in the draft manifesto. He told her he thought any one of them could go off, but he did not know which one. They were:

1. The abolition of free school meals in primary schools for the well-off, with a free breakfast for all primary children substituted.
2. Ditching the 'triple lock' on state pensions, which had been widely

anticipated, and replacing it with a 'double lock', to rise with earnings or inflation.

3. Changing the structure of social care payment.

4. Instituting a social insurance system.

5. Means testing winter fuel allowances, taking £300 p.a. away from wealthier pensioners.

May's team thought the most likely backlash would come over the fuel allowance change, and that social care had played well in focus groups when tested, Crosby approved of it and Textor told him, 'I love all the social care stuff.'

A hand grenade did go off, and it went off that day in May's sitting room. The sceptic was Hill, who was about to launch into the most bitter disagreement with Timothy during their time together in No. 10.[59] The cost of social care had been a long-standing worry for government. The proposal in the manifesto had been developed in the Policy Unit, in close alliance with Hunt and the Department of Health and the Cabinet Office. A key question was whether the general public should pay, or those who benefited from the social care. John Godfrey had invested considerable thought in the policy and came to regard the failure to settle on a properly evidence-based social care funding model as 'the biggest single regret of my time in government'.[60]

The policy was not straightforward, but this is it in summary. It sought to raise the asset floor above which an individual fully pays for domiciliary care from £23,250 to £100,000 (the floor was increased from the initial level of £50,000 during the policy meeting at Sonning on Sunday 14 May) but to include the value of their home in total assets, as was already the case for residential care.[61] So that elderly people paying for domiciliary care would not have to sell their house during their lifetime to afford care, as was happening under the current system, payments were only collected from the estate after death. May's team viewed a floor as fairer than the cap proposed in the 2011 Dilnot Report, as it would make the distributive effects of the social care changes more progressive; a floor would protect those with modest assets, whereas a cap would have protected those with significant assets.

Social care was one of the few manifesto policies about which May expressed strong feelings. Tanner says:

> What really motivated her were the occasions when people felt let down by politicians. On social care, she believed that despite thirteen White Papers and reports since the 1990s, no reform had been implemented. She was strongly opposed to the Dilnot recommendation of a cap on care costs. She felt there should be redistribution within the system based on the principle of fairness, her guiding passion.[62]

While Heywood was sceptical of the specific policy (he preferred the Dilnot approach, mixed with other policies), he supported its inclusion in the manifesto – it would not pass through Parliament otherwise – and the focus: he knew social care was a major national issue which needed a new solution.[63] Heywood was typically fired up by big-ticket, big-spending items and had been actively pressing for social care reform since May entered No. 10, having set up a project team in the Cabinet Office to develop policy. Gummer himself had been converted to it after he became Minister for the Cabinet Office.

The gloves were off as Hill and Timothy went head to head in front of May in her sitting room, disagreeing vehemently. Gummer didn't take sides but told May, 'You promised social care would be a big policy area in your premiership and it will look odd if you merely offer blancmange or the promise of a Green Paper.' Gummer had earlier gone through his five potential grenades with Hammond, introducing them one by one and leaving social care till last. Hammond had told him, 'I can see the rationale for having it in, but you'll have to make a political call.' That was exactly the debate they were having now. 'It's ridiculous not to have it in,' said Timothy, but Hill remained inflexible in her opposition. May said, 'I promised people that I would sort out social care, what else can I do?' She had earlier said on social care, 'I know I'll have to use up some political capital, but this is the time to do it.' So at the meeting at her home, the last Gummer had with her, he told her he thought that this was indeed the time to spend political capital, that there might be a bad week after the initial announcement but that she would get through it. One present heard May saying to Timothy on the decision, 'Nick, this is madness; this is what difficult feels like.'

When Gilbert and Crosby arrived at her Maidenhead home on the Sunday, they were shown into another room, aware that the Prime Minister was still in heated conversation with Timothy, Hill and Gummer: 'It was very odd for them to be discussing it and us waiting outside, as if they didn't want to have our views.' Gilbert and Crosby had stated that they favoured a light manifesto, and that afternoon was the first time they realised the full extent of how weighty it would be. 'It broke the clear rule that the electorate wouldn't like the idea of us pushing through a tough domestic agenda when they were told the election was going to be about Brexit,' says a CCHQ source. When eventually they were shown in to see her, the atmosphere still fraught, they expressed reservations about school meals and the triple lock changes; Timothy and Gummer agreed to change the wording on various passages, including on Brexit, the environment and over-seas aid. A proposal to guarantee minimum service levels for strikes in transport and other key public services was dropped. May herself vetoed the social insurance proposal, on which she said, 'Not over my dead body.' But despite the staunch disagreement of Hill, the other four grenades, including social care, were left in.

Hill left Maidenhead very unhappy, with a deep sense in her bones that what was being proposed wouldn't work. She couldn't sleep that night and got up at 4.30 a.m. to go into the office on Monday 15 May. A colleague described her as 'ghostly white': she foresaw what was going to happen. 'Nick always has had a thing about capital versus earned wealth: he forgets that much inherited wealth is in the hands of lower middle classes in their homes,' says one critic of his line. Hill decided to act. Assembling the senior team at CCHQ as the document was going off to the printers, she told them bluntly, 'This isn't going to happen on social care.' Hill called Timothy and told him that she and Penn were going to see May to tell her to take out the policy. He was furious and hurried over to Downing Street to lobby the PM. Hill asked for an impromptu meeting to be convened in May's No. 10 office. 'If I don't have it in my manifesto, it will become an empty manifesto,' said May. 'Good,' Hill retorted. May banged her fists on her desk, had tears in her eyes and was distraught at finding her two closest advisors on opposite sides of such a major argument. 'We're going to do this,' she said defiantly. 'Fine,' replied Hill. 'But you'll have to phone every newspaper editor, or they'll hit us hard. It's going to be bumpy and nasty.'[64]

On Thursday 18 May, the Conservative manifesto, 'Forward, Together', was published in Halifax, Yorkshire. The location had been the cause of another row between the Downing Street team and Crosby, the latter favouring the launch at a RAF base, which made the others wince. 'World War II bombers were hanging from the ceilings!' Timothy remembers.[65] The five key themes for the next government were listed: a strong economy, Brexit, healing social divisions, the ageing society and technological change. Key policies apart from social care included real-terms increases in NHS spending, an expansion of free schools, a revival of grammar schools, an extra £4 billion spending on schools by 2022, an increase to house-building targets, and net migration to be cut below 100,000 per annum. On Brexit, the manifesto committed Britain to leaving the single market, the customs union and the jurisdiction of the ECJ, and pledging to keep agricultural subsidies at EU levels while 'taking back control' of British fishing waters. Osborne's tax lock, which prevented government from raising tax for the course of the parliament, was retained until his promised date of 2020 but was to be dropped afterwards.

The introduction, called 'Five Giant Challenges', written by Timothy, was a statement of the philosophy he expected to dominate government thinking for the next five years. 'Conservatism is not and never has been the philosophy described by caricaturists. We do not believe in untrammelled free markets. We reject the cult of selfish individualism. We abhor social division, injustice, unfairness and inequality. We see rigid dogma and ideology not just as needless but dangerous.'[66] No one, not least himself, anticipated it was to be his swan song.

REASON 3: THE SOCIAL CARE U-TURN

The initial reaction to the manifesto was positive. Matthew d'Ancona in *The Guardian* said it 'represented the most adventurous restatement of Conservatism since Margaret Thatcher'.[67] But it was the social care policy, and above all the way she handled it, that more than anything unravelled May's credibility with the nation, and thus unpicked the entire early election strategy. The first salvo came from Andrew Dilnot himself, who, that morning on Radio 4's *Today* programme, said that the proposed changes would leave the elderly 'helpless' until their assets reached £100,000. 'The analogy is a bit like saying to somebody, "You can't insure your house against burning down; if it does burn down then you're completely on your own, you have to pay for all of it until you're down to your last £100,000 of all your assets and income."'[68] By lunchtime on launch day, the phrase 'dementia tax' was in widespread use across the media to describe the social care policy. Labour, still raw from being accused by the Conservatives of a 'death tax' in the 2010 general election when introducing a similar initiative, pounced. Hill's warning to May was proving eerily prescient.[69] By the end of the day, the broadcast media was awash with callers phoning in, worrying about what might happen to their savings/house/pension under the policy.[70] May did nothing to stem the tide of concern in the days to come. When asked on television how she could guarantee that people would not lose their homes and be bankrupted, she did not communicate or defend the policy with conviction: nobody would lose their homes during their lifetime and they would be left with at least £100,000, she could have said.[71]

On Friday 19 May, the flood of criticisms became a torrent, and over the weekend of 20–21 May, the phone lines at CCHQ were clogged by furious Tory MPs asking, 'What the hell is the Prime Minister thinking of?' Gilbert repeatedly tried calling May, but she wasn't picking up. In desperation, he called Timothy and told him, 'Look, I need to sit down with her urgently and talk this through.' A message eventually came back to Gilbert to say, 'The Prime Minister is unable to talk to you, she will be spending the weekend with Philip. But she'll be happy to talk to you at the end of the weekend by telephone.' Deep in her bunker of two, May was having a bad turn. She was having her first intimations that the early election idea, which she and Philip had agonised over, was about to explode in her face. Gilbert, a veteran of many Conservative campaigns, expressed concerns to colleagues about how strange it was for a party leader not to see him during a campaign emergency. He spoke again to Timothy. Despite being the staunchest advocate for the policy in the senior campaign team, Timothy now favoured a U-turn after its obvious failure with the electorate. He remembers, 'I felt I had to support it. By the weekend, our MPs were ready to burst into flames. We had to change direction.'[72] Hill told Gilbert the same: for her, the U-turn couldn't come a moment too soon. He spoke to several Cabinet ministers, including David Davis, at this point clearly the most influential. 'Make the U-turn, do it now' was the polite gist of the message he received back.

Crosby, unimpressed also that May wouldn't talk to him, now said that the policy could cost the party the general election – despite his having no objection to it at Sonning. But he too counselled acting at once: changing the policy would involve taking a hit, but it would pass in one day.[73] Any lingering doubts about whether a change was needed were countered by the Sunday press, even grimmer than Friday and

Saturday, with a YouGov poll in the *Sunday Times* putting the Conservative lead down to single figures. The first poll in the campaign to do so, it placed Labour on 35 per cent, up four points on its showing under Ed Miliband in 2015.[74]

May had recovered her nerve by Sunday and accepted she would have to make a U-turn, and she prepared to re-enter the world after her withdrawal during the critical thirty-six hours. When Gilbert, Timothy, Hill and Crosby eventually saw her on Sunday evening at CCHQ, Tom Swarbrick saw her going into the meeting and was struck by 'how very stressed and tired she looked. There was something different about her.'[75] When Gilbert told her in his capacity as the official head of the campaign that the change had to be made, she said, almost robotically, 'Really, I have to do this?' It struck those present that she was almost lifeless. There was no debate, no argument. She was merely told, 'Yes, you've got to do this.'

Monday 22 May saw a listless May launch the Welsh Conservative manifesto in Wrexham. She argued that the social care policy had been misrepresented by Labour with 'scaremongering' and that the Conservatives were absolutely right to face up to the social care and other difficult decisions, which the country needed to tackle. She said the policy was to change: there would be a consultation leading to a cap on care costs, the policy Dilnot strongly advocated. This would change the social care policy to favour the rich, with very few paying more than the likely cap for social care of £100,000, but the regressive change was generally not picked up on by the press. The real damage came after her speech. She was visibly riled under a barrage of fierce media questions. From Channel 4: 'Doesn't this show that you are really weak and wobbly, not strong and stable?' From the BBC: 'You have just announced a significant change to what was offered in your manifesto ... that doesn't look so strong and stable, does it, Prime Minister?' Each question saw her becoming noticeably more needled. She snapped when Christopher Hope from the *Daily Telegraph* asked,

'Will anything else in the manifesto change between now and June 8?' 'Nothing has changed!' she barked, with Thatcher-like certainty.

Why had she said something so utterly gauche? Some close to her speculate whether she said 'nothing has changed' because she hadn't engaged with the detail of the policy over the weekend, and, cut off and alone with Philip, no one had the chance to brief her properly. Crosby was horrified with the words, calamitous to the image of her being strong and stable. He believes that had she said, 'I've listened to you: I won't let Labour scare the elderly,' she could have come out of it on top.[76] Instead, May's team now floundered to defend this comment, trying in vain to claim that the manifesto had promised a Green Paper and that a cap could have come up as one of the solutions. This wouldn't work. In briefings to journalists before the manifesto, the media had been told that getting rid of the cap was a fundamental part of her new social care policy.

To CCHQ's fury ('typical left-wing bias', they claimed), the BBC led the charge on May. Norman Smith, the assistant political editor, had been told by Tory sources before the speech that there would be no rowing back from the controversial cap. He thus said the Prime Minister was now effectively ripping up the manifesto commitment. Osborne, vastly enjoying her distress, tweeted (in a reference to Ed Miliband's notorious pledge tablets in 2015): 'At least this manifesto wasn't carved onto a stone.'[77] CCHQ fought back, saying that wild talk of a 'dementia tax' and people having to sell their homes was 'shameful'. Laura Kuenssberg was not impressed and was merciless in her analysis. Hill blamed May for fastidiously ignoring Kuenssberg during the campaign, along with other key figures in the media, and thought that she sacrificed goodwill as a result.[78] The way the U-turn was executed focused the nation's attention on May personally. It was her biggest test of leadership and character to date. She either had to hold her nerve or retrace her steps with candour and style. She did neither. She failed to step up.

REASON 4: RESPONSE TO THE MANCHESTER AND LONDON BRIDGE
TERRORIST ATTACKS

On the evening of Monday 22 May, the American singer Ariana Grande had just finished her concert at the Manchester Arena when a radical Islamist, Salman Abedi, detonated a shrapnel-laden home-made bomb, killing twenty-three people, including himself, and injuring 139, more than half of them children, with several hundred more suffering psychological distress. The youngest child to be killed was just eight years old. It was the deadliest terrorist attack since the 7/7 bombings on London transport in 2005, which killed fifty-six people, including the four bombers. May promptly spoke to Corbyn, and they agreed to suspend the election campaign.

Issues of national security brought out the best in May. She promptly convened a COBRA meeting with the Chief Constable of Greater Manchester, Ian Hopkins, present, announcing that the UK's terror threat level was being raised to critical, the highest level. It remained there for a further four days amid widespread concern of an imminent fresh attack. Five thousand soldiers were drafted in to support armed police protecting vital parts of the country, with troops deployed to guard government buildings in London. ISIS claimed responsibility, saying the attack had been carried out by a 'soldier of the Khalifa'. A vigil organised in Manchester was attended by Corbyn and Liberal Democrat Leader Tim Farron but not May herself, who, having visited victims of the bombing in Manchester's Children's Hospital, had returned to London to chair a second meeting of COBRA. Those on the inside intelligence and security track spoke with admiration of how well she oversaw the governmental response to the outrage. But the public noticed her absence, not her skill behind the scenes.

Natural leaders, like Thatcher after the bomb attack on the Grand Hotel in Brighton on 12 October 1984 or Blair after Princess Diana's death on 31 August 1997, rise to the occasion at great moments and find the words that speak to the nation. May was unable to do this – or perhaps unwilling. She read out, in a dispassionate way, the speech written for her by Timothy and Wilkins in her statement from Downing Street at 11 a.m. on 23 May: 'Today, let us remember those who died and let us celebrate those who helped, safe in the knowledge that the terrorists will never win – and our values, our country and our way of life will always prevail.' Wilkins, who had children himself, felt the anguish of the families very personally, as did many across the nation. The text that he wrote for her was: 'Today, let us remember those who died … and let us hold those we love a little closer.' She did not feel comfortable with such language and struck it out.[79] The decision not to engage with social media, driven by Hill, was also criticised. While Corbyn tweeted his sympathies at midnight on the Monday, there was no statement from No. 10 until the early hours of Tuesday, allowing others to fill the vacuum.[80] Craig Oliver interpreted the refusal to resort to social media as another deliberate attempt to distance themselves from the style of the Cameron era.[81]

Had May not been so discombobulated by the social care saga, she might have been thinking more clearly. It was an opportunity to assert her own strength on law and order, highlighting Corbyn's vulnerability, given his previous association with terrorist groups, while at the same time deflecting media attention away from her own U-turn. Here was the opportunity for her to be statesmanlike – strong and stable, indeed. But she refused to use the suspension of the campaign to exploit the opportunity to come across as prime ministerial. She was right to avoid using the tragedy for political gain, but social media went into overdrive. CCHQ staff identified some forty organisations that 'all hate the Tories' who were setting the agenda on social media in the vacuum.[82]

Critical days were lost, during which the perception of May personally, and the polling for the Conservative Party, dropped dramatically. Nor did she manage to look prime ministerial when she went to a G7 summit in Sicily on Friday 26 May. Rather than scoring points for being photographed with world leaders, using the opportunity to make eye-catching statements, people wondered why she was abandoning the country at such a fragile time. From Sicily, May castigated Corbyn for saying 'that terror attacks in Britain are our own fault … I want to make something clear to Jeremy Corbyn … there can never be an excuse for terrorism.' But a new narrative was now taking root: cuts in the police numbers, which she herself had argued for, were being portrayed as in part responsible for the vulnerability of the British public to terrorism. It may not have been fair, but many believed it. The last thing she needed, with nerves so frayed, was a second terrorist attack.

On Saturday 3 June, just after 10 p.m., three terrorists drove a van into pedestrians on London Bridge, killing two, before running to nearby Borough Market, where they began to attack anyone in their path with twelve-inch knives. In all, eight people were killed, and another forty-eight injured in the bloody attacks. All three attackers were shot dead by police. Again it was decided, against Crosby's advice, to suspend national-level campaigning for a day. On Sunday morning, May delivered a strong statement from behind the podium of No. 10, with all the imagery of state power behind her. She spoke about the terrorist attacks, which she claimed were 'bound together by the single, evil ideology of Islamist extremism that preaches hatred, sows division and promotes sectarianism'. She added, 'There is – to be frank – far too much tolerance of extremism in our country, so we need to become far more robust in identifying it and stamping it out.' Then, in a memorable phrase, she said, 'Enough is enough.' At last, May had risen to the hour and given a strong prime ministerial speech. But neither change nor follow-up was seen to flow from it.

This second attack supported the narrative begun after the Manchester bombing about May's attitude to the police and thus to public safety. A former Metropolitan Police officer said in an interview on Sky News that the government was lying about the number of armed police available, which was circulated on social media 7.5 million times. Another clip, of May as Home Secretary telling the Police Federation in 2015 that they were 'scaremongering' about the impact of spending cuts on police effectiveness, was also widely circulated. On Monday 5 June, just three days before polling, May came under intensive questioning by the media over the cuts. London Mayor Sadiq Khan, who had not been conspicuous in campaigning for Corbyn so far in the election, swung into full gear, attacking the government over spending on the police in London, while the head of the Metropolitan Police, Cressida Dick, said that the police would be seeking 'more resources'. A worse start to the final week of the campaign for the strong and stable former Home Secretary could not have been imagined.

REASON 5: FOCUS ON THERESA MAY HERSELF

The Crosby–Textor strategy of focusing the campaign on May herself might have worked had she been able enough to carry the performance. But the long campaign cruelly exposed her unusually inflexible and introverted character, which had been shielded from the public by Timothy and Hill in her first ten months at No. 10. Now, without her two chiefs constantly directing her every move, and with cameras and journalists probing her relentlessly, she began to crumble. Timothy, Hill and Wilkins, who had foreseen what might happen, had argued forcefully for the campaign to focus on the wider ministerial team. They knew her vulnerability. Crosby and Textor, who didn't, prevailed, leaning on their analysis that Cabinet was too weak and that their polling saw her as a major asset. May herself was ill at ease with the phrase 'strong and stable', and with being made the focus of the campaign. She said with increasing anger as the campaign went on, 'I'm the leader of the Conservative Party, not a presidential candidate. I'm not comfortable. I don't want it to be about me.' She bitterly resented that Crosby had persuaded her to be the centre of the campaign.

As early as Sunday 30 April, she was challenged by Andrew Marr on his BBC One programme about her repeated 'robotic' use of the phrase 'strong and stable'.[83] Marr's description of her would soon become commonplace. A clip went viral of her speaking later in the campaign in such a manner: though a satirical compilation, many felt it expressed a truth about her. Mid-campaign, but too late, Crosby changed tack. He decided to drop 'strong and stable'. 'Clearly, it was a mismatch between her demeanour and the way she was conducting herself,' he reflects now.[84] May entered the election campaign not with the boundless belief and confidence of a natural leader, many of whom have far bigger egos, but riddled with anxiety about herself and the result. With each passing week, she became more withdrawn and hesitant. Crosby began to note the stark contrast with Cameron and Osborne, who were always 'interested with how things were playing out, taking part in multiple meetings and constantly asking questions'. In contrast, 'she didn't engage much. She'd be on the morning call and turn up to meetings, but she wasn't an active participant in the campaign. She was in a cocoon.'[85] May had been advised not to come into CCHQ because of germs during a prolonged flu epidemic. To colleagues, she seemed to jump on this as an excuse for being AWOL. With the media, too, she became increasingly withdrawn as the polls slid – the very opposite of what was needed. She had never enjoyed engaging with them, but in the final ten days of the campaign, as they became acrid, she reached new heights of awkwardness with them.

Hill became so alarmed by May's state of mind that she effectively switched from being communications director at CCHQ to minding May, travelling with her on the bus to be at her side. She was shocked at what she found:

The journalists didn't like her. She was surly and not particularly pleasant. She was very quiet and seemed unhappy. I asked her, 'Have you been down to talk to the journalists at the front of the bus?' She replied, 'Why should I?' I said, 'Because we're campaigning and you have to tell them the story.'[86]

Throughout the campaign, May had been petrified of saying anything that came from deep inside her, of being caught out offering unprepared thoughts or feelings, so she stuck relentlessly to the scripts she was handed, and she sounded ever more wooden. In desperation, her team implored her, 'Look, whatever you say will be fine. If it creates difficulty, we can clear it up. It really doesn't matter.' She was eventually persuaded to walk down to the media's end of the bus on 2 June, and spoke about her manifesto ambition to cut immigration to less than 100,000 a year by 2020 in a desperate attempt to capture some positive headlines in the final days. But then on BBC's *Question Time* that evening, David Davis contradicted her when he said that 'we can't promise within five years' to achieve any particular target.[87] She was then 'doubly cross' that her initiative had gone down so badly.[88]

Crosby was surprised by her inability to campaign as the election went on. 'She wasn't good. She would say she liked general election campaigning, but she didn't. What she liked is knocking on doors. She didn't like handling the national media and came over as a reluctant Leaver. As soon as she had anything off-piste to say, she came across poorly.'[89] Her constant complaining about the campaign – 'This is not what I believe in. I want to be out campaigning' – began to alienate senior staff. 'I couldn't imagine any other Prime Minister complaining in the way she did,' says one. Another recalls, 'She was a terrible campaigner. She came across as grumpy, entitled and expecting to win, and then visibly irritated when she came under scrutiny.'

Not taking part in the TV debates contributed further to the impression of a leader self-centred and entitled. Her advisors were unanimous that she shouldn't take part in them, for obvious reasons. But to the electorate it only highlighted her weakness. A stronger leader would have risen to the challenge, difficult though the debates are for an incumbent Prime Minister, and led from the front. Instead, she didn't even lead from behind. Her team looked for opportunities where she could be prominent in front of cameras, hoping these might compensate. They searched in vain to milk what their polling had shown, that the electorate saw her as a calming influence, a grown-up after Cameron and Osborne, as someone who was neither a right-wing nor an aloof Tory. There were some good performances, notably her initial announcement of the general election outside No. 10 on 18 April. After returning from Buckingham Palace to inform the Queen that Parliament had been dissolved on 3 May, she delivered a strikingly antagonistic speech about the EU from Downing Street. Responding to the leaks in the German press about her ill-fated dinner with Juncker the night before, she urged voters to 'give me your backing to fight for Britain'. She accused European politicians of intentionally misrepresenting her stance and making 'deliberately timed' interventions to affect the result of the general election. 'We continue to believe that no deal for Britain is better than a bad deal,' she said, adding, 'But we want a deal. We want a deep and special partnership with the European Union, and we want the EU to succeed.'[90] Even though she didn't go as far in attacking the EU as some had counselled her, it was to make her life more difficult when she returned to negotiating in Brussels in June. Nevertheless, it was her strongest performance during the campaign, along with her words after the London Bridge bombing.[91]

For the seven-way live debate of party leaders on 31 May, Amber Rudd deputised for May very ably, despite her father having just died (she didn't let this be known). Five times during the debate, May was attacked for not being present herself. It made her look weak. May did, however, appear on a special edition of BBC's *Question Time* on 22 May. Aides report how extraordinarily nervous she was before she went on: 'Terrified beyond belief,' says one. Another thought that she had lost her confidence after the social care U-turn, and it never fully recovered. May was the first to be questioned by the studio audience, and, according to Kavanagh and Cowley, 'struggled both over her failure to participate in the earlier debates and over domestic policy'.[92] Two particular moments stood out. A nurse complained about her pay not rising for many years, to which May responded, 'Being honest … there isn't a magic tree that we can shake that suddenly provides for everything that people want.' Factually true, maybe, but a failure to respond empathetically, a lapse underlined further when responding to a question from a woman, close to tears, who had problems with mental healthcare. May again showed her inability to respond in a human and personal way despite mental health being a core issue for her. Next up was Corbyn, who himself came under pressure, particularly on questions over his attitude to the IRA and nuclear weapons. The event wasn't judged a disaster for May by her team. But if avoiding a disaster was where her team set the bar, it only highlighted the folly of placing her centre stage.

May rose to her long-awaited keynote speech on 1 June, urging the electorate to embrace the 'promise of Brexit'. Set speeches were a strength, and it helped steady nerves. It served to remind the electorate of the primary reason that she called an election: to obtain a solid majority in the Commons so she could ensure a strong Brexit in the national interest. But throughout the campaign, she had nothing new to say on Brexit; nor did she give any indication about what it would look like, or about what she would do with powers returning from Brussels. The newspapers on Sunday 4 June were nevertheless positive, with the *Sunday Times* and the *Sunday Telegraph* talking about planned tax rises by Labour. It helped May go into the final week with an average of nine lead points, down from an average of twenty points at the start of the campaign. It suggested that hopes of a great Tory landslide like in 1959 or 1983 were receding, but she was still in line for a majority of some forty to fifty seats.[93]

REASON 6: A CATALOGUE OF ERRORS

Political research is insufficiently sensitive to pinpoint the exact impact of any one change on the voting intention of the electorate. We know little, therefore, about the precise significance of any of the multiple woes, many self-inflicted, that the Conservatives faced during the campaign. But we know that the cumulative impact was devastating. Here are some of the more significant ones. On Friday 12 May, the electorate heard about a computer virus known as WannaCry, which encrypts data on infected computers and demands a ransom payment. It was the largest cyber-attack to affect the NHS in England. The media was awash with the potentially serious implications for the NHS in its ability to provide care for patients, and it contributed to a sense that, on this most sensitive of areas, the government was failing to look after its citizens.[94]

By deliberate intent, none of the Conservative policies in the manifesto were costed, which gave little confidence that a Conservative government would have the cash to combat austerity and pay for the new policies Timothy wanted to appeal to voters in the Midlands and the north. Hammond had won the day, including added fiscal flexibility with the removal of the triple lock on pensionable benefits. It left the field open to Labour with its promise to increase spending.

Corbyn emerged as a far better campaigner than the Conservatives had imagined, while Labour's own manifesto, which had been leaked maliciously in advance by a Scottish Labour activist, had the inadvertent effect of giving it two bites of media exposure.[95] The manifesto itself chimed far more with the electorate, and addressed its disillusion with the Westminster establishment. The first big spike in Labour support came just after the leak; the second, immediately after the Conservative manifesto was published. Corbyn's announcement that Labour would scrap university tuition fees wrongfooted the Conservatives and proved very popular with students, who were already disenchanted with the government over Brexit. CCHQ constantly castigated the BBC for not probing Labour sufficiently on how it would pay for university fees, and more generally for not questioning Corbyn more rigorously. If these accusations were true, it was in part because Corbyn was the underdog, and Labour were trailing a long way behind. CCHQ believed the BBC was intent on probing the party most likely to be in government. Because, as Crosby feared, the electorate thought that the Conservatives would win easily, they were less motivated to vote and more likely to be swayed by local campaigns on schools and hospitals, where Labour were often strong.

The absence of a credible third party, with Tim Farron unable to galvanise the Lib Dems, meant that votes piled up for the two main parties, which had not been anticipated. 'We didn't catch onto how we would suffer with the vote divided between just the two main parties,' admits McLoughlin. Ever since the 1970 general election, third-party voting had increased, but in 2017, 82.4 per cent of the votes cast nationally were for the two main parties. The Tories lacked a strategy for dealing with this shift.[96] The length of the campaign – seven weeks – also proved a severe handicap for the Conservatives: the team blamed May's indecision in calling the election, which meant the window for having a short campaign had closed due to the Whitsun holiday. Parties that are ahead almost invariably prosper with a shorter campaign, while their weaknesses are probed when longer. Here was a mistake Baldwin did not make in December 1923: his snap election had a snap campaign, just three weeks.[97]

As the Conservative lead slipped in the polls like a barometer with winter approaching, the Conservative team, never properly constituted in the first place, now began to split apart fatally over messaging. Wilkins, Gummer and Timothy were locked out by Crosby for their focus on policy, which Crosby continued to believe was anathema to the success of the campaign. 'It will increase the salience of Labour issues. Stop banging on about policy, let's keep to the message. The only thing you have is May and Brexit,' he would intone. Hence, more complex policies such as changes to social care and free school meals were not properly communicated to either the press or the electorate, and too little was done in advance to prepare for them. May's team thought that Crosby's singular focus on Brexit meant that 'by the end of the campaign, we were made to look like a bunch of Brexit-obsessed, English right-wing nationalists', as one comments. 'The trouble with "the Australians" is they're much more right-wing than us,' Hill would say. Timothy was incandescent when the *Financial*

Times carried a headline blaming him solely for the social care policy, spreading suspicions about who was leaking. No one found out. Soon the chiefs began to wonder whether Crosby even wanted to win. As divisions between May's chiefs and Crosby–Textor grew, so too did divisions between Hill and Timothy, exacerbated by disagreements over social care. The bitterness between the different arms of the campaign continued long after the election result, with claims about selective briefing to journalists and writers. Crosby admits it was not his most glorious campaign in Britain: 'We obviously all need to accept some responsibility for the campaign ... I don't absolve myself of guilt.'[98]

ELECTION DAY AND AFTER

May met her close team at 8 a.m. in her kitchen above Downing Street on polling day, Thursday 8 June. She hadn't been keen to meet but had been prevailed upon to do so by Williamson, who was anxious about the result. 'Do we really need to meet?' she had asked. 'Yes, we do,' he replied. 'It's what David Cameron did in 2015. We need to check that we have everything in place for all scenarios.' Williamson nevertheless cautioned that if the majority was low, they would be in deep trouble because Conservative MPs were going to shout: 'Really? Were the last seven weeks really fucking worth it? Why have you put us through this long torture, used all this time and money, just to get the same number of seats?' He enquired whether any overtures should be made to the DUP in case the worst happened. But May was not interested.[99] Williamson's pessimism was not widely shared. Internal Conservative predictions on polling day suggested a majority of between fifty and sixty, comfortably sufficient to have justified calling an election, if short of the landslide they had hoped for when the campaign commenced. Throughout the day, intelligence from CCHQ, which had proved accurate on polling day in 2015, suggested that their position was strengthening with a lead of 8 per cent over Labour, who were predicted to fall to just 203 seats, down from 232 in 2015.[100]

That evening, May visited CCHQ and was reassured to hear there was nothing to worry about. As the close of poll approached, the mood became more buoyant and a staff party to celebrate the end of the long campaign cautiously began. The release of the exit poll at 10 p.m. thus came as a profound shock: it predicted that the Conservatives would win just 314 seats and Labour 266. 'They're wrong. They're definitely wrong,' said Messina. Hill, who had had the result leaked to her shortly before the broadcast, shared the figures with Timothy. Both were reeling, not knowing what to think. David Dimbleby, fronting the BBC's election night programme, said that May had called the election because she wanted certainty and stability, 'and this doesn't seem, at this stage, to look like certainty and stability'.

When the exit poll was announced, Crosby, Gilbert, Timothy and Messina were in the green room at CCHQ. Messina, whose data sheets were predicting a sixty- to seventy-seat majority, remained optimistic. When the Sunderland vote came in, contradicting the exit polls, Crosby said, 'See, this shows the exit polls were wrong.' Textor was very quiet. Gilbert took Timothy on one side and said, 'Look, I hate to say this, but the exit polls are never wrong.' May, who knew the same, called Timothy, palpably upset. He advised, 'Let's not worry too much about them. Let's see what happens. Lynton and Jim are saying that they're wrong.'

'Oh fuck,' read a text from Deputy Chief Whip Julian Smith to Williamson, who recalls now, 'I didn't think he meant that in the sense of it being amazing.' Even Heywood was lost for words: 'Blimey,' he texted a colleague in the middle of the night. Heywood had been typically cautious in the run-up to the general election, making sure to meet Corbyn during the campaign and keeping in regular contact with his senior team, including MP Jon Trickett. He was aware of the need for the civil service to be seen as politically neutral in order to avoid the institutional clash that folklore says happened with Blair in 1997, despite regular contacts before the election between Labour and mandarins (Labour had been as strongly tipped to win then as the Tories were now). When he had spoken to the top 200 officials and business leaders that year, Heywood had said very publicly that Labour would, in the next ten to fifteen years, judge the civil service by the way they were treated in the transition. As the results began to pour in, the Cabinet Office sent a precautionary message to Karie Murphy, head of Corbyn's office, 'in case we needed to talk', but received no reply.[101]

To May, the exit poll had confirmed all her worst apprehensions. She spent the night of the election in the company of her head of operations Richard Jackson, affectionately known as 'Tricky', who did his best, as ever, to manage her. While Timothy remained with Wilkins in the boardroom at CCHQ, May texted Hill and asked if she could come up to join her at Maidenhead. 'I've thought a lot about why she asked me to be with her, but I'll never know unless I ask her, and I never will,' Hill reflects now. 'My God, it's all going wrong,' she thought at the time, as she was sped in the early hours of the morning by car through west London.[102] When she saw May, they hugged and the Prime Minister burst into tears. Philip looked ashen faced and grim. Hill accompanied them to the declaration in Maidenhead just after 3 a.m. At the count, journalists shouted at May, 'Are you going to resign?' Her team had hurriedly prepared some words for her, to say she had called the election because the country needed stability and that if the Conservatives emerged as the largest party, it was incumbent on them to provide that stability. The next two hours were some of the worst May endured as Prime Minister, with nine government ministers losing their seats and Rudd looking as if she might lose hers in Hastings and Rye. Just before 5 a.m., and after a full recount, the BBC reported that Rudd had crawled home with 346 votes.

Shortly before, at about 4.30 a.m., May arrived at CCHQ from Maidenhead. Hill and Timothy looked at each other, knowing that everything was over. 'Well, that's it,' they said. They knew what was coming. May asked, 'Might we need to talk to the DUP? We must keep Corbyn out.' The chiefs told her that people would want blood. 'We should resign to protect you,' they said. 'You will have to meet Cabinet ministers in the morning to hold this together. We mustn't be there. You must look after yourself.'[103] May didn't seem to be taking it all in. Crosby, who'd received livid texts from both May and Hill, was subdued. May complained bitterly that she had done exactly what they had told her to do and this was the result. She had visited constituencies that they had told her were winnable and almost none of them flipped Conservative, while Labour had made gains in constituencies that she had been told were safe. After an acrimonious and unpleasant hour, she emerged to address staff at about 5.30 a.m.

Gilbert encouraged her to say a few words, conscious when introducing her that he didn't want to say too much because it might tip her over the edge. 'The Conservative Party is the best political party in the world,' she told them. 'We continue to be the best political party in the world and continue to fight another day.'[104] She said how sorry she was, and tried to make a joke about the awful plates of cheesy pasta the team had eaten that night. 'This hasn't gone the way we wanted it to,' she said. When she finished, barely anyone applauded. Those present wondered whether she was going to make it to the end of her speech without bursting into tears. Philip, everyone noted, was conspicuous, a staunch presence at her side.[105]

She left to return to Downing Street at about 6 a.m. as the news confirmed that, after Labour held Southampton Test, the UK had a hung parliament. The final results were the Conservatives on 317 seats (down thirteen), and Labour on 262 (up thirty). The biggest loser of the night was the SNP (down twenty-one). Corbyn emerged as the moral victor, May the clear loser. The result was through the floor of even the party's most pessimistic predictions.

Hill remembers standing alongside Timothy in CCHQ, as he told

May again, 'I think I need to resign.' May was fidgeting with her phone, responding to the occasional text message. She responded coldly, 'I think you both need to resign.'[106] A distraught Hill went back home, turned off her phone and slept for the rest of Friday. Timothy desperately tried to call her, saying that he thought he should resign quickly. He was worried about the media storm brewing and the impact on his family. Hill said she needed time to think it over, so Timothy waited. Another row erupted between them over the phone on Saturday morning when Timothy refused to delay any longer and said that he was going to throw in the towel. Davis and Johnson had both called Hill, saying, 'Don't go.' 'You've got to stay,' Davis told her. Hill held on, but later that morning May called her and insisted, 'No, you have to go.' 'I'm not sure that I do have to resign. DD said I shouldn't,' Hill retorted, anxious to avoid a second sacking by May. The Prime Minister then told her down the phone, 'I'm sorry, but you come as a pair.' Hill felt at that point she had no choice but to issue a resignation statement in public. Davis called her, angrily asking why she resigned. Hill replied, 'I didn't resign, she made me.' 'Oh. So it was not your choice.'[107]

The media storm against Timothy and Hill had begun with Katie Perrior's appearance on Radio 4's *Today* programme that Friday morning. Keen to stick the boot in, Perrior said the atmosphere would be 'great' in meetings when they were absent, but 'terrible' when they attended, and spoke of the tight grip they held over No. 10. Fury from Cabinet ministers poured out over the next few hours, in particular from Hammond, still livid about briefings during the campaign that he would be removed as Chancellor after the general election and believing May wanted him replaced with 'somebody who would be totally compliant, and do what he was told'.[108] For many, this was payback time. Javid told one aide on his reappointment, 'These two people are pure poison,' reflecting the anger that he had suppressed against Hill in particular for many months. Though Hill may not have been responsible for the failures of the election campaign, her and Timothy's abrasive conduct with ministers and MPs would seal their departure.

May decided that she had to wash her hands of her chiefs altogether. Unlike Cameron with his departing team, there were to be no promotions to the Lords and no help finding another job. They were hung out to dry and were treated not as the people who had made her Prime Minister, nor those who had helped forge her agenda in the first few months, but as pariahs. Both had known May for over a decade, but neither would see her for the remainder of her premiership. When May went to the 1922 Committee just after the general election, she said, 'I can show you that I've changed, I've gotten rid of my drivers.' That the drivers, not May, were at fault, was a theme many were to echo in the months ahead. Now she was heading out into the night on her own, without them.

The fault was not her 'drivers': she was the driver. Until May began to accept her own responsibility, for her staff and for her failings, she was not going to grow in the job and become her own person.

PART TWO

THE
UNRAVELLING
OF THE
PREMIERSHIP

INTRODUCTION TO PART TWO

THE UNRAVELLING OF THE PREMIERSHIP

By the morning of Thursday 8 June 2017, despite all the mayhem of the election campaign, Theresa May was still predicted a majority of fifty to sixty seats. Friday 9 June, however, was to be the first day in the unravelling of her premiership. The following fifteen chapters in this second part often just focus on one episode culminating in her departure from Downing Street on 24 July 2019, and the difficulties that, for all her efforts, she left in her wake.

May begins this section of her premiership at her lowest ebb. Her strategy, team, credibility and confidence all lie in tatters. Ironically, the more her premiership unravels, the more she grows as a person and a leader. If her story was one of tragedy, by the end it had become a heroic tragedy as she gains in wisdom and recognises what she should have known all along, that a Brexit led on tribal grounds would never secure the votes it needed to get it through the Parliament she found herself facing. The quality of her leadership in her final year was un-recognisable to what had preceded it.

We crave villains, and the millions of words that have already been written, and the tens of millions of words that will be written about this period will have villains aplenty. This book takes no side, but lays out who did what and why in the unravelling of the premiership.

The story of the unravelling opens on 9 June, the second most important day of Theresa May's premiership after 12 July 2016.

May was utterly shattered by the general election result. Her husband Philip provided constant support, an indispensable rock throughout her premiership.

CHAPTER 6

'NOTHING HAS CHANGED'

9–11 JUNE 2017

Friday 9 June was a day on which British history pivoted. Theresa May was hanging onto her premiership on the end of a very thin piece of rope. A challenge that day from one of the big beasts would have severed it. In the early hours of the morning, a Jeremy Corbyn-led government, unthinkable when the election was announced just seven weeks before, did not appear an impossibility. The Conservative Party was in shock.

The civil service and Buckingham Palace, meanwhile, were worrying about the impact of all the uncertainty on the markets, on the delicate state of negotiations with the European Union, and on the country's political stability. All eyes were on Theresa May. Would she be able to stay on? Would she even want to?

PICKING UP THE PIECES: FRIDAY 9 JUNE

Any doubts concerning her resolve would soon be answered. Theresa May had absolutely no intention of giving up a job she had yearned for many years to acquire, with so many of her ambitions in office still unfulfilled. The job was her life. She was full of resolve as she was driven into Downing Street at 5.30 a.m. from CCHQ and went upstairs to the flat with Philip. Some things she knew. The results were terrible and realised her worst fears. She had made few friends in Cabinet over the past year. She knew that the two pilots of her first ten months, Nick Timothy and Fiona Hill, had to go. Who could she turn to for advice? She texted Gavin Williamson to come in to see her. The Chief Whip was being driven down from his South Staffordshire constituency when he received her message, and gave instructions to go to 70 Whitehall, where he entered No. 10 discreetly through the connecting internal door from the Cabinet Office. No. 10 was still ghostly quiet. As he entered, he bumped into May's still new Principal Private Secretary, Peter Hill (they had not yet met because of the election campaign), and explained that the PM wanted to see him upstairs. The private office couldn't reach her, though; neither she nor Philip was picking up their messages. It was decided that he would go up to the flat, knock on the door and wait outside to see if he could gain admission. In no time, Philip opened the door and ushered him through to the kitchen, where, less than twenty-four hours before, they had talked about scenarios in the event of a hung parliament.

Williamson was aware of history on his shoulder:

I had been churning over in my mind on the journey what I should say to her. Should I say she should go or stay? I decided to frame it in a way where I asked her what she herself wanted to do. 'What do you want to do now?' I asked. 'I want to carry on,' she shot back at me calmly and clearly. I've thought a lot since about what I could have said differently, although I think she would have stayed even if I'd said I thought she ought to go. I think she would have found others who would have given her the answers she wanted, and ignored my advice.[1]

At the front of Williamson's mind that morning was the thought shared by many senior Conservatives: 'My complete concern was that we should at all costs avoid a Corbyn government. My worry was that, if she couldn't get a Queen's Speech passed, it would lead inevitably to Corbyn, and at all costs we had to stop that from happening.'[2] Corbyn may not have scared the electorate, but that morning he was certainly spooking Tory MPs.

As May and Williamson sat down at the kitchen table, they ran through her options for staying on. A coalition with Labour would obviously never happen. Neither would a coalition with the SNP, which had itself done badly in the election. The Lib Dems, they agreed, would not want to repeat the experience of the 2010–15 coalition government, though their twelve MPs would have carried her over the line. That left the DUP with ten as the only option on the table to provide the numbers needed to pass the Queen's Speech. So they agreed that that was their best – indeed, their only – chance. Williamson saw himself that morning as 'the Praetorian Guard', doing his utmost to secure the position of the government and the Prime Minister. A friend of Williamson recalls him saying to them after his sacking in 2019, 'I had been with David [Cameron] until the end and I thought I would be with her until the end too. If she had to go, I wanted it to be as humane a dispatch as possible, a good death.'

While they were discussing how they might best approach the DUP, David Davis burst through the flat's door at 6.45 a.m. and into the kitchen. 'You've got to stay, Prime Minister,' he spluttered. She responded emotionally to his plea, affirmation from one of the few politicians she regarded as a friend at the time. 'She really wasn't thinking straight at all,' as pent-up feelings burst through at last, Davis recalls. He was completely clear, telling her, 'I'll support you. It's your duty to stay on.'[3] After she left to pick up a call, Davis turned to Philip and asked, 'Does she understand how tough this is going to be?' 'Yes, she does,' he replied quietly. Davis left the flat with Williamson, who accompanied him on the walk to his office at DExEU, telling him of the need to get the DUP firmly on board in order to stabilise the government. Davis replied that he'd keep in touch but needed to travel back to his constituency in East Yorkshire. Davis left London at 8 a.m., turning down all requests from CCHQ and from the media to be interviewed. No. 10 wanted him to be on standby to walk up Downing Street on his reappointment later that day. 'Sorry, I'm on a train back home,' he told them.[4] He had done his bit for the day.

By the time he had spoken to May that morning, she had already decided to stay. Davis was later to be blamed by some for propping her up at a critical time, however. He didn't consult any of the big beasts, not even Michael Fallon, who had proposed him for the leadership in 2005 and knew him well. 'She was at her weakest that morning,' Fallon says now. 'David never spoke to me about propping her up.'[5] So why did Davis act as he did when 10 Downing Street appeared ripe for the taking?

> Because I'm built like that. I didn't think that there was a proper alternative at the time. Had Boris stood, I would have blocked him. But if I had challenged her, it would have all been over for her. But I took the decision that the Brexit negotiations were so sensitive that the job was to keep the ship on an even keel and get on with it. My hero was William Marshal, the Anglo-Norman statesman who served no less than five English kings.[6]

Davis's colleagues are less convinced of his high-minded motivations. Twice he had run for the Conservative Party leadership (coming fourth in 2001 and second in 2005), and his long-standing ambitions for the top job were no secret. One Cabinet colleague says:

The reason DD told her to stay on, I suppose, was he wanted to stand as leader and he knew that his best chance was that if he was known to be loyal. The Sunday papers were full of reports about how he tried to make her stay on. The leak to the press didn't come from her...

Boris Johnson had also texted her that morning to reassure her of his backing. Again, his motive, given his appetite, was positioning himself. 'All possible challengers that day had in mind the folklore that "he who puts the knife in doesn't inherit the crown",' says another Cabinet minister. 'But there was also a feeling abroad that she was so weak that she wouldn't survive, so nobody needed to put the knife in anyway.' The 'Big Five' – Davis, Johnson, Hammond, Rudd and Fallon – did not talk as a group. Individual messages passed, including between Hammond and Johnson, suggesting that Hammond would support Johnson if he were to stand against her.[7] Rudd recalls talking to Hammond that evening:

> I was slow to realise how vulnerable she was. I had just got my majority of 346 in my constituency, that was really where my focus was. I spoke to Philip Hammond, who brought me up to date. He told me that he had said to her that Nick and Fi had to go. He was really giving her the conditions for him staying on, but the ERG lot were joining forces round her and being polite to her. They hadn't yet given up on her, and at the time the ERG didn't really like Boris. I certainly wasn't looking to move her on.[8]

Not one tried coordinating a joint effort to unseat her, wary of being seen as the ringleader – May knew she would need to move quickly to reassure them of her strength and their positions to pre-empt any such move.

Another factor was running in favour of May's survival. None of her challengers, least of all Johnson or Davis, had anticipated such an election result. None had their campaigns and teams lined up ready to go. 'They were caught entirely with their trousers down,' says one insider. Johnson had looked totally devastated when May announced the early election because he saw his chances of taking over in the near future going down in flames. With no time to prepare, and the DUP closing the windows fast, the challengers were less powerful than they appeared.

DEVASTATION IN DOWNING STREET

'It was very odd,' says Williamson. 'The top of the house was in tears; the bottom in shock.'[9] At 6 a.m., Jeremy Heywood convened a meeting in Room 103, his large oblong office in the Cabinet Office. He had followed his usual general election routine of returning to his house in Clapham for a short sleep between 12 and 5 a.m. and was ready for action. In the room were his most senior Cabinet Office officials: Sue Gray, in charge of government propriety; Lucy Smith, responsible for the constitution, devolution and inter-governmental relations within the UK; and Peter Hill. Heywood was not himself in shock – he never was – but the result was certainly not what he had expected. One insider contrasts the deadly quiet Cabinet Office that morning with the buzzing atmosphere in 2015, when officials were up all night in the expectation of a hung parliament: 'We were always fighting the last election,' he says ruefully.

Heywood had nevertheless taken great care during the campaign to keep in regular contact with the Labour leader's office, in part to pre-empt allegations that he was *parti pris*. He was far from calm as he saw the results from the constituencies sway the likely outcome one way

and then the other. He had been in the lead figuring out how to make
the coalition government work in 2010, and for its subsequent five
years. He knew the acute difficulties. Providing a stable government
was his prime objective. 'Jeremy was all about stability,' says a civil
servant who worked closely with Heywood. 'He thought, "There's a
hell of a lot to deal with here, but the country comes first." Even then,
he was certain the PM would come back.' He worried, too, about the
markets (the Bank of England was monitoring them closely), about
the position of the Queen, and about the soon-to-recommence negotiations with Europe. Christopher Geidt, private secretary to the
Queen, was also in contact with No. 10 – suggestive of the constitutional concerns of the hour. 'That morning, there was a sense of
massive instability,' one of May's team recalls.

Heywood was in communication with May from early morning – he knew she would not resign – and they discussed what had
to happen next. 'You are the Prime Minister,' he told her. 'With
the Cabinet behind you, you will be fine.' An arrangement with
the DUP being her only feasible option for staying in power, Heywood was clear that there were two practical relationships that the
Conservatives could form, one of which he favoured, a confidence-
and-supply arrangement, and one of which, a coalition government,
he did not.

At 9 a.m., a formal meeting was convened in her study around the
oval table, with May in her usual position and officials gathered all
around her – Heywood, Peter Hill, Will Macfarlane and James Slack
principally among them. The absence of political figures was startling.
One attendee recalls:

> There was a gaping hole around the table where the chiefs and the
> other political advisors used to sit. The Prime Minister was exhaust-
> ed, falling asleep in front of us. It was awful to watch. I had never

seen her that way. Her eyes kept closing in front of us, then she'd jolt herself awake. Jeremy Heywood was very much in the lead, thinking above all about stability and how a stable government could be formed.

Peter Hill had been in office for only a few days, and although he was the senior official within the Prime Minister's office, he was happy for Heywood to call the shots, given that the Cabinet Secretary had cross-governmental responsibility. They debated whether she would be forming a new government or continuing with the old one. It was decided that, even though under the Fixed Term Parliaments Act she did not need to go to Buckingham Palace to see the Queen, it would show her in a strong light if she was filmed going on the well-worn track to see Her Majesty.[10] The paramount need to keep the monarch above politics was not the only concern for Buckingham Palace: May's involvement in the Queen's Speech, and any relationship with the DUP, was also of great interest – hence Geidt's presence in No. 10.

At 10.10 a.m., after the meeting in her room broke up, a formal announcement was made that the Prime Minister would be going to see the Queen. At 10.30 a.m., May spoke to DUP leader Arlene Foster, and, despite no details yet having been agreed, an announcement was rushed out that there would be an agreement with the DUP. Stabilisation was the motive for releasing the news so quickly. The message crafted, as agreed upon at the 7.15 meeting, had one aim and one aim alone: to deliver stability to the country. As one official present recalls:

We didn't think much about the need for her to give a political message, to acknowledge it was her fault, that she was aware of the pain and harm caused to so many, especially the MPs who had lost their seats, and she had got it wrong. We were not thinking of that audience. We were thinking of a different audience.

The officials trooped into the office, where an exhausted Wilkins was slumped over his desk, and, according to his account, they dictated her statement from written notes, which he then typed out on his computer and printed off for them. 'Basically, the civil servants had taken control,' he says.[11] The civil servants present strongly dispute this version of events, and take issue with the story of 'shellshock' which appears in Tim Shipman's *Fall Out*. 'It's not at all my memory of what happened,' recalls one.

> I gave Wilkins the five to six bullet points we had agreed with the Prime Minister, asking him to turn them into a statement. But Wilkins drafted it. The idea that it was all down to the civil servants is entirely a post-hoc narrative to exonerate himself from the lack of messaging in the statement.

Shortly after 12.15, May was driven to the Palace, where she reassured the Queen in a fifteen-minute audience that she was confident she could form a government, on the basis of conversations with the DUP. At 12.50, she returned and delivered her speech outside Downing Street.

> I have just been to see Her Majesty the Queen, and I will now form a government – a government that can provide certainty and lead Britain forward at this critical time for our country. This government will guide the country through the crucial Brexit talks that begin in just ten days and deliver on the will of the British people by taking the United Kingdom out of the European Union.
> It will work to keep our nation safe and secure by delivering

the change that I set out following the appalling attacks in Manchester and London ... What the country needs more than ever is certainty, and having secured the largest number of votes and the greatest number of seats in the general election, it is clear only the Conservative and *Unionist* Party has the legitimacy and ability to provide that certainty by commanding a majority in the House of Commons.

As we do, we will continue to work with our friends and allies in the Democratic Unionist Party in particular... This will allow us to come together as a country and channel our energies towards a successful Brexit deal that works for everyone in this country – securing a new partnership with the EU which guarantees our long-term prosperity ... Now let's get to work.

The speech lasted just under three minutes. With Philip standing to her left, she gave a confident enough performance in front of the cameras. Before she had left for the Palace, Macfarlane had asked her, 'Are you happy for the staff to clap you back in? We would like to do so.' She replied, 'Yes.' And they, ever loyal to her, did.

But the country did not applaud the speech. 'What the fuck was that speech on the doorstep? No contrition, no humility, nothing,' said one special advisor.[12] A concerned George Hollingbery, her Parliamentary Private Secretary, arrived in the building to see her, but was told by JoJo Penn that he would have to wait until later in the day. He passed on to her the comment from fellow MPs that 'the speech ... seemed as if it might have been drawn from the wrong pocket and was actually the speech for an eighty-seat victory'.[13] Tim Shipman quotes a senior Tory MP telling ITV's Robert Peston, 'We all fucking hate her. But there's nothing we can do. She's totally fucked us,' and a senior backbencher adding, 'Most colleagues want her to go but I want her to dangle from a rope.'[14]

May spent some time alone with Philip up in the flat over lunch.

In the early afternoon, Philip came down the steps to say that he and the PM had talked it over and decided that the speech outside hadn't gone down well, and that she needed to say something afresh to address concerns of MPs. So the decision was taken for her to record a message that afternoon in her office. In it, she accepted blame: 'I'm sorry for all those candidates and hard-working party workers who weren't successful, but also particularly sorry for those colleagues who were MPs and ministers who contributed so much to our country and who lost their seats and didn't deserve to lose their seats.'

The message soothed some of the anger, but it was her earlier speech that stayed in the minds of MPs.

At 3 p.m., a meeting was convened in the Cabinet Room to discuss the detail of talks with the DUP, at which Williamson volunteered to go across to Belfast immediately to talk to their senior politicians. May readily agreed.

By this time, Jeremy Heywood had received a difficult call of his own. After his morning meeting with the Prime Minister, his GP had rung. The doctor had his X-rays – taken because Heywood had developed a cough – and wanted him to see a cancer special-ist. Heywood's health had been good until the spring of 2017, but in early April he had started to become breathless. During the elec-tion campaign, he had a succession of appointments with doctors but was always blasé about them: 'I've always had trouble with my lungs,' he would say. He was thus not too worried when he returned to his office to phone his specialist at 4 p.m. But he was told that his doctors were worried about recent tests and wanted to conduct far more invasive explorations. This was the first time he realised that it could be lung cancer. One of his officials says, 'I'll never forget how focused Jeremy was after hearing the news on such a day, when he put the survival of the government, and what he needed to do for the Prime Minister, above all other considerations.' Aside from the personal worries for Heywood, with three children of school age, he knew he had to steer the country through one of its greatest periods of turbulence in modern history, made none the easier by his determination that nobody, bar the tightest of circles, should know his news.

By mid-afternoon, May's position was beginning to strengthen. Stabilising the team of special advisors, the vein through which the political blood at the centre of Whitehall flows, was now vital if May was to recover confidence. With talk rife of Nick Timothy and Fiona Hill departing, and other names being mooted for the chop, the atmosphere was febrile. At 4.30 p.m., Alex Dawson, while in the car on the way to Northolt Airport bound for Belfast, established a WhatsApp group. It included Wilkins, Penn, Ed de Minckwitz, Liz Sanderson, Tom Swarbrick and Stephen Parkinson. He gave the group the title 'Rough DS staffers list'. Some semblance of order was returning to 10 Downing Street.

At 5.30 p.m., Hollingbery was finally able to see May, together with Philip. He had phoned Philip earlier, encouraged by his own wife, who suggested the Prime Minister would be 'exhausted, deflated and feeling horrible'. He was spurred to do so too by reports that none of her Cabinet had yet heard from her. He made three points to Philip over the telephone, which he elaborated on when they met:

> First, in essence, all MPs in their heart of hearts knew there was no alternative, at least for now, but for her to carry on. The principal aim therefore had to be to make it as easy for them as possible to forgive her for what had happened. Everything she did from now on must be consultative and open and she had to be seen to listen to her Cabinet and colleagues. Second, however much we both knew Nick and Fi were talented and very able people, they had to be dismissed or resign, and as professionals they would know that anyway. Finally, Gavin Barwell should be the new chief of staff.

Hollingbery left for Downing Street with a food hamper for the Mays including a fish pie from the freezer and vegetables from the garden. His wife warned him, 'Be prepared ... She will cry.' When they met in the late afternoon, he elaborated on why he thought her speech outside Downing Street had landed wrongly. His advice was for her to see 'a procession of grey beards', senior leaders in the party who had taken it through difficult times, including Major and Hague, and said that she 'must have a government of the most talented people' – including Michael Gove.[15]

A further task that day was the announcement at 5.15 p.m. that the Big Five would all remain in post: Hammond at the Treasury, Rudd at the Home Office, Johnson as Foreign Secretary, Davis as DExEU Secretary and Fallon as Defence Secretary. May did not have time to call them all in, but she did speak to them. Fallon told her, 'The style of government has to change. You have to involve colleagues more.'[16]

The No. 10 press office released the names in good time for the Saturday papers, as further evidence that her premiership was stabilising. Heywood's attempt to persuade May to reappoint the previous Cabinet in its entirety, in the name of stability and continuation, was roundly countered by Williamson, who told her it was 'a dreadful decision'. After an argument, Williamson agreed to her appointing these five names, but said 'absolutely no more'.[17] More appointments would have undermined his bargaining position with the DUP on coalition places for their big hitters, as well as limiting her manoeuvrability in replacing the more ineffective ministers with others who could shore up her Commons support.

The long day was coming to a close for May, and after Hollingbery left there was little more she could do but prepare to go to bed, having had no sleep since early Thursday morning. At 11 p.m., however, she spoke to Trump and Macron, both of whom congratulated her on remaining in office. The single most testing day of her premiership had come to an end, and a way forward was beginning to emerge.

ALL CHANGE AT NO. 10

May had no prior thought of dropping Timothy and Hill at the general election, so there was no plan for possible replacements. Two candidates had lost their seats and had the right qualifications: Ben Gummer and Gavin Barwell. It was made very clear to May on Friday, though, that the former's role in the manifesto and his closeness to Timothy made it impossible, and even if he was offered the role Gummer would have seen it as a step down and rejected it.[18] That left Barwell. At least three people suggested his name to May that day, including Heywood as early as 9.30 that morning. Williamson was a keen advocate. And Hollingbery mentioned his name to Philip on the telephone at midday. Barwell was the ideal, if the only, choice on the table. He had joined CCHQ in 1993 from Cambridge, where he had read natural sciences and served as president of the Union. He rose to become chief operating officer at CCHQ, as well as serving as a local councillor in Croydon. Entering Parliament in 2010, he rose swiftly as a PPS, a whip and finally a successful Minister for Housing from July 2016. He was due to be elevated to Cabinet after the election and possessed the essential benefit for the time of being liked across all sections of the party.

By 10 a.m. on Saturday, there was still no formal news about Timothy and Hill going or Barwell being appointed. With Williamson away in Belfast, Deputy Chief Whip Julian Smith picked up the reins and invited Barwell up to London to meet him. While they were together at Smith's flat, they had a call from Downing Street to say the Prime Minister wanted to see Barwell in Sonning. He was embarrassed to have to admit that he had just given a broadcast interview criticising the election campaign, but nevertheless set off from Paddington by train to Reading, where Philip met him at the station. 'Something's a bit awry when the husband of the Prime Minister has to drive to the station to pick up the new chief of staff,' remarks Smith.[19] When Barwell arrived at the Mays' home at Sonning, they talked from 3 p.m. until well after 6 p.m., covering a wide range of topics, including what had gone wrong in the campaign, her relationships with her senior colleagues, how she wanted to move forward, the state of the negotiations with the DUP, and how to manage the back benches. To Barwell, the meeting was incredibly important: 'It set up our relationship for the next two years.'[20]

That evening, he went straight into No. 10 after leaving her to talk to Peter Hill. His appointment was announced late afternoon and was reported in the Sunday papers, another plank in the bridge to May's safety. The appointment went down well with the civil service, who believed his experience in Parliament would be key to achieving the Brexit votes to come. One official comments:

In the White House, the chief of staff has often been a legislator or figure with a strong personal history, or an independent figure of standing. In No. 10, Barwell has been the only chief of staff to be an MP, as well as a whip and minister, and would have been in Cabinet if he hadn't lost his seat. His experience of the legislature would, we thought, be useful.

Penn survived the transition, endorsed strongly by Barwell. She provided continuity with the old regime, and while she was not popular with some for being seen as the agent of Timothy and Hill, she had not angered ministers to anything like the same extent, and was seen as reliable and loyal, if not a major player herself. Several figures like Perrior and Loudon had already left No. 10 at the start of the campaign. John Godfrey came back in after the election and spoke to

Heywood about how the job of head of the Policy Unit would now change. He, as well as many others, had realised it would become very narrow due to Brexit, so he decided to quit.[21] Will Tanner was offered the job of head of Policy Unit in his place, but similarly declined the offer: 'It was clear that the head of policy role would not be the same and policy would be subordinate to Brexit, so I decided to quit.'[22] Chris Brannigan, director of government relations and the liaison between 10 Downing Street and the business lobby, would be another to leave No. 10 that month. The post would not be filled for another year.

Wilkins found himself in a dilemma about what he should do. On Saturday morning, he texted May to say, 'What a disaster. Can I come over to Sonning? What would you like me to do?' But he had no reply. Some had suggested to him on Friday that he would be chief of staff, but then he saw the news on Saturday afternoon about Barwell's appointment. On Sunday he received a message that the new chief wanted to see him in No. 10 the next day. 'The PM wants you to stay on. Can you take over as director of communications?' Barwell asked him. Wilkins was in no fit state to decide, asking to think it over for a week so he could talk about it with his family. He soon decided he would accept the job vacated by Perrior, on top of his existing job as head of strategy. But when he spoke to Barwell a week later, he was told that the director of communications job was no longer on offer. He could read the runes and decided to leave, requesting a meeting with the Prime Minister before he did so. 'That's a bit of a surprise that you want to go,' she told him. 'Not really, it's right I should go,' he told her. 'I'm sorry for the way it worked out. I know I was one of those who counselled holding the general election.' 'Don't worry about it,' she replied. 'It was my responsibility.' That was it. No farewell kiss or hug. 'I don't think I ever kissed her,' he reflects now.[23] Nor was there any recognition or honour for Wilkins, any more than there was – at this moment in time – for others who departed.

Not all left in the cull: Alex Dawson, heavily embroiled in the Belfast discussions, stayed on as political director, as did Stephen Parkinson as political secretary and Liz Sanderson as head of features, and Hollingbery as May's PPS. The latter offered his resignation, but May refused point-blank to let him go. Robbie Gibb, former chief of staff to Francis Maude in opposition, and recently head of BBC Westminster in overall charge of the BBC's political programmes, was appointed director of communications on 7 July. The brother of Schools Minister Nick Gibb, he shared with his sibling a belief in Brexit and a single-minded focus on the task. 'Damian Green had suggested me,' says Gibb. 'I was a lifelong Tory. Nick and I are very close: he had a big influence on my development.'[24]

No. 10 changed greatly in the next two years. Staff report that it became a much friendlier and more open place, taking its character from the leadership of Barwell, and with Peter Hill becoming an urbane presence across the building. The tone was set by the first meeting Barwell convened in the Cabinet Room at 8 a.m. on Monday morning, 12 June. Sitting in the PM's chair, the new chief told the packed room, 'We are here to support the PM and get through the next few weeks. We are in the Grand National taking each fence as it comes. The culture in No. 10 will change. It needs to be actually enjoyable.' He added, gesturing to Penn, 'She speaks for me.' No. 10 became much quicker at making decisions, and its relations with Westminster and Whitehall improved. But would the policy drive be as effective under the new team, with the parliamentary arithmetic now more precarious and the PM palpably weakened? David Davis was one of the first to identify the significance of the change for Brexit. He remembers:

There was a huge difference in her advisors before and after the general election. Nick was a robust Brexiteer who was backed up on Europe by Fi, who deferred to him on it, even though she was a moderate Remainer. So you changed from them being all-dominant to one where the closest advisors are 100 per cent pro-Remain: Barwell, JoJo, Denzil Davidson, the entire civil service team … The only one who wasn't a Remainer was Parkinson.[25]

BUT CABINET CONTINUES IN PLACE…

May had spent much of Saturday 10 June phoning the MPs who had lost their seats and talking to Barwell about the future. With talks still in train with the DUP, the reshuffle was delayed until Sunday, when an appointments meeting was convened at 10.30 a.m. at No. 10 to plan the details. In attendance were Barwell, Williamson, Penn and Hollingbery, with Sue Gray stepping up in Heywood's absence (he worked from home over the weekend). 'She knows the insides of every ministry, gets feedback from all the private offices and knows how departments get on with their ministers,' records one present of Sue Gray.

Prior to the election, it had been widely assumed that the reshuffle would be a 'cleaning out of Nick's enemies', including Hammond. With May separated from her two chiefs for much of the election campaign, however, little detailed thought had gone into the composition of her post-election reshuffle. The identity of the figure pencilled in for Hammond's replacement would be intriguing to know, but it would appear no firm name had been identified: 'She never wanted to talk about the reshuffle,' says Timothy. 'She never indicated she wanted any particular new figure, though Boris was definitely safe.'[26] Now, in the cold light of a lost majority, and with Timothy and Hill packing their bags, the scene looked very different. It was immediately apparent to the group meeting that morning that 'pretty much the same people would stay on in post, as the PM's not strong enough to do much else'.[27] Leadsom was the one candidate considered ripe for sacking: she was not seen to have performed well enough as Environment Secretary and, given the department's exposure to Brexit, a minister better equipped for handling policy detail was deemed necessary. All bar Williamson thought she should go; he thought it a 'shit decision' because of the optics of the PM removing her leadership challenger from the previous year. So she was left in the Cabinet on the argument that 'it was deemed wrong to sack just one person'. She was appointed instead Leader of the House of Commons, very upset at the demotion but placated with promises of a more prominent media role. Liz Truss was the next to be considered for a move, judged to be in the wrong job having lost (or never gained) the trust of the judiciary after she failed to defend them against the tabloid media branding them 'enemies of the people' following the Supreme Court's ruling on Article 50 in the spring. The decision was taken to move her to Chief Secretary to the Treasury.

Among the beneficiaries, David Lidington was promoted to Justice Secretary to succeed Truss, while David Gauke was promoted from Chief Secretary to Work and Pensions Secretary. Damian Green was another winner, brought in to succeed Gummer at the Cabinet Office but with the added title of First Secretary of State, a similar role to William Hague's under Cameron, and Michael Heseltine's under Major. May had not initially wanted to have any sort of Deputy PM figure but was pushed by Williamson to appoint one on the grounds that she needed someone by her side to compensate for her own lack of persuasive ability. When Green emerged as the front-runner for such a post, her opposition to the idea softened. Her new team thought he would be the ideal foil, helping to project her strength, albeit falling short of the influence that Osborne had enjoyed for six years. But it didn't fall short enough for Hammond, who had what was described as 'a massive tantrum' when he learnt about the appointment because he had always seen himself as May's *de facto* if not *de jure* deputy. Sensitive handling was required to re-assure him that he would retain prominence after the appointment. Much was made in the press briefing of Green's friendship with May, and of his wife, Alicia Collinson, having been May's tutorial partner at Oxford. In truth, the relationship between Green and May was never as close as portrayed. The three promoted – Green, Gauke and Lidington – were all considered competent by the civil service and respected by the party. They were shrewd promotions, giving May fresh loyalist support from three figures seen as technical-but-boring, none of whom were after her job, for the anticipated battles in the months ahead.

They were also all Remainers, if not of the ardent tendency, and further adjustments were needed to balance them if May was to pla-cate Brexit backbenchers. Barwell and Williamson argued strongly for the return of Gove. May needed some persuading, still distrusting Gove after his actions in the leadership race a year earlier and their clashes when she was Home Secretary before that, but according to a senior No. 10 official, 'In the end it was agreed that he should replace Leadsom at DEFRA as the challenges faced by the government in Brexit were felt suitable for his ability.' So the call went out from No. 10 to Gove in the late afternoon to come in to see her. He recalls the experience:

> On the Sunday after the general election, most appointments had been made. I didn't think I was going to make it. I was then called in my constituency home. I thought it may have been a joke. I was told to drive in my car to Sloane Square Tube station, where I'd be met by an official, Becca Hogg, and then taken to No. 10. I thought it sounded like a TV stunt. TM said, 'I'd like you to join the govern-ment. I want you to become Environment Secretary. There's going

to be a big job to do after Brexit.' I said, 'Thank you very much, Prime Minister, I'd be delighted.' I think the two principal advocates for me were Gavin Barwell and George Hollingbery. I then went to see [civil service ethics chief] Sue Gray. She asked me if I had any conflicts of interest and whether I was a vegetarian. I said, 'I own nothing and I eat meat.'[28]

Brexiteer nerves were soothed equally by the appointment of chair of the ERG, Steve Baker, who became Parliamentary Under-Secretary of State at DExEU under Davis. Anne-Marie Trevelyan was one of several members of the ERG to receive first-rung promotions to the post of PPS, in preparation for Brexit talks reopening on Monday week. The message to the ERG was plain: play ball with the government, and you can expect to be rewarded.

The rest of Sunday saw May juggling awkwardly apologetic calls to former MPs with reappointing the new Cabinet. Aside from Hammond remaining at the Treasury, the main beneficiaries of Timothy's departure and May's failure to achieve a strong majority were Greening at Education and Javid at Communities and Local Government. May's allies remained in post too: Hunt at Health, McLoughlin as party chair, Clark at Business, Bradley at Culture, Brokenshire at the Northern Ireland Office and Williamson as Chief Whip. May saw them all in the Cabinet Room or in her study, and after the conversations they went to have a chat with Sue Gray about propriety, then had the traditional mugshot taken, before an official escorted them to the front door. 'All those who had been briefed against by the party chiefs were in a state of complete fury and rage, which poured out of them on that walk,' reported one on door duty. 'Liz Truss said that she had food poisoning, but in fact she was seething. Sajid [Javid] looked at me and said, "Those people are pure poison." This resentment had built up over nine months and just came out like a torrent after the result. There was no way they could have survived.' Their rage was directed against Timothy and Hill, not against May. Another plank on the bridge.

THE THREAT OF A CHALLENGE FADES

Plank by plank, May was building her bridge to safety. One explosion would have blown it to smithereens: a challenge from Johnson. A message came into No. 10 on Friday that he was 'on manoeuvres'. He had texted May in the early hours of Friday morning pledging his support, but a text is a text. And Boris, she knew, was Boris. The pressure for him to challenge her was considerable from many quarters within the party, and from Osborne outside. Headlines in the *Evening Standard* on Friday, including 'Queen of Denial', expressed his pent-up rage and contempt.[29] Looking back on the day now, he describes it thus: 'The obvious missed moment to have gone for her was when she lost the majority. But the party bottled it. If you ask leading members of that government, they will say it was a mistake not to have challenged her then, probably DD would have got it.'[30] One of the great unanswerable questions, a less obvious missed opportunity, is whether Osborne himself might have been able to launch a challenge to May at this point had he stayed in Parliament and played the same patient game as Gove had after the events of July 2016.

The threat of a challenge was being frantically countered on Friday and Saturday by Williamson in Belfast and Julian Smith in London, holding the fort in the Chief Whip's absence. Smith says, 'Our main motive on Friday and Saturday was to keep Corbyn out. That was the big thing. My role was to get the whips' team up and ensure that the operation was intact.'[31] Johnson was desperate not to be seen to be agitating himself or undermining May. So he let his lieutenants test the water, dangling the prospect of government jobs and positions in No. 10. Karen Bradley phoned No. 10 on Saturday to report that 'several contenders' were sniffing around, particularly Johnson. Davis was watching Johnson and his acolytes very carefully too from Yorkshire. When asked whether he would have sought the role if May was displaced, he says:

> Had the Prime Minister fallen, I would have stood, because there was nobody else to do it. There was no plethora of candidates like in 2019. It was Boris or me. It would have been over very quickly. We were in the midst of the biggest negotiation of modern times with Brexit and we had to batten down and get on with it. So I would have stood.[32]

That said, Davis didn't reckon that MPs would welcome her departure that weekend and risk getting Corbyn at another general election: 'All those guys who had just got home in their constituencies would have been very nervous.' He was one of many to think that if Johnson himself thought he had a strong chance, he would have gone for it. So when Williamson was being driven in from the airport after getting back from Belfast on Saturday evening, he sent a message to Johnson to say he wanted to see him urgently. Johnson walked from the Foreign Secretary's official residence in nearby Carlton Gardens across to the Foreign Office to meet him. Because Johnson's office was locked, they sat in the gracious Locarno Rooms, just the two men alone in the vast space. 'You're not going to be moving against her, are you?' the Chief Whip asked the Foreign Secretary. Had Williamson meant that as a question or a threat? 'I was trying to guide him,' he says. Johnson spouted out his ready backing and assured him that 'I won't do anything to undermine her. I'll be completely supportive of her.' The meeting lasted just twenty minutes, but it gave vital reassurance. No. 10 were very relieved when Williamson relayed the news.[33] Later that evening, Hollingbery had a private conversation with Johnson's close confidant, Lancashire MP Ben Wallace, who gave him the same reassurance.

Despite a lack of movement from Johnson, if not some of his acolytes, the press were in a frenzy, and rumours of a challenge did not cease that weekend. Johnson expressed outrage late that evening when the *Mail on Sunday* blazed a headline from the following day's paper: 'Boris set to launch bid to become PM as May clings on'. He tweeted in response, 'Mail on Sunday tripe – I'm backing Theresa May. Let's get on with the job'.[34] The time for a challenge looked to have slipped away. His hesitancy to be the one caught holding the knife meant the window had passed.

By Sunday evening, May was in a stronger position, which had seemed impossible sixty hours before. She had appointed a refreshed Cabinet, and no one had refused to serve. The contrition in her broadcast interview from the Cabinet Room on Friday and her subsequent phone calls had reduced some of the anger against her in the party, as had the departure of Timothy and Hill and their replacement by Barwell. But May's premiership had just suffered from the equivalent of a massive heart attack. She was strengthening, but she still had a long way to go. The next plank on her bridge to safety was to secure the DUP in a firm understanding to ensure she would have a majority in Parliament. The DUP, sensing their hour had come, were going to be no pushover.

The significance of the three days covered by this chapter is that she survived as Prime Minister in the wake of the election. For how long, and to what purpose, would now be decided partly by the DUP. She had been able to rule with an iron fist for the first ten months because she had momentum from the beginning, and when she called the general election everyone expected her to get a big majority and make a decisive reshuffle. Ministers had been constrained and under the cosh. The moment the general election result was known, the corks came off and they felt they could at last say and do what they wanted. Tory

MPs at large were now much stronger too – as was Jeremy Corbyn. He had been a far from impressive figure in the eyes of the public since he succeeded Miliband in September 2015, but now, having defied expectations and denied May a majority, he was strong, self-confident and had an enlarged group of MPs behind him in the House of Commons. The EU, too, gained in strength. It looked across the Channel to May in London and thought, 'Our leverage has increased enormously.'

The agreement with the DUP gave May the ten MPs to allow her to govern. But it came at a heavy price. Here, Arlene Foster enters 10 Downing Street during the June 2017 confidence-and-supply negotiations.

CHAPTER 7

A DEAL WITH THE DUP

9–26 JUNE 2017

May was still far from home. Procuring a deal with the DUP, the Conservatives' only viable partner, was essential if she was to get her Queen's Speech through Parliament. In the general election, the Conservatives had secured nine seats short of the 326 needed for a majority. The DUP had ten seats, sufficient to get her over the line. If she was to have any hope of surviving, bringing Brexit to a successful conclusion and passing her domestic policies, some form of a relationship was essential. Because she had not been willing to countenance the possibility of anything other than a comfortable victory, she had not prepared the ground for talks, and was having to battle with extreme fatigue when taking the critical decisions on Friday 9 June. Even if successful, a deal with the DUP would come at a price in terms of the demands that the party would extract and the restrictions it would place on the government's freedom of action. What she did not foresee was its influence over her Brexit plans.

AN OFFER FOR ULSTER

The final election result – Conservatives 317 seats, Labour 262, SNP 35, Lib Dems 12, DUP 10, Sinn Féin (not taken up) 7, Plaid Cymru 4, Green

1, Independent 1 and the Speaker 1 – was going to impact heavily on May's plan for a progressive government. It would inevitably swing the balance of power to a handful of malcontents and ideologues on the left and right wings of the party, who knew that she would depend on their support to maintain her fragile majority that Friday. Gavin Williamson was in his element: 'It was really exciting, an amazing opportunity to do something big. One reason I was able to have so much influence over the DUP deal was that everyone in No. 10 was still in a state of shock.'[1]

Heywood was more than a match for Williamson, supported by the Cabinet Office including Shona Dunn, head of the Economic and Domestic Affairs secretariat; Lucy Smith, responsible for the constitution and devolution; and Brendan Threlfall, formerly of the No. 10 private office. They considered two possible plans: a full-blooded coalition or a confidence-and-supply arrangement, in which the DUP would guarantee to support the Conservatives on all confidence motions (thereby avoiding another general election) and on key financial measures. Heywood clashed with Williamson, the other dominant figure in No. 10 that day, on several issues. The Cabinet Secretary worried that Williamson risked being an unguided missile and was especially nervous about what he might say about a formal coalition. The closer the eye he kept on Williamson, who was fired up about the prospects of a relationship with the DUP, the better. So he was nervous when Williamson told him, 'I'm going to Belfast.' Williamson added, 'I need a constitutional expert, a special advisor who knows about Northern Ireland, and I'm not going to pay for the flight.'[2] Dunn and Threlfall were enlisted to go with him ('to make sure he was properly advised'), while Lucy Smith remained the point person in London. For political input, Williamson asked Alex Dawson – who lacked real expertise on Northern Ireland – to accompany him. He had not at first envisaged going himself, imagining a figure like David Gauke heading up the Conservatives' team, but he believed 'there was nobody else who had as close a relationship with the DUP as me and, frankly, no one else who wanted to take the risk'.[3] One person he did not contact, however, was Jonathan Caine, a veteran spad in the Northern Ireland Office – much to Caine's surprise. 'As one of the few people around who had experience of successfully negotiating with the DUP, I thought Gavin or somebody from No. 10 might call and at the very least ask for a few tips,' he recalls. 'Not a word.'[4]

The DUP had waited many years for such largesse to come their way. Founded by the Protestant Reverend Ian Paisley at the height of the Troubles, it had consistently been seen as a largely negative force in British politics. Chiefly known in England for its opposition to gay marriage and to extending abortion to Northern Ireland, it was also firmly pro-Brexit. Williamson knew that its wish to see Brexit happen, and its grave distaste for Corbyn and fear of a Labour government, would be his strongest weapons in securing a deal. The DUP's natural allies were thus the Brexiteers in Parliament, with the caveat that they were vocal opponents of any form of border between Northern Ireland and the rest of the UK. The DUP were seasoned negotiators. Representing an economically diverse collection of constituencies, they were united, too, in wanting far higher government spending in Northern Ireland. As other parties had ruled out the prospect of a coalition, they knew that they were the Conservatives' only prospect of remaining in office, which further emboldened them.[5]

Arlene Foster, the DUP's leader; Nigel Dodds, her deputy; and the Chief Whip, Jeffrey Donaldson, greeted the news of the party of four flying over to see them with tense anticipation. The RAF plane touched down in Belfast shortly after 5 p.m., and the group were driven to the Northern Ireland Office in Stormont. Dodds and Donaldson kept them waiting for an hour after the time agreed for the meeting. The London party were famished but a promised Chinese takeaway failed to materialise, with the exception of a plate of prawn crackers.

Williamson brushed aside any irritation when they eventually met sometime after 7 p.m., launching in with the question, 'Do you want to make this work?' The response from the DUP was that they very much did, and after a fairly short discussion, they agreed to meet the next day with Arlene Foster to go into the details.[6] Williamson's colleagues on the trip were struck by his 'grasp of the politics and the personalities'. A coalition government seemed the most attractive proposal to the DUP that evening, with talk of the offer of a Secretary of State position, possibly Trade, or Chief Secretary to the Treasury.

The mood music was generally positive after Dodds and Donaldson rubbed home the poor performance of the Conservatives in the election, losing thirteen seats, compared to their own, which saw them gaining two. After the meetings broke up at about 10 p.m., Williamson repaired to the bar with Dawson. Although neither had been to bed since Thursday morning, they stayed up planning till 1 a.m. A day which had begun so terribly was concluding on a more optimistic note.

MIXED MESSAGES

Talks did not begin until 11.30 on Saturday morning, in a farmhouse owned by a DUP supporter in the village of Blackskull, twenty miles south-west of Belfast. Arlene Foster now joined Dodds and Donaldson, but they were far less accommodating than they had been the evening before, the first flush of excitement having worn off. 'They came back in a different mood in the morning,' says one present at the talks. 'They'd spoken to their party. We hadn't really factored in their need to do so, with their various MPs and supporters outside.' The DUP knew they had time on their side: 'We felt the clock ticking heavily all the time in our ears, the urgent need to get a positive answer back to London to stabilise the political position, but for them time was no problem at all. They just wanted to get more and more out of us,' one official says. The DUP had pound signs in their eyes, and they knew exactly the kind of bonanza they wanted. In the run-up to the 2015 general election, they had produced a 'Northern Ireland Plan' to be ready for post-election haggling in the event of a hung parliament. 'It was basically a shopping list … It even had the prices marked up,' one negotiator said at the time.[7] They began talking a lot about history, using it to justify their demands for extra money, according to one attendee: 'With the DUP, it was always about history.'

Overnight had seen a change of heart in London, too. Buckingham Palace had not been pleased. 'They were annoyed as we had jumped the gun on confidence-and-supply,' says one in No. 10. Jeremy Heywood was not happy, and 'had got to the Prime Minister', according to one political figure involved. The implications of a coalition were his particular worry. 'You have to remove the coalition offer from the table,' May said to Williamson on the telephone. 'No, I won't,' he replied defiantly. 'You agreed to it yesterday, and my word is my bond. I'm going to leave it on the table.' He comments now:

> I often found I had to be very blunt with her. I insisted that unless we appeared to be generous and taking them seriously, it wouldn't work. Jeremy was always, frankly, the best politician in Downing Street, but he could be a bugger when he didn't like something. He worked on the PM when I was away, telling her ten times that the coalition couldn't be done.[8]

Rumblings were also reaching No. 10 from senior Conservatives about their unhappiness with a formal link with the DUP in any shape. Former Prime Minister Sir John Major, who had laid the groundwork for the Good Friday Agreement in 1993–97, later made his views known on the BBC, saying, 'I am concerned about the deal … for peace process reasons.' He worried that if the peace unravelled, the 'hard men' would return to violence:

> A fundamental part of that peace process is that the UK government needs to be impartial between all the competing interests in Northern Ireland … The danger is that, however much any government tries, they will not be seen to be impartial if they are locked into a parliamentary deal at Westminster with one of the Northern Ireland parties.[9]

Among serving politicians, Scottish Conservative leader Ruth Davidson was the most vocal Tory figure on the airwaves on Saturday. Northern Ireland is the only part of the British Isles where same-sex marriage remains outlawed, with the DUP controversially using a voting mechanism designed to protect minority rights at Stormont to prevent it from being legalised. Davidson, who'd become engaged to her partner, Jen Wilson, in May 2016, tweeted a link to a speech she had given in favour of marriage equality, noting, 'As a Protestant unionist about to marry an Irish Catholic, here's the Amnesty Pride lecture I gave in Belfast.' Davidson, emboldened by the Conservatives taking thirteen Scottish seats, the party's best performance north of the border since 1983, had a frank conversation with May on the telephone. Afterwards she told the press:

> I was fairly straightforward with her and I told her that there were a number of things that count to me more than the party. One of them is country, one of the others is LGBTI rights … It's an issue very close to my heart and one that I wanted categoric assurances from the Prime Minister on, and I received [them].[10]

For a while, it seemed as if the talks might stall. The pressure was all on one side to start with, but the DUP quickly became alarmed by the prospect of failure. Williamson's insistence that the coalition offer remained on the table rapidly became superfluous. The penny dropped that if the DUP were in formal coalition with the Conservatives, it would mean signing up to policies which would have resulted in endless acrimony with their supporters. Recognising the fragility of May's position, the risk of a Corbyn government if she fell and the opprobrium of their supporters if they were to reject the Tories and the offer of money that would come their way, the DUP fell in behind the confidence-and-supply option. On Saturday afternoon, with the negotiations coming to an end, Williamson texted May to say, 'The deal is done.'

By about 4 p.m., the negotiators from London were concluding that the DUP's body language was good, and they started turning to a joint press statement to release later that afternoon. A draft was sent to the No. 10 press office, who replied, 'We're going to release this unless we hear from you to the contrary in a few minutes.' The pressure to get the story out was intense – too intense for the deliberative processes of the DUP. 'You cannot send it out' were the last words Williamson said before the plane door slammed on the way home. But that message did not get back to London.

By the time they landed, a statement had been released by No. 10: an agreement with the DUP had been reached on a confidence-and-supply motion which was going to be discussed with the Cabinet on 12 June. The DUP 'went utterly apoplectic'. So did Williamson. So too did May. Accusing Williamson of bad faith, and of bouncing them into a premature agreement before they had squared all their supporters, the DUP suggested they'd break off all relations. Frantic messages flew to and from Belfast, forcing No. 10 to retract. Sky News reported that Downing Street's earlier statement about the deal had been 'issued in error' and that talks between the Conservative Party and the DUP were still ongoing.[11] The precipitous official from the press team was roundly 'bawled out' by Williamson, while May told him more gently, 'That caused me some heart attacks in the night. Let's try and avoid that again,' she said with a smile, according to a contemporary account.

The DUP conceded that they had to issue a statement that the talks had been at least 'positive', though it was announced that the Queen's Speech, due to have been delivered on 19 June, might be delayed to give both sides more time to finalise their partnership. The BBC commented that, while not all DUP politicians strictly observed the Sabbath, enough did so to make it party policy to avoid being seen to negotiate on a Sunday: 'It was no coincidence that a DUP statement effectively denying that any final deal with Theresa May had been reached was published at midnight exactly, not one minute past.'[12]

By the Sunday morning, calm had returned, as No. 10 grew more confident that the DUP would come to an agreement, albeit with much haggling expected before that point was reached. The decks were sufficiently cleared for May to continue with the remainder of her Cabinet reshuffle. The Cabinet Office, which had been frantically looking back at the 2010–15 coalition and the rationale behind the posts offered to the Liberal Democrats, breathed a sigh of relief. 'There had been talk about the Chief Secretary to the Treasury going to the DUP. We were asking ourselves all kinds of questions, but it was a slightly crazy idea, way ahead of the official advice we had given Williamson,' says one official – though Cabinet posts were on offer if the DUP opted for the coalition agreement presented to them. That afternoon, May duly appointed the rest of her senior team, all Conservatives, some of them still loyal to her, with not a DUP member in sight.

By Tuesday 13 June, however, frustration and worry were setting in on both sides. At the 8.30 morning meeting at No. 10, George Hollingbery notes:

We decided we needed to get tough with them. The Queen's Speech had already been delayed from the 19th, but no date had yet been given. So we decided at this meeting that it would be Wednesday 21 June, to apply at least some pressure on the DUP, and that Gavin Williamson would take a slightly harder line.[13]

Around the same time, Caine received a call from the DUP – Arlene Foster, Nigel Dodds, Tim Johnston and Jon Robinson were in London and wanted to meet him. 'They were very angry,' he recalls, when he found them at the Royal Horseguards Hotel. 'They said the document – which I still hadn't seen – looked like it was drafted in Dublin.' Caine suggested adapting the 'much more pro-Union language' of the Northern Ireland version of the Conservative manifesto. They said they would pursue this idea and later, around lunchtime, Caine received another call – this time from No. 10 – asking if he could go over that afternoon, at the request of the DUP.

Later that day, Foster stated that discussions were going well and sources indicated there were 'no outstanding issues left'.[14] But the following day, as news emerged of a devastating fire engulfing Grenfell Tower in west London, the party said it would be 'inappropriate' to announce a deal. Discussions that week ran with Foster, Dodds and Donaldson in the lead for the DUP, with both sides finding the other awkward. According to one special advisor present, the officials at the negotiations 'freaked [the DUP] out', so 'we shifted the venue to Gavin's Chief Whip's office so they wouldn't be spooked'. Williamson gave No. 10 regular updates on progress.

On 15 June, No. 10 felt sufficiently confident for Andrea Leadsom, in her first week as Leader of the House of Commons, to announce that the Queen's Speech would take place on Wednesday 21 June, thirteen days after the general election. David Davis similarly confirmed that Brexit talks with the EU would officially commence as planned on Monday 19 June. May herself announced that a two-year parliamentary session, rather than the traditional one year, would begin on the same date, a move that was immediately denounced by Labour as an attempt to shore up her position after failing to win a majority.[15]

Despite agreement on the Queen's Speech, talks dragged on into the week beginning Monday 19 June, with a four-hour meeting required to clear all remaining issues. For the DUP, their key concern was not God – abortion and gay marriage – but Mammon, i.e. extra funding for Northern Ireland. They eventually settled at £1 billion of extra spending for health, infrastructure and education, a figure Williamson claims he'd conceived from the outset.[16] The final agreement, as Kavanagh and Cowley note, went wider than just a confidence-and-supply agreement, 'if not as wide as the Lib-Lab pact of 1976–78'.[17] After negotiations were whittled down to two teams of two – Williamson and Caine on one side, Dodds and Donaldson on the other – the document was eventually signed at No. 10 by the two Chief Whips, Williamson and Donaldson, in the presence of the two party leaders on Monday 26 June. It guaranteed support on all motions of confidence, the Queen's Speech, the Budget, finance Bills, legislation relating to Brexit and to national security, and was to remain in place for the entire parliament, but to be reviewed every parliamentary session. ('Interestingly,' Caine recalls, 'one of the revisions that had later significance was dropping, at the DUP's insistence, the word 'all' in respect of supporting EU legislation.') The Conservatives pledged no change either to the pension triple lock or to the winter fuel payment, and included a statement of their ongoing commitment to the union of Great Britain and Northern Ireland. Both parties agreed further to adhere to the provisions of the Good Friday Agreement, to work towards the formation of a new Northern Ireland Executive, and that votes relating to other matters in the Commons should be agreed to on a case-by-case basis.

'With the DUP on board, the PM was safe,' says Deputy Chief Whip Julian Smith. 'Gavin had done a great job.'[18] Indeed he had, and – while Caine's quieter role was also crucial – it was a real moment of triumph for the Chief Whip. The deal guaranteed the government a working majority of thirteen in the Commons on all matters relating to Brexit, though not on the domestic legislation, and not in the House of Lords. Without the deal, May and the government would have fallen. But even with the deal, her domestic agenda, as well as her Brexit strategy, would be severely hampered. The reaction was predictably caustic. Corbyn said, 'This Tory–DUP deal is clearly not in the national interest, but in May's party's interest to help her cling to power,' while outgoing Liberal Democrat leader Tim Farron added, 'The public will not be duped by this shoddy little deal.' The most ferocious reactions came from Scotland and Wales, angry that Northern Ireland was benefiting from government largesse at the expense of the other devolved nations, who branded the deal 'shabby' and 'a straight bung'.

The first DUP skirmish came as early as September, when they broke with the government in support of binding Labour motions on university tuition fees and pay for NHS employees. But it was to be the relationship between the DUP and the European Research Group (ERG), unforeseen in June 2017, that was to present the biggest problem for May. The DUP bond breathed renewed life into her premiership after the general election debacle – but it was also to take that oxygen away altogether two years later.

May's slow response to the Grenfell Tower fire on 14 June contributed to the perception from the general election that she lacked the instincts of a natural leader. But her response, albeit late, saw her discover new strengths as Prime Minister.

CHAPTER 8

THE WEEK AFTER: THE 1922 COMMITTEE AND GRENFELL

12–18 JUNE 2017

Many myths surround the May premiership. In this chapter, we look at two: the first Cabinet following the election, and her first 1922 Committee, both deemed to have been all-important in saving her premiership. In reality, her premiership had been saved earlier, by the failure of a challenger to emerge in the first twenty-four hours after the general election, and by the commitment to the DUP deal. In the absence of an alternative leader presenting themselves capable of uniting Conservative MPs, neither Cabinet nor her MPs were ever going to bring her down. They did want public hangings, however. These came in the form of heaping the blame onto Timothy and Hill. They were far from guiltless, but by making them the sole scapegoats for the campaign's disaster, deeper malaises were insufficiently examined. Then came Grenfell, which revealed starkly how disorientated May still was, with enduring damage for the rest of her premiership.

POLITICAL CABINET: MONDAY 12 JUNE

By Sunday 11 June, May was safe. Even Osborne describing her as 'a dead woman walking' on that morning's BBC's *Andrew Marr Show* failed to have the desired impact. He suggested that 'we could easily get to the middle of next week and it all collapses for her', and expressed his fury at the loss of socially liberal seats such as Bath, Brighton Kemptown and Oxford West, undoing his and Cameron's work over the past ten years. Defending Lynton Crosby, he blamed Timothy and Hill squarely for the defeat, but said that May herself must bear primary responsibility.[1] The irony was that had Osborne acted differently, not resigned his seat and played the loyalty game as Gove had done, he could have been succeeding her that weekend. 'It's one of the great possibilities of history,' a close Cabinet colleague believes. More likely, though, with memories of his feisty pro-Remain leadership in the referendum, he would have split the party.

No. 10 was at work early on the morning of Monday 12 June. At 7 a.m., Barwell, Williamson and Hollingbery met to finalise Minister of State and other outstanding appointments in the reshuffle. At 8 a.m., Barwell called the political team for his pep talk to political staff, and at 8.30 a.m., the morning meeting in May's room assessed the week ahead and the decisions that needed to be made. At 11 a.m., leaders from both Houses of Parliament came in to discuss the forthcoming legislation and the Queen's Speech, and which Bills would have to be dropped. Would anything be left bar Brexit? The DUP agreement ensured no changes to the pension triple lock or the winter fuel payment, and the team hurriedly surveyed other items that would be unlikely to pass given the new parliamentary arithmetic. They agreed that the two big-ticket items for the Queen's Speech should be Brexit and counter-terrorism policy, both of which were guaranteed DUP support, while the shake-up of education policy, including new grammar schools, was among the many domestic casualties.

At 2 p.m., ministers gathered for a political Cabinet, with no officials present to take notes, and with senior special advisors in attendance. One observer confided to his diary that it was the interpersonal politics that made a lasting impression: 'There is a certain protocol about who sits where at Cabinet, and since Damian Green had been made First Secretary of State he had to sit opposite the PM, so it meant Philip Hammond would not be opposite her. PH was not best pleased to say the very least.'

Indeed, so great was the fuss created by Hammond that, when Cabinet convened the following day for its regular 9.30 a.m. Tuesday meeting, Hammond was placed next to May herself, with Jeremy Heywood on her other side. May had gone into the political Cabinet with the reassurance that she had the backing of the Big Five: Davis, Johnson, Hammond, Rudd and Fallon. 'She was utterly safe by then. The moment had passed,' says Fallon.[2] The meeting should thus be seen as a bloodletting rather than a trial. It was not the big beasts whose day it was, but that of the second eleven. Javid, one of the four most embittered by the chiefs, launched in, telling May:

Prime Minister, your problems didn't begin when we called the election. They began the day you became Prime Minister and you appointed these two people. These chiefs of staff and their behaviour cost us this election ... When you should have broadened contributions, you narrowed things down because of them ... One of the abiding lessons of this election result is that we didn't talk about our fundamental strength, which is the economy. Now is an opportunity to dump all those anti-business policies that we had in our manifesto.[3]

The big beasts listened quietly, biding their time, while the May cheerleader role was given to party chair, the widely respected Patrick McLoughlin, to remind attendees that the party had increased its vote in the general election from 36.9 per cent to 42.4 per cent and had done surprisingly well as a result in many constituencies.[4] May soaked up the comments, using them as a way of calibrating what she might say to the more important meeting coming up later that day, with the 1922 Committee.

1922 COMMITTEE: MONDAY 12 JUNE

At 4 p.m., May met with Barwell, Penn and Hollingbery to go through what she might say to the assembled 1922 Committee. The political team had prepared some draft words for her, but Barwell was adamant that the words had to come from her. Hollingbery's notes from the time record what happened:

> [The PM] had made her own notes to work from. She came up with the line 'I got us into this mess and I'll get us out of it.' I threw into conversation whether or not she should finish with an acknowledgement that her position was in question ... [Gavin Barwell] suggested the shape of the words that would be her final phrase: 'And I will serve as long as you want me to,' and TM came up with the context of her enormously long service to the party, starting with her delivery of leaflets at the age of twelve and all the jobs she had held in government and opposition.[5]

With Williamson tied up with the DUP talks, Julian Smith came into his own. 'I don't think people at the 1922 Committee were wanting her to go. There was no one else to step up. She could have been challenged by Boris or DD, or any other Brexiteer, but they hadn't come forward,' he says now.[6] It was Smith who decided to overrule advice from some quarters in No. 10 not to manage the 1922 Committee. 'Under Cameron, the 1922 Committee had been manipulated to ensure the right people spoke first to set the tone. Julian was adamant that we had to do the same, to get a Leaver and then a Remainer to speak first and second after the PM. So we fixed that,' says one of the team.

The meeting had been due on the Tuesday but had been brought forward by a day in response to the demand from backbenchers, who wanted to know more about talks with the DUP. Brushing off a media question in the corridor outside about whether she was nervous, she entered Committee Room 14 at 5 p.m., flanked by her aides and security. The room was full to bursting with backbenchers and ministers. They banged their desks in their traditional way, albeit for only twenty-five seconds, 'considerably less than the ovation offered to David Cameron after his shock 2015 victory', as the *Daily Mirror* noted.[7] Some MPs remembered the last time they had met, seven weeks earlier, when she had announced there would be an election, to resounding chants of 'Five more years' as she entered the room.

May opened, 'a little nervously and a little wooden. For a moment, I thought she would not carry it off. But then she found her stride with clear emotion,' recorded one of her colleagues at the time. For the first time since early April, she was meeting MPs face to face, many of whom had seen their majorities slashed and their friends lose their seats, and who felt cheated that the reason that she had given for calling the election had failed utterly.

But words and her softer tone slowly drew the sting. Barwell, sitting at the table by her side, and Hollingbery, sitting behind her, anxiously scoured expressions to read their reactions. Hollingbery had his eyes on two MPs in particular: 'Watching faces carefully, Anna Soubry and Nicky Morgan in particular, showed that she had carried the day.'[8] MPs noted the stark contrast between her robotic responses to the media during the general election campaign and now, in front of her own, when she was personable and responsive. Some twenty questions rained down, with particular anger over the manifesto's social care policy, as well as cuts to school budgets and the failure to increase public sector pay. She avoided mentioning Timothy and Hill by name but said pointedly, 'I have changed my team.' When she introduced Barwell, the room erupted into cheers. She reassured MPs that the DUP would get no veto on gay marriage or abortion and told them that the negotiations were 'getting there'.

When the subject of Europe came up, she suggested there might be a softer Brexit, with a move away from the 'no deal is better than a bad deal' position, and a softening of her stance on immigration to pave the way for a closer economic relationship with the EU.[9] *The Guardian* reported a Cabinet minister saying that work was underway on a new approach to the EU27 in light of the more finely balanced parliament, with the prospect of seeking areas of compromise with other political parties, while reports in the *Daily Telegraph* and the *Evening Standard* claimed that secret talks had already begun between Cabinet ministers and some Labour MPs. Her speech closed with the two very significant rehearsed phrases: 'I got us into this mess, and I'll get us out of it' and 'I'll serve as long as you want me to'. In an interview with Sky News that evening, she vowed to carry on as Prime Minister but did not give a straight answer to the question about whether she would serve the full five years.

One former minister spoke just after the 1922 Committee meeting, saying, 'A broader backing for Brexit has to be built, and I think she recognises that.' Ardent Remainer Heidi Allen, who had declared just after the election that May would be gone within six months, commented after the meeting, 'I saw an incredibly humble woman who knows what she has to do, and that is be who she is and not what this job had turned her into. She has lost her armadillo shell and we have got our leader back.'[10]

The active support of 1922 Committee chair Graham Brady had been pivotal in getting her through. At one point he asked if she had time to answer any more questions, to which she replied, 'Don't worry, I told you I have changed,' a nice parody of her tone-deaf 'nothing has changed' comment on social care, which looked spontaneous. But critics of May were cross with Brady, with one observing now, 'You'll notice that he was made "Sir" Graham Brady before the election and "Rt Hon." afterwards. That kind of patronage was pretty obvious. He was holding her up and stayed loyal for some long time after.'

May was smiling as she left Committee Room 14, and so were her team. The aim of the game that evening was not her political survival – that was not in doubt – but giving MPs the grounds on which they could forgive her and reset a new relationship. She did her bit, and they did theirs. MPs who had been urging Davis to stand against her over the weekend, and who were disconcerted when he had dismissed such attempts as 'self-indulgent', came up to him afterwards to say he had been right after all. Cabinet the next morning was a much more relaxed occasion for May. A visibly relieved Prime Minister crisply handed over to Angela Leadsom to outline the legislative programme agreed the previous morning. 'Unfortunately, she seemed not to have briefed all Secretaries of States as to those Bills that had to be cut down substantially or even removed,' recorded one notetaker. 'Michael Fallon was particularly furious about the fact that he was completely unsighted.' The second item was introduced by Davis, who outlined the thinking on the Brexit negotiations, due to open the following Monday. Remainers were disappointed that there was little evidence of a fresh approach.

The window on fresh thinking was indeed slammed shut by the DExEU Secretary no sooner than it had edged open. Cabinet ministers observing her acutely that morning saw a very different Prime Minister. No longer a leader they feared, heading for a stonking majority and with their futures in her hands; now they saw a weak and humbled woman who had told them the night before that she would serve only 'as long as you want me'. Her future was now in their hands.

GRENFELL TOWER: 13–17 JUNE

A happier Theresa May than she had been for many weeks left London for Paris on Tuesday 13 June. On Sunday, her political team at No. 10 had leaked her visit to see the new star on the world stage, President Macron, to show that 'here was a government getting back to business'. The visit had been personally requested by Macron, just one month into his presidency. He had been deeply moved by the terrorist attack in Manchester on 22 May and walked the short distance from the Elysée to the British Embassy to express personal condolences, with memories of the terrorist attacks in Paris in November 2015 and in Nice in July 2016 still fresh in his memory. Macron told the British Ambassador he 'wanted to reach out to Theresa May and invite her to Paris so they would show joint solidarity'. When the London Bridge attack came in early June, he redoubled his efforts.

So different in personality, the two leaders chimed on their common cause: standing up for democratic values against those who would try to destroy them. Once at the Elysée, they spent some time getting to know each other; it was their first bilateral. 'We're quite happy if you change your mind and stay,' said the President with a smile. At the press conference in the grounds of the Elysée Palace afterwards, May stuck to script, speaking about the close trading and security relationships between both countries, and concluded on Brexit, 'We want to maintain a close relationship and a close partnership with the EU and individual member states into the future ... The timetable remains on course and will begin next week.'[11]

The two leaders were then sped through Paris to the Stade de France for a France *v.* England football match. Out of respect for British victims of terror, Macron arranged for the Oasis song 'Don't Look Back In Anger', which had become a symbol of the Manchester spirit, to be played as the players emerged onto the pitch, and for 'God Save the Queen' to be played last. The television cameras picked up a boyish

Macron readily rising to his feet as a Mexican wave swept through the stands, and, too many moments later, an off-guard May attempted to follow suit. 'As badly timed as the election', was the *Evening Standard*'s verdict.[12] Despite England's 3–2 loss to France, it was a contented May who flew back to London that night, returning to No. 10 in the early hours.

At exactly the same time, just before 1 a.m. on Wednesday 14 June, a fire broke out in the kitchen refrigerator of a fourth-floor flat in Grenfell Tower, a 24-storey tower block in north Kensington, west London. Within minutes, the fire, helped rather than retarded by new external cladding, raced up the outside of the building and spread to all four sides. By 3 a.m., most of the upper floors were alight. The high-rise building, built in 1974, contained 120 homes. London Fire Brigade were called at 12.54 a.m. Within a short time, forty fire engines and more than 200 firefighters were on the scene. They were unable to have much impact as fire engulfed the block.

After a short night, May had completed her boxes and was down in her study for her 8.30 a.m. meeting. Top item on the agenda was Williamson providing an update on the talks with the DUP. A long conversation proceeded about how to inject urgency into the negotiations. When Grenfell Tower was brought up, visible on the TV screen in her room, there was 'agreement that it looked very bad'. The civil servants reassured those present that 'we are across it' and would keep her updated during the day. One present recorded, 'I was surprised that that was it.' The media equally took time to understand what a profound story Grenfell would become. May then dashed off to Brexit committees, where she was ensconced for most of the day. In the early evening, the office tweeted from her official account: 'I am deeply saddened by the tragic loss of life at Grenfell Tower. My thoughts are with all those affected and the emergency services.' It very quickly became apparent to May's media staff that 'that wouldn't do it' – especially after the newly reinvigorated Corbyn said on LBC Radio, 'Tomorrow is the day for the searching questions,' but then, much to the chagrin of those in No. 10, ran through a list of those questions, including 'the provision of fire safety equipment, the provision of sprinklers and the support the emergency services need and must have in all circumstances'.[13] May's team thought this had immediately politicised the incident, all the more awkward for the government because Gavin Barwell had been Housing Minister and was being implicated in a delay in a review into fire safety.

On Thursday 15 June, the fire, which had seen the numbers of casualties rising steadily, was the number one discussion item at May's 8.30 a.m. meeting. They were told, 'The advice from security was for the Prime Minister not to see residents herself as it would involve taking police away from their duties.' One present recalls, 'Seconding them to us didn't seem right.' A more experienced or confident political team in No. 10 might have overruled the official advice. Even Heywood gave May assurances that the crisis was in hand. After the meeting broke up, she went to Grenfell, speaking as advised to emergency services rather than to the survivors of the tragedy. In contrast, Corbyn visited the scene concurrently to see members of the local community and volunteers, and was filmed hugging and engaging emotionally with them. One resident of the tower told him, 'May was here and she didn't speak to any of us. She was shit.'[14]

On her return to Downing Street, May said, 'I want to reassure the residents of Grenfell Tower, all of whom are in our thoughts and prayers ... that the government will make every effort to ensure that they are rehoused in London, and as close as possible to home.'[15] Neither the message nor the announcement that a full inquiry would take place into the causes of the inferno ('if there are any lessons to be learned they will be') quelled public anger. That afternoon, No. 10 was besieged by calls from journalists demanding, 'Where's the Prime Minister? Why is she not down with the residents in Grenfell?' The answer was that she was in the Cabinet Room all afternoon, talking to the Northern Ireland parties in attempts to re-establish the Northern Ireland executive. The television coverage that evening was bleak and showed no sympathy with the difficulties of handling multiple, simultaneous government crises: the only journalist her press team thought was remotely balanced was her old Oxford contemporary Michael Crick on *Channel 4 News*.

On Friday 16 June, the morning's press was universally brutal. The 9 a.m. meeting took place without May, and heard reports from George Hollingbery that 'MPs are openly calling for her head', and about their anger that 'they're getting grief locally for her handling of it'. Barwell, still in his first week in the job, convened a meeting of the press and events team immediately afterwards, with Alastair Whitehead and Lorna Gratton from the private office in attendance. Even with the DUP negotiations still taking place, and it being the final working day before the Brexit talks resumed, there was only one priority for the Prime Minister. 'You can have all her diary time you need. Go,' said Barwell. While they prepared for a visit to a hospital for May to see victims, a Cabinet Office Briefing Room meeting was convened. Michael Fallon, the Defence Secretary, wrote a note to hand to the chair to say clearly that Kensington and Chelsea Council weren't coping and that the army should be brought in. But with senior figures from the NSC participating remotely, he held onto the note, later saying in a Cabinet meeting that it was 'the biggest regret of his career' not to have insisted. When one of the political team asked about bringing in the army, officials thought the suggestion ridiculous, as one reflects: 'Bringing in the army was never a serious proposition and would not have helped. The problem was Kensington and Chelsea Council and the time it took central government to realise that [the local authorities] simply could not cope.'

May spent an hour at Chelsea and Westminster Hospital, which did nothing to arrest the growing criticisms that she had failed to show humanity in 'refusing' to talk to residents when she had visited

Grenfell the day before. She was filmed at the entrance to the hospital, but cameras were not allowed into the building, and her interactions with patients and her empathy were not recorded. So the events team arranged for her to visit St Clement's Church in Kensington to meet survivors. On the way, Tom Swarbrick, head of television in No. 10, called the BBC to tell them about the visit, relaying police advice from earlier that day that 'if she goes to the scene of the fire, she will start a riot'. This time it was the residents themselves who had asked for film crews not to come into the church to witness her meetings. So he asked the BBC if they could film her arriving or leaving. But the location was leaked, as a result of which angry crowds were already building up by the time she arrived.

Once inside the building, May spent time with the bereaved and other survivors, hugging them and holding their hands: 'She gets it, all the things the media said she couldn't do or feel, she did,' said one of the team with her. At 3.30 p.m., her team took a message from security to say, 'A riot is coming. You must leave in ten minutes.' So they broke it to the PM, who told the residents, 'I'm really sorry. I want to see you again. Can we find a time to do this?' She was then bustled out of the meeting and into her car, ringed by her security team shouting, 'Get back, get back' to the surging crowds, who were bellowing 'Coward' at her. In the confusion, she was separated from the rest of her team, who were left behind as the prime ministerial convoy shot off, escorted by police bikes through the Kensington streets. From her car, Richard Jackson messaged her team left behind to say, 'She's going to Sonning.' 'No way, we'll be lynched if she doesn't say anything,' they replied. So they arranged for her to detour to BBC's New Broadcasting House to make a statement.

Journalist Emily Maitlis was hurriedly organised by the BBC to interview her. Without her team to prepare her, and unnerved by it all, the PM was back to the Theresa May of the general election campaign, startled by the questions and evidently unable to respond with anything other than prepared answers. Maitlis began by asking why she hadn't been prepared to give the interview at Grenfell itself but had come to the BBC. Her response that the government was making £5 million available for the residents was given short shrift by Maitlis, who asked her, 'There is a need for the public to hear you say in words of one syllable … "Something has gone badly wrong. It is our fault. We acknowledge that and accept responsibility."' May visibly wilted under the ferocity of the questioning: 'Something terrible has happened. This is an absolutely awful thing that took place. People have lost their lives.'[16] The interview was a disaster for the Prime Minister. It was a perfect storm: an exhausted and unprepared May against one of television's most incisive and ferocious interviewers, full of the indignation of the nation. It was no contest. 'They took massive advantage of her,' says one No. 10 source. A bitter argument with the BBC ensued about their handling of her, and its description of the hospital visit as short: 'No one at the BBC knew how long the visit was. They made it up.' The team who had returned to No. 10 then found themselves under lockdown until after 11.30 p.m. because of the mob in the street outside. They thought the BBC was being unfair to them. The press the next day was even worse, with damning headlines about her utter failure to respond in a human way.

Late on Friday night, Heywood texted a fellow official in No. 10 to say, 'We failed her. We deserve the blame for this, not her.' For Heywood, it was a scarring experience. He determined that the government's response would be swift and the commitments made would be honoured. His team was struck by how, even during his hospital visits, with a drip in one arm, he was still using his BlackBerry in the other, dictating operations. Another official says, 'It was our fault. We knew how to respond to terrorism but not to this. Our immediate response was to set up an inquiry, but the Home Office said no. She should shoulder no blame.'

That Friday night, something happened to May. She visibly grew and returned to being the more open person she had shown MPs in the 1922 Committee at the start of the week, rather than the closed person she had been for much of the previous year, culminating in the general election campaign. 'She came to the realisation that she herself had to reach out to the Grenfell families. She turned it around that Saturday,' says an official. Damian Green and Jeremy Hunt were two she spoke to about how she should respond, and who helped draft the statement that she wrote on Saturday afternoon, while Liz Sanderson from her political team helped oversee a visit from Grenfell residents to Downing Street earlier that day. Afterwards, a press release was issued from No. 10 to say:

Earlier today I met with victims of the Grenfell Tower tragedy and the volunteers and community leaders who are working so hard to help people rebuild their lives... The response of the emergency services, NHS and the community has been heroic. But, frankly, the support on the ground for families who needed help or basic information in the initial hours after this appalling disaster was not good enough. I have heard the concerns and I have ordered immediate action across the board to help victims' relatives and the survivors. People lost everything in the fire and were left in only the clothes they were wearing.

She spoke about the public inquiry, the £5 million emergency fund, how she had decided that she herself would be responsible for implementing the findings of the inquiry, and that she had ordered other councils to complete urgent safety checks on similar high-rise blocks to Grenfell. She concluded, 'The fire at Grenfell was an unimaginable tragedy for the community, and for our country. My government will do whatever it takes to help those affected, get justice and keep our people safe.'

She had spent two and a half hours earlier talking to sixteen survivors being 'angry' and 'passionate' with her. Their harrowing accounts moved her to well up, they later said. Reverend Mark O'Donoghue told Sky News that 'somebody began to sob beside her and she just held her hand for the next twenty minutes, which wasn't quite the caricature most of us have of the Prime Minister'.[17] Damian Green, in one of his first major public acts as First Secretary, said that she had been 'as distraught as anyone' about the fire, and that all the criticism of her had been 'terribly unfair'. 'She has the same degree of sympathy and horror at these events that we all have.'[18] But it was O'Donoghue's words that made the impact.

By late afternoon on Saturday, the narrative shifted. 'We saw the mood begin to change and stabilise from about 5 p.m. or 6 p.m.,' says one Downing Street insider. For many with her in the building, as for she herself, Grenfell, and the reaction to it, was the hardest time they had to endure. She was scarred by the episode, continuing to take a close interest in the Grenfell children and Grenfell United, the survivors and bereaved group founded soon after the fire – though she failed to satisfy the demands of many, not just at Grenfell, but in similar towers across the country. Till the end, she had drawings in her room by the Grenfell children, alongside a paper crown they gave her at a garden party she held for them at No. 10. In one of her final Cabinet meetings as Prime Minister, on 11 June 2019, in the week of the second anniversary of the fire, she said with passion, 'I may be gone shortly, but the people at Grenfell and their families will still be there. You have a duty to do what we pledged to do and to deliver the truth of what happened.'

Grenfell had made her dive deep into herself. Her initial response was terrible, and it rekindled memories of her robotic general election performances. The question was: would she be able to continue as the more empathetic and independent-minded figure who began to emerge after the Grenfell tragedy, or would she retreat to her earlier incarnation? Her problem was that many had already reached their verdict, and it wasn't in her favour.

The EU27 entrusted Brexit to their chief negotiator, Michel Barnier. He provided a more united front throughout than Brexit Secretary David Davis, who had just one country to represent but many factions within it. Here, they enter Downing Street together during Brexit negotiations, 5 February 2018.

CHAPTER 9

HARD ROAD TO HELL
JUNE–SEPTEMBER 2017

The prime cause for May calling the early election, casting aside all that she had said about waiting until 2020, had been her hope of securing a large majority to push through the Brexit legislation she had outlined in her party conference and Lancaster House speeches. If she had difficulties getting her initial Brexit steps through the Commons before the general election, with a majority of thirteen, how would she fare now, with no Conservative majority at all?

As the battle to get her deal through Parliament continued for month after month from late 2018, people inevitably asked, why had she and the government not reappraised their position in the days after the general election and reached out to other parties earlier? It was clear there was no longer a majority in Parliament for the type of Brexit she had advocated before the election, so why did the government's strategy and rhetoric change so little? Still others ask why serious preparations for no deal hadn't begun at once, given May's rhetoric of 'no deal is better than a bad deal'. The decisions taken – and, more importantly, those not taken – in the pivotal three weeks after the general election shaped the Brexit story over the following two years.

A RECALIBRATION

'No one was calling for a rethink on softening Brexit in the days and weeks after the general election. Nobody but Anna Soubry,' is the view of one senior figure in No. 10. 'Arguing so is to rewrite history.' Conservative MP Anna Soubry, who would leave the party over Brexit in February 2019, had indeed said, 'I know that [Theresa May] understands the need to build a consensus and that everything has changed after the general election in June.'[1] But to cast her as a lone figure calling for a rethink is a mistake: some insiders were arguing this very case at the time. As we saw in the previous chapter, on Monday 12 June, just four days after the general election, a Cabinet minister told *The Guardian* that work was underway on how to achieve a deal with the EU27 that could pass through a much more finely balanced parliament, involving seeking areas of compromise with other parties. That very day, insiders added that one of the ideas being actively considered in order to win backing across Parliament was 'not to major' on the controversial 'no deal is better than a bad deal' stance adopted by May in her party conference speech, reinforced at Lancaster House and in the election manifesto.[2]

Many on the Remain wing of the party believe that the hardline Brexit stance had cost them seats in the general election in areas like Battersea, Kensington and Twickenham while failing to win sufficient numbers of target seats from Labour in the north of England. Denzil Davidson, the EU specialist within the political team at No. 10, commented to Barwell after the general election that there was now a majority in the House of Commons in favour of a customs union arrangement, but May's team declined to respond positively to this point, or to others making similar appeals to think afresh about what was politically possible. George Bridges, junior minister at DExEU until the general election, became the unofficial leader of those who sought a rethink: 'You just can't carry your vision of Brexit as if you hadn't lost the majority,' he told Davis and No. 10. Bridges regarded it as 'delusional' for May to plough ahead regardless.[3] Jonathan Hill, Britain's former European Commissioner, argued along the same lines but similarly found himself running into a wall. These were people of influence: both had been senior advisors to Major, still a respected figure in May's No. 10. Oliver Letwin, sacked by May in June 2016 as the PM's Europe advisor, was another who tried to encourage No. 10 to rethink how to play Brexit, though 'it became very quickly clear that she did not warm to the idea'.[4]

The Queen's Speech contained the following crucial statement: 'My government's priority is to secure the best possible deal as the country leaves the European Union. My ministers are committed to working with Parliament, the devolved administrations, business and others to build the widest possible consensus on the country's future outside the European Union.'[5] But none of this materialised at any point before the 29 March 2019 deadline set by Article 50. What happened to her thoughts about building a 'broader consensus' on Brexit?

Many leading Conservatives look back to the weeks after the general election and see a lost opportunity. Chief Whip Julian Smith says:

We called the general election to get a majority to make Brexit easier. When we didn't get it, we could have recalibrated our approach. I spent eighteen months trying to get a deal through, but we could have reset the thinking after the election. No Brexiteer had stepped up to challenge the Prime Minister on it: there was little pressure from that side at the time. But instead of saying, 'Let's look at this again,' we made the red lines even redder. Instead of opening it out, we held to the same approach, even though we didn't have the majority for it. No one was thinking long-term.[6]

One Cabinet minister says:

With hindsight, we should have done more thinking, given the new arithmetic after the general election, about exactly the type of Brexit that we could get through Parliament. If we had made the change then, if we'd engaged cross-party, we could have ended in a very different position. We could have reached out to all parties, small and large, saying that the task is now to find a parliamentary solution. We could have said that the type of hard Brexit we went into the election to achieve was no longer possible. It didn't have to be one speech: it could have been progressively rolled out. Instead, the ERG let itself think it could get exactly the type of Brexit it wanted, and it wasn't told until eighteen months later that it simply wasn't going to happen.

Commons deputy leader and de facto Deputy Prime Minister David Lidington thinks similarly: 'My own view is that, with hindsight, we could have done more then to rethink our Brexit position. She did speak in the Queen's Speech about talking to other parties, but it was never followed up.'[7]

Many officials, too, questioned the strategy. 'It is very striking', says one, 'that despite the parliamentary arithmetic and political landscape changing completely at the election, her approach to the negotiations didn't change at all.' One senior civil servant who sat through the post-election discussions recounts:

We didn't really have that discussion. The PM's focus was on how she was going to get the Cabinet to agree to any of the policy we would pursue. It seemed near-impossible. She had this hope, as did many in the Cabinet, that it would be possible to move the EU from the position it started out with, i.e. presenting us with a series of third-country models, to the position that she wanted, which was her own model. No one in Cabinet thought that it was the wrong thing to do. They all thought we would get more flexibility from the EU. Nobody was saying in Cabinet that the EU would never buy it. Of course Ivan [Rogers] had given his lectures, and some people did read those, but some regarded it as a cracked record and the same old story. So nobody heeded [his advice] at the time and it took another year for people to realise how difficult it would be. It was still not clear to the PM at this stage where she would end up. She still felt until relatively recently that she could persuade her Brussels colleagues.[8] Her focus wasn't on how to bring the Cabinet forward from non-negotiable positions to getting to a position where she could get something negotiable.

A greater stateswoman than May might have found a way through the morass. A more composed No. 10 might have recognised that it was heading into a fast-approaching hurricane, with no clear idea of how it would get out the other side, and attempted to find a new route through. Arguments aplenty, however, dictated that she keep relentlessly to her set course, even if it would end in disaster. At the most visceral level, she was battling for her survival. Some worried that an appeal to dilute the purity of the hard Brexit vision would have damaged her, possibly irreparably. 'Had overtures been made then, it would have finished her off,' admits David Lidington.[9] The Conservative Party had banked on the Brexit vision of Lancaster House, one entirely outside of the single market and customs union, and there was little clamour from former Remainers to revisit her stance. They might have hated Brexit, but they were resigned to it. One Remain-voting Cabinet minister had been surprised at how meekly accepting many in the Remain wing of the party had been: 'I woke up the morning after Lancaster House and I was amazed at how the party had simply accepted it without protest. She would have been toast if she'd tried to go back on it after the election.' Denzil Davidson identifies the lack of rethinking as a constraint imposed by the ERG, who, even then, would have reacted with 'the most virulent kickback'.[10]

David Davis, too, would have been resistant to any change. He had told May that he would brook no watering-down of the British stance: he would drive it through root and branch as it was, regardless of the general election result. Davis had had enough of being pushed around by No. 10 and Olly Robbins in May's first months. He was insistent that he was now the undisputed Brexit supremo, heir to a Conservative Eurosceptic tradition which looked back to Thatcher's Bruges speech in September 1988, first inspiring the revolt against the EU which now engulfed the party. He was insistent: Brexit would happen in his way. Nor was May herself in favour of deviation from or flexibility in the position she had outlined before and during the election. The electorate had spoken, MPs had stood on her Brexit policy, and she was inherently cautious about changing her position. Keeping Cabinet together was her top priority. She had deliberately chosen a balanced Cabinet so she knew that if she carried them, she could carry the party, and Cabinet was in no mood in June 2017 to revisit her red lines.

Crossing party lines to seek an agreement may also have proved difficult for May personally. She was a very tribal Tory, and Cameron's No. 10 had regular battles with her during the coalition government emanating from tensions between her and the Lib Dems. As Letwin says, 'It was not natural to her to negotiate with any other political party, especially not Labour, and most definitely not a Labour Party led by Jeremy Corbyn.'[11] One official adds, 'The idea of reaching out to the Labour Party was anathema to her, especially a Labour Party that she regarded as outside of the political norm. So there was absolutely no thought after the general election of going in that direction.' Negotiation with the Labour leader would indeed be political suicide after the hostilities of the general election and given the Conservatives' attitude to Corbyn; her new chief of staff Gavin Barwell had once publicly commented that Corbyn 'poses a far greater risk to our security than any other Labour leader in my lifetime'.[12]

Other factors further militated against reaching out to a wider base on Brexit. Had May made overtures to Labour in June or July 2017, it is unlikely that they would have agreed to participate in seriousness. Corbyn and Labour were at the very height of their confidence, believed they had May on the run, and were looking for ways to undermine her to precipitate another general election. Individual Labour MPs who might have been interested in such an overture would have had no support from the leadership. No. 10 had a jaundiced view about the prospect of success, as one Downing Street figure outlines:

> At no stage in her last two years was Labour ready to make a compromise and enter into discussions on Brexit in good faith. Look at what happened when we involved them in April 2019. All they ever wanted under Corbyn was to force a general election. They offered chaos theory from Day 1, not a serious attempt to achieve Brexit.

Martin Selmayr, chief of staff to European Commission President Jean-Claude Juncker, and later to become Secretary-General of the Commission, recounts his concern with Corbyn's approach to Brexit:

> I remember my first meeting, and this was after the negotiations on the withdrawal agreement had been concluded, where I listened most to [Corbyn] and asked him only one question: do you have the mobile phone number of the Prime Minister? And he said no, and that made me deeply worried. I know the British constitution and political system is different, but in such an existential division, I would have expected that the leader of Her Majesty's opposition and the Prime Minister might speak at least two or three times a week on the phone personally and have a standing communication line to solve this matter, and this was not the case. He was even surprised that I even asked this question.[13]

The negotiation needed to be with someone other than Corbyn. Labour's divisions were sufficiently deep, in particular over Brexit, to allow May to talk to those MPs who were not front-bench loyalists. A bloc of Labour MPs including the likes of Lisa Nandy, Gareth Snell and Caroline Flint saw the need to complete Brexit and avoid a no-deal scenario, many wary of their Leave-voting constituents if they failed to support the outcome of the referendum. Some estimated their number at around thirty, although in private No. 10 saw this as optimistic. Giving these MPs skin in the Brexit deal that they would inevitably have to vote on would have significantly boosted May's chances of success at passing a withdrawal agreement. But she lacked the statesmanship, the candour and, most importantly, the bravery to make a bold move as a solution to a problem she would not have to face for a year and a half. Her cautious, partisan nature would win out. The Conservative Party was her life, and, ultimately, she believed that Conservative MPs would hold and vote together behind her, and she could bind the party together. According to one senior EU figure, her approach bemused EU leaders:

> Several Prime Ministers in the European Council meetings asked Theresa May why she hadn't consulted Labour earlier, and she explained that the UK system is different; it is more antagonistic, this is not the normal way of doing things. But then many people responded, 'Well, this is not a normal situation; sometimes you have to do something else. You found a coalition with the DUP, it was not normal when we had a Tory–Liberal coalition, so why in such an existential situation can someone not do this?' I think the failure on this one was certainly on both sides of the aisle, because I think the constructive existentialist observation was not there on both sides. People were fighting people and whenever we appealed to both sides to sit together and come to an agreement, that didn't succeed.

The sheer panic of the early days after the general election damaged any prospect of a rethink, less because the DUP made an ideologically pure Brexit a pre-condition of the pact, more because the depleted No. 10 team had its attention fixed wholly on securing a deal in the critical ten days after the general election, when the window might have been open for a rethink before negotiations. Perhaps that explains too why No. 10 didn't take on Hammond and the Treasury head-on in the flush of his relief at being reappointed, and insist they funded no-deal preparations beyond contingency planning. George Bridges, who resigned as junior minister at DExEU just after the election, says, 'She could have started to make the case for no-deal planning just after the general election. I sent memos to No. 10 to do this. But nothing changed.'[14]

From July, May cleared her diary so that she could focus on Brexit as her no. 1 priority. Only once she did so would she be able to turn her attention back to the causes she most cared about: her social policy and domestic agenda. One official recalls:

> Those who tried to manage her diary found it very difficult to find any time for domestic policy from the summer of 2017 onwards. She would come in on Monday morning for the staff meeting at 10 a.m., and from that point onwards, Europe was dominant. Tuesday saw Cabinet at 9.30 a.m. and officials would be reluctant to put any event in before lunchtime, as meetings often overran. On Tuesdays and Wednesdays, she would be preparing for PMQs, and by Thursday she was preparing to leave, either for the constituency or abroad. It was a total drain on her diary throughout her final two years.

Davis had been a constant worry for May. Before the general election, he had threatened to resign over Olly Robbins, whom he considered to have excessive authority. May had been powerful then and told him to 'sort it out between the two of you'. But now she was weak. So when he marched in to see her after the general election, insisting on the purity of the original vision without equivocation, and threatening to resign unless Robbins was moved, she had no option but to act. 'The last thing she wanted was to lose her DExEU Secretary,' says an insider. She talked it over with Heywood, who told her, 'I have a way forward.' His plan was to move Robbins out of his current role as Permanent Secretary of the fast-growing DExEU and have him report directly to her. The move came as a relief to Robbins, because the relationship between May and Davis had become so strained. Fiona Hill told Davis that he was 'crazy' to cast Robbins out of DExEU into the clutches of May, and that he would lose control of Brexit as a result.[15] But in the short term he was only happy that Heywood had 'got Robbins out of his hair', and he was confident he could ensure that May remained true to the vision.[16]

LOSS OF CONTROL OF THE TIMETABLE

Mid general election campaign, Davis had brazenly attacked the EU's firmly established timetable for Brexit talks, laid out in April 2017, which maintained that Britain's withdrawal from the EU must be negotiated first, and only then could negotiations begin about Britain's future relationship with the EU. On 14 May, he had promised that both sets of talks could be held in parallel, and that getting his way would be the 'row of the summer'. Conducting the negotiations in parallel would theoretically give the UK a stronger hand, allowing them the flexibility to leverage the trickier aspects of withdrawal against concessions which could be made on the future relationship. Yet when Davis and Barnier agreed to a schedule of five rounds of negotiations when talks began in Brussels on Monday 19 June, the EU successfully insisted that the exit Bill, dealing with the rights of EU nationals and the issue of the Irish border, should all be settled before talks on a future trade deal began. The British government insisted that 'nothing had changed' in its ambition. But there was no doubting that a climbdown had taken place – even if it was an inevitable one. 'The "row of the summer" did not even get to midsummer's day. It was instead the row-back of the summer,' as the *Financial Times* put it.[17] Ministers tried to say that it was a 'compromise' and described it as a 'concession'. But it was neither. It was a setback not just for Davis but also for May, who had similarly said before the general election that both stages should be negotiated in parallel. Indeed, her Article 50 letter had said, 'We believe it is necessary to agree the terms of our future partnership alongside our withdrawal from the EU.' Both now lost face.

The denial of any U-turn from DExEU received short shrift on both sides of the Channel. 'There is no doubt that the UK has had to back down from its original demands,' said *The Guardian*.[18] The *Financial Times* was more scathing, especially about Britain's cavalier approach:

> The U-turn … demonstrates the disparity in clarity and transparency between the two sides. The EU has been unafraid to be open about its approach. The UK government, on the other hand, seems to think it can get away with publishing almost nothing. That it can make do with ministerial boasts and official misdirections … The government is so used to improvisation and secrecy, it is wrong-footed by the EU's diligence and candour.[19]

Before the general election, the British government had regularly underestimated the EU, believing that it would eventually see reason and come around to the British point of view because it would be in its interest to do so. But the EU had always had its own priorities: to keep the EU27 together and maximise its interests, and to negotiate in an orderly fashion in line with all its agreed procedures. Fallon was one of many in Cabinet who think an opportunity was lost on sequencing: 'Why did we have to accept the EU's diktat on sequencing for the money and citizens' rights to be agreed to first, before we could even mention trade and the economic relationship? It was a major error.'[20] To a previously Remain-supporting Cabinet minister, the big mistake was losing control over sequencing, which led to the backstop, which led to May's downfall. Only later did [David Davis] say that we should have been far more insistent on not accepting their sequencing. If we had been able to control the sequencing, we wouldn't have had to have the backstop, and we would have left the EU on time.

Bridges says, 'She should never, never have accepted the EU's insistence on sequencing. They truly trussed us up, and it led to the horror of the backstop.'[21] On the British side, there was a lot of support for changing the sequencing – but few, if any, could provide details of how exactly it could be achieved, or why the EU would concede. Davis is adamant that he went to Brussels on 19 June with the intention of having his way on sequencing, only to find once there that May had already conceded to the EU's demands. 'I thought, "Do I overrule No. 10?" but then I thought that if I did so the consequences would have been the EU openly accusing her of negotiating in bad faith,' he says now, adding that if he had done that, 'I think she would have also fallen as Prime Minister'.[22]

No. 10 was not so convinced that Davis's approach would find success, given the EU's approach to negotiations. As one Downing Street Brexit official explains:

DD thought at some point that someone, probably himself, had merely to go off to Brussels, have a massive row, leave the room and the Commission would come to their senses, become contrite and malleable and concede that they were wrong and they would change their mind on the sequencing. The Commission had said no negotiations until Article 50 was triggered, and that we had to get agreement on the terms of the exit before we could discuss the future relationship. But Whitehall officials and lawyers didn't see anything in Article 50 that would divide the negotiations up cleanly into these two halves and therefore we argued that the discussions should cover both simultaneously – but the Commission said very clearly that it had to be in both parts.

This was new territory for the Commission, as they'd never conducted an exit, and according to EU officials they felt that the UK

> had to be held to account very clearly for issues like the money they owed, the budget and the commitments we'd already entered into and we had to sort out the detail of this before we could talk about the future relationship. [The UK] were completely fixated on that [future relationship].

Martin Selmayr reflects on sequencing and Davis's approach:

> In my personal view I never sensed that sequencing could ever be up for discussion because of the logic of Article 50 and it's also the psychological logic of the divorce metaphor. If you stay friends afterwards, it depends whether you have settled the divorce fairly. You cannot say that we stay friends afterwards but refuse to pay for the children. I don't think that is going to work. Had David Davis gone into it more deeply, he would have understood about sequencing. He never really made the argument strongly because he was only in Brussels for very short periods of time. He came in, the meetings were short and then there was a press moment and he left again. There were many more words spoken by him outside than inside the room. I don't want to be negative about DD, as he certainly had his political reasons, but I never had the feeling he was taking charge of the negotiations, doing his homework. I don't think he was there with the idea to deliver this.[23]

The No. 10 Europe team's view was that Davis's stance was fundamentally misguided, as one member recalls:

> There was still this lingering belief from people like DD that they could persuade the Commission that we should be able to talk about both simultaneously. What some politicians forgot was that

a deal with Britain was not the principal objective of the Commission's negotiating team. What mattered to them is keeping the EU together and that was obvious from the word go. The Commission thinks in terms of treaty-based negotiations and they want to maintain the integrity of those treaties and of the European Court of Justice. It took ministers a long time to realise that this was their approach. Therefore, DD's big row never took place. I don't think he ever marched in to tell them. We never made that case.

In contrast to the beliefs of her party, May felt she had little choice but to agree to the EU's timetable. She had told Robbins just after the election that he needed to engage urgently with Barnier, so he went to see him for lunch in the week beginning 12 June, with his colleagues Germany's Sabine Weyand and France's Stéphanie Riso. It became clear to Robbins that had Davis persisted with his unilateral insistence on trying to get the EU to reverse their position, it would impede the success of any serious discussions. The agreement made was that talks on the future relationship could begin once 'sufficient progress' had been made on the outstanding issues of, in particular, the UK's financial settlement and EU citizens' rights in the UK. What exactly constituted 'sufficient progress'? It had yet to be determined. But the agreement was sufficient to bring Davis to the table, and for talks to commence on schedule on 19 June.

ALL CHANGE IN NO. 10

On 18 September 2017, Robbins ceased to be Permanent Secretary at DExEU and officially became the Prime Minister's Europe advisor and chief negotiator on Brexit, retaining his additional role as the Prime Minister's Sherpa. Some in DExEU had been worried that he would take the cream of their staff to his new base in the Cabinet

Office, hurting a department already suffering from one of the highest churn rates in the civil service. Indeed, Robbins quickly built up a high-quality team around him, including Kay Withers, his deputy, Matt Baugh, Catherine Webb and a team of highly intellectual individuals, to be joined shortly by Jonathan Black from the Treasury.

The switch suited both Robbins and Davis personally. Davis had found Robbins irksome and ideologically unsympathetic. Robbins, with his razor-sharp intellect, found Davis's failure to grasp detail and unwillingness to engage with EU treaties and processes equally irritating. As the relationship between Davis and May wore thin, so too did that of Davis and Robbins, the civil servant finding it difficult to represent both the Prime Minister and Brexit Secretary's interests and broker between them. The arrangement had become unsustainable. For the next two years, Robbins held an iron grip on Britain's negotiations, the undisputed master of their intricacies, arousing suspicions among the Brexiteers that he had gone native in Brussels and become 'Ivan Rogers 2.0'. Worse for them, there was no figure like Timothy left in No. 10 to bend May's ear and hold her to the pure Brexit flame. In Timothy's place came Barwell, a Remain supporter, as were many other of her senior staff, including Penn, Davidson, Dawson and James Marshall, the new head of policy. As for the officials, they were regarded by Brexiteers as unrepentant Europhiles. The only senior Brexiteer in No. 10 was Robbie Gibb, with Parkinson more junior.

And so the die was cast. There was to be no recalibration of the government's Brexit strategy after the general election, even had such a change been politically possible. Britain lost the argument over sequencing, had it ever been up for negotiation, with everything that followed from that on the backstop. No urgency was given to plans for no deal. And the dominant figure in Britain's negotiations at May's right hand was no longer David Davis but Olly Robbins. May's preference for secrecy was now to be reinforced by Robbins's own predilection for the same modus operandi.

May's moment of greatest public humiliation came when she was handed a mock P45 form during her speech at the 2017 Conservative Party conference, only worsened by her subsequent coughing fit and the lettering collapsing behind her.

CHAPTER 10

RE-FINDING HER AGENDA

JULY–OCTOBER 2017

The anguish for May, as month followed month after the general election, was that Brexit ate into her time to achieve anything domestically, and that Philip Hammond, whose wings she had clipped in her first term, was manoeuvring himself into the position he sought, to be like Osborne under Cameron, a key figure on the domestic stage and driver of the fiscal agenda. What from her manifesto did she have a mandate for domestically, if anything? What was to be her own and the government's purpose, besides Brexit?

QUEEN'S SPEECH

The core text laying out May's *raison d'être* was the Queen's Speech. Not everything a Prime Minister might do requires legislation through Parliament, but a sizeable part of any government's work does, and she was ill-prepared to compose a bustling legislative programme.

The Queen arrived at Parliament on Wednesday 21 June by car, not the traditional horse-drawn carriage. Indeed, the whole Queen's Speech process had been rushed through at great haste to show that May had rekindled her cause and could command a parliamentary majority. 'This is a major moment for Theresa May,' said the *Daily Telegraph*, 'as she tries to assert her authority by showing that she has a substantive programme to push on with as Prime Minister.'[1] With the DUP talks still going on, a series of very rushed meetings had taken place in No. 10, whittling down the manifesto, dropping many items and ensuring that all twenty-seven Bills in the speech had DUP support. Eight of the Bills related to Brexit; the remaining nineteen, including three in draft form and three finance Bills, were a mixture of new proposals and legislation carried over from the last parliament – cut short by the surprise election. The process was hamstrung by May having no head of policy at No. 10 in place. John Godfrey left after the election, and his successor, James Marshall, did not arrive until 27 June, six days after the Queen's Speech had been delivered. The principal innovation, as we have seen, was that the programme would cover a two-year period rather than the conventional one, purportedly to give MPs more time to debate legislation. But the real reason, as Gavin Williamson says, was:

> We didn't want to create another point of vulnerability before Brexit, and by styling it as a 'Brexit session', it took away the need to carry over Bills. Our thinking was that most of the Brexit Bills would be ready for later in that first year, and it would make it smoother and safer for us under the circumstances.[2]

May spoke in the Commons of seizing 'this moment of national change', and said the country was split 'between red and blue, young and old, and Leave and Remain'. Parliament's challenge was thus 'to heal those divides'. Intriguingly, and largely escaping notice, she promised to work with 'anyone in any party' on Brexit (and on other issues) 'in the national interest'.

As a programme for domestic legislation over the next two years, it was a very pale shadow of the vaunting – with hindsight, hubristic – ambition of her inaugural doorstep speech, with its rallying cry to tackle the country's 'burning injustices'. There were no new Bills on health or education, nor extra money for social care. A meek promise of 'a review' of mental health, as well as a 'digital charter' to enhance safety online escaped the knife. The main proposals included a civil liabilities Bill, a domestic violence and abuse Bill, and a tenants' fees Bill – hardly a moral crusade for two years' work.

What was cut from the Timothy agenda? Casualties of the election result included plans to expand grammar schools, end free school lunches for all infants, scrap the winter fuel allowance for well-off pensioners and end the automatic 2.5 per cent pension rises, while a commitment was made to consider the controversial reforms on funding social care through consultation (which would never be published in May's time as PM), and plans for workers on boards and enhanced corporate responsibility were equally kicked into the long grass. The industrial strategy, the centrepiece of May's economic agenda, was watered down in a White Paper published in November 2017, prison reform plans were shelved, and proposals for a free vote on the future of fox hunting to take place in government time were also scrapped. Never had a manifesto been so quickly dumped by an incoming government. What, then, had the general election given May the legitimacy to do as Prime Minister?

On Brexit, the so-called Great Repeal Bill was included in the Queen's Speech, intended to repeal the 1972 European Communities Act and to end the jurisdiction of the European Court of Justice. It would carry all EU laws over into British law, with Parliament deciding which were to remain. The eight Brexit Bills covered immigration and trade, as well as particular economic sectors, including farming and fisheries. But it had no fresh thinking on Brexit and provided no extra certainty on what the government hoped to achieve from the EU, nor how it would pass the eight Bills, given Conservative divisions and reliance on the DUP, each of which would require careful parliamentary handling.

Ominously for the Conservatives, Jeremy Corbyn reached new levels of assuredness and effectiveness in his response to May in the debate on the Queen's Speech, exhibiting 'far greater flair and confidence in his speech than any he [had] made since 2015', in the eyes of *The Guardian*. The paper's assessment of the Queen's Speech was, to recall an expression used by Norman Lamont of Major in June 1993, that it showed the Conservatives were 'in office but not in power'. It was 'a government without a clear mandate, lacking a clear plan and led by a prime minister whose stock is on the floor', who had produced a 'radically emaciated version' of the Conservative manifesto.[3] It was hard to disagree with that verdict.

SUMMER 2017

By early July, May's position had stabilised, and the remaining weeks until the summer recess passed smoothly, with the Chief Whip helping to ensure that contentious votes, which would have called the DUP relationship into question at its outset, were avoided. Corbynmania was on the rise, and thanks to his popularity and appeal to young voters, the word 'youthquake' became the Oxford Dictionaries' word of the year for 2017. The Conservatives appeared to have no answer. On 24 June, Corbyn took to the main Pyramid stage at the Glastonbury festival and, to deafening applause, said Trump 'should build bridges not walls'. Is it right, he asked repeatedly, that Conservative policy should punish the vulnerable, including those caught up in Grenfell Tower? The previous year, Corbyn's Glastonbury appearance had been cancelled amid concerns over his political survival.

The Spectator's summer party on 13 July, meanwhile, was a low point for May, with contempt for her and cynicism about the Tories' prospects widespread among the well-heeled revellers. In contrast to Corbyn's rise, here was the same woman who, just seven short months before, had won *The Spectator*'s 'Parliamentarian of the Year' award, now brought low. Misgivings were shared openly about why MPs hadn't dumped May straight after the election, and why Davis and Johnson, both very evident at the party, had bottled it.

May herself was exhausted, and Philip and her team in No. 10 insisted she have a proper holiday. She agreed to take three weeks, and left for five days at Lake Garda in northern Italy on 24 July, returning to northern Europe for commemorations of the centenary of the Battle of Passchendaele in Ypres, Belgium, on 31 July, which she found 'profoundly meaningful'. Afterwards, she went walking with Philip in the Alps for two weeks, returning to No. 10 on 16 August after the longest break of her premiership.

In early September, when the No. 10 team reassembled, they were in a much better frame of mind, with everyone from the Prime Minister down rested and optimistic. Downing Street had become a much friendlier and less anxious place since the general election. But it had also lost an edge. The Prime Minister's authority, which for ten months had held Whitehall in an iron grip, had suddenly been relaxed. It was no longer evident to May, beyond survival, and Brexit, where the government was heading. 'The PM had suddenly become relatively powerless. Cabinet ministers revelled in the newfound freedom and were beginning to realise that if they didn't like a policy the Prime Minister wanted, they could block it. It made for a dangerous autumn,' says an official. The big beasts were out of the cage. A reprieved Hammond was even more intent on keeping a tight grip on the nation's finances in preparation for his Autumn Budget. Hunt was on the prowl, angling for more money for an ambitious NHS investment. Johnson was licking his wounds and contemplating his next move. With the DUP deal in the bag, and the prospect of anarchy looming in the party, Williamson was becoming restless. After the conflict over grammar schools, Greening was determined never to be pushed around again by No. 10, and had her plans for action. Gove, the most successful of Cameron's ministers, was back in the game at DEFRA – but would he be an unguided missile or a loyalist?

Within the building, three key figures were establishing themselves as the new drivers of policy, each with their own take. Gavin Barwell was channelling his recent experience as Housing Minister into devising new housing policy, while the new director of communications, Robbie Gibb, was hatching ideas on student finance with JoJo Penn. Alongside them, Alex Dawson and James Marshall, the new head of policy, were becoming increasingly influential. Marshall wanted to see a dynamic agenda from his Policy Unit, with the NHS and the environment a top priority: 'Conservatives should be about conserving the environment. We needed to show young people we had an active policy on it beyond obsessing about fox hunting.'[4] On the NHS, Marshall worked closely with Dawson to shift the focus away from corporate structure to workforce, patients and technology. Revisiting childhood obesity was an early focus, as was mental health. The drive bore fruit months later in the NHS Long Term Plan. All the time, Marshall wrestled with the question: 'What was the status of the election manifesto, given it hadn't won a majority? How much should it be a guide to the future?' May's party conference speech in Manchester would have to pull all the emerging ideas together and land well if her authority was to be restored. But a succession of events conspired to ensure that this was not to be: Johnson deciding to show his pro-Brexit core base a bit of leg, squabbles with ministers over policy, her own speech backfiring and, at the end of conference week, an attempted coup.

PRE-CONFERENCE MINISTERIAL SQUABBLES

A major lesson all four of May's lieutenants drew from the general election campaign was that more needed to be done for young people.

'Coming out of the general election there was a definite sense from the Prime Minister and No. 10 that we needed fiscal loosening, that the electorate were just seeing the Conservatives as an office to cut the deficit,' says a No. 10 advisor. 'Hence the commitment to do more for public services, and most immediately, for schools.' In mid-September, Greening thus announced 'historic' changes to the school funding formula in England to make it fairer and more transparent, to address 'inequities in funding that have existed for far too long', targeting resources 'where they are most needed'.[5]

No. 10's focus then switched to university students, in light of Corbyn's announcement early in the election campaign that he would scrap tuition fees, envisaging a return to 'free university education' for all. The Conservatives had panicked at this pledge, and Timothy had inserted a sentence into the manifesto late in the day promising a review of student fees. 'I'm not certain the Prime Minister even knew it had gone in, but the Conservatives wanted to show that they had a positive agenda for the young, to counter Corbyn,' says a Treasury official. Greening had resisted the insertion at the time but was easily outmanoeuvred.

After the election, the initiative inside No. 10 was driven by Penn and Gibb, who thought that the revolt of university students had lost the Conservatives their majority at the election. Alison Wolf, the influential academic, had shaped thinking in No. 10 with her argument that further education needed much more investment in Britain, and should be dealt with in association with higher education. Her scepticism, too, on the value of non-Russell Group universities and some of the degrees they awarded found ready supporters in Downing Street and beyond. But in the early days after the election, the case for a review of HE and FE lost traction.

Fervour to take action was reignited when Damian Green, flush with his newfound status as May's 'top aide', announced on 1 July at a Bright Blue conference in London that student debt was a 'huge issue' and Conservatives should 'change hard' to woo the young. His words had not been cleared by No. 10, but they spurred it into action.[6] Research conducted after the election by James Johnson revealed to May the three key planks for Conservative policy if they wanted to improve public perception and reinforce core values: educational standards, increased housing and protecting the environment. No. 10 would drive for a review of tuition fees.

Greening's team in the Department for Education was hotly opposed to a review, while the Treasury was ambivalent. It believed that Universities Minister Jo Johnson (younger brother of Boris) had done a good job neutralising the issue by challenging Labour's promises head-on, which led them to backtrack. The Treasury nevertheless agreed to look at various options, concluding that, in the short term, the most effective way to help students, with minimum cost to the Exchequer, was to change their repayment threshold. No. 10 agreed but wanted the full review of student finance too, as had been promised in the manifesto. So it set up a joint project with the Treasury to explore how a review might take place, despite Greening's opposition. While she regarded the whole subject as a distraction from her primary concerns – schools and social mobility – Jo Johnson was more bothered about the unpredictable consequences of any such review, which he described as 'a can of worms', including how differential student fees might damage more expensive university courses, including STEM subjects, if it emerged as a recommendation. Johnson submitted a paper to No. 10 in mid-September, arguing for a reintroduction of maintenance grants for poorer students and a change to the interest rate that students paid. While May rejected his ideas, he had a sympathetic audience with Hammond, which angered Greening, who thought Johnson was going over her head to introduce a policy she hadn't approved.

The issue came to a head on Friday 29 September, on the eve of the party conference. While May was recording an interview with Andrew

Marr, to be broadcast on his BBC One programme that Sunday, in which she talked about the review being set up, Penn was in another room trying to talk Greening down from resigning. A promise that she would have a significant input into the review helped to calm the situation. But when the programme was broadcast on Sunday, Greening's office issued a statement indicating that it did not have her support. May nevertheless went ahead with her planned confer-ence speech, including setting up the review into university funding and student financing, alongside a freeze in the cap on tuition fees at £9,250 and a higher earnings repayment threshold of £25,000. But again Greening's team briefed that the policy did not have her sup-port. To the intense irritation of No. 10, the education press noted the stark difference of view.[7]

No. 10 decided it had little option but to put the review on hold until it could remove the blockage, i.e. the Education Secretary. On 8 January 2018, Greening was moved on and her successor, Damian Hinds, was appointed Education Secretary on the condition that he backed the review. The following day, Jo Johnson, the other blockage, was made Minister of State for Transport and Minister for London, with Sam Gyimah taking over as Universities Minister. Terms of ref-erence were then agreed between No. 10, the Treasury and the DfE. The Treasury wanted the review done internally but No. 10 insisted that it was done outside Whitehall, and it was agreed that it should take place in two phases: the review and then the government's re-sponse. The banker Philip Augar emerged after much haggling, and at the suggestion of Jeremy Heywood, as the chair; the Treasury, who didn't know him, was happy to go along with the idea. Some insiders thought he was chosen because he knew the Mays and played golf with Philip. In fact, it was another Heywood solution.

Housing was the other major general election legacy issue that No. 10 wanted to address urgently, fortified by some values research undertaken over the summer in No. 10. They focused on four elements: building new homes, the private rental sector, social housing and rough sleeping. Again, May and the Treasury were on opposite sides of the argument. No. 10 pressed the case to appeal to younger voters by helping them buy their first home. There were prolonged exchanges. In the end, No. 10 secured some modest announcements and Hammond offered – with characteristic caveats – a £10 billion extension of the Help to Buy scheme for first-time buyers. Together, the housing and student changes constituted an £11 billion package of pre-conference announcements. However, the impact of the initiatives, over which No. 10 had laboured so hard, was eviscerated by Boris Johnson, who knowingly sucked up much of the media attention in the run-up to the conference.

BORIS ON MANŒUVRES

Boris was not a happy man in the summer of 2017. The Foreign Office bored him, a sideshow that failed to engage his full interest. He wanted to influence Brexit, the biggest show in town, but all the action was in DExEU and No. 10, not his Foreign Office. Worse, he saw himself increasingly sidelined in the post-election Cabinet, with Damian Green elevated to First Secretary of State, a re-energised Hammond scoring runs at the Treasury, and arch-rival Michael Gove back in the Cabinet, the darling of sections of the right-wing press. Younger stars were emerging on the right, too, some more articulate and persuasive than himself, like Jacob Rees-Mogg; others better on the detail, like Steve Baker. That August, Johnson was a bear with a sore tooth. His cherished ideal of Downing Street was slipping away. He determined to make a speech in September about Brexit. But No. 10, with the PM's Florence speech coming up, flatly forbade him.

The week before her speech, he thus resorted to his Fleet Street home, the *Daily Telegraph*, who cleared space on 15 September for a 4,200-word article. 'Once we have settled our accounts, we will take back control of roughly £350 million per week,' Johnson wrote. The money would go, as stated in the referendum campaign, direct to the NHS. The UK should not continue to make new agreements with the EU post-Brexit, he added, while ongoing membership of the customs union and the single market would make a 'complete mockery' of the referendum result. His peroration was about how the UK could be 'the greatest country on earth'.[8] His article rekindled uncertainty about May's future, as intended by author and newspaper. In early September, May's successor in pole position was no longer Johnson but Amber Rudd, who used her appearance on *The Andrew Marr Show* on Sunday 17 September to remind the public of her strengths, accusing Johnson of 'backseat driving', deftly adding that she hadn't read his piece because she had 'rather a lot to do', responding to a terror attack at Parson's Green.[9] Nevertheless, Johnson's article, not her put-down, drove the news the following week.

Johnson's antics placed No. 10 in a difficult position. He was the Foreign Secretary: making no response risked emboldening him, while challenging him head-on would heighten his popularity, given May's lack of it. So Barwell decided it would be better to ask Johnson for help with the final drafting of her Florence speech, while asking Gove for his comments too. Her words in Florence nevertheless left Johnson chuntering, and in *The Sun* on the Saturday before the party conference opened he spoke off-piste about the 'red lines' for the forthcoming Brexit negotiations. The transition period had to be a maximum of two years, the UK must refuse any new EU or ECJ rulings in that period, no payment for single market access during the transition period should be paid, and the UK must not agree to shadow EU rules to gain access.[10]

No. 10 was livid. Johnson had achieved his objectives at the expense of their own. In the space of a month, he'd changed from being yesterday's man to being the reminder of everything that she was not

– bold, optimistic, and unyielding to the EU. As delegates assembled in Manchester, Boris was on the tip of all their tongues, while a ConservativeHome leadership survey placed him front-runner to succeed May.

Johnson captured headlines once more that week, if less intentionally, when he spoke at a fringe meeting, saying that all that was required for the war-torn Libyan city of Sirte to become a world-class destination like Dubai would be to 'clear the dead bodies away'.[11] No. 10 leapt on the gaffe, saying it was a matter for Johnson as to whether he should apologise, but 'we did not feel it was an appropriate choice of words'. Johnson's comment provoked international condemnation, but it made no dent in his support within Conservative circles. Indeed, the more Corbyn rose in popularity, the more they thought that only a charismatic figure like Johnson would counter Labour's ever more celebrated leader.

MAY'S SPEECH: 4 OCTOBER

Much hinged on the impact of May's speech, and she knew it. She'd reflected on what she might say over her long summer break and determined that she would, against her nature, reveal more about herself. Her team encouraged her to do so, recognising that putting words in her mouth, which had reached nemesis-point in the election campaign, did not work. She needed to show that, despite the lack of a popular mandate, and despite her reliance on the support of the DUP, she had a coherent agenda of her own and deserved the party's and the country's support. Wilkins recalls the process:

I came back in mid-September just to write it. It was the most personal speech she ever tried to deliver. My approach was to ask her,

'What is it you want to say? Why are you in politics?' It took about two weeks to bring it together. We spoke several times, as I worked her ideas up into a narrative.[12]

The speech was in good shape when May boarded the flight for Tallinn in Estonia for an EU digital summit on Friday 29 September. Though the focus was on the digital economy and society, Junker and Tusk led a discussion about the future of Europe over the coming years. Britain would not be part of that future, and the summit broke up early, with May announcing she would like to see the famous Alexander Nevsky Cathedral, which crowns the hill above the compact city. On the way up, she bumped into a rowdy group of Englishmen on a stag do. Her security detail feared the worst, but, rather than meting out abuse, the revellers came over and asked for selfies, a rare moment of public affection. On the plane back to London, though, her staff noticed for the first time that her voice was becoming croaky, the first sign of a hacking cough.

By the time she reached her hotel in Manchester for the party conference on Sunday, she was already losing her voice. But the desire to rebuild relations after the general election propelled her into a tireless programme of receptions, meals, coffee sessions and speeches. She managed to find some time on the Tuesday evening to run over her speech in a special room set aside for her, and her team thought she was in reasonably good shape. Expectations thus ran high, and her speech began promisingly. She explained why she entered the Conservative Party, reminding people that it lay at the very heart of her life, before going on to apologise for the general election.

A little over forty years ago in a small village in Oxfordshire, I signed up to be a member of the Conservative Party. I did it because it was the party that had the ideas to build a better Britain ... It had at its heart a simple promise that spoke to me, my values and my aspirations: that each new generation in our country should be able to build a better future. That each generation should live the British Dream. And that dream is what I believe in.

But what the general election earlier this year showed is that, forty years later, for too many people in our country, that dream feels distant ... I called that election. And I know that all of you in this hall – your friends and your families – worked day and night to secure the right result. Because of your hard work, we got 2.3 million more votes and achieved our highest vote share in thirty-four years. That simply would not have been possible without the long days and late nights, the phone calls, the leaflet drops. The weekends and evenings spent knocking on doors. So for everything you do, let me say – thank you.

But we did not get the victory we wanted because our national campaign fell short. It was too scripted. Too presidential. And it allowed the Labour Party to paint us as the voice of continuity, when the public wanted to hear a message of change. I hold my hands up for that. I take responsibility. I led the campaign. And I am sorry.

The major theme of her speech was the promise of a 'British Dream' for young people, a strong echo of Labour leader Ed Miliband's promise in 2014. It had been picked up by Corbyn, who promised that Labour would build a million new homes, half of which would be council houses. As she warmed to her theme, May struck an unusually personal note, saying, 'It has always been a great sadness for me and Philip that we were never blessed with children. It seems some things in life are just never meant to be. But I believe in the dream that life should be better for the next generation as much as any mother.' The major announcement in her speech that the government would invest £2 billion in affordable housing came on the back of announcements by Hammond and Javid earlier in the conference to extend Help to Buy and to give more protection to tenants. She then turned to health, and the launch of a review into how the NHS and other public services deal with those suffering from mental health problems, announcing that distinguished psychologist Simon Wessely would conduct a review into the Mental Health Act to improve existing legislation. The lack of equality in access to mental health, she said, was one of the 'longstanding injustices' that still motivated her in politics, repeating a refrain throughout her speech that 'that's what I'm in this for', to remind her audience that she still had the appetite for power. Her announcements on student finance – the review into higher education and change to the repayment threshold – were the most important of her speech, thought Marshall, while to Barwell it was her housing initiatives that took centre stage.

With the Florence speech having taken place the week before, May had little fresh to say about Brexit, dealing with it in just eleven short paragraphs, in which she repeated promises about a new 'deep and special partnership' with the EU and urged negotiators to reach a deal on the rights of EU citizens quickly. As in 2016, she wanted her keynote speech to be about her domestic agenda, including an attack on 'rip-off energy prices', with the promise of a new cap on bills, honouring another manifesto commitment. Holding the party together was a core objective. She laid off attacks on Johnson, who repaid the compliment by saying that he agreed with 'every syllable' that she had uttered in Florence. She made a clever dig at Osborne early in the speech when she said, 'I know that people think I'm not very emotional … And I don't mind being called things like the Ice Maiden – though perhaps George Osborne took the analogy a little far'– a reference to his comments about putting her chopped-up body in his freezer. But she built bridges with him too, praising his Northern Powerhouse initiative and the economic record of Cameron's coalition.

The biggest irony of her whole speech came with her statement, shortly to be tested to destruction, that 'the test of a leader is how you respond when tough times come upon you'. Shortly afterwards, a comedian called Simon Brodkin interrupted her mid-flow to hand her a fake P45 with the words, 'Boris asked me to give you this.' Few of her staff knew who he was; she definitely didn't, 'and it spooked her', says one. 'She would never say it, but she was thinking, "Where are my security team?" They just let it happen and it destroyed her momentum.' With commendable sangfroid, May said afterwards, 'There was nothing about his body language that gave me cause for alarm,' but her team were furious that he'd obtained a security pass and was allowed to approach her at such a sensitive moment.

The anxiety the gag caused her provoked her cough, latent all week, to break through. Her team, watching her speak from No. 10, were in despair as they saw that she still had nine long pages to get through before the end, while her team watching from the green room in Manchester wondered whether they should intervene to give her a break to recover. But on and on she battled. Rudd encouraged Johnson to his feet for a standing ovation, and when Hammond passed her a cough sweet, she joked, 'It's the Chancellor giving something away for free.'[13] Then disaster struck again, this time when the slogan behind her saying 'Building a country that works for everyone', attached to the wall with magnets, began to fall off, letter by letter. One Tory aide says, 'It could have been worse: I thought the "o" might fall off the word "country".' 'God, when is this going to finish?' thought Seema Kennedy, Hollingbery's successor as May's Parliamentary Private Secretary. Sitting next to Philip May, the agony of watching it all unfold reminded her of childbirth.[14]

Philip, visibly suffering for his beleaguered wife, went up to her on stage afterwards and whispered consoling words in her ear. As she left the stage to go back to the green room, she summoned all those who had helped on the speech to come for sandwiches and cake bought from Waitrose. Without a trace of self-pity, she said a few words thanking everybody. Only then did her team realise that she had been unaware about the letters falling down behind her. But she made light of that too as she was escorted out of the building to return to Sonning. Every person present was struck by how, at the most humiliating moment of her premiership to date, she was blaming no one, and tried to keep everybody upbeat and positive. Only in the seclusion of her official car did the pent-up emotion at last get the better of her as she broke down.

A LITTLE COUP

As she feared, the mishaps dominated media reports of her speech, crowding out the robust agenda she had tried to discuss. The *Financial Times* encapsulated her predicament: 'The Conservatives had been looking to Mrs May to map a path out of their post-general election malaise. Instead, her accident-strewn speech capped a conference that only highlighted the party's problems and revived speculation about how long Mrs May can remain as prime minister.'[15] Her speech, with its theme of a 'British Dream', may have been hackneyed and lacking in a dynamic new mission for government, but the momentum it did offer was crushed at birth. Despite his gaffe over Libya, Johnson, not her, was the undoubted star of the 2017 party conference, highlighting her inability either to sack him or to wrench the political narrative in her own direction. Jacob Rees Mogg, the rising star of the ascending ERG, was a threat not just to Johnson but, increasingly, to May herself, with his talk of the 'real Conservative' policies needed to counter the conviction of Corbyn, who had led an electric party conference the previous week in Brighton.

The *Financial Times*'s verdict was that 'many party activists ... remain unconvinced that she has either the verve or the ideological clarity to lead them out of their malaise'. 'Coughing and spluttering – May's British Dream turns into nightmare' was the judgement of *The Guardian*, while *The Times* ran with 'May on final warning after speech shambles'.[16] The *New Statesman* thought that she failed on the most pressing issue of the day, housing, dismissing the initiatives at the conference as 'about as effective as fighting a house fire by chucking a few fireworks through the letterbox and arming yourself with a water pistol'.[17] Gavin Williamson's verdict was:

Until she spoke, there was a slight sense of relief that the conference hadn't been any more difficult. We'd been anticipating slow hand-clapping and worse. After her speech, I was getting messages in the Whips' Office saying, 'Go, go, go. Let's get shot of her now.' There was a real tidal wave approaching. It felt like she'd had nine months of amazing luck when nothing could go wrong. Now, nothing could go right.[18]

Before the summer, Grant Shapps, Cameron's party chair, had been covertly agitating to oust May. With support from some twenty MPs, he fell well short of the forty-eight required by the 1922 Committee rules to challenge her. Many MPs thought the moment had passed in the early hours after the general election defeat; others queried whether Shapps himself, with a colourful past and questionable success as party chair, was the right person to head the charge. As chair, he had made an enduring enemy of Nick Timothy by ensuring he did not become a candidate to become an MP: that did not matter, because Timothy was history, but he had equally prevented Stephen Parkinson, the influential aide in No. 10, who did matter. There were scores to be settled.

Williamson had known about the rumblings around Shapps for several weeks, but after May's speech, it suddenly became an urgent issue, especially because he started hearing 'from MPs who were never usually difficult, who spoke about "the legacy of the general election and the sense that it was just all not meant to be"'. So, after her speech, he searched out 'the best place I know where you can be really confidential, a café in a department store', taking with him his Deputy Whip, Julian Smith, and Assistant Whip, Christopher Pincher.[19] As delegates filed out of the conference hall, the three slunk off to Manchester's Deansgate, to the top floor of Kendal's department store, to discuss 'how we steady the ship'. Getting the plot out into the open, they decided, was their best resort, knowing how shallow support for Shapps was and how quickly it would evaporate if exposed quickly. So they spoke to journalists they knew they could trust.

By the end of the week, Sam Coates of *The Times* was writing about how 'Theresa May appears to have seen off the immediate threat of a coup attempt led by Grant Shapps'.[20] A series of MPs were lined up to speak out against him. Tim Loughton said Shapps needed 'burying in the sand', while Nigel Evans added, 'There is only one direction that the Shapps band-wagon is going to roll ... and that is over him.'[21] Influential MP Nicholas Soames, grandson of Winston Churchill, tweeted, 'Winner of nominees for the person one would least like to go to war with: unanimous decision @grantshapps #shutup'.[22] Mark Pritchard, former secretary of the 1922 Committee, wrote in an article for PoliticsHome:

> The current plot against Theresa May will fail. Fail, because the main protagonists are unconventional, precipitous, and just far too keen ... The truth is, the Prime Minister has got more political balls than most male MPs. She is tenacious, a fighter, not a quitter, someone shaped in the real world, not in an avatar world of self illusion.[23]

Meanwhile, Johnson himself was persuaded by No. 10 to make supportive comments. A furious Shapps responded about his shock at the 'abuse and bile' and 'deliberate attempt to vilify those who wanted to speak to the Prime Minister' to express concerns that many shared across the party.[24] 'The Chief Whip did a really good job in closing it down,' says a No. 10 source. 'It wasn't that big a deal.'

The party wasn't yet in a mood to ditch her. David Lidington recalls, 'Given the instability, there was a slight worry it could move into something bigger.'[25] But MPs remembered her words to the 1922 Committee on 12 June: she would serve as long as MPs wanted her. 'Frankly, no one saw it as a serious challenge,' says another Cabinet minister. 'There was a sense of "let her deliver Brexit". Then the party would look again.'

Williamson had another worry that weekend. No. 10, in the form of Gibb and Barwell, were toying with a reshuffle as a way of restoring order. To pull this off, they had needed her to have a strong week in Manchester to refuel her authority. At the end of a long week, Williamson saw red and, according to sources, texted May: 'You haven't a clue, thinking about a reshuffle, and not consulting the Chief Whip. It's an insult.' He thought she now lacked the political strength for a reshuffle of any significance, so went on the warpath to stop it, marching into No. 10 to demand: 'You're not going to have a reshuffle. There's no way the government is in a strong enough position to burn goodwill.' Williamson considered that he himself was the figure who had dug May out of the mess at the end of the week, not her aides, and he was damned if he was going to let them float a shuffle in the papers. May had no choice but to go along with Williamson, though she did agree to give Tim Shipman, to whom the prospect of a reshuffle had been leaked, an interview in the *Sunday Times* on 8 October. She put particular thought into how to come across as a leader in command. 'I am a very determined person so no, I didn't,' she replied when asked if she had considered leaving the stage during her speech that week. 'One minute journalists are accusing me of being an ice maiden or a robot, then they claim I'm a weeping woman in dire need of a night's sleep,' she said. 'The truth is my feelings can be hurt, like everyone else, but I am pretty resilient.'[26]

By the following week, May's team in No. 10 were reporting that things were looking quite good. She had a rare good coup, emerging the stronger for it. But her ability to drive through her domestic agenda overall had been weakened. Coming up on the slate in the next few weeks, they had the Withdrawal Bill, the Autumn Budget and the European Council. They were reasonably confident that brighter days lay ahead.

At a famous lunch with EU Commission President Jean-Claude Juncker on 4 December 2017, May is forced to break off after she receives a call from Arlene Foster withdrawing her support for the Irish backstop.

CHAPTER 11

DAWN DASH TO BRUSSELS: THE DOUBLE-EDGED JOINT REPORT

JUNE–DECEMBER 2017

The starting gun had been fired. The government was opening negotiations with the EU for Brexit with a shrunken majority post-election – but no change either in the substance of what it sought or in its relationships with other political parties. For all May's dismissal of labels, this was undoubtedly going to be a Conservative Brexit and a hard Brexit, one leaving the UK firmly outside the customs union and single market. Nor would any changes be made to the sequencing upon which the EU insisted: only once 'sufficient progress' was made on Phase 1 and its three principal points of contention – citizens' rights, the financial settlement and the Irish border – could negotiations move on to Phase 2 and a detailed discussion on the future UK–EU relationship and transitional arrangements.

Brexiteers repeatedly asked why the timetable had to be adhered to so fervently, but, as Guy Verhofstadt explains, legally there could be no other way. 'It was absolutely clear in Article 50 that you did the divorce first and then the future arrangements second,' he says, turning to the same metaphor as Martin Selmayr.[1]

But if negotiations were to be like a divorce, it wouldn't be an ordinary one: it was fast becoming clear that there were more than two parties. On the UK side, it wasn't just a matter for May and her team: a Withdrawal Agreement Bill needed to pass through Parliament as well. MPs had not yet forced the government's hand into giving them a 'meaningful vote' on the agreement with Brussels, but they were still involved with the ratification process.

In the wake of the election result, no-deal preparations were not to be given any significant boost. It was business as usual, more or less. May was captain of the ship sailing off into the night, without a clear idea of either its final destination or the course it would take. The ship had been much weakened by the general election result and the weather report was worsening. But the government was going to journey forth one day at a time.

THE SEARCH FOR 'SUFFICIENT PROGRESS': JUNE–SEPTEMBER 2017

A rhythm of four-day meetings in four-week cycles was scheduled from the outset. Round 1 was from 19 to 22 June, the second from 17 to 20 July and the third from 28 to 31 August. Of the three issues to be discussed as part of the terms of withdrawal, the financial settlement – rather than Northern Ireland or citizens' rights – was predicted to be the main source of hard haggling. This miscalculation became a foundational error in the government's Brexit strategy. As one DExEU insider recalls:

> In the run-up to the October 2017 Council, our attention was on the financial settlement. All our intelligence was that Northern Ireland was going to be easy, as it would be in Dublin's interest to find a solution to it. But then Northern Ireland erupted as the difficult area. The odd thing was that it wasn't planned that Northern

Ireland would be in the withdrawal agreement as one of the pillars. Initially, there were only the two main pillars of the financial settlement and the citizens' rights, but the British pushed for Northern Ireland to be there as we thought that it would be helpful for us to start talking about Phase 2 if we inserted it because we'd have to be thinking about the future, but the way it worked out was backwards. Dublin wanted to find a solution to all the issues and wanted to know where it would end up in the withdrawal agreement, which caught us off guard.

David Davis was announced as chief negotiator for the UK, and seasoned French politician Michel Barnier for the EU. Davis from the start was eager to move on as swiftly as possible to Phase 2 – namely, talking about the future relationship and transitional arrangements – and to convince the EU that its insistence on 'sufficient progress' had been satisfied. But he was determined to fight the British corner hard on all three aspects of Phase 1.

Progress proved more difficult than Davis expected, with the British side labouring under a number of handicaps. Davis and Olly Robbins, the two principal figures, did not see eye to eye. Their joint meeting with May just after the election proved difficult. Davis thought the EU could be pressured into giving Britain what it sought; Robbins explained that it was not going to be that straightforward. A pattern was adopted whereby Robbins would see May first and talk through a paper with her, and then the three of them would meet, with May and Robbins having to awkwardly pretend it was the first time it was being discussed. Robbins and Tim Barrow, the UK's senior diplomat in Brussels since the departure of Ivan Rogers, marshalled an army of British officials, which at the high point reached up to 100 Brussels-based staff, the largest number of British officials working in another capital since Washington in the Second World War. In the cycle of talks, the key discussions in Brussels were chaired by Robbins for the British and Sabine Weyand for the EU. The British team kept in close touch with Davis, who would then turn up on the final day, rounded off by a press conference in a tightly choreographed sequence. The cream of the British civil service had been mobilised for the operation, but they struggled to match the team from the EU, whose depth of knowledge and long exposure to the intricacies of trade negotiations could not be bettered. The EU team was single-minded and strong – and they knew that their counterparts carried a weak Prime Minister and a divided country, with no clear line on what the final settlement might look like.

The British negotiating position was made no easier by the sizeable and influential bloc in Parliament, spearheaded by the ERG, which seemed to crave a dramatic showdown with Brussels. They were emboldened by powerful friends in the media, above all at the *Daily Telegraph* and the *Sunday Telegraph*, and often created the impression that May's team were either going soft or led by traitors. No politician was more effective in this cause than Steve Baker, the MP who had corralled colleagues to campaign for Leave during the referendum. Baker had been ERG chair from November 2016 until the election in June 2017, when he was appointed junior minister at DExEU; his place was taken by Suella Braverman, a determined but more consensual leader. The ERG exerted great and growing pressure on a Prime Minister very conscious of her lack of majority and determined to hold her party together. The group also stiffened the resolve, if indeed it was needed, of Davis himself. The attitude to the withdrawal agreement on the hard Leave side was: 'Why the hell should we give the EU a single penny?' To many in the ERG, any concession would be as good as capitulation.

Officials had long struggled to convince Davis of the importance of reaching an agreement on the 'divorce bill'. Jeremy Wright, long-serving Attorney General from 2014 to 2018, was one of those who helped explain the legal position to Davis, whose attitude on the financial settlement slowly shifted to one of reluctant acceptance, from 'We shouldn't pay them anything' to 'I can see there's no way round this, but let's make it as small a sum as possible'. As one insider says, 'It was always much easier to convince [Davis] of any argument if it was not being put to him by the Treasury, and particularly not by Philip Hammond.' The lobbying began to bear fruit. But still the right of the party, including many in Cabinet, believed that Britain's best strategy was to fight the EU hard on money, and use threats rather than diplomacy.

May was anxious to unblock the problem. Shortly before the third round of talks opened on 28 August, Robbins was invited to Chequers to see her, accompanied by Heywood, Barrow and the No. 10 team, but without Davis or other ministers. One civil servant recalls, 'As before the general election, she liked to have meetings with officials so she could work out in her own mind what she thought and wanted to do, before she opened it up to the politicians.' It was the first attempt to explore exactly what a financial settlement for the withdrawal looked like. Robbins argued that holding out on reaching a financial settlement would be 'toxic' if the EU thought that Britain was doing so to gain concessions. 'What kind of negotiator would recommend that?' May asked. He was blunt with her: 'Too many in SW1 think of the financial settlement purely in terms of leverage. This view is corroding the negotiations, and the longer it carries on, the more corrosion it will cause. Only once we commit to our financial liabilities will progress be made.' May didn't like what she heard, and she was worried by the expectations of easy financial wins on the right of her party. One Chequers attendee says, 'She was cross with the world, cross with the position she found herself in, her head frequently resting on the table.' Heywood came to Robbins's support, as he always did, and calmed the fraught atmosphere: 'You've got to listen to him, Prime Minister. Our current strategy of holding out is not working.'

In early September, a follow-up meeting at Admiralty House saw May soften her resistance. But she still worried that, with the party conference coming up, a large figure for the financial settlement would be a hard, if not impossible, sell. To make matters worse, May was under great pressure from the other side as well, with the Treasury and BEIS demanding a speedy resolution so that talks could move on from Phase 1, to discuss the future relationship and the transition period. Behind the scenes, a Treasury team led by Mark Bowman was battling with their opposite numbers from the EU Commission, bringing down the figure of €100 billion, which was initially on the table. Here, at least, the civil service was every bit the equal of their EU counterparts, living up to their historical reputation as the Continent's 'best negotiators', in Selmayr's view.[2] They drove down the figures, relentlessly challenging the assumptions that the EU were outmanoeuvring them on detail.

When Davis made a statement to Parliament on 5 September about the progress of negotiations after the first three rounds, he was optimistic. Far more so than Barnier, at least, who declared that there had been 'no decisive progress on any of the principal subjects' and expressed scepticism that 'sufficient progress' would be made by the time of the European Council, set for 19–20 October. The pressure on May grew greater: going into the fourth and fifth rounds of negotiations – scheduled for 25–28 September and 9–12 October – the second phase felt as far away as ever.

FLORENCE SPEECH: 22 SEPTEMBER

With progress blocked in Brussels and London, it was decided that May should give a speech in Europe – both to help get the backing of the October EU Council and to take hold of the domestic debate. Unlike her two earlier major speeches on Brexit, at the party conference and Lancaster House, this would be the first without a partisan British audience. 'She tried really hard to think through how to appeal to a European audience and make a connection with them,' says an official. A European city seemed ideal, with Italy chosen because it was neither Germany nor France, and because 'we wanted to show our relationship with Europe was based on shared history and culture, and not just on the existence of the EU', according to Gibb.[3] Her text was written and rewritten by Denzil Davidson and Robbins, who didn't get much sleep over several days writing it. Breaking with how she had prepared for her previous two speeches, May also went through the message with her ministers at a two-and-a-half-hour Cabinet meeting on 19 September. She then left for New York, for the United Nations General Assembly, where she told the visiting press that Cabinet was 'absolutely united' on what she would say. Johnson nevertheless made a public denial that he was on the verge of resigning over the speech, following his 4,200-word article giving his views on Brexit in the *Daily Telegraph* the previous Saturday. 'We are a government working together,' said Johnson. 'We are a nest of singing birds.'[4] Philip Hammond was not in singing mode, though, and neither was Davis: as all three went to join May in New York, the tension on the plane over was palpable. As Hammond worked his way through a huge pile of Treasury cuttings, he glared periodically across the aisle at Johnson, whose disobliging comments were reported on his lap.

The key element of May's speech, delivered on 22 September, was to tell the EU that Britain would play ball on its financial contribution. 'The UK will honour commitments we have made during the period of our membership,' she told her audience. She avoided mention of a precise figure, but £18 billion was reported in the press, which excluded EU pensions and debt commitments, so the final sum was likely to be double, albeit a long way short of the £70–100 billion that the EU was initially said to be eyeing up.

May spoke about the transition period, bridging the gap between

Britain leaving the EU in March 2019 and the beginning of a new trading relationship, which she envisaged lasting 'around two years' and which would allow 'people and businesses ... to adjust to the new arrangements in a smooth and orderly way'. She acknowledged that any such transition would mean abiding by EU rules, as per the EU's insistence, including the jurisdiction of the ECJ and free movement. At home, her speech appealed to both hard and soft Brexit camps. On the one hand, the 'strictly time-limited period' gave Hammond and others on the Remain side the gradual exit they had been demanding since the election, avoiding a regulatory cliff-edge for UK business. On the other, Brexiteers were calmed by the assurance that Britain was well and truly on the way out of the EU.

The speech also saw important movement on citizens' rights. May's earlier decision not to unilaterally recognise EU citizens' rights but to use them as a negotiating tool – if only to ensure the reciprocal protection of UK citizens' rights in the EU – had been controversial on both sides of the Channel. May saw the uncertainty as strengthening her hand. As one No. 10 source recounts, 'She thought that if you take any aspect of the negotiation and deal with it in its own right, it gives away some negotiating strength.' In many ways, this simply mirrored the EU's stance of 'nothing is agreed until everything is agreed'. Yet in her Florence speech May included important concessions on the issue, offering to write legal protections for EU citizens living in the UK into the exit treaty, rather than letting MPs vote on them independently. 'I want to incorporate our agreement fully into UK law and make sure the UK courts can refer directly to it,' she said. Accepting a role for the ECJ in settling rights disputes marked a further concession: 'I want the UK courts to be able to take into account the judgments of the European Court of Justice with a view to ensuring consistent interpretation.'

Florence saw a fudge on two issues, however, both to become of seminal significance. First, the EU wanted clarity about how Britain would solve the problem of the border between Northern Ireland and the Republic of Ireland once the UK left the customs union, having previously dismissed the government's thinking as 'magical'. May declared, 'We have both stated explicitly we will not accept physical infrastructure at the border,' but she gave no suggestion of how the Irish border would work out. Second, no clarity was provided on the future relationship and single market access that the UK might want. The options available were either to cut loose altogether and seek a free trade deal such as the EU had recently secured with Canada, as the Brexiteers wanted, or to agree a deal similar to Norway, remaining close to the EU in regulatory terms but at a cost in sovereignty and money. Barnier had already dismissed as a 'fantasy' the idea that Britain could have a bespoke 'halfway house', with Norway-style benefits and Canada-style low costs. But what Barnier called 'having your cake and eating it', May called common sense. Choosing one option over the other was 'stark and unimaginative', May said, and not 'best for the UK or best for the European Union'. Whereas a Norway-style deal would represent 'a loss of democratic control', a Canada-style deal, May argued, would be 'such a restriction on our mutual market access that it would benefit neither of our economies'.[5]

Overall, the speech landed well in both Brussels and London, with both Remain and Leave wings of the Conservative Party relatively content. May and her team were in high spirits when they left Florence, though there were some worrying signs: Johnson spent the journey 'chuntering away' in his seat, evidently unhappy with what May had said. But Barnier was convinced that the British would agree the financial settlement, so long as they could say they had got something out of the negotiation. He tried hard in the final week of September to come up with a plan to allow discussions to move forward in the October–December period, so both sides could have a win.

It wasn't to be. Barnier had not reckoned with the steely Committee of Permanent Representatives in the EU, who had, according to one member of the British negotiating team, 'cut him off at the knees and told [him] that he had exceeded his mandate' through none other than the French Ambassador to the body. Their undermining of him, at the instigation of Macron, who wanted the British to be given a rough ride, meant that Barnier's efforts to convince the forthcoming EU Council that sufficient progress had been made were much diminished.

But any internal division experienced by the EU paled in comparison to the UK, where the gulf between hard and soft Brexiteers was widening. May frantically tried to hold both sides together, and rival EU leaders weren't making her task any easier. On 11 October at PMQs, May said, 'We are preparing for every eventuality. We are committing money to prepare for Brexit, including a no-deal scenario … The Treasury has committed over £250 million of new money to departments.' But Macron claimed, 'At no moment has Theresa May ever raised a "no deal" as an option,' rejecting what he termed 'noises, bluffs, false information by secondary actors or spectators' on the possibility of no deal.[6]

At the Council on 19–20 October, leaders of the EU27 duly declined to say that 'sufficient progress' had been made. Negotiations would not yet move onto the transition and future relationship. Tusk, in his capacity as President, nevertheless saw reasons to be cheerful. He said that EU leaders had agreed to start 'internal preparatory discussions in relation to the framework for the future relationship and on transitional relationships', and that this step would not have been possible 'without the new momentum given by the Florence speech of Prime Minister May'.[7]

TOWARDS A JOINT REPORT: OCTOBER–DECEMBER

The cold shoulder from the Committee of Permanent Representatives made Robbins and Sabine Weyand, the German deputy to Michel

Barnier, determined to work much more closely together. 'Up to that point, it was all smoke and mirrors, but from the bust-up with the French Ambassador onwards, Sabine and Robbins worked so closely in carrying the EU27 that they even started thinking similarly,' says one close observer. Their determination was to produce a joint report between the EU and UK on all three Phase 1 pillars, ready to convince the EU27 at the December Council that sufficient progress had indeed been made to allow progress to Phase 2.

November proved a low point on that journey. With reports of the wrangling of Cabinet ministers regularly reaching the ears of the EU27, Barnier issued an ultimatum in late November. The UK had two weeks to stop arguing and come up with proposals that would satisfy the EU on the three pillars; in the case of the Irish border, the government of Ireland needed to be satisfied as well. One UK official became so worried about the rumours that Britain would be staying in the customs union, and the violent backlash from the ERG it would provoke, that they texted Heywood to ask for his views. 'WE WILL NOT BE IN A CUSTOMS UNION,' he texted back. While tempers frayed in May's team, officials in Brussels – on both sides – quietly beavered away.

By the week ending 1 December, the joint report, which included a summary of the negotiations over the previous five months towards a legally binding withdrawal agreement, was all but complete. On citizens' rights, both teams had reached a 'common understanding', providing reciprocal protection for EU and UK citizens exercising 'rights derived from Union law and based on past life choices'. An independent national authority in the UK and the European Commission would monitor the implementation of citizens' rights. On the financial settlement, it was agreed that none of the EU27 would pay more nor receive less by dint of the UK withdrawing from the EU, and Britain would pay its share of the current EU budget, which was to run until 2020, alongside some payments to be made after that date, based on average UK contributions. The figure of £35–39 billion was confirmed in the House of Commons by May on 11 December, subject to there being an agreement on the next stage and the partnership for the future. Several outlets, including the *Financial Times*, had previously suggested the final bill could be as high as £100 billion, a measure of the success of the Treasury arm of the British negotiating team, led by officials Mark Bowman and Jonathan Black.

The difficulty, however, came over the third pillar, the Irish border. Only that autumn did it dawn on the two negotiating teams in Brussels quite how complicated the issue was going to prove. For many in Britain, the realisation would not come until the following year, or even 2019. The joint report said the Good Friday Agreement of 1998 would be upheld, and a hard border between Ireland and Northern Ireland – 'including any physical infrastructure or related checks and controls' – avoided. But should the withdrawal agreement be unable to prevent a hard border, the UK would propose 'specific solutions to address the unique circumstances of the island of Ireland'. Were there to be no agreed solution, the UK would maintain 'full alignment' with the rules of the single market and customs union in support of North–South cooperation. Little detail was given about how all of this might be achieved, but it piqued intense interest and concern from the DUP and the right wing of the Conservative Party.

On Thursday 30 November, when presented with the draft joint report by EU officials, Robbins began to have his first doubts about the section on the Northern Ireland border. Together with Simon Case, May's former Principal Private Secretary and now director general for the UK–EU partnership, he pushed back hard on the text. The only solution they could see to help solve the Irish border problem was for Northern Ireland to remain in the customs union and single market. The following day, they flew back to London to see May, who according to Downing Street aides was extremely upset and worried: 'She could see at once that it would effectively entail a border down the Irish Sea.' Another comments, 'It was partly because she anticipated how concerned and negative the DUP would be when they heard about it, but she also felt upset because she was such a strong Unionist herself, and she felt the lure of the Union in her bones.' One No. 10 figure recalls the realisation of how difficult Northern Ireland would be at this point:

> After the Commission came up with the first version of the NI protocol, their proposal was greeted by consternation from us in No. 10. Olly, as he does, worked on it on his own and we didn't understand how deeply dug in the Irish were. It was a shock to pro-Remainers like Philip Hammond to see how intransigent the Irish were being and how our early hopes of making progress on the border were going to come up with problems, and how the Irish were going to insist that there would be no change to the border. Nobody understood how serious and intractable this problem would become.

While Robbins returned to Brussels to eke out more concessions, May went to work to win round her colleagues. The stakes were high: unless the wording was agreed, those two magic words on which everything relied – 'sufficient progress' – would remain elusive, and with them any sense of certainty over Britain's future. On several occasions that weekend she phoned Irish Taoiseach Leo Varadkar, but when his office told him who was trying to speak to him, he refused to pick up her calls. 'This was upsetting for May, but it was perfectly rational from his position, because he knew if he got embroiled with the Prime Minister, it would create problems with the Commission and put him in a very difficult position,' says one insider.

On Sunday 3 December, May called Davis to say, 'We've agreed the language, but you might have concerns over a number of details that I want to talk over with you.' Davis asked to hear what they were. On the first front, regarding the future relationship with the ECJ, Davis said he 'did have an objection, but not fatal'.[8] But on the second, which could have seen Northern Ireland remain aligned with the Republic of Ireland and not mainland Britain, he was deeply concerned. 'Prime Minister, you can't do that,' he said. 'You have said repeatedly in your speeches that we won't have full harmonisation.' 'No, no, no,' she replied. 'It's merely harmonisation on *outcomes*, not regulations.' 'Prime Minister, are you sure about the language?' he replied, knowing how crucial the language would be. She said, 'We've made progress, David, and that's important.' 'Prime Minister, I'm worried about it. Can I think about it overnight?' On Monday morning, he called her to say, 'It'll be bloody difficult, but on the basis [that] you've agreed it, we'll try to find a way forward.'[9]

A FRAUGHT WEEK: 4–8 DECEMBER

Juncker invited May, Davis and Robbins to lunch in Brussels that Monday. Davis suspected that Juncker was making it a high-profile event because he wanted to revel in the successful conclusion of the long autumn odyssey producing the joint report. The media had concluded that the deal was done, and expectations were running high about a major announcement being made. May was a worried woman when she boarded the British Aerospace 146 from RAF Northolt for the short flight to Brussels. Holding her party together always dominated her thinking, and she worried she'd lose the DUP, or ERG, over the Ireland proposals. Robbins tried to reassure her it would all be all right. He had worked hard over the weekend to ensure that he'd extracted all the compromises on the table. The financial settlement and citizens' rights had fallen into place. The issue that worried him was how far into the future the ECJ would continue to hear cases.

Robbins and Barrow went to the airport to pick her and the team up for the lunch, driving through the perimeter and onto the tarmac. But nobody came down the gangway. 'Can you come and get her off the plane?', texted a member of her staff on the ground. 'The Prime Minister is finding it difficult to finish all the material,' an official on the plane replied. She had only been given the final draft text that morning, and she was poring over every word in a state of increasing agitation. 'When she read the latest draft on the flight over, she foresaw with ghastly premonition all the difficulties she'd run into with her party,' says one. Davis, as he often did, made light of the drama and tried to jolly her along. 'There's still all to play for, and the important thing is to move on to the broader conversation with the EU on Phase 2,' he told her. The ECJ extension period, but still more the Northern Ireland text, weighed heavily on her, but she was eventually coaxed off the plane and into the waiting car.

'I'm not sure this is going to work,' she confided to her team as they sped through the outskirts of Brussels. Juncker was in a jovial mood when he greeted her for the long-awaited lunch to confirm whether 'sufficient progress' had been made on Phase 1. The conversation at the outset was whether they could settle on eight years for the timeframe for the ECJ. Mid-meal, and before any conclusion on it had been reached, her team received a call from Julian Smith, who had taken over as Chief Whip from Williamson a month earlier when the latter had been promoted to Defence Secretary. 'We have very big problems here,' Smith said down the line. He had been under huge pressure to secure the support of the DUP for the joint report, and regretted that the tight timeframe had meant that May had left for Brussels without their signing up to it. 'We'd had intelligence from the Chief Whip the night before that the DUP were huffing and puffing, but we still thought they would get us over the line,' says one present at the lunch.

While May carried on talking to Barnier, distantly aware of the growing consternation among her team, one of them left the room to find out more. It transpired that Arlene Foster had declared on television that morning that 'any form of regulatory divergence' separating Northern Ireland from mainland Britain was totally unacceptable to her, and No. 10 worried that she might abort the confidence-and-supply agreement if it went ahead. A note was passed to May to say that there were grave problems with the DUP. She visibly reeled but carried on for a while talking about the ECJ timeframe, before she became so distracted that both she and Juncker agreed to pause their conversation. 'Look, I can see this is very difficult for you. You can have the room,' Juncker told her. 'I'll go to my office for the afternoon, and if you receive the news that you need to allow you to go ahead, let's pick up from there.' 'You have to give it to him,' says one of the British party. 'He could not possibly have been more gentlemanly or considerate. I can't speak too highly about him.' After Juncker left the room, May called Foster to get her onside. Foster was angry about leaks of the proposed text of the joint report earlier in the day, and she vented her anger on May. One official describes it as a 'pretty difficult conversation'. May decided she had no choice but to return to London that afternoon. 'It was all very embarrassing for the Prime Minister,' says Smith, who offered up his Chief Whip's office at 9 Downing Street for government and DUP talks to begin the following day.[10]

The timetable was incredibly tight. The Council was being held at the end of the following week, 14–15 December. Juncker confided in May that he had to go into hospital for a medical procedure on Friday 8 December, but he could see her for breakfast if she came to Brussels that morning to secure his final blessing that sufficient progress had indeed been made. That gave her just three days to hammer out an agreement with the DUP, who were in little mood for compromise. The DUP's team in London consisted of Nigel Dodds, Sammy

Wilson, Emma Little-Pengelly, Timothy Johnston and Gavin Robinson, with Jeffrey Donaldson turning up for one or two sessions, and Arlene Foster in Belfast. While they fought over changes to the text with the Conservative team – Jonathan Caine, Julian Smith, Gavin Barwell and Simon Case – Robbins was in Brussels, working in parallel to secure concessions from the Commission.

Tuesday morning began badly, according to one civil servant close to negotiations: 'The DUP explained their beef with the process. They felt they had been bounced, taken for granted in the confidence-and-supply process and, frankly, treated like children.' May's team in turn were less than impressed with their Northern Irish interlocutors, as one recounts: 'It appeared to us, frankly, that dignity, tactics and face were more important to them than the substance and importance of the negotiations' – there was a sense that the DUP were treating it like any other negotiation in Northern Ireland, whereas May's team were adamant it wasn't. The talks appeared to be going nowhere. In Brussels, Robbins managed to extract some changes – substantive improvements, in some eyes; simply DUP-friendly phrases in others. This included inserting the now notorious Paragraph 50 into the joint report, which talked about Northern Ireland's secure place within the United Kingdom without a border down the Irish Sea. With its insertion, Wednesday saw a better atmosphere in 9 Downing Street by the evening. On Thursday, the negotiators were summoned to 10 Downing Street, where May told the DUP team, 'You've got some big wins here. Please take it back to Arlene in Belfast and please ask for her to support it.' But the movement in Brussels still failed to satisfy the DUP.

While the DUP team were in the air en route to Northern Ireland on Thursday evening, May made her first call to Foster at 8 p.m. 'I hope you will get behind this, Arlene. We have been over all the text and made significant concessions,' she said. It was a 'difficult' conversation. A frosty Foster told her, 'I'll talk to my team when they're back and I'll speak to you later.' She wanted to understand the urgency – why they couldn't carry on pressurising Brussels, with a week still to go to the EU Council. While May and her team waited anxiously for Foster to call, aware that the clock was ticking, and with the BAe 146 plane on standby at Northolt ready to fly at any time, the No. 10 Christmas party was in full swing across Downing Street. Robbie Gibb recalls:

> It was all rather surreal. The PM was downstairs in her study at the back of the building, and in the outer office, officials were working hard on the text. But in the rest of the building, including above them in the state drawing rooms, Christmas events were going on in different rooms, including karaoke. The PM would periodically go off and join in the festivities while they waited for the call back. Then, famously, whether by accident or not, the record 'Come On Eileen' came on. I still don't know if it was deliberate.[11]

At 11.30 p.m., May could wait no longer and picked up the phone to Foster. 'Switch', as the Downing Street switchboard are called, got hold of Foster but were unable to patch May through so that all the team could hear the conversation. Instead, May spoke from one of the phones on the desk of a private secretary in the outer office. Foster reported that she was still talking to her colleagues but had been unable to secure their unanimous support. 'It's very difficult for us, Prime Minister,' Foster would say, adding little more. In the end, she would confirm neither her support nor her opposition, and May decided to go for it. 'Well, Arlene, I hear you. You are talking from the point of view of Northern Ireland, but as Prime Minister I have to do what I think is in the national interest. I will travel to Brussels shortly and say what I have to say.' Foster gave no answer, and as May replaced the phone, spontaneous applause burst out all around her from her team. She had said what many had wanted her to say for a long time. As the room cleared, May went back into her study with Barwell. They debated whether she should go to Brussels. 'This is a decision of country versus self-interest,' he said. 'If you go, it will be a risk, as you are not certain that you will have the DUP or the Conservative Party behind you. But if you don't go, we'll not be able to move on to Phase 2, and the timetable is already under great pressure.'[12] In the two years he spent with her, Barwell always found that if he framed any decision by signalling one of the options as the right thing to do for the country, she would always take that option. The calculation they both made was that although the DUP were clearly still not happy, they wouldn't want to risk bringing the government down over it. The card that May didn't play that night was to confide in Foster one of the main reasons for the urgency: Juncker had told her in confidence about his medical condition, which had put him out of action in the critical few days leading up to the EU Council the following Friday. But she never betrayed his trust.

May decided she should go. Messages went from No. 10 to the airport to say she would be leaving shortly. En route, she called in on Sonning and then went on to the airport, boarding the plane at 3 a.m. with the ever-present Richard Jackson at her side. Smith and Case were left behind in London, putting in calls to individual DUP members from the early hours trying to get them onside. At 5 a.m., messages came into No. 10 that Foster would be saying that morning that she supported the deal and announcing that the DUP had achieved significant gains. But was she really giving May the DUP's full support? No one could be entirely sure. To Case, the previous ninety-six hours had been the highest drama and tension of his entire time in Downing Street, possibly of his career. Slack, too, had felt the tension, and when he took the lobby meeting that morning, the journalists clapped him in. 'At the time, it felt like a very good moment indeed,' he says.[13]

At six o'clock on Friday morning, a tired but resolute Theresa May landed in Brussels. Aides thought she was a completely different woman from the one earlier in the week. 'Do you still think you can't do this?' Robbins asked her, as they were driven from the airport. She smiled. It said it all. Given that May was now confident of her hand, the breakfast meeting was barely needed: 'It could have lasted just six minutes, because the language had all been agreed and settled in advance,' a member of the British negotiating team says. But it was nevertheless important that they had a meeting together. It was vital that Davis was seen to be supporting May all the way, and with him onside, she was secure on her right flank. 'No. 10 made certain, step by step through Phase 1, that Davis's hands were in the mangle,' says one. The breakfast was one of the most convivial that May, who had developed an unexpected regard for Juncker, was to experience in Brussels.

Because the media had been led to expect an announcement the previous Monday, No. 10 had been careful to play down hopes of any deal on Friday. So when Gibb came in to Downing Street at 5 a.m., he was surprised to find his staff dotted around the communications office at No. 12 in sleeping bags because they'd been working so late through the night. He made them tea and then called the *Today* programme to say, 'You might want to make some changes to your running order, as some important news is going to be breaking when you are on air.'[14] Thus did he confirm that the UK–EU joint report had been agreed, and that the 'sufficient progress' criterion had been met, allowing the negotiations to move on to Phase 2 in January 2018. The report called for 'an agreement as early as possible in early 2018 on transitional agreements', with another separate mandate required for negotiations on the future trade framework in late March 2018.

Game over, or at least Round 1 over, May's team thought, for a few glorious days. But Davis had spotted a catch, as one of the negotiating team recalls:

On the question of the language on Ireland, he would often ask what the words precisely meant in practice. It was impossible to give him a precise answer. We tried to reassure him, but what we were really doing was letting him believe what he wanted to believe about the language, until it came back to hit us all. Language got us through Friday and the following week into the December Council, but in time we were all brought down by it.

Liam Fox was concerned too, but, as he recalls, 'When they lobbied us about it, Gavin Barwell said, "We're only putting in the backstop so we can take it forward, don't worry, you'll never have to vote on it." It was a technical step to allow us to move on to the next stage.'[15]

Thus it was that May committed herself to the backstop on Northern Ireland: a de facto insurance policy in Brexit negotiations that would protect the open border in Ireland, whatever deal was decided (or not). The Commission had inserted this contingency plan into the text, giving No. 10 little time to consider it in the drafts they'd produced at the end of the previous week. 'The PM felt that if we didn't accept the backstop as an insurance policy, progress would have come to a complete halt, and that it would have a damaging effect on the economy. The PM had to take a calculated risk,' says Denzil Davidson.[16] Davidson was one of those who believed it was an error, if an understandable one, that the government didn't produce its own version of the backstop. But British officials were wary of producing a bespoke version because they thought that it was a legally operative text and as such any version they produced could not be both politically acceptable in the UK and credible with the Commission.

No single event was more significant in the unravelling of the May premiership than her apparent triumph in early December 2017. 'The absence of full DUP agreement cast a major shadow over the whole process and meant that Brexit became much more difficult early in 2018,' says Julian Smith. 'For the following eighteen months, we tried to get the DUP into a position of acceptance, but we never fully locked them in. The whole genesis of the DUP's lack of support was the December 2017 joint report.'[17] Smith knew the difficulties the backstop would pose and had spent the day before phoning Cabinet ministers, ensuring they were on board. As Rudd recalls:

I remember thinking how odd it was, back at the end of December 2017 at the time of the joint report, I got a call at about 11.30 p.m. from Gavin [Barwell] and Julian. They'd called all of us and they clearly felt they needed to handle everybody and to make certain they had the support for the next day. That, of course, was the beginning of the backstop.[18]

The backstop brought down May's Brexit deal, and it brought down May. The Brexit story has indeed been the story of Northern Ireland. Many are responsible for not seeing earlier how much of a problem Northern Ireland was going to become in 2018 and 2019. The EU can be criticised too for being insufficiently sympathetic to the Unionist community in Northern Ireland and for demanding a formula that would work in all circumstances within their own carefully prescribed legal framework. Hardliners within the DUP became steadily more inflexible, as individual MPs vied with each other for position, and the party worried about the advance of Sinn Féin, making them more and more obdurate in a bid to secure their base in the face of competition from their rival Unionist party, the UUP. The hardliners within May's own party were just beginning to flex their muscles. And within a month, the moderate Suella Braverman would be promoted to a junior minister, clearing the way for the far more uncompromising and determined Jacob Rees-Mogg to succeed her as chair of the ERG.

But for a while May and No. 10 basked gloriously in the applause of the EU December Council, as the Commission announced 'sufficient progress' had been made. On 15 December, the EU Parliament adopted a resolution recommending the EU27 agree to move on to Phase 2. A visibly relieved May and No. 10 went off for their Christmas holidays in a better frame of mind than they had been at any point since the general election six long months before.

May was never able to craft the Cabinet she wanted, or to dismiss Chancellor Philip Hammond, who proved a constant thorn in her domestic and EU policy. Here she is in Cabinet on the day after her botched reshuffle, alongside Hammond.

CHAPTER 12

PARADISE LOST: A BOTCHED RESHUFFLE

OCTOBER 2017–JANUARY 2018

The party conference at the start of October 2017 had spectacularly failed to give May and No. 10 the lift-off into the autumn they had been hoping for. A strong riposte to Corbyn was required, with a convincing stance on the NHS, policing, industrial strategy and the environment to win young people back. Above all, May needed a calm autumn, devoid of difficult votes in Parliament and party squabbles, rounded off by a Budget to show her clear commitment to the more equitable Britain that she had always spoken about. None was to happen. Worst of all, the reshuffle, one of the few shots she had left in her locker, backfired spectacularly, leaving her considerably weaker.

WESTMINSTER SEX SCANDALS: OCTOBER–DECEMBER 2017

In autumn 2017, the hashtag #MeToo began to spread on social media in response to the sex abuse allegations against American film producer Harvey Weinstein. The American actress Alyssa Milano encouraged victims of sexual harassment to tweet about it to 'give people a sense of the magnitude of the problem'. High-profile responses came from actresses Gwyneth Paltrow, Jennifer Lawrence and Uma Thurman, among others.

On Friday 27 October, a story broke in *The Sun* that a WhatsApp group had been set up naming sex pest MPs, including Cabinet ministers. A major scandal loomed. Two days later, International Trade Minister Mark Garnier became the first minister to be named and shamed, after admitting he had asked his secretary to buy sex toys. Former Work and Pensions Secretary Stephen Crabb was reported to have said the same day that it had been 'foolish' to send explicit messages to a nineteen-year-old woman whom he had interviewed four years before. The floodgates opened when Guido Fawkes revealed that thirty-six MPs had been named on the WhatsApp group. That Sunday, May, for whom such conduct was utterly alien, wrote to the Speaker to call for a binding code of conduct for all MPs, saying it was 'vital' for Parliament to retain the confidence of its staff and public.

On Monday 30 October, the frenzy exploded, with fresh names circulating around Westminster and the media. Leader of the House Andrea Leadsom said, 'I am setting the bar significantly below criminal activity,' warning that ministers could be fired, MPs could have the whip withdrawn, and staff could lose their jobs. So far, no big beasts had been implicated. But Defence Secretary Michael Fallon would soon be the first Cabinet minister in the firing line, following reports that he had touched the knee of a journalist fifteen years before. There were calls for the whips to open up their 'black book' on misdemeanours by senior MPs and ministers.[1] Inside No. 10, Gavin Barwell was coming under enormous strain. A series of women had called him to say, 'I'll tell you something that happened to me, but I don't want you to do anything about it.' One of them was *Observer* journalist Jane Merrick, who a week later decided to break her silence. 'Michael Fallon lunged at me after our lunch,' she wrote.[2] By Wednesday 1 November, Fallon considered his position had become untenable, and resigned, saying his behaviour had 'fallen below' the standards expected of him. His departure had been hastened by suggestions from Leadsom herself that he had made inappropriate comments to her when she complained of having cold hands.

It was the Leadsom allegations that proved fatal. Heywood's advice from early on was that Fallon would have to go, but May was torn. She was determined that she wanted to champion women, but she didn't want to lose loyal ministers to a media storm without proven evidence. She spent two days mulling over the decision before deciding. Heywood was forceful at the 8.30 a.m. meeting on Tuesday, but only later in the day did she make up her mind. 'When one Cabinet minister says they've been sexually harassed by another, they have to go,' says a No. 10 source, adding, 'Most embarrassing of all the resignations was that of Michael Fallon.' Prominent female Conservative MPs, sensing that Downing Street might try to close down the scandal for fear of destabilising the Prime Minister, began to speak out. Justine Greening said anyone who felt they'd been sexually harassed should contact the police, while backbencher Nadine Dorries said, 'No male predator should be given cover. In order for women to reach their potential, the corridors of power have to be free from all forms of sexual harassment and intimidation.'[3]

Fallon's departure was a blow for May, as she lost a loyalist and sound performer, if not a star. But the choice of his successor affected her much more. In Fallon's place, she appointed Gavin Williamson as Defence Secretary, the subject of considerable contemporary comment. One senior backbencher described the promotion as 'unbelievable. Ludicrous. Astonishing,' while a former minister said, 'I thought the secret of naked ambition was not to make it so obvious.' Some of the anger was motivated by jealousy, but some emanated from a concern that the Whips' Office had for years been complicit in covering up bad behaviour by MPs until the point at which it erupted.[4]

Some MPs wondered whether Williamson had manoeuvred Fallon out. In any case, he certainly wasn't bashful about suggesting himself as his successor. Cynics suggest that Williamson had sniffed the wind of the new parliament, contemplated the parliamentary arithmetic and the gargantuan challenges on Brexit up ahead and decided to move before it became nasty. May lost a formidable Chief Whip: like Cameron before her, who had appointed Williamson as his PPS, she had found Williamson's political instincts astute, detailed and decisive. His knowledge of the DUP was a particular strength at such a delicate time. Following his appointment as Defence Secretary, Deputy Chief Whip Julian Smith was promoted into his place. Formidably hard-working and loyal, Smith was to perform the job under the most difficult of circumstances over the following eighteen months. Williamson's departure tipped the balance in the key Strategy and Negotiation (SN) Cabinet Committee towards the hard Brexiteers. As Chief Whip, Williamson had been mostly reticent about his pro-Brexit views, but in the powerful position of Defence Secretary, with a seat on the critical Cabinet committee, he decisively pivoted away from Brussels.

Fallon's departure only fanned the flames of Westminster's #MeToo movement further. No. 10 was determined to get ahead on the sex scandal in a way that it thought it had failed to do during the expenses saga under Gordon Brown in 2009. The *Daily Telegraph*, which had been at the centre of that controversy, had already predicted, 'Sex scandal could be worse than expenses'.[5] No. 10 seized on a speech May was due to give to the Confederation of British Industry on Monday 6 November, using it as a call for a 'new culture of respect' in public life, ahead of the meeting that she had convened with fellow party leaders to discuss a collective response to the sex scandal. In the speech, she said change was needed so 'everyone can feel confident that they are working in a safe and secure environment'. She noted, 'Political parties have not always got this right in the past. But I'm determined to get it right for the future.'

Little came of the leaders' meeting. 'Labour wouldn't play ball. They said we didn't need any new parliamentary declaration: all we needed to do was work through the trade unions,' says a No. 10 source. But May also arranged a meeting with parliamentary researchers and staff, on a cross-party basis, to hear first-hand from those affected.

Any hopes that May's words or meetings, well-intentioned though they were, would close down the furore were misplaced. Tory whip Chris Pincher was next to go, after allegations of inappropriate behaviour, while fellow MP Charlie Elphicke was suspended from the party when 'serious allegations' against him were referred to the police. Meanwhile, two other Conservative MPs, Daniel Kawczynski and Dan Poulter, both of whom denied wrongdoing, were referred to the party's disciplinary committee, alongside Stephen Crabb. All three were later cleared. It wasn't just Tory MPs under suspicion. Labour MP Kelvin Hopkins was suspended by his party. A separate investigation was launched after a Labour activist said she'd been raped by a more senior party member at a party event in 2011 but had been discouraged by a senior official from reporting the attack.[6]

On Wednesday 8 November, International Development Secretary Priti Patel resigned for very different reasons: she had failed to be candid with May about unofficial meetings with Israeli ministers, businesspeople and a lobbyist. May met Patel for just six minutes. Patel admitted that her actions had fallen 'below the high standards that are expected of a Secretary of State'. 'The most ridiculous of all the cases was that of Priti Patel,' says a source.

It caused great upset with Whitehall and in the FCO. She gave us a list of the meetings she had, and the PM asked her, 'Are you sure there are no others you saw?' 'There are no others,' she replied. But within a couple of days, another name emerged. It had to happen.

Patel's resignation came after six days of headlines about alleged meetings that might or might not have taken place. It damaged May's authority and made a reshuffle inevitable – one she had little political authority to execute.

Boris Johnson now came into the firing line over a sensitive case involving a British-Iranian charity worker, detained as she tried to leave Iran in 2016 with her daughter. On 1 November, Johnson said, 'If you look at what Nazanin Zaghari-Ratcliffe was doing, she was simply teaching people journalism, as I understand it, at the very limit.'[7] Three days later, she was returned to court in Iran, where Johnson's statement was cited as evidence against her for allegedly plotting to 'topple the Iranian government'. Johnson's inept comments were roundly condemned, and pressure grew for May to sack him, a call which, for reasons of political expediency, she was unable to implement. The departure of Patel, a standard bearer for the Brexiteers, made Johnson even safer, given May's constant article of faith about balancing Brexiteers and Remainers in Cabinet.

Damian Green was the figure who, more than any other in her Cabinet, May did not want to lose. Appointed First Secretary of State in the reshuffle after the general election, he had been conspicuously successful in his first five months. 'He was one of the Prime Minister's most loyal allies. They were close friends, he was her No. 2, he'd only recently been appointed, she could rely on him completely, and losing him so soon after his appointment she knew would impact on her credibility,' says a No. 10 source. Green was accustomed to scandal, dating back to November 2008 when he was arrested and held by the Metropolitan Police over his potential involvement in the leak of confidential government documents. His home and offices were searched – 'heavy-handed tactics', in the critical words of David Cameron, which would later prompt an internal review at Scotland Yard. Green seemed to be in the clear until, in 2017, a 31-year-old writer and academic, Kate Maltby, made suggestions that Green had inappropriately touched her knee in a pub and subsequently sent her a 'suggestive' text message. May promptly responded by asking Heywood to investigate. In the attention that followed, new concerns emerged about pornography that police had found on one of Mr Green's parliamentary computers during the 2008 investigation. Green's case rumbled on for the rest of the month until, on 1 December, a former Scotland Yard detective told the BBC he had been 'shocked' by the amount of pornography found at Green's office in 2008. The Cabinet Office's head of propriety and ethics, Sue Gray, spent vast amounts of time in December ploughing through the evidence before reporting on 18 December. She found that Green had breached the ministerial code. Green continued to fight on, believing that there was no hard evidence against him and the allegations were unfair and based on hearsay. But Gray's conclusion that Green had given incorrect evidence about the pornography when questioned was fatal. He had to go. He was extremely unhappy with the outcome, having lost a dream job, and believed he had been unfairly treated. But he apologised to Maltby for making her feel uncomfortable, while May herself expressed 'deep regret' at his departure.[8] There was to be no return to the limelight for Green. The dominant political force in government after May was completely extinguished.

A CONTESTED BUDGET: 22 NOVEMBER 2017

Hammond was another figure under pressure that autumn. Eurosceptic Cabinet ministers, Johnson, Fox and Davis in particular, alongside the increasingly vocal European Research Group, were targeting him for his 'pessimistic' approach to Brexit and refusal to invest properly in planning for a no-deal Brexit. They wanted him replaced by Michael

Gove, whom they regarded as far more economically literate, and who would offer a positive vision about Britain after Brexit. Further attacks on Hammond came from the other flank, with ministers such as Communities and Local Government Secretary Sajid Javid and Work and Pensions Secretary David Gauke believing, as had Nick Timothy before the general election, that he was starving the country of the money needed to invest in the future, specifically into housing and universal credit. Ministers and MPs with marginal seats were no less keen to see some serious government spending.

In the weeks leading up to the Budget, the press was briefed that Hammond was proposing a 'revolutionary Budget' that would make a 'big offer to the nation' on housing, tax, welfare and more. Plans for a 'safety first' Budget had been abandoned, the briefings said, to make way for 'bold solutions' to appeal to younger voters, to combat Corbyn's success with them, as the Tories' answer to 'intergenerational unfairness'. In Cabinet, Hammond was urged to boost investment, to see the housing supply kickstarted, and to allow more building on the Green Belt.[9] With few friends, the Chancellor was vulnerable. But as long as he had May's support, he was secure, and she had no plans to change her Chancellor. The replacement of Timothy, an arch-critic, by Barwell, who had a more positive relationship with Hammond, was key to his survival. Will Macfarlane, May's Deputy Principal Secretary, had worked closely with Hammond's Principal Private Secretary, Stuart Glassborow, to ensure that the relationship between Prime Minister and Chancellor worked better than it had before the general election, not least by rationing May's and Hammond's encounters only to those occasions when they needed to meet, and by ensuring that the ground had been properly prepared beforehand to minimise fisticuffs. 'Barwell had an open and trusting relationship with most everybody, and that changed the tone in No. 10 and made for a much better relationship with the Treasury,' says an insider.

Tensions resided below the surface, however. Hammond had been furious when Javid went on BBC One's *Andrew Marr Show* on Sunday 22 October and said the government should be taking advantage of record-low interest rates to boost housing, arguing, '[It] can be the right thing if done sensibly.' It came at the end of an eight-week campaign on housing initiated by Javid, in which he called on the industry to offer solutions to meet the demand for new homes. Hammond was furious that May refused to slap Javid down. That autumn, housing became the subject of extensive briefing and counter-briefing, even more intense than earlier spats over social care and higher education funding. Hammond furiously resisted all attempts at what he considered to be inappropriate and excessive spending. Few Chancellors in the past twenty-five years have chimed so closely with the Treasury's own views – so much so that he bought their long-standing argument that the Budget should be rolled in with the Autumn Statement, which took place on 22 November.

Hammond won many of the arguments in a conservative and dull Budget. The NHS was the main priority for No. 10, who wanted to see £4 billion in extra funding, as Simon Stevens, the influential NHS England chief executive, and the King's Fund had been arguing. But Hammond would grant just £2.8 billion, to include £350 million immediately to address the winter crisis and a further £1.6 billion to be given in 2018/19, with the rest in the following year. 'It ended up riling the NHS rather than pleasing them,' says Alex Dawson.[10] The Policy Unit, Penn and Dawson had argued for £4 billion, but they ran straight into resistance from May, who argued, 'The problem with conceding to what Simon Stevens is always demanding is that we end up putting the money into short-term solutions like reducing waiting lists rather than seeing systemic improvement, or into preventative medicine or mental health.' Hunt backed her up, concerned that annual increases produced no political capital and limited forward planning. Outflanked this time, the Policy Unit decided to bide its time and put all its effort into a major drive for extra funding in 2018 which could be coupled with a long-term plan.

Housing was No. 10's next priority, with Barwell joining forces with Javid, his former boss. The new accord with Treasury officials bore fruit, with stamp duty reduced for the majority of first-time buyers for properties worth up to £300,000. Hammond agreed to increase the construction of new homes to 300,000 a year by the mid-2020s, up from 217,000 in 2016, facilitated by the government providing at least £44 billion of capital funding, loans and guarantees over the following five years. No. 10 and Javid were disappointed that Hammond wouldn't go further, but they felt confident that they had at least made some progress. Universal credit, introduced by Iain Duncan-Smith under the Cameron government, continued to be a source of grief. Hammond unveiled a £1.5 billion package to ease its problems, targeting funding for the areas worst affected by the housing benefit freeze.

Any lift from the November Budget fell far below No. 10's hopes. Hammond refused to do more to support May's industrial strategy, the linchpin of her domestic policy. The Department for Business, Energy and Industrial Strategy had been created in July 2016 expressly to give industry a boost, with No. 10 always suspicious that the Treasury was lukewarm to its initiatives because it saw BEIS as a threat to its near-monopoly over economic policy-making. Nor was Hammond willing to allocate specific funding to raise public sector pay, despite intense pressure to do so from across the political spectrum. The furthest he would go was to say that he would allocate additional funding if independent pay bodies were to recommend it. The failure to make a decisive move away from austerity disappointed many. Hammond argued that the economy was going to grow more slowly than he had expected at the time of the March 2017 Budget, with half a percentage point shaved off his growth forecast, slowing to 1.5 per cent in 2017, and down to 1.4 per cent in 2018 – though the government was still on course to meet its target to cut the deficit to below 2 per cent of GDP by the end of the parliament. A series of lesser measures, including a freeze in petrol and diesel duty, a reduction in business rates rises, and the ditching of plans to reduce the VAT threshold for business, passed largely without comment. Hammond was in a more light-hearted mood for the country's first November Budget since Brown had moved it to spring after Labour came to power in 1997. It included seven jokes (people counted), the best of which was the rehearsed stunt in which Hammond received some cough sweets from May, accompanied by the line, 'I did take the precaution of asking my right honourable friend to bring a packet of cough sweets just in case,' a visible (if contrived) indication of an improved relationship since the nadir during the general election.[11]

BOTCHED RESHUFFLE: JANUARY 2018

The Conservative Party had been expecting that a reshuffle would come after the general election, and then again in October. Both had been scrapped due to May's lack of political capital. 'Then suddenly, out of nowhere, between Christmas and the New Year, No. 10 started briefing to the media that a reshuffle was imminent. It got everyone very anxious,' says Justine Greening.[12] Williamson had succeeded Fallon as Defence Secretary, and Penny Mordaunt had been rapidly promoted to succeed Priti Patel as International Development Secretary on 9 November. But Damian Green's long, drawn-out departure on 20 December had left May no time before Christmas to fill such an important post. A reshuffle could be put off no longer.

No. 10 wanted to use it to freshen up the government and to produce new impetus for 2018. The Brexit team was to be unchanged, but dynamism was sought in domestic departments, as well as more women, young talent and black, Asian and ethnic minority (BAME) ministers, 'to make it the most diverse Cabinet in history'.[13] The day before the reshuffle, No. 10 briefed out that May wanted 'to make sure the government reflects the modern and diverse country we live in',[14] a passion of the Chief Whip, who spoke of a 'talent pipeline'. 'We knew we couldn't change the top jobs, but we wanted to gain momentum, and get a better gender balance into the Cabinet,' says Barwell.[15] In addition to finding a successor for Damian Green, a dynamic replacement was needed for Patrick McLoughlin as party chair, who, unfairly or not, took some of the blame for the general election and the 2017 party conference debacle. James Brokenshire at the Northern Ireland Office, who resigned unexpectedly due to needing surgery to address a lesion in his lung, also needed replacing. All three were staunch May loyalists and their replacements would require serious consideration.

Why no changes at the top? No. 10 would far sooner have lost either Johnson or Hammond than these allies. May was unimpressed by her Foreign Secretary's record: she would have loved to have replaced him, but the risk of moving or firing him was considered too great, and, according to an insider, 'We couldn't get rid of Philip Hammond, because if she'd sacked him, she'd have had to have sacked Boris to maintain the balance in Cabinet on Brexit, and stabilisation of Cabinet was all-important to her.' She was snookered. So Johnson was left to continue to bluster and undermine her, and Hammond to block her attempts to build her domestic agenda while failing to be the ally she needed on her emerging Brexit strategy.

The No. 10 political team, supported by Jeremy Heywood and Peter Hill, put considerable effort over the holiday into how best to execute this reshuffle, with Gavin Barwell and Julian Smith the chief architects. Moves were mapped out in detail on a whiteboard, originally in the Cabinet Office and then in the No. 10 private office. Heywood was a reshuffle veteran and had seen even the best-planned of them go pear-shaped; he helped the team design a detailed choreography for the day. Rumours emanating from the centre about who might be moved flew around over the news-light Christmas and New Year period, with McLoughlin, Greening, Clark and Leadsom all mentioned as for the chop. Gove, already seen as the star departmental performer at DEFRA under May, as he had been at Education under Cameron, was tipped for an even bigger job. All looked set for a smooth reshuffle.

It didn't take long for such optimism to unravel. Barwell had briefed CCHQ on the morning of the reshuffle that Transport Secretary Chris Grayling was to succeed McLoughlin as party chair. When Penn and Gibb realised the plan, they said it was 'crackers' to imagine that Grayling had the skills required, and No. 10 changed course. But nobody had told CCHQ. When they saw Grayling walking into Downing Street, it was tweeted that he was party chair. A panicked No. 10 instructed them to delete the message, but it had already been widely noted, creating an air of incompetence before the reshuffle had even begun.

With little room for manoeuvre, the principal ploy to re-energise the government was to swap Jeremy Hunt and Greg Clark, given it was deemed unwise to dismiss the solid Clark, a loyalist and a strong advocate of Remain, which would have unsettled the large cohort of Conservative Remain MPs. Hunt was seen as having been at Health for long enough: it was over five years since he had replaced Andrew Lansley back in September 2012. May thought he had done well, but his strengths lay in reforming and galvanising a department and setting out a new strategy. With no further NHS reorganisation planned, his skills would be wasted. Clark's strengths, meanwhile, were not dynamism (May blamed him for the slow progress of her industrial strategy at BEIS) but rather for affirming stakeholders, and a job needed to be done at Health to placate junior doctors after their prolonged dispute. 'Everyone got on well with Greg, and he would soothe the NHS after Hunt,' says a No. 10 source.

The augurs looked good. Hunt had spoken to No. 10 before the general election about wanting to be moved in the post-general election reshuffle. However, he had begun to change his mind without notifying No. 10. He had become excited about the possibilities of significant extra funding for the NHS to be announced at its seventieth anniversary in July, which became the NHS Long Term Plan later in 2018, and about the prospect of becoming the longest-serving Health Secretary in history. 'So, Jeremy began to think he wanted to stay, or at least not go for the option we presented him with, which gave us one almighty problem,' as a No. 10 advisor says. When Hunt was called into No. 10 that morning, May tried to inspire him, telling him her industrial strategy lay at the heart of her domestic vision, and she badly needed his business and leadership skills to at last drive it forward. But Hunt, deeply ambitious, had his eyes on a bigger prize than becoming Business Secretary, however attractively she presented it.

Discussions continued for almost an hour. No vacancies were available at the Treasury, Foreign Office, Home Office or Defence, but he had reason to believe that he might become Green's successor as First Secretary, a rumour that had been in wide circulation. 'He'd been very loyal and had her trust: it was clear to us he wanted to be second in command,' says an official. But May could not allow it for fear of destabilising the delicate balance at the heart of her government. None of her big beasts would have been happy to see a leadership rival grow politically closer to May, with a contest perhaps not many months away. So, she bought him off by offering the additional responsibility for social care, a poisoned chalice after the disaster of the election manifesto, but a problem that badly needed gripping by government (which was to remain unsolved).

Worse was to come when Greening refused point-blank to be moved sideways from Education to succeed David Gauke as Work and Pensions Secretary. The team in No. 10, according to one insider, thought she had good aspects to her, was committed to social diversity, to young people, but she had to go because she was blocking us on the report into higher education. So, we sought an equivalent rank, and said she could take her equalities brief with her, about which she was passionate.

But because of briefings over the holiday that she was going to be sacked, the source continues, 'she turned up at No. 10, looking incredibly tense and thinking she was in for the chop, so she wasn't even listening to what the Prime Minister offered her'. Greening herself recounts:

I'd told Julian Smith twice over the holiday period that I was not going to move from Education. So when I went in to see the Prime Minister, she told me that I'd done well with the schools funding formula and at Education, but she wanted me to move. I replied, 'I'm very grateful, but I care about social mobility and education so much, that I'm off to the back benches.' Frankly, I saw the government falling apart and I really didn't want to be part of it any more.[16]

Greening was very deeply upset and offended by the offer. Education was a job that she passionately loved. She spent considerable time in the room opposite the Cabinet Room composing herself – and convincing herself she was making the right call – until she was certain of her decision and felt ready to face the world, a reminder of how cruel ministerial life can be. Later that year, from the back benches, she established the Social Mobility Pledge, to broaden social mobility and opportunity in Britain, and in early 2019 founded a new group with Dominic Grieve to campaign for a second referendum.

Her departure created space for the biggest surprise of the day: Damian Hinds, a relative unknown as a Minister of State at DWP,

was to succeed her as Education Secretary. An old friend of Barwell –
they had entered the Commons in the same year, 2010 – Hinds was an
enthusiast for technical and apprenticeship education. He says:

> I couldn't have been more surprised or happier. It was already early
> evening when I was called in to see her. 'I'd like you to take over
> at Education,' she said. The HE review was implicitly part of my
> accepting that job, but she gave me no specific instructions. I then
> sat down with Gavin Barwell after, and we ran over the priorities,
> including the HE review, and it was clear what I was signing up to.[17]

David Lidington was the other surprise of the day. Realising they
daren't appoint a big hitter to take over from Green, Lidington was
judged to possess the skills of competence, loyalty to the Prime Minister and acceptability to both wings of the party. He remembers:

> I had no hint at all that I would get the call. She saw me in the
> Cabinet Room, with just Gavin Barwell present, and said, 'Thank
> you for doing Justice. I'd like you to become Chancellor of the
> Duchy of Lancaster and Minister at the Cabinet Office.' She didn't
> expressly mention me becoming First Secretary of State, but she
> did say, 'You'll be No. 2 in the government, you'll sit opposite me
> in Cabinet, and you'll come to my 8.30 meetings.' At the end, she
> added that I'd also be overseeing devolution, the constitution, and
> she'd like me to help out on the European negotiations as well.[18]

Barwell was responsible for suggesting Lidington, thinking he had
done well as Justice Secretary and as Leader of the House previously,
when he oversaw the government response to the terrorist attack on
Westminster Bridge in March 2017. Barwell and May decided that
they needed a figure similar in age, profile and mindset to Green,

rather than a 'firebrand' like Matt Hancock. Importantly, it had to be someone she could trust – someone who wouldn't be sniffing after her job.

Esther McVey, a Deputy Chief Whip who had lost her seat in 2015 but re-entered Parliament in June 2017 in George Osborne's Tatton constituency, was another major gainer. She had been slated to become Immigration Minister until Greening refused to move to DWP; now, with a Cabinet chair to fill and little time to think, May handed McVey the position of Work and Pensions Secretary. Even before McVey's resignation over Brexit in November 2018, the unsuitability of the match would become apparent.

Barwell said at the time that the reshuffle would be judged not on the short-term dramas but on how the new ministers performed, and he had particularly high hopes for Damian Hinds and Matt Hancock. The latter had been promoted from Minister of State to become Culture Secretary, which gratified him a great deal, as it did his patron, George Osborne. No. 10 was glad, too, to appoint Karen Bradley to succeed Brokenshire at the sensitive Northern Ireland post, given the careful handling the DUP required. Most pleasing of all to May's team was the appointment of outsider Brandon Lewis to party chair. Seen as doing a good job as Immigration Minister, his non-public school, hands-on dynamism was just what was needed to supercharge the moribund party organisation. Lewis was delighted: 'I have to say it was a dream job. The Prime Minister was phenomenal to me, and let me run the party, never interfering, always backing me up and supporting me, always there when I needed her driving through the change.'[19] Lewis's impact on the party organisation, and in devising a much more strategic and competent party conference that autumn, was quickly felt.

Javid was a minor gainer, given the beefed-up title of Secretary of State for Housing, Communities and Local Government (HCLG), to reflect May's priority of addressing the housing crisis. Barwell had wanted to announce the change in title to HCLG at the party conference in 2017, but it was considered premature.

The reshuffle did little overall, though, to boost the position of women and ethnic minorities. Ardent Brexiteer Suella Braverman was the highest-profile BAME figure to be promoted, to junior minister at DExEU (resigning as chair of the ERG in the process). Among other women to be promoted, Caroline Nokes succeeded Lewis as Immigration Minister, while Claire Perry became Clean Growth and Energy Minister, also with the right to attend Cabinet. The changes only slightly improved the gender balance in Cabinet. At junior ministerial level, May tried to promote a young and diverse team of recently elected MPs, including Kemi Badenoch, who had spent part of her childhood in Nigeria, and James Cleverly, whose mother was from Sierra Leone.

May's biggest reshuffle can be seen as a microcosm of her entire premiership: constrained by parameters, with little wiggle room, and damaged by ministers refusing to follow her instructions or to hold their counsel from the press. The damage was initially done by the speculation and expectation aroused over the Christmas holiday, and by No. 10 failing to clear its lines beforehand. In the short term, the reception was negative. Key figures with ethnic minority backgrounds, like Nusrat Ghani, Rishi Sunak, Seema Kennedy and Bim Afolami, either stayed put or received low-level advancements. But the much deeper damage was that it showed the world May's inability to sack any minister and impose her will: coming on the heels of her minimalist June 2017 reshuffle, when she was unable to sack Hammond, Javid, Leadsom and Greening, the harm was immense. Openly mocked as 'embarrassing' by some of her MPs, it was characterised by a senior minister as 'the reshuffle that never was, it's bizarre. It just looks weak.'[20]

'Her shambolic reshuffle' was how the *Sunday Times* assessed it, stating that it had 'provoked fury by promoting only the youngest MPs, while thwarting the ambition of those in the middle ranks who might have been a greater threat to her'. One minister commented that, as a result, 'people are realising that she won't go of her own accord and will have to be forced out'.[21] Gavin Williamson, seen by elements in the press as one of May's preferred successors and still regarded as an éminence grise despite no longer being Chief Whip, took some blame for the failure to promote rising stars to favourable positions in which they could grow. They included Dominic Raab, Rory Stewart and Tom Tugendhat, the first two being handed challenging briefs (Housing and Prisons respectively) and the last receiving no promotion at all. For Liam Fox, 'the January 2018 reshuffle was the big turning point for her as Prime Minister. After it, ministers felt they could get away with openly defying her.'[22]

The reshuffle damaged Cabinet collegiality, too. From January 2018, as the Brexit negotiations began to impinge seriously upon Cabinet, it would break down altogether. Significant ballast was lost with McLoughlin's departure: he was 'the sheet anchor that held us together', according to one former Cabinet minister. Green was a very significant loss too, not least for his communication skills, though Lidington proved a successful replacement. ('I think my position became stronger over time: I played fair with people on all sides and my position emerged as stronger and stronger,' he comments.)[23] At different times, Gove, Hammond and Rudd played key roles trying to hold Cabinet together, as did Julian Smith and Brandon Lewis. Cabinet became steadily more leaky from early 2018 onwards. Cabinet ministers did not hesitate to place the blame for leaks on particular colleagues, with Liz Truss ('You could tell when she was responsible for a leak because she'd always be painted in a favourable light,' says one minister), Sajid Javid, Gavin Williamson and Boris Johnson regularly mentioned as 'the four big leakers'. Leadsom was seen as a leaker too, but mostly towards the end, when she became exasperated. With Gove, it was his team who were blamed for leaks. A senior official who sat in on Cabinet says, 'Leaking started slowly, but got gradually worse from the general election. From early 2018, it became a torrent. It became pointless for the Prime Minister to start a meeting with the words "please stop leaking" because it made no difference, it merely diminished her authority.'

Stories of leaking were legion. Geoffrey Cox said he didn't want to speak in Cabinet and read his comments in the papers tomorrow. Fox says he'd never seen anything like it in twenty-seven years in politics, and when on a trip to the US in October 2018, he learnt more about what was said in Cabinet in the media than in the official record.[24] The damage to May, the head of the leakiest Cabinet in history, is unquestionable.

Karen Bradley believes May lacked the authority a Prime Minister needs with Cabinet from the start. 'The damage had been done by David Cameron's suspension of Cabinet responsibility for the referendum. For the first few months, Nick and Fi, and Gavin as Chief Whip, kept a tight grip. But once it fell apart, she never recovered her authority.'[25]

MAY AND THE MEDIA

Not since Clement Attlee had there been a Prime Minister so out of tune with the way the media works. She was one of the least avid readers of newspapers and headlines of any Prime Minister in the modern era. Unlike many Prime Ministers, she would not look at the first editions before going to sleep. If back at the flat in time, she'd watch BBC One's *News at Ten*, but not *Newsnight* on BBC Two.

When she awoke, again unlike many PMs, she didn't listen to Radio 4's *Today* programme. She had all the papers in her outer office and would sometimes flick through. Only *The Times* and the *Daily Telegraph* were on her desk in the morning, and she read the latter less and less, raising her eyes upon seeing its regular pro-Boris spin. May would refer to *The Times* most often of all the newspapers. 'Every so often she'd try and catch us out by talking about something she saw in the business section of *The Times*,' says one of her team.

May enjoyed rockier relationships with the proprietors of major newspapers than most of her predecessors. She stayed well clear of the Barclay brothers, owners of the *Telegraph* titles, who she thought were – from very early on in her premiership – conducting a war against her in favour of Johnson. Some in her team considered the *Telegraph* to be a hollowed-out newspaper, a shadow of its former self, but they accepted that many Conservative voters read it, and that many ambitious Tory MPs saw it as the natural outlet to air their views. May's team made repeated attempts to persuade editors Chris Evans of the *Daily Telegraph* and Allister Heath of the *Sunday Telegraph* of the virtues of her Brexit deal, but they were repeatedly told that *Telegraph* readers didn't believe in it. Neither did she meet personally with Rupert Murdoch, who owned *The Times* and *The Sun*, nor with the Rothermeres, who owned the *Mail*.

Her strongest relationship with an editor was with Paul Dacre at the *Daily Mail*. She was less close personally to his successor, Geordie Greig, who took over in September 2018. She respected the *Financial Times*, as did Philip, and she would see editor Lionel Barber occasionally at the party conference, where she might also bump into John Witherow of *The Times* and Martin Ivens of the *Sunday Times*, neither of whom rated her highly. *The Times* was more supportive than the *Sunday Times*, though was often exasperated with her. The columnists most likely to give her a fair wind were Peter Oborne and Stephen

Glover in the *Daily Mail*, William Hague in the *Daily Telegraph* and Daniel Finkelstein in *The Times*, who would write sympathetically about her predicament and help with her PMQs briefings. She was close to *The Sun* and saw its editor, Tony Gallagher, several times. Right up until 29 March 2019, the paper remained supportive of her, helping her against even the ERG.

Until the end, May remained uncomfortable being interviewed by the press and broadcasting, though she would never decline if she thought it important to make her case. Emily Maitlis, who gave her the most excoriating interview of her premiership at the height of the Grenfell tragedy, was surprised by how inflexible her responses were.[26] On the radio, she was at her happiest being interviewed by Nick Ferrari on LBC, though even then, she was never fully at her ease. The contrast with her performances in the House of Commons, where she improved steadily over the three years, was stark. Robbie Gibb, director of communications for the last two years of her premiership, became progressively more exasperated by the media. He says:

> There was a very different narrative in Westminster to the rest of the country. For a period, I would say to the commentators and journalists, 'Have you ever spoken about the Prime Minister to people across the country, outside the bubble, and asked what they think?', but I would get nowhere.[27]

Gibb reserved much of his frustration for the BBC's comment (not its bulletins, which he thought fair), as had most holders of his position before him. But he accepts that May's own awkwardness in live interviews didn't help her cause:

> The Prime Minister stuck firmly to her script. The reason she did that is because she set so much store by getting the message absolutely right. She knew that if she was quoted out of context, it could

damage the work of the government or the Brexit negotiations. She never wanted to take a risk or let the side down. I know the journalists thought she was robotic and inflexible. But when she relaxed, she could be extremely good.[28]

The autumn lift-off had failed, and May's reshuffle in January 2018, one of the final weapons left in her locker, had backfired. She needed a success badly if she was to survive. The party wasn't yet ready to drop her, with no clear successor in the wings. But surviving because there is no one to succeed is never a good long-term strategy for a Prime Minister. Standing up to the DUP over the joint report in December 2017 had brought her short-term relief. As she entered 2018, her own survival, and the success of her project, whatever exactly that now was, flapped in the wind.

May proved a much more respected and adept figure on the world stage than many expected. Here, she addresses members of the media during a news conference at 10 Downing Street following air strikes in Syria, 14 April 2018.

CHAPTER 13

AUTHORITY REASSERTED: SALISBURY AND SYRIA

JANUARY–APRIL 2018

'**W**e'd had six months since June learning how to walk again after the general election fiasco, and there was a sense within No. 10 over the New Year that we now really needed to move on. It was now or never,' says one insider. The dawning of 2018 gave No. 10 a chance to put crisis management behind them and carve out a domestic policy beyond Brexit. May's New Year message promised that she would 'get on and deliver a good Brexit', but added, 'That is not the limit of our ambitions … The first step to a better future is getting a place at a good school … We will build more homes … And we will protect and enhance our natural environment for the next generation.'[1]

May appeared on *The Andrew Marr Show* on BBC One on Sunday 7 January to impart a sense of momentum. A wide range of speeches had been planned: on the environment (with her 25-year plan and initiatives on plastics), on housing, on the industrial strategy, and on higher, further and technical education. The speech she was unable to give was on the NHS, as she was still unable to extract the money from Hammond to make the announcement No. 10 wanted, though she did visit Frimley Park Hospital in Surrey on 4 January to signal a greater personal priority for health. Away-days were planned to galvanise thinking. On 22 February at Chequers, the focus was on domestic policy, while the Europe team in mid-January and again on 12 April went to Admiralty House to discuss planning for Phase 2 of Brexit – the future relationship.

TURNING POINT IN BEIJING: 30 JANUARY–2 FEBRUARY

May's first official trip to China had taken many months of hard graft and planning. It was delayed by the rebuff China felt at her pausing Hinkley Point in her first weeks as Prime Minister, and the deliberately cool attitude emanating from No. 10 towards China, chiefly from Nick Timothy, in direct contrast to Cameron and Osborne. In reality, she was no more suspicious of China than most of her predecessors as Prime Minister – Cameron had been the exception – but equally she was no natural Sinophile. She saw the importance of the relationship, especially regarding China–Britain trade post-Brexit. But when she arrived in Beijing, she was not in the happiest frame of mind, given the intense pressure she had faced in the previous two months. Liam Fox, who accompanied her to drum up trade, told broadcasters that 'her middle name is Resilience', urging backbench Tory MPs to witness what she was achieving on the world stage.[2]

In China, however, May was not able to achieve much. The Chinese government was in no mood to be helpful, especially after she sidestepped the Chinese push for a formal endorsement of its $900 billion Belt and Road Initiative. Her decision not to sign the memorandum of understanding soured the trip, as did her raising human rights in Hong Kong with President Xi. She was only able to announce some soft power initiatives, like an extension of an existing scheme to send British maths teachers to learn Chinese, and the sale of distribution rights to the BBC's series *Poldark*. Tame stuff, compared to Xi's visit to see Cameron in 2015, when deals were signed with a value of £40 billion. And scant return: May had with her the largest business delegation that her office had ever taken on a foreign trip. May's absence of momentum thus continued. But as James Slack, May's official spokesman, says:

> At the time, her trip to China was the moment her fortunes began to change for the better, if only for a few months. After the long and difficult autumn and winter, she hoped for a fresh start. Yet when she boarded the plane, I took her to speak to the journalists, and every question they asked her was about her survival. It was a real low point. But she built steadily from then.[3]

WOMEN IN POLITICS

Theresa May was only the second female Prime Minister in Britain out of fifty-four, and she took her role of advancing the position of women more deliberately than Thatcher. 2018 brought the 100th anniversary of women gaining the vote, providing an ideal platform for her. She had yet to recover from the party conference speech the previous October. On 13 November 2017, she had tried to give a resounding speech in favour of capitalism, taking the fight to Corbyn, but had struggled to find her authentic voice and escape the drafting by civil servants, so it had come across as wooden.

So, she wanted her two speeches on 6 February 2018, marking 100 years of women's suffrage, to set a new standard. She began the day in Manchester, where – with a nod to the suffragettes' colour – she wore purple as she made the case for why more women were needed in politics. 'For women, politics can be as much about listening and learning from others as it is about broadcasting your own views and opinions,' she said, perhaps with a subtler nod to her sparring Cabinet. She ended with a stirring image: 'Each day in Downing Street when I pass the framed portraits of my fifty-three predecessors, fifty-two of whom were men, I focus not on what I can say but on what I can do to make our country a better place.'

Later, at Westminster Hall, May stated:

I'm the 54th person to be Prime Minister of this country, but only the second to be a woman. Women make up half the population of this country, yet only a third of its MPs. I've long campaigned to get women into public life at all levels. It's not about appearances, or even just about giving women an equal chance to get on. I want to see more women in politics and government because greater female representation makes a real difference to everyone's lives. The same is true of … people from minority ethnic groups, members of the LGBT community, people with disabilities, or those from less privileged backgrounds. At last year's election, the proportion of MPs who were educated at comprehensive schools reached a record high, but it's still just 51 per cent.

Here was the authentic voice of May. These were the most passionate speeches she had made since her doorstep speech on 13 July 2016. It helped restore a sense of purpose – and gave her the confidence to continue.

SKRIPAL

No. 10 were banking on regaining initiative through progress on Brexit, domestic policy successes or an implosion by Labour. What May hadn't anticipated was a good crisis. Yet that is what she was about to experience. On Sunday 4 March, at 4.15 p.m., Wiltshire Police received a call from a member of the public concerned about the welfare of a younger woman and an older man in a park in Salisbury. Emergency services were called, and the two were promptly admitted to A&E at Salisbury District Hospital. Neither Sergei Skripal nor his daughter Yulia had any obvious sign of injury. Suspecting foul play, Wiltshire Police immediately began an investigation and the following day declared a major incident.

On Tuesday, the Metropolitan Police were called in and they decided that the case should be transferred to the National Counter Terrorism Policing Network. Samples from the victims' tissue were tested at Porton Down, the top-secret laboratory for testing chemical and biological weapons. On Wednesday, the Met revealed that the Skripals had been exposed to a nerve agent and that the incident was being treated as attempted murder. A police officer who had attended to them was in hospital suffering from the same ailment. Professor Dame Sally Davies, Britain's chief medical officer, said there was a low risk to the public, and May reassured the nation that Britain had world-leading emergency response teams well equipped to meet the challenge of chemical, biological and radiological attacks.

Home Secretary Amber Rudd then made a statement to the House of Commons on Thursday 8 March, saying, 'The use of a nerve agent on UK soil is a brazen and reckless act. This was attempted murder in the most cruel and public way. People are right to want to know who to hold to account.' But she stressed that it would be unwise to speculate about who the perpetrators might be, and that the police and investigating authorities should be allowed to examine the facts unhampered until it became completely clear who was responsible.

Behind the scenes, May was coming under pressure, in particular from her Foreign and Defence Secretaries, Johnson and Williamson, who favoured making an early and dramatic response against the likely country responsible: Russia. The incident was an important stage in May cementing her relationship further with Mark Sedwill, the National Security Advisor, whom she had brought in from the Home Office to fill the post in April 2017. The experience of Russian dissident Alexander Litvinenko in 2007 was high in the minds of the intelligence and security community. On that occasion, two assassins had put polonium into Litvinenko's tea. Prime Minister Gordon Brown had expelled four Russian diplomats in protest at Putin's refusal to extradite Andrei Lugovoi and Dmitri Kovtun, the two suspects, but Britain was considered to have acted prematurely. As one civil servant recalls, 'Whitehall has a folk memory that we had acted too early in the Litvinenko case, before we had the full facts.' The ever-meticulous May wanted to be certain that she knew where they stood before they acted. Working with Mark Sedwill and his deputy, Christian Turner, she handled it, in Rudd's eyes, 'with great confidence and skill'.[4]

The weekend of 10–11 March saw intense work behind the scenes while the intelligence services and government scientists examined the nerve agent. On Monday 12 March, May chaired a meeting of the National Security Council, before telling the House of Commons that it now seemed 'highly likely' that Russia was responsible for the poisoning of Sergei Skripal, a former Russian military officer and double agent, and his daughter Yulia, and that Britain would not tolerate such a 'brazen attempt to murder innocent civilians on our soil'. She said they had been targeted by a 'military grade nerve agent of a type developed by Russia', describing it as an 'indiscriminate and reckless act against the United Kingdom'. The Foreign Secretary, she said, would be summoning the Russian Ambassador to demand an explanation by the end of the following day.

The Russian government immediately hit back, calling May's remarks a 'provocation' and describing the event as a 'circus show in the British Parliament'. Lugovoi, one of the two men accused of assassinating Litvinenko, now a Member of Parliament in Russia, described May's response as 'at a minimum, irresponsible'.[5] May said there could be just two plausible explanations: 'Either this was a direct act by the Russian state ... or the Russian government lost control of their potentially catastrophically damaging nerve agent and allowed it to get into the hands of others.' May was in no mood to equivocate, describing the attack in Salisbury as coming against 'a backdrop of a well-established pattern of Russian state aggression', listing the annexation of Crimea, cyber espionage, meddling in elections and the killing of dissidents outside Russia. She went on, 'Should there be no credible response [by Wednesday], we will conclude that this action amounts to an unlawful use of force by the Russian state against the United Kingdom.'

Corbyn found himself in an awkward position. He described the attack as 'deeply alarming', before cautioning against a complete break-down with Moscow: 'We need to continue seeking a robust dialogue with Russia on all the issues ... currently dividing our countries.' May's stronger statement received praise from across the House of Commons. She delivered her strongest performance in Parliament that Wednesday, after PMQs. Speaking slowly and deliberately, she said:

> Mr Skripal and his daughter were poisoned with Novichok – a mili-tary grade nerve agent developed by Russia. Based on this capability, combined with Russia's record of conducting state-sponsored assassi-nations – including against former intelligence officers whom it regards as legitimate targets – the UK government concluded it was highly likely that Russia was responsible for this reckless and despicable act ...
>
> The Russian government have provided no credible explanation that could suggest that they lost control of their nerve agent, no explanation as to how this agent came to be used in the United Kingdom, and no explanation as to why Russia has an undeclared chemical weapons programme in contravention of international law. Instead it has treated the use of a military grade nerve agent in Europe with sarcasm, contempt and defiance.
>
> There is no alternative conclusion other than that the Russian state was culpable for the attempted murder of Mr Skripal and his daughter and for threatening the lives of other British citizens in Salisbury, including Detective Sergeant Nick Bailey.

At the National Security Council that morning, it was agreed that im-mediate action should be taken to dismantle the Russian spy network in the UK, to ensure that those seeking to carry out such actions could not enter the UK. High-level contacts between the UK and the Russian Federation were to be suspended. Twenty-three Russian diplomats who had been identified as undeclared intelligence officers were required to leave within one week, the biggest expulsion for over thirty years, with May saying the ejection would 'fundamentally degrade Russian intelligence capability in the UK for years to come'.

Behind the scenes, a major international effort was taking place, with May, No. 10 and the National Security Council in the lead. Security and the defence of the country were the domains where May was at her most comfortable and her emotions most strongly engaged. Talking to her officials after a disappointing response at the Foreign Affairs Council on Monday 12 March, they decided that she would need international support to put pressure on Putin, and that meant harder evidence. Officials declassified a dossier the following day to share with allies. While Sedwill went to Brussels to lobby NATO (which eventually bore fruit), May hit the phones.

By the end of the week, she had called Trump, Merkel, Macron and Trudeau. When she spoke to them, the full picture was still not completely clear, so her opposite numbers had to take a certain amount on trust. She briefed them on what she knew and what had already been established by British intelligence, what her expectations of the Russians would be and what actions she would take if the Russians did not respond. 'We believe this to be in our national interest,' she told the leaders. 'I'm sure you'll want to do what's in your national interest too.'

Trump was not happy. Indeed, insiders described it as 'easily her worst call ever with the President'. He was particularly negative about Merkel, whom he disliked, and bleated about how no one in Europe pays their way. May's team were left wondering if they'd be able to count on him. Building a coalition of support against Putin was still far from certain. However, by the time she spoke to Hungarian President Viktor Orbán and others the following week, the picture was becoming clearer. An internal debate took place over whether she should speak to Putin himself, but the verdict was that there would be little value in doing so and some risk of worsening her position.

It was Putin's misfortune that an EU Council opened on Thursday 22 March, at the height of the crisis, which gave May the opportunity to build support among her fellow EU leaders. May felt sure of her ground when she arrived in Brussels on the Thursday evening with an official who carried a locked briefcase containing the details of Russian culpability. 'Russia staged a brazen and reckless attack against the United Kingdom,' she told her fellow leaders on arrival. 'It's clear the Russian threat does not respect borders and indeed the incident at Salisbury was part of a pattern of Russian aggression against Europe and its near neighbours.'[6]

May began a systematic lobbying exercise, choreographed with great care. She started with the Baltic States, who were the most anxious about Russian intentions, and soon gained their agreement. She then spoke to Merkel and Macron, knowing both might be difficult, for different reasons. She appealed to Macron's vanity, but also to his genuine horror of terrorism. He was an increasingly influential force in the EU, and he concluded their talk by saying, 'We have to be with you at your side on this.' Merkel took her lead from Macron. In her private bilateral, she said, 'We need to show you solidarity as well.' In the view of one insider, 'These words were absolutely critical in allowing us to get the rest of the Europeans to get on board too.' By dinner, May had nine onside, and after working in the Council chamber through the night, she had eighteen with her by 5 a.m.

More work was required to convince the more dovish states, Greece, Slovakia, Hungary and Bulgaria, that the EU could roundly blame Russia for the attack. Putin was keeping up intense pressure on those states, and targeted Boris Johnson for comparing Russia's hosting of the FIFA World Cup in the summer of 2018 with Hitler's hosting of the Olympics in Berlin in 1936. However, before they left on Friday, EU leaders declared unanimously, 'We stand in unqualified solidarity with the United Kingdom in the face of this grave challenge to our shared security.'[7] Some even considered taking their own action in expelling Russian diplomats.

On Friday, the White House was told the EU were all on board: 'That was what was needed to get Trump onside,' says a No. 10 aide. May announced early the following week in the House of Commons that the response from the EU had exceeded her own hopes. Over 100 Russian diplomats across the EU were told to return to Moscow in a coordinated response to its use of chemical weapons. May said it was 'the largest collective expulsion of Russian intelligence officers in history', adding:

I have found great solidarity from our friends and partners in the EU, North America, NATO and beyond over the past three weeks … Together we have sent a message that we will not tolerate Russia's continued attempts to flout international law and undermine our values… If the Kremlin's goal is to divide and intimidate the western alliance, its efforts have spectacularly backfired.

Germany, France and Poland each decided to expel four Russian diplomats with intelligence backgrounds, while other states expelled fewer numbers, and the US ordered the expulsion of sixty Russian officials.

It marked the high point of May's success as Prime Minister. Stephen Bush of the *New Statesman* described it as

unquestionably a diplomatic coup for Theresa May … It is impressive even to have got this far, given the diplomatic constraints the UK operates under. It adds to the growing mood at Westminster that the PM might have got her groove back … If she can get a good Brexit deal, there will be no real pretext to get rid of her. Another defensive reshuffle in which no plausible better candidate emerges and you can just see how she might end up fighting the next election after all.[8]

Praise was almost unanimous across the UK and the international media. It was not a foregone conclusion that she would have played it well. But she listened carefully to her advisors, particularly Sedwill, refused to act precipitously, was in command of all the detail and had a compelling case to put to the world leaders on the phone and in person. Most strikingly, she knew the subject better than any politician on either side of the House, and she commanded authority. The question now was: could she maintain this momentum?

SYRIA: APRIL–JULY

On Sunday 8 April, news came into No. 10 that dozens of innocent citizens had been killed in a suspected gas attack in a rebel-held area of Douma near Damascus. The gas, at the time believed to be chlorine, had been dropped on homes and makeshift bomb shelters that evening. Photographs and videos taken inside hospitals and houses showed images of children foaming at the mouth.[9] May was shocked when she heard about the use of chlorine against civilians, who were hiding in cellars, unable to escape. Much as Cameron had been when news of chemical weapons attacks in Syria first emerged in August 2013, she was physically and morally sickened by the details of the inhumanity and deliberate cruelty. Numbers said to have been killed varied between forty and fifty, many of them children, with up to 500 severely affected. It was the deadliest chemical attack in Syria since sarin had been dropped on Khan Shaykhun in April 2017, killing more than eighty. That episode had prompted the US to fire Cruise missiles at the airbase used to launch the attack.

Trump was quick to respond to the latest attack on Twitter, calling Assad an 'animal' and condemning Russia and Iran for their support for the regime. Johnson leapt onto the airwaves to say it was 'deeply disturbing ... Those responsible for the use of chemical weapons have lost all moral integrity and must be held to account.'[10] This placed May under immediate pressure to take a strong stance, especially as reports began emerging that Macron was 'egging on' Trump and that, unlike the French President, May had been unable to speak to Trump himself.[11]

Frantic efforts took place between London and Washington to calm the President down, and to prevent the situation escalating unstoppably towards armed conflict. US Defense Secretary James Mattis was a key figure, warning Trump of the risks and telling him to scale down the rhetoric. At the UN in New York, the Russian envoy claimed that the atrocity was 'fake news', designed to distract the world's attention away from the Salisbury nerve attack, which Britain had 'muddled up'. Ratcheting up the pressure on May, Johnson spoke to his counterparts in France and the US, seeking to keep Britain in the running for joint military action. While visiting Scandinavia, May urged caution, conscious of Britain's position as a guarantor of international law. 'It took a full forty-eight hours for the true picture to clarify about what had really happened,' says an insider. On Wednesday 11 April, Trump warned Assad and Russia that he had 'nice and new and smart' missiles which 'will be coming'.[12]

Cabinet was divided by the prospect of military action. Those demanding a strong intervention included Matt Hancock and David Gauke, while Gove, a strong advocate for military intervention against Syria in August 2013, played a more passive role.[13] On the other side, Davis and McVey were among those who wanted May to make the case for military action in Parliament. The Commons was not due to return until Monday 16 April. May's team debated whether she should recall Parliament, as Cameron had done in August 2013. Advice was received that 'the Prime Minister had reserved power to take such action' and the very urgency demanded a quick decision without resorting to Parliament. But would that be enough to convince her colleagues? Memories of August 2013 were still very fresh in everyone's mind, in which Cameron suffered a humiliating loss in the House of Commons to Miliband's Labour over the government motion for intervention in Syria. May would be open to attack for slavishly following Trump, at the height of his unpopularity in Britain, if she did support the American attack, and would be accused of letting down the special relationship and appearing weak if she didn't.

The evidence, which had not solidified, was presented to Cabinet on 11 April by Charles Farr, chair of the Joint Intelligence Committee, and Mark Sedwill. Attorney General Jeremy Wright advised that a strike on a plant used in the production of chemical weapons would be legal on humanitarian grounds.[14] May stressed the need for secrecy, given that service lives were at risk, and revealed that military strikes were likely to take place that Friday or Saturday. Cabinet listened and, for once, didn't leak. Ministers criticised Trump's pugilistic tweets as 'unhelpful', making it easier for Putin to paint the West as the aggressor, and for Corbyn to claim that she was in a rush to war as a poodle of the President, much as Blair had been accused of being Bush's poodle during the Iraq War. May told Cabinet that the decision over whether to recall Parliament would be taken the next day. On Thursday, she spoke to Trump to discuss the planned airstrike. He was visibly more subdued than earlier in the week and told her, 'We're going to do it and we're going to do it well.'[15] Listening in to the call, aides detected a nervousness from him when faced by the actual prospect of putting American lives, and lives of those on the ground, at risk, a nervousness that was evident again in June 2019 when he pulled back from airstrikes in Iran.

After a ring-round of MPs by the Chief Whip, May decided that she would authorise action without a recall of Parliament. Anxiety ran high: 'If it all goes wrong and the Russians bomb Cyprus, or use nerve gas against a British expat in Paris, or launch a cyber-attack that disrupts the NHS, it will be down to the PM and she will have to go,' said one Tory backbencher. 'If Parliament has voted for it, we are all culpable. If [not], it's all on her.'[16]

Friday 13 April was decision day, and due to operational security,

May banned ministers from giving broadcast interviews. A No. 10 aide said, 'She was adamant that we had to give our boys the best chance of getting in and out in one piece.'[17] At 5 p.m., May and Williamson spoke on a secure line to confirm targets, and she then went to Chequers, where, at 11 p.m., she recorded a video announcing her decision, to be broadcast at 2.10 a.m. on Saturday 14 April. At midnight, she called Corbyn, the Lib Dem leader Vince Cable, and her two immediate Tory predecessors as PM, Cameron and Major, to talk them through her decision. Throughout the evening and night, she spoke to fifteen world leaders, finishing the marathon at midday on Saturday.

In the early hours of Saturday, four RAF Tornado GR4 aircraft, each armed with two Storm Shadow Cruise missiles, took off from the Akrotiri base in Cyprus and entered Syrian airspace. They launched their attacks on a facility fifteen miles west of Homs, which had been identified by intelligence as the place where the Assad regime housed its chemical weapons. Williamson wrote in the *Sunday Times* that 'history teaches us to defend the global rules that keep us safe and that failure to do so has grave consequences'.[18]

May was back at No. 10 by 7 a.m. on Saturday morning, and emerged into Downing Street to say that the 'co-ordinated and targeted strikes' had taken place to degrade Syria's ability to make chemical weapons and deter their future use. 'This collective action sends a clear message that the international community will not stand by and tolerate the use of chemical weapons ... We cannot allow the use of chemical weapons to become normalised – either within Syria, on the streets of the UK or elsewhere.' Mindful of claims made in the recent past about Iraq, she said that the government had judged it 'highly likely' that Syria had used chemical weapons, and that it was 'clear' that the Assad regime was responsible for the attack on civilians on 7 April. 'No other group could have carried out the attack,' she said, taking pains to stress that Britain's action was 'not about interfering in a civil war and ... not about regime change'.

May emerged strongly from the events of those two weeks. She avoided the crude triumphalism of Trump, who tweeted, 'Mission accomplished!' on 14 April, a gauche echo of the words of George W. Bush's premature declaration of victory after the first phase of the Iraq War. The President had often seemed distracted by attacking the 'slime ball' former FBI director James Comey over his memoirs, rather than focusing on Syria.

It was May's gravest test as a foreign leader and one where her painstaking, methodical handling of the data and arguments paid off. When she made her statement on Monday 16 April, she dealt firmly with concerns from MPs, justifying her decision to authorise action without recalling Parliament, and refusing to give the Commons a retrospective vote. Chocolate for her diabetes had to be smuggled into the Chamber as she answered MPs' questions for over three hours. She did not finish until 10 p.m., when she returned to No. 10 to catch up on her overflowing red box. The next day, Windrush exploded.

CORBYN LOSES THE INITIATIVE

The Salisbury and Syria crises shifted national politics onto more favourable terrain for May, bringing an end to arguably the strongest period of Corbyn's leadership. Since becoming Prime Minister in July 2016, May had enjoyed popularity ratings way above Corbyn, who slipped steadily in the polls from July 2016 to April 2017. But from the moment she called the early election until June 2017, Corbyn's ratings soared while May's fell. He remained comfortably ahead of her, albeit falling slightly until September, when the successful Labour Party conference contrasted with her own poor performance at Manchester the following week. He maintained a significant gap over her until February 2018. During the spring of 2018, however, May became the more popular leader, with a ten-point net favourability lead over

Corbyn in April. Corbyn's response to the poisoning of the Skripals in early March, and criticism from prominent Labour figures of his standing up for Russia, were significant factors in his decline – whereas 61 per cent thought May had done a 'good job' handling the UK's relations with Russia. The *New Statesman* noted that Corbyn always fared badly when there were questions of national security and defence, a particular strength of May's.[19] According to YouGov, 53 per cent of Britons thought that May had handled the Salisbury crisis well, whereas only 18 per cent said the same about Corbyn.[20]

Two weeks later, Labour's antisemitism row erupted, prompted by Corbyn's comments on an allegedly antisemitic mural in 2012. It brought the issue back into the public eye at the very time when Corbyn's judgement and fallibility were being questioned again. The first major episode in Labour's antisemitism row under Corbyn occurred when it came to light that, before she became an MP for Bradford West, Naz Shah had shared a graphic showing Israel superimposed on a map of the US under the headline 'Solution For Israel–Palestine Conflict: Relocate Israel To The United States'. Underneath the image she had commented, 'Problem solved.' The same month, March 2016, long-term Corbyn supporter Ken Livingstone was suspended from the party's membership after making incendiary comments about Hitler and Zionism. This resulted in the establishment of the Chakrabarti Inquiry, which in June 2016 found that Labour was 'not overrun by antisemitism, Islamophobia, or other forms of racism'.

But allegations of antisemitism continued to plague Corbyn's leadership, and he was never able to free himself from suggestions that his dislike of the state of Israel bled into antisemitism. A YouGov poll in early 2018 found that only 15 per cent of Britons felt that Corbyn had handled the issue of antisemitism well, compared with 46 per cent who believed he had handled it badly.[21] By mid-April, a YouGov poll was placing the Conservatives and Labour neck and neck on 40 per cent each. The negative image of Corbyn was feeding through into the popularity of the party, with Labour's net popularity score falling from -8 in January to -17 three months later. The same poll found that while 26 per cent of people asked thought that Corbyn would make the best Prime Minister, 37 per cent said May (and 37 per cent 'don't know').[22] Suddenly, May looked like a winner again. Her many critics in the parliamentary Conservative Party began to view her in a new light. The 'Oh, Jeremy Corbyn' chant of Glastonbury in June 2017 started to seem a long time ago. In spring 2018, momentum was now, once again, with May.

NHS LONG TERM PLAN: JANUARY–JULY 2018

Even amid her foreign policy achievements in the New Year, May knew she needed a big domestic policy success to prove her purpose. The challenge was where and how. She was blocked on schools as, according to the new Education Secretary, Damian Hinds, 'everything was defined by implementing the Gove reforms'. There was no question of her doing anything radical in schools that would require more money or legislation.[23] She had the review of universities in train, but that was all No. 10 could do on education. She'd made her push on housing in her party conference speech and Autumn Budget, while social care was dead in the water after the manifesto debacle. May had already made her play on the environment, while her industrial strategy was blocked in BEIS. So that left just health.

May always maintained that the party had got itself into a 'ridiculous position' on the NHS. Lynton Crosby had decreed in the 2015 and 2017 general elections that it couldn't be talked about, and her first financial event as PM, the 2016 Autumn Statement, had been silent on the NHS. A plan to announce an inquiry into the NHS at the end of her speech, similar to the inquiry on HE, had been overruled by the Treasury. May wanted to break out but didn't know how. The NHS five-year plan – or 'Five Year Forward View' – was approaching its final stage, and many NHS leaders, including Simon Stevens, felt it was already obsolete. She'd been sceptical at the time of the November 2017 Budget about further spending on the NHS without the promise of reform, which is why only £2.4 billion was granted, rather than the £4 billion figure that some of her advisors suggested.

But in late 2017, her thinking began to change. NHS topped the polling on the public's political priorities, and May knew that – with the winter months ahead – the NHS's performance was bound to come under scrutiny. Corbyn's pressure – despite his poor polling – was hurting the government. The NHS's upcoming seventieth anniversary in July would only attract more attention and public affection, and May did not want to find herself on the wrong side of the national mood.

In October 2017, before the Budget, Penn had written a note to May about what it would take to get onto the front foot on the issue of the NHS. On 8 November, May had met with Hunt and Hammond to review spending for the following year. By Christmas 2017, plans were coming into shape – not to unpick the still controversial Lansley reforms head-on, but to secure the NHS's future funding and incremental reform. James Kent, the former doctor and NHS lead in the Policy Unit, was the key figure, with Penn, Alex Dawson and James Marshall strong advocates. Sarah Wollaston, the Conservative MP who chaired the Health Select Committee in the Commons, began to call for a Royal Commission, which scared No. 10 – and, for different reasons, No. 11 – witless, not least the prospect of ceding the initiative to Parliament. The realisation began to dawn that unless spending increased, per capita spending would fall in real terms.

On 7 February 2018, Hammond and Hunt came to May's office in the House of Commons, where Dawson presented them with polling evidence to show that the public regarded the NHS as second only to the monarch as a source of national pride and would be prepared to pay extra taxes to fund improvements in it.[24] Jeremy Heywood, sensing he had been overly mean in the autumn in arguing against more spending, set up a group in the Cabinet Office to look at the minimum funding the NHS would need over the following five years, reporting to May, Hammond and Hunt on 8 March with a recommended figure of 3.04 per cent in real-terms growth. Suddenly the NHS was becoming the top domestic priority, with much legwork done by special advisors, Duncan McCourt and Tim Pitt reporting to Hammond, and Ed Jones to Hunt. They helped bring Hammond onside. As James Marshall puts it, 'It had taken five months of intense struggle to convince him from November to April.'[25] The pressure for a long-term settlement to allow the NHS to plan ahead with a degree of confidence was becoming overwhelming, not least from the influential health think tanks. Rather than being regarded as bowing to pressure to increase spending, why not seize the initiative? May began to realise that she could reform the NHS in the same way that she had driven through reform of the police force. A No. 10 source says, 'By this time, the PM started to think that the NHS leadership needed to be treated in the same way as the police: it needed reform to become much more biddable.'

May spoke passionately about the NHS on 17 March at the Conservative spring forum, emphasising how much it meant to her. 'I rely on the NHS every day, and I'm eternally grateful to them,' she told delegates, adding that, along with all Tories, she cared deeply about public services.[26] She reminded her audience that the Conservative Party created the modern police force, county councils and universal schooling, and while Labour may have created the NHS seventy years before, 'Conservatives backed its key principles then and have supported them ever since'. She spoke about her personal appreciation for the service, saying, 'When I was diagnosed with diabetes, the NHS was there for me. Skilled and compassionate, helping me every step of the way to manage my condition and live a normal life.'

Later that month, May appeared on the Liaison Committee, where she declared her intention to reform NHS funding. In the war with No. 11, May's team hail this as a decisive moment: finally, they found themselves on the front foot. 'For the NHS to plan and manage effectively, we need to get away from those annual top-ups of the budget,' she said. 'We do need to have a sustainable, long-term plan that should build on the work of the Five Year Forward View – but we should look beyond it to a plan that allows the NHS to realise greater productivity, to realise efficiency gains.'[27] This language was deliberately designed to chime with Stevens, whose legacy was the Five Fear Forward View, and to steer clear of anything that sounded like Lansley. But May's announcement was clever in a second sense. She stressed that the NHS reforms should be 'clinically led and locally supported' – increasing both the freedom and responsibility of NHS officials for whatever happened next. 'Essentially, we were trying to increase the agency for the NHS around the plan – if they fully owned it then we could hold them to account for delivery,' a No. 10 insider says.

May's pronouncement played well in the press. The message was given out that May was planning to plough 'billions of extra pounds a year' into health spending as part of the 'birthday present' to mark the anniversary. Boris Johnson proved a useful ally, anxious to show that the Vote Leave pledge of £350 million a week diverted to the NHS was not an idle promise. On 25 May, Hunt backed up her words with a plan to train more than 3,000 extra midwives over the following four years and to bring down A&E waiting times, which were the worst on record. The media was briefed that May would be making the NHS the 'centrepiece' of her strategy over the following year, demonstrating that the government had a dynamic domestic agenda post-Brexit.

By mid-June, the long struggle with the Treasury was over. Hammond had held out for a three-year settlement but came to accept that it would be five. On 17 June, May announced an extra £20 billion a year in real terms by 2023/24 as a '70th birthday present' for the NHS,[28] which according to No. 10 was the biggest fiscal event outside of the Budget that the country had seen. It meant that the £114 billion annual budget would rise by 3.4 per cent annually, albeit less than the

3.7 per cent average since its founding in 1948. May provoked criticism when she said it would be funded in part by a 'Brexit dividend', but also suggested that an increase in taxes might be necessary. Paul Johnson of the Institute for Fiscal Studies tweeted that 'there is no Brexit dividend', while Sarah Wollaston described the idea as 'tosh'.[29] The announcement also meant extra money would be available for Scotland, Wales and Northern Ireland. Speaking to Andrew Marr on BBC One from Chequers the day before her speech at London's Royal Free Hospital, May acknowledged that pressure on the NHS had been growing, but said her plan would be about 'securing its future'. She said, 'We're going to ensure there's a ten-year plan for the NHS. It will be a plan for world-class healthcare – more doctors, more nurses. It means extra money, significantly more money, going into the NHS.' It was a real achievement that owed much to May's personal push in the face of detractors. It also marked her greatest personal victory over Hammond in her long, difficult battle with the Chancellor. Hunt then went off on a tour of the country, exploiting the breakdown of collective responsibility that would come as a result of internal Brexit disagreements to highlight, not unfairly, his own role in securing the plan.

The NHS Long Term Plan was published on 7 January 2019, setting out priorities for healthcare over the following ten years. It marked the official abandonment of the policy of competition in NHS England, which had been established in the Health Act 2012 – and, on the whole, it was well received by the press and the health sector. The plan moved resources out of hospitals into community services and primary care, in particular to improve mental health through support in schools and 24-hour access to mental health teams. The main disease priorities it named were cancer, cardiovascular disease, stroke, diabetes and respiratory disease, with particular emphasis on digital access.

For a brief moment, it gave the government respite from Brexit

– although not without criticism. Negative responses to the plan focused on the overall 3.4 per cent increase, which was not just below the historic trend, but below that in many developed countries, where spending has been rising by 4 per cent a year. It was criticised too for failing to address the shortage of clinicians, and for unclear prioritising of objectives. A solution to the long-term problem of social care was also left hanging. Heywood, who had worked hard on the plan before the 2017 general election (not without reservations), continued to chair meetings on social care, but he knew his own plan was dead: Ben Gummer, the principal protagonist, had lost his seat. It was one of many long-term problems May bequeathed her successor. But the plan brought the NHS more stability. Significantly, May's most noteworthy domestic policy achievement had not been mentioned in the 2017 manifesto.

TWO DEPARTURES

On 25 June 2018, Heywood took his leave from his office owing to illness, with an official bulletin saying he would temporarily stand down but would return after the summer holiday. Heywood remained in constant touch with the office, sending emails at almost the same rate as when fully fit. However, in October it was announced that he would be standing down altogether. On 4 November, he passed away.

Gavin Barwell describes Heywood's loss as 'catastrophic both for his family and for the country', saying, 'In domestic policy, he helped us bind departments together, giving us strength standing up to the Treasury. It couldn't have come at a worse time.'[30] Heywood had indeed given 'equality of arms' to No. 10, with a unique ability to giving opposing sides at least a sense of equal opportunity. The NHS Long Term Plan was one of his final achievements. He knew the Treasury inside out and could always out-argue it. The civil service missed him too: he took his role as head of the civil service seriously, investing enormous intellectual energy, clarity and firepower into it, as well as being its fiercest champion. No single official missed him more than Olly Robbins, who came under increasing attack, Heywood had thought wholly unfairly, from Brexiteers. Unable to answer back, Robbins had been given cover by Heywood. After Heywood stepped down to undergo treatment, Mark Sedwill stepped up to the mark, initially as temporary successor and then full-time, without civil service competition given the unusual circumstances. Sedwill's expertise was in security and diplomacy, and his impact as National Security Advisor was felt with the Skripal and Syria cases two months before he became Acting Cabinet Secretary. May knew and trusted Sedwill from when he had been her Permanent Secretary at the Home Office: no other Permanent Secretary had his authority or confidence. Heywood had wanted him as his successor, but, as we shall see, not everyone in the senior Conservative circles felt similarly.

Shortly before this, May had lost another loyal figure, when Amber Rudd resigned in the wake of the Windrush scandal that April. Rudd had stood squarely behind May since her appointment as May's successor at the Home Office in July 2016. While not uncritical of some of May's policies and methods, Rudd was a loyalist, a supporter of the Prime Minister on Brexit (despite being a Remainer and often siding with Hammond and Clark), and she was an admirer of her, particularly on terrorism:

She was fantastic on counter-terrorism, the first Prime Minister to take such an interest in security briefs, incredible throughout on security matters. She was very supportive of me on tough decisions. She understood all the details and what we were up against. After the Manchester terrorist attack in May 2017, the level of terrorist activity escalated. She was with me all the time.[31]

On 18 April, the Windrush scandal exploded, puncturing the buoyancy in No. 10 from successes over Salisbury and Syria. The Windrush generation – named after the *Empire Windrush*, which landed at Tilbury Docks, Essex, in 1948 – immigrated to the UK from Caribbean countries in the two decades following the Second World War, responding to Britain's post-war labour shortage. In 1971, Commonwealth citizens already living in the UK were given indefinite leave to remain. In 2018, however, when faced with the government's 'hostile environment' policy towards illegal immigration, they struggled to prove their legal status. Tens of thousands of the Windrush generation were thought to lack documentation, particularly those who had travelled as children, although many had lived and worked in the UK for decades.[32] As documentation of their legal status was not kept by the government, and the landing cards belonging to the migrants were destroyed by the Home Office in 2010, they found themselves in the crossfire, sparking a public outcry.

May supported Rudd during ten days of intensive probing by Labour and the media. The attacks built to a crescendo during the week beginning Monday 23 April. May spoke to Rudd that Friday and encouraged her not to leave. Rudd admits that she was completely wrong-footed by the fury of the attacks on the government's immigration policy, which vented pent-up frustration, not least with May's very restrictive immigration policies since she had taken over as Home Secretary in 2010. 'I was slow, to be honest, to realise the extent of the problem, as were No. 10, who hadn't wanted me to make a statement. I'd never encountered anything like this before.'[33]

Rudd told May she'd think about her future over the weekend, but after the hostility of the papers on the Saturday and Sunday, which repeatedly challenged her over her role in the treatment of the Windrush-generation migrants, she decided on Sunday that she would have to go. 'Are you sure you want to do this?' May asked her. Rudd recalls that May was 'very kind and thoughtful', adding, 'I was not cross with her, I didn't blame her. The whole hostile environment had built up until it had become impossible.'[34] Rudd announced her resignation on the Sunday evening. Losing the second most powerful woman in Cabinet was a blow, not least after three months of steady progress, but May took it stoically, as she always did.

The next day she announced the appointment of Sajid Javid, the son of Pakistani Muslim parents, to the role of Home Secretary, an appointment designed in part to show critics that the government was aware of how damaging the issue had been for community and BAME relations, and for trust in the immigration system. The mini-reshuffle was smartly executed, with Brokenshire, who had recovered from the removal of his tumour, coming into Javid's job at Housing, while International Development Secretary Penny Mordaunt took over the role of Minister for Women and Equalities from Rudd.

Javid's arrival marked a change at the Home Office. While Rudd had been content to follow many of the policies that had been outlined by May herself between 2010 and 2016, Javid wanted to take the Home Office in a wholly new direction. More immediately, his appointment changed the balance within the key Cabinet Brexit Strategy and Negotiation Committee, tilting it in favour of the hard Leavers. His arrival made a difference within three days, at one of the ugliest and most acrimonious ministerial meetings of the entire Brexit saga, which might never have occurred had Rudd still been Home Secretary.

That conflict, more than any other single event, ended the short months of May's newly acquired authority. Poison had helped kick it off; a different kind of poison helped kill it off.

Theresa May's Cabinet meet at her Chequers country retreat to discuss Brexit, 6 July 2018.

CHAPTER 14

CHEQUERS: JOURNEY INTO OBSCURITY
JANUARY–JULY 2018

2018 had begun full of promise for May on Brexit. The joint report of December 2017 felt to May's team like a 'big moment which allowed us at last to move forward, with the nightmare of sequencing and budget discussions over, into Phase 2'. Cabinet remained relatively united, and leaking was not yet at industrial levels. The country was still supportive of the two main parties, backing either Corbyn's Labour Party or May's Conservatives, with UKIP in the wilderness and the Brexit Party not even a twinkle in Nigel Farage's eye. Brussels had barely begun to bare its teeth. A quiet sense of optimism was in the air. May just needed to confirm her deal with the EU, get it past Cabinet and Parliament, and Britain would be out of Europe and she could start her domestic premiership in earnest.

It had been eighteen months since the June 2016 referendum, but few questioned that Britain was on an orderly course for departure in fifteen months' time. The first six months of 2018, however, saw the realisation dawn for many in Cabinet and the Conservative Party that Brexit would not be easy, that the platitudes the Brexiteers had allowed themselves to believe were just that, that the December joint report had been a fudge, and that the question of Northern Ireland presented almost impossible choices – choices that May would have trouble communicating, let alone confronting.

Not until the end of February, when the EU translated the Northern Ireland section of the joint report into legal language, did MPs at large begin to wake up to the full significance of the backstop, and, for the first time since the referendum result, the tone in Westminster began to turn seriously ugly.

THREE FRACTIOUS MONTHS: JANUARY–MARCH 2018

The expectation in No. 10 in January was that the EU would let the government move straight on to Phase 2. But three months of bitter haggling ensued until the March Council. An excited group of No. 10 staff went to Admiralty House for an away-day in January, with the purpose of working out what the joint report meant in practice and what their vision for the future British relationship with the EU might look like. May stuck by her determination to reject the EU's models of a future relationship, including Canada, EEA and EFTA. To Oliver Letwin, it was a 'fatal error' for the government to refuse to accept Barnier's judgement 'that any bespoke model Britain might come up with which would create frictionless trade from the outset would not be workable'.[1] 'They have to realise there won't be any cherry-picking,' Barnier told *Prospect* in December 2017.

A debate did take place within Whitehall on whether the government should produce its own text on the backstop or Northern Ireland protocol. Political advice favoured publication, but civil service advice did not, and the latter won the day.

Attention focused instead on clearing up all remaining impediments to moving onto Phase 2, including outstanding issues on the financial settlement, citizens' rights and a solution on Northern Ireland. Paragraph 49 of the joint report had laid the last of these out with great clarity – 'The

United Kingdom remains committed to protecting North–South cooperation and to its guarantee of avoiding a hard border' – while Paragraph 50 said the government 'will ensure that no new regulatory barriers develop between Northern Ireland and the rest of the United Kingdom', and it would continue to enjoy 'the same unfettered access' to the whole of the UK. Politicians who'd never given the intricacies of Brexit much thought were beginning to realise that there were only three options for the border between Northern Ireland and the Republic. First, a bespoke arrangement for Northern Ireland, creating in effect a set of barriers in the Irish Sea; second, regulatory and customs alignment for the whole of the United Kingdom; and third, a hard border, which would entail physical infrastructure along the entire Irish border.

January saw tempers flare on other topics, too, including the implementation period post-Brexit. Some Brexiteer ministers flatly denied that any implementation was needed. Conscious of the growing power and disquiet of her right wing, May sat impatiently while officials explained to her the risks of leaving without any transition period. She hadn't fully factored it in and had to be persuaded that one was needed. So too did Davis, though once convinced, he became a strong advocate. On 20 February, he delivered a speech to businessmen in Vienna, as part of a mini-series of 'The Road to Brexit'[2] talks by senior ministers. Johnson was the biggest sceptic of any need for a transition period, and the most reluctant to engage with the detail: 'What? Is a transition period really necessary? Can't we just get on and take all the benefits of Brexit coming our way rather than waiting?' he would regularly demand. Hammond, on the other side, was the strongest advocate, and argued that the longer the transition period, the better for British business and the economy.

May had a major speech scheduled for 2 March, her fourth on Brexit, and she was determined to use it to bring her Cabinet colleagues together on the kind of Brexit deal Britain should have. Hammond had tried to bring the issue to a head, asking ministers to rank in order their priorities, including an independent trade policy, frictionless trade, an end to free movement and an end to financial contributions, to help steer them towards trade-offs and the decisions they would inevitably have to take sooner or later. With attitudes on both sides beginning to harden, two meetings of the Strategy and Negotiation Brexit Cabinet Committee had failed to secure agreement, so May summoned its ten members to Chequers on Thursday 22 February for a prolonged session, which lasted eight hours, to knock heads together. The membership of the SN Committee was deliberately balanced, with Hammond, Rudd, Clark, Lidington and Bradley the main soft Brexiteers, and Johnson, Davis, Fox and Gove the principal hard Brexiteers. Williamson, Defence Secretary since November, increasingly leant in the latter's direction. Two days before the meeting, sixty Tory MPs who were aligned with the ERG wrote to May with a list of demands in an attempt to stiffen her resolve. The signatories felt they had, albeit reluctantly, accepted some compromises, including the £39 billion financial settlement and transition period, but they wanted to impress upon her that they would go no further. As the BBC's Laura Kuenssberg put it, the ERG 'made it clear they are not up for budging'.[3]

May played a long game at the February Chequers meeting, letting ministers talk throughout the long sessions, and then continuing the discussion over dinner till everyone felt 'talked out'. No. 10 claimed that she had 'played a blinder' keeping both sides together, achieving the consensus she sought for her speech. Both sides briefed that they'd come out victorious, with the hard Brexiteers claiming British sovereignty was guaranteed, and promises of flexibility extracted by the other side, including for the car industry, on which Greg Clark spoke with great passion. May herself had advocated for what was termed 'three baskets', with different parts of the British economy to be treated in bespoke ways by the EU. Industries that ministers believed should remain fully aligned to EU rules and regulations, including aerospace and cars, constituted the first basket. The second covered areas of shared goals between the UK and EU, as over the preservation of consumer rights and the environment, while the third specified areas where the UK specifically wanted to remove itself entirely from the EU parameters, above all agriculture and fisheries.

The speech that May delivered on 2 March was the most conciliatory of her four main Brexit speeches, with No. 10 feeling that they needed to try to move the debate on. Gavin Barwell sketched it out, with Denzil Davidson and other officials filling in the content. Early drafts of the speech spelled out the hard choices Britain would have to make, and the need for compromise. Conscious that the speech would be for ever known for the location in which she delivered it, a venue was scouted out in Newcastle, a city that voted Remain in a region that voted Leave – a statement in itself that this wasn't more Westminster solipsism. Late in the day, the conciliatory tone was dialled down, for fear of upsetting the hard Brexiteers, but the biggest blow came from 'the Beast from the East'. As a snowstorm engulfed the country, the location was forced closer to home: Mansion House in the City of London.

May said her aim was to seek an 'ambitious economic partnership' with the EU and that the UK would become a 'champion of free trade' following Brexit. Her most telling phrase was, 'This is a negotiation and neither of us [Britain and the EU] can have exactly what we want.' She outlined her own five tests: any agreement reached with the EU must respect the referendum result, including the UK regaining control of its borders, laws and money; the new arrangement must endure and not entail a return to the negotiating table; it must protect jobs and security; it must be consistent with British values, including being open, modern, outward-looking, tolerant and democratic; and finally, it must strengthen rather than weaken the Union within the UK. One member of No. 10's Europe Unit recalls the speech:

> In Mansion House the PM was essentially acknowledging that there
> would need to be compromise between two irreconcilable objectives
> – frictionless trade with the EU and a fully autonomous trade policy

with the rest of the world. The extent to which these hard choices were laid bare was inevitably watered down through the drafting process, but the message that hard choices would indeed have to be confronted, and compromise would be needed, was still at the heart of the speech. Hammond had asked the Cabinet to rank their priorities at a Cabinet meeting in early 2018 ... so that we might be able to clearly construct a policy, but the suggestion was not taken forward and really the moment never came when ministers had an honest and objective debate about the trade-offs that were inevitably going to be necessary. The PM's great strength – and what would prove her fatal weakness – was that all Cabinet ministers felt sure she wanted to deliver on their personal top priority right until the end.

Mansion House was the high-water mark of May's ability to be reasonable and accommodating to both sides. Immediately following it, as part of No. 10's media strategy, ardent Remainer Nicky Morgan and champion of the ERG Jacob Rees-Mogg wrote orchestrated articles praising her speech. Brexiteers 'will have concerns with Mrs May', Rees-Mogg wrote, 'but now is not the time to nitpick'.[4] Also writing in the *Daily Telegraph*, Morgan said May's speech was a 'welcome dose of realism. The EU can't say they don't know what the UK wants any more.'[5] Her words may have landed as intended in London. They did not in Brussels. The more the EU looked at May's hopes of 'mutual recognition', the more it thought it neither mutual nor sustainable. More work would have to be done to bring the EU onside on regulatory alignment and customs, as eventually emerged in the Chequers plan.

Two days before May gave her Mansion House speech, a bombshell landed on Whitehall. Since early January, the Commission had been hard at work. On 28 February, it published its draft withdrawal agreement between the EU and the UK, translating into legal text the joint report of December 2017. The government knew that the text would pose political problems in Parliament and tried to convince the

Commission in the days leading up to the publication how difficult an uncompromising text would prove at Westminster. May found Leo Varadkar in Dublin helpful at this time, but the Commission was anything but. According to one No. 10 figure, 'It simply would not accept how difficult it was for us. They absolutely refused to share any text with us in advance.' The day before publication, Olly Robbins marched into Sabine Weyand's office in Brussels. 'The government's strong advice is not to publish at all,' he told her, 'but if you must, you could at the very least share it with us in advance.' 'Sorry, no,' was the gist of her reply.

The EU's document insisted that 'citizens with settled status' were entitled to bring over non-EU partners they met after the exit date, while British citizens in other member states would be able to enjoy EU rights only in their current countries of residence. On transition, it advocated suspending the benefits of the single market for the UK in the event that it did not fulfil its obligations. It was most incendiary, though, in regard to Northern Ireland. The only way to avoid a hard border between North and South, the text said, would be for Northern Ireland to remain within the EU customs union and 'maintain full alignment' in areas including livestock and agriculture.

May's response was unequivocal. 'No Prime Minister could ever agree to it,'[6] she pronounced, while Arlene Foster's verdict was that it was 'constitutionally unacceptable' and 'economically catastrophic'.[7] The Commission would blame Britain for the difficulties that ensued after May's round rejection of its draft text. The British government in turn blamed the Commission for high-handedness, lack of consultation and lamentable handling, placing the Prime Minister in a position where she had no option, given her deep commitment to the Union, but to distance herself from the proposal. 'The times I've seen her most unhappy have always been to do with the Union: she's passionate about it. The EU's withdrawal agreement touched a very raw nerve within her,' says one close advisor.

Two weeks of tortured diplomacy followed, resulting in the

Commission and the British government publishing an amended version of the draft withdrawal agreement on 19 March, highlighting areas of agreement and disagreement, employing a green, yellow and white colour-coding system. A key point not picked up at the time lay in the preamble, where negotiators agreed that the backstop arrangements would apply 'unless and until' another solution was found. This cemented the backstop in a way the joint report had not – and it received barely any attention.

On the same day, May wrote a seminal public letter to President Tusk reiterating her commitment to a legally operative backstop solution to the withdrawal agreement to avoid a hard border. Orchestrated by Dublin and Brussels, it provided an opportunity for Varadkar to say that progress on the Northern Ireland issue must not be neglected. A paper was then steered through Cabinet ahead of the March EU Council, securing agreement to the legal text on the transition period and rounding off some remaining items on citizens' rights and the financial settlement. Progress had been made, or so it seemed at the time.

EU COUNCIL: 22–23 MARCH 2018

The March Council was a key marker in the Brexit story, with the EU27 finally approving guidelines for the negotiation of future relations with the UK after Brexit, allowing Phase 2 to properly begin. With the UK on track to leave in March 2019, the expectation was that an agreement would be reached by October, just six months away, allowing the EU and UK Parliaments time to consider the settlement before agreement was reached by the New Year, in time for final preparations before 29 March 2019. Tusk said that 'positive momentum' was needed to settle outstanding issues over Northern Ireland, with the hope that the EU27 would decide in June whether 'the Irish question' had finally been resolved. May, who was not present when her fellow leaders discussed Britain and Brexit, said she believed that there was a 'new dynamic' to the negotiations, and that 'it is in the best interest of both the UK and the EU that we get a deal that actually is in the interests of both'.[8] The EU27 then endorsed the arrangement, finalised earlier in the week, that the transition period should last twenty-one months, between Britain leaving in March 2019 and December 2020.

Spain's repeated demands for concessions over Gibraltar led to the EU's inclusion of a reference to their position on the Rock in the legal text, which stipulated that Spain would have to reach a separate deal on it with the UK. The critical issue that the March Council left on the table was how to avoid a hard border on the island of Ireland, with the EU insisting on a backstop for Northern Ireland, which in effect meant it would remain in the customs union. Varadkar said he wanted the agreement to keep 'as close as possible' to the UK. But any form of customs union was anathema to May's right wing. According to No. 10's Europe experts, the EU had deliberately designed the timetable following the March Council knowing that the UK would have to confront the question of Northern Ireland, which it was convinced would entail the UK opting for some form of customs union.

Davis had pushed hard to get the agreement to move on to Phase 2. But relations between him, May and Robbins had become seriously strained again. He wanted no-deal planning to be made public, so businesses would have a year to prepare should it occur. But he found himself up against the Treasury and BEIS, as well as No. 10. Davis recounts, 'I could have outwitted the other two, had No. 10 not opposed me, whose argument was "You'll worry businesses if you start talking about no deal." I thought that was nonsense. I was beginning to think that No. 10 was losing its nerve.'[9] Not for the first time, Davis found himself in a quandary, split in two directions. Part of him was a purist on sovereignty and wanted the same pure form of Brexit envisaged by the ERG; but he was also a loyalist and a pragmatist, and he knew that some form of compromise with the EU would have to come if Britain was to secure a negotiated deal. The previous summer had seen him firing from all guns about sequencing – the question of whether Britain and the EU needed to settle the basics of the divorce before moving onto their future relationship – only for him to yield to Brussels. He had equally conceded on several points in early 2018, including no-deal planning, and No. 10 was becoming nervous about how far he could be pushed.

Despite his pugnacious style, the EU did not always take Davis seriously – and they felt sympathy for May's predicament. 'May developed a vision over negotiations, I think Olly Robbins had a vision, but I don't think that David Davis had a vision,' the then Secretary-General of the European Commission Martin Selmayr reflects now. 'I don't want to be negative about Davis, as he certainly had his political reasons, but I never had the feeling he was taking charge of the negotiations. I don't think he was there with the idea to deliver this.' According to Selmayr, Davis 'never really made the argument strongly: he came in, the meetings were short, and then there was a press moment and he left again – Robbins did most of the work. But he wasn't an actual politician, so he couldn't achieve the same in Parliament.'[10] Guy Verhofstadt, chief Brexit representative for the European Parliament, shared this view. 'We always regarded Olly Robbins as the real negotiator,' he says.

> We thought he was very able and good. If anyone deserves blame, it wasn't officials but those on whose judgement the officials were acting. David Davis had a small engagement at the start, but by the end he became more involved. We took the view his main task was to tell the Brexit story in the UK.[11]

But Britain's problem was that it could not get its story straight – what resonated with Conservative MPs often rang hollow with the EU. Jeremy Heywood, still serving as head of the civil service at the time, watched the unfolding drama with apprehension. While many in the Cabinet Office thought the government was heading for the major showdown in the summer, he thought it would come in the autumn. Heywood remained the key player in these early months of 2018, pushing the discussion along and ensuring the Treasury, No. 10 and Cabinet Office were all as aligned as he could encourage them to be.

PIVOTAL CABINET COMMITTEE: 2 MAY

Following the March Council, May convened another Europe away-day at Admiralty House on 12 April. Her team were worried about the ticking clock, as there was still no solution to the backstop, and her Cabinet ministers seemed to be diverging rather than converging. She then lost the best part of a week from 16 to 20 April to the Commonwealth Heads of Government Meeting (CHOGM), hosted by Britain and held at Lancaster House, with festivities at Buckingham Palace and Windsor Castle. The only CHOGM of her premiership had been planned to be held at Vanuatu in the South Pacific Ocean at the end of 2017, but it had been moved to the UK because of the impact of Cyclone Pam on the island and postponed to April 2018 because of other pressures. A royalist, a patriot and a firm believer in the Commonwealth, May approached her leadership and hosting role with typical diligence, but it took up much of her time (the biennial CHOGMs almost always seemed to occur at pressure points for PMs). The leaders' statement that Prince Charles would be the next head of the Commonwealth was one of the most significant of the outcomes.

The event had meant delaying a crucial meeting of the SN Cabinet Committee, to discuss the government's customs arrangement to put to the EU, until 2 May. Tempers frayed as the Wednesday meeting approached. The ERG sent out a warning that they would not tolerate anything that smacked of a customs union. Briefing on both sides became so intense that May debated with her team whether it was wise to let the meeting go ahead: 'There'd been so much pre-briefing, but we decided it would have been a loss of face if we had postponed it,' says one insider, who emphasises another factor: 'Theresa May's bloody-mindedness. She had her favoured solution and she was convinced that she could persuade her Cabinet colleagues.' What she hadn't anticipated, though, was Rudd's resignation as Home Secretary on Sunday 29 April. Her successor, Sajid Javid, despite voting Remain in the EU referendum, had become an avowed Eurosceptic – weakening May's standing within the SN Committe and emboldening the hard Brexit cause.

May's plan was to get overall agreement from Cabinet by June at the latest before the EU Council that month. Achieving the support of the SN Committee, which was more Eurosceptic than the Cabinet at large, was the necessary precursor. Her favoured model was known as the 'hybrid', or New Customs Partnership (NCP), originally worked up in the Treasury by Jonathan Black and Jeremy Heywood in 2017. It provided May with just the solution she needed, offering the promise of keeping the borders open, of frictionless trade in Northern Ireland, and of an independent trade policy, while also seeing Britain leave the single market and customs union through the UK and EU establishing two separate sets of tariffs under a common regulatory framework similar to the customs union. It had first been pitched to her the previous autumn, and 'she bought it as it appeared to square the circle', according to her No. 10 Europe advisors. But, crucially, Davis didn't like it. He questioned how far it would be acceptable to Brexiteers, and personally he wanted no such relationship with the EU and wished to diverge on regulatory standards. He worried too that World Trade Organization (WTO) lawyers would recognise it as a customs union, sending a message anathema to his side, who demanded a more perfect sovereignty. Instead, he had his own favoured option, known as 'maximum facilitation' (or 'max fac'). Such an agreement would rely on technology-based solutions to enable a reduction in frictions to trade while establishing the scope for regulatory divergence from the European Union. He argued that this was how customs systems operated for third-party countries, and that building on existing facilitations would work in the best interest of the UK. Davis argued strongly for his own model, which he admitted might involve some friction on the UK–EU border, and particular difficulties on the Northern Ireland border, but which he believed could be made to work in time. Like others on his side at the meeting, he thought May's hybrid model might work intellectually but was not politically appetising. Members of May's team felt the opposite was true: it was Davis's model which relied on hypotheticals – untested technology and ungrounded hopes that the necessary infrastructure would not breach the commitment to no related checks or controls. The expert consensus was overwhelmingly against Davis's proposal: the technology would not be ready in time for its implementation in January 2021, and the EU would reject it out of hand for its failure to maintain the legal order of customs without significant physical infrastructure on the Irish border, something the UK had already committed to avoiding in the December 2017 joint report. The EU were sceptical about the NCP too, but, according to No. 10 Europe advisors, Brussels were at least willing to discuss it as a possibility.

These practical concerns motivated May's approach, but she knew what she was up against. She came down to the 8.30 meeting that Wednesday morning with two sheets of paper, written on in her fountain pen (she liked to use disposable Pilot V-pens). Aside from PMQs, when she would bring blank A4 paper for comments as they came, she would only rarely draft her own words; far more often, she would read through the speaking notes in her overnight red box and write notes as an aide-memoire for herself on them. 'But that morning,' according to a senior member of the UK negotiation team, 'she was very determined and very clear, and had mastered the detail to the highest degree.'

'Very unpleasant' was how one observer described the SN meeting that followed; 'awful' was the verdict of another. May opened, and outlined her plan, but it was clear early on that she was facing determined opposition. Javid was one of the first to speak out against it, telling her that he had 'significant concerns' with her proposal. Davis was clearly very unhappy, while Johnson grumbled throughout, staring out into the Downing Street garden on a very hot summer's day. The argument went from side to side in the hot Cabinet Room. Williamson claimed to keep a tally of the number of ministers speaking for either side – although May's team believe he deliberately misrepresented the figures. He slipped Johnson a note to say that while only five were supportive of May's plan, six were against, mostly in favour of Davis's max fac scheme. 'Prime Minister, there's a majority against you,' Johnson shouted out, becoming suddenly very animated. She tried to bat him aside but he came straight back at her and shouted out, 'It's 6–5 against you, 6–5 against.' May refused to take a formal vote on either side, saying that several of the views expressed were nuanced, so reducing it to such a simple matter of a vote would be wrong. A No. 10 source with a transcript of the meeting suggests that a more accurate breakdown would have been four ministers vocally in favour, three vocally against and four on the fence. 'Williamson was setting this up from the off,' the source says. 'Ironically, had a vote really been forced, I strongly suspect the PM would have won it.'

The angry meeting broke up shortly after, with ministers across the board unhappy with May. 'Within minutes, details of the discussion were briefed out to the media. Her authority never recovered fully after that meeting. It was a key turning point in her premiership,' recalls one official. Williamson identified it as a key staging post in the loss of her authority with her Cabinet colleagues, and in the shattering of any remaining vestige of collective responsibility:

The problem for the Prime Minister was that ministers were beginning to realise that no one had a stake in her. It became less and less valuable for them to back her plans and invest in her politically, and for anyone to go out of their way to support her, because there was less collateral and little emotion for her. Two years before, when Michael Gove had come out against David Cameron on the referendum, he had tortured himself. Nobody now tortured themselves about speaking out against Theresa May.[12]

May was now under considerable pressure. Brussels were demanding progress before the June Council, and a solution to the Irish border problem. In the House of Commons, meanwhile, Tory rebels were threatening to force the government into a customs union unless it came up with a viable plan acceptable to them, and the ERG were bolder than ever. May knew she had to act swiftly and, after talking to Barwell, Penn and her officials, decided to set up two working groups, each with a mixture of ministers from the SN Committee from both sides of the argument. One group would explore the merits of her hybrid model; the other, max fac. One No. 10 civil servant thought it a revealing play: 'It demonstrated one of her characteristics, which is not to be defeated, but to push things into the future in the hope that a solution might come up. One could have argued that nothing would happen to change ministers' minds, but she was set.' Barwell and Robbins put considerable thought into who would sit on each group. Two advocates would be asked to join the working group examining the plan they opposed. Fox and Gove were thus asked to sit on the group examining the hybrid option, while Bradley and Clark were asked to be on the max fac group. The idea was pure Micawberism: hoping against hope that 'something will turn up'. But what else could she do? If she had killed max fac outright, it would have angered the Brexiteers, risked resignations and prolonged the split. If she accepted it in spite of her belief that it would not solve the border issue, it would have upset her soft Brexiteers and risked the loss of support of the DUP, and nor would it have been acceptable to the Commission. She hoped the working groups would expose the truth of the matter.

The thinking was that both groups would visit Northern Ireland, holding a series of discussions with key players on the spot. But, as often happened with Cabinet committees, there was little time, and plans rarely worked out as intended. Six to eight weeks were lost while the groups met, argued and fell out. Meanwhile, the timing of the Cabinet debate on the two options, which was planned to be held at Chequers, was pushed back week after week. It meant even less time was left to convince Parliament and the country of her plan, assuming she could get agreement in full Cabinet. As the working groups ground on, a new quarrel emerged. To the more savvy among her ministers, the groups increasingly appeared a fix, as it became obvious May would never back the max fac option (which morphed into the Highly Streamlined Customs Arrangement, or HSCA) because she thought the EU would never agree to it and the timeframe to deliver frictionless trade was too long. Gove had been the first to recognise that the groups had been set up for one reason alone: to reach one conclusion, the Prime Minister's conclusion. 'Is this an honest exercise?' he asked. The whole reason the two groups had been set up, he said, was because of May's failure to convince Cabinet of her own preferred solution, which she was not prepared or able to force through. According to one No. 10 insider, when Gove was presented with max fac's negative RAG rating – a common project management method for scoring status reports – he tore it up in front of officials.

Davis continued to maintain that, with technological advances, facilitations and exemptions, the HSCA plan could deliver a solution that would satisfy the Northern Irish. He had support from Brexiteers, but he was losing ground. Hammond and Clark argued forcefully that his plan was unworkable, it wouldn't deliver for business and it would take far too long to come about. Behind the scenes, Robbins kept reminding No. 10 that max fac would never get through Brussels. The truth was that No. 10 did indeed see the two groups as an exercise to get Davis, as well as Johnson, Fox et al., to engage with reality and recognise that his dreams of perfect sovereignty and free trade were incompatible with the need to seek a resolution of the Northern Ireland problem. A corrosive cynicism was kindled, not subdued, by the working group exercise, which came back to haunt May when she eventually convened full Cabinet.

Hidden from both working groups, May had authorised a covert third strand, which was worked up within the Treasury and HMRC, looking at the merits of both schemes to see if there was a middle way that might hold both poles together. Heywood set himself up to challenge and quality-control this whole covert process. The exercise produced a new model, with yet another acronym: the Facilitated Customs Arrangement, or FCA. The fact that it was much closer to May's hybrid model than to max fac, though it had some of the facilitation and techniques of the latter scheme, was never going to endear itself to May's troublesome priests on the other side. Playing Micawber wasn't working.

CRISIS OVER THE BACKSTOP: 6 JUNE

On Wednesday 6 June, the seventy-fourth anniversary of D-Day, May welcomed the stars of Soccer Aid for UNICEF, including Olympic athletes Usain Bolt and Mo Farah, and Soccer Aid co-founder Robbie Williams, to a reception at No. 10. Downing Street staff, as always happens when celebrities come to the building, were politely star-struck. May gave a speech in which she talked about 'honour[ing] the promises that we have made to the poorest in the world'.

Earlier in the day, she'd had a meeting with Davis. Thanks to several briefings to the newspapers – which May's team presumed to have come from one of Davis's special advisors – trust had already frayed between the pair. Now his anger and disappointment at her proposals on the customs component of the backstop unnerved her. 'You can't let this happen. It will cripple our negotiations and be in breach of your promises. The party will never accept it,' he told her.[13] Under threat of his resignation, she offered to make some concessions. But they proved insufficient to assuage him. Their meeting broke up inconclusively.

May was desperate to move beyond this, but she had a busy schedule ahead. Davis returned for a second meeting. May listened, and then met with aides to discuss his concerns. She went to the Soccer Aid reception, and then onto the Palace for her audience with the Queen. Her team worked towards trying to settle Davis's fears. That evening, May had a rare theatre trip planned with Philip –but in the car back from the Palace, she spoke with JoJo and they decided she couldn't go. May didn't want to cancel, and she apologised to Philip – but she knew Davis's resignation would split her Cabinet and disrupt the hard-earned progress of the previous few months. Under intense pressure, May and her team agreed to last-minute changes to her plan, sufficient to appease Davis (they met the following morning), but which were to lead to significant difficulties with Dublin.

The immediate crisis may have been averted, but the writing was on the wall. Davis sensed the influence of Robbins behind her backstop proposals, and he didn't like it. Neither did he like being told by May that he couldn't, as DExEU Secretary, publish his own White Paper. 'Not yet,' she told him again and again, to his mounting frustration. Of the two factors influencing Davis, the one pressing for a more perfect sovereignty was beginning to win out over the voice that said he should help his Prime Minister deliver a Brexit solution to which all Cabinet could sign up. 'There was nobody in No. 10 I could talk to about it,' he says now. 'In the old days, I could talk to Nick and Fi. I was beginning to realise I couldn't stay on board for much longer. I pressed ahead with writing my White Paper, but I realised my time was coming to an end.'[14]

THE BUILD-UP TO CHEQUERS: 1–5 JULY

The Chequers meeting scheduled for Friday 6 July, the most important of her premiership, could be delayed no longer. The clock was ticking: she needed to secure agreement from her Cabinet and then present the proposals to Parliament and secure agreement with the EU by the autumn. Still to be resolved were the regulatory issues she had aired at Mansion House and a final way forward on customs to provide a workable solution on Northern Ireland. 'Our thinking was that all of Cabinet would come together on a big away-day,' says an aide. 'Far too much political effort and time had been expended on it. We needed to get the fingers of the entire Cabinet in the mangle. The EU was under no time pressure: but we were.' Another says, 'Heywood and Barwell felt strongly that we had to find a way to let everyone in Cabinet have their say before moving on.' The fudge of the joint report could not continue indefinitely. Parliament, too, was becoming an increasing worry, with the Trade Bill, whose passage was always going to be difficult, coming up later in July, and with a clear answer needed on trade. The growing risk was that Parliament might try to take authority into its own hands.

Off radar, Robbins had been hard at work on what became May's White Paper, led by DExEU, which was debated at Chequers and published on 12 July. His initial hope was to get an agreed text on separation issues through the June Council so that they could move on to the discussion on the future framework. But when that deadline passed, Robbins kept working away, sharing elements of his text with No. 10 and integrating their comments. The final text was cleared with May only in the week ending Friday 29 June. The proposal, an iteration of FCA, was much closer to the NCP and retained its most controversial element: that the UK would collect duties on imports at its borders at the rate of the EU's Common Customs Tariff, opening it to be attacked as Britain playing the role of 'EU's tax collector'. But ahead of Chequers, crucial details of Robbins's proposal – on trade and customs – were still to be decided.

As details of the plan seeped out, however, it presented the hard Brexiteers with a difficult choice. They could challenge her and resign en masse, which would almost certainly lead to her failing and her replacement by an unknown successor; they could work up a new proposal, as Davis favoured, with max fac back on the table; or they could opt for a no-deal option. May's deal seemed to them to be BRINO (Brexit In Name Only), described by Robert Peston as their 'worst nightmare'.[15] They were snookered. They were divided over no deal. A Canada-style free-trade deal gave them many of the benefits they sought but risked the break-up of the Union by separating Northern Ireland from the rest of the United Kingdom. A Norway option of staying within the single market would mean accepting freedom of movement, which they and May both believed would be a repudiation of the referendum result. In this sense, May had the initiative. Her enemies in Cabinet were divided over what course of action to favour over hers, and who, if anyone, to pit against her as the next leader.

On Monday 2 July, Davis came back to No. 10 to talk to May, which he describes as 'the beginning of it going seriously wrong'.[16] No. 10 judged him their biggest risk. She needed to win him over. But he hit the roof at the plans she unveiled to him that morning, which included 'a common rulebook'. This was even worse than what he'd had to swallow on the backstop four weeks before. A bitter row broke out between them. 'What you have here, Prime Minister, is incompatible with what you said in your conference speech and in your manifesto,' he said, with a new edge in his voice. Davis explains, 'The meeting broke up with it being clear to me that she was not going to budge.'[17] Their fall-out had been long in the making. They had both made assumptions about each other, based more on wishful thinking than on the hard reality of the other's position. Davis always believed that he could win May round to the logic of his own cause, in part because he thought he had the big beasts with him – not just the usual suspects of Johnson and Fox, but also Javid and Gove. 'Right up until the Friday of Chequers, he believed he could find a way to bring

Cabinet behind him and find a way forward on the future relationship based on his ideas with which they could all live,' says an aide.

From Monday, ministers began receiving a series of papers explaining why the different models hypothetically on offer wouldn't work. Norway and the European Economic Area would fail to meet May's red lines. The paper that most riled the ERG was one which explained why a no deal would cause profound economic damage to the country. The drip-drip of papers was No. 10's device to soften up the ground for the delivery of May's paper, the one that would best meet their objectives. But the process led, almost inevitably, to suspicion, leaks and threats.

May found herself in an almost impossible position, needing to convince both wings of her own party in Britain, as well as Belfast and Dublin, not to mention the EU27. On Tuesday 3 July, she flew to see Dutch Prime Minister Mark Rutte at his official residence, the Catshuis, in The Hague. On a long walk with him alone around the garden, she discussed her strategy and need for positive praise for it from the EU. She couldn't risk another EU rebuff, as had happened after Mansion House. The support of Rutte, an influential and well-disposed figure in the EU, she regarded as vital. Over breakfast at a long table, with both Prime Ministers and their staff on either side, Rutte said, 'The Prime Minister is on the eve of taking her proposal to Cabinet,' and invited his team to interrogate their British opposite numbers to 'try to poke holes in the argument'. To the British team, it was 'an incredibly helpful and valuable exercise'. At the end of it, the lead official of the Dutch Foreign Ministry turned to Rutte and said of May's plan, 'It works.'

Wednesday 4 July was a more difficult day. Chief Whip Julian Smith had a meeting with some forty MPs from the ERG, who told him that the Prime Minister and her plan would be 'toast' if it 'welched' on the Brexit promises of Lancaster House and beyond. For good measure, they added that the £39 billion 'divorce bill' should only be paid to Brussels on the condition of getting a deal.[18] Andrew Bridgen said that if May went ahead with her plan, 'it would be probably terminal', while reports circulated that at least six MPs were writing to Graham Brady, chair of the 1922 Committee, to say that they wanted a leadership contest (under party rules, forty-eight letters expressing no confidence in the current leader were required to trigger a vote). At noon, Davis sent a counter-proposal into No. 10, but heard back at 2 p.m. in a message from Barwell of May's 'blanket refusal' to consider his text. Davis promptly convened a meeting with his ministerial team and special advisors about what he should do next. Suella Braverman was supportive and empathetic to his plight, Robin Walker was non-committal, while ever-zealous Steve Baker agreed with Davis that he had no option but to resign. Davis thanked them and said he would hang on in the hope of swaying his Cabinet colleagues on Friday. 'I expected to lose the argument, but I was determined that I would be able to put my points across,' he says now.[19]

Not to be outmanoeuvred, Johnson convened a meeting at the Foreign Office that afternoon of senior fellow travellers, including Davis, Fox, Gove, Leadsom, McVey and Mordaunt, to discuss their concerns. Javid was invited but didn't turn up. Davis spoke about presenting his alternative plan at Chequers on Friday. This was applauded by Mordaunt, but support for Davis – a leadership rival to Johnson – was far from universal. Grayling said that they should swallow their reservations and accept May's deal.[20] Their anxieties about maintaining a common rulebook with the EU on food and farming standards, and the difficulties of striking future trade deals with countries such as the US, quickly leaked.[21] May's team were becoming increasingly exasperated at the blatant disloyalty and decided to raise the heat on the swelling opposition. At the same time, in an effort to bring Dublin in behind them, Hammond and Lidington met Irish Deputy Prime Minister Simon Coveney, who also acted as Foreign Affairs and Trade Minister, and meetings were held with the two most sympathetic

Fleet Street editors to her plan, Paul Dacre of the *Daily Mail* and Tony Gallagher of *The Sun*.

Thursday 5 July saw MPs on both sides becoming increasingly vocal and exasperated. Forty-six Conservative MPs, including eleven former Cabinet ministers, wrote to May urging her to listen to business voices ahead of Chequers, and not to succumb to pressure from her own right wing.[22] On the other side, former Cabinet minister Owen Paterson said that if reports of May's plan were accurate, it would be in 'complete breach' of the 2017 manifesto, while Andrea Jenkyns, who'd resigned as a PPS over Brexit in May, said she was ready to vote against a Brexit deal on such terms. David Jones, the former Brexit Minister, said her plan, if the reports of it were true, would 'lock the UK into the customs union and single market in perpetuity'.[23]

Johnson convened a second meeting of his informal group in the Foreign Office on Thursday evening to discuss their strategy for the following day. Gove describes the meeting thus: 'The PM looked like she was coming to conclusions and we were worried about the level of alignment with the EU that she was going to be proposing. We spoke about it, and what we might be able to do about it.'[24] Support for Davis's idea to put forward an alternative proposal at Chequers had lost ground in the thirty hours since they had last met. Johnson himself was in a quandary. He was the Foreign Secretary, but he also wanted to become the leader. Tim Shipman records one MP saying, 'I told Boris on Tuesday evening that anyone who harbours leadership ambitions, if they accept this very bad deal, it's going to be very difficult for them. He had a look of dead fear in his eyes.'[25]

May spent a large chunk of Thursday flying to Berlin to see Merkel. It would help her credibility significantly the following day if she was able to say that the Chancellor was on board with her plan. So she pitched her proposed solution to Merkel, who turned to her colleagues and asked for their thoughts. They questioned May and Barwell, much as Rutte's team had done, before concluding, 'What is being proposed is a significant step forward in the Prime Minister's position.' The exact words she wanted to hear. No. 10 was able to claim that the talks had been 'constructive', with Merkel saying in public that a political framework for a future relationship needed to be clear by October.[26] May's efforts were further rewarded with support from Barnier, who said in a speech the following day that he would be ready to compromise, if Britain would too, to reach a final agreement.

May returned to London relieved, but on her return immediately had to get to work to keep her colleagues on board, holding a series of conversations with Davis that evening, trying to edge him towards acceptance and prevent him from resigning. Earlier on, Cabinet had at last been sent May's proposal for the following day. The aim was to give them the minimum amount of time to leak it, which No. 10 knew would be likely to occur – but this required, by necessity, giving them the minimum amount of time to read it. Together with Chief Whip Julian Smith, No. 10 had resorted all day to employing sticks and carrots, offering some Brexiteers, including Raab and Braverman, the prospect of promotion in a reshuffle, while warning others of the dire consequences of rebellion and emphasising their political vulnerability at such a significant moment.

That evening, unhappy Brexiteer MPs stayed up late talking to each other, agreeing that the May deal was a bad deal, but divided over how to respond. To protect existing supply chains for business and to keep the UK within the EU's economic orbit, May was proposing a degree of regulatory alignment which they found wholly unacceptable, not least for opening up the UK to continued rulings of the hated European Court of Justice. The gains that they had always championed from Brexit, with the UK being able to set its own standards and product tariffs and to be a significant operator on the global trading stage, would all be sacrificed.[27] The success of her plan was still in the balance. May went to bed on Thursday evening unsure whether she had done enough to get it over the line.

CHEQUERS AWAY-DAY: FRIDAY 6 JULY

Ministers were invited to arrive at Chequers between 9.30 and 10 a.m. for coffee. Tempers were frayed at the outset thanks to some heavy-handed instructions from No. 10, which included ministers having to hand over their mobile phones (as in the Cabinet Room) and not being allowed their special advisors, and with rumours circulating that No. 10 had a 'reshuffle plan prepared in the event of resignations'. The most Machiavellian tactic, tipped off to the Politico website, was that business cards for a local Buckinghamshire taxi firm had been left in the Chequers foyer for any minister who decided they would resign, because they would no longer be able to use their official car to take them home.[28] Gove recalls it as an 'unfortunate briefing…, which didn't get us off to a good start'.[29] Davis was more emphatic: 'What the fuck,' he said. 'The children have taken control of the kindergarten,' he told Julian Smith, who listened and was apologetic.[30] Barwell was furious about the taxi story, worrying that it would undo the exhaustive work that the political team had put in over the previous few days to try to bring ministers onside with her deal. 'The political team had put in a huge amount of work talking through concerns with each member of Cabinet to bring them onside,' he explains.[31] Fox wryly comments that it was all rather pointless, as the email telling them about the taxis would not be read, since 'we'd all had our phones confiscated before the message arrived'.[32]

As the day began, No. 10 was most worried about two figures: Davis and Gove. The lobbying of Davis had been intensive and inconclusive. So too had it been with Gove. 'Michael had made us nervous,' says an official. 'We had a number of one-to-ones with him but none of us knew what he would say at the meeting, and which side he would come down on.' In the final few days, May had a bilateral with him. So did Barwell, and so did Robbins; they could do no more. They made no similar attempt to lobby Johnson, an unguided missile in their eyes, while they were reasonably confident of support from other known hard Brexiteers, including Fox, Leadsom and Grayling. Gove recounts telling Barwell in the morning:

'I think it will be easier, as the day goes on, if you can acknowledge the disquiet that some colleagues have, like Andrea Leadsom, and show willingness to amend the proposal.' 'We can't do that,' I was told, quite abruptly. 'That's rather disappointing,' I replied. 'Why can't this happen?' I was told, 'Because it's all been signed off.'[33]

At 10.15 a.m., ministers were directed to the wood-panelled Hawtrey Room for a series of presentations and Q&As. Party chair Brandon Lewis gave a presentation on polling and how much damage was being caused by the perception that the party was disunited. Greg Clark, who had done much in the previous few weeks to encourage companies like Jaguar Land Rover and Nissan to make public their private warnings of the dangers of a hard Brexit,[34] spoke about how the car industry might be affected under different Brexit scenarios, and how the proposal offered by May would be the best for industry overall. 'The morning meeting was clearly a general rallying cry designed to make it look like the Prime Minister's option was the only option,' says Davis, adding, 'Boris was quite agitated, but I was quiet, biding my time.'[35] Olly Robbins and Tim Barrow outlined the arguments and answered questions from Cabinet. Then Smith, fatigued from weeks working with his team to bring MPs onside, gave a stark warning about the dangers of rebellion, warning that Remain MPs would back an amendment to the Trade Bill later that month to keep Britain within the customs union if they didn't get a move on. When May called on him to speak, Johnson apparently groaned, 'Oh God,' to which she replied, 'The Chief will always like that as an introduction!'

During what one present described as a 'six-minute moan', Johnson dismissed May's plan as 'a big turd', which he had thought was dead but which had re-emerged 'zombie-like from the coffin'. If EU rules were to be accepted on the sales of goods, it would, Johnson said, leave Britain a 'vassal state' and fail to honour the referendum pledge to 'take back control of our laws'. Defenders of her proposal, he said, would be 'polishing a turd', as he referred to a recent visit to Whipsnade Zoo, where he had viewed similar activities. 'I see there are some excellent expert turd polishers here,' he added. It was vital for Britain not to 'surrender' on immigration or money, he said towards the end of his tirade.[36]

At 12.30, ministers broke for lunch, with the mood still positive despite the diatribe. Over a buffet of barbecued chicken thighs and other meats, 'ministers actually spent an hour talking to each other without texting any of their friends in the press to say what was happening. It was marvellous,' says an official. The break provided the opportunity for Barwell, Robbins and members of the political team to chat to individual ministers and offer reassurances where they could. At 1.30 p.m., ministers were directed upstairs to the Grand Parlour for what was intended to be a three-and-a-half-hour Cabinet meeting but which didn't finally break until 6.45. It was another immensely hot day, as the fateful SN meeting had been. One minister joked that even the weather had been enlisted by No. 10 to ensure that ministers would be perspiring so much they'd be desperate to reach agreement, even if it was to May's plan. May was visibly apprehensive as she called the meeting to order, still unsure whether she'd carry the day. She was taking no chances. 'I know that a lot of you want to speak on this subject, but I'll come to you and ask you to speak in order,' she said as she opened the meeting. 'It was one of those meetings where she had spoken to the Chief Whip before and they decided who was going to talk and in what order,' says one. After she had reprised the arguments ('very strong on detail, as always,' remembers an official), David Lidington spoke, filling out points she had made and speaking passionately in support.

Then it was David Davis's turn. Everyone leant forward and started to listen very attentively. His tone was typically polite and respectful (no mention of turds). 'We liked David Davis; he didn't generally brief the media, and he had a lot of respect for the PM, which was mutual,' says a No. 10 source. He told his fellow ministers:

> You know, Prime Minister, that I am the odd man out on this. You have made a very good case. But I want now to put a counter-argument. If we go with your proposal, we'll be agreeing to a European rulebook, not to a common rulebook. This would not matter so much if we were talking only about existing industries, be it automobile or steel, but it will apply also to new areas like AI, life sciences and genetics, where Britain could be in the lead globally if we were not hamstrung by making them subject to European regulations. I don't like us being dictated to by the EU. Stop giving ground to the EU and stand up to them. They will take it. We should be telling them what we want, not the other way around.[37]

Johnson spoke next, but he hadn't expected to be called then and hadn't properly collected his thoughts, so he was not at his best or most persuasive. Nevertheless, he made a robust argument in favour of rethinking her whole strategy. It was now Gove's turn. Again, ministers leant forward, sensing that what he would say would matter. As he spoke, the clocks showed 3.15 p.m. It was the most dramatic moment of the day. His was to prove the most influential speech of the afternoon. Whitehall should be doing more to prepare for a no-deal Brexit, he said, and he expressed surprise at the changes in May's proposal from what she had said at Mansion House and before. He had recovered from his irritation at the way the process had been choreographed, however, and ultimately came out in favour of her deal: 'There's an awful lot in the Prime Minister's proposal that I find hard to swallow. But ... there are really only two choices that we are left with: we could reject it, or we could accept it, and I have decided to argue that we should accept it.'[38] With his DEFRA hat on, he said May's was the right solution on agriculture and food, though he was unhappy about whether it was right for EU rules to apply to other goods as well. His support threw Davis, who also hadn't known on what side he would land, and who explains now, 'Michael was one of those who I thought might have been expected to back us.'[39] One minister present later told the press, 'His speech pulled the rug from under Boris and David Davis's feet,' while another said, 'His was the decisive voice.'[40]

After that, none of the interventions mattered very much. Fox clearly disliked the plan but had decided beforehand that he would not resign: 'The specific reason I didn't go was I never thought her deal would prove acceptable to the EU. My more general reason was that you can't influence events once you're out.'[41] Javid was next up, asking for reassurances that there'd be no backsliding on the promise to end unlimited EU immigration, as well as arguing for a technical solution (which turned out to be unworkable), but nevertheless he was broadly supportive of the Prime Minister. Leadsom was another figure to disappoint Davis and Johnson. She began by attacking May's proposal, before concluding, 'The most important thing we do is to find common agreement, so I will be backing the proposal.' Two other Cabinet ministers who spoke most strongly against May were McVey, who took a populist viewpoint, stating that the electorate would not understand her deal, and Mordaunt. '[Mordaunt] was the most important person on my side,' says Davis. 'The remainder were mostly against me.'[42] Hammond expressed irritation at the length of the Brexit talks, saying, 'We have wasted time during this negotiation.' May was often at her most assertive when challenged by Hammond, and after he had spoken for some ten minutes, she said in a tone reminiscent of Thatcher, 'Is there a question?'[43]

May summed up the meeting by saying there was a clear majority in favour of her proposal but that there had been 'too much discussion outside Cabinet about what has been said, which is a continuation of the suspension of collective responsibility authorised during the referendum campaign. We have to make certain this ends now, and that we work together.' For those who were behind her, it was a profoundly unifying moment. For the six or seven who had spoken out against her plan, it sounded menacing. She said she would no longer tolerate breaches of the convention of collective responsibility, with the clear implication that ministers would be sacked for doing so. Davis alone refused to sign the joint Cabinet statement, but it was clear long before May closed the meeting that she had won. As the BBC's Laura Kuenssberg put it, 'The Brexiteers ... are not happy but they are also not united.'[44]

As they broke up for pre-dinner drinks, the mood suddenly lifted, with ministers toasting each other, as did the staff team in a separate room. Some ministers suggested they go out for more occasions together. Cabinet sat down at round dinner tables, to be served Chequers' best – cured Scottish salmon, Oxford beef fillet and marmalade bread-and-butter pudding.[45] Discussions took place on how they could bring the Europeans onside and convince the nation of the deal. Davis and Johnson were asked how they would sell the deal. Davis stood up to speak, with several positive suggestions, while Johnson offered thoughts from his chair – and even, according to one No. 10 source, offered a toast to what had been agreed. Several on both sides of the debate arranged to write joint articles for the Sunday papers, including Clark and Gove's jointly authored piece for the *Mail on Sunday*, which would bear the headline 'We're friends reunited for the battle for Britain!'[46]

Gove had declared; now the figure whose face No. 10 staff scrutinised most that evening was Davis. It was clear that he was far from happy, but none of them knew exactly what he was thinking, or which way he would jump.

Earlier that evening, at 7 p.m., while the ministers had been chatting over drinks, still without their mobile phones, the government had published details of its plans, which included a new 'facilitated customs arrangement', with the UK to apply UK tariffs to UK goods and the EU applying EU tariffs to EU goods; a common rulebook with a free trade area for goods, but different rules for services; continued harmonisation, with Parliament free to diverge; and a joint institutional framework to interpret the common rulebook. May's statement said:

> Today in detailed discussions the Cabinet has agreed our collective position for the future of our negotiations with the EU. Our proposal will create a UK–EU free trade area which establishes a common rule book for industrial goods and agricultural products … As a result, we avoid friction in terms of trade, which protects jobs and livelihoods, as well as meeting our commitments in Northern Ireland.

RESIGNATION OF DAVIS AND JOHNSON: 8–9 JULY

Davis was tired but in good spirits, fellow ministers thought, when he left Chequers on Friday evening to be driven up to his home in Yorkshire. He called his special advisor, Raoul Ruparel, from the car and conveyed the impression that he had still not decided to resign but was certainly minded to do so. To another colleague, he said, 'If I was Secretary of State of a different department, and didn't agree with the Brexit policy, I could put my head down and get on with my main job. But if I'm Brexit Secretary and I'm not happy with Brexit, it's just not sustainable.' He spent Saturday quietly in his Yorkshire constituency, reflecting on the time when, in June 2008, he resigned from Cameron's shadow Cabinet and as an MP, to provoke a wide debate on the erosion of civil liberties, about which he cared passionately. He says now:

> I'd spent three days mulling over my resignation in 2008, and I wanted to do the same thing here ten years later. I wrote out a 'logic tree' on a clean piece of paper with a map of all the scenarios that could happen, which helped me understand what I wanted to do. I concluded I would have to go.[47]

He had come close to resignation at several earlier points, often sparked by his unhappiness at Robbins's influence on the Prime Minister and what he saw as the steady erosion of the promise of a full Brexit that her own speeches had aroused. He had come within a whisker of resigning on 6 June over the backstop. Now, the Rubicon had been crossed. On Sunday 8 July, Davis took his daughter to the British Grand Prix at Silverstone, wanting to spend a quiet day with her without them being pursued by the media, as would have occurred if the news had already broken. His phone was repeatedly ringing. Earlier on Sunday, while driving to the racetrack, he had spoken to Johnson to tell him. He was always wary of doing anything that might further Johnson's ambitions; he regarded Johnson as a very different animal from himself. 'Are you certain you want to resign?' Johnson asked him. 'Yes, I am, Boris,' he replied. 'Because if you go, I'll have to go too,' came Johnson's voice jabbing down the line. Davis wasn't certain why Johnson said he would have to follow suit but speculated that it was because he had not resigned on 21 June, when junior Trade Minister Greg Hands did, in opposition to the planned expansion of Heathrow Airport. Johnson was the highest-profile opponent in Cabinet of the Heathrow expansion, once pledging to lie down in front of bulldozers to stop it happening. 'If Johnson has a backbone or a shred of credibility left, he will join Greg Hands in resigning,' Green MP Caroline Lucas had tweeted.

Davis spoke next to McVey, who was strongly supportive of his resigning, and to Fox, who said, 'I understand why you are doing it.' ('I always rated Liam: he always behaved very properly,' says Davis.[48]) Late on Sunday afternoon, with the race over (a win for Sebastian Vettel over Lewis Hamilton), Davis texted Julian Smith to ask to speak to the Prime Minister. Receiving no response, an hour later he texted again. After a while, Smith responded to say, 'Can we talk?' 'There is no point in us talking. I have made my mind up,' Davis texted back. The next text was from director of communications Robbie Gibb. 'Can we talk?' asked Gibb. Davis decided it would be best to come down to London and meet up with Gibb and Smith in person. The latter suggested the Chief Whip's office in 9 Downing Street. 'You can't go, you're too important,' they both told him. 'We know you've been badly treated. We know you were on the wrong end of the policy and we're sorry.' They offered him two jobs. The first was Leader of the House, the post occupied by Leadsom, who, though she had her doubts about Chequers, would not resign over it. The second was Foreign Secretary – offered to Davis before No. 10 knew Johnson would resign. Barwell was messaging Davis at the same time, making the same offers.

They all knew what a serious blow it would be if he left. Davis wanted to be helpful, but he had run out of road and did not want to be seen to have been bribed into a post which would require Johnson's sacking. 'It's too late for any of that,' he said finally. According to Gibb, 'It was hopeless. He told us he'd already spoken to his constituency chairman.'[49] To show there was no bad feeling, he went off for a pint with Gibb at the Red Lion pub on Whitehall, almost opposite the front gates of Downing Street. He retired to the flat of his friend and former Cabinet minister Andrew Mitchell, as the media would not know where he was and he wouldn't be doorstepped.

Davis had already written a careful resignation letter. 'If David Davis had gone for the Prime Minister and made it personal, there was a risk he might have taken her down, which he didn't want to do, so instead, he made his focus on policy,' says an aide. Davis sent the letter in to No. 10, with the idea that it would be released to the media at 11 p.m., though No. 10 decided to leak it some moments before. As they did so, he received a call from the Prime Minister. 'I'm very disappointed,' she said. 'That may be,' he replied, 'but I'm not going to alter my decision.' She said again, 'I am very disappointed, David.' The conversation was clearly going nowhere and lasted no more than a couple of minutes. Shortly after, he received a call from Radio 4's *Today* programme: would he go on the following morning? Davis explains:

> That's what I'd been aiming for. It was deliberately timed to avoid the story being in the morning papers. As there's not a single news-paper in the UK which is less than partisan on Europe, I didn't want my resignation to be used as part of their polemical mission. I wanted to do it in my own words, so I took the 8.10 slot on *Today* and arranged a talk with Laura Kuenssberg and Robert Peston af-terwards, so I could get my own account out across on the BBC and ITV, and then the papers would report my words on Tuesday.[50]

His letter of resignation was indeed respectful, citing the 'common rulebook' as a principal cause for his resignation, but also noting, 'This is a complex area of judgement and it is possible that you are right and I am wrong.' May's reply was equally respectful, and an opportunity for her to restate her own position.

As May's team had suspected, Davis's departure put the heat on Johnson, who hadn't anticipated Davis resigning. Johnson called his PPS at the Foreign Office, Conor Burns, from his car on his way home from Chequers. Burns recalls, 'He was not in a good place. He thought it was a terrible proposal May had produced. He said he would mull over his future that weekend, but I had no doubt he'd no longer be a minister by close of play on Monday.'[51] When Michael Gove spoke to Johnson on Sunday, before Davis had called him, 'he gave no indication that he was about to quit'.[52] Waiting Foreign Ministers and dignitaries were stood up by Johnson at a West Balkans summit he was supposed to be hosting while he secreted himself away in the Foreign Secretary's official residence in Carlton House Gardens, not taking any calls, composing his resignation letter – and calling in a photographer for good measure. Anxious to deter him, May tried to speak to him. Several attempts from Switch at No. 10 failed, but eventually they got him on the line. 'What are you planning to do, Boris?' May asked him. He kept avoiding her question, going round in circular arguments, and only at the end of a long and swirling conversation did he confirm that he would be leaving. As Foreign Secretary, he had not developed into the thoughtful figure, with gravitas at home and internationally, that May had exhorted him to become almost exactly two years before, on his appointment. Now, she was livid at his resignation. While May and her team at No. 10 understood and respected the reasons for Davis's resignation, Johnson was 'a different matter'.[53]

On the Friday evening at Chequers, Johnson's mood was described as 'ecstatic and highly relieved', and he was reported as saying, 'At least we have stability and can move forward on a common position.' His rapid U-turn was despised in No. 10. 'We were left with a contrast between David Davis leaving over a genuine difference that we respected,' says Barwell, 'and Boris Johnson leaving, thinking not about the country but about his own narrow position.'[54] His antics, according to *The Economist*, had rendered the Western Balkans summit 'like a scene from one of the *Carry On* films'.[55] When the Foreign Ministers learnt that the reason the British Foreign Secretary had kept them all waiting was not because he was attending an urgent government security meeting sparked by the death of a British woman who had come into contact with Novichok, but because he was resigning as he thought May's plan would leave Britain a 'colony' of the EU, some apparently 'burst out laughing'.[56]

No. 10 moved quickly to fill both their places. Suspecting that Davis's resignation was on the cards, they'd already lined up Dominic Raab, who had performed well as Minister of State for Housing since the January reshuffle and who had Brexit credentials in abundance, a core requisite for the job of succeeding Davis. A brief discussion had taken place about bringing back a Brexiteer big beast – IDS was one who might have considered it[57] – but No. 10 quickly closed that window. 'Will you sign up to my policy?' May asked Raab on his appointment. 'Because we'll need to be in this together.' 'Yes, Prime Minister,' he replied. For Johnson's successor, a gift fell into May's lap. Back in January, Jeremy Hunt hadn't wanted to be moved until he had steered through the NHS Long Term Plan. Now he was eager to move to a bigger position, and he accepted the post of Foreign Secretary with alacrity. Hunt had become a convert to the Brexit cause, but he had voted Remain in the referendum, as had the other three holders of the great offices of state: Prime Minister, Chancellor and Home Secretary. Matt Hancock was promoted to Health Secretary in Hunt's place, with the Attorney General Jeremy Wright replacing him as Culture Secretary, and backbencher Geoffrey Cox, who was to play a seminal part in the story, becoming Attorney General. No fewer than eight Cabinet ministers had now departed since the general election just a year before: in addition to Davis and Johnson, there was Fallon, Rudd, Green, McLoughlin, Greening and Patel. Not a good omen, least of all with May about to fly into some heavy turbulence.

THE SIGNIFICANCE OF CHEQUERS

May had expended considerable political capital on the whole Chequers process, with the aims of making decisive progress towards Britain's exit from the EU, ensuring that she would keep Brussels onside, and strengthening her own authority in the Conservative Party by restoring Cabinet unity and the doctrine of collective responsibility. None of these goals was to be achieved. On 12 July, the government published the long-awaited White Paper, entitled 'The Future Relationship Between the United Kingdom and the European Union', which envisaged a close future relationship on a range of areas, from economic cooperation to security, data, science and innovation. It anticipated the UK remaining in a number of EU agencies, including those involved with aviation, chemicals and medicine, with the UK also remaining close to the EU's energy and transport markets. A temporary customs arrangement (TCA), which had been published a short while before, dealt specifically with the backstop and foresaw it being applied UK-wide so as to avoid any checks on the Irish Sea, as well as avoiding a hard land border on the island of Ireland. It envisaged the backstop being temporary but could not say it would be time-limited.

The initial signs from the EU were positive, similar in the tone to the comments by Rutte and Merkel in May's meetings with them in the week leading up to Chequers. Barnier, too, softened his tone from earlier in the year, saying that the EU remained ready to change its Brexit offer if the British government itself shifted its red lines on freedom of movement and the role of the ECJ. 'All the models are available, customs union, customs union-plus, Norway, Norway-plus. We can work on all these.'[58] But, to May's torment, over the summer the EU hardened its position. Hostility built up against allowing Britain as a third country to be a full member of EU agencies, especially as they operated under the jurisdiction of the ECJ. On the backstop, both the European Commission and Dublin became increasingly unhappy at any suggestion of it being time-limited. Haggling with the Commission continued throughout August, with Robbins arguing that the TCA was a viable alternative to the EU's own backstop proposal. They were still arguing in September, with another valuable six weeks lost.

The delayed timing of Chequers meant that only two weeks of parliamentary time remained before Westminster and the EU went off on their holidays, and when the leaders of the EU returned after August, their mindset had changed back to thinking of the integrity and strengths of the EU27 first, rather than leaning over to be helpful to a state that wanted to exit on its own terms. The prospect of achieving agreement by the stated date of the October Council was beginning to slip away. 'Had the EU maintained their initially positive reception of Chequers, it would have made a big difference. But they didn't,' says a No. 10 source. 'For a long time, the PM continued to hope for more from the EU27, and from the Commission, than they were prepared to give.' No. 10 blamed the Commission for being obstructive. The path was paved to a markedly unpleasant encounter with its President, Donald Tusk, at Salzburg in the autumn.

Chequers also marked the point when the ERG turned on May, destroying the relationship between backbenchers and government. The Brexiteers had backed her Lancaster House speech and thought Britain was on course for a free-trade, Canada-style Brexit. Chequers came as a severe shock to them, and they worried that in the long term Britain would end up in a customs union. May went before the 1922 Committee on the evening of Monday 9 July, buoyed by a chorus of support from the great and good in the party, including former leader Michael Howard and former Foreign Secretary William Hague. She was cheered at the meeting, per convention. But the applause was wearing thin. It was increasingly a question not of whether the forty-eight signatures would ever be acquired, but when. One Cabinet minister reflects, 'Once Boris and David Davis went, it started the bandwagon rolling. We were playing catch-up from that point onwards. After Chequers, we were never on the front foot again. There was never any real optimism.'

After Chequers, few believed that May would ever have the votes to pass her Brexit plan. James Forsyth of *The Spectator* was one of the first to acknowledge that, even if she did manage to get the EU to accept her plan, she would never have the support of Parliament.[59]

After Chequers, both wings in Parliament – the hard Brexiteers in the Tory Party and the pro-European Conservative and Labour MPs – began to believe that their interests might be better served by voting her deal down. The former thought that by doing so, Britain would default to leaving the EU without a deal and trading on WTO terms. The latter equally saw no incentive to vote for May's deal, believing that, if it was defeated, a softer version of Brexit would have to come forward, or even no Brexit at all. Chequers failed finally to restore collegiality in Cabinet. Indeed, it was a significant staging post towards the worst deterioration of collective decision-making since the doctrine emerged in the eighteenth and nineteenth centuries. By the time Cabinet returned in September, there were hardly any loyalists left. Brokenshire, Bradley and Lidington were May's only totally loyal supporters. Many others, like Gove and Javid, supported her deal but continued to harbour significant reservations about her capabilities as Prime Minister. If one throws in the toxic mix of leadership challengers, spearheaded by Johnson overtly campaigning as her successor, one can understand how the internal party battles of June and July were just a preliminary skirmish and how, as Jeremy Heywood had predicted, the real struggle would come in the autumn.

May was determined to show strength and character at the 2018 Conservative Party annual conference, after the previous year's debacle. To the surprise of many, she came on stage to ABBA's 'Dancing Queen'.

CHAPTER 15

INTO THE EYE OF THE STORM
JULY–NOVEMBER 2018

May's long-delayed Brexit plan had had a bumpy start: her Brexit and Foreign Secretaries had resigned, her Cabinet was restless, her MPs divided. If her plan was to have any prospect of passing through Parliament, she needed a summer and autumn of mounting unity behind her and her deal. What she did not need was to be repeatedly attacked by a Conservative contender for the leadership, nor by Britain's prime overseas ally, both of whom proffered an alternative version of Brexit which called into doubt her own and whipped up Tory MPs against her. Fighting on both fronts, she limped through to the end of July, but the attacks started again in earnest in September. Her speech to the party conference quelled the unrest, but for days rather than weeks. Yet she showed no indication of taking stock of her parlous parliamentary position and broadening the support behind her plan.

TRUMP'S FIRST VISIT: 12–16 JULY

The trouble began long before President Trump touched down at London Stansted on Air Force One at 1 p.m. on Thursday 12 July, fresh from a NATO summit in Brussels where he had grandstanded and blustered about how member nations all needed to pay more, entertaining the idea that the US might even leave NATO, before changing tack and smothering the bemused organisation in gushing rhetoric. No. 10 had consistently sidelined Johnson from May's relationship with Trump, not inviting him on her first US visit in January 2017, nor wanting him to be a participant in the irregular monthly calls between the two leaders. Records of the conversations show May constantly trying to stick to her script, while Trump veers off in all directions. In a call earlier that summer, Trump flew off in a romantic solipsism about how much he loved Ireland. May listened to it for as long as she could stand, but eventually, conscious that she was not making the progress she wanted on the written notes in front of her, arrested him mid-flow: 'Donald, why are we talking about Ireland?'[1] May could happily be forceful with him, as she had been in Washington in January 2017 over the US commitment to NATO and in March 2018 when persuading him to stand up to Putin after the Salisbury attack, and as she would be again in her final weeks in office.

On a personal level, Trump didn't know what to make of May, nor May of Trump. It was a case of extreme incompatibility of personality types. Throughout her premiership, May was receiving reports from the British Embassy in Washington telling her how erratic and dysfunctional a leader Trump was. The last thing she wanted was her own dysfunctional and erratic Foreign Secretary teaming up with the US President – a constant threat. Shortly before and during Trump's visit, reports from right-wing sources began to appear in the press questioning their relationship. 'Aides and diplomats … have come to fear that May's inability to flatter Trump has damaged Britain,' ran one article in the *Sunday Times*, citing a source who said, 'She has no small talk; all he has is small talk.'[2] Many on the right argued that Prime Minister Johnson would represent Britain much better to the President, man to man, and negotiate the kind of trade deals and relationship Britain would need in the future.

A month earlier, comments had been leaked, allegedly uttered by Johnson, saying he was becoming 'increasingly admiring of Donald Trump' and 'convinced that there is method in his madness'. Johnson then homed in on the British crisis: 'Imagine Trump doing Brexit … He'd go in bloody hard … There'd be all sorts of breakdowns, there'd be all sorts of chaos, everyone would think he'd gone mad. But actually you might get somewhere. It's a very, very good thought.'³ Another thought was that his own name could be substituted for Trump's on 'Brexit made simple'.

In the final week of June, Iain Duncan Smith, a long-time friend of Trump's National Security Advisor John Bolton, invited the American to a meeting of right-wing MPs including Bernard Jenkin and Bill Cash, where Trump's enthusiasm for a trade deal after Brexit was discussed. After the meeting, Duncan Smith told the BBC's *Sunday Politics* that Bolton was 'very pro the idea of a trade arrangement as quickly as possible and the general view was that they could get it done within two years if the British really wanted to do a real push on it'.⁴ The press reported that Bolton spoke to an ERG meeting to undermine May, which Duncan Smith denies: 'It was just an informal conversation with old friends.'⁵ Nerves in No. 10 were frayed anyway in the run-up to Chequers at the end of the following week, and when No. 10 read reports in the media about a senior member of Trump's team having a secret meeting with those who were trying to destroy her deal, they felt angry and betrayed.

The ground was prepared for an extremely fractious visit from Trump in the critical week after Chequers. The President and the First Lady were whisked away by helicopter from Stansted to Regent's Park in central London, the official residence of US Ambassador Woody Johnson. Indeed, a helicopter was the chosen method of transport throughout the trip to avoid the protests against his visit. Anger against the President had built in Britain since his election in November 2016, focusing on his proposed wall along the Mexico border, his hostility to Muslims, his rejection of the Paris climate deal, and, in the weeks before his arrival, new reports of migrant children being separated from their families and held in detention centres. Thousands took to the streets of London as a large 'Trump Baby' balloon depicting the President in a nappy, complete with mobile phone and tan lines, flew above the protesters. 'I guess when they put up blimps to make me feel unwelcome, no reason for me to go to London,' Trump responded.[6]

No. 10 sought out locations that would please the President safely away from London, settling on Blenheim Palace, built for the Duke of Marlborough in the early eighteenth century and the birthplace of Winston Churchill, as the venue for the dinner on the first evening. Knowing how impressed Trump had been by the French military band in Paris the year before, his arrival was greeted by the Scots, Irish and Welsh Guards. Trump was invited to sit in the chair used by Churchill, his hero, which he duly tweeted. Business leaders from both countries were guests, designed to impress upon him the reality of the relationship today. At the dinner itself, he sat next to May. Kim Darroch, the British Ambassador, thought it the most relaxed and easy conversation they were ever to have. Both leaders totally ignored those on either side: 'I was very embarrassed for the rest of the table,' Trump said.[7] The President was in his element as he tucked into the first course of smoked salmon followed by Hereford beef fillet, rounded off with strawberries and cream, after which May presented him with a gift of an illustrated ancestral charter of his Scottish heritage. No expense or care spared.

But behind the scenes, all was not well. As Trump was arriving at 7 p.m., James Slack, May's official spokesman, took a call from *The Sun*, from which he learnt that editor Tony Gallagher and political editor Tom Newton Dunn had travelled to the NATO summit the previous day to interview Trump. As a courtesy, the paper wanted to let Slack know they would be leading on it the next day, and it would not make good reading. As Slack ended the call on the front steps of Blenheim, he wondered whether he should tell May now, and risk spoiling her dinner, or delay. In a split-second decision, he chose the latter. During the meal, her team assessed Trump's words, which they considered unbelievably rude, ungracious and problematic.

The headline in *The Sun* the following morning, already online, was 'May has wrecked Brexit... US deal is off!'[8] Beneath it, Trump's words: 'I would have done it much differently. I actually told Theresa May how to do it but ... she didn't listen to me.' Instead, Trump said, she 'went the opposite way' and the results had thus been 'very unfortunate'. He disparaged her Chequers deal, saying, 'If they do a deal like that, we would be dealing with the European Union instead of dealing with the UK, so it will probably kill the deal.' He added that her plan 'will definitely affect trade with the United States, unfortunately in a negative way'. Turning to Boris Johnson, Trump said:

> I like him a lot. I have a lot of respect for Boris. He obviously likes me and says very good things about me. I was very saddened to see he was leaving government and I hope he goes back in at some point ... I am not pitting one against the other. I am just saying I think he would be a great Prime Minister. I think he's got what it takes.

For one leader to have undermined the other in such a way was unprecedented in the 100 years since a US President first met a British Prime Minister face to face, when Woodrow Wilson met David Lloyd George at the end of the First World War. The Blenheim dinner broke up all bonhomie. May was excited by the animated conversation.

She was briefed only when the President's helicopter took him away. 'She took the news stoically,' one civil servant says. But inside she was seething at the humiliation.

Friday 13 July was set to be a very difficult day between the two leaders. Speaker John Bercow had overruled the plan for Trump to address both Houses of Parliament, a regular invitation for visiting US Presidents, on the grounds that it was 'not an automatic right [but] an earned honour ... and my view is that he has not earned that honour'.[9] The atmosphere was icy when the President's helicopter landed at the Royal Military Academy at Sandhurst. The venue had been picked to appeal to Trump's love of the military and tradition, and in a place where he was as secure as one can be anywhere in the country. Trump was without shame. He couldn't escape mentioning the interview, but the closest he came to an apology was: 'I said a lot of nice things about you, Theresa. We've got the tape. It's all nonsense. It's all fake news.' May's team noticed, however, that, as he began to relax, he was polite and civil with her and even that 'he often disparaged himself: we hadn't seen that before'. They talked it over as they watched a joint US–UK Special Forces display, emerging from a Chinook helicopter and attacking a mock Daesh stronghold. After it was over, they met the troops face to face. One official says, 'The President didn't actually know a lot about what our joint forces do. Seeing the soldiers with their Union Jacks and Stars and Stripes on their uniforms seemed to make a deep impression on him.'

By the time he flew off to Chequers, relations had recovered, and she'd even convinced him that her Brexit deal need not stop a good US–UK trade deal. Once at the PM's country retreat, Trump was briefed on the latest news on the Novichok poisonings in Salisbury. Two members of the public, Charlie Rowley and Dawn Sturgess, had recently been admitted to Salisbury District Hospital after encountering traces of the nerve agent used to poison the Skripals, which resulted in Sturgess's death on 8 July, four months after the initial incident. Trump told May that he would take a tough line with Putin when he saw him immediately after the UK visit.

The joint press conference, held in the open air, was remarkable for the oddity of Trump holding May's hand as they walked towards the podium, which became the topic of much ridicule and some ire. The first question they received, inevitably, was about the *Sun* interview, from Sky News. Trump transferred blame onto the *Sun* journalist for writing the interview up in a biased way, because he had said 'very good' and 'tremendous' things about May, and then reported that he had said to her that morning, 'I want to apologise because I said such good things about you.' Trump recounted how May had told him earlier that morning, 'Don't worry, it's only the press,' commenting that he 'thought that was very professional'. Observers in May's team noticed how his charm was suddenly switched on. He said he had come to know her 'much better' during his visit, and what an 'incredible woman' she was, who was 'doing a fantastic job'. 'She's a very smart, very tough, very capable person. And I would much rather have her as a friend than my enemy, that I can tell you.' The charm then switched suddenly flicked back off when questions came in from the American networks. 'CNN is fake news. I don't take questions from CNN. Let's go to a real network.' Then he clashed with a reporter from NBC, which he described as 'possibly worse than CNN'. May repeatedly batted away questions about his comments on her and her Brexit plans, avoiding anything that could be construed as critical. One of Trump's ploys backfired when he dismissed the *Sun* interview as 'fake news', which prompted the newspaper to publish the full audio recording online, with a front-page headline: 'Fake Schmooze'.[10]

Trump continued to embarrass his host. When asked about his comments about Johnson, the President replied, 'He'll be a great Prime Minister. He's been very nice to me. He's been saying very good things about me as President. I think he thinks I'm doing a great job. I *am* doing a great job, that I can tell you – just in case you haven't noticed. But Boris Johnson, I think, would be a great Prime Minister.'

Trump's comments gave the audience in Britain a further insight into the way his mind worked. He knew he had to talk up the prospects of a trade deal with Britain, and the US–UK relationship, so in he went: 'We have just a tremendous opportunity to double, triple, quadruple [trade].' May and her team breathed a sigh of relief. But then he launched himself off to Planet Zog: 'I would say I give our relationship, in terms of grade, the highest level of special. So we start off with special. I would give our relationship with the UK – and now, especially after these two days with your Prime Minister – I would say the highest level of special. Am I allowed to go higher than that? I'm not sure. But it's the highest level of special, they are very special people.'

That afternoon, the Trumps went to Windsor Castle, where the President inspected the Guard of Honour, watched a military march pass and had tea with the Queen. Trump was the twelfth US President the Queen had met, and, for him, it was the highlight of the entire trip. So he was dismayed when he breached protocol by walking in front of the Queen when reviewing the troops. But a much greater breach followed with his revealing details of their private conversation in an interview with Piers Morgan. Asked if he had discussed Brexit with the monarch, Trump said, 'I did. She said it's a very – and she's right – it's a very complex problem. I think nobody had any idea how complex that was going to be. Everyone thought it was going to be [simple].'[11]

The collective sigh of relief in May's camp was almost audible when Air Force One lifted off on Friday, initially for Scotland and then on to Russia, leaving dismay and bemusement in its wake. For all the deft footwork exhibited in managing such a controversial visit, with the President's disobliging comments before, during and after it, the harm it did to May's authority, and her chances of getting her deal through, is undeniable. An editorial in *The Spectator* captured the mood when its headline asked: 'The worst thing about Trump's outbursts on Brexit and NATO? That he's right.' The article continued, 'It was undiplomatic, but not wrong, for Trump to have described Britain as a country "in turmoil" this week. How else could you describe the government's failure even to agree a negotiating position on Brexit, let alone persuade the EU to accept it?' Of Chequers, it said:

> The resignations of two cabinet ministers might be seen as a price worth paying if Mrs May had discovered a route for a successful Brexit ... [but she] has ceded power to Europe at almost every turn. Her memoirs, if they're ever written, could be called 'The Art of a Bad Deal'.[12]

Tim Shipman, writing in the *Sunday Times*, suggested that May's situation was as dire as ever: 'In the end it was not Trump's erratic style that was the problem but the substance of his complaints about the Chequers deal,' he wrote. 'This weekend, the details of that deal mean the prime minister's future is still in the balance, with Eurosceptics – unlike Trump – not planning to row back on their criticisms.'[13]

In a bid to regain the initiative after the trip, May went on BBC One's *Andrew Marr Show* on Sunday 15 July, 'with her premiership at its most vulnerable point since the disastrous snap election', in the view of *The Spectator*'s Katy Balls.[14] She was in feisty form, as often happened when backed into a corner. When asked what advice Trump had given her on Brexit, she replied, 'He told me I should sue the EU,' letting out a slight laugh as she did so. The interview confirmed that she had absolutely no intention of changing her mind on Chequers, despite the pressure from all quarters. When asked about the possibility of a no-confidence vote and talk of the rising number of letters to the 1922 Committee to trigger a leadership election, she replied that she had absolutely no intention of going quietly and would fight to get the deal through, and for her own survival. The lady, she might have said, was not for turning.

PRESSURE MOUNTS IN SEPTEMBER

May knew that only a very strong speech at the party conference would steady nerves, not least with memories of her 2017 fiasco still very fresh. 'Things were very edgy in the run-up to the 2018 conference,' says a senior party member. 'There was lots of speculation on what Boris was really up to, and a belief that some MPs would push for a no-confidence vote just after the conference.' Her words had to land perfectly. The task of writing was entrusted to a team of four, with Keelan Carr and Alex Dawson joining Barwell and Penn. They put the first note into her red box shortly before she went off on holiday in late July. She and Philip had planned a similar trip to 2017, a week by Lake Garda, then a hop across to France for the latest First World War centenary event, this time for the Battle of Amiens, followed by two weeks walking in Switzerland. They broke off early to visit Macron on 3 August at the French President's retreat near Toulon, Fort de Brégançon, on a small island off the Mediterranean coast, to lobby him about Chequers. Macron's voice was becoming the most influential among EU leaders, and he was the most sceptical. The trip was a damp squib: he was gracious but non-committal, his office briefing that the dinner 'does not substitute' for official discussions with Michel Barnier.[15] The reception of her plan in Brussels and what she would say at the party conference were the two uppermost thoughts in her mind that August.

An early theme to emerge for her conference speech was that the mounting use of abrasive language towards politicians wasn't good for the country. This attempt to portray herself as above the fray eventually became the passage in her speech where she decried the trend for those willing to serve in politics to become 'targets', and that 'rigorous debate between political opponents is becoming more like a confrontation between enemies'. She highlighted a far-left extremist who shouted abuse at Jacob Rees-Mogg's children as 'sickening' but went on to say the abuse was rife across all parties.

> The first black woman ever to be elected to the House of Commons receives more racist and misogynistic messages today than when she first stood over thirty years ago. You do not have to agree with a word Diane Abbott says to believe passionately in her right to say it, free from threats and abuse.

Keelan Carr remembers that May had two particular objectives in mind for the speech: 'I want people to go away from it proud to be Conservative' and 'I want people to leave the conference feeling good and optimistic about the future of our country.'[16] When May left for a three-day trip to Africa on 28 August, to include meetings with the Presidents of South Africa, Nigeria and Kenya, the speech was already in outline. With her on a chartered RAF Voyager was a trade delegation to boost Britain's post-Brexit trade prospects. It was the first visit by a British Prime Minister to sub-Saharan Africa for five years, and the first to Kenya for thirty. In South Africa, she met President Cyril Ramaphosa, visited Robben Island and danced in front of a crowd of students in Cape Town, repeating her dance routine in Kenya. The New York Times noted how 'the vicar's daughter, known for her devotion to duty and wooden campaign style, busted out first in South Africa and then in Kenya'.[17] British politics followed her throughout the journey, including in some surprising places, when Uhuru Kenyatta, President of Kenya, ridiculed Boris Johnson, feigning to forget his name and then referring to him as 'the bicycle guy'.[18] Nigeria and South Africa are the UK's two biggest trading partners in Africa, and the continent's two largest economies, with Kenya ranking ninth. The trip was a political and commercial success, even if the media was more interested in subjects other than May's trade and security agenda.

By the time May flew to New York for the UN General Assembly, where she was due to speak on 26 September, her conference speech was two-thirds written and she was regularly commenting on drafts. Keelan Carr recalls:

> She was to open with a subject to unify the country: World War One and the centenary commemorations, climaxing that year. The text then moved on to unifying the Conservative Party, which is when she spoke about Tory values and criticisms of Labour. Then, having built up goodwill, that was the moment to discuss Chequers, which we wanted as neither the first nor the last item in the speech. The final portion was to be about how we would move as a country beyond Brexit.[19]

The political tom-toms beat louder and louder throughout September as the party conference approached. Nigel Farage raised adrenalin levels when he announced that he would be returning to frontline politics to 'fight back' against May's 'fraudulent' Chequers deal, which he described as 'a betrayal of everything people voted for'. His attacks were destructive and very personal: 'She doesn't believe in Brexit, she doesn't believe in Britain, she doesn't believe we're good enough to run our own affairs.'[20] The ERG were quick out of the blocks, too, when Parliament returned for two weeks on 4 September, offering a 140-page document laying out its alternative to Chequers. When Johnson declined to back it in public, the plan lost some momentum,[21] though Steve Baker, who had resigned as a DExEU junior minister after Chequers, claimed up to eighty MPs would vote her plan down and argued she therefore needed to produce a new solution at the party conference.[22]

Johnson was a changed man after the summer: more focused, ambitious and tidy. Two figures above all were responsible for the transformation, both wanting to see him installed as PM at the earliest opportunity: new girlfriend Carrie Symonds, and Dominic Cummings, with whom he'd been in constant touch since Vote Leave. After a few months of brooding, he burst back in the *Mail on Sunday* on 9 September, describing May's deal as 'a suicide vest'. He wrote, 'Under the Chequers proposal, we are set to agree to accept their rules – forever – with no say on the making of those rules … We look like a seven-stone weakling being comically bent out of shape by a 500lb gorilla.'[23] While FCO Minister Alan Duncan attacked his former boss's suicide vest comments as 'one of the most disgusting moments in modern British politics',[24] to the ERG they were a spur. Baker said opposition to May had swelled over the summer, and he warned of an autumn with 'a tremendous amount of political crisis and rupture' if she didn't ditch Chequers.[25] Conor Burns, Johnson's PPS at the FCO, who resigned with him, continued to work with him, energetically raising his profile. 'Boris was not trying to get rid of her,' he says now, 'but he was wanting to keep himself in the eye of the party.'

Attention shifted to Johnson's private life, with the announcement that he and his wife Marina Wheeler were divorcing. A 4,000-word dossier full of allegations of Johnson's sex life was passed to the *Sunday Times* which 'contain[ed] a catalogue of lurid allegations about Johnson's sexual liaisons … and damning assessments of his character'.[26] No. 10 flatly denied that it had anything to do with circulating the document, originally drawn up by one of May's team during the Conservative leadership election in 2016, when Johnson had been seen as her fiercest rival. The story prodded the hornet's nest but didn't damage Johnson unduly: his infidelity had already been factored into people's estimation of him. The following week, Johnson used his new weekly column in the *Daily Telegraph* to return to the subject of Chequers, writing, 'The whole thing is a constitutional abomination … It would mean that for the first time since 1066 our leaders were deliberately acquiescing in foreign rule.'[27] Reports circulated about supporters of Johnson wanting to trigger a leadership contest, with Lynton Crosby set to run his campaign. No. 10's riposte – that Johnson had signed up to the joint report, the backstop and, on the day, to Chequers – got nowhere.[28]

'The Prime Minister's got ten days to come up with a new plan and reset Brexit and her leadership, or men in grey suits will be dispatched to tell her to go,' one Brexiteer told Tim Shipman. 'It's now shit or bust.'[29] Johnson called the Chequers plan 'deranged' and questioned whether she believed in Brexit at all any more. 'Unlike the Prime Minister, I campaigned for Brexit. Unlike the Prime Minister, I fought for this, I believe in it, I think it's the right thing for our country and I think that what is happening now is, alas, not what people were promised in 2016.' Shipman's view was that 'Johnson's intervention marks the start of a public beauty contest between the pretenders to May's crown at the Conservative Party conference'.[30] Indeed, possible contenders – Gove, Hunt and Javid among them – were already sniffing the autumnal air.

PARTY CONFERENCE: 30 SEPTEMBER–3 OCTOBER

For the second annual party conference in a row, Johnson was doing his best to unnerve and probe May. In an interview in the *Sunday Times*, which delegates read as they arrived in Birmingham, he expanded his criticisms beyond the Prime Minister's Brexit policy to encompass her plans on public services, saying, 'I think we need to make the case for markets. I don't think we should caper insincerely on socialist territory. You can't beat Corbyn by becoming Corbyn.'[31]

The interview was a warm-up act for Johnson's speech to a ConservativeHome fringe event, which saw queues forming three hours in advance, with activists blocking stairways and corridors in the hope of obtaining a place. The front row was filled with Johnson's parliamentary supporters, including Iain Duncan Smith, Zac Goldsmith and even David Davis. The former Foreign Secretary opened with his best joke of the day, saying how good it was to be back in Birmingham, 'where so many thoroughfares in the city are already named after our superb Conservative Mayor, Andy Street'. Moving on to the Chancellor, he said, 'I want to congratulate my friend Philip Hammond for predicting that I will never become Prime Minister ... That is the first Treasury forecast in a long time to have a distinct ring of truth.' After the slapstick, he moved onto the Chequers plan as his main target. The EU may have been good for Britain in the 1970s, he said, but 'it makes less sense in the globalised economy of today, when 95 per cent of the world's growth is going to be outside the EU ... That is why it is such a mistake for us to leave on the Chequers terms, locked in the tractor beam of Brussels.' May's deal was neither pragmatic nor a compromise, he said: 'It is dangerous and unstable, politically and economically ... This is not what we voted for.' May had let them all down, he said, by abandoning the Lancaster House vision, and they should 'back Theresa May in the best way possible, by softly, quietly and sensibly backing her original plan'.[32] The audience applauded to the room's steel girders.

In stark contrast, at a Campaign for Conservative Democracy meeting, May was booed by delegates when she mentioned her Chequers deal: 'It was a wave of grumbling, really. The party leader normally gets a standing ovation at the end of the meeting, but after the Q&A, Mrs May just walked off,' said one attendee. 'This is my 55th party conference and I've never seen that happen before.'[33] Nerves were not calmed when news then emerged that Brexiteer MP and former FCO Minister James Duddridge had submitted his letter of no confidence in the Prime Minister to the 1922 Committee, writing, 'There comes a point that blind loyalty is not the right way forward. We need a strong leader, someone who believes in Brexit and someone to deliver what the electorate voted for. The Prime Minister seems incapable of doing this.'[34]

May at least was in better physical and mental shape than she had been for Manchester the year before. Her team had persuaded her to avoid many of the conference receptions, sending colleagues in her place, so she could rest her voice and prepare fully for the speech. On the Monday evening, she had celebrated her sixty-second birthday. A diabetic birthday cake had been baked for her, and a small party convened on the top floor of the Hyatt Hotel in Birmingham, to which her senior political team were invited, as well as loyalist MPs including Karen Bradley, James Brokenshire and Seema Kennedy, her PPS.

Whereas in 2017 luck ran against her, two devices now worked in her favour. The first was Stephen Parkinson's ploy of asking the new Attorney General Geoffrey Cox, appointed in July, to give a rousing warm-up act for her, employing to the full his resonant barrister's tones in a rallying cry for the party to unite behind the Prime Minister in her task of taking Britain out of the UK. Cox recalls:

I have no idea why they asked me, but I was happy to do it. I wanted to rouse the audience and tell them it was not a done deal. To seize the prize required single-minded energy and a willingness to compromise, and we all thus needed to get behind the Prime Minister's plan.[35]

'Absolutely superb speech from new Attorney General Geoffrey Cox. Richard Burton voice; Churchillian style; Rumpole humour. A hidden star! Standing ovation,' tweeted MEP David Campbell-Bannerman.

No one, not even her team, was prepared for what happened next. To the music of ABBA's 'Dancing Queen', this most surprising Prime Minister danced onto the stage. One of her choices on *Desert Island Discs* in November 2014, the song was certainly one she liked, and she had casually mentioned to her team at the top of the Hyatt that she might just possibly dance on. None of them knew if she was serious. For a risk-averse and unusually shy Prime Minister, and no natural dancer, it was a brave move. But it went down a storm. 'Let's all dance to May's tune' was the headline in the *Daily Express*, while the *Daily Mail* renamed her 'Mamma May-A!' and declared she had 'danced her way back to authority'.[36] May's telling delegates that if she coughed during this speech it was only because she was up all night securing the letters to the backdrop was another winner. 'The combination of Geoffrey Cox, the dance and the joke meant everyone was on her side from the first moments,' says one of her team. 'The voluntary party always loved her, recognising her as one of their own,' says a Conservative Party board member, who had deliberately helped conceive a much more energised conference, in contrast to the lacklustre 2017 event which prompted the Shapps coup.

The speech was deliberately light on policy announcements but high on emotion. Lifting the cap on local authority borrowing to build more council homes was a rare announcement, as was freezing fuel duty for the ninth consecutive year, but it was hardly the stuff to get Tory pulses racing. Just before the conference season, early forecasts had been shared with the Treasury by the Office for Budget Responsibility (OBR) showing that tax receipts were higher than expected, giving Barwell confidence about the Budget to come and allowing May to make a bold claim. 'A decade after the financial crash, people need to know that the austerity it led to is over and that their hard work has paid off,' she said to huge applause. More tentatively, she pinned the blame for the loss of seats in the general election on austerity. The most poignant moment came when she spoke of her pain at the death of her goddaughter from cancer, as she unveiled a blueprint to save 55,000 people from the disease over the coming decade. Visibly emotional, she described the agony of 'losing a loved one before their time'.

Her team knew that she had to find the right response to Johnson, in a way that didn't raise hackles. So she adopted a subtle tack: 'While she never mentioned his name, almost every passage was a rebuke to Mr Johnson ..., who is now openly intriguing against her ... Her scorn for him was obvious,' said the *Financial Times*.[37] She stressed that the

Tories were here to 'back business', a clear put-down to Johnson, who in June was reported to have dismissed business's concerns over Brexit with the words 'Fuck business'.[38] Johnson's popularity plummeted following the conference. A YouGov poll taken ten days afterwards saw his net favourability decline from -28 on the eve of the conference down to -35, while May stood at -21.[39]

May had pulled it out of the bag. Katy Balls wrote in *The Spectator*:

> For the first time in months, Downing Street have little to worry about from today's papers. After delivering one of her best speeches since becoming Prime Minister, Theresa May is enjoying some of the best front pages she has had since the disastrous snap election. Each paper carries photos of a happy PM dancing – with her promise to 'end austerity' after Brexit making the top line.[40]

The party still didn't love her Chequers plan, but she had seen off the challenge from Johnson and the ERG, strengthening her grip on the leadership, at least until 29 March 2019, if not for much longer. Johnson's putsch had failed, but the anger and contempt for her and her deal had far from died. The part of her speech that riled the ERG and other critical MPs was the suggestion that, if MPs backed her Brexit plan, she would pursue the ending of austerity, which suggested to them she had no plans to leave on or soon after 29 March. Remaining at No. 10 was not part of their reckoning. 'She was only good in our eyes until she delivered Brexit. Then she would be toast,' says one.

TORRID OCTOBER

May's escape at the party conference was to prove short-lived, as if the very success of her speech bred resentment among her MPs, who were palpably unhappy when the House returned on Tuesday 9 October. May was about to enter the most difficult month in her time as Prime Minister to date. Attacks came from multiple quarters, with claims that the numbers of signatories calling for a leadership contest had now crept up to forty-six, two short of the magic number. Although likely an exaggeration – No. 10 suspected the real number was two thirds of that figure – it was still unnerving. While Johnson's supporters went into a depressed state after the conference, sensing that his moment may have passed, Davis's star was in the ascendant, with his backers encouraging Johnson's to see if their man would stand aside, given his own attempt had collapsed.[41] Those Brexiteers still inside the government were becoming increasingly outspoken. DExEU secretary Dominic Raab was openly saying he could not support signing up to a customs union without an end date. Four Brexit Cabinet ministers were said to be planning to resign together in a bid to force May out: if so, their combined force would almost certainly have achieved the end that they sought. While some Brexiteer MPs shifted their tactics to speaking about voting down the Budget unless May took a tougher line with Brussels,[42] May was coming under pressure from her other flank too. On Saturday 20 October, some 700,000 protesters descended on central London for the People's Vote March, amid talk of up to fifty Conservative MPs, including five ministers, wanting to back a second referendum. Hammond was incensed by May's comments about ending austerity: he visualised his hard work over the previous two and a half years going up in flames, and her taking credit. The better relationship that they'd enjoyed in the fifteen months since the general election came was coming under serious threat.

Sunday 21 October was a particularly bleak day for May. Johnny Mercer, the former army officer who had been an MP since 2015, and who had voted Remain in the 2016 referendum, used a newspaper column in the *Sunday Times* to say that he could not 'continue to support an administration that cannot function'. Having branded the government 'a shit-show' earlier in the week, he recounted how he had received 'overwhelming support' from MPs, including ministers. In the article, he attacked 'an abject failure of this government to govern'. What was required, he said, was 'courage, fight and conviction ... We need technocrats and managers ... but at this defining moment in our history, Britain cannot be led by them.'[43] Mercer was not a hothead but a respected figure: it showed how mainstream Conservatives were moving to oppose May and her deal.

The language now reached new levels of intemperance. May was 'entering the killing zone', said one ally of David Davis's, while an ex-minister compared the Prime Minister to a 'lame cockroach' and another said, 'The moment is coming when the knife gets heated, stuck in her front and twisted. She'll be dead soon.' Still another told a reporter that May should 'bring her own noose' to a meeting on 24 October of the 1922 Committee.[44] At a time of mounting knife crime, and following the murder of MP Jo Cox by a far-right extremist, the incendiary language was irresponsible yet indicative.

The Celtic fringe posed further worries. May's thirteen Scottish MPs were rucking over any extension to the transition period, principally due to concerns over fishery policies, while the DUP, under heat from their own rivals, the UUP and Sinn Féin, were seeing even less need to be obliging, and becoming unrecognisable from the biddable band who had teamed up with May the year before. 'Are these the last days of Theresa May?' asked the *New Statesman*'s Stephen Bush, noting, 'This morning's papers are full of plots and ultimatums to the Prime Minister unless she changes her Brexit strategy.'[45]

Anger at such articles, informed by briefings by disgruntled Tory MPs and ministers, was top of the agenda at the 1922 Committee meeting on Wednesday 24 October. May blasted in with an emotional and personal speech about why her deal was the best and only way forward for the country. Her MPs bought it. One MP declared the meeting was an 'outbreak of unity ... not one dissenting voice', adding, 'Well, you look over the cliff, consider the alternative, and then think, hmmmm, perhaps not.'[46] What had happened to all the noise about her being on her last legs? By disproportionately quoting malcontents, the press had given a distorted view of the power of her enemies. By this stage, some fifty to sixty MPs wanted a leadership challenger to replace her, but many were hesitant to submit their letters at the wrong time lest she survive the vote. The 1922 confirmed the verdict of the party conference exactly three weeks before. Conservative MPs at large were not ready to drop either May or her deal. Yet.

HEYWOOD'S DEPARTURE AND PEAK HAMMOND

Wednesday 24 October was also the date when news was released that Jeremy Heywood had resigned officially as head of the civil service because of his cancer, and that Mark Sedwill would succeed him. The departure of Whitehall's most senior and experienced figure left an enormous hole at the heart of Whitehall, and at the most perilous of moments. When he first stood aside in June, the plan was for Treasury Permanent Secretary Tom Scholar (who had briefly been chief of staff to Gordon Brown as Prime Minister) to take over some of his work, convening the Budget negotiation between the Treasury and No. 10. But much of Downing Street was preoccupied with other matters, and his mission lapsed. Heywood's departure meant the loss of his unique ability to challenge the Treasury and provide counter-arguments for May against Hammond. Peter Hill, May's tenacious Principal Private Secretary, was a Foreign Office rather than a Treasury appointee, unusually, and Mark Sedwill, although an economist, had not worked in the Treasury. Will Macfarlane, the Treasury official who had been the

Prime Minister's private secretary for economic affairs since 2015, had seen this problem early. He had tried to grow Treasury experience in No. 10 – Lorna Gratton and Imran Shafi in the private office, Patrick Curry and Will Davis in the Policy Unit. But there was no second Heywood at hand.

This was one reason why the October 2018 Budget was substantially made in the Treasury – although, in light of May's recent announcements (on the NHS, austerity and the health of public finances), the Autumn Budget was bound to be less contentious. May's mind was on political firefighting and the EU. 'We really just wanted the Budget out of the way,' says one No. 10 official. According to a Treasury official, 'A whole series of planned meetings did not take place or were cut short.' Macfarlane and Barwell continued to work with Hammond and his team, but a confrontation was the last thing May's team wanted. It made for the most harmonious of Hammond's four Budgets. Unusually, it was held on a Monday, 29 October, again reflecting Brexit as the dominant issue. Throughout the Sunday, every senior Treasury civil servant was in the office advising the Chancellor on how to spend the remaining cash at his disposal – the vast majority already taken up by the NHS Long Term Plan. No. 10 were simply 'kept informed' in the final stages, and the customary wrangles with departmental ministers were equally minimised. Decisions on the finer details of health and education were taken deep into Sunday evening.

'We have reached a defining moment on this long, hard journey,' Hammond told the House, building on May's conference speech in declaring that the 'era of austerity is finally coming to an end'. He described it as a Budget for 'the strivers, the grafters and the carers', promising a 'brighter future' at last after a decade of constraint, with a slight but significant increase in growth forecasts, from 1.3 to 1.6 per cent for 2019, and better-than-expected borrowing figures.[47] The principal features were changes to universal credit, to reduce the numbers losing out when moving to the new system, an extra £1 billion for defence, £650 million for social care, £500 million for housing and £400 million for schools. 'It's far from spend, spend, spend,' said Laura Kuenssberg, 'but it is certainly the promise of a change of direction.' She added, 'It's a claim from Philip Hammond and Theresa May that they can, while in office, reverse the political pendulum.'[48]

Her party conference speech and the Budget had again bought May time. The question was, for how long? She was flying into the eye of a storm with her eyes closed, with no idea how she would magic up the votes to get her deal through Parliament. 'I gave it a 50:50 chance that I'd be out of a job by Christmas,' says a senior No. 10 aide. To many, that sounded optimistic.

Dominic Raab (left) succeeded David Davis as Brexit Secretary from July to November 2018, clashing strongly with the EU, as well as with May's own Brexit advisor, Olly Robbins (right).

CHAPTER 16

BREXIT: NO WAY THROUGH

AUGUST–DECEMBER 2018

With the EU and parliamentary clocks now firmly against her, May had three challenges in the autumn of 2018. She had secured the backing at Chequers in July to her plan. Now she had to secure the EU's agreement, to take the deal back with any revisions to Cabinet, and then to see it through Parliament. The first proved unexpectedly difficult, the second still more so, and the third, ultimately, impossible. By Christmas, many had come to think her deal was dead, at least in its unamended form. Holding faith in this doomed deal rested on the shoulders of one person: the Prime Minister. She never gave up believing in its ability to secure the parliamentary support needed to take Britain out of the European Union.

The arithmetic refused to add up. Her withdrawal agreement might have been acceptable to the EU, and to a majority in a deeply divided Cabinet, but it was never going to pass through Parliament. Amending it to embrace a customs union was popular within the EU, and may have secured a majority in Parliament with the help of Labour votes, but her Cabinet would never back it. Adapting it to rest on the possibility of alternative facilitated customs arrangements might have carried Cabinet, and maybe, at a stretch, Parliament, but it would not pass muster with the EU. Only at the very end did she come to realise that the hardest struggle over Brexit was not with the EU, but with politicians at Westminster, and her team's dreams of a secret ballot, where MPs could vote without worrying about their whips, were never realised.

But despite repeatedly being told that the numbers in the Commons didn't stack up, May continued to believe that the nearer the clock ran down to 29 March, the more the pressure would build on the various factions to vote it through. Perhaps, her advisors wondered, MPs would reject the Bill the first time and then, having rebelled once, accede. But the hard Brexiteers in the ERG were clock-watching too, gaming events to ensure no deal passed through the House, making no-deal Brexit inevitable. 'People like Gavin Barwell were forever saying that they would get the deal through Parliament,' Verhofstadt says. 'They always believed that, somehow, they could hold the Conservative Party together. But that was never going to happen.'[1]

STRUGGLE #1: ACHIEVING AGREEMENT WITH THE EU

May had cut short her summer holiday to visit Macron in his Mediterranean retreat, the Fort de Brégançon, on 3 August, in what proved a forlorn attempt to gain his understanding. He was among the most sceptical of all the senior EU27 leaders, who together found themselves in a dilemma on how to respond to Chequers. While in private they felt May was being overly demanding, they were wary of coming down too strongly against her, jeopardising her premiership and letting Johnson in – an eventuality that, in their eyes, seemed increasingly plausible. Besides, many saw real signs of progress. 'Juncker and his closest team saw Chequers as a positive step going in the direction of a future partnership formed on a free trade area,' says a senior Commission official closely involved in the Brexit negotiations. 'We welcomed it.'

In the run-up to the Chequers summit, May had taken encouragement from her visits to Rutte and Merkel that the EU supported her deal. But in August and September, when May's ministers and officials made more efforts to persuade other individual EU leaders and key figures in Brussels, she was discomforted by what she saw as a hardening of their opposition. She still did not appreciate that the EU were truly worried by parts of her plan, especially the common rulebook, in which the UK followed some but not all parts of the single market, and the proposed customs arrangement, in which the UK would collect tariffs on behalf of the EU and be able to set its own rates. She was pressing for precisely the cherry-picking approach that Barnier had chastised. August had seen EU leaders off on their holidays, but on 2 September Barnier sprang into action with an interview in the German newspaper *Frankfurter Allgemeine Zeitung* in which he came out openly in 'strong opposition' to May's plan, above all for trying to split the single market. On 4 September, the day the House of Commons returned, Barnier appeared before a committee of MPs and said in measured tones that the trade proposal in the White Paper 'does not seem workable to us'.[2] Juncker reiterated this same message in his annual State of the EU speech in Strasbourg.

May's mind remained set that the EU could be persuaded by her plan, if only they understood it properly. An EU emergency summit, hosted by Austrian Chancellor Sebastian Kurz in Salzburg, had been called because the EU didn't want Brexit discussions to bleed over into the October Council. 'We want to see more realism from the UK across the piece,' she was told. They were not the only ones trying to land that message. Before the summit, Dominic Raab had a glass of wine with May as they enjoyed a rare leisurely discussion. 'I think we have a 40 per cent chance of getting the deal agreed in Salzburg,' the DExEU Secretary told her, knowing at the time that he was exaggerating the odds. 'It was fairly clear to me from Chequers onwards that her plan would crash and not get through the EU, but I thought it would be too damning if I put the odds any lower,' he admits, adding, 'I needed her support getting the backstop changed.' 'We have a much bigger chance than 40 per cent,' she shot back at him, looking surprised and offended.[3]

Raab found himself increasingly at a loss to understand her thinking, which, in his view, was constantly gravitating towards the EU. He had no doubt who was responsible: the Treasury, intent on diminishing the 2016 referendum result in its eagerness to remain close to the EU. In contrast, he found the views of the Foreign Office and its Permanent Representative to the EU, Tim Barrow, more realistic. 'The Foreign Office had been sidelined in the whole Brexit process but had a far more acute understanding of how Brussels operated and the way the EU thought,' he says.[4]

Among EU officials, however, May had the opposite reputation – in their eyes, her mind was always drifting back to Britain, refusing to fully appreciate the EU's side. On Tuesday 18 September, she boarded the plane to Salzburg, realising she had a difficult task, but confident of success. Either she had still not absorbed the warning signs, or the advice had failed to truly convey how and why the EU were unhappy with Chequers – and this sense of dissatisfaction was deepening, as the EU's internal position moved towards one of confrontation rather than concessions. The atmosphere would have been hostile enough without May publishing a pugnacious article in the German newspaper *Die Welt*. 'We are near to achieving the orderly withdrawal that is [an] essential basis for building a close future partnership ... [but] to come to a successful conclusion, just as the UK has evolved its position, the EU will need to do the same,' she wrote.[5]

The 'evolution' of the EU's thinking that May sought was not on offer, and the insinuation that only Britain had been compromising, and it was now the EU's turn to bend, did not sit well – with good reason. The article set fraught foundations for the conference from the off. 'Suddenly when EU leaders and their teams arrive in Salzburg,' a senior Commission official recalls,

> there's an article that May published the same morning which was rather tough – the wording didn't feel in line with the constructive atmosphere we had developed over the past months. Basically it said that the EU now has to give in to finally help us. This was considered by anyone who read it to be unhelpful and inappropriate.

That evening, May was given the floor at the end of dinner. When she most needed charm, cordiality and conviction, she made another ill-judged move, attacking Barnier in an ill-conceived, and poorly delivered, speech to EU leaders. The speech had, as one of her EU advisors recalls, 'a slight note of impatience, a rare miscalculation on her part. May knew at once that it hadn't gone well, but it's not in her nature to apportion blame, recognising we'd all misjudged the tone.' The speech led to glum faces and some awkward and considerably irritating conversations that evening. 'To keep saying, "This is what I've said and I'll keep saying it" – they felt hectored,' said Frans Timmermans, the Commission's Vice-President.[6] Another senior Commission official, closely involved in the Brexit negotiations, called it 'a mistake', adding, 'She read out speaking points which were basically identical to the article [in *Die Welt*], and she didn't look people in the eyes when delivering her message – there was great unrest at the time.'

Thursday 20 September saw no thaw. Macron, increasingly the leader of the EU hardliners against May, had also been infuriated when he heard reports that she told Varadkar over a private breakfast that it might not be possible to reach a compromise on the Irish border by the October Council deadline. May was pointedly excluded from a lunch of the EU27 leaders, where tempers frayed. Macron spoke out against her, and after the meal openly attacked Brexiteers who claimed that an easy Brexit was possible on terms favourable to the UK, branding them liars.[7] The British press, as ever, hadn't helped matters. Unsubstantiated media reports alleged that the Belgian and Dutch Prime Ministers were ready to give May ground – forcing both leaders to declare these reports were fake. 'This further hardened the sentiment in the room,' the senior Commission official says.

> So when Tusk came out of the meeting, people who had called for something a bit more open were not supported. There was so much frustration – and he got clear instruction from the EU leaders to give a tough statement without any sign of openness, using anti-Chequers language. Without the original atmosphere, the situation would have been softer, if not fundamentally different.

May had held a brief private meeting with Tusk, who had told her what to expect. She was given an hour to prepare for what she was warned might be a hostile encounter. But she later said that she received no indication of quite how abrasive it would be. An official travelling with her says, 'We had no idea, we didn't see it coming. The EU leaders really didn't understand the difficulties under which she was labouring.' Whatever animosity the EU felt towards May was now more than mutual: 'We strongly felt that Tusk had not behaved properly,' another No. 10 official says.

Tusk launched into her at the press conference, saying the EU could not support Chequers, and embellished his remarks with other disparaging comments. He followed it up by mocking her negotiating strategy on Instagram. At the summit, he had ushered May over to a tray of cakes and invited her to partake, ensuring a photographer captured the scene. After proceedings closed, he posted a picture on Instagram of May and himself at the cake stand with the caption: 'A piece of cake, perhaps? Sorry, no cherries,' a reference both to the running joke, or irritation, across the EU that (in Boris Johnson's words) Britain wanted to 'have its cake and eat it', and to Britain's doomed desire to 'cherry-pick'.[8] May suspected Merkel was no longer willing to go out of her way to support Britain, while Macron's views on Britain, hardening all the time, were similar to Barnier's: British Brexiteers to him were like Trump, Orbán and Le Pen, and in the view of one Brexiteer Cabinet minister, EU officials saw themselves as 'involved in a Manichean struggle against the forces of populist darkness, to which they had to take a strong stand'.

No. 10 was incandescent with Tusk. Even his 'A piece of cake?' stunt was deemed insensitive to a Type-1 diabetic. A conversation ensued between staff in London and Salzburg on whether May should walk out. Sober voices prevailed. Raab thought the treatment of her was 'extraordinarily rude and unacceptable'. The headlines the next day, 21 September, read: 'May humiliated as European leaders tell her: your Brexit plan won't work' (*The Guardian*), 'Humiliation for May as EU rejects Brexit plan' (*The Times*), 'The Salzburg disaster' (*i*) and 'EU dirty rats: Euro mobsters ambush May' (*The Sun*). Raab recalls feeling 'my strongest sense of loyalty to May throughout my entire time at DExEU was after the way she was treated at Salzburg'.[9] The EU, too, knew that it had behaved poorly, and became more emollient over the following weeks.

May needed a robust response. Her team decided to bring television cameras into No. 10's state dining room for her to hit back. 'It was the one occasion when she kicked the tables over emphatically,' says director of communications Robbie Gibb. 'There's an argument for saying she should have done it more often.'[10] At her most defiant, May demanded that the EU show the UK respect and understand that she would not 'overturn the result' of the EU referendum, nor would she sign off any plan the EU foisted on her that would 'break up my country'. Climbing onto the moral high ground, she made an unconditional offer to the three million EU citizens living in the UK that they could remain, even in the event of no deal. 'Throughout this process, I have treated the EU with nothing but respect,' she concluded. 'The UK expects the same.'[11]

In the short term, there was a silver lining from the EU's rebuff. 'After her speech she gave one of her best Q&As ever,' says one of her team. It boosted her standing among Brexiteers, and recovered some ground lost at Chequers, while Conservative polling ratings picked up (from 40 per cent in late August to 42 per cent in late September, according to YouGov). The shared sense among EU leaders that they may have overstepped the mark was also expected to work in May's favour. But the narrative that May was 'standing up for Britain' and was a Brexit hero barely survived the weekend. By early the following week, the ERG was back on the warpath, apportioning blame for Britain's humiliation on Robbins in increasingly personalised attacks.

On Monday 24 September, a group of Brexiteer ministers, including Leadsom, Mordaunt and McVey, launched an initiative for a Canada-style free trade agreement for Britain to leave the EU and secure its own trade deals. Rees-Mogg said it was the 'obvious solution', but others opposed to Chequers thought it would not work as it failed to solve the Northern Ireland conundrum. All options were under review at No. 10, including calling a snap general election to capitalise on Corbyn's growing unpopularity in opinion polls. But it was promptly ruled out – among many other things, the anger it would engender in the party, which was readying for her departure, would be severe. Thus went the only option to change the parliamentary arithmetic and regain personal standing with the EU, Cabinet and public opinion.[12]

The party conference, finishing on 3 October, bought May precious little breathing space. The following week saw a difficult Cabinet meeting on Tuesday 9 October. The day before, she met early with Graham Brady, on his request, who warned her that – if press briefings about her deal were true – she had a 'massive problem'. At lunchtime,

Denzil Davidson and Raoul Ruparel were sent to Brady's office to give him a full briefing. 'All my worst suspicions were confirmed,' he says. 'I asked for another meeting the next day before Cabinet and told her there was no earthly way it would get through the Commons.'[13]

Later, during the Cabinet meeting, Leadsom openly flirted with resigning and Mordaunt and McVey were palpably unhappy at the compromises May was apparently planning for. In Parliament, the Prime Minister faced angry dissent from the ERG and the DUP, who were now finding common ground, as well as from rebel Remainers. Even moderates like Jo Johnson, Transport Minister and brother of Boris Johnson, were dismayed by her Brexit position and oscillating stance – and he would resign a month later, saying the public was being offered 'an agreement that will leave our country economically weakened … [Her deal] will inflict untold damage on our nation.' To Jo Johnson, the country was being presented with a choice between 'vassalage and chaos', making it 'a failure of British statecraft on a scale unseen since the Suez crisis'. The two brothers had not always been politically close, so Jo's words that 'my brother Boris, who led the Leave campaign, is as unhappy with the government's proposals as I am' opened up a new front.[14]

May found herself caught up too in an increasingly acrimonious stand-off between her Brexit Secretary, Dominic Raab, who kept telling her what Conservative colleagues wouldn't stand, and her Europe advisor, Olly Robbins, who kept telling her what the EU wouldn't stand. Both identified the Northern Ireland backstop as the major issue still to be settled with the EU, which could sink the deal in Parliament if not resolved. Robbins was determined to try to find a solution. Told in late September that Sabine Weyand from Barnier's team thought he was annoyed with her after the Salzburg debacle, he arranged to go out for dinner with her in Brussels to try to find a way forward. They planned for their teams to convene for a week's hard slog to prepare the ground ahead of the October Council, from which emerged Weyand's tentative agreement to shift on the backstop to a solution closer to what they hoped would satisfy the British government and the DUP. She had indicated the EU was open to the idea of an agreement in which an all-UK customs union was included in the terms of exit to deal with the issue of Northern Ireland, ensuring there was both a frictionless land border and no customs border along the Irish Sea. It was known as 'the backstop to the backstop'.

Robbins presented it remotely to a meeting of the Cabinet's SN Committee in early October. 'It's good news, Prime Minister, we have most of what we want,' said his flickering face on the screen. Geoffrey Cox, who had been appointed Attorney General in July, asked the critical question: 'Am I wrong to think that what you propose isn't going to be legally enforceable?' The text Robbins had negotiated with the EU lacked the clause necessary to force Brussels to adhere to their promise of a UK-wide customs union. 'The Attorney General is right,' Robbins replied. 'This is completely unacceptable then,' said May. She knew that any risk of a Northern Ireland-only backstop, without a clear end point, would threaten staunch opposition from the DUP, who would baulk at the idea of any regulatory divergence from the UK, as well as from Brexiteers.

With the EU Council just days away, and under pressure from all sides, with no spirit of compromise in the air, May still had no solution. *The Spectator* captured her predicament:

> The papers are filled with Cabinet resignation threats, rumoured leadership bids and a warning from the DUP that 'no deal' is now the most likely outcome ... If last week was 'hell week' for Theresa May, the next few days could be classed as the Prime Minister's trip to the ninth circle. With problems over the Irish border backstop unsolved, No. 10 are fighting a war on multiple fronts ahead of the crucial EU Council meeting on Wednesday.[15]

In Brussels, May did her best to present her case for more compromise, spending fifteen minutes lobbying the leaders at the October Council on the evening of Wednesday 17 October with a 'message of goodwill'. But the EU leaders were not buying it, saying that she offered 'nothing new', which was self-evidently true. They promptly cancelled the emergency summit that had been planned for November to finalise Brexit, in the hope that it would 'avoid another spectacle in front of the world's media', as *The Guardian* put it, while giving negotiators space to hammer out an agreement away from the limelight.[16] On her return to the UK, May tried to reassure MPs when she made her post-Council statement on Monday 22 October, insisting that '95 per cent of the withdrawal agreement and its protocols are now settled'. The remaining 5 per cent, she admitted, was a 'considerable' sticking point, namely the Irish border, with May reiterating her opposition to Brussels' favoured Northern Ireland-only backstop. No British Prime Minister, she told MPs, could accept the consequences: namely, a border down the Irish Sea. She said that a new spirit had come into the negotiations since Salzburg: 'The EU are now actively working with us on this proposal.' But she knew, fundamentally, that the EU was showing the UK little goodwill.

In truth, May and the EU were both guilty of a lack of sympathy. She underestimated Brussels's existential commitment to the sanctity of the single market and the EU's fundamental freedoms, while the EU failed to appreciate fully the difficulties May encountered in finding a solution to Northern Ireland, and her lack of room for manoeuvre in her own party and in Parliament. The EU still believed that if it pushed hard enough, time pressure would force her to adopt one of its favoured 'off-the-shelf' models for Brexit. It was impatient with May, believing it had told her all along that any workable Brexit would necessarily involve a customs union, and was growing tired of what they saw as vague proposals and promises which sought to appease every side. To Barnier, Brexit could not be a win–win. It was lose–lose. And if other member states who might be considering their own exit from the EU saw how long and painful it was, well, that would be no bad thing.

A breakthrough nevertheless came in the following two weeks. Barnier, after heavy British lobbying, agreed to drop his opposition to a UK-wide customs union being written into the withdrawal agreement, which meant that the Northern Ireland-only backstop was dropped. But – and this was the hitch – the UK-wide customs union that came in its place had significant conditions, which were to pose very serious problems for May when she tried to sell her withdrawal agreement, first to the Cabinet and then to Parliament. The most significant was a guarantee to Ireland that Britain would not leave a UK–EU customs union backstop unless the EU was first satisfied that arrangements were in place to avoid a hard border, either through a trade deal or through a successor plan for Northern Ireland. Exit from the backstop was to become the issue that was to dominate the next twelve months in British politics.

May at last had her deal agreed with the EU. It may have only been the beginning – her next task, getting it past Cabinet and Parliament, would be the greater challenge – but it was a genuine achievement. May was a tougher negotiator than she is often given credit for – and the EU's position, far from being set in stone, gave much more ground than is often acknowledged. The backstop effectively kept the UK in the customs union without having to accept all the obligations of membership – cherry-picking plain and simple, albeit not all the cherries Britain would ideally have chosen.

'I think they're wrong, those who say she should have been tough from the start,' Martin Selmayr says. 'Anyone who believes that Theresa May or Olly Robbins were not tough negotiators is profoundly mistaken – they were, often even extremely inconvenient negotiators. She negotiated it skilfully, with a profound understanding of detail, much deeper than many Prime Ministers on the Continent.'[17]

STRUGGLE #2: ACHIEVING AGREEMENT WITH CABINET

May's battles with the EU were etched deep into her consciousness. She knew she wouldn't get more from a Brussels that had grown very tired of what they saw as her endless requests for further concessions. But many in her Cabinet and among her MPs simply didn't believe she had achieved the best terms, and thought she just had to batter them for a better deal, or break from the EU without a deal. Robbins, as the principal official conduit, was blamed for the message that the EU would not budge further, and DExEU Secretary Dominic Raab was the champion of those who were saying, 'Go back, be tougher.' Forced to choose one advocate over the other, May felt she had no choice but to back Robbins's judgement. She had made the same choice before, preferring the judgement of Robbins over David Davis, ultimately precipitating his resignation. It was nothing to do with their personalities: she liked Davis, and she liked Raab. It was simply her judgement that Robbins had achieved the best negotiable result if the EU was to agree her withdrawal terms and Britain was to avoid the cliff edge of a no-deal exit. A Prime Minister with stronger authority and advocacy skills would have done more to explain the difficulties Robbins faced working with the EU, and the skills he displayed. At this most difficult moment, another factor made his life more difficult: Heywood, his most powerful supporter in Whitehall, retired because of cancer on 24 October. With little cover, Robbins became the target of ERG ire as never before. And in the new DExEU Secretary he had a far less urbane sparring partner than Davis.

A practicing solicitor at Linklaters at the start of his career, with law degrees from Oxford and Cambridge, a stickler for correct form and with limitless self-belief, Raab had been surprised to find on his appointment on 9 July that the key meetings between Davis and Barnier, and between the British and Weyand's teams, had not been properly minuted. He became concerned that Robbins was keeping him out of the loop. One insider (a Brexiteer) recounted how

Olly would at times deliberately circumvent the PM's box process. He would insert things late at night with decisions required within just a few hours, when it would not be possible to obtain a balanced view on the other side. He repeatedly delivered documents late, which meant the PM was left with an overwhelming balance of advice just from his side, rather than Dom's. The PM's private office was worried about what was happening, and several figures went to Gavin Barwell to say it had to stop.

According to Nikki da Costa, May's senior legislative aide, 'The more it became just Olly and Gavin in the room, the narrower the decision-making, and the more pro-EU the decisions went.'[18] Reports flowed back to Raab that Robbins had been complaining to May behind his back, hearing that 'Raab will torpedo these delicate negotiations if we don't stop him' – a view that was caught on BBC Four's fly-on-the-wall television programme *Brexit Behind Closed Doors*.[19] Raab believed May was allowing Robbins to hold technical conversations offline on the backstop, on which he was consistently more hardline, deliberately excluding him, and he was 'frozen out of discussions'. After Salzburg, he found himself refused permission to go to Brussels: 'She chose to listen to Olly Robbins rather than me.' He says, 'Olly used Salzburg to cement his grip on No. 10 and cement his relationship with the PM.'[20]

Raab became concerned too by the balance of opinion within No. 10, regarding Stephen Parkinson as the only serious Brexiteer in the building. While Robbie Gibb had been a committed Leaver, and was passionate about the cause, he was also a loyal believer in May's plan. Raab found Barwell too ready to agree to the EU line, while her other key Brexit advisors in the No. 10 Europe Unit – Denzil Davidson, Ed de Minckwitz and Raoul Ruparel – were all, in differing ways, Europhiles. (Although at least one of them preferred the label 'reality-based', and another pointed to how much the meaning of Europhile had changed after the Brexit vote – encompassing anyone, they said, who was not a 'true believer'.) The advice Raab thought May was receiving was thus far too much on one side. He had accepted the line that No. 10 gave out after Chequers, which was 'it is this far, but no further towards Brussels'. So he was constantly on the alert to prevent any further slippage.

May had indeed been on a journey since the general election, away from the hard Brexit she had articulated in her 2016 conference and Lancaster House speeches, towards recognising that a customs union in some form was inevitable. If a no-deal was to be avoided, an accommodation had to be struck with the EU. So she found herself at odds with the ERG, and increasingly with her middle-ground colleagues in Cabinet like Javid, Hunt and Gove, who kept telling her she needed to be tougher with the EU to get what Britain needed, as Thatcher had been. She put her faith in Robbins as the man to say what kind of deal was possible with Brussels. In so far as she was aware of the rising cacophony of criticism of Robbins from Brexiteers, she never let it disturb her trust in him. He did have an individual working style that grated with some, especially those who either thought the PM was neglecting their advice or believed Robbins was overstepping his remit. He did fight fiercely to protect his channel to her, because he worried about what he saw as partisan and ill-informed advice damaging delicate discussions and progress he had fought so hard to make in Brussels. He was more concerned about what would be acceptable to the EU than what would pass through Parliament – but he would say he was her EU advisor, not her political advisor. He knew he was becoming the bogeyman, as he had foreseen on his appointment, but he stuck to his task, holding fast despite an increasingly ugly atmosphere around him.

The EU had given May an agreement deadline of 21 November. Her team were very conscious too of the fast approach of 29 March 2019, now less than four months away. She had to first get the meaningful vote through, then the Withdrawal Agreement Bill through its Commons stages, then take it through the House of Lords (where the majority of peers were pro-Remain), then have it ratified in Europe, before Britain could leave. The timeframe gave her precious little time to canvass support, with cracks growing all the time. Even within her citadel of No. 10, divisions were festering, with Gibb and Parkinson believing she could do more to stand up to the EU, as she had famously done after Salzburg.

The critical Cabinet meeting, long delayed and already putting the timetable under considerable strain, was due the following week. The Friday before saw frantic work in Brussels to confirm the final text. The French lobbied at the last minute to tear up concessions that the British had already been granted, while Robbins fought hard to get them back onside, which resulted in him having to insert a clause into the political declaration to 'build on and improve' the customs arrangement agreed in the withdrawal agreement. At 11.57 a.m. on Monday 12 November, Robbins sent May's senior team at No. 10 his final version of the text, incorporating all the last-minute amendments they had sent him. Ruparel was one of those who, when he read the submission, became immediately worried that it did not address the lack of a time limit on the exit clause to the backstop. It raised the question, which the ERG and DUP would inevitably alight upon, about whether the EU might dictate Britain's future. He worried too that the ERG would rebel at the prospect of a permanent customs union and would argue that the UK was paying out too much for very little in return. That evening, he sent Barwell an email: 'My assessment is that this won't get through Cabinet and Parliament.' Equally, as he acknowledged, 'I don't know what the alternative is, if there is one.'[21]

After the 8.30 a.m. meeting in May's room the following day, Tuesday 13 November, what became known as 'Small Group' convened after more junior staff left. 'This is it,' May said. 'The negotiations with the EU have come to the end of the road, and we now have to get it through Cabinet and put it to Parliament. We have got as far with the EU as we can get.' Those present noted how unusually weary she looked, with a sense of foreboding that things might not go well.

Throughout the day, her senior team worked on the final details and a strategy to put to Cabinet and Parliament the next day. Hunt asked to see May alone mid-afternoon on Tuesday, but she was accompanied by Penn. As Foreign Secretary, he knew what was in the deal, and he felt he had to speak out. He recalls:

I told her, 'Prime Minister, if you go ahead with this deal, your premiership will be over. It won't get through Parliament and you will fall. The backstop is the killer. You need your Maggie Thatcher moment. Show the country you are batting for Britain and stare down the EU. That's the only way you'll do it.' But she told me, 'I don't think I can do more.'[22]

At 5 p.m. that day, a meeting was convened between Barwell's and Robbins's teams. Nikki da Costa, director of legislative affairs at No. 10, said she would like to pose a question: 'You are asking the senior team to help sell the proposals, and yet we don't know exactly what's in them. We need to see them in order to do our jobs.' She had not been on the distribution list the day before, and over the previous weeks she had become increasingly concerned whether Britain was slipping into a customs union, losing space for manoeuvre, and with no mention of no deal as a fallback. Barwell was visibly unhappy with her but agreed that a reading room be established in No. 10's Europe Unit, so that designated individuals could go there and read the proposal.

In the torrid atmosphere, leaks even in No. 10 had become a real fear, hence the wish to restrict access to a bare minimum. Da Costa feared the worst. She was strongly against a customs union. But she was not fully prepared for what she was to read: 'I felt shocked about what the document said about regulatory alignment, new elements on the backstop which had not been shared with the wider senior team, and I worried about what it meant for the relationship with Northern Ireland and the UK.'[23]

She was cross too that she had been isolated from decisions taken within the building. 'It seemed to me that the decisions had been taken tighter and tighter within a group of the senior team,' she says.[24] Like many, she thought that Geoffrey Cox's legal advice would be critical, and by 7 p.m. on Tuesday she had secured a copy. Despite being told earlier in the day by Barwell that 'I think the Attorney General will be helpful with Cabinet', she thought the legal opinion 'punchy' and felt it might not achieve the response from Cabinet ministers that the Prime Minister imagined. Da Costa went home that evening feeling very conflicted, frustrated that her views weren't being heard, and concluded – not for the first time – that she had to quit. Early on Wednesday morning, she saw Barwell to say, 'I am sorry, but I am going to have to resign. This leads to being stuck in the customs union.' '*A* customs union,' he responded. He said he was sorry and that the PM would certainly want to see her personally. She wrote a letter of resignation at once, saying she would do it very quietly (the fact of her leaving was leaked to blogger Guido Fawkes, but her letter did not). The next morning, she collected her personal possessions and quietly left the building: 'I thought I could live with Chequers, but further ground had been conceded in the summer and now again. I just felt I'd been pushed too far from where I thought we were meant to be and what we had said publicly.'[25] The loss of a No. 10 aide at such an acutely sensitive point was a worry – and a harbinger.

When Cabinet had eventually been allowed to see the legal advice in 70 Whitehall and make notes, several communicated their reservations, with Raab one of the most worried; Barwell went to see him in his room in the House of Commons to try to reassure him. The bilateral exit mechanism, Raab told him, was insufficient and it would be a 'national humiliation' if the UK was to sign up to it without unilateral control. What he objected to the most, though, was the text that he believed that Robbins had slipped into the political declaration at the last minute, suggesting that the basis for the future relationship would be the backstop. 'So, suddenly, having not seen the papers until the night before, I found the backstop had changed from a temporary device to the basis that would be the building block of the entire future relationship in effect, the hybrid customs union model.'[26] Others who worried most were the expected voices: Leadsom, Mordaunt, McVey, Javid and Fox; Gove was concerned but more hopeful than some of finding a collective way through. They all learnt only on Tuesday afternoon about an emergency Cabinet meeting to thrash it all through, called for the following day, Wednesday 14 November.

Gove and Raab were prominent in wanting to hear Cox's legal opinion on the deal before the meeting. Since succeeding Jeremy Wright as Attorney General in early July, Cox had been immersing himself in the documents, and he had devoted much of August at his Devon constituency home to probe what had been agreed. His conclusion was that the December 2017 joint report and May's March 2018 letter to Donald Tusk had entered Britain into commitments which he suspected neither May herself nor Cabinet, which included Johnson and Gove, could have fully comprehended at the time. The agreements were bound to leave Northern Ireland within the single market for goods, and with the backstop came the oversight of the EU Commission and the ECJ, with all the ramifications that it entailed. He concluded that either Cabinet had not had the implications explained to them at the time or, if they had, they didn't fully understand. From September, he began to explain the position to May and her team, and she asked him to try draft legal changes to the backstop which Robbins could then negotiate with Brussels before the door closed. He cautiously agreed. 'We're trying to find a way out of this, but I'm not sure it will be possible,' Cox said.

Cox explains the background to his legal advice thus:

My advice for the 14 November Cabinet was on the backstop and the backstop only. I wrote the advice myself, and then I tested the conclusions and reasoning with other senior lawyers. It said that, if the talks broke down, there would be no way out, and it could become indefinite. However, I said at the Cabinet meeting itself that I thought it was a risk worth taking if it meant we could get out on 29 March 2019. I believed then, and I still believe, that the withdrawal agreement was the mechanism which, for all its flaws, would allow us to leave. It had disadvantages, obviously, but it had advantages too, like avoiding an abrupt departure and risking damage to business. [It was] the deal that gave Britain the chance to adjust.[27]

The ground was prepared for a tense Wednesday Cabinet meeting, which lasted five hours. It proved even more fraught than the Chequers Cabinet in July, with discussion just as tightly choreographed. To Brokenshire, 'it was the most fractious Cabinet in my three years under Theresa'.[28] Gove thought one reason for the tension was 'because May was in a much weaker political position than she had been in back in July'.[29] Chequers, in contrast, seemed like a gentle evening breeze at the end of a hot summer's day.

McVey grew noticeably agitated as the meeting went on, and asked if there could be a formal vote. Julian Smith told her, 'We are not going to be doing that,' to which Cabinet Secretary Mark Sedwill added, 'Voting is not the way that the proceedings happen.' The Attorney General concurred that the Cabinet Manual does not indicate an obligation for the PM to hold a vote. McVey was clearly not happy. The balance of opinion flowed one way, then the other. Several ministers felt they were being taken for granted. Attendees were not sure May would carry the day. But then Gove spoke up. As at Chequers four months before, he proved the decisive swing voice. He said he was worried that 'the Lancaster House vision was being diluted constantly, and the nature of the proposed backstop would profoundly affect relations with Ireland'. Nevertheless, he said he would back her deal and spoke up positively for it. Cox pitched in too to say he thought it an 'ugly sister' of a deal, a life raft lashed together with bamboo and oil drums and with a plastic sail to get them through the shark-infested waters out into the open sea. He concluded that his legal advice was just 'one feature of the landscape', and that if Cabinet didn't go for this deal, it could mean no deal – or worse, in his eyes, no Brexit. Despite his and Gove's eloquence, it became increasingly obvious to those present that the ocean between ministers was unbridgeable, and that Raab and McVey, and potentially others, might resign.

'Raab and I met in an empty room afterwards outside the Cabinet Room, and I tried to dissuade him,' says Smith. 'But he was pretty set on what he was doing.'[30] 'Please can you wait, though?' Smith asked him. Out of respect for the Prime Minister and his colleagues, Raab said he'd delay his resignation until after the Radio 4 *Today* programme the following morning, to allow May the best chance of putting her own vision of the withdrawal agreement forward without news reports being overshadowed by his own resignation. 'The truth was that in terms of the undertakings given to me on my appoint-ment, the process of me trying to do the job had been shabby, and I felt I couldn't continue,' he says.[31] 'Dominic's resignation made a big impact,' Karen Bradley says, because 'it said to the ERG, "May's deal is BRINO." After it, the ERG never trusted her again.'[32] It provoked cold fury in May's team. As one member says:

> We understood DD's resignation, which was on principle. Domi-nic's we saw as ruthlessly calculating – he had known exactly what he signed up for and jumped ship the moment he judged it was no longer in his personal interest to be on board. Dom could have been a historical figure who delivered a good Brexit for the nation: instead, he'll be an obscure answer to a pub quiz question.

May brushed aside the Cabinet's noise and strode confidently out into

Downing Street to make a brief statement. 'The choices before us were difficult,' she said. 'But the collective decision of Cabinet was that the government should agree the draft withdrawal agreement and the outline political declaration.' Despite having just chaired a draining and challenging five-hour Cabinet meeting, she spoke without notes and conveyed a sense of confidence.

McVey's resignation followed hard on the heels of Raab's. In her resignation letter, she said:

The deal you put before the Cabinet yesterday does not honour the result of the referendum. Indeed, it doesn't meet the tests you set from the outset of your premiership … We have gone from no deal is better than a bad deal to any deal is better than no deal.[33]

May's team inside the building held their breath: 'I was frankly surprised more didn't resign,' says one. Amid the ministerial resignations there were fears too that other officials and aides in Downing Street might follow Da Costa. Parkinson had serious concerns about the deal, but he was a loyalist to May, and, like some others, he bit his lip. Would any MPs resign the whip? With the lack of a majority, it was a further worry. May faced a torrid time in Parliament on Thursday, much of it from her own MPs. One, Julian Lewis, referred to it as a 'Hotel California Brexit deal which ensures we can never truly leave the EU'. Anger was building, but no others jumped ship, yet.

May needed a new Brexit Secretary, and quickly, to head off growing unrest. This one had to stay put. She couldn't afford to appoint a fourth. May called Gove at home on 15 November. 'I would like you to become my Brexit Secretary,' she said. 'That's very kind indeed of you, Prime Minister,' he replied. 'Can I come back to you after I have spent the day reflecting on it?' A long and hard talk with his wife, journalist Sarah Vine, as well as his close political team, followed. He spoke confidentially to Hunt, too, whose views he respected, before making his mind up. The next day, he went to see May and told her that, if he was to be her Brexit Secretary, he had to be very honest with her, saying, 'I don't think you'll be able to get the deal as it stands through the House of Commons. I think we should cancel the planned summit, go back to the EU and say that we cannot accept the agreement that has been reached with you.' May listened politely and replied, 'I am not going to do that, Michael. I am determined to go ahead with it. I can only do it my way.' 'I completely understand that, Prime Minister, in which case, I'll have to consider my own position.'[34]

Suddenly May found herself in one of her most perilous positions as Prime Minister. The prospect of losing her Environment Secretary, respected both by Brexiteers and Remainers, was terrible to her. 'I need you to stay and do this job,' she said to him, fearing the Cabinet could well collapse if she lost him. So he went back to talk to Sarah and his special advisors, and they rehearsed all the arguments. His future membership of Cabinet, May's fate and her deal all hung by a thread. Julian Smith anxiously contacted him to persuade him to stay, and again Gove spoke to Hunt. When he woke up the following morning, his mind was made up. He would not resign.

Gove rang May after breakfast on 16 November and said, 'Please forgive me, Prime Minister, but I would like to stay as Environment Secretary, if you'll let me. I will put out a statement to confirm it because speculation has been rife about what I might do.' Gove reflects now, 'I was in a major dilemma. It was very difficult. Dominic and Esther had spoken out very clearly and I was supportive of their viewpoint.' But, as he admits, he was also thinking, as a historian, of his reputation in history.

In 2016, as result of my decision to campaign for Vote Leave, David Cameron lost his job. He was a close friend and it affected me greatly. Then I took the decision soon after to withdraw my support from Boris Johnson, which may have prevented him from succeeding as

Prime Minister that year. If I were now to have withdrawn my support from Theresa May, then it would be another Prime Minister who I had effectively seen off. I did not want to be the person that cannot settle down with his party and puts his own ego ahead of the team. So that was why I decided that I would not go and I would stay at DEFRA. I didn't want to gain a reputation as the person who brought down Prime Ministers.[35]

Had he resigned in the wake of Raab and McVey, it would not necessarily have brought May down, though it would certainly have weakened her. 'Who knows what chaos it might have led to if I resigned?' Gove says.[36] A source close to the minister says:

> His difference at the time with Boris on the withdrawal was that [Boris] thought that if you 'break a leg' you can never mend it, i.e. we could never go back to the EU once we left. Michael believed, however, that we could and would go back to them again and secure a better deal after leaving.

So Gove decided to stay, setting out his reasoning in a long article in the *Daily Mail* at the end of November. If the British government was resolute, he said, and deployed a skilful negotiating team, it could use the backstop to Britain's advantage against the EU.[37] 'The longer the backstop lasts, the more difficult it will be for Europe,' he wrote. He took head-on his fellow Tories 'who would prefer a clean break', arguing that a 'no deal would cause considerable dislocation and disruption in the short term'. He aired his pent-up trauma of coming out against his long-standing friends Cameron and Osborne at the referendum, the heavy 'personal cost' it entailed, and addressed the criticism of him for being dismissive of 'experts'. It was an elegant and erudite argument, shaped in part by conversation with Geoffrey

Cox, whom he regarded as a fellow traveller. The article reflected too the journey Gove had taken on no deal. Since becoming Environment Secretary, he had heard first-hand the damage that no deal would do to the farming industry and beyond. Few of May's ministers evolved their thinking – in the light of expert opinion, indeed – more than Gove.

The departures of Raab and McVey prompted a mini-reshuffle. Stephen Barclay, the pro-Brexit Minister for Health, was promoted to DExEU Secretary, while McVey's departure provided the opportunity for Amber Rudd to return to Cabinet, which she eagerly seized. Both figures had the maturity, competence and loyalty that May badly needed. In that respect, at least, the reshuffle was a boon to her. She at last had the support of her Cabinet, more or less. But could she gain the support of Parliament?

When May travelled to Brussels for a special summit on Sunday 25 November, the omens were good. The summit was convened to sign off on the future relationship: Juncker said no one should be 'raising champagne glasses' at the prospect of the UK leaving. While saying he was anxious not to tell MPs how to vote, Juncker stressed that 'this is the best deal possible … This is the only deal possible,' a sentiment echoed by Varadkar, who said, 'Any other deal really only exists in people's imagination.'[38] The EU, proceeding by consensus, approved the terms of the political declaration, on the future relationship (twenty-six pages) as well as the withdrawal agreement (585 pages), without a vote. May's concluding statement gave a firm statement of her intent and hope that Parliament deliver on what she had negotiated: 'The British public don't want to spend any more time arguing about Brexit,' she said.[39]

That might have been her hope, but it did not accord with the reality. She was about to face the biggest parliamentary struggle of her political career.

STRUGGLE #3: PARLIAMENT

Following the party conference and her difficult week that followed, beset by tensions in Cabinet, over the weekend of 13–14 October Julian Smith took stock of the support her deal might achieve. The whip's ring-round suggested ninety-seven out of 314 Conservative MPs would not vote for it, with a further forty-seven uncomfortable about doing so. He wrote May a letter that Sunday suggesting, 'We are going to be in trouble.' At Cabinet on 16 October, he told ministers he envisaged a rebellion of 150. Rather than constructive appraisal, he 'got roundly bollocked' by No. 10, according to one present. The backstop had emerged as the principal concern of Conservative MPs, and the whips repeatedly flagged to No. 10 that autumn that the DUP wasn't on board. Smith became convinced that only fresh wording on the backstop would secure the DUP's support. So worried did he become that on one dark October evening he travelled to St Pancras International to talk to Raab before he caught the Eurostar to Brussels to fight for change. With Raab, he was pushing at an open door, but not with May's team, who worried that too abrasive a stance would alienate the EU. Back off, was the message he received. But he continued to advise that her deal would not pass through Parliament, bringing him continued opprobrium from No. 10: 'I took a pasting that autumn and was regarded as a serious irritant by the PM's team,' he says.[40] 'This is the deal, your job is to deliver the votes on it' was the message back, to which his response was: 'I am supporting the PM by trying to get more out of the EU to achieve a better deal on the backstop, to enhance the prospects that MPs would vote it through.'

Her team believed that the changes Robbins had secured with the EU in early November on the backstop would make it much more sellable to the DUP once Northern Ireland realised that it would have full and frictionless access to both UK and EU markets.[41] But, slowly, the confidence May had displayed outside Downing Street after Cabinet on 14 November began to evaporate. One senior No. 10 advisor says Robbins must bear some blame: 'There were hard political constraints on what would be possible at home, but it did not feel like Olly always took them seriously – he treated them as opinions held by those who wanted a harder Brexit rather than the political reality of what would pass Parliament.'

The ERG was in the vanguard causing difficulty. The day of the critical Cabinet meeting, the steering group of the ERG met in Iain Duncan Smith's office. Jacob Rees-Mogg, the group's chair and one of its more persuasive voices, called for 'the gloves to come off', comparing May's Brexit deal to the Suez crisis of 1956. Since Chequers, the ERG had been in the lead coordinating efforts to secure the forty-eight letters to trigger the no-confidence vote in May's leadership. Smith reported to No. 10 that the ERG had been running its own whipping operation since at least July, but its activity intensified greatly after Raab's resignation in November. May had appointed him because of the credibility he carried with the ERG as an authentic Brexiteer. The ERG felt his resignation personally. In total, seven Conservatives quit, including two private secretaries and two junior ministers, Suella Braverman and Shailesh Vara. May and her team always found Rees-Mogg civilised, and saved their ire principally for Steve Baker, who had become the ERG's deputy chair to Rees-Mogg when he resigned as a DExEU Minister in July.[42] Lidington was one of May's loyalists to regard Baker as more influential than Rees-Mogg: 'We thought he was the organiser and the tactician and less pragmatic and reasonable than Jacob.'[43] To one MP senior in the party, Raab's resignation was the moment the ERG stopped being biddable. Afterwards, it started to create a party within the party, drawing on a phalanx of the old guard including Duncan Smith and Bernard Jenkin, who prided themselves on seeing off two earlier Prime Ministers (Major and Cameron) and were intent on seeing off May. They found mutual common cause with the DUP and began to work closely in Parliament.

Within hours of the resignations, unhappy Cabinet ministers began meeting to discuss the courses of action open to them. Most conspicuous was the 'Gang of Five', Leadsom, Fox, Grayling, Gove and Mordaunt, dubbed the 'Pizza Club', meeting over takeaway pizzas in Leadsom's office. Largely escaping media attention was another group which began to meet more or less weekly from November in Javid's Commons office, with Hunt, Raab and Gove. 'Our main purpose was to press the Prime Minister to extract much more out of the EU than she'd done so far,' Hunt says. 'We were set up in part to counteract the influence on her of Philip Hammond and Olly Robbins.'[44] Pressure climaxed at the end of the week with talk of possible challenges to May, resulting in more terrible headlines and press for her over the weekend of 17–18 November. There were calls from Steve Baker and co. for Barwell and Gibb to resign, along with May's Europe advisors, Denzil Davidson and Ed de Minckwitz.[45]

Smith – whose mantra always remained 'Make your argument strongly but leave enough room to change your opinion' – felt the vote would fail but stayed coy, but May and her team continued to push for it in the hope that MPs would eventually allow it to pass. The tempo picked up in the week beginning Monday 19 November. The following day, a 7 a.m. meeting was started in No. 10, which met on some Saturdays and Sundays, unofficially called 'the hub', with the official title 'the meaningful vote meeting'. The meaningful vote had been necessitated by Dominic Grieve's December 2017 amendment to the EU (Withdrawal) Bill, which Da Costa helped draft and made the final deal subject to a majority vote in the House of Commons. The hub had started meeting informally two weeks prior and lasted until just before the first meaningful vote (MV1) in January. Brandon Lewis says:

I always felt we were playing catch-up on it. We were always trying to get ahead of the curve, but we never could. We met to see how we could get MPs to see that the deal was a good thing, and to see how we could sell it to the country, to gain a momentum and a feeling of 'let's get it done'. But it was hard work with MPs, while businesses across the country didn't seem keen to get involved and to make the public pronouncements we wanted in favour of the deal.[46]

In parallel, a 'war room' was set up in a large room on the first floor of the Cabinet Office with some thirty to forty staff under the overall direction of Barwell and Gibb, to campaign to get the meaningful vote passed in the House of Commons, and to provide instant rebuttals and tailored briefings for MPs when addressing the media. Tory MPs were offered a range of incentives to win them round, including scrapping hospital parking charges and plans to ban men from cross-examining victims in domestic violence cases. Mistrust ran high. It reached a peak in Cabinet on 21 November, with May forced to deny rumours in circulation among Brexit MPs that she was about to reach out to Corbyn and offer a general election in exchange for Labour's support, which she dispatched as 'outrageous and untrue'.[47] Not totally untrue, in fact, as Labour figures including Stephen Kinnock and Lucy Powell had been talking to Lidington since September in strictest secrecy to say that under certain circumstances some Labour MPs would vote for her deal.

On 25 November, May officially launched her two-week PR blitz to convince the nation of the merits of her plan, writing an open letter to the electorate in which she spoke of wanting to see 'a moment of renewal and reconciliation for our whole country'. The time had come, she said, to put aside the labels of 'Leave' or 'Remain' for good and to 'come together as one people. To do that we need to get on with Brexit now by getting behind this deal ... I will be campaigning with my heart and soul to win that vote.'[48]

The meaningful vote was scheduled for Tuesday 11 December, after five days of debates, beginning the previous Tuesday. Any hopes May had for a calm debate before the vote rapidly dissipated. Trump, whose National Security Advisor John Bolton was in regular touch with the

ERG, chose this moment to respond to their whistle. The President told reporters that the withdrawal agreement 'sounds like a great deal for the EU', implying it wasn't for the UK, and that it meant it might not be possible to get a trade deal with the US.[49]

A trip to the G20 in Argentina from Thursday 29 November to Sunday 2 December was the last thing May needed at this point. Four crucial days were lost when she might have been planning and lobbying for support at Westminster. On the fourteen-hour flight travelling to Buenos Aires, she signed Christmas cards and distracted herself with a sudoku puzzle when not working and sleeping. The G20's priorities – the future of work, infrastructure and sustainable food – were not hers at the time. But while there, she campaigned hard to make progress on the environment, notably on plastics, and she had what one official present describes as a 'blunt and difficult' conversation with Saudi Arabia's Mohammed bin Salman over the murder of journalist Jamal Khashoggi in October, as well as the conduct of the war in Yemen.

There would be no break in the relentless battering her deal was taking in the media at home, with Universities Minister Sam Gyimah resigning on 30 November and dismissing her withdrawal agreement as 'a deal in name only', saying he wanted to be free to campaign for a second referendum on Brexit.[50] May's team again braced themselves for further resignations. To regain some initiative, they briefed on Sunday 2 December that she was willing to challenge Corbyn to a live TV debate, which was pencilled in with the BBC for 9 December. More time was lost in the pointless ploy – they had not expected Corbyn to respond positively, and several days of wrangling followed over the format, and over which broadcaster should screen the debate, before the initiative fizzled out in general disagreement.

Further turbulence came with the row that erupted in early December over the secrecy of the legal advice that the Attorney General had given Cabinet on the withdrawal agreement on 14 November. Shadow

Brexit Secretary Keir Starmer brought the government under considerable pressure to release what Cox had said before the meaningful vote in the House of Commons on 11 December. May's advisors were divided. Smith argued that the advice should be released, but May, on civil service advice that it would create a precedent and make the conduct of government unworkable, resisted. No. 10, worried that, if published, the legal advice might inflame pro-Brexit MPs concerned that the backstop arrangements could become permanent, hoped to get away with publishing a summary, which it presented to the Commons on 3 December. A forlorn hope. On 4 December, Starmer resorted to a historic parliamentary procedure called a humble address to prise Cox's full legal advice out into the open, and, after two lost votes, Leader of the House Andrea Leadsom announced that it would be published in full. In the process, the Commons found the government in contempt of Parliament for the first time since the 1970s.

Cox thinks it 'contemptible' that, as a result of Starmer's campaign, the advice was wrenched out of the government:

> I was standing up for a vital constitutional principle, which was that the Attorney General could offer confidential advice to the Cabinet about the key issues of the day. If that advice comes out subsequently, it will mean that the Attorney General in the future might not be willing to give brutally honest advice, and will always temper it. But I was also an MP, and I felt the public interest in the dignity of the House of Commons at this time, so it was important that their view was upheld too.[51]

On Wednesday 5 December, a six-page document containing the legal advice was released to Parliament in which Cox conceded, as he had in his summary on Monday, that the UK could find itself indefinitely trapped in the backstop, with 'protracted and repeated rounds of negotiations in the years ahead'. Starmer said, 'It's obvious why [the legal advice] needed to be placed in the public domain ... [What] this advice reveals is the central weaknesses in the government's deal.'[52] It was not the ideal curtain-raiser to the meaningful vote.

PULLING THE MEANINGFUL VOTE: 7–10 DECEMBER

Tension mounted steadily towards Friday 7 December. Some in Cabinet started talking openly about delaying the vote to the following Tuesday to avert an almost certain defeat. Over the weekend of 8–9 December, many spoke out against the EU for not giving the UK enough, saying that, if brought under pressure, it would give more to allow the government to present fresh concessions to the Commons on the Monday, bringing more MPs over the line. Hunt advised May to hold the vote the day before the Christmas recess having extracted concessions from the EU on a time limit to the backstop.[53] May made a frantic round of phone calls to the EU that weekend, including her staples of Merkel, Rutte, Varadkar and Tusk. She pleaded for last-minute adjustments on the withdrawal agreement. But she was told flatly that the 585-page document would not be reopened: 'This deal is the best and only deal possible. We will not renegotiate the deal that is on the table right now.'[54] Smith, whose latest advice was that up to 150 Conservative MPs would vote against, refused to give up all hope:

As the vote approached on 11 December, the feeling was that the prospects were not great, but it was not impossible, and we needed to fight hard for changes. We were driven by the need to get the legislation through, with so much else that needed to happen before 29 March.[55]

Smith had been speaking to Cabinet daily with Hunt and Williamson, the strongest advocates for pulling the vote. May's team's worry was that, if the vote went ahead and she suffered a bad defeat, it would trigger a no-confidence vote and a leadership challenge. But other voices counselled taking the hit in the hope it would bring Tories back to their senses and the party back together in the New Year. A ring-round of Cabinet on Friday and over the weekend saw ministers more or less unanimous: the vote should be pulled. The press became increasingly confident that May could not go ahead: in the *Sunday Times* on 9 December, Tim Shipman predicted that it would be pulled. Nevertheless, in the absence of a definitive story from No. 10, Gove went on the *Today* programme on Monday 10 December, and loyally adhered to the media handling line. Asked whether the vote was 'definitely, 100 per cent going to happen', he replied, 'Yes.' When pressed further, he again stated, 'The vote is going ahead.' He confirmed that May was trying to seek new concessions from Brussels, though there was always a risk of her, or indeed another leader, returning with a worse deal. While declining to rule himself out of succeeding May if she was ousted, he said it was 'extremely unlikely' that he would do so.[56] Gove was the fifth government minister in five days to confirm the vote would be going ahead, the next most recent being Barclay, who had told Andrew Marr on BBC One on Sunday morning, 'The vote is going ahead, and that is because it is a good deal, it's the only deal.'

Yet, seven hours after the *Today* programme, near the end of the fourth of the five-day debate, May announced that she would be delaying the meaningful vote as she admitted the deal 'would be rejected by a significant margin', and she needed more time to secure reassurances from the EU on the backstop. MPs reacted angrily, and the Speaker confirmed that Labour would be allowed to express its disapproval in a three-hour emergency debate the following morning. At the end of a torrid debate, Labour MP Lloyd Russell-Moyle marched forward to grab the mace in what he called a 'symbolic gesture' of protest at the government's decision. May announced that she would be setting off on a tour of European capitals to hold talks with the EU on the delayed vote, which could be held in January. While EU leaders reiterated that they would not re-enter negotiations, May grasped at a morsel of hope from Tusk, who tweeted, 'We are ready to discuss how to facilitate UK ratification.'

Lidington is one of those who regrets the decision to delay:

With hindsight, the postponement was a big mistake. The pragmatic MPs just wanted the whole issue settled, and they thought postponing it was prolonging the agony and making it worse for them in their constituencies. The delay was greeted with horror in Brussels and in the major EU capitals. It made it more difficult for us to obtain further concessions, and made them ask whether the British government could be trusted any longer. They felt that we had agreed to a deal and a timetable and received assurances that they had given enough to get it over the line. Clearly, they hadn't.[57]

CONFIDENCE VOTE IN MAY: 12 DECEMBER

This was the ERG's moment. The group went into overdrive on 11 December, vocally campaigning for MPs to submit their letters of no confidence in the Prime Minister to chair of the 1922 Committee Graham Brady. 'Are you sure you want to do this?' Rudd asked Rees-Mogg. 'Yes, we just cannot take the lack of trust any more,' he replied. 'We feel completely misled by her.'[58] May meanwhile flew off on the Tuesday to The Hague to see Rutte, to Berlin for talks with Merkel, and to Brussels to see Juncker and Tusk to explain her position. Throughout the day, she was given regular updates on machinations in Westminster. The numbers of letters (sometimes emails or other forms of messages) had been steadily creeping upwards. Brady recalls one or two had been in his possession since before the general election. They leapt up in June 2017 just after the vote, but then steadied, and some were withdrawn in late 2017 and early 2018. The Chequers summit and publication of her deal in July then saw 'an immediate increase', with numbers steadily building through the autumn.[59] As tensions rose in November, Steve Baker went public to say that by his numbers forty-three letters had been received, which Brady later confirmed was the precise number. But then it fell back to the high thirties: submissions and withdrawals ebbed and flowed. When, in mid-November, staunch Brexit MP Andrew Bridgen accused Brady of withholding the fact that forty-eight letters had been received, Brady found it 'deeply offensive', but decided against suing Bridgen as it 'would have been difficult to prove without opening the safe'. On 21 November, Brady had been on the verge of pulling out of a trip to Scotland, suggesting the number was on forty-six or forty-seven, but then a couple of letters were withdrawn, and the immediate crisis passed.[60]

The delay of MV1 was the final straw. Early on Tuesday, the forty-eighth letter was handed to Brady in the corridor, only to be followed a short while later by another MP withdrawing their letter. He was in a dilemma which was solved when further letters arrived that afternoon. Brady claims that not even his wife Victoria, nor his 76-year-old secretary Sybil, who had worked with him for twenty-two years, nor the 1922 executive, knew the tally. He sat down alone and planned the next move, asking Sybil to call No. 10 to request an imminent meeting with the Prime Minister, who was still abroad. Within the hour, he was besieged by phone calls from the media. Even today, he doesn't know who leaked the meeting request, which was immediately interpreted as his telling her the hour had come. 'I'm pretty certain it wasn't Sybil,' he says, adding, 'She has worked for me for twenty-two years and has maintained absolute confidentiality at all times.'[61] Suspicion fell on No. 10, eager to get the news out and to hold the vote at once, before her enemies on the 1922 executive leaked it to the ERG to give them a head start with lobbying.

As soon as May's plane touched down at Northolt, she phoned Brady. 'Prime Minister, I'm telling you the forty-eighth letter has now been received,' he said. 'I think we should do this as soon as we reasonably can,' she replied. A clinical conversation. Brady decided to hold the vote the next day, which Baker and Mark Francois thought reasonable, but others discontented with May's leadership thought it gave them insufficient time to mobilise support. 'I thought they were pretty disingenuous,' Brady says now, 'as they had been organising and campaigning for the numbers for many months.'[62] A meeting was rapidly convened in May's office while she was still in transit from the airport to debate how they would get MPs to come out and support her on social media so they could claim 50 per cent support as early the next day as possible. May walked in near the end of the meeting, quietly determined, almost relieved that the moment had come after months of intermittent letter-waving from rebellious MPs.

'Every day, we had been expecting the forty-eighth letter to arrive, and we were prepared,' says speechwriter Keelan Carr. 'I got in early on the Wednesday morning and wrote a short, sharp statement for her to deliver. She was in good form. My draft was based on my knowledge of working with her, and what I thought she would want to say.'[63] Few changes were made as she walked out onto the steps of Downing Street on the morning of the vote, Wednesday 12 December, to rehearse her history as a Conservative activist, councillor, MP, minister and now Prime Minister, vowing that she would contest the challenge 'with everything I've got'. With a Brexit deal now 'within our grasp', she urged her MPs not to 'put our country's future at risk', saying, 'The only people whose interests would be served are Jeremy Corbyn and John McDonnell.'[64]

During the day, with Philip watching from the gallery, she did PMQs, starting nervously when Corbyn asked her what improvements to the deal she had managed to secure on her visits to see EU leaders the previous day. When vocal pro-EU backbencher Ken

Clarke announced that the leadership challenge was 'unhelpful, irrelevant and irresponsible', a large section of MPs behind her remained ominously silent, failing to provide the braying support she needed to lift MPs' sentiments. Late in the day, she brought them to life, mocking Labour's Barry Gardiner as 'the inconstant gardener' ('a Danny Finkelstein special', one of May's aides calls it).

The ERG, denied a contest on their preferred date, the following Monday, were on the back foot. The initiative was with No. 10, but still they found themselves under huge pressure as the ring-rounds revealed a mixed picture from her MPs. Some hated her personally, but many felt indifferent to her and simply believed that only a true Brexiteer PM could now deliver. The whips suspected that 'some of our MPs simply couldn't handle the fact of a woman sorting out Brexit, while others didn't have it in their hearts to make any compromises and were trying to bully her out'.[65] To a Cabinet minister who later went on to serve as a member of Johnson's government, the vote was driven by the ERG. They were not concerned about getting the numbers for a deal: they were motivated purely by getting a new leader who would be one of them. An intensive operation was run out of Duncan Smith's office to persuade MPs to vote against her; the former Tory leader had been compiling spreadsheets since August for just this eventuality. Having finessed the campaign, he was confident the ERG would mount a serious challenge.[66] But would it be enough? The whips thought she would win comfortably: all that was required was a simple majority, 158 MPs, which would prevent her being challenged for another year. But the bigger her margin, the more secure she would be. Ninety-five were on the government payroll, with a further forty-one parliamentary private secretaries, giving her a reasonably large voting base. Anything under 200 would have made life very difficult for her; she needed over 220 to be secure.

May had to cancel her visit to Varadkar in Dublin to be present for the result. She spent much of the day talking with colleagues face to face and on the phone. The whips organised a cascade system, with loyalist MPs and spads lobbying the undecided. One of their core arguments was that there was no logic in changing the Prime Minister now, as it would not change the discussion with the EU. Other lines they used were the damage it would do to the party removing another leader, their dislike at having the ERG dictating to the wider party, and this being the wrong moment for it. 'The ERG buggered up the timing,' says Rudd. 'If only they'd waited until the meaningful vote had been defeated in Parliament, they'd have got a different result. There was not always the EQ, frankly, in the ERG to go along with their high IQ. Too many were overly emotional. They screwed it.'[67]

The results were due at nine o'clock that evening, and May did not stop driving for votes until the last minute. When she appeared before the 1922 Committee at 5 p.m. in Room 14, she pledged to step down before the next general election in the hope of swaying the still undecided. The room was not overfull, and her performance was underwhelming. A number of MPs told Brady she'd have done better not to have spoken. Grant Shapps saw Johnson on the other side of the room. 'God!' he texted him in despair at her painful impact. 'She's awful,' Johnson texted back.

When May herself went to vote, she was required to produce ID. Her PPS, Seema Kennedy, noted that rather than being impatient, she reached calmly into her bag: 'I think I have my passport here.'[68] The result, 117 voting against her and 200 for, was known by the 1922 executive several minutes before the published time. No one leaked it. When Brady called her to give her advance notice, he was surprised – given the level of opposition to the motion – to detect 'a note of relief' in her voice. Lidington was watching the declaration with Lewis in his office: 117 was at the top end of their fears – they had not expected it to go any higher. An impromptu party was quickly convened outside the Cabinet Room. When she appeared with Philip, applause rang out. A sense of relief washed over the building, Barwell hugging Gibb;

even the Prime Minister hugged some of her colleagues, a rare occurrence. But the jubilation jarred with some of her staff: 'She had 117 voting against. What was there to celebrate?'

Martin Kettle of *The Guardian* described it nevertheless as a 'decisive' victory: 'It's a better result for May than when she won the leadership against Andrea Leadsom and Michael Gove in 2016 (she got 199 back then; against their 130).'[69] May had survived, but she had suffered significant harm. Pulling the vote had achieved little other than raising an almost impossible expectation that she could achieve more from the EU. No one had a workable plan for converting the likely 150 Tory opponents into supporters of her deal. May's own self-belief was not going to do it. When, in July 1995, an earlier Conservative Prime Minister, John Major, had been challenged by leading Eurosceptic John Redwood, Major had received more votes: 218 (66.3 per cent) against Redwood's 89. He had remained at No. 10 another two years, but he never recovered. His critics were not subdued but emboldened. Most damaging of all, May's announcement that she would stand down before the next general election was an open advertisement, if any were needed, for her rivals to be even more brazen in their campaigning for her job. As the *Financial Times* put it, 'The race for the Conservative party leadership was underway whatever the outcome of Wednesday's confidence vote.'[70] May had no plan, and no way through in sight.

For much of May's final year, the streets of Westminster were awash with demonstrators on both sides of the Brexit divide, symbolising the clash between direct and representative democracy. This photograph of pro-EU campaigners was taken on 15 January 2019, the day of the first meaningful vote.

CHAPTER 17

FIRST ATTEMPT AT PARLIAMENT: MAY'S QUEST FOR A DOMESTIC LEGACY

DECEMBER 2018–JANUARY 2019

May went into the Christmas break in 2018 with two dominant thoughts. How would she get the withdrawal agreement through Parliament, with little more than ninety days left until 29 March? And – like Cameron before her – how could she ensure that the rest of her premiership would not be defined by the European Union? The EU did not set her pulse racing, as it did some Conservatives, and she had so much more she wanted to achieve. But first, she had to get her deal through Parliament. She announced before Christmas that the meaningful vote would take place in the week beginning Monday 14 January.[1] Her staff deliberately kept work away from her over the holiday to let her recharge her batteries. She began 2019 with a bang. In her New Year message, she said, 'New Year is a time to look ahead, and in 2019 the UK will start a new chapter … If Parliament backs the deal, Britain can turn a corner.' This, she said, would be the year 'we put our differences aside and move forward together'. It was an optimistic aspiration. But she would need much more than that to convince MPs to change their minds.

THE SEARCH FOR A WAY THROUGH PARLIAMENT

May had postponed the vote on her withdrawal deal on 11 December because she knew that it would be defeated disastrously. Some 150 Conservative MPs, perhaps more, had been prepared to vote against it. Lidington recalls the thinking:

> The hope was that by deferring the vote we'd get people to calm down, relax over the holiday and get behind the deal. But by the end of the Christmas period, it was clear that had not happened. If anything, our MPs were moving the other way … They were irritated and annoyed and not in any sense ameliorated.[2]

May had lost one Foreign Secretary and two Brexit Secretaries and was fighting to keep her other Cabinet ministers around the table. She had not sought to broaden her support in Parliament, despite the parliamentary arithmetic after the 2017 general election suggesting that was exactly what she would need to get her deal through. She was now staring at the inevitable result.

She was almost completely boxed in. The party was divided, with the ERG and DUP on one side demanding further concessions from the EU or else no deal, and the other wing of her party wanting a customs union or second referendum as the way forward. At a pre-Christmas party at No. 10 for MPs, one ERG member was very frank: 'The PM's deal will never get through. We'll keep stringing it along, but it will end in no deal.' 'What really depressed me', says the aide to whom this opinion was imparted, 'was I knew he was right. I thought I'd be out of a job in the New Year. Many of us did.'

May's ministerial team was divided, Cabinet was divided and Whitehall was divided. No. 10 was increasingly divided too between different factions with their own solutions. Even May was divided in her own mind about the right course of action. Where did she go now? On 2 January, she held a meeting with her Cabinet, cutting short ministers' Christmas holidays by five days to bring them in to discuss the way ahead. The return of the meaningful vote was only two weeks away. On the BBC's *Andrew Marr Show* on 6 January, she announced, 'If the deal is not voted on … then actually we're going to be in uncharted territory.' A bewildering range of options were open to her. She had secured the agreement of her Cabinet to the With-drawal Bill, but ministers were bound together by the most fragile of ribbons, with only a mixture of self-interest, fear and loyalty to her and to the party holding them together.

A defensive strand of thought was that if the Bill was defeated in the House of Commons in mid-January, it would send a powerful message to the EU that she had tried and been rebuffed, and it needed at last to get real. Only something as dramatic as that, it was believed, would shake the EU out of its complacent hostility and force it to make concessions. Anxious itself to avoid a no deal, the EU would then come back to her, with beatific Brussels smiles, and give her what was needed to secure a majority in the House of Commons. That, at least, was the theory.

May herself believed she could secure better terms from the EU before the meaningful vote came back to the House. The soundness of her belief was questioned by some around her, but they went along with it. The belief that the EU would yield if only spoken to harshly enough was so widespread among political circles, who were they to contest it? May had set off with high hopes to the EU Council in Brus-sels on Thursday 13 December, buoyed by surviving the confidence vote by her own MPs the day before. The Council had considered Brexit on its first day, but had been in no mood to be sympathetic. Juncker expressed surprise that May was even bothering to ask her fellow EU27 leaders for help, all of whom had repeatedly stated that there was nothing further they could do to help her. Juncker was emphatic: 'We do not want the UK to think there can be any form of renegotiation whatsoever.'[3] The statement at the end of the Council could not have been more unequivocal: 'The Union stands by [the withdrawal] agreement and intends to proceed with its ratification. It is not open for renegotiation'. The official record reconfirmed the conclusions it had reached on 25 November, namely that the EU endorsed the withdrawal agreement and approved the political declaration, with no further change. Yet still the message didn't sink in fully in London.

One idea after Christmas was for No. 10 to back a parliamentary amendment to signal to the EU the precise nature of the concessions that might be needed. Hence the idea for the UK to leave the backstop within twelve months unless a trade deal had been put in place to ensure no hard border in Ireland, and with the ECJ giving an opinion confirming that the backstop would only be temporary. But Jacob Rees-Mogg put an end to that when he heard about the plan: an aide told the *Sunday Times*, 'I'm not sure that asking the ERG to accept the word of the European court, the institution they least trust, is the way to win this.'[4]

Double-barrelled lobbying in Brussels in early January proved more fruitful, in the form of a joint letter from Tusk and Juncker laying out their 'firm commitment' to working towards the backstop being deployed for 'the shortest possible period'. Limited though it was, the accommodation, engineered by Merkel in one of her sparse interventions to support May, persuaded Varadkar to soften his inflexibility on the backstop and gave desperate people in London some hope. Less helpful – and more honest – was Tusk and Juncker's repetition of the EU position: it was not going to change the terms of the deal that they had negotiated with the Prime Minister. Period.

That placed the onus on getting the vote out in the Commons.

Between the delay of the vote on 10 December and it taking place on 15 January, No. 10 threw its weight behind the strategy of securing the votes of all ten DUP MPs, biddable members of the ERG, and targeted Labour MPs in Leave seats in the Midlands and the north of England. The dream scenario was a domino effect: if the DUP vote could be secured, that would help lock in most of the ERG, and then with the DUP and most of the ERG on board, Labour Leave MPs might be willing to take the risk and openly vote for it in the Commons, believing it would pass.

Much rested on the Chief Whip and his success in delivering the strategy. Smith knew time was short, and from his home in his Skipton and Ripon constituency, he hammered the phones all the way up to Christmas Eve, and was back on the phone from first thing on Boxing Day through into the New Year: 'I knew how critical and close it was going to be. I was talking all holiday to Labour Leave MPs, the DUP and Conservatives, drumming up support, trying to protect the PM,' he recalls.[5] As soon as Parliament reconvened, a fresh charm offensive was opened, with every Conservative MP invited to drinks receptions in Downing Street on 7 and 9 January. The hope in No. 10 that week was that they could whittle down the opposition to just some thirty to forty hardcore MPs in the ERG, those who would never forgive May after Raab's resignation in November.

May became personally involved too in the overtures to Labour MPs to back her deal, reminding them that 80 per cent of the House of Commons (i.e. all the Conservative and Labour MPs) had stood on manifesto pledges in 2017 that they would deliver Brexit. Most were disillusioned with Corbyn's lead, or lack of it, on Brexit, and she sought to capitalise on their disenchantment. Just before the Christmas break, in one of her best lines of the year, May had mocked Corbyn's vacillation: 'I know it's the Christmas season and the pantomime season ... He's going to put a confidence vote. Oh yes he is!

Oh no he isn't! ... I've got some advice. Look behind you! They are not impressed and neither is the country.'[6] In early January, a loose cross-party coalition of sixty Midlands MPs, including Labour's Jack Dromey, convened to persuade the government to rule out no deal because of the damage it would do to their local industry. May would not agree to their wish, ever cautious of the anger it would arouse in the ERG. The best way of preventing such damage, May argued, would be to vote for her own deal.

No Members received more attention than the ten DUP MPs, who were all too aware of the power they held. They became increasingly assertive, ramping up their pressure for legally binding changes to the backstop, and May was unable to assuage them.

Lidington was one of many to grow weary of them: 'The DUP wanted their pound of flesh and were increasingly demanding. They dug in more and more against the backstop, giving any variety of reasons. It meant that we'd be heading for an almighty defeat in January.'[7] The DUP's deepening relationship with the ERG was also worrying. Northern Ireland Secretary Karen Bradley found herself often close to despair at their lack of cooperation, which she puts down to several factors:

> They're neither Conservatives nor supporters of the Conservative Party; some of my colleagues failed to appreciate that and thought that what was in the interests of the DUP was necessarily also in the interests of the Conservative Party. Their policies are Unionist in its widest sense, but they are not Unionists in the sense that the UUP or Unionists in Scotland and Wales might be; it might be more correct to define their approach in many ways as Ulster nationalists. And often their approach is one of short-term tactics over long-term strategy, with a desire to keep short-term popularity with their own base, even if it leads to long-term losses for those same voters.

Though they presented a united face to the outside world, they had no clear leader between Belfast and Westminster, which made negotiations difficult. Remember, too, they have a Presbyterian history which means that for them, the text of documents, notably the backstop, was all-important and is read very literally.[8]

The range of views within the ten MPs was extreme, too, from those like Emma Little-Pengelly, who was more inclined to compromise, to Sammy Wilson, who wanted a very hard Brexit. Neither Arlene Foster, official leader of the DUP since 2015, nor Nigel Dodds, deputy since 2008, could guarantee a uniform view among the ten MPs. Besides, they had their own party politics to play. In the 2017 general election, the DUP had secured 36 per cent of the popular vote, to 29 per cent for Sinn Féin, 12 per cent for the SDLP and 10 per cent for the UUP. May always argued that she headed a national party, representing the whole UK, and believed she had the best deal possible for Northern Ireland, as anywhere else. But as their election rivals the UUP started gaining popularity, the DUP only dug their heels in deeper. Another factor in the difficult relationship went all the way back to November 2017 and the change to the Chief Whip. Gavin Williamson had negotiated the deal with the DUP and considered himself a master at handling them. Smith had less experience, and – in the eyes of his critics, at least – his appointment coincided with an increasing lack of cooperation from the DUP. But it was always going to be a hard task – for all their professed Presbyterian fastidiousness, the Conservative Party's election partners were all too ready to cut corners and bend the rules. And, like May, Smith was never willing to countenance the DUP's desire for a return to direct rule in Northern Ireland, convinced it would damage the Union.

When it became apparent that the chances of building a majority for May's deal on 15 January were minimal, the opposing sides only began pushing their respective causes even harder – an unhappy inversion of the intended 'domino effect'. Gauke, Hammond and Rudd pushed again for an indicative vote on a second referendum to break the impasse in Parliament, believing the idea would now secure enough votes in the Commons to pass. But their main obstacle was a significant one: the Prime Minister, who remained implacably opposed, despite Barwell and Lidington encouraging her to keep her mind open to it. They remained in touch with MPs across the House about it nevertheless, and were heartened by a YouGov poll on 11 January which found that 36 per cent of voters thought May should indeed hold a second referendum, as opposed to 31 per cent who favoured a no-deal Brexit – and just 11 per cent who thought she should hold a Commons vote to force her deal through.[9] Dominic Grieve was another actively campaigning in Parliament for a second referendum, and on 17 January co-founded the group Right to Vote.

Barwell was desperate to consider any serious option that might allow May to retain the initiative. Oliver Letwin was one of the 'great and good' whose counsel he sought. May spoke to David Cameron about her options, while Smith was in regular touch with William Hague, a figure respected by all sides. For a short period, Barwell was convinced the answer could be a customs union, despite the ERG's hostility, because it provided a solution to the backstop. But this belief wavered in mid-January when 'it became clear Cabinet would not support any softening of her deal', as Lidington says. 'We might have got it through six or twelve months earlier, but with a leadership election coming even closer by January, those figures who might have once supported it in Cabinet regarded it as anathema.'[10]

Meanwhile, the government also accelerated no-deal planning, hoping to put pressure on Brussels by stoking anxieties about the eventuality they wanted to avoid. At the final pre-Christmas Cabinet on 18 December, it had been decided to greenlight the preparations. Given

Hammond's resistance to spending any more money on no-deal planning than was absolutely necessary, the decision was taken to cull manifesto commitments, including reforms to social care, to divert money towards planning. May took personal charge, chairing a new Cabinet committee to be called EUXT(P) (European Union Exit and Trade (Preparedness)) to ensure Britain was ready in the event of a no-deal exit on 29 March. DExEU's preparations included launching a radio advertising campaign, while DIT went into overdrive to secure bilateral deals with other third-party countries – aware that their trading relationship would no longer be covered via the EU.[11] Unsurprisingly, such no-deal planning received a mixed reception from MPs. On 8 January, two cross-party groups, one led by Labour's Yvette Cooper, the other by Lib Dem leader Vince Cable, sought to tie the Treasury's no-deal powers to MPs voting explicitly for this outcome (which, given the composition of the parliament, it never would). And, despite all the government's efforts, Brussels still sensed a bluff. 'We have seen what has been prepared on our side of the border for a hard Brexit. We don't see the same level of preparation on the other side of the border,' said Martin Selmayr, chief of staff to Juncker, and the Commission's éminence grise.[12] 'We never saw no deal as a credible threat,' he adds now.[13]

By now, the remaining vestiges of May's authority were vanishing before her eyes. A self-evident lack of respect emanated from several in the Cabinet, openly flouting collective responsibility, proposing their own Brexit solutions and plotting their leadership campaigns. David Davis, who had lost a stone and a half through jogging, saw himself briefly as a serious contender again, while Javid, Leadsom, Raab, Rudd and James Cleverly had longer-term intentions.[14] Behind the scenes, Johnson, supported by the ubiquitous Conor Burns, Grant Shapps with his forensic analytical methodology, and Williamson with his unparalleled knowledge of Tory MPs, was quietly strengthening his base week by week. Meanwhile, the contempt coming from the backbenchers wasn't quiet at all. The 117 MPs who had voted against May in the confidence motion refused to concede defeat, and were only riled up further by the insistence that there could be no second official challenge for another year.

May's sense of being besieged by all sides was only compounded by the House of Commons trying, as ever, to assert its own authority on the Brexit agenda – whether by voting on suspending Article 50, out-lawing a no-deal Brexit or proposing alternative deals. In Parliament, Grieve was at the heart of May's troubles, tabling two amendments – the first on 4 December and the second on 9 January – which meant that, if May lost the meaningful vote, scheduled for 15 January, the Commons would hold 'indicative votes' on alternative approach-es, including a second referendum and a customs union. Speaker Bercow, who had enjoyed a good relationship with May for much of her premiership, changed long-standing parliamentary convention to permit the amendments to go ahead – incensing No. 10 and many Conservative MPs. His ruling led to a fierce exchange between Speak-er and Chief Whip, with the latter alleging Bercow's action was 'totally out of order' and was 'throwing centuries of precedent in the bin'. Bercow responded that Smith was trying to 'bully' him.[15]

Amid this hostile atmosphere, May didn't have many options. She could delay the vote again – after all, the DUP had declared the gov-ernment's hard-fought concessions on the backstop were insufficient. But the belief that more time might see their will soften, along with that of other MPs, was pure hope, no expectation. Buying more time with an extension to Article 50 was also possible. At this time, even those closest to May, including Barwell and Penn, didn't know ulti-mately what was in her mind, any more than Timothy and Hill had on how she would vote in the EU referendum. Did she even know herself how she would get her deal through? Running down the clock was certainly one of her thoughts. She hoped against hope that the closer it came to 29 March, the more likely the approaching cliff edge would waken MPs to the reality as she saw it: her deal, no-deal or no Brexit. Of this triumvirate, May's team reasoned, surely her deal struck a sensible middle ground? But until that decisive moment, it was too easy for opposing – and minority – factions to indulge the idea that, if they held tight, their dream outcome would come to pass.

As the vote on 15 January approached, with no evidence that it would be won, tempers frayed among May's aides. The finger of blame was pointed at Smith for the continuing difficulties in winning MPs over. Some thought he had been insufficiently strategic or decisive, too willing to bend with the wind – right with the ERG and then left again with Anna Soubry and her centrist supporters who were calling for a second referendum. All that happened through the swaying was a slow dissolution of May's authority. Others simply missed the boundless optimism and can-do spirit of Gavin Williamson, against which Smith's slower, more cerebral approach seemed lacklustre. They wanted Williamson's thumping certainty, and his announcing, 'Prime Minister, you've got to do this' – forgetting how much they often resented his stridency at the time. Still others thought it was shifting the blame to pick on Smith. He was given an impossible task and worked frenetically at it nevertheless.

What became apparent to some around May was that, despite her drive and unrelenting self-belief, not only was there no clear plan for how her deal would pass; there was no sense either of what would happen in the increasingly inevitable event of defeat.

MEANINGFUL VOTE 1: 15 JANUARY

On Thursday 10 January, before the 8.30 morning meeting in Downing Street, Julian Smith broke it to May that their intensive lobbying operation had completely failed. Last-minute lobbying continued all weekend but, the following week, the Whips' Office were predicting a loss by some 200 votes. She took it stoically. Publication of the Juncker and Tusk letter on Monday about the backstop proved a damp squib, a disappointing return for all the effort that went into procuring it. On the morning of the vote, both at her 8.30 a.m. meeting and at Cabinet, May seemed distracted, her state of mind difficult to read. She said she was determined to deliver on the referendum result, but without giving her colleagues any clear indication about what the next step would be when the expected defeat came.

The Attorney General had been asked to open the debate, warning Conservative MPs that if they did not accept the deal, they risked condemning Britain to the chaos of a no-deal Brexit: 'It would be the height of irresponsibility for any legislator to contemplate with equanimity such a situation.' Should it come to no deal, he said, members of the public would say to their MPs, 'What are you playing at? What are you doing? You are not children in the playground. You are legislators and this is your job.'[16] Six months later, as if to make amends for an unsuccessful pitch, he says, 'You have to understand, I'm basically a courtroom lawyer. Much in Parliament is still unfamiliar to me. I'm learning all the time. I'd been at the dispatch box barely a handful of times before.'[17] Conservative backbenchers queued up after him to lay into May's withdrawal agreement, confirming No. 10's worst fears: few if any MPs had changed their minds. A last-minute hope of the whips was that MPs would merely abstain rather than vote against the government. A forlorn one, as it turned out.

But however expected the defeat itself, the scale of it surpassed all predictions: 432 MPs voted against the agreement to 202 MPs for. The 230-vote margin constituted the worst defeat in modern parliamentary history, comfortably beating the largest previous rebellion, when 139 voted against Blair over the invasion of Iraq in 2003. Only

196 Conservative MPs out of 316 voted for the government, as did three Labour MPs (Ian Austin, Kevin Barron and John Mann) and three independents. All ten DUP MPs and no fewer than 118 Conservative MPs voted against the deal – almost matching the 117 who voted against May in the 1922 no-confidence vote. May had her words ready for the certainty, if not the scale, of the defeat: 'It is clear that the House does not support this deal,' she told MPs. 'But tonight's vote tells us nothing about what it *does* support.' She made it clear she was not going to quit. She said she would deliver on the result of the referendum – 'I believe it is my duty to deliver on their instruction and I intend to do so' – but she didn't say how.

NO-CONFIDENCE VOTE: 16 JANUARY

Eager to seize what little command of events she could, May said she would welcome a vote of no confidence in her own government – threats of which had been simmering away for some time – and would make time for it the next day. Corbyn, who had been equally well-prepared for this eventuality, quickly confirmed that the motion had indeed been tabled, with the support of leaders of all opposition parties: 'This is a catastrophic defeat … The House of Commons has delivered its verdict on the Prime Minister's Brexit deal and that verdict is absolutely decisive … The Prime Minister's governing principle of delay and denial has reached the end of the line.' If she survived the vote, May said that she would hold cross-party meetings with senior parliamentarians 'to identify what would be required to secure the backing of the House'.

The DUP immediately made it clear that they would return to supporting May in the no-confidence motion, while a representative of the ERG said that they would 'of course' be backing the Prime Minster. 'We're Conservatives – we're going to support the Conservative government,' said Steve Baker.[18] They didn't fancy the prospect of a Corbyn victory, and with Labour rising again in the opinion polls, the ERG had no intention of precipitating a general election, any more than the DUP wanted to do anything to let republican-sympathising Corbyn through the front door of No. 10. The polls had the Conservatives sitting on around 35–40 per cent, with a few even suggesting Labour had a lead of 1–5 points, far too close to risk a general election, not least with the party vulnerable to charges that, after thirty months, Brexit was still unsolved. The risk of a revived Farageist movement taking votes from disenchanted Brexit-inclined Conservatives impatient at the lack of progress was all too real.

In No. 10, concentrating on how to win the no-confidence motion focused minds away from the gargantuan loss and how to take May's Brexit strategy forward. Barwell called Gove mid-evening to ask him to wind up the debate the following day. He took his task very seriously, and recalls now:

I sat in the Chamber throughout the no-confidence debate on Wednesday. My team had been doing research on Jeremy Corbyn's different positions and would bring in periodic notes as I wrote the speech on Commons notepaper, making bullet points as I did so. After the divisive day on Tuesday, I thought it would be good to remind Conservative MPs who the enemy truly was and get on the front foot, rather than to continue internal fighting. I was delighted by the result, although I think we would have won whoever spoke.[19]

Gove gave an eviscerating speech, considered by MPs on all sides one of the most eloquent of the three years of May's premiership, pummelling Corbyn again and again, and whipping up Tory MPs to rare cheers and whoops of delight:

When this House voted to bomb the fascists of ISIS, in order to defeat fascism … I'm afraid he was not with us. Similarly, when this House voted to take the action necessary when Vladimir Putin executed an act of terrorism on our soil, many Labour MPs stood up to support what we were doing, but not the Leader of the Opposition … How can he possibly protect this country? … No allies, no deterrent, no army – no way can this country ever allow that man to be our Prime Minister and in charge of our national security.

For a short time after, good humour and unity returned to the Tory benches. As expected, May carried the day, winning by 325 to 306. Had the DUP voted against, she would have lost by one.

After the result, as promised, May invited leaders of all parties to hold meetings with her on the way forward on Brexit, beginning that very evening. The leaders of Labour, the Lib Dems, the SNP and Plaid Cymru were invited to approach the conversation with a 'constructive spirit', with May announcing, 'We must find solutions that are negotiable, and command sufficient support in this House.' Corbyn, who had earlier dismissed her as leading a 'zombie' administration which had lost the right to govern, said she needed to rule out a no-deal Brexit before any 'positive discussion' could take place. Other party leaders were more accommodating. Ian Blackford, the SNP leader in Westminster, met with her shortly after to examine a way forward. Vince Cable said it would be 'silly not to talk' but added that the Prime Minister had to display a 'willingness' to discuss a second referendum.

All-party talks were the easy next step for May to announce, and they brought her a little time. But where might they lead? To a second referendum? She would never agree to that. To taking no deal off the table? She knew that would lose the ERG. To a customs union? Ditto and more, because it prevented the independent trade policy the majority of her party wanted. All other options, including a Norway-style economic partnership, were fraught with danger. As Liam Fox went on the record to say, 'a customs union means no independent trade policy', and would lead to a 'major reduction in the benefits of Brexit'. He added, 'As the Prime Minister says, Brexit has to mean Brexit, not a different relationship that doesn't actually deliver on Brexit.'[20] The way forward was unclear. May's lack of a Plan B suddenly made her look vulnerable – and, worse, ill-prepared. Officials in No. 10 recognised that the vote might have to go back to Parliament several times. One recalls, 'The thinking was it would take time for MPs to show they were voting with their hearts before eventually their heads and reason took over.'

Before the meaningful vote debate had opened on Tuesday, May had said, 'This is the most significant vote that any of us will ever be part of in our political careers.' The decision, she continued, 'will define our country for decades to come'. But where was the strategy to lead the country through the impasse? As it dawned on May that, in all likelihood, her hard-fought Brexit deal was doomed, and with it her own premiership, she turned her mind to what might define her own premiership apart from Brexit. Would she be remembered for nothing other than catastrophic defeats: losing a winnable general election and then failing to take Britain out of the EU, with the biggest parliamentary rebellion in history? It was a bleak and haunting prospect.

BURNING INJUSTICES: MAY'S DOMESTIC POLICIES

The text of May's July 2016 speech on the doorstep of No. 10 hung both in the Downing Street waiting room and outside her private office, constant reminders to the Prime Minister and her staff of the slow progress on her domestic agenda. In calling the general election, May wanted more than just a bigger majority for steering Brexit legislation through Parliament: she craved five secure years to make her mark domestically. As it happened, her days were numbered – and with the clock ticking louder and louder, she went to work with what power and time she still had.

It wasn't much, in either case. She had no majority after June 2017, for a start, and the votes of the DUP could not be relied upon for some of the domestic changes she wanted to make. Her authority with her Cabinet was shot, and Timothy and Hill, her two feisty policy brains who knew her mind, had gone. Her social policy aspirations did not resonate with her MPs in Parliament. Her Chancellor remained as obstructive after the general election as he had been before. A senior member of her political team described him as 'the biggest single obstacle' she faced as Prime Minister. However, her officials tended to take a more nuanced view – May was more sympathetic to the prudence of her Chancellor than her political team really accepted, they reasoned, and tension between No. 10 and No. 11 on domestic policy was natural, even healthy. The 2017 manifesto carried little credibility, and though much of it was to be enacted, it didn't provide the clear road map that Cameron's government had with the coalition agreement after 2010 or the Conservative manifesto after 2015. Her instability – surviving from month to month, sometimes week to week – meant it was difficult for her policy team to plan long-term, and gave another reason for the Treasury to deny the funding: why risk putting money into projects of a Prime Minister whose position was so precarious? And, finally, surely an even bigger obstacle than the Treasury: Brexit, which took up more and more of her time and political capital.

From 2018, however, May was determined to forge ahead. She convened the first of what she wanted to be twice-yearly domestic policy away-days at Chequers on 12 January 2018, and then another on 14 September. When Brexit prevented the first away-day of 2019 happening, a lengthy discussion was held in Downing Street in its place. Fortnightly meetings with her policy team were also begun after the January 2018 away-day, not dissimilar to Blair's regular domestic 'stock-takes' in No. 10. They often fell through – pushed aside by other priorities – but those who attended noted how much she enjoyed getting her teeth into topics that were anything other than Brexit. 'They reminded the Prime Minister why she was in the job,' says one senior Policy Unit official. Even when the pressure was most on May's political survival, her thoughts never left her domestic agenda for long. She had little interest in economics – her heart was in social policy. It was here that her Christianity, which she never wanted to talk about in public, became most visible, in her genuine concern for the powerless.

She was as determined to see through business begun under Timothy and Hill as she was to seize upon new initiatives that came to her mind subsequently. JoJo Penn became the key figure in May's inner court, driving forward her domestic agenda, as Barwell was sucked into managing Brexit and Parliament. Two linchpins were James Marshall, John Godfrey's successor as head of the Policy Unit, and Natalie Black, who was one of the civil service's powerhouses in May's No. 10.

Black focused on the modern industrial strategy, one of May's key strands, with Giles Wilkes taking over as the policy specialist after Neil O'Brien became an MP in June 2017. She chaired regular meetings which brought together the key players, maintaining tempo, with the drive coming more from No. 10 than from BEIS. The Treasury was sceptical – as ever – of the modern industrial strategy, and whether No. 10 and BEIS were developing the right policy ideas. Hammond was particularly suspicious, regarding May's elevation of BEIS as an attempt to create an 'Economics Ministry' whose policy platform was the modern industrial strategy. According to a senior member of May's team, Hammond's message was essentially: 'All attempts to take on the Treasury are doomed.' They pushed ahead on its strategy of 'sectoral deals' and identifying 'grand challenges'. Inspired by Mariana Mazzucato of University College London, these involved four major cross-cutting themes: artificial intelligence and data; the ageing society; clean growth; and the future of mobility. In March 2017, May had announced a review, in association with BEIS and

DIT, to boost Britain's AI sector, which resulted in extra funding for doctoral research and retraining for business – coupled with a new digital charter, which followed in 2018, May was determined to make Britain 'the best place in the world to start and run a digital business but also the safest place in the world to be online'.[21] May's speech on science and the modern industrial strategy at Jodrell Bank on 21 May 2018 touched a nerve when she challenged scientists to help transform Britain after Brexit. Her communications team always struggled to gain media interest in her domestic policy, so this was a rare exception, helped by her eye-catching claim that 'in cancer, our ambition is that within fifteen years we will be able to diagnose at a much earlier stage the lung, bowel, prostate or ovarian cancer of at least 50,000 more people a year'.

May worked hard throughout at her relationship with business. She was not naturally at ease with people from the sector in the way that Cameron and Osborne had been, and neither did she have a figure like Andrew Feldman (party chair from 2010 to 2016) to act as a bridge builder. Lingering damage had been caused by her bold if risky agenda under Timothy to make business more corporately responsible and democratic. Businesses complained regularly about the constant flow of new regulations billowing out of government, such as the gender pay gap reporting and national living wage. But its biggest beef was Brexit, where the endless uncertainty was taking its toll. May could offer no reprieve, but at least in Hammond business had a ready ally arguing their case against the perils of no deal. In her final nine months, bridge-building was enhanced, especially with financial services, by the appointment of veteran banker William Vereker as 'business envoy', another recommendation from Heywood, backed too by George Hollingbery. Her institution of five 'Business Councils' from early 2019 onwards also helped, institutionalising links with Downing Street.

May's work on modern slavery bore fruit in her speech at the United Nations General Assembly (UNGA) on 20 September 2017, in which she helped internationalise a cause which, under the inspiration of Hill, had been one of her earliest campaigns. She threatened to withhold money from the UN if she didn't secure its support to move modern slavery up its agenda, achieving the UN's first agreement on it as a result. At the same UNGA, drawing on her experiences as Home Secretary, she demanded giant technology companies remove extremist material within two hours of it being posted, gaining support from fellow leaders, including France and Italy.[22] May's deep sense of herself as being a guardian of national security, keeping the country safe, was one of the leitmotifs of her premiership.

Under Matthew Taylor, Blair's former head of policy, she set up a review on modern employment, published in July 2017 with the title 'Good Work'. Taylor received some flak from trade unions and traditional Labour supporters for chairing the review, and he himself was not uncritical of the response his work received from No. 10.[23] But his report helped produce a more thoughtful and better-informed conversation on the digital economy and work, and introduced some protection for gig employees.

The Race Disparity Audit, another first-term project, came to fruition in May's second term. Launched at Downing Street the week after the party conference in October 2017, the ethnicity website saw significant stakeholder involvement. In a similar vein, she instituted the gender pay gap reports, published every April, with the 2018 report revealing that 78 per cent of firms had a pay gap in favour of men. The BBC was the most high-profile institution on whose practices the report shone a light, with the difference in pay between male and female presenters drawing significant coverage. Domestic violence was another first-term issue never far from her mind. Just one week after the first meaningful vote was defeated, the draft Domestic Abuse Bill was published, which sought to offer greater protection to victims.

It was one of several issues No. 10 pushed that caused friction with Conservative backbenchers, albeit not on the same scale as Cameron's quest to introduce same-sex marriage. 'There was constant tension between No. 10 and our MPs on this: they never saw her social policy agenda as big retail, but she stuck with it,' says James Marshall.[24]

May's initiatives on the environment came almost entirely post-election. For all her love of walking, it was not natural territory for her, any more than it had been for Thatcher, whose late conversion to green issues owed much to the influence of diplomat Crispin Tickell. Always a tribal Conservative, May associated the green agenda with the left, and she worried that Tory MPs, whom she was trying so hard to keep onside, regarded it as another pretext to bash capitalism. But when No. 10 recommended using the language of 'clean' and 'efficient' rather than 'green', she began to change her mind and gradually became an enthusiast. Several factors came together to push it up her domestic agenda, none more important than Gove being appointed to DEFRA in June 2017. Within a month of his appointment, he had set out his agenda in a speech, 'The Unfrozen Moment', at the World Wildlife Fund's Living Planet Centre. The appointment of former Conservative MP and whip John Randall as her environment advisor within the Policy Unit in August 2017 further galvanised her, as Randall brought with him strong relationships with stakeholders. Marshall, an enthusiast, was able to exploit Ben Gummer's pivotal insertion into the 2017 manifesto of the passage on building a cleaner and 'better' environment, with a pledge to be the first generation 'to leave the environment in a better state than we inherited it'. Robbie Gibb, another enthusiast, was delighted for the Conservatives to have something to say on the environment other than about fox hunting. He welcomed the announcement at the party conference of 2017 of plans to increase the maximum sentence for animal cruelty to five years. A powerful facilitator behind the scenes was the BBC's screening in the autumn of 2017 of David Attenborough's *Blue Planet II* on marine life, which saw many Conservative MPs take to Twitter to voice their support.

On 11 January 2018, May spoke at the London Wetland Centre in Barnes to launch the 25 Year Environment Plan, foreshadowed in the manifesto. She argued that preserving the environment was a natural stance for Conservatives – and while she could certainly have done more during her premiership to affirm this belief, she nevertheless took some steps. At the Commonwealth Heads of Government Meeting in London three months later, she pushed the fifty-three member states to be more active on plastics and on adopting a protocol for cleaner oceans. Late in the day, she set up the first major review of the UK food system in nearly seventy-five years, led by Henry Dimbleby; announced an Environment Bill in July 2018; and declared Britain's intention to become a net zero carbon emissions nation by 2050 – becoming the first major country to do so. May's environmentalism showed that, despite critics saying she was inflexible and robotic, she could adopt new positions with enthusiasm.

Support for the LGBT community was another area which saw May do just this. She had happily gone along with Conservative opposition to much of the equality legislation passed by Labour between 1997 and 2010, including reducing the age of consent for gay sex, allowing gay couples to adopt, and introducing civil partnerships for same-sex couples. Her views subsequently softened. In 2013, not only did she vote in favour of same-sex marriage but, in her role as Minister for Women and Equality, she and Lynne Featherstone co-launched the initial government consultation which led to the question being put before Parliament. In the same role, she also introduced civil partnerships in religious settings, as well as a scheme to clear criminal records for people convicted of offences that were no longer illegal once homosexual acts were decriminalised.

As Prime Minister, May's transformation continued. On 19 July 2017, the annual Pride reception in Downing Street marked fifty years since the Sexual Offences Act 1967 was signed, which decriminalised homosexual acts in private between men aged over twenty-one. 'Like millions of other people in this country, I have changed my own mind on a number of the policy issues which I was confronted with when I first became an MP twenty years ago,' May said. 'If those votes were today, yes I would vote differently.'

She was at pains to stress at the reception that the new confidence-and-supply relationship with the DUP would not alter her commitment to the gay community, despite their well-known opposition to same-sex marriage. Her speech was well received. Later, she was told by a member of her team, 'I asked someone in the garden what they thought of your speech. He was gay, in his thirties. He said, "Well, it was the kind of chat you had with your mum – or at least, the one you wished you'd had."'

A year later, on 3 July 2018, Downing Street's Pride reception marked a different anniversary. 'Thirty years ago, in a room that overlooks this garden, the government of the day took the decision to support the introduction of Section 28,' May said, gesturing to the Cabinet Room. Many were impressed by her willingness to confront the mistakes Britain – and, in some cases, specifically the Conservatives – had made. The actor Simon Callow tweeted, 'It was indescribably moving. She spoke with warmth and generosity to an audience of seasoned campaigners – Michael Cashman, Chris Smith, Peter Tatchell, whom she singled out for special honour – and LGBT kids and supporters plus a handful of ministers. A milestone, I thought.' He was struck by how she 'apologised for the past – her own and her party's – and promised new action to counter present injustices'. Justine Greening, who came out in June 2016, was less convinced by May's commitment to the LGBT cause. 'May felt she was vulnerable because of the DUP's hard-line position on LGBT, so I would say she allowed progress on gay issues to develop rather than pushed it.'[25]

On mental health issues, May continued with the same sense of purpose that had set in during her time as Home Secretary. Back then, she had been struck not just by how many of those in prison were suffering from mental illness, but by how many people with mental health issues were being incarcerated in the first place, with prison cells being used as 'places of safety' – hardly the right environment to recover. In her last weeks as Prime Minister, she sought to make the Mental Health Act 'fit for modern society', preventing people with mental illness from being detained.

As Prime Minister, her understanding of mental illness became even more deeply felt. It was one of her 'burning injustices' in her doorstep speech. 'If you suffer from mental health problems, there's not enough help to hand,' she'd said on 13 July 2016. Then came her groundbreaking speech on 9 January 2017. As with the environment, this partly reflected society-wide shifts: hers was just one of several voices pressing in the same direction, with the royals, particularly Prince Harry, performing a galvanising role on mental health aware-ness similar to David Attenborough's on the environment, both of whose efforts she applauded.

Hunt, who had taken on the mental health brief as Health Secre-tary, was a fellow enthusiast, and suggested that Poppy Jaman, found-er of Mental Health First Aid, and Simon Wessely, president of the Royal Society of Medicine and former president of the Royal College of Psychiatrists, address Cabinet on 10 October 2017. The last item on the agenda, they were given forty-five minutes. May introduced the topic, and most ministers asked questions, apart from Johnson, who gave the impression that he thought it was all nanny-state stuff and made *sotto voce* asides throughout. Wessely focused on stigma and the value of people being open about their difficulties. Liam Fox, a doctor, asked searching questions, while the mental health of students was the most common topic, Wessely suspected because so many ministers had children at universities.

After Matt Hancock succeeded Hunt in July 2018, he set up a

White Paper, with a particular focus on the BAME community, given the disproportionately high number of that community who were sectioned. An aim of the health professionals working on the paper was to make it 'Boris-proof' in the event that he became Prime Minister. In 2017, Wessely had been invited to conduct a review of the Mental Health Act of 1983, and produced its final report in December 2018, with its main theme being that the voice of the patient should be heard far more than in the past. No. 10 ensured that both Hancock and Simon Stevens, chief executive of NHS England, appeared at the publication to ensure that both the Department of Health and NHS England were fully bound in. What struck Wessely most about May was that she took a particular interest in the most intractable aspect of mental health, one in which there were the fewest votes: severe mental illnesses. 'No senior politician, at least not since Stephen Dorrell in the 1990s, had taken such a real interest in that most difficult part of the whole spectrum,' Wessely says.[26] May was helped by having two Secretaries of State, Hunt and Hancock, who championed the cause. The latter had been influenced by writer and one-time sufferer Rachel Kelly, and he spoke movingly and personally about it at the launch of her book *Singing in the Rain* in January 2019. There was also the Farmer–Stevenson review into mental health in the workplace. 'We really wanted to make sure we were addressing every facet of the issue,' Penn says.[27]

The NHS Long Term Plan was May's biggest single domestic achievement – and there, too, mental health was made central. The plan included a commitment that spending on mental health would increase as a proportion of overall health spending in each and every year. The funding would also be tracked, because a frequent complaint had been that when more money was allocated to mental health, it was often diverted by local health trusts. By the end of her premiership, May had developed a deep understanding of the issue and its harrowing impact on sufferers and their families.

But the larger story was one of incompletion. Many aims, such as boosting the status and funding of further education, could never be carried out. On school policy, after her plans for grammar and faith schools hit the sand, she decided this was an area which offered little scope for fresh thinking other than consolidating Gove's pioneering work as Education Secretary. Her attempts to boost school funding in her final months hit the roadblock of the Chancellor.

May had a similar lower-middle-class, earnest background to Thatcher. She strove more consciously than her only female predecessor to advance the position of women, encouraging them to become involved in politics from at least her time as party chair onwards, founding Women2Win with Anne Jenkin in 2005. As Prime Minister, she sought in both her July 2016 and January 2018 reshuffles to promote more women and BAME ministers. Rudd thinks 'she tried to make women's lives better, not least on domestic violence and modern slavery. She did have an impact, more so probably than Margaret Thatcher.'[28] In her final PMQs, May was praised for her 'integrity, her commitment to public service and her dedication to this country' by Mother of the House Harriet Harman, while newly elected Lib Dem leader Jo Swinson said she had been 'inspiring' to young girls growing up in her constituency.

If social care became too touchy a subject after the election debacle, May hoped at least to explore the question of helping parents with childcare. She had Heywood's support but – in what became a recurring theme – ran slap up against the Treasury, who responded to the Policy Unit's requests for new money with challenges on whether the system also needed reform. Stalemate ensued. May's policy team had some sympathy but found that its blanket refusal went too far. On the issue of support for child funerals, for example, the sums seemed small compared to the difference it would make and distress it would save. May's team had stand-up rows with Treasury officials but lost. The Treasury were so focused on the 'sacred gospel of their financial rules', in the words of one aggrieved member of May's Policy Unit, it gave them little room for flexibility. But there was genuine tension between the fiscal approach May and Hammond agreed early in her premiership and the spending ambitions that emerged further down the line. The issue of school funding also led to fraught, frustrated discussions, testing relations both within and between No. 10 and No. 11 even further.

Nothing was made easy for May. Not only was she tasked with one of the most riddled projects in British history, but it actively impeded her from enacting more straightforward proposals: she had neither the time nor the support. May displayed some flexibility in her thinking about social issues, forgoing larger reforms to do what she could in introducing incremental improvements. The question was, could she be as nimble in her thinking about the Withdrawal Bill through the House of Commons? Or had the moment already passed?

Two figures toiled to get the second meaningful vote on 12 March over the line. Attorney General Geoffrey Cox (left) sought legal changes on the backstop from the EU, while Chief Whip Julian Smith (right) looked to get the numbers in the Conservative Party to pass the withdrawal agreement. Neither was successful.

CHAPTER 18

THE SECOND ATTEMPT AT PARLIAMENT

15 JANUARY–14 MARCH 2019

May had been warned the numbers would be high, but she was still shaken by her record-breaking parliamentary defeat on 15 January. Her self-belief, however, hardly wavered: she was determined to press on. Turning such a large defeat into a victory, with seventy-four days left to 29 March, was not going to be easy. So she said she would entertain any idea to get the deal through and, once that happened, return to her domestic agenda and to strengthening the Union and the Conservative Party. She was never one for throwing in the towel. Rumours circulating in Westminster that she was on the verge of resigning – because of health, exhaustion or the advice of Philip – were not true. Defeat, reversal and contempt were only making her more determined.

DIVISIONS WITHIN MAY'S TEAM AFTER MV1

May found herself uncomfortably caught between two camps, each of which responded to the MV1 defeat in different ways. Barwell thought fresh thinking was required, and wanted a permanent customs union and talks with Labour back on the table. Qualified support came from

David Lidington, increasingly influential as May's deputy, as well as from Hammond, at the height of his brief influence on Brexit, and from Robbins and Letwin. Julian Smith, supported by Brandon Lewis and Robbie Gibb, was deeply opposed because he thought it would split the parliamentary Conservative Party even more deeply than it already was. The moment for a permanent customs union had passed. 'By January, there was no hope of getting it past Sajid or Jeremy: their eyes were on the leadership election coming ever closer: anything smacking of a customs union wouldn't fly,' says a senior colleague. Smith et al. wanted to stick by the tripartite strategy they'd deployed in the first meaningful vote: Conservative MPs, DUP MPs and Labour MPs in Leave seats. The initial 230-vote rejection made it an uphill struggle: just three Labour MPs had voted for the deal out of the group of twenty the Conservative whips thought biddable. All ten of the DUP had voted against, and 118 Conservatives had rebelled against the whip to vote it down too, roughly 110 of whom were ardent Brexiteers. Getting a majority from these figures, if it were possible at all, would require careful balancing of the Conservative Brexiteer, DUP and Labour Leave blocs. As neither faction could give her a majority on their own, she needed to convince MPs of mutually contradictory outcomes from their actions: for the Labour MPs, that voting against her would result in the UK leaving the EU without a deal, and for Conservative and DUP MPs, that voting against her would result in no Brexit at all. If May looked too far from victory then Labour MPs would not expend their political capital to vote with the government, but in order to gain credibility by acquiring a significant portion of those 110 Brexiteer Tory votes, she would have to harden her stance considerably. To make matters worse, any concessions made in favour of Labour risked scaring away the ERG and DUP, and vice versa.

For the plan to work, further concessions on the backstop would be needed, to pacify the ERG and the DUP, and inducements would need to be given to Labour, too. For the supporters of this strategy, it was a price worth paying. For its opponents, it was a pointless exercise: Barwell and his backers believed this approach had been tried and failed on MV1, and that it would never succeed in bringing enough members of the ERG round to May's plan – they were a lost cause. 'Gavin felt we had to move on, we would be wasting our time, twenty to twenty-five ERG members would always refuse to vote for the deal, and we'd be best just to accept that,' says one aide, who thought the ERG were just gaming the system – holding out till no deal became inevitable. The only option, on this view, was to go cross-party.

As May picked herself up, this divided opinion in her inner sanctum was the last thing she wanted. In all the difficult times earlier – the general election defeat, the Chequers Cabinet, the fraught Cabinet on 14 November – her team around her were united in support. May worried that Downing Street, which had remained almost impervious to leaking over the previous two and a half years, was now becoming porous. Reports appeared in the press of Barwell's enthusiasm for a permanent customs union.[1] Was there a leak in her 8.30 a.m. meetings? It was one factor that made her tighten her circle after MV1. One close to Barwell says:

> The press made out that Gavin was obsessed with the customs union for ideological reasons, particularly as he'd been a Remainer and had held a London seat. The truth was that his stance was motivated by pragmatism. His main preoccupation was to avoid the PM having to face another defeat as huge again on MV2.

On Wednesday 16 January, talks opened with Labour, overseen by Barwell, Lidington and Gove, with soundings taken too with the SNP, Liberal Democrats and Plaid Cymru. 'Julian wasn't remotely happy,' says one, but he accepted that the process needed to be worked through. When Robbins too pushed for cross-party engagement, straying into areas some felt more akin to when he was Principal Private Secretary to the PM between 2006 and 2007, it sparked resentment from some, admiration from others. Deep inside No. 10, the viability of pledges to enhance workers' rights after Brexit were examined, to help convince Labour MPs, led by John Mann and Caroline Flint, to bring more Labour recruits over to the Conservative side. May watched the outcome nervously. As expected, Labour quickly came back and said they'd only be willing to vote for May's deal if she promised a second referendum – interpreted as a cynical response to maximise Conservative divisions.

The EU had been waiting for May to make this move for a long time. 'We were always trying to press them into talks with Labour,' Guy Verhofstadt recalls. 'Every time I came over, I tried to get them to do that.' But they lacked real conviction and drive, and by the end of January, it became clear that the strategy of courting Labour was going nowhere, which placed the tripod plan back on top of the table. Reports appeared in the press of there being 'daggers drawn' between both factions, noting of an overheard argument between Barwell and Smith in a House of Commons corridor: 'It was not a pleasant conversation. They were like a couple of stags facing each other.' Rumours circulated of Philip May intervening to convince Barwell that his plans to reach out to Labour MPs would be divisive and unworkable.[2] Suspicions in No. 10 were that Smith had been talking to Tim Shipman, who duly reported his comments in the *Sunday Times*.

In this febrile atmosphere between MV1 and MV2, such fallouts within No. 10 were not uncommon. But Barwell, a collegiate rather than an abrasive chief of staff, restored order, focusing everyone's minds on the tripod strategy.

Robbins was duly dispatched back to Brussels in late January, to explore possibilities for changes to the backstop in an attempt to bring the DUP and ERG back onside. Support for a second referendum was aired by Barwell and Lidington in February, if all else failed. But May closed it down: 'I'm not going down that path,' she said at an

8.30 a.m. meeting in February. An early general election was another option discussed among May's team, though not with any enthusiasm. Three Cabinet ministers told the *Financial Times* that they thought an early election was possible,[3] including Hunt, who believed one might be necessary to honour the result of the 2016 referendum if May was unable to secure the votes in Parliament to see her deal through.[4] Some macho voices suggested that going to the polls in June, after a successful Brexit, would secure the mandate the Conservatives didn't achieve in June 2017.

Reports of an early general election as the only way out were slapped down by May's team, worried the talk would inflame hostility within the party. Besides, CCHQ still hadn't recovered from the trauma of 2017, the party was short of cash, and wide-ranging reforms being pushed through by Lewis were far from complete. Will Tanner, the former No. 10 policy deputy, produced research from his think tank Onward which concluded that an election would be a huge risk: 'It would take a tiny swing for Labour to sweep dozens of seats to become the largest party – with 40 Conservative constituencies held with a majority of just 5 per cent or smaller.'[5] But Mark Sedwill still thought it prudent to hold discussions with Permanent Secretaries in January and February to plan for such an eventuality, given the instability caused by the MV1 parliamentary defeat, the thinness of the majority and its dependence upon flaky DUP support, and Corbyn's relentless quest to precipitate the early calling of a general election.

THE MALTHOUSE COMPROMISE AND THE BRADY AMENDMENT

May's mind was darting all over the place, desperately searching for a way forward. After the MV1 defeat, there was a sense among Tory MPs that they now needed to work together or they would let Corbyn in. Could she capitalise on the goodwill? She decided to try again with her ploy from before Christmas, when, following her decision to delay MV1, she had brought together various factions of the party, including figures like Rees-Mogg, Baker, Letwin and Welsh MP Guto Bebb, to remind them of what united them. Nicky Morgan was at work in her constituency on the morning of Saturday 19 January when her mobile rang. 'Look,' May said, 'I don't know what you're doing tomorrow, but could you come to Chequers for lunch to talk about things?' 'Yes, of course,' Morgan replied, with no idea why she was being invited or who was going to join them. She arrived to find a company of six around the lunch table: the Prime Minister and Penn (Barwell was on a family engagement), along with Green, Rees-Mogg and Baker.

May's idea, it transpired, was to enlist their support for the Withdrawal Agreement Bill (WAB), discovering what it was that was stopping Baker and Rees-Mogg and the ERG from agreeing to it, and what Morgan and Green from the other wing thought could be done to win round those hankering after a second referendum. 'There was a general sense from Jacob and Steve that they wanted to hold the party together, support the deal if they could, and we talked over the problems that they had, principally the backstop and anything that smacked of a customs union,' Morgan recalls.[6] She found the Prime Minister the most relaxed and open that she'd ever seen her in post. The lunch concluded with general bonhomie, and a sense from the guests that the Prime Minister was in listening mode.

The following morning, inspired by the same strand of thinking for fellow Conservatives to find common ground, government minister Kit Malthouse convened a meeting in his room in the House of Commons, where Morgan, Green, Rees-Mogg and Baker were joined by ministers Robert Buckland and Stephen Hammond. The meeting was genial (they ate through his children's Christmas chocolate) and they agreed to meet at least once a day for the following week to hammer out an agreement which eventually became the Malthouse compromise. Despite its name, the plan was very much conceived by the ERG, namely Shanker Singham and Baker, but it got heavyweight backing from Remainers like Nicky Morgan as well. At 1.45 p.m. on Thursday 24 January, the group marched in to see May in her House of Commons study to share their thinking. They proposed that the government renegotiate provisions in the WAB relating to the back-stop and replace it with a mixture of max fac provisions, exemptions and hypothetical technologies which, in the eyes of critics, had already been rejected by the EU. According to the proposal, if the attempt at renegotiating the backstop failed, Plan B was clear: a 'managed no-deal'. 'Baker et al. were cock-a-hoop that they had brought some high-profile Remainers into backing what they and we knew to be unicorns,' one of May's close advisors says.

May was taken aback: this was not what she had expected when she had instigated the Chequers lunch four days before. Julian Smith, who was at her side, was 'sniffy and negative', though apologised later. 'What the PM had wanted from the Chequers lunch was to bring us all behind her deal. She hadn't expected us to come up with our own proposal,' says Morgan.[7] But neither did she dismiss the idea out of hand. She told them she would 'think on it'.

The story broke in the *Daily Telegraph* on 28 January and then it was open news that both wings of the party were trying to find another way forward before the second meaningful vote.[8] Joined by Duncan Smith at a further meeting on 31 January, and by Robbins with his team at May's request, her Europe advisor went meticulously through their plan and explained how different elements of it would be difficult or impossible to negotiate with Brussels. Duncan Smith spoke about his own conversations with Barnier in October, which envisaged the possibility of the backstop being completely eliminated in favour of new technologies, and said that he thought it should be seriously explored. 'IDS repeatedly mistook courteous diplomatic rebuffs as genuine interest in his proposals,' one of May's advisors says.

But May set up three long meetings on concurrent days from 4 February with DExEU officials, at which they tried to hammer out a way forward. 'The problem was that May wouldn't listen, and because she didn't, she blew it,' says Duncan Smith.[9] In the eyes of May's team, it was Duncan Smith who wasn't listening: either to May or to the EU.

May considered the proposal but ultimately pushed it aside. 'To this day, I don't know why they were not willing to play ball with us,' says Morgan. 'We felt that Steve Barclay was sympathetic, but we simply couldn't get the buy-in from No. 10.'[10] The EU's anticipated resistance and May's own well-founded reticence towards anything that boosted the possibility of no deal – a reticence which intensified after her seminal visit to Belfast on 5 February, the day after the DExEU talks opened – were the two most decisive reasons.

More successful was the so-called Brady amendment. Raoul Ruparel, who had now joined No. 10's Europe wing, was an important figure, having established reasonable relationships with Brexiteers during his time as Davis's special advisor. This is one of the reasons Barwell wanted to keep him in government after Davis's resignation. Shortly after the MV1 defeat, he wrote an email to Barwell exploring a way out of the impasse May found herself in, around which MPs might coalesce. Ruparel then spoke to Smith over the weekend of 19–20 January, who liked his thinking, which utilised the concession won by Grieve earlier in January that MPs had the right to bring forward amendments on Brexit.

Though the EU had repeatedly agreed that if alternative arrangements could be implemented to enable a frictionless border in Northern Ireland they would replace and obviate the need for the backstop, Brexiteers still harboured suspicions that the backstop would not be removed but instead become the backbone of the future relationship. To address this, the Brady amendment would call on the government to renegotiate the backstop with the EU, eliminating it in favour of implementing the alternative arrangements without requiring the

UK to remain in a customs union if technological solutions to the border could not be found. But who should propose the amendment? '[Graham] Brady's role was to say "Yes" by giving his own name to the amendment, and then to take it forward,' Smith says. The hope was that it would send a very clear signal to the EU that the backstop was the only issue blocking the deal, suggesting simultaneously that the deal was all but finished (reassuring Brussels), at the same time leaving room for negotiation (reassuring Brexiteers).

The plan, though, was fraught with doubts. It was uncertain until the last minute whether May herself would back it, Cabinet would support it, Bercow allow a vote on it, and, if he did, whether it would pass the Commons. Robert Peston thought that May was, 'almost certain to be humiliated' in any vote,[11] while the *Financial Times* thought it 'likely to fail'.[12] When May went in to address the 1922 Committee on Monday 28 January, she was still undecided on whether to give her backing to the amendment. But while on her feet for more than an hour, excited by the prospects she saw of a collective solution, she made a rare on-the-spot decision to say that the amendment would be whipped the following day, announcing her verdict 'there and then'.[13]

Why had she done this? The ERG had conducted its own analysis of the MV1 defeat, noting the increasing desire of the Commons to take over the direction of policy, and the momentum building in favour of a second referendum which might delay Brexit indefinitely, both of which were threats to them. So Rees-Mogg and senior ERG figures had been to see May on Thursday 24 January and told her that they might be willing to vote for the WAB, as long as she vowed never to extend Article 50 and could achieve meaningful change on the backstop. They wanted Geoffrey Cox, in whom they had particular confidence as an accomplished Brexiteer, to provide legal advice that would reassure them on any changes.[14] It helped give May the confidence to think she should throw her weight behind the Brady amendment.

Tuesday 29 January, the day of the vote, opened with a political

Cabinet at 8.30 a.m. at No. 10. Gove, again proving himself the decisive voice, encouraged May to show enthusiasm about the amendment and a new spirit of compromise when she spoke in the debate, and to say how pleased she was to see MPs working together. After the meeting, however, she spoke to Juncker, who told her that it would be utterly pointless to come to Brussels if she intended to reopen the text. Despite the rebuff, she went on to the House of Commons, where she 'directly said what the ERG needed to hear'[15] – she would be reopening the withdrawal agreement with the EU to rewrite the backstop. It irritated Brussels, Paris and Berlin, but it irritated and worried the Irish government even more, as it went back on what they saw as a clear understanding in the joint report, for which they had lobbied so hard in late 2017. The Irish began to think that the government was reneging on its word and couldn't be trusted.

Dublin's fury seemed a long way away when, to the surprise of many across the House, the Brady amendment passed by 317 votes to 301. May promptly pledged to return to the Commons and put a revised Brexit deal, if she was able to achieve one, to the vote by 13 February. To her relief, the Cooper amendment extending Article 50 beyond 29 March was defeated the same day, though an amendment to reject a no-deal Brexit was passed with a majority of eight.

Tuesday 29 January thus appeared to be a rare good day for May. Had the House passed Cooper's amendment, she would have lost control of the Brexit agenda, but by passing Brady's, it allowed her to retain the initiative, albeit for a limited time. Isabel Hardman wrote in *The Spectator* that 'the Brady amendment gives Theresa May the strength to kick the can down the road',[16] while James Forsyth said it left the Prime Minister 'in a stronger position than anyone would have expected – especially after her 230-vote defeat on the withdrawal agreement a fortnight ago'.[17] It meant, despite Juncker's brush-off, another attempt at persuading the EU she wanted to reopen negotiations on what she had described as the 'only possible' deal a short while before. Her message to the EU was: agree alternative arrangements that remove the backstop, and I'll have the support I need in the House of Commons to get the deal through.

Robbins was not pleased, and nor was he confident of success. Emails he wrote to No. 10 on 28 and 29 January were leaked, suggesting that the latest foray to Brussels would be futile and might even heighten the risk of a no-deal Brexit.[18] 'The EU will be rightly angry and confused,' agreed one of her team, adding, 'They must think we are completely crazy.'[19] But she was committed to the course of action and had to go through with it. The first two weeks of February thus saw her in prolonged conversations in Brussels and on the phone to EU leaders. So off she went into the dark Brussels night, armed with little more than her self-belief that, this time, they would listen.

A HISTORIC VISIT TO NORTHERN IRELAND:
5 FEBRUARY

Her immediate problem did not come from Continental Europe, however, but from Northern Ireland. When Karen Bradley heard reports about May announcing to the 1922 Committee that she was going to whip through the Brady amendment, she froze. Had anyone considered how the idea of replacing the backstop with alternative arrangements would be received in Belfast? She immediately sought out Lidington and told him about the damage that would be done by the word 'replacing'. Had it said 'amending' the text by the 'alternative arrangements', that would have been a different proposition, she told him. She was due to have dinner with Irish Foreign Minister Simon Coveney later that week, but received a curt message that the dinner was off, and she was summoned to the Department of Foreign Affairs in Dublin, traditionally the least pro-British institution within the

Irish government (and which had clashed with Raab and, still more, Davis in their time as DExEU Secretaries). For thirty minutes, Bradley absorbed a rant in which she was told that the British were not the colonial rulers any more, that they didn't now run the country, and that any hope of support from Dublin for the restoration of talks in Northern Ireland were at an end.

Bradley contacted May at once and tried to persuade her to come over to Ireland to repair the damage, suggesting she watch the Six Nations rugby match that Saturday, 2 February, between England and Ireland. May was open to the idea but was overruled, to Bradley's irritation, by advice from No. 10. So Bradley went to the match alone and spoke to Varadkar, to be roundly beaten up a second time for 'the arrogance of the British'. Varadkar's mood was not improved by a famous England victory (32–10) against an Ireland side which had won the Six Nations in 2018 and expected to win this time. Bradley was immediately back on the phone to May and told her she had to come urgently to restore trust across Northern Ireland after her support for the Brady amendment. So, after Cabinet on Tuesday 5 February, they flew together from Northolt to Belfast: 'What you have to understand', the Northern Ireland Secretary explained to the Prime Minister, 'is how strongly the Irish feel about the backstop and the security it gives them.' The dominant view in Northern Ireland, she explained, was: 'We understand why you are doing Brexit, though we didn't vote for it. But please do it in a way that doesn't hurt us, and the backstop is our guarantee that we won't be hurt by Brexit.'[20] May held a series of meetings that afternoon, including in nationalist areas, in which she stressed that she wanted to make alterations to the backstop, not removing it, and she was committed to avoiding a hard border.[21] 'I had rarely seen her as moved as after the last meeting,' one advisor says. 'Later that day, she made a speech where she reaffirmed her personal commitment to Northern Ireland and the Union, and I think it answers so many questions about the decisions she took in the last year. The Union was always her first priority.'

In the early evening, a private meeting took place in the Northern Ireland Office in Stormont House, Belfast, that was to make up May's mind on no deal. Naturally risk-averse, she was always cautiously against this outcome. But after her time across the North Channel, she now settled upon that stance with urgent conviction. Accompanied by Bradley and Barwell, but without officials, she met locals. The meeting had been scheduled to last twenty minutes, but she kept shooing away her minders who were trying to keep her to timetable, saying she needed longer. She understood perhaps for the first time how precarious the continuation of the Union was, and the sense of betrayal that residents across the communities felt, and how its continuation depended upon support for it from the minority nationalist community. She saw how a no-deal Brexit could sabotage the delicate balance on which the security of the Province depended. As Philip Hammond says:

> She came to understand what it meant on that trip to Northern Ireland. It saw a real step-change in her thinking. She realised a border poll [as enshrined in the Good Friday Agreement] was a real possibility. She had not appreciated how the Union relied upon the Catholic voters, and they wouldn't continue their support if there was to be a hard border. Her dislike of no deal was thus its knock-on impact on the Union. For me, it was primarily the economic danger of no deal.[22]

They flew back that evening, with May still absorbing what she had heard. At the 8.30 a.m. meeting the next day, she said, 'People in Westminster need to hear what I heard with their own ears. It's now completely clear to me the damage that reneging on our commitments to the backstop could do.' She explained to those present how the trip made her realise that she could never support no deal, as it would entail the return to direct rule in the Province, which would jeopardise peace in Northern Ireland, with a possible knock-on effect on Scotland, upsetting the delicate balance in favour of Scotland remaining within the Union. She quoted with feeling a moderate nationalist who had said, 'It's not the borders on the land but the borders in our mind that you need to worry about, and that's what the Good Friday Agreement was about.' After the meeting, Barwell and Bradley privately agreed that it was rare for May to be as moved by a meeting as she had evidently been the evening before in Belfast.[23]

Back in Brussels, as expected, neither Donald Tusk nor fellow EU leaders were in any mood to be helpful. Following talks with a still irate Varadkar in Brussels, Tusk spoke of a 'special place in hell' for 'those who promoted Brexit without even a sketch of a plan of how to carry it out safely'. No. 10's carefully calibrated response to his comments, that it was a question for the Council President 'whether he considers the use of that kind of language helpful', disguised its anger and disappointment.[24] Still more so the following day when, most unhelpfully, Tusk said of Corbyn's Brexit plan, which included establishing a permanent customs union, that it offered a 'promising way out' of the stalemate. Following Tusk's comments, May held 'robust but constructive' talks with him and EU leaders in Brussels.[25] They advanced her cause not a metre.

Neither was her task helped when, at the start of the following week, Robbins was overheard by a reporter from ITV in a Brussels bar suggesting that her strategy was to hold the vote back until late in March, thereby presenting MPs with a stark choice: support her deal, or accept a long extension to Article 50. If MPs 'don't vote for the deal, then the extension is a long one'.[26] Ah ha, said Brexiteers: just what we suspected. Robbins reportedly also said that the difficulty with the backstop was that the government initially intended it as a bridge to a long-term trading partnership, but it has become 'a safety net' – a view with which many agreed. Tensions with Robbins ran high, and the episode gave licence and opportunity for the venom to seep out into the open. Since Chequers, Robbins had become a divisive figure within May's team, with even middle-ground figures like Hunt, Javid and Gove thinking that he was overly cautious about what might prove acceptable thinking in Brussels. But they were angrier still with May for accepting his advice meekly that 'the deal on the table is the best we'll get out of Brussels' rather than telling him to 'go back and get a better deal'. May found herself becoming irritated with Robbins, as she had in the autumn, asking herself whether his advice that there was no other way was right. It was a long time since a civil servant had been so identified with a disputed policy. Some Brexiteers – the spectre of the Second World War never far from their minds – even drew comparisons with the counsel Neville Chamberlain received from his senior official Horace Wilson on Europe policy, specifically recommending appeasement.

To the ERG, Robbins, who they never thought believed in Brexit, and would have settled for a customs union, was always the *bête noire*. One Brexiteer said, 'The trouble with Mr Robbins is that he is a draughts player in a chess world.' Baker's comment, or caution, after the leak was: 'As a consummate civil servant, Mr Robbins is likely to be appalled by this story. Officials advise. Ministers decide.'[27] Back in the Commons, May ran into angry comments from MPs that she was merely playing for time, with just forty-five days left until 29 March. The second meaningful vote was still expected before the end of February, and MPs were making it clear that they wouldn't brook another delay.

THE DECISION TO DELAY MEANINGFUL VOTE 2

Aside from the Grieve motion, May had committed to hold a vote in the Commons every two weeks. On 29 January, it was the Brady amendment. On 14 February, another vote was due, thought to be routine. The government tabled a motion confirming May's approach of going back to the EU for better terms, as endorsed on 29 January. But this time the ERG abstained, on the argument that the motion ruled out a no-deal Brexit. The rapprochement with the ERG, which had held for a period after the MV1 defeat, was beginning to shatter. Defeat, by 303 to 258, was deeply embarrassing for May, and damaged her case in Brussels to be speaking for a majority in Parliament. The pain was exacerbated by May, who, for almost the first time on such a contested vote, slipped out of the building and did not respond herself, 'fueling the impression across the House that she is not in charge of Brexit', according to Jane Merrick in a report for the US broadcaster CNN.[28] It was May's tenth defeat in the Commons on Brexit.

Instead of sending a message to Brussels that the UK was at last getting its act together on Brexit, the vote confirmed the EU's worst thoughts: that the government was unable to deliver. May was left with the almost impossible task of producing something fresh to offer MPs to persuade them to vote for the deal before the end of the month. Richard Harrington, a junior minister at BEIS, exploded with anger when he heard reports about the ERG drinking champagne to celebrate May's defeat at their hands: 'I read that Nigel Farage is setting up a new party called "Brexit" and if I were them I'd be looking at that, because that seems to reflect their views more than the Conservative Party does.'[29] Indeed, with Farage's Brexit Party formally announced on 20 January, the fear was precisely of ERG supporters crossing over to it. May and her team were quietly seething with the ERG.

On Friday 15 February, Baker sent a WhatsApp message to ERG members, which now numbered as many as 100 MPs, saying that May was only pretending to negotiate with the EU, while 'working together to run down the clock to force [her] deal through' with few changes, and that the Brussels negotiations were 'a complete waste of time'.[30] May's response came on Sunday 17 February, in the form of a letter written to all 317 Tory MPs, urging them to unite behind her Brexit deal. 'History will judge us all,' she warned. She told MPs that her aim of achieving concessions from Brussels was still the policy, she would be returning to see Juncker in Brussels in the week ahead, and she would be speaking to every single leader of the EU27 by phone over the coming days to win concessions on the backstop. 'The decision of dozens of them to abstain on the vote on Thursday was thus disappointing,' she wrote. 'I do not underestimate how deeply or how sincerely colleagues hold the views which they do on this important issue – or that we are all motivated by a common desire to do what is best for our country, even if we disagree on the means of doing so.' But she said that if they failed to compromise, they would be collectively guilty of failing to deliver on the result of the referendum and 'will let down the people who sent us to represent them'.[31]

More difficulties came for May the following week. On Monday 18 February, news broke that seven MPs, including Luciana Berger and Chuka Umunna, were breaking away from the Labour Party, which they said under Corbyn 'no longer exists'. For a day, it seemed like good news for the Conservatives, especially as revulsion at Corbyn's failure to lead on antisemitism was one of the rebels' motives. But smiles were rapidly wiped away when Nick Watt reported the next day on BBC *Newsnight* that three Conservative MPs – Heidi Allen, Anna Soubry and Sarah Wollaston – had gone 'very, very silent'.[32] Indeed, on Wednesday, all three MPs crossed the Commons floor to sit alongside the now eight Labour MPs (the original seven joined by Joan Ryan) who formed what they called The Independent Group (TIG). Worse, Allen said that 'a significant number' of Conservative MPs might be joining them but were holding back for fear of sparking a general election at this 'critical juncture'. Their unhappiness went far wider than Brexit, they said, accusing May of throwing away the modernisation agenda begun by Cameron. Soubry said, 'The right-wing, the hard-line anti-EU awkward squad that have destroyed every leader for the last

forty years are now running the Conservative Party from top to toe.'
She urged fellow One-Nation Conservatives as well as 'like-minded
Lib Dems' to 'come and join us'. May responded that she was 'saddened' by the resignations, while insisting that she was 'delivering on
our manifesto commitment and implementing the decision of the
British people' to leave the EU.[33] She heard the news in the middle of
her 8.30 a.m. morning meeting on Wednesday. Julian Smith says:

> The Prime Minister and I were extremely upset about the defec-
> tions. I can't overstate how devastated she was about the loss of the
> three MPs. She had campaigned with them and helped them and
> she felt, 'This is what they've done for me.' I'd been speaking to
> them too to try to stop them. For a Tory Party leader to lose MPs
> to another party is a massive thing. She saw it at once as a threat to
> the party, and the fact that they were holding a press conference she
> thought was awful.[34]

The defections heightened interest in leadership challenges, further
weakening her position. Concurrently with the defections, Javid was
seen to be taking a hard line at the Home Office, exploiting a wave of
press-fuelled righteous indignation over Shamima Begum, a former
student at Bethnal Green Academy in London who'd left the UK to
join ISIS in 2015. Pregnant with her third child, she wanted to return
home. Javid removed Begum's British citizenship. His militant stance
was designed to boost Javid's 'prime ministerial ambitions', said Roy
Greenslade in *The Guardian*.[35]

With the second meaningful vote expected that week, and with
nothing fresh from Brussels to soothe MPs, May announced on
Sunday 24 February that she would delay the vote until 12 March
to allow more time for negotiations. As often happened for PMs at
moments of high tension, she had to leave for an international conference. May could have done without the meeting of the EU–Arab

League in Egypt's Sharm el-Sheikh. 'We still have it within our grasp to leave the European Union with a deal on 29 March and that's what I am going to be working at,' she said before she left.[36] The two-day conference, the first between the EU and the League of Arab States, saw discussions on Syria, Yemen and the evolving threat from Daesh. But it gave May the chance to hold meetings with Tusk, Juncker, Merkel and Varadkar, the most fruitful being breakfast with Merkel: 'She really was trying to help,' says an official, who comments, 'Overall, the conference was grim, soulless conference centre, not what anyone needed.' Before flying home, May said she had confidence that we could 'find a way through which allows the UK to leave the EU in a smooth and orderly way with a deal'.[37] She didn't elaborate on the grounds for her optimism, but on the plane home she was relaxed enough to enjoy an animated game of cards with her team. Once she landed, she hoped she had one last card to play – but it all depended on a mission the Attorney General had undertaken at her request.

SCRAMBLE FOR VOTES: COX'S LEGAL ADVICE

The delay to the Commons vote, while inevitable, merely cranked up the pressure on May to deliver this time. Johnson started holding conversations with MPs with a view to giving the Prime Minister an ultimatum: 'The idea is that unless she agrees to go immediately after Brexit, the group would go on strike and refuse to vote for any government legislation,' reported Tim Shipman, quoting an ally of Johnson's.[38] One of those whom Johnson reached out to was Amber Rudd, who had abandoned her own leadership ambitions and was exploring ways of securing a deal. Highlighting May's continuing difficulties in putting together a winning coalition behind her deal, a survey of Tory MPs compiled by the People's Vote campaign found that ninety-six Tory MPs demanded changes to the deal which looked impossible for her to deliver, forty-three wanted a complete removal of the backstop, thirty-four demanded a strict time limit on it, and thirty-one called for a unilateral exit mechanism from the backstop. Given that some MPs fell into more than one category, it added up to a minimum of 108 Tory MPs who were not going to vote for May's deal.[39]

May's strategy for the final two weeks leading up to the second meaningful vote on 12 March was to throw everything she had at the tripod strategy. To woo Labour MPs, conversations were stepped up to discover exactly what it might take to secure their vote. With Labour's leadership office and whips looking increasingly threatening, the MPs demanded real gains to compensate for the ire. Workers' rights and environmental standards emerged as two policy changes that might entice Labour MPs. As Stephen Bush noted in the *New Statesman*, however, the problem was that there was only a 'very, very small pool' of no more than '29 votes, including a number of sitting shadow ministers', who at best might abstain on May's deal.[40] John Mann, whose constituency was a former coal mining area in Nottinghamshire, told May, 'Show us the money,' calling for 'transformative investment' in areas that had voted to leave.[41] In response, May launched the Stronger Towns fund, a £1.6 billion government fund to boost less well-off communities in England after Brexit, with more than half, spread over seven years, going to the Midlands and the North. When the predictable outcry came from Northern Ireland, Scotland and Wales about preferential treatment, the government promised that additional announcements would be made 'in due course' for deprived areas in each of the other three nations too.[42] Smith redoubled his efforts with Labour, preferring to talk to Caroline Flint, who he felt, as a former minister and candidate for deputy leadership, had more credibility and reach across the party than Mann.

By early March, with no good news from Brussels, Smith was becoming desperate about the numbers, which still didn't stack up. He clung to the hope that most Conservative MPs would in the last analysis vote for the WAB. It wouldn't be enough, but if all ten DUP members voted, just some twenty Labour MPs would be sufficient to get the government over the line. The message he kept receiving from Flint and Mann was that 'you have to convince us that the numbers are going to go up, because we're taking such a huge risk if we vote with the government'.

Confidence that the DUP and ERG could be brought onside took a knock in early March with an initiative between both parties, which marked the high point of their collaboration. To secure their support in the vote on 12 March, they announced the government must meet 'three tests'. A group of eight ERG lawyers (inevitably dubbed the Star Chamber), chaired by Bill Cash, had to satisfy themselves that a 'legally binding mechanism' had been put in place to escape the backstop, that there would be a clear 'exit route' for the UK, and that the language of the government's legal advice would be rewritten.

By early March, May was beginning to turn inward, relying on fewer and fewer advisors. The 8.30 a.m. meetings were losing their impact, as decisions were increasingly taken in 'small group', with Barwell, Penn, Smith and Gibb, as well as her three senior officials, Sedwill, Robbins and Peter Hill. Brandon Lewis complained that he was no longer being invited, while even Cabinet ministers like Lidington and Gove, as well as Bradley, Brokenshire, Clark, Gauke and Rudd, who had loyally supported May, felt they were being excluded, and they were cross. 'She had become very controlling and micro-managing. She lost trust in MPs, then her Cabinet, then even her allies and aides,' says one. As she was wont to do when her back was against the wall, she lashed out. On 8 March, in Grimsby while on a tour of Labour Leave areas, she spoke about her frustration with the lack of flexibility from the EU:

Just as MPs will face a big choice next week, the EU has to make a choice too. We are both participants in this process. It is in the European interests for the UK to leave with a deal ... The decisions that the European Union makes over the next few days will have a big impact on the outcome of the vote.[43]

It was unusual for May to be so blatant, and her comments were not well received. The response to No. 10 from Brussels was 'less than lukewarm'.[44]

All eyes were now fixed on Geoffrey Cox, MP for Torridge and West Devon since 2005, Attorney General since July 2018, and an almost complete unknown till he stormed into public consciousness as the warm-up act to May's speech at the 2018 party conference. May had first approached him in mid-February to work with Barclay to see what could be done to find changes on the backstop that would allow sufficient MPs to vote for the WAB to get it over the line. Cox was everything the ERG thought Robbins wasn't: a Brexiteer, a Conservative and a sceptic about Brussels bureaucrats. Cox was all too aware that, given the high profile his legal advice had received following its public exposure in January, his opinion could prove all important in MPs' deciding whether to vote for MV2. He now found himself being launched at Brussels as the secret weapon which, at five minutes to midnight, could win the war.

In truth, Cox never thought his mission would succeed: as he saw it, both the December 2017 joint report and the Prime Minister's letter to Tusk in March 2018 made plain that life on the Irish border would be unchanged. This meant he would be seeking a change in the very nature of the backstop which had already been agreed and concluded. May and the Cabinet had signed up to Northern Ireland being in the single market for goods, subject to oversight by the Commission and the ECJ – there was no changing this. As many times as he told May this basic, incontrovertible fact, she didn't seem to listen. Cox began attending the 8.30 a.m. meetings from January and hoped that someone else would get the message across: a change to the backstop could not, in the current context at least, be fulfilled. When Olly Robbins tried, May became irritated and impatient: 'Well, Olly, how do you propose to get us out of this?' There was a sense that May was simply suspending disbelief, hoping for the best without any reason why.

Nevertheless, Cox went off with Barclay, in whom Barwell vested high hopes. A trusted friend of his, Barclay's appointment meant that for the first time May's team had a DExEU Secretary they felt confident to let into the inner sanctum. In Cox and Barclay, they had their dream team. The pair arrived at the Berlaymont building, headquarters of the European Commission in Brussels, on Monday 18 February for a series of meetings, armed with a briefing from Cox specifying the minimum changes the EU would need to make to allow him to change his legal advice. When they met Sabine Weyand – callously, and childishly, described by a member of the British team as being '4 foot 8 with a pudding bowl haircut' – they proposed a complete change in approach from the EU, because, at present, all the risk and the need for adjustment in the legal order was being carried by the UK and none by the EU. The votes had shown it was intolerable to the House of Commons, they said. Unless some of the risk was transferred to the EU, they told her, the withdrawal agreement would never pass through Parliament. Building on the abortive work of Robbins in attempting a breakthrough, Cox produced his own proposal, stress-testing it 'with some of the best legal experts in the country'. The exit mechanism he proposed would, he believed, offer sufficient security to the DUP, with whom he was in touch every two or three days, to gain their support.

By the end of the first week in Brussels, it was clear that progress would be slow, which fed into May's decision to delay MV2. They worked flat out for a second week (25–28 February), but began reporting in to May's 8.30 a.m. meetings that neither Barnier nor Juncker were being as available or as cooperative as they needed. Robbins had cautioned that he and Barclay would have to gain face time with them, and that their whole mission would be very heavily and intentionally choreographed by the EU. By Friday 1 March, they had still not made sufficient progress. The vote on 12 March was now little more than a week away. Cox had been advised by Robbins to take away the documents after the two first conversations with Weyand and her team at the Berlaymont, because the British had discovered they couldn't trust them not to leak the detail.

But on Monday 4 March, Cox noticed that the atmosphere in meetings with EU figures had become even more tense, the talks less constructive. Cox is unable to identify what caused the change, but speculates that it had been May's statement in the Commons the previous Tuesday that she was prepared to countenance a vote to rule out no deal if the meaningful vote on 12 March failed.[45] Cox left Brussels for the final time on Wednesday 6 March. Before he did so, he spoke by video conference to May in London: 'I've tried for nearly three weeks to get the EU to understand and agree to the minimum changes it would take, but they have not been prepared to move nearly as far as necessary,' he told her and her staff, gathered in one of Downing Street's video conference rooms. 'I must warn you, Prime Minister, that I will not be able to change my legal advice,' he said firmly. For May's team, these dreaded words were not welcomed, confirming their fears.

On Thursday 7 March, while Olly Robbins and the negotiating team continued to talk to their counterparts in Brussels, Cox saw May in No. 10 and repeated to her in person that, based on the reports he had seen of Robbins's discussions, he would be unable to change his opinion, as he told her again on Saturday and Sunday. May still hoped that Cox would deliver the legal opinion she sought. 'Prime Minister,' he said, 'I must reiterate that nothing I have seen from Olly Robbins will enable me to change my mind. None of what is being proposed changes the legal equation, and I will be obliged to say that the risk of indefinite detention in the backstop has not changed.' He felt like a lawyer giving a client advice they did not want to hear. As he spoke, he had an image in his mind of a runaway train heading towards a wall. Racking his brains for a way ahead, he raised the idea of putting forward a unilateral interpretive declaration, binding it in international law, with the hope that it would not be objected to by the EU and so give the UK the ability to argue that it had the right to withdraw from the backstop. May was positive, but on Sunday, Robbins's unit in the Cabinet Office came back to say that, while they would keep on working on it, they didn't think that they'd be able to square the idea with the EU without retaliation, and certainly not in the time available. When something was agreed, it did not reflect the original intention – more surface than substance.

With two days to go until the vote on Tuesday 12 March, and a defeat in the order of 150 on the cards, May was staring at oblivion. Hunt was one of several in Cabinet who thought she needed to tell Brussels, 'We're not settling,' and let the talks break down to bring them to their senses.[46] Over the weekend, Cox had pleaded with her:

> Prime Minister, you must take the fight yourself to Brussels. If we continue on the present trajectory of the talks, I will have to say we don't have the legal changes necessary. You will lose your credibility because you'll be seen to have meekly given in to the EU and you will not get the vote through in the House of Commons. Some in this room will tell you it can't be done, but it can. Tell the German Chancellor yourself what is at stake: we're only asking for a modest change.[47]

For a moment, his eyes met May's and he felt that she was responding. Had she understood that he was trying to help her? There was a silence before she replied, 'I don't think that's possible at the moment. I've spoken to Macron and Merkel and I don't believe there's any prospect of them changing their minds.' Cox immediately replied that if the EU didn't cut the government some slack, even if there was an Article 50 extension forced on the government, the EU would be unable to move on and they would find they had thirty to forty Farageist MEPs elected in the European elections in May. He urged her to say, 'All they needed to do was to give us what amounted to a fire escape from the backstop, a small thing to ask given the alternatives.'[48]

Sceptical though she was, instructions were sent to Northolt for her plane to be placed on standby to take the Prime Minister to Europe to finalise the text before the vote. Juncker, the key to unlocking progress, was in Strasbourg, not Brussels, which meant a longer flight in the government's 33-year-old BAe 146 jet. Three times she came near to leaving; three times she put off the trip. She spoke to Cox again later on Monday, as she was pondering whether to make the flight. 'I don't think you should go ahead,' he told her. 'The current text of the draft documents cannot change the legal analysis, and if I don't change my opinion, you haven't a hope of getting it through the Commons.' When May decided to make the dash to Strasbourg, Barclay was in constant touch with him about the document they would be discussing when they arrived. When Cox saw the final text of the document, containing no mechanism for the UK to exit the backstop without EU agreement, either in the form of a time limit or as a unilateral exit clause, he texted the DExEU Secretary at 8.30 p.m. to say, 'This will not work. You must not sign these documents. They will not pass the House of Commons.' Barclay handed his phone to May so she could read his text for herself. 'I've just shown her your message,' he replied to Cox, who wondered whether it had sunk in. But the next thing he heard was that she'd signed the document. Cox felt that she was like a doomed prisoner going to the scaffold and resting her head on the block. He would have to repeat to the Commons his legal findings: the risk of indefinite detention in the backstop had not changed. May nevertheless eventually decided early on Monday evening that she had to give it a go. Once in Strasbourg, she spent three hours arguing with Juncker, during which he smoked continuously, aggravating her sore throat. At the press conference at the conclusion, May announced that she had secured legally binding changes in the joint instrument, sufficient, she hoped, to convince MPs to back her deal. With May desperate to get home to prepare for the vote the following day, she had to wait while Varadkar at his most argumentative objected to the text. The length and intensity of these discussions showed how much was at stake, and the UK won substantive – if unflashy – new concessions. The EU reiterated its commitment to replacing the backstop with alternative arrangements and, more importantly, signed a joint legally binding instrument agreeing a formal dispute process against the EU if they kept the UK tied into the backstop against its wishes, with the aim of 'reaching a mutually agreed solution', declaring it inconsistent with the obligations of both parties to act with the objective of applying the backstop indefinitely. But these were far from the cast-iron guarantees Cox and backbench Brexiteers wanted. The negotiations took their toll in another way too. Only in the early hours of Tuesday 12 March did May get away, finally getting to bed utterly drained at 2.15 a.m.[49]

MEANINGFUL VOTE 2: 12 MARCH

Julian Smith was about to have the most stressful week of his career as Chief Whip, culminating in him exploding and contemplating resigning. Over the weekend, he'd been trying to contact Cox in Devon, but had been unable to do so – he had been told the line was bad, and then that he was out to dinner with his wife. He was desperate to ascertain what the legal advice was going to be, but had started fearing the worse. 'My sense was that the Attorney General was moving against giving us the advice that we'd hoped,' he says.[50] All weekend and throughout Monday, the whips had been drumming up support. Securing the backing of David Davis was a significant moment because he brought some MPs with him. Smith spent time himself talking to Raab, Johnson and Rees-Mogg, urging them to 'show some real leadership'. He still believed that 'if they all came out for the deal, we might just have enough votes'. But, equally, he knew that a reason Davis had decided openly to declare his support for MV2 was because his own leadership aspirations were over; for the others, they weren't, and supporting MV2 was unlikely to help their prospects.

'Dies irae, dies illa', Rees-Mogg tweeted on Tuesday morning, fore-telling a day of political wrath and anguish for the Prime Minister. At the 8.30 a.m. meeting, May reported back on the Strasbourg trip: the signs were that the Brexiteers might be responsive to the assurances she gained. But it all hinged on Cox's final advice, which he had stayed up much of the night writing, based on the latest text that May had extracted from Strasbourg. He presented it in the form of a letter, which May read after the 8.30 a.m. meeting had finished, but before Cabinet at 11 a.m. It can't have come as a surprise.

Smith recalls:

> I was with the Prime Minister in her office when she heard the advice. She was sitting at her desk. She wasn't at all happy. I think we both knew the significance of that moment. Geoffrey Cox had been up all night. I'm not sure what had been on his mind. His advice wasn't what we had hoped, or needed.[51]

Those of May's colleagues who had been pinning their hopes on his advice were bitterly disappointed. Cox had been told his advice would result in fury and some ugly briefing, but he was still taken aback by the ferocity. 'I can't see any future government bringing in such a figure again,' says one prominent Conservative.[52] A remark he was alleged to have made was circulated to disparage him by suggesting he put profession above country: 'I have to keep my reputation in the Middle Temple,' one Cabinet colleague recalls Cox saying. Cox disagrees with this account: 'I said in response to suggestions I would not be objective that I valued my professional reputation at the Bar too much not to give an honest opinion on the issues of law.'[53] Many of his colleagues respected his predicament, but they still felt he could have left out the final paragraph which caused the damage, which pronounced that 'the legal risk remains unchanged', adding that the UK had 'no internationally lawful means of exiting the Protocol's arrangements, save by agreement'. 'Geoffrey thought he was giving legal advice rather than statecraft,' says another Conservative. 'It did great damage.' One of May's closest advisors even complains about how Cox ordered the paragraphs. Building up to this conclusion 'maximised the negative impact', he says. 'Had the content been identical but the emphasis through the ordering of the argument different, who knows what might have been.'

Cox was sleep-deprived and not in a good mood on Tuesday morning, so when at 10 a.m. television journalist Jon Snow asserted on Twitter that, after rejecting May's deal, Cox had 'been told to go away and find a way to say YES: a cohort of lawyers has been summoned'. Cox tweeted back, 'Bollocks'.[54] The first paragraphs in his letter were reassuring, saying that the changes that May had managed to secure 'reduce the risk that the UK could be indefinitely and involuntarily detained within the Protocol's provisions'. But the final paragraph indeed packed the killer blow. May was visibly disconcerted when she went into Cabinet. Even though Cox tried to give Cabinet as upbeat a gloss as he could on his letter, it was clear that the assurances that the Star Chamber were demanding were not there, and that support from the ERG would not be forthcoming. The mood in Cabinet was sombre. After it was over, Cox had a five-minute conversation with Smith, who was in despair about the prospects for the vote.

May rose in the Commons shortly after 2 p.m. to appeal for MPs' support. Her voice had almost gone, and she'd been sucking Strepsils all morning. Philip watching from the gallery above like an anxious partner at Wimbledon, the low attendance and lack of excitement told him what to expect. With cracked and frail voice, May pleaded, 'This is the time – time for us to come together, back this motion and get the deal done.' Her one joke fell flat: 'You should hear Jean-Claude Juncker's voice as a result of our conversation,' she said, before adding that if the motion were defeated, 'it would be no good blaming the European Union. [The] responsibility would lie with this House.' May was exhausted as she waited for the result. The news was worse than she expected: the motion rejected by 391 to 242, a defeat of 149 votes, the fourth worst for a government in history (albeit an improvement, of sorts, on the 230 defeat on MV1 in January). Nine Conservative MPs switched their votes since MV1, David Davis being the biggest prize. But only three Labour MPs supported the government, while all the DUP MPs and many ERG supporters were among the seventy-five Conservative rebels. After the defeat, May immediately rose to her feet to say she 'profoundly regretted' that, for the second time, her deal had been rejected. MPs, she said, would be given the opportunity the following day to debate whether the UK should leave the EU in seventeen days without a deal on 29 March. MPs would then be given the opportunity to delay Brexit by requesting an extension to Article 50 on Thursday. Donald Tusk, who'd been following events closely, warned that he expected to hear a 'credible' reason if Brexit was to be delayed: 'Should there be a UK reasoned request for an extension, the EU27 will consider it and decide it by unanimity.'[55] Then a further humiliation and twist of the knife came on Tuesday evening, when an amendment from Tory MP Caroline Spelman to rule out no deal in more robust terms than the government's motion passed by four votes. At that point, amid general exhaustion and confusion, the government changed its voting strategy and whipped its MPs to vote against the motion the following day, ordering them to vote to keep no deal as an option.

FINAL TWIST OF THE KNIFE: CABINET ROW: 14 MARCH

Three May loyalists, Clark, Gauke and Rudd, had over the months regularly expressed their concerns in Cabinet about the risk of Britain leaving on 29 March with no deal. Hammond felt as strongly as them about the damage no deal would inflict but, to their irritation, preferred to keep his head down. On Monday 18 February, the three had gone in to see May in her office in No. 10 to seek her private assurance that no deal wouldn't happen. They'd agreed beforehand what they'd each say. 'All that was necessary was for her to say that she was not contemplating no deal, and that she could confirm that to us confidentially,' says Clark. 'She listened to us, but we all felt she said nothing of any substance to reassure us.'[56] Even though the meeting occurred two weeks after her Damascene visit to Belfast, she still didn't feel she could give her closest supporters the comfort they sought. Barwell tried explaining to them that whereas she was privately committed to avoiding no deal, she didn't feel able to say it in public, or indeed behind closed doors. The reason was that her now tight team didn't trust it not to leak, which would lose her the votes of ERG-inclined MPs.

The reassurance was not enough for them, so they decided to take their case direct to the public in the form of a joint article in the *Daily Mail* that Saturday. In the piece, they applauded the 'extraordinary determination and resilience' that May was showing to implement the result of the referendum but warned that a no-deal Brexit would 'severely damage' the economy.[57] No. 10 was 'extremely angry' with them. It highlighted the box in which May found herself: deeply opposed inwardly to no deal because of the risk it would pose to the Union, but unable to say so in public or in private, even to those she once trusted.

On Wednesday 13 March, the vote came to the House ruling out no deal, which, even though it was non-binding, was to be a whipped vote. Nevertheless, thirteen government ministers, including Clark, Gauke and Rudd, joined by Scottish Secretary David Mundell, defied the whips to abstain on the vote, which passed by 321 to 278, a majority of forty-three ruling out no deal as an option. Sarah Newton, a junior minister who had voted against the orders of the whips, promptly resigned. 'This is now a crisis,' said Laura Kuenssberg. 'The rules that traditionally have preserved governments are out of the window. The Prime Minister has been defeated again. Her authority – if not all gone – is in shreds.'[58] That evening, allegedly under pressure from the ERG, Smith asked Gauke to resign. Some were puzzled why the ERG had picked on Gauke as the target. 'No one', one of them says, 'knew who on earth David Gauke, the Lord Chancellor, was outside Westminster. It was very odd.' The abstainers thought Gauke was being victimised and decided to stick together: 'Our response was that they would not just have the four in Cabinet resigning, but a further nine ministers as well. They could obviously not withstand twelve resigning, so the whips backed down over David. It was a very satisfactory moment,' says one of the rebels. As Rudd recalls:

> Having written the big piece in the *Daily Mail* in February, we bided our time. When the issue came back to the House, we decided together that we would abstain, and rather than resigning, we decided we'd wait to be pushed if that was going to happen. We knew we were taking a big risk and that we were making it very difficult for the Chief Whip, who was in the firing line. But we felt that those on the left of the party were always very nice and only those on the right could play hardball. So we decided it was our time to make a stand.[59]

So Gauke and the other abstainers remained in office. Smith, torn and exhausted, knew when he was broken. Cold fury broke out across both wings of the party. By Wednesday evening, May and her team, after all the humiliations and disappointments of the week so far, were more ragged and angrier than ever. It was decided the time had come to convene an emergency Cabinet meeting on Thursday 14 March, where she would forcibly assert her authority. Described as 'a bloodbath', the meeting saw May 'dressing down the rebels'. There could be no more excuses, the Chief Whip made clear, and no one in Cabinet should be breaking collective responsibility by abstaining on a government vote. Sarah Newton, by contrast, was praised for doing 'the honourable thing' by resigning.[60] May was particularly scathing of Clark when he replied that he had not been clear what the line was due to changes in the instructions from the whips. Smith, who felt his professionalism was under personal attack, exploded. Shouting, 'Don't lie,' he stormed out of the room with the words 'Read your text messages, Greg.'[61] It was the closest Julian came to resigning: one of his colleagues in the Whips' Office told him, 'If you go, we'll all resign too.'

May rounded on her colleagues and upbraided all of them for leaking Cabinet discussions, for not providing the quality of leadership that was expected of them, for being self-serving and concerned more with their own leadership prospects than with the big discussion. She risked a mass walkout from ministers rebelling at being treated like naughty schoolboys. Geoffrey Cox tried riding to the rescue with his *mea culpa*: 'I know that as a Leaver I may have said some things that will have caused upset and for my offence I apologise.' But Cabinet was not for soothing with eloquence. Nor for listening to lectures on leaking. One of them promptly leaked the discussion, picked up by Tim Shipman, who cited one saying, 'She's moving imaginary armies in her head. It felt like *Götterdämmerung*.'[62]

But some thought she hadn't gone in hard enough. One loyal Cabinet minister says that May's failure to make all the rebels resign marked a significant turning point:

The fact that she didn't take away their jobs enraged the ERG, but also the party and the country. The parliamentary party was extremely angry. At the Cabinet, she spoke about the damage that had been done and the need to reassert collective responsibility, but took no action. The fact that she didn't punish them was really the beginning of the end.

Gove was one of the many loyalists perturbed by the damage she had sustained. 'I spoke to a group of MPs from marginal seats after the vote, who were all incredibly angry.'[63]

In the Commons that day, the whips were in a dilemma about how to handle the vote on a motion to ask the EU for a short delay if Parliament could not agree on a Brexit deal by the following week, or a longer delay if no deal could be agreed in time. 'We didn't know how to whip it, and even those close to the Prime Minister didn't know exactly what she thought. So we decided that we had to back a free vote because otherwise we could have risked mass resignations.' Parliament decided by 412 to 212 to support the motion, making clear what was already obvious, that the 29 March departure date, mentioned 109 times by May at the dispatch box, was likely to be missed.

May had less than two weeks until that date, she had a Cabinet more openly divided than ever, an increasingly fractious and exhausted team around her, and little hope that a final vote would be successful. There had been a tentative hope – much debated among May's team and Cabinet – that, by narrowing the number of options and forcing no-dealers to give in, it would boost May's deal. 'Only when it was a binary choice and one camp's preferred outcome was gone would that camp get behind leaving with a deal,' the reasoning went.

But the vote to rule out no deal further weakened her, as she had always feared it would. The prospect of no deal made May's middle road more attractive to many MPs. When its possibility was nulled, many thought they would sooner have a second referendum or start over with a new negotiation than back her deal. Whether or not it also weakened her bargaining power against the EU remains hotly debated. 'Brussels was *terrified* of no deal happening: it was a huge worry to them,' says Jeremy Hunt. 'As soon as Parliament took no deal off the table, Brussels relaxed. We lost our leverage with them.'[64] One of May's close advisors disputes this logic. 'I very much doubt it did,' he says.

> The EU always believed that Parliament would stop no deal, and could read the parliamentary arithmetic from the 2017 election. For many in the EU, too, any threat to the integrity of the single market and the autonomy of the EU's legal order was, they thought, a greater danger to their national interest than a no-deal Brexit.

Olly Robbins is of the same opinion: 'Brussels was not terrified. Long before the votes in Parliament, they simply did not believe Parliament would entertain no deal.'[65]

For May personally, the MV2 defeat was a decisive blow. Few knew her mind as a politician longer or better than Bradley, who recalls:

> Until MV2, she had a decent chance of having nearly twelve more months in office. She wanted to do the G7 in Biarritz in August, the party conference in early October, then go. After the second massive defeat, many more said she had to go. She couldn't deliver it. It was the final hope.[66]

May was staring into an abyss. No time. No plan. No Brexit.

Brexit protesters amassed on 29 March 2019, the date on which this photograph was taken, and the date on which Britain was supposed to be leaving the EU. Instead, it saw the withdrawal agreement defeated in the House of Commons for a third time.

CHAPTER 19

THIRD AND FINAL MEANINGFUL VOTE

15–29 MARCH 2019

'Oh gods! Who is't can say, "I am at the worst"? I am worse than e'er I was … And worse I may be yet,' says Edgar in Shakespeare's *King Lear*.[1] There were elements of tragedy of Shakespearian proportions about May, reeling from blow after blow, stretching her own and her team's endurance and sanity to the very limits as she struggled to carry her Brexit deal over the line. Britain was facing its greatest domestic challenge since the constitutional crisis of 1909–11, with Cabinet, the Conservative Party, Parliament and the country all deeply divided and with no evident way forward. Assailed from all sides, May had said more than 100 times in the previous two years, as politicians and the press delighted in reminding her, that she would not delay Brexit beyond 29 March: but that is exactly what seemed bound to happen. Wednesday 20 March marked 1,000 days since the referendum of 23 June 2016. And things, as Edgar feared, were about to get a lot worse.

THE SPEAKER ROARS

John Bercow had been elected Speaker in June 2009 and had made it his mission to restore the authority of Parliament, which had been steadily eroded by government over many years. Given as he was to making striking and surprising announcements, few were more so than his announcement on Monday 18 March, which threw the Prime Minister and No. 10 into confusion. Bercow declared that he would not allow a third meaningful vote in the coming days on 'substantially the same proposition' as the one twice rejected by MPs. 'We're in a major constitutional crisis here,' said Robert Buckland, the Solicitor General (deputy to the Attorney General). 'There are ways around this – a prorogation of Parliament and a new session – but we are now talking about not just days but hours to 29 March.'[2] May initially had no idea how to respond. That afternoon, at the regular briefing for journalists, her spokesperson said, 'The Speaker did not forewarn us of the content of his statement or the fact that he was making one.'[3] Over the weekend, intensive discussions had taken place getting the DUP back on board after MV2. An announcement about it was planned for Monday afternoon. 'It was a tremendous blow,' says an official. 'It shattered the momentum and confidence that we could bring it back to the House in time. It damaged the fragile understanding rebuilt with the DUP, and made it impossible to get it moving thereafter.' But one of May's close advisors said her team's perception of Bercow's decision wasn't so clear-cut, even if the briefing to the press was one of outrage. 'I would be cautious of misreading the significance of what the Speaker did here,' the advisor says.

> We were aware of this risk before the ruling and we certainly hadn't resolved on the timing or strategy for bringing an MV3 forward. There were quite a few of us who thought the Speaker did us a favour – all the blame and anger for not being able to hold MV3 and for the extension was directed at him rather than us.

Bercow rested his case on that bible of parliamentary procedure Erskine May, asserting that 'a strong and long-standing convention' dating back to 1604 and confirmed many times, including in 1864, 1870, 1882, 1891 and 1912, made it clear that the same question 'may not be brought forward again during that same session'. He added, 'One of the reasons why the rule has lasted so long is that it is a necessary rule to ensure the sensible use of the House's time and proper respect for the decisions that it takes. Decisions of the House matter. They have weight.' The earlier two meaningful votes, on both the withdrawal agreement and the future partnership (with only some minor differences to the two propositions), had been comprehensively defeated twice, he said, and the motion could not go forward a third time unless significantly changed.

His intervention prompted fury from the tabloids. 'B****cks to Bercow', said *The Sun*, a reference to his wife's 'Bollocks to Brexit' car sticker, which had caused widespread offence earlier. (When attacked on the sticker in January, Bercow had said that he was sure his inquisitor 'wouldn't suggest for one moment that a wife is somehow the property or chattel of her husband?'[4]) 'The Brexit destroyer' was the headline in the *Daily Express*, while the *Daily Mail* contented itself with 'Smirk that says: Brexit be damned'.[5]

May was visibly disgruntled at Cabinet on Tuesday 19 March, the first since the MV2 defeat and the explosive meeting that followed it, when she explained she would be going back to the EU to ask for a delay. Pro-Brexit ministers were in no mood to make her life easy, insisting firmly that any delay be for the shortest possible dimension, aware that their chances of getting rid of her before the exit were slim. The departure date she set was 30 June, believing this would be enough time for a renegotiation. 'You do understand the consequences of what you have said?' Barwell asked her after the Cabinet. 'If we can't get a deal by that date, we'll be out.' 'What more can I do?' she replied. 'We can't extend it indefinitely.' For a few days, officials concluded no deal had become the likely outcome. The day following the meeting, her spokesman said, 'The PM won't be asking for a long extension ...

The people of this country have been waiting nearly three years now. They are fed up with Parliament's failure to take a decision and the PM shares their frustration.'[6] May delivered the same message to the Commons that afternoon. She would be seeking an extension only for three months, until 30 June: any longer, and Britain would have to participate in the elections for the European Parliament on 23 May. She blamed MPs for the predicament they found themselves in, and said any longer delay would provide 'endless hours and days of this House carrying on contemplating its navel on Europe and failing to address the issues that matter to our constituents'. The thesis she was honing was that it was not herself or her office, but Parliament itself which was responsible for the chaos: 'The British people … deserve better than this House has given them so far.' Jeers and hoots of derision greeted her comments, most significantly from her own MPs. The mood had already turned ugly before she made a further and more pointed speech later that evening.

MAY BLASTS MPS

May's team decided that she needed to get on the front foot. One of the most important powers a Prime Minister has is the ability to speak to the nation on prime-time television at a moment of their own choosing. Now, they thought, was the time to deploy this weapon. Her broadcast from the State Dining Room was delayed because she was locked in a meeting trying to lobby twenty Brexiteers for their support. Backbencher Ben Bradley told her that,

> having had forty-odd conversations with colleagues over the weekend since MV2 … they don't have trust in you, Prime Minister, to re-establish Cabinet responsibility and to have the right plans to

get a better long-term relationship. The only way it is likely to get through is if you agree to leave in the summer.[7]

The tone and text of her speech was principally the work of Robbie Gibb, though it was the joint response of a beleaguered and exhausted team who, after weeks of being humiliated, felt bitterly let down and frustrated. They wanted to reassert her authority by shifting the blame firmly onto Parliament. The text was 'a collective howl of pain from across the building'. The tone was wrong, but the substance was not without justice. The broadcast opened as an apprehensive May came to the lectern, with two Union Jack flags prominently displayed behind her. Her words reveal much about her thinking:

Nearly three years have passed since the public voted to leave the European Union. It was the biggest democratic exercise in our country's history. I came to office on a promise to deliver on that verdict. In March 2017, I triggered the Article 50 process for the UK to exit the EU – and Parliament supported it overwhelmingly. Two years on, MPs have been unable to agree on a way to implement the UK's withdrawal. As a result, we will now not leave on time with a deal on 29 March. This delay is a matter of great personal regret for me. And of this I am absolutely sure: you the public have had enough. You are tired of the infighting. You are tired of the political games and the arcane procedural rows. Tired of MPs talking about nothing else but Brexit when you have real concerns about our children's schools, our National Health Service, and knife crime. You want this stage of the Brexit process to be over and done with. I agree. I am on your side. It is now time for MPs to decide.

The speech lasted barely four minutes. She recounted that she'd written to Tusk earlier that day requesting a short extension of Article 50 to 30 June, but she disparaged the notion of a longer delay, or holding a second referendum. 'I don't believe that is what you want – and it is not what I want.'

No. 10 expected a reaction, but not the intensity of the backlash that followed. 'The initial reaction on social media was that she'd said nothing new: but then the narrative changed into her denigrating MPs,' says Gibb.[8] Many viewed it as the worst-judged public intervention of her premiership. 'It was an attack on liberal democracy itself,' said Labour MP Lisa Nandy that night on ITV's *Peston* programme. 'There's absolutely no chance she is going to win over MPs in sufficient numbers after that statement ... I will not support a government that takes such a reckless, dangerous approach.'[9] MP Wes Streeting went further, describing it as 'incendiary and irresponsible', adding, 'If any harm comes to any of us, she will have to accept her share of responsibility.' Attacks did not just come from Labour. Former minister Sam Gyimah said, 'Democracy loses when a PM who has set herself against the House of Commons then blames MPs for doing their job.'[10] Memories of Jo Cox, the Labour MP murdered during the referendum campaign by a far-right activist, were cited by some as evidence of the folly and lack of judgement of May's words. With many MPs reporting intimidation, threats of violence, and abuse on social media, the failure to foresee how her words would be interpreted was a serious lapse of judgement.

For a Prime Minister who prided herself on her approach to national security, the criticisms wounded her deeply. None more so than the words of Dominic Grieve, who, during a debate in Parliament, described it as 'the worst moment I have experienced since I came into the House of Commons'. The fact he spoke in sadness rather than anger made his words penetrate all the further: 'I have known her for many years and we have a personal friendship ... but I have to say that I could have wept to see her reduced to these straits.' The *New*

York Times put its finger on an irony: a Prime Minister castigating the political games of MPs when she had deliberately sidelined them, waiting as late as she could to let them vote on her deal, hoping to apply as much pressure as she could. She never explored the possibility of a cross-party consensus on a softer Brexit deal, which would have secured the endorsement of the EU and minimised economic disruption but still ensured that Britain left the EU.[11] Reflecting on it eight months later, Greg Clark, one of her biggest supporters in Cabinet, says:

> It was a disastrous intervention. We had been not far off getting a majority, and Labour MPs were willing to come onside, but as a result of the speech, we lost them. We'd been getting the trade unions onside. I immediately sent a text to Gavin Barwell to say, 'What on earth do you think that achieved?'[12]

Barwell received many angry texts that evening and throughout the next day, as did Julian Smith and Graham Brady. Why had she given the speech? Smith had been saying to May for several weeks that she needed to make a public announcement to put her side of the case direct to the nation. She seized on his idea but didn't let him see the text till an hour before she delivered it, to his fury. She alone must carry responsibility for the error of judgement. One blessing for her was that, had it happened at a quieter moment in politics, the furore would have rumbled on for days, possibly weeks, but in these days of high drama it was largely forgotten within twenty-four hours.

On Thursday 21 March, May went to Brussels to plead the case for a three-month extension. She was granted a ninety-minute slot to make her pitch to the EU27 leaders. By general accounts, her delivery was flat, the fresh content low, and her response to the predominant question her fellow leaders had – what was her Plan B? – evasive.

Never before had a British Prime Minister appeared weaker at an EU Council. The *Financial Times* reported:

> Emmanuel Macron ... arrived in Brussels giving Theresa May a 10 per cent chance that she could save her Brexit deal and probably her premiership. By the time he had listened to a haunted Mrs May address the European Council, he had revised his opinion: he gave her a 5 per cent chance. Donald Tusk ... said Mr Macron's 5 per cent chance was too generous.[13]

After her presentation, May was asked to leave and departed for five hours while the EU leaders debated in her absence how they should respond. They debated whether she was finished and might only last a few days longer, and whether her tactic was to set up the EU as the guilty party in a blame game.

With May and her team still waiting – they had dinner on their own in the UK's delegation room – the EU leaders discussed various dates for the UK's extension: 12 April, 1 May, 23 May, even 31 December, some conditional on May's plan passing the following week, others not. In the end, 23 April was knocked out because it was St George's Day in England, while 7 May was deemed unsuitable because it was the eve of commemorations of the end of the Second World War in Europe. So they settled on 12 April, the date May mentioned herself as the last day for a decision before Britain must commit to taking part in the European Parliament elections. When she was allowed back to join them, at 11 p.m., the verdict was delivered: they agreed to postpone the exit date until 22 May, as long as the Commons voted for a deal at the end of March: if not, it would be 12 April.

The media reaction in the UK and across Europe was scathing. The *Guardian* splash was 'May's appeal falls flat as EU seizes control of Brexit date',[14] while the *Financial Times* thought that Britain now faced a 'national emergency' with her authority in tatters.[15] Most scathing of all was an editorial in *The Times* which castigated May for 'her stubbornness, her tin ear, her lack of imagination and empathy, her inability to charm, cajole or persuade. Too often she is intransigent when she needs to be flexible, dithers when she needs to be decisive and has stoked division when the country urgently needs to be brought together.'[16]

May's team judged the outcome differently. 'The EU did what we couldn't do for ourselves: it got us out of a complete impasse with Cabinet and gave us the best possible chance of getting her deal over the line,' says an official. They singled out Merkel for being the figure who came to her rescue: even though far from the force she once was, she still knew how to work the EU27, motivated as she was by a desire to avoid Britain crashing out with no deal.

On Friday 22 March, and in an effort to rebuild trust after the broadcast, May wrote to MPs, setting out four options that she believed Britain now had left in light of the decision by the EU to extend the deadline. First, revoking Article 50, which she labelled 'a betrayal' of the Brexit vote. Second, leave without a deal on 12 April, with all the risks that that entailed. Third, pass her deal in a vote next week. Finally, if there was insufficient support, she could go back to the EU and ask for a second extension, this time beyond 12 April, but that would require participation in the European elections in May, which she said 'would be wrong'. Her letter pointed to option three being the best choice: 'I hope we can all agree that we are now at the moment of decision,' she wrote.[17]

One Cabinet minister believes her deal might have secured a majority vote had her tactical handling been more adroit in March:

I thought that we could get it through, but then she flip-flopped in mid to late March and my confidence turned to despair. She tried to keep all three doors open: no deal, deal, delay. She then flipped from to delay or deal, then to delay or no deal, then she went back to delay or deal. Then at the end she flipped back to no deal just as the Labour votes were coming over: Remainers thus thought by voting down her deal they'd get no Brexit, and the Leave side thought voting it down meant leaving with no deal. No. 10 were in a spin and had panicked.

The final weekend before Friday 29 March saw an explosion of activity. A mass protest in London by the Put It to the People campaign on Saturday 23 March claimed more than a million joined the march, putting it on a par with the biggest march of the century, against the Iraq War in 2003. It finished up in front of Parliament, with protesters carrying EU flags and placards demanding a public vote. The same day, the pro-Brexit March to Leave, which had started in Sunderland the previous week, reached a village near Nottingham. Nigel Farage told around 200 Brexit supporters that Mrs May had reduced the nation 'to a state of humiliation', as he said that those marching in London did not represent the majority.[18]

Conservative MPs, who had already used their trump card of the confidence vote on 12 December, were tearing their hair out thinking how they could dispense with May. Smith, at the end of his tether, demanded a meeting between him and his fellow whips and May alone, because 'he felt sometimes Gavin failed to comprehend the full depth of backbench frustration'. Some of the whips represented marginal constituencies and had 'watery eyes' as May was told she had to go and that MPs were hardening against her deal: 'They felt they had done all they could to protect her,' says an insider. The name of David Lidington, her de facto deputy, was now mooted in Westminster as a possible caretaker Prime Minister around whom the left and right in the party might unite. The *Sunday Times* reported that no fewer than eleven Cabinet ministers contacted said they wanted May to make way for another leader, and at least six were supportive of installing him.[19] Lidington himself says:

> It was a function of the febrile atmosphere in Parliament, with people wondering how on earth we were going to find a way through, a time of plots and non-plots, of factions and gossip. Some people, on both the Leave and the Remain wings, wondered whether men in grey suits would go and see her, or even that she might stand down. But I never thought any of that was going to happen. I thought it was just talk.[20]

For all his sangfroid, he was forced nevertheless to come out in public and tell reporters in his Aylesbury constituency, 'I don't think that I've any wish to take over from the PM who I think is doing a fantastic job.'[21]

BACK TO CHEQUERS: SUNDAY 24 MARCH

May was determined to hold a vote on 29 March (even though it was a Friday, which would rile MPs), knowing that it may well not pass. But she wanted to show that she'd done everything possible. She was still pursuing the tripod strategy of trying to win over the ERG, DUP and Labour Leave MPs. So she gave fresh instructions for new overtures to the ERG via Steve Baker, seen as the linchpin of the group: under what circumstances, if any, might he be willing to support her deal the following Friday? He said he'd 'certainly be prepared' to examine a way forward, motivated in part by his desire to keep Corbyn out and the Conservative Party together. At the end of the week, he went to see Smith in the Whips' Office. 'We all recognised we were heading for a political crisis,' Baker says, and they were bound together by common interest at a grave point in history. So he agreed that, as long as there was a material change to the substance of the deal, especially on the backstop, as well as a change of Prime Minister to allow another figure to take forward Britain's future relationship with the EU, he would be willing to canvass colleagues to see if they'd be prepared to vote for it.[22]

Thus it was that Baker, along with Johnson, Davis, Duncan Smith, Raab and Rees-Mogg (the 'Eurosceptic Sanhedrin', as Gove describes them[23]) found themselves driving to Chequers to talk to the Prime Minister on Sunday 24 March. There was little sense of what was planned. Duncan Smith, like the others, thought he'd been summoned to a private meeting with the Prime Minister. He arrived in his Morgan sports car. Rees-Mogg brought his son, while May arrived the night before with a ferocious determination to bring the ERG behind MV3. Her guests included Lidington, Gove, Smith and Alistair Burt, a junior minister at the FCO. Seven different participants at the meeting subsequently provided eight different accounts of what happened. But the outcome was clear. 'We were lobbying the ERG to see if they would support us,' recalls Lidington. 'If they didn't, we would be in a very difficult position.'[24] May's team found Rees-Mogg the most accommodating, and Baker the most adamantly opposed. 'Jacob already indicated that he might be moving over to our side, and by the end of the day, we were hopeful of the others, and possibly even getting Dom Raab and IDS over the line, but we were not certain about Steve,' says Barwell.[25]

It fell to Duncan Smith, as the senior figure present, and as somebody who had known May well for several years, to convey the hard message that the ERG thought she needed to hear. On two occasions, the first during a break-out session and again later in the day, he singled her out. 'It was a very difficult thing for him to say,' recalls Baker. 'Iain is a decent and civilised man and he'd been badly treated himself when leader, but he was very brave in what he said.'[26] Duncan Smith recalls what happened:

I told her MPs didn't trust her any more and that she would have to stand down so that someone could continue with the negotiations that needed to take place urgently. Only a new leader would be able to say that there are elements of the deal that we can't agree to. 'No one believes that you are capable of making the changes required, you've run out of road. You know what has to happen. You have to say that you're going to go and that you're not going to be part of the future process.' She responded that she was reconciled to leaving but didn't want to quit until the party conference. 'You can't announce that you're going to be going and then stay on for five months,' I said. 'There are some acceptable parts of your deal, but other parts need to be changed, and urgency is vital.' I saw her again at the end of the day, but she hadn't changed her views.[27]

MAY SAYS SHE WILL QUIT: 25–27 MARCH

For the two years since the triggering of Article 50, May had known that the week beginning Monday 25 March would be one of the most important in modern British history. She kicked it off with an emergency Cabinet in which she robustly defended her intention to hold a third vote. No indication of how she would deal with the 12 April deadline, were the vote to fail, was given. In the build-up to the meeting, Westminster's gossip had been about Cabinet ministers openly telling her that she would have to go. But Downing Street rapidly put out word that no minister raised the question of her leadership at the meeting.[28] That afternoon, she had a difficult conversation with Arlene Foster. She badly needed the DUP to fall into line, because the

ERG would only back her if they did. Considerable work had been taking place deep in Downing Street, with a team including Julian Smith and Cabinet Office official Brendan Threlfall looking at ways to accommodate the DUP's concerns. 'We came so close to getting the DUP onside that week,' says Barwell.[29]

Tuesday had been a more optimistic day. Rees-Mogg told a meeting of the ERG that he would back May's deal as long as the DUP was on board. That evening, speaking to a packed audience at Central Hall Westminster, Johnson said, 'I'm not there yet,' but added, 'If we vote it down again, for the third time, there is now ... an appreciable risk that we will not leave at all.'[30]

Pressure was building from multiple quarters: a cross-party group of MPs voted, by 329–302, to pass an amendment proposed by Oliver Letwin and Labour's Hilary Benn, known as the Letwin amendment, to change the rules to allow the Commons to set the timetable for debate and subsequent votes on alternative outcomes. The latest gambit to take power away from government and give it to MPs allowed backbenchers to hold a series of 'indicative votes' on alternatives to the Prime Minister's Brexit deal. May worried greatly that if a majority voted for a second referendum or customs union, it could be very dangerous, and Smith and Penn shared her fears. But a silver lining for No. 10 would be if the indicative votes, to be held on Wednesday 27 March, were to panic some Brexiteers into backing May, fearful that calls for a softer Brexit or a second referendum might receive majority support. May was concerned also by the loss of a further three ministers, including Burt, among twenty-nine Tory MPs who rebelled to vote for the amendment. But she had bigger fish to fry.

May had one card left, her trump card: to announce that she was going to resign. 'Her resignation gambit had been knocking around in the drawer for some time,' says an aide. On Wednesday, MPs, enabled by the Letwin amendment, voted on eight possible options, from no deal through to a Norway-style deal to a permanent customs union and a second referendum. None commanded a majority. The option that secured most votes was the permanent customs union, beaten by the very slimmest of margins, 272 to 264. Brexit Secretary Stephen Barclay capitalised quickly on the results to announce, 'There are no easy options here. There is no simple way forward. The deal the government has negotiated is a compromise, both with the EU and with members across this House.'[31]

May had asked to see Duncan Smith earlier in the day. When they met, he found that she was still unwilling to give a precise date for her departure but said she still wanted to carry on to the party conference. 'But how can you?' Duncan Smith asked her again. 'Once you've said you're going, you have to go.' He spoke to Barwell afterwards and told him that she would face a simple question at the 1922 Committee later that day: 'When are you going?' Duncan Smith explains, 'All she had to say is, "I'm resigning in weeks." But she still wouldn't say when exactly it would be.'[32]

The 1922 Committee met as usual in Committee Room 14. A visibly emotional May stood up in front of MPs and said, 'I've heard very clearly the mood of the parliamentary party. I know there is a desire for a new approach – and new leadership – for the second phase of the Brexit negotiations, and I won't stand in the way of that.' Then she dropped her bombshell: 'I am prepared to leave this job earlier than I intended to do what is right for our country and our party [but] I ask everyone in this room to back the deal.' There was a gasp of surprise. Brady thought 'it definitely shifted some votes': some MPs said openly they would now support the deal.[33] But she did not mention a precise date for her departure: she was damned if she was going to be forced out by the ERG while she still believed she could get her deal through and have time for her domestic agenda. Duncan Smith, who had reassured the ERG that she would be naming a date in the near future, felt bitterly let down. When ERG members left the meeting, 'They were muttering to themselves: "There you go again, you can't trust the Prime Minister. Iain was gullible. Her assurances are valueless."'[34] By the time No. 10 sought to clarify her intentions, albeit still without a date, he thought her opportunity to win them round had passed.

Neither had she said enough for the DUP, who had their own worries. Shortly after the 1922 Committee, it released a statement to say it would not support the government if it tabled a fresh meaningful vote, because 'the necessary changes we seek to the backstop have not been secured'.[35] Raoul Ruparel wondered whether her announcement of her departure had in fact damaged the prospects of bringing the DUP on board: 'The irony was that when she said she was going to resign, the DUP became very alarmed, as they worried who her successor might be, and whether they might be as amenable to them. So they rang around various leadership contenders, got cold feet, and withdrew their support.'[36]

May was playing her cards very close to her chest: neither of her two longest-serving allies in Cabinet had known what she was going to say. Brokenshire knew only when he saw the face of Seema Kennedy, her Parliamentary Private Secretary, as they entered the room: 'I realised then that the game was up and that she'd be standing down.'[37] Bradley thought she'd damaged her cause: 'She gave away her premiership at that meeting without getting anything back.'[38] In the endgame, she was still confiding only in the very tight group of Barwell, Penn, Gibbs and Smith on the political side, and Robbins, Sedwill and Peter Hill as her most trusted officials. Will Macfarlane remained at the heart of things until he left for Brussels, becoming the UK's Permanent Representative to the EU. Other influential officials she trusted were James Slack, her official spokesman, Raoul Ruparel and Christian Turner, the omnicompetent Deputy National Security Advisor. Cabinet ministers whom she continued to confide in, albeit still not in the inner group, were Lidington, Gove and Cox. Figures whom a Prime Minister would be expected to rely upon in a squeeze, including the Leader of the House and party chair, were now outside the ring.

THE VOTE ON 29 MARCH

To pave the way for the vote, Lidington and Geoffrey Cox had been to see the Speaker to present the argument for why a third vote should be allowed. Lidington remembers, 'The Speaker listened to us carefully and said he'd think it over and he'd come back to us, which he did later in the day to say he agreed.'[39] Their gambit, which secured Bercow's consent, was to put only half the Brexit deal to Parliament, stripping it of the political declaration, which satisfied him that it constituted a different motion. The hope too was that by omitting the political declaration, it might induce more Labour MPs and ERG members to soften their opposition. But would it still be sufficient to satisfy the EU's criterion that the Bill had passed, and thus would Britain avoid leaving on 12 April? The political declaration was much shorter and lacked the binding legal weight of the withdrawal agreement, which included the all-important backstop, lethal to the chances of the DUP and to many in the ERG supporting her.

May had to make one of the most critical decisions of her premiership: did she have another vote on 29 March, knowing it might be defeated? 'We felt that if we couldn't get MPs to vote for Brexit on what was meant to be Brexit Day,' one advisor recalls, 'then we never would.' But the evening before, the whips still didn't know how Baker would vote: 'We knew that whatever he went for would have a domino effect.' Gove counselled her to hold the vote; Smith advised it might be defeated; she decided to go for it, believing MPs should make a decision on Brexit Day itself. Thursday 28 March thus saw the government tabling a motion for the following day, asking the House to approve the withdrawal agreement. Frantic lobbying, briefing and plotting took place. Andrew Percy, Conservative MP for Brigg and Goole, was one of many to be disconcerted about the timing. He had been asked to be best man at a wedding on the Friday, and the Whips had told him, 'You're staying put.' When No. 10 was informed, May wrote a personal letter to the bride and groom to apologise.[40] Cox opened the debate on Friday at 9.35 a.m. by apologising to all Members for calling them in on the day. But, he said, with it being the original deadline day, 'the government have taken a view that it would have been wrong to allow that time and date to expire [eleven o'clock that evening] without giving this House the opportunity' for debate. Shadow Brexit Secretary Keir Starmer dismissed the motion as 'desperate', noting, 'The argument is thin,' and warned that 'once you strip the political declaration off … you have no idea what you are really voting for'.[41]

At 2.11 p.m., May rose to deliver one of her most impassioned speeches:

Today should have been the day that the United Kingdom left the European Union. That we are not leaving today is a matter of deep personal regret to me, but I remain committed to the United Kingdom leaving the European Union, and that is why I brought this motion to the House today. There are those who will say, 'The House has rejected every option so far. You'll probably lose, so why bother?' I bother because this is the last opportunity to guarantee Brexit. I say to all those who campaigned to leave, who voted to leave, who represent constituencies who voted to leave and, indeed, to all of us who want to deliver on the vote to leave: if we do not vote for this motion today, people will ask, 'Why did you not vote for Brexit?' By voting for this motion today, we can send a message to the public and to the European Union that Britain stands by its word and that we will leave the European Union on 22 May.

Speaking at the close of the debate, Corbyn said, 'The government have run down the clock in an attempt to blackmail MPs at every turn. The government are in chaos, the country is in chaos, and the responsibility is the government's and the government's alone.' Without his or his Chief Whip Nick Brown's knowledge, a group of ten Labour MPs had slipped into the PM's room behind the Speaker's chair during the debate for forty minutes. Some were in tears, all were fearful, vexed, aware of the risk they were taking in supporting the motion. Barwell, with her in the room, recalls, 'Had she won them over it would have transformed the position and she would have been able to do Phase 1 of Brexit.' The Labour MPs told her, 'If we can be certain the vote will be won with our help, then at least we'll be risking our political careers for something, but if it goes down, we'd have run that risk for no benefit at all.' Barwell says, 'In the end, she simply couldn't give them the assurances they sought.'[42]

When the vote eventually came in the early afternoon, 344 MPs voted against the motion, 286 for, a majority of fifty-eight, a considerable improvement on the 230 and 149 on MV1 and MV2. But at a time of such great national uncertainty, thirty-four of her own backbenchers had voted against the motion, as well as the entire DUP. For all the Herculean efforts, only five Labour MPs voted for the motion, up from three on MV2. Lidington's verdict was:

> We went into the vote sensing the numbers were against us, but that there was a chance. The PM weighed it up and decided to go for it, saying we needed to get it out into the open if we were not going to leave. It became clear to us during the day that Nick Brown was taking a very hard line with his MPs if they didn't support the leadership, and it ebbed away from us.[43]

Responding to the defeat, May said:

I fear that we are reaching the limits of this process in this House. This House has rejected no deal; it has rejected no Brexit; on Wednesday it rejected all the variations of the deal on the table; and today it has rejected approving the withdrawal agreement alone and continuing a process on the future.

The dismay in May's team was intense. As Barwell recalls:

That was the closest we got. We were so close. The ultras could have gone for it, but at the end of the day, we simply couldn't get all the people to go through the hoops at the right time. There were always some who clung onto the notion of the ideal, and we couldn't persuade them. We were so very close to getting the support of the ERG, DUP and a group of Labour MPs.[44]

Duncan Smith, Johnson, Davis, Raab and Rees-Mogg all, despite their qualms, voted for the government. But Baker did not. 'If we had only secured his vote, we knew he would bring others in the ERG and the DUP with him. Losing him cost us the motion,' says one. And with the motion, so too May's deal. No. 10 never knew how close they had come to persuading the man they regarded as the pivot. That afternoon, Baker had sat down with Rees-Mogg and they agreed with heavy hearts to vote for the government, fearful of the unknowable consequences of a defeat. They walked together to Nigel Dodds's office to share their thoughts: 'This is the best we can do. It's not what we want but we've decided that we have to vote with the government.' Baker was 'three quarters' of the way through writing an article for Paul Goodman for ConservativeHome, explaining the agony of his decision to vote for her, intending to finish it off shortly and email it to him. When they knocked on Dodds's door, they found his room empty. It is possible that their decision might have persuaded Dodds and the DUP to vote the same way: we shall never know. Baker and Rees-Mogg then went their separate ways, agreeing to talk later. On his way to the House of Commons Library, Baker passed Suella Braverman, who was 'revolted' that he intended to vote for the deal, making it clear to him that it was something she would never do. He then recalls bumping into another strongly pro-Leave Conservative MP, Julia Lopez, who 'grimaced' at him in revulsion at his intentions.[45] Dodds's absence, combined with his chance encounters with Braverman and Lopez, made him think again. The idea that both his fellow MPs felt that 'even Steve Baker was giving in' was agonising for him.

He met former Vote Leave director Chris Montgomery, and they went for a two-hour walk, with Baker using him as a sounding board to weigh up the risks of voting for and against. 'It was much the hardest decision of my entire political career,' he confesses now.[46] Much more agonising indeed than his decision to vote against MV2, when he was filmed with tears in his eyes by Laura Kuenssberg for her BBC television documentary.[47] Baker was a deep thinker and a committed Christian; even those who disagree vehemently with him couldn't deny the depth and sincerity of his thought. His chance encounters that day might have tipped British political history. On such flutters of a butterfly's wings do great events hinge.

MANY DOORS: NO COINS

As one door closed, others opened. Too many doors for a majority to walk through just one, as was needed. MPs were to take part in the second round of indicative votes on Monday 1 April to see if Parliament could find its own way forward. As it had failed to find a consensus the previous Wednesday, hopes were not running high.

A general election, which needed two thirds of MPs to vote for it, was an option talked about increasingly. Within No. 10, Gibb and Parkinson saw merits, if only as a stick with which to beat Tory MPs back into the pen.[48] Or Britain could leave on 12 April, just two weeks away, with no deal, as the Pizza Club wanted, claiming they had 170 MPs in support. But that would have prompted the resignations of at least Rudd, Clark, Hammond and Gauke from the Cabinet. A no-confidence vote, called by Labour with support from some Conservative rebels, was another possibility being mooted, giving two weeks to install a new Conservative leader capable of winning a confidence motion in the House; if it failed, Corbyn would have been invited to try to form a government. May herself could have resigned. But despite the persistence of rumours, she never contemplated it. She could have been pushed, as many wanted, but that would have had to rely on persuasion rather than procedure, given that there were still nine months till the next vote of the 1922 Committee. Within No. 10, the favoured option was introducing a fourth vote on the withdrawal agreement without further change, which entailed reaching out to Labour in a new way, favoured by Barwell and Lidington, in the hope of securing a majority. At the time, with the cohesion of the Conservative Party in question, with leadership challengers swirling above the wasting if still defiant body of May, and serious threats to pro-Remain Conservatives like Grieve of being deselected by their constituencies, they were prepared to consider anything.

'Peace, prosperity and friendship with all nations' was the wording to have been on a commemorative 50p coin to mark the UK's departure from the EU, as well as the date, 29 March 2019. The coins were not minted, though the idea survived for another day. The pro-Brexit marchers, who had set off two weeks before from Sunderland, stopped in their tracks. The champagne corks remained in the bottles. The balloons were put back in the cupboard. The TV networks, preparing for months for special programmes, hastily re-planned their schedules. Eleven o'clock on the evening of 29 March was to have been the biggest single moment in May's premiership, the chance for the nation to celebrate or to commiserate. She was in bed. So too was much of the nation.

All political careers end in tears. May's proved no exception as she announced her resignation on 24 May 2019.

CHAPTER 20

THE LAST THROW OF THE DICE: TALKS WITH LABOUR

1 APRIL–26 MAY 2019

Britain had not left the EU on 29 March. At once, May faced the greatest challenge of her leadership. A lot needed to change. Renowned for her intransigence, she now had to show flexibility: her original approach had failed. Renowned for her tribalism, she now had to reach across the aisle of the House of Commons: her party and its partner, the DUP, could not be relied upon for a majority. Renowned for her introversion, she now needed all her powers of persuasion – to convince a sceptical EU that she had a plan, her own MPs that she still had value as their leader, and Labour that they should work together in the national interest. It ended in tears, but, as so often in her premiership, events might have gone another way.

On Sunday 31 March, she took the unusual step of phoning all four of her living predecessors as Prime Minister to seek their advice. Once a Prime Minister, you join an elite club. No one else in the country knows first-hand what the job is like. At this moment of grave national crisis, she wanted to hear their thoughts. The idea came up because Blair had made it known that he would like to speak to her, and she felt bound to speak to the others – Major, Brown and Cameron – as well. All were happy to be consulted, and offered their thoughts. Did the experience make her think that they were a resource she could have drawn on more? Like most PMs, she was reluctant to listen to wise voices within and across parties. They prefer, until too late, to rely on an ever-narrowing group of trusted advisors. The former PM she connected with most – surprisingly, perhaps – was Brown, who shared his thoughts not about how to play Brexit but about the importance of her burning injustices agenda, which planted a seed in her mind. Committed to social reform, Brown was also the child of a vicar, introverted, tribal, and a missionary whose time was cut short.

A HISTORIC CABINET MEETING: 2 APRIL

The Cabinet meeting at 9.30 a.m. on Tuesday 2 April had been intended to take all morning, but it lasted over seven hours. It ranks as one of the five most historic in May's premiership, along with 6 July 2018 on her Chequers deal; 14 November, where she unveiled the withdrawal agreement; 14 March 2019, where she tried and failed to restore collective responsibility; and 21 May, where she was unable to secure continued support for the withdrawal agreement.

Following the defeat of MV3 on 29 March, May had rallied quickly and found within herself new reserves of strength and willpower. She steadied herself over the weekend: she was not going to allow herself to be defeated by her own MPs, nor was she going to desert the country without first taking it out of the European Union. Monday 1 April was a torrid day, with four indicative votes put before the House of Commons, none of which secured a majority. Closest to passing – indeed, the closest vote ever under May – was on the customs union, defeated by 276 to 273, a majority of just three, tighter than the defeat of the same proposition by twelve the previous week. It showed beyond doubt that the Brexit option that the greatest number of MPs supported was remaining within a customs union, which, given the closeness of the referendum result in 2016, would have chimed with the consensus view across the country. But the idea was summarily brushed aside. The defeat of a Common Market 2.0 proposal tabled by indefatigable campaigner Nick Boles, among others, led to his resignation from the party. 'I have given everything to an attempt to find a compromise,' he said. 'I have failed chiefly because my party refuses to compromise. I regret, therefore, to announce that I can no longer sit for this party.' As he left the Commons chamber, some MPs shouted, 'Don't go, Nick,' with a mixture of regret and irony, while some from other parties applauded him.[1] 'April Fools' was the *i* newspaper's headline the day after MPs had rejected every alternative plan for Brexit for a second time.[2]

May now faced an almost insurmountable challenge across the English Channel. 'The mood in Brussels was one of disbelief that the UK still does not seem to know what it wants,' said the BBC's Europe editor, Katya Adler.[3] Scorn, derision, pity and anger had been growing across the EU over the previous weeks. For some, the frustration at their 'awkward partner' had been festering for years. Now it exploded in a chorus of disbelief. None of them had foreseen quite what a mess Britain would make of Brexit.

May found herself having to defend Julian Smith, in trouble over Laura Kuenssberg's BBC documentary *The Brexit Storm*, which aired that evening, intended to be screened at the start of Britain's first full week outside of the EU. Smith, thinking Britain would be safely beyond Brexit, said he thought that ministers had shown 'the worst example of ill-discipline in British political history'. Worse in the eyes of Brexiteers was his comment that the parliamentary arithmetic suggested they should have opted for a softer type of Brexit.[4] May gave him a rap over the knuckles, which was briefed out to assuage the anger, while privately agreeing with much of what he said.[5]

May and Smith determined, with negotiations entering a new era, that Cabinet on 2 April would see a step-change in discipline and a return to collective responsibility. The political Cabinet met first, and then the broader Cabinet met after lunch. It began with the familiar routine of ministers being checked to see that they had handed over their electronic devices before meetings. Not just the logistics but also the substance of the meeting had been carefully choreographed to ensure that it secured the outcome they wanted, and that the Brexiteers, who had repeatedly thwarted May, should not this time emerge on top.

She opened the discussion by saying there were just three serious options on the table: further indicative votes, a managed no deal, and talks with Labour – and by the end of the meeting they had to agree collectively on one. The first option had its supporters among the centre and Europhile wings of Cabinet, but May herself talked it down, saying there was no guarantee that it would settle anything, and she didn't want to cede control to the legislature with no guarantee where it would end up. A managed no deal was advocated strongly by Leadsom with support from Grayling, Truss, Fox and Mordaunt. Now it was Gove's turn to speak out strongly against it, saying that Parliament would always block it and it would cause untold damage to farmers and others economic interests. Vocal attacks on it came too, as over the previous months, from Hammond, Rudd, Clarke and Gauke. It rapidly became clear that Cabinet would never agree to it.

Brandon Lewis, who had been readmitted to the inner circle, took over Hunt's seat for the meeting, a symbolic gesture of intent. He crisply dismissed a general election and a second referendum. The former, he said, was 'out of the question', given the current state of polls (in which the Conservatives had suffered a dramatic drop) and the state of the party's finances, while the latter would be inconclusive.[6] That left talks with Labour as the 'least disagreeable' option left on the Cabinet table. The idea was vigorously opposed by Williamson, as well as by Grayling, Leadsom and Truss. Before the meeting, Smith, who saw talks with Labour as a way forward, had spoken to Cox, who shared with him his own thoughts about reaching out to Labour. Smith seized on it, and May, who was deeply sceptical it would work but had no Plan

B, assented. Gove was supportive too of talking to Labour. Thus it was that the two loyalist Leave ministers, Cox and Gove, who had so often ridden to her rescue, did so again. 'The Attorney General was more persuasive about the case for opening talks with Labour,' says Gove. 'I merely argued that we had to at least get the Withdrawal Bill through, and that there were a group of serious Labour MPs including Lucy Powell and Steven Kinnock with whom it would be worth exploring common ground.'[7] Cox then gave ministers a powerful speech in which he told them, though it pained him to say so, that 'the price of amending our red lines would be worthwhile if it meant we could get the Withdrawal Bill passed', and here he returned to his earlier metaphor of going through 'the choppy waters and out into the open sea'.[8] Cox proposed nothing less than a 'big generous offer' be made to Labour. Hunt, who considered Cabinet was in a 'fatal pickle', was wryly amused by 'what appeared to be Geoffrey's brainwave on the spot'.[9] But this time, not even Cox's eloquence could becalm the choppy waters in Cabinet.

With no agreement reached by lunch, the decision was taken to continue the meeting at 1.30 p.m. after a short break when sandwiches were brought up to the State Rooms. Ministers who had to cancel their plans for that afternoon, with no prospect of an end of the meeting in sight, were not in good humour when they came back down the stairs to resume. Williamson was the most outspoken, saying that reaching out to Labour was a 'stupid idea' which would damage the Conservative Party, have no effect because Labour was so tribal, and that, as they'd spent the entire time decrying Corbyn since he became leader in 2015, to now say that he could help them solve Brexit lacked all credibility. For Williamson, the key to Britain leaving lay, as always, with the DUP, who would come on board if only concessions could be made to the backstop. He repeatedly asked to check that his comments were being recorded by Mark Sedwill and his officials, highlighting the lack of trust that many Brexiteer ministers now had in the Cabinet Office, its objectivity and its ability to act independently of the will of the PM.

Gove countered Williamson's comments by saying that, while it would obviously be good to get the DUP back onside, they'd tried many times before, as they had with the ERG, but without evident success. It was thus their duty to explore fresh ideas. Hunt and Javid helped swing the conversation by saying that they should try to reach out to Labour, though they stressed that they shouldn't go too far on the customs union. Hammond too weighed in heavily, saying that the time had come to work with Labour, so eager was he to reduce the risk of no deal. Leadsom and Truss were clearly still very unhappy, while Mordaunt was 'the most obviously discombobulated' by the direction the meeting was taking, according to Cabinet sources. When she – like Leadsom – didn't turn up for drinks after the marathon, fear spread that she would follow the route of Davis and Raab and walk. Ministers were clearly becoming impatient with the time that was being taken, as May, sensing the disquiet about a 'fix', spun it out to let all contribute who wanted to speak. Exacerbating her task was the jockeying for power between the leadership candidates around the table, to whom the events of 29 March had given such a considerable boost.

When it became clear that the meeting was winding down, May's team slipped out to prepare the statement that she would shortly deliver on the street outside No. 10. Because of the opposition voices, May was going to be unable to say that the decision in favour of talks with Labour would be unanimous – 'collectively' was agreed to be the more prudent word. The mood did not lighten towards the end. The Brexiteers knew they had been roundly outflanked, and they did not like it. They had lost out on the length of any extension before Brexit. May simply said that any delay beyond 12 April should be 'as short as possible'. They had lost out on the talks with Labour, which despite their fierce opposition were going ahead. The final insult was the agreement that, should the cross-party talks fail, there would be a decision by the Commons between her thrice-rejected deal and an alternative deal, so far undefined but clearly entailing a customs agreement with the EU, an outcome that Hammond, Clarke, Gauke and Rudd as well as Barwell and Smith favoured. As the *Financial Times* put it, when the Prime Minister had to pick a side, she came down against the Eurosceptics.[10]

The meeting finally over, ministers remained locked inside the building, as some – most, in fact – were no longer trusted not to leak. While they were served drinks ('a rather nice Rioja', says Lidington), May went to her office, where she read over the draft her team had prepared, made changes and, because of the rain outside, walked upstairs to the State Rooms to deliver it. 'This is a decisive moment in the story of these islands and it requires national unity to deliver the national interest,' she said. 'I have always been clear that we could make a success of no deal in the long term, but leaving with a deal is the best solution.' She announced that she would therefore be asking for a further extension of Article 50 at a special EU Council the following week.

The right's reaction at hearing that their cause had been so roundly squashed at Cabinet, and, with it, hopes of Britain having a no-deal exit on 12 April, was ferocious. 'This is an utter disaster,' said Duncan Smith. 'We are just about to legitimise Corbyn.'[11] Rees-Mogg, when asked if his support for her would continue, said, 'I wouldn't hold your breath, I'm not a Marxist in case you haven't noticed.'[12] MP Michael Fabricant tweeted a poster which read, 'We trusted you', saying, 'I feel ashamed #Brexit'.[13] Two resignations followed at 6 p.m., Welsh Minister Nigel Adams and a Brexit Minister, Chris Heaton-Harris, taking the tally of resignations over Brexit since June 2018 to nineteen. May now had six ministerial positions to fill and a dwindling pool of those willing and able to do so. Fury was not limited to the ERG wing, with even moderate MPs referring to a ConservativeHome survey that week that found that 75 per cent of party members now favoured a rapid no-deal solution.[14] Tory members across the country cut up their Conservative membership cards on social media, while John Strafford, chairman of the Campaign for Conservative Democracy, said, looking ahead to the local elections in May, 'The feeling is that this is a complete disaster.'[15]

When May entered the Commons on Wednesday 3 April, the lack of support for her action was palpable. PMQs saw the anger topple over, with the government benches silent as she delivered lines against Corbyn which would usually buy cheap applause. Instead of posing helpful questions from her own benches, angry Tory Members queued up to disparage her new strategy. Julian Lewis asked why she'd taken no deal off the table when she had repeatedly told them that 'no deal is better than a bad deal'. Lee Rowley asked, 'What qualifies Corbyn now for his involvement in Brexit?', while David Jones asked her, 'Does it remain the position of the Prime Minister that the Leader of the Opposition is not fit to govern?'[16] After this hour-long grilling, May took refuge in No. 10.

She lost much of the press, too, that had still been loyal to her to the point, notably *The Sun*, whose headline the next day was 'Tory MPs launch bid to kick Theresa May out TODAY'.[17] Newspapers that had always been critical of her stepped up their attacks. An editorial in the *Financial Times* said that a cross-party Brexit 'should have happened at the start of the withdrawal process – or when the government lost its majority in 2017 – not as a final, desperate step'.[18] Nothing summed up how precarious her predicament was than the reaction to her holding out a hand (and little more) to Corbyn's Labour: for some, it was too little, too late; for others, it was far too much to take. It made perfect sense; it was beyond the pale – and there was May, as ever, right in the middle.

The EU were great supporters of cooperating with Corbyn, but even they had their doubts. 'I saw Jeremy Corbyn several times in our office in Brussels. I didn't see anything near any vision or concept either, or deep understanding of what Brexit means or should be,' a senior Commission official says.

I asked him about the interaction between the withdrawal agreement and the political declaration. But he couldn't answer them. He merely wanted to use the meeting for his audience at home. He didn't have any particular clarity, nor did he have a sense that this is a moment where national unity is needed.

Despite May's calls for unity, Parliament was as divided and deadlocked as ever. On Thursday 4 April, there was a dead tie in the vote over a proposal by Benn to have a third round of indicative votes: 310 MPs for, 310 MPs against. The Speaker cast his deciding vote, in line with precedent, against. The last time Parliament had been unable to reach a decision was in 1993, over the ratification of the Maastricht Treaty, a reminder that Europe had divided Parliament down the middle for over a generation. The Commons then passed, by one vote, a Bill tabled by Yvette Cooper and Oliver Letwin, requiring the PM to propose a further extension beyond 12 April, as a further step to avert no deal.

THE EU AGREE TO SECOND EXTENSION

May wrote to Tusk on Friday 5 April, asking for Brexit to be delayed until 30 June to allow time for talks with Labour, while also pledging to make preparations for the European Parliament elections on 23 May in the event that a longer extension was needed. The talks with Labour began with little fanfare or expectation. Gove had been intended to be the lead figure for the government, but after Labour made it clear they didn't trust him for ideological and political reasons, Lidington and Barclay picked up the baton, with Keir Starmer and Rebecca Long-Bailey for Labour. Letwin was one of those who thought the talks had come too late:

A chess player can make the right move, but if it is not at the right time, it is useless. Timing is all important, as was shown here. A sensible solution would have been to start talks in 2016, or even in June 2017. The Tory left, the ERG, the EU and even Labour might have been willing to compromise then. But over the following months, the arteries hardened and positions were toughened. On Labour's side, suspicions grew. Had a big overwhelming offer been promptly made, even as late as the start of 2019, a positive outcome might have occurred.[19]

May made her latest begging mission to Brussels, in search of a second extension, on Wednesday 10 April. After five hours of talks lasting into the early hours of Thursday, the EU27 agreed a 'flexible' extension until 31 October, with a chance to 'take stock' in June. 'I know that there is huge frustration from many people that I had to request this extension,' May said. 'The UK should have left the EU by now and I sincerely regret the fact that I have not yet been able to persuade Parliament to agree a deal.' It was a victory of sorts for May. Merkel, though, had been less than amenable, and Macron as sceptical and demanding as ever. EU leaders at large displayed barely concealed pleasure mixed with contempt at Britain's discomfort, demanding to know how an extension might bring closure to the three-year-long process.[20] On her return, May had an uncomfortable day in Parliament on Thursday 11 April, with angry Tory Brexiteers demanding that she quit over her 'abject surrender' to Brussels. Bill Cash said that she should resign, while the DUP's Sammy Wilson accused her of having 'rolled over' for Brussels. May was heartily relieved that the 11th marked the beginning of the eleven-day Easter break. She said it was a time for MPs to 'reflect' on the decisions needed as part of their 'national duty' to 'find a way through this impasse'. The break had not come a moment too soon.

CHALLENGES FROM THE GRASSROOTS, 1922 AND FARAGE

While May was away walking in Snowdonia with Philip over Easter, No. 10 had to issue an official denial that, unlike after her walking holiday there two years before, she was not about to announce a general election.[21] On her return, she faced attacks on at least three fronts. First, grassroots Conservative activists wanting to force an extraordinary general meeting to allow a no-confidence motion in her from party members. 'They are livid, they are fed up,' said rising Tory star Johnny Mercer, 'but not as fed up as I am having to come up and work here.'[22] The National Conservative Convention, the most senior body of the party's voluntary wing, was bound to hold such a meeting if the chairs of more than sixty-five Conservative associations called for it. The expedient had never been used in the past, and members would require at least twenty-eight days' notice, but it was an unpleasant threat hanging over her, the suspicion in No. 10 being that it had been orchestrated by the ERG.[23] 'The ERG put pressure on the voluntary party, which had always loved Theresa May but had started to turn against her after the 29 March postponement. Baker was in the vanguard, aided by Francois,' says one.

Second, Farage's still new Brexit Party was enjoying a surge in support in the run-up to the EU elections, boosted by Rees-Mogg's sister Annunziata, a former Conservative parliamentary candidate, crossing over to join them. By the end of April, Farage suggested that as many as twenty-eight Tory MPs – a group known as 'the Spartans', led by Baker and Francois, who vowed never to back May's deal – would not face Brexit Party candidates standing against them. In 2014, he had persuaded two Conservative MPs, Douglas Carswell and Mark Reckless, to defect to UKIP, causing Cameron considerable distress. Was history about to repeat itself?

The 1922 Committee was the third pressure on May. The Whips' Office and No. 10 suspected that Brady was coming under intense pressure from his executive, notably Bernard Jenkin and Sheryll Murray, to change the rules to allow MPs to mount another no-confidence vote before 12 December 2019. The eighteen-member executive held a private vote on 24 April, narrowly coming out in favour of retaining the rules. But when one of them leaked the news, the executive came under intense pressure to hold another poll. No. 10 thought the more ardent Brexiteers, above all Jenkin, had bullied Brady to hold a second vote, which he did on 22 May, this time a secret ballot. In between both votes, the local elections had been held on 2 May, which saw the Conservatives lose 1,330 seats and the Lib Dems gain 704. Brady put the executive's voting slips in an envelope, which he sealed, saying he would *only* open it if she didn't announce that she was definitely leaving office on 12 June.[24] 'It's still unopened,' he says some months later.[25]

When Brady went to see May at No. 10 to inform her of the pressure for a rule change, she tore into him, visibly angry: 'You told me that if I promised the 1922 Committee that I would give up being Prime Minister, I'd get the withdrawal agreement through on 29 March. I promised I'd go, but I didn't get the withdrawal agreement through. You have let me down.' Relationships turned toxic. May's team, who had recommended Brady for a knighthood in January 2019, thought they had listened endlessly to him but now could no longer trust him. She had him in for a 'smoothing-over' conversation, following their contretemps, but there was no way back. No. 10 instead began to work closely with Brady's vice-chair, Charles Walker, whom it found sympathetic to May's predicament.

DROPPING OF THE PILOT: DEPARTURES

On 18 April, the day before Good Friday, Lyra McKee, a prominent gay journalist in Northern Ireland, was fatally shot during rioting in the Creggan area of Derry. The following day, party leaders from across the political spectrum, but not May, went to Creggan in a show of unity against violence. No. 10 advised the PM it would be too big a risk for her to go to the funeral, to be held at St Anne's Cathedral, Belfast, on 24 April. But Northern Ireland Secretary Bradley, who thought May should attend, deliberately went over No. 10's heads and texted her directly. May heeded her suggestion. Bradley recalls:

> It was an absolute no-brainer. She's at her most comfortable in church. Here was a gay journalist, young, passionate. It was a real moment for the PM when she could show the world who she was and to let her humanity out. She came, and was so good with everybody at the funeral, with Lyra's family, with the mourners. She tuned into the whole situation, was deeply moved, and was adamant afterwards that talks had to be urgently restarted, and the laws on same-sex marriage changed.[26]

Father Martin Magill spoke the words, 'I commend our political leaders for standing together in Creggan on Good Friday. I am, however, left with a question. Why in God's name does it take the death of a 29-year-old woman with her whole life in front of her...' Before he could complete his sentence, spontaneous applause rang out from mourners in a standing ovation. May rose to her feet, albeit with some awkwardness, but showing how far she had travelled in the two years since Grenfell.

She found it harder to deal with news that broke just before the funeral, that confidential information had been leaked from the National Security Council (NSC), which she chaired, about the Chinese tech company Huawei being allowed to help build the UK's 5G network, the next generation of mobile networks. Barwell was furious and said that if the leaker was found, regardless of rank, they would be dismissed. Leaking had become endemic in Cabinet and Cabinet committees, but never before from the NSC, regarded as sacrosanct due to the sensitivity of the material discussed and its importance to national security. After a week of investigation, May announced on 1 May that, despite his strenuous denials, Defence Secretary Gavin Williamson was responsible and would be dismissed. The investigation and decision were extremely painful for May. She knew, of course, that he was a

significant briefer and leaker from Cabinet, and that he was helping
Johnson with his leadership campaign. But she still liked and trusted
him, and he'd always been very loyal to her personally and looked out
for her. No other Cabinet ministers had done so much for her: he had
helped her become PM in 2016, and had been by her side, as Chief
Whip, then Defence Secretary, for thirty-four months. Now he was off.

She was cautioned against announcing the sacking the day before
the local elections. 'I can't leave it until afterwards,' she said. 'It will
look as if I'm diverting attention away from me and the bad results.'
Williamson was a big figure, larger than life, and she worried about
replacing him, about what he would do, and whether he would hurt
her, as reports suggested he might do. May loyalists and centre-ground
ministers in Cabinet were pleased to see him go and thought the move
bolstered her authority: Williamson had overstretched himself. Had she
not sacked him, after all she'd tirelessly said about Cabinet security, her
credibility would have been in tatters. 'But then he began to see himself
as the man who could deliver on Brexit for Johnson, and began openly
organising for him. That made life very difficult for her,' says a May
loyalist. Johnson's own intentions were becoming similarly blatant. 'I'm
not resigning,' May told Johnson during a couple of angry exchanges.

Williamson's departure equally brought the spotlight onto Mark
Sedwill, the Cabinet Secretary. Jeremy Heywood had been regularly
singled out by conspiracy theorists, populists and the right-wing press
as the very epitome of the unelected state, blocking their Brexit. Now
it was Sedwill's turn. He was accused of using underhand methods to
clamp down on leaking to restore Cabinet conventions. Williamson
and his allies blamed Sedwill more than May for his departure. With
Williamson now openly coming out in support of Johnson, and with
Johnson a sceptic of the civil service, bolstered by his experience of
the FCO, it created new elements of uncertainty at a moment of maximum volatility. When, on 16 May, Johnson publicly declared that
he would be standing for the leadership, Sedwill's future became a

matter of public debate. 'Sir Mark Sedwill "facing the axe as Cabinet Secretary" if Brexiteer becomes Prime Minister', said PoliticsHome.[27]

PRESSURE MOUNTS ON MAY TO QUIT

It became a toss-up by mid-May whether the first to plunge in the knife would be the Conservative grassroots (who gave notice that an extraordinary meeting of the National Conservative Convention was to be held on 15 June),[28] her Cabinet colleagues, the 1922 Committee, or her leadership rivals. Six or seven in Cabinet were toying with resigning to focus on their campaigns. Hammond was the only top figure not to have designs on her job.[29]

First off the blocks was the executive of the 1922. On Thursday 16 May, it made a decisive move, spurred on by May's announcement two days before that she would be putting the withdrawal agreement to a vote in Parliament in the first week of June. To the 1922 Committee, it was a further prevarication, denying the opportunity for a leadership election before the summer recess. That day at 11.30 a.m., the executive trooped in to see her in her office behind the Speaker's chair in the Commons. They were met by a stony-faced Prime Minister, flanked by her Praetorian Guard: Barwell, Smith and Lewis. With tears never far away, she explained that she regarded it as her duty to see through Brexit. 'Tears welled in her eyes as she made her argument for just a little longer in Downing Street. She dabbed at her nose with a handkerchief. Yet the sympathy and patience of the 1922 Committee had run out,' said one report.[30] The epic encounter, which lasted over an hour, saw her out-argued and outmanoeuvred. She had no alternative but to sit down with Brady and Lewis in the first week of June to agree a timetable to appoint her successor. The 1922 executive promptly briefed out, 'We have agreed to meet to decide the timetable for the election of a new leader of the Conservative Party as soon as the second reading has occurred and that will take place regardless of what the vote is on the second reading – whether it passes or whether it fails.'[31] 1922 treasurer Geoffrey Clifton-Brown told Sky News, 'The sooner the better, and that's not being unkind to the Prime Minister. I just think the longer this goes on, it's not in the nation's interests, it's not in the party's interests.'[32]

The next day, 17 May, she received an official letter from Corbyn to say that, after forty-two days of talks, they had gone as far as they could, but had reached an impasse due to 'the increasing weakness and instability of your government'. Corbyn later said that, with a Tory leadership battle imminent, he had no confidence in the government's ability to deliver any compromise agreement, adding, 'She is not going to be Prime Minister for much longer anyway.'[33] May had entered the talks reluctantly, viewing them as an inevitable next step, but without high hopes. The question in her mind throughout was: 'Can Jeremy Corbyn and Seumas Milne deliver on the Labour side? Will the price that they will likely extract, i.e. moving towards a customs union, prove too much for my Cabinet ministers teetering on the edge of resignation?' But she saw no choice but to go for it. For Keir Starmer, it was too little too late. 'Talks began not at the eleventh hour, but after the twelfth hour,' he says. 'In my view, there had been a moment when we could've got a soft Brexit through, but leaving it so late made it very, very difficult. I think Labour was serious on our side and I didn't think that the government was merely going through the motions. I think it was real.' Barwell and Gibb continued to believe in the value of the talks, with the latter in particular thinking that Corbyn and Milne were serious, as long as the government could deliver what they were demanding. Gove too initially thought there was a prospect of success. However, as he says now,

The closer we came to the European elections, the more it appeared that the talks were not working. Keir Starmer did not seem to be serious. They wanted to avoid being blamed for the breakdown, so they continued talking. But there just wasn't buy-in from Corbyn's office. The message Labour's negotiating team was receiving from it was: 'Don't push the agenda.'[34]

May took stock over the weekend of 18 and 19 May. With her No. 10 team, she ran over the questions for the nth time that had been at the forefront of their minds for the previous six weeks: 'Are Labour serious about reaching an agreement? Are we at risk of giving away too much? Is there a landing zone? Might we risk tearing the party apart?' 'It got close,' says an official, 'but then Corbyn's team thought they needed a second referendum. Had talks begun two to three months earlier, it might have worked.' It was looking increasingly impossible to hold her premiership together, with agitation from all sides of the party, and a drubbing expected in the European elections that Thursday. 'By this point, Cabinet had started caving in,' says Lidington. 'You had the Johnson and Raab campaigns up and running, and some colleagues saying, "If we don't start campaigning ourselves, we're going to be overtaken by them."'[35]

Rapidly running out of road, May tensed herself for a crunch Cabinet on Tuesday 21 May, for one final run at the hurdle to get Labour back in to the talks and, with their support, to push the withdrawal agreement through the House of Commons.

CRUNCH CABINET AND ANNOUNCEMENT OF RESIGNATION: 21–24 MAY

May opened the Cabinet meeting on Tuesday morning not knowing if or how she would survive. An amended Withdrawal Agreement Bill had to be published later in the week, and choices needed to be made. Ministers were presented with a paper which listed options, from a customs union through to a second referendum. A Downing Street official recalls the meeting:

By the time it started, it was already clear no one was in favour of any [of the available options]. It was one of those occasions where no one knew what they did want, but all knew what they didn't want. Most Cabinet ministers, though, didn't want to negotiate on anything related to a customs union or second referendum.

They were divided clean down the middle on whether to support the Prime Minister in her continued efforts to find a way forward with Labour. Loyalists, to different degrees, included Lidington, Hammond, Gove, Smith, Gauke, Lewis, Wright, Barclay, Hinds, Hancock and Rudd, but increasingly they believed, as did Brokenshire and Natalie Evans, that the time had come for her to go. Those most opposed to her continuing were Leadsom, Javid, Hunt, Truss, Mundell, Mordaunt, Grayling and Alun Cairns, who was particularly unhappy about the European elections. Even Cox had begun to despair. As May made the case for talks to continue, it was clear that support was seeping away. Discussion became fractious while May outlined her thinking. Rudd recalls, 'Various parts of it were agreed, but other parts weren't, with particular conflict over the issue of the second referendum, and whether we would allow for a debate on it. But when Cabinet broke up, I thought it would probably be all right and hold together.'[36]

Leadsom was the most sceptical. Since she had stepped down as a leadership contender in July 2016, paving the way for May to become Prime Minister, she saw herself as responsible for delivering Brexit, all the more so after she became Leader of the House in June 2017. She held regular meetings with Rees-Mogg and others to try to bring them round and to mediate their concerns back to May, whom she would phone on Sundays to discuss ways of holding the party together. But the two months since 29 March had tested her. At the Cabinet, she argued that they should forget a meaningful vote and go straight to the withdrawal agreement and, if they could get it through the second reading, then both left and right would have the opportunity at that stage to come forward with their amendments. She thought that was what had been agreed when the Cabinet meeting broke up.

May spoke about what Cabinet had agreed, as she saw it, at the HQ of consultancy firm PricewaterhouseCoopers, when she outlined a new ten-point offer. MPs, she said, had 'one last chance' to deliver Brexit, and she urged them to vote for what she promised was a 'new deal'. A negotiated deal would be 'dead in the water' if they rejected the proposal. 'I have compromised, now I ask you to compromise too,' she added, reminding her audience that she had even 'offered to give up the job I love earlier than I would like' to see the deal through. Extending the Brexit deadlock risked 'opening the door to a night-mare future of permanently polarised politics', she continued. She offered a guarantee of a Commons vote on whether to hold another referendum on the government's final deal, with a promise to honour the outcome, as well as a vote on alternative customs arrangements, including a government proposal of a temporary customs union for goods, and a legal obligation for the UK to 'seek to conclude alterna-tive arrangements' to replace the backstop by the end of 2020.[37]

The speech went down poorly. To her team, anxiously watching her speak, they knew it was a gamble, but there was no other card left in her hand. 'Even while she was delivering it', says one of her team, 'it became clear to us she was dead in the water, with Labour MPs tweeting it didn't go far enough, and Tory MPs outraged she'd gone so far.' After she finished, Labour claimed she was merely offering a 'rehash' of exist-ing plans. Johnson said that 'we can and must do better', adding that the proposals contravened the party's 2017 general election manifesto, while Rees-Mogg said that her proposal was 'worse than before'.[38] None was more unhappy at her comments than Leadsom: 'I felt uncomfortable with the speech because I didn't think it entirely reflected what had been agreed in Cabinet,' she says now. 'So I told No. 10 that, as Leader of the House of Commons, I wanted to see the draft of the Bill that I would be introducing on Thursday.'[39] At first she was told that would not be possible. Then, when she persisted, she was handed a copy. She was most exercised by the implication in the Bill about facilitating a vote on a second referendum and – while May's team were confident they would win such a vote – she worried that it could be interpreted as the Cabinet legitimising a second referendum. Ministers at large were invited to a secure Downing Street room to view the draft text of the amended WAB. But when they saw the language, they too were unhappy. 'Almost all refused at the fence,' says one. 'By mid-afternoon it was clear the Bill was dead, and with the Bill dead, so too was her premiership.'

On Wednesday, Leadsom sent several text messages to Barwell and Smith, as well as to May herself, saying, 'Please don't go ahead with this Bill. It will be a total disaster.' She received no reply. She told her team that if at 5.30 p.m. she returned from her Privy Council audience with the Queen, which she attended in her capacity as Lord President, without any response coming, she felt she would have no option but to resign. So she picked up the telephone to tell May, a strange bookend to the call that she had made almost exactly three years before to begin her premiership. She recalls:

> I told her, 'I'm sorry to say this, but I will have to resign.' The Prime Minister replied that she was genuinely very sorry, and she tried to dissuade me. 'I'm very sorry, but I've reached the end of the road, there's no way back,' I told her. 'What you said in your speech wasn't my understanding of what had been agreed at Cabinet, and I can't in all conscience introduce the Bill in the House tomorrow.'[40]

Wednesday 22 May was one of the most painful days for May personally, in a premiership not short of difficulties. At PMQs, she took a savage battering from her own MPs about historic allegations during the Troubles in Northern Ireland, revealing new levels of derision towards her. The premiership was unravelling in the most public of ways. The 1922 Committee was discussing new moves against her. Cabinet ministers were considering resigning. At this point, Fox sent Barwell a text: 'Gavin, what is confirmed in the draft bill is not what we agreed in Cabinet. I cannot agree to it being published.' He recalls now:

> It was a heart-tugging moment sending that text to Gavin. It effectively meant I was withdrawing my support from her and that she wouldn't have been able to carry on, because if I went, there would be no more support for her from the Brexit wing of the party. I knew that my resignation would greatly weaken her position and perhaps even bring her down.[41]

No ring-around or formal poll of Cabinet ministers was conducted by Smith that day, to ask if they still had confidence in her or whether she should go. But it became apparent over the course of the day that her time was up. 'I think we're probably close to an end now,' Barwell said to Lidington late in the day. Rudd recollects:

> The conversation in the corridors had been: 'Can she survive another week?' And the reply would always come back, 'She survived the last one, so who knows?' But we had come to the tipping point. It hadn't been obvious to me at the Cabinet on Tuesday that something had changed, but there was so much dry wood, and what that meeting did was to light a match that ignited the tinder.[42]

Javid and Hunt both requested meetings with May on Wednesday to explain their unhappiness with the Bill and with her leadership, but their request was declined, though she agreed to see them on Thursday. Mundell and Mordaunt also made their acute discontent known. Then, that evening, Leadsom's resignation was announced, with a public warning that she no longer believed that Cabinet was capable of delivering on the referendum result. The impact was devastating. 'Leadsom resigning was the critical factor in the Prime Minister going,' says Lidington, 'because Andrea was always honest and straight with the PM. She had strong views, but for the greatest part she had been loyal. It was a real moment.'[43] It was the thirty-sixth ministerial resignation under May, twenty-one of them over Brexit.[44] Gove, so often the supporter of May over the previous twelve months, was having doubts too: 'I was beginning to think that, given that MPs would not vote for it, we would need a prorogation and a new Queen's Speech to introduce the Bill, and I thought that should be a job for a new Prime Minister.'[45] News also broke late on Wednesday that Brady had demanded an audience to see May on Friday to tell her that she must leave.[46]

Thursday 23 June was voting day in the European elections, with Farage's Brexit Party expected to damage the Conservatives considerably. (When the results were declared, the Brexit Party achieved 31.6 per cent of the vote to the Conservatives' 9.1 per cent. The Tories placed fifth, behind the Lib Dems, Labour and the Greens, the worst Conservative result ever in a national poll.) May was merely thankful that the announcement of the results was delayed, to allow declarations to be synchronised across the EU.

She had decided on Wednesday afternoon, without telling anyone apart from Philip, that she couldn't go on if she couldn't bring the WAB forward for a second reading, and with Cabinet disintegrating, she told Barwell later that afternoon. Gibb had been advising that, given it was now all but an inevitability, she would do better if she kept control of the agenda by making an announcement imminently. Doing so would mean she would be able to oversee the Trump visit and the seventy-fifth anniversary celebrations of D-Day, and remain as Prime Minister with a calm and dignified exit. Late on Wednesday afternoon, Barwell called May's closest team into the Cabinet Room to plan the choreography of her resignation announcement. With the next day being polling in the European elections, that was not an option, so they decided to announce it on Friday. That evening, May went to see the Queen for her usual weekly audience. In line with custom, none of her team were told whether she had notified the monarch of her intentions. Her hopes of remaining Prime Minister until the party conference, in part because she wanted the opportunity for the next generation, like Rory Stewart, to lay out their platforms, were squashed. As Philip May told Lidington on Friday morning, 'We'd seen it coming for some months, it was just a question of time.' Lidington adds, 'I don't think she was intending to go on any later than the party conference in October 2019, so we were only fighting over a matter of months.'[47]

On Thursday morning, before the 8.30 a.m. meeting, she informed her closest Cabinet colleagues, including Lidington, Smith and Lewis, of her intentions. But she didn't speak to her loyalist allies, Bradley and Brokenshire, until Friday morning: 'She realised she couldn't go on, it was all too much,' Bradley says.[48] When May saw Hunt and Javid that afternoon, she listened to them politely but didn't reveal her intentions, believing it would leak. 'She was brilliantly po-faced,' says an aide. Mundell was another to request a meeting with her, very unhappy about what was being offered to the DUP, and the risks it posed for Scotland.

May spent the rest of Thursday 23 May making preparations for her departure, and that evening she went with Philip to Sonning for space to prepare herself for the next day. She'd taken with her a copy of the resignation speech written for her by Keelan Carr. He recalls:

We'd spoken often, and I had an idea of what she might want to say. She herself wanted certain words inserted, including 'I am the second female Prime Minister, but I won't be the last'. She wanted to include the words 'compromise is not a dirty word', spoken to her by British humanitarian Nicholas Winton. The draft contained the text about 'the country I love'.[49]

She and Philip were back in No. 10 by eight o'clock on Friday morning. She approved the final text of the speech and other details of the day, and then at 9 a.m. Brady came in for his meeting. She had been prepared carefully. With Barwell, Lewis and Smith beside her, she told the chair of the 1922 Committee that she was leaving, obviating the message that he was about to deliver. Then, as Brady recalls, she 'hit me with a bombshell', saying:

> Before you leave the building, I want you to tell me whether you're going to be a candidate. She wanted my answer there and then, because she would shortly be making a statement about the leadership election process and who the returning officers would be, and if I myself was going to be a candidate, I couldn't be one of them. So I went off to the waiting room opposite her study, made a couple of calls, and I decided there and then that I would recuse myself from the chair, and told her so.[50]

The conversation lasted twenty minutes and was described as 'formal more than polite'.

After the deed had been done, she was joined by Philip, Barwell, Penn, Slack and press secretary Paul Harrison, putting the final touches to her speech. They then left her alone for ten minutes, as she liked to have before delivering any major statement. She then walked down the long corridor without Philip and out into the street, where she said:

> Ever since I first stepped through the door behind me as Prime Minister, I have striven to make the United Kingdom a country that works not just for a privileged few but for everyone, and to honour the result of the EU referendum ... I negotiated the terms of our exit and a new relationship with our closest neighbours that protects jobs, our security and our Union. I have done everything I can to convince MPs to back that deal. Sadly, I have not been able to do so. I tried three times ... But it is now clear to me that it is in the best interests of the country for a new Prime Minister to lead that effort. So I am today announcing that I will resign as the leader

of the Conservative and Unionist Party on Friday 7 June so that a successor can be chosen … It is, and will always remain, a matter of deep regret to me that I have not been able to deliver Brexit. It will be for my successor to seek a way forward that honours the result of the referendum.

She listed the 'progress' that she felt that she had made over the previous three years, including almost eliminating the deficit, building more homes, protecting the environment and announcing the NHS Long Term Plan and Race Disparity Audit, before concluding her speech:

I will shortly leave the job that it has been the honour of my life to hold – the second female Prime Minister but certainly not the last. I do so with no ill will, but with enormous and enduring gratitude to have had the opportunity to serve the country I love.

As she spoke the final words, the strain suppressed for far too long welled up to the surface, and she choked up. As she came back into the front hall, and the door swiftly closed, her staff surrounded her in a cocoon of support. She turned to Barwell and said, 'I'm sorry for crying.' As if in a valediction to her entire premiership, he told her, 'Don't apologise. You have nothing to apologise for.'

May enjoyed her final two months at Downing Street. She was never happier than when she invited the England cricket team into No. 10 to celebrate their victorious World Cup campaign on 15 July 2019.

EPILOGUE:
THE LAST DAYS OF
A PREMIERSHIP

25 MAY–24 JULY 2019

May didn't have the premiership she wanted, but she had the exit many Prime Ministers dream of but are denied. A reason so many Prime Ministers (as well as their staff) suffer trauma post-premiership – from Anthony Eden and Harold Macmillan through to Gordon Brown and David Cameron – is that they suddenly find themselves thrust out of the job and building with no time to prepare, to adjust themselves psychologically, or have any kind of closure. In this regard, if in no other, May was a fortunate Prime Minister.[1]

For the nation, the nine weeks between May announcing her resignation on Friday 24 May and Johnson becoming Prime Minister on Wednesday 24 July had an autumnal hue. It gave a moment of much-needed respite after six months of incessant political turmoil, before the noise resumed with Johnson's dramatic arrival in Downing Street. In the little time she had left, May displayed the same zeal on her domestic agenda that she had shown when trying to force her deal through Parliament. She eschewed self-pity and recrimination, made peace where she could with Cabinet and parliamentary colleagues, who had for months been trying to oust her, and seemed determined to enjoy herself.

THE RACE TO SUCCEED MAY

In the wake of her resignation, no fewer than thirteen MPs put their names forward to succeed her, making it the most crowded leadership race in the party's history. The battle formally opened on Friday 7 June when she officially stood down as Tory leader. This was the same day as the results were announced in the Peterborough by-election, in which the Conservative candidate, Paul Bristow, saw his vote plummet by 25 per cent, pushed into third place by Nigel Farage's Brexit Party, which narrowly failed (by a margin of 683 votes) to gain its first elected seat at Westminster. The judgement was clear: 'The desertion of Conservative voters to Mr Farage's party was a reflection of Mrs May's failure to accomplish her principal task as Prime Minister: to deliver Brexit,' said the *Financial Times*.[2]

By the time the race got formally underway on Monday 10 June, the thirteen had whittled down to ten, with James Cleverly, Sam Gyimah and Kit Malthouse dropping out. May's attitude towards the contest was one of insouciance. The next to fall were Harper, Leadsom and McVey, eliminated in the first round. Hancock then dropped out, while Raab fell in the second round. When asked at the 8.30 a.m. meeting on Tuesday 18 June if she was going to be watching the BBC One television debate that evening between the remaining candidates – Gove, Hunt, Javid, Johnson and Stewart – May replied, 'I know everything I need to know about these people: I don't need to know any more.' Not even her close team know how she voted, though she was meticulous always in casting her vote. The most likely choice was Stewart, but it's only a hunch because she'd been eager to see younger talent come forward. She had no rapprochement with Johnson even after he became front-runner. On the morning of the final ballot of MPs, 20 June, when the parliamentary party decided which two of Johnson, Hunt and Gove would go forward to the membership in the country, Johnson turned to his colleague Conor Burns, who had supported his campaign in Parliament since mid-2018, and asked, 'Conor, how often have you and I gone through this walk of shame?', adding, 'There are two people I credit for my emergence as front-runner: Theresa May for her failure to deliver, and Nigel Farage, who exploited the position left by her failure to deliver.'[3]

TRUMP VISIT, D-DAY ANNIVERSARY AND INTERNATIONAL FAREWELLS

President Trump provided bookends to May's premiership, as the host of her first successful overseas trip in January 2017 and the last major overseas leader to visit London before she resigned. Surprisingly, perhaps, she was looking forward to the visit, and she would have hated having to leave office before it happened. Before leaving the US, Trump expressed his admiration for Farage and Johnson, saying that they were both 'very good guys' as well as 'very interesting people'.[4] 'A great woman' is how he described the Queen, who hosted a state banquet for him at Buckingham Palace on Monday 3 June.

Tuesday saw a switch from the royal theatre to the political, with the President spending the morning in Downing Street. For two hours, he and May spoke across the Cabinet table on difficult issues, including Iran, free trade, Huawei, Yemen, the Middle East and Syria. 'She found it hard to get a word in edgeways. He basically took over,' says one observer. She was punchy with him, as she was when she presented him with a symbolic gift: Churchill's own draft of the Atlantic Charter of 1941, one of the foundational texts of the UN. The choice of document was intentional: Trump's constant antipathy towards multilateral organisations and the rules-based international order had jarred with May, and they repeatedly found themselves at opposite ends of the ideological divide.[5]

The afternoon press conference in the Foreign Office saw a thaw, at least for public consumption, in Trump's attitude to May, when he said, 'She's probably a better negotiator than I am,' joking that she should 'stick around'. 'Nice try,' she shot back: 'I'm a woman of my word.' He praised Johnson, though less effusively than last time, so as not to embarrass her. 'I know Boris, I like him, I've liked him for a long time,' he said. 'I think he would do a very good job.' He said the same about Hunt. This time, he saved his scorn for his favourite UK target: Mayor of London Sadiq Khan, whom he blamed for anti-Trump protests on the streets of London, which had marred his visit the previous summer. The President described him as 'not a very good mayor' who had 'done a very poor job', implying he had damaged the relationship between the US and the UK. Trump's suggestion that the NHS would be on the table in future trade deals stirred some controversy. He also claimed to have turned down a request for a meeting with Corbyn.

On Wednesday, the D-Day celebrations opened with the naval tour of Portsmouth. May played host to fifteen world leaders, including Trump, to honour the largest naval, land and air military operation in history, with figures from every country that had fought alongside the UK. The National Security Council team had worked on the D-Day proclamation, a joint statement pledging to ensure that the 'unimaginable horror' of the Second World War would never be repeated, and committing each country to working together 'to resolve international tensions peacefully'. At a ceremony on nearby Southsea Common, Trump read out the prayer spoken by President Roosevelt in a radio message ahead of the D-Day landings, while Macron read out a letter from a member of the resistance.

May recited a letter written by a soldier, Captain Norman Skinner, who was among the 156,000 Allied troops who set sail exactly seventy-five years before to take part in D-Day the following day:

> My darling, this is a very difficult letter for me to write. As you
> know, something may happen at any moment and I cannot tell

when you will receive this ... My thoughts at this moment, in this lovely Saturday afternoon, are with you all now. I can imagine you in the garden having tea with Janey and Anne, getting ready to put them to bed ... There is so much that I would like to be able to tell you ... God bless you and keep you all safe for me.

He died two days later, letter in pocket.

May hosted a lunch for the leaders. Behind them lay a map that General Eisenhower, the senior Allied Commander for D-Day, had himself used. The only leader of a major country involved in the fighting not to be present – excluding Russia – was Jacinda Ardern from New Zealand, still caught up in the fallout from a terrorist attack at Christchurch. Over the meal, Trump sought to antagonise Merkel, whom he disliked more than most European leaders. 'Well, it was clearly all the fault of the Germans, Angela,' he said. May jumped in, 'Donald, you're not allowed to say that today. It was the Nazis.' Canadian Prime Minister Justin Trudeau lightened the mood. 'Be careful, all of you,' he said. 'Theresa can say anything she likes today and there's nothing any of us can do about it.' At the meal's end, a bottle of 1945 vintage port was produced, the last from the British government's capacious cellars. Merkel didn't want to partake, but Rutte piped up, 'You must, Angela, we can't leave it for Boris to drink.'

On Thursday, the anniversary date itself, May took part in commemorations in Normandy. Speaking under a new bronze statue by sculptor David Williams-Ellis depicting three British soldiers charging up the beach on D-Day, she said, 'These young men belonged to a very special generation, the greatest generation. A generation whose unconquerable spirit shaped the post-war world. They didn't boast, they didn't fuss: they served.' It was the last time she saw Macron in person, the affinity between them palpable, despite his being a constant thorn agitating the EU to stand up to Britain over Brexit. She appeared to forgive him. While waiting for the Prince of Wales for a service at Bayeux Cathedral, she spent over an hour talking to veterans, making each one of them feel that she was giving them her personal attention: May at her best.

On 28 and 29 June, she was in Japan for the G20 at Osaka, called to discuss the eight themes in global sustainable development. Her grittiest moment came on the first day, a forty-minute bilateral with Putin, their first formal encounter since the Salisbury attacks in March 2018. It was a closed session, with interpreters but no officials. She laid into him, telling him there would never be 'normalisation' of relations between Britain and Russia until Moscow halted its 'irresponsible and destabilising activity' around the world. She insisted that the two primary Salisbury suspects be 'brought to justice'.[6] She was very determined and very firm with the Russian leader, challenging comments he had made earlier in the day that liberalism was now 'obsolete'. Britain, she said, would continue to 'unequivocally defend liberal democracy' as well as to 'protect the human rights and equality of all groups, including LGBT people'.[7] For the second half of their bilateral, which also lasted forty minutes, their staff joined the meeting. 'It was immediately clear to us', says a member of May's team, 'that she had delivered a very stern message to the Russian leader. The atmosphere was not easy.'

Putin may have recalled unpleasant memories of a similar ear-bashing from Blair in his own final weeks in power on the last day of the G8 at Heiligendamm in Germany on 8 June 2007, when Blair had a 'very private, very pointed message' to deliver to Putin, telling him that, if he continued to conduct himself on the international stage as he had been doing, his ability to form working relationships with other world leaders would be considerably reduced. After it was over, Blair expressed himself satisfied with the outcome to his Principal Private Secretary and Sherpa for the G8, Olly Robbins.[8] May had a far more congenial bilateral with Erdoğan, despite their considerable differences in personality and outlook. As it ended, he told her, 'I respect you for the way you have conducted our relationship over the last three years.'

May had a brush with Trump, too, who tried to snub her efforts to persuade the leaders to sign up to an international commitment on tackling climate change. Why should I put America at a 'permanent disadvantage' in comparison to the rest of the world, he protested? It had been a fractious summit and only at the eleventh hour did the eighteen other leaders join May in putting their names to the agreement, without the US.

They were to clash twice more – starting with the last crisis May encountered. On 7 July, the *Mail on Sunday* published confidential messages sent by the British Ambassador to the US, Kim Darroch, to London, which criticised the Trump White House as 'clumsy and inept'. The President responded the following day with furious tweets: 'I do not know the Ambassador, but he is not liked or well thought of within the U.S. We will no longer deal with him.' He turned his fire on May too, less than a month after she had hosted him in London, saying, 'What a mess she and her representatives have created,' and on Brexit specifically, 'I told her how it should be done, but she decided to go another way.' It was, among many things, a sign of how deeply the special relationship had disintegrated. The British government responded by lamenting the regrettable leaks, which it said 'do not reflect the closeness of, and the esteem in which we hold, the relationship'. Trump was unimpressed: 'The good news for the wonderful United Kingdom is that they will soon have a new Prime Minister. While I thoroughly enjoyed the magnificent State Visit last month, it was the Queen who I was most impressed with!' Never in the hundred years since the Anglo-US relationship was forged in the First World War had there been such open rudeness.

Johnson came under pressure to give his own verdict, but he refused to be drawn on whether he would keep Darroch in Washington if he became Prime Minister. Then Foreign Office Minister Alan Duncan could not contain himself, saying that Johnson had effectively thrown the ambassador 'under the bus'.[9] On 9 July, May wrote a private letter to Darroch, urging him to remain in post, but in the leaders' debate on ITV that evening, Johnson repeatedly refused to guarantee that he would keep the ambassador. After a sleepless night, Darroch phoned FCO Permanent Secretary Simon McDonald at 4 a.m. to say that he was quitting. May was incandescent. 'I've worked with her for two years and I've seen her furious less than a handful of times: this was as angry as she gets,' says an official. Payback time came a week later when Trump tweeted that four Democratic congresswomen who 'originally came from countries whose governments are a complete and total catastrophe' should 'go back', despite three being born in the US and one entering the country as a child refugee. May instructed James Slack, her official spokesman, who had shone in the post, to go out in front of the lobby and 'wallop the President'. He duly did so, saying that the Prime Minister found Trump's words 'completely unacceptable'.[10]

Most unusually with an outgoing Prime Minister, there was no final telephone call with the President. Throughout her premiership, she had bitten her tongue at Trump's rudeness and breaches of protocol as she tried to work with him in the interests of Britain. But she was not sorry that she had come out so strongly in public with him in their final encounter. Indeed, she found it thoroughly cathartic. It sparked some hostility within the UK from voices who said that her own rhetoric on immigration had been divisive too, but she gained international plaudits: 'Britain's departing Prime Minister Theresa May was among the first world leaders to condemn President Trump's racist tweets,' said the *Washington Post*.[11] But any feeling of catharsis vanished when it was confirmed who would succeed her. May thought Johnson morally unfit to be Prime Minister. She was in anguish about having the job taken from her, and distraught that it would be him to follow.

DOMESTIC SQUALLS

The episode further cemented May's relationship with Sedwill, one of the sheet anchors of her ministerial career. One motive for the leaks was said to have been to damage Sedwill's chances of succeeding Darroch as ambassador. May's staunch defence of the civil service ethos and national security chimed with Sedwill. They'd bonded over the dismissal of Williamson as Defence Secretary, which she had found so painful. He repeatedly defended her against Cabinet ministers who were saying that her summing up in Cabinet was not reflecting the balance of opinions shared. Not since Ted Heath, the Prime Minister who took Britain into Europe, had there been a PM more comfortable in the company of officials than with fellow politicians. In particular, she liked the company of very bright male officials, like Sedwill, Heywood, Robbins, Peter Hill and Deputy National Security Advisor Christian Turner.

No relationship with a Cabinet minister was more difficult than that with Hammond, and in her final two months, the relationship deteriorated to its barely functioning state of late 2016 and early 2017. Just after announcing her resignation, she carefully wrote out the policy priorities that she wanted to advance with what time remained. These included carbon net zero legislation, progress on the higher education review, spending on schools, mental health, parental leave consultation, the Domestic Abuse Bill introduced, the disability strategy developed, an office for tackling injustice established, and speeches on the Union and the deterioration of political discourse. She took the decision that she would not involve herself any further in discussions on Brexit, and neither would she give her successor problems by talking about a prorogation of Parliament. Her sole focus was to be on domestic matters.

With less legislation going through the House, and Brexit off the table, Tory MPs became more biddable, many positively excited at the prospect of having, at last, a 'Brexit Prime Minister'. She spoke to Hammond several times in the week beginning Monday 3 June, thanking him for his support on projects for the 'just about managing' families. But he told her firmly that he was unwilling to dip into any of the £27 billion fiscal pot he had set aside to help the economy cope with the impact of a no-deal Brexit, his so-called war chest, until a Brexit deal had been approved.[12] May fought hard throughout June for a three-year funding deal to build new schools and pay teachers higher salaries, but the Chancellor repeatedly resisted. Eventually, in early July, he told her that he would fund an extra £3–5 billion for schools, buildings and teacher salaries, but only if she allowed Conservative MPs a free vote in attempts to stop a no-deal Brexit.[13] She came back to him to say that, if those were the terms, she could not accept the money because it would be quite improper for her to do so. As relations plummeted, she made no secret of her fury at him. Hammond says:

> I never came close to resigning throughout the three years. But had she forced the education spending at the end, I might well have considered doing so, because I considered it completely wrong for an outgoing administration to make such a significant strategic financial decision with a new government just about to take office. I was also unconvinced by the argument that further spending was the answer: Britain has the second highest school spending in the G7, but the second worst outcomes.[14]

The dispute left a bitter taste in both their mouths: Hammond fell out not only with May but also with Barwell, who together with Macfarlane (now in Brussels) had been responsible for the much-improved Chancellor–Prime Minister relationship since the general election. Sedwill was drawn into the dispute, siding with the Treasury view on spending. Implementing the higher education review and schools aside, May was able to significantly advance her designated target list of legacy projects, which brought her much satisfaction.

She wanted to make a final curtain call with the media, notwithstanding her awkward and distant relationship with it over the previous three years. The *Daily Mail* was chosen as the newspaper to conduct the exit interview with her, while the BBC was selected as the broadcaster for her final television interview, in recognition of the two key media influences on her last two years, Robbie Gibb (ex-BBC) and James Slack (ex-*Daily Mail*). Laura Kuenssberg tried with limited success to get May to open up in an interview in the Downing Street flat, encouraging her into admitting that she should have taken part in the TV debates during the general election, and that she had failed to appreciate that the real Brexit battle would be not against the EU but against her fellow Conservatives. But for all the broadcaster's skill, she still couldn't make May relax and be herself. She nevertheless allowed May to talk about her successes, including the NHS Long Term Plan, the net zero announcement on carbon emissions, the lowest unemployment and the highest house-building levels 'for many years'.[15] The interview was a personal closure of kinds too: Kuenssberg had probed May relentlessly throughout her three years, No. 10 felt unfairly. Then again, it has never felt well treated by the BBC.

May poured more of herself into a speech, her last substantial one as Prime Minister, given at London's Chatham House on 17 July. She had become animated in her final weeks about the theme of compromise. This was the subject she chose to air in her swansong. She had become 'worried about the state of politics' and the 'coarsening [of] our public debate', she said. Intended to be a powerful defence of liberalism and compromise as the driving forces that sustain democracy, the speech provoked criticism from those who said compromise is precisely what she was not willing to display towards the 48.1 per cent who voted Remain: 'She made no attempt to bring the country together, to seek the sort of compromise she so lauded today ... Theresa May bemoans the rise of populism, but she should look in the mirror,' said Sky.[16] The speech, a very rare personal meditation by May, deserved more attention, and had echoes of a similar speech given by Blair, who also enjoyed a long endgame, when on 12 June 2007 he attacked the 'feral' media, saying, 'The fear of missing out means today's media, more than ever before, hunts in a pack ... just tearing people and reputations to bits.' May would have echoed that sentiment.

May followed the cricket World Cup intently from the first match on 30 May to the final on 14 July, within a week of her leaving No. 10. The six-week arc of matches by the ten teams of the tournament nicely mirrored her entire final period in office. On edge for the semifinal at Edgbaston between Australia and England on 11 July, she was monitoring progress closely. 'It's all going well, Prime Minister,' Peter Hill shouted through the double doors between his private secretary's office and her study. 'Shut up, you'll jinx it,' she fired back. The long farewell and the removal of pressure gave May the opportunity to spend a weekend watching sport: Saturday at Wimbledon on 13 July for the ladies' final (an easy victory for Simona Halep over Serena Williams) and Sunday at Lord's, where she was in her element. So much so, she invited the victorious England squad into Downing Street for a reception the following day. 'In three years, I never saw her happier,' says one of her aides. The team recognised her as a genuine enthusiast for the game, and listened while she spoke to them:

> The final was not just cricket at its best but sport at its best – courage, character, sportsmanship, drama, incredible skill and even the odd slice of luck ... Yesterday, we saw a final for the ages. And here today we have a team that will be spoken of in awe for generations to come.

'Talk about resilience,' one of the players said. 'She's the one who had it.'

THE FINAL TWO DAYS: 23–24 JULY

The morning of Tuesday 23 July saw May's final Cabinet. Two items of business were dispatched smartly, Hancock talking about the NHS and Lidington about the implementation of government policy over the previous three years. All eyes then turned to May, to utter her final words in the Cabinet Room. Even her harshest critic recognised that they were witnessing history. She spoke about what she had done as PM, her hopes for the future, and that the next Cabinet under her successor would protect the Conservative Party and the Union. As she did so, she began welling up until she could carry on no further. An awkward pause, the ministers collectively stood up and gave her a standing ovation to get through it. Lidington then gave a short speech, saying the three facets that most characterised her were: first, her trying to help those who were not the winners, mentioning modern slavery, the gender pay gap, rough sleepers and mental health sufferers; second, her commitment to the Union; and third, her 'deep sense of public duty and service'. At that point, Gove slipped out of the room and came back with the two gifts. He'd texted Cabinet ministers earlier in the week to ask for a £20 donation from each of them – Smith said they should all give £50 – and Gove's wife Sarah was asked to select the gifts, a Liberty bucket bag and a Lalique necklace. As they all clapped while she unwrapped them, her team sitting in chairs around the room had a bitter taste in their mouths, thinking, 'That's all a bit rich, for the last two years many of you had been truly awful to her.'

May's team bade farewell to her that afternoon. Liz Sanderson had bought her a vase, which she gave her in an impromptu party in the Cabinet ante room. This was the farewell that meant the most to her – these were the people who had stuck by her all the way through – and with tears in her eyes she held the vase up in the air for all to see, as if it was a football trophy.

At 11 a.m. the next day she went off for her final PMQs in the Commons. As she walked into the Chamber, Tory MPs erupted in loud cheers, including Duncan Smith, very obviously waving his order paper and smiling support. Rees-Mogg paid tribute to her 'remarkable public service'. Her best line was against Corbyn, who remained rebarbative to the end. 'As a party leader who has accepted when her time is up,' May said, 'might I just suggest that perhaps the time is now for him to do the same?'

She returned to Downing Street for lunch, and then at 2 p.m. she went upstairs to the Pillared Room: staff across the building crowded in to listen to her say that she felt they'd achieved a huge amount, 'if not everything they sought to achieve', that she always felt they'd 'worked together as a team' and was very proud of having worked with them. She went down for a final time to her study to collect her thoughts while her staff lined up in the corridor leading out to the front door.

Her closest team, who had been with her without a break for two years, had gathered in the front hall immediately behind the door. She stopped to say a few final words to them, and then Philip spontaneously thanked everybody. When her eyes welled up with tears, the team followed suit. The world's press on the other side of the door waited while the Mays were shuffled across into the No. 11 entrance hall to compose themselves for two or three minutes. When she was ready, the door opened and she walked over to the lectern, where her leaving speech was waiting for her, gently blowing in the afternoon breeze.

ACKNOWLEDGEMENTS

First and foremost, I would like to acknowledge my thanks to principal researcher and associate author Raymond Newell, who has been a superb support, working without a break since we began this project together in February 2019. Raymond achieved a brilliant first at the University of Buckingham in December 2018 and has a maturity, knowledge and understanding way beyond his years. He has been an inspirational colleague throughout. I can see him going very far in life. He is among the most impressive 21-year-olds I have ever met. I must thank too his parents, Bob and Elizabeth, and his girlfriend Jessie, for allowing me so much of his time.

We were blessed with a team of exceptional researchers, including Ed Dolley, Peter Gallagher, Natasha Hornby, Daniel Oakey, Morgan Proverbs and Lindsay Singh, all students from the university. Ian Kelly provided excellent research early on, as did Saskia Pain and Lily Rosengard in later stages. Alice Billin proved a master at producing coherent text. A special thanks go to Sam Earle, who helped in the latter stages of preparing excellent chapter briefs and updating the text. Angela Reed of Wellington College, the doyenne of heads' PAs, was always at the end of a phone for any names and other information.

Sarah Sayer was a constant support at my side throughout writing this book, helping me hugely through some very weary and hard times.

Fellow university leaders have been uniformly supportive, none more so than Alistair Jarvis, chief executive of Universities UK. Nick Hillman and Mary Curnock Cook have been wonderful counsellors.

At the University of Buckingham, my thanks go to my council, headed by our superb chair, Rory Tapner, and deputy chair, John McIntosh. My senior colleagues were also extraordinarily understanding and supportive of a VC who tried not to miss a day but was periodically tired: Jane Tapsell, John Clapham and Emma Potts. I'd like to thank them as well as my executive, Deba Bardhan-Correia, Chrissa Beaumont, Sandra Clarke, Ian Creagh, Paul Jennings, Barnaby Lenon, Alistair Lomax, Alan Martin, Chris Payne, Harin Sellahewa, Greg Simons, Karol Sikora. I must thank my humanities colleagues in particular, including Nick Rees, Paul Graham, Anthony Glees and Alan Smithers, Jane Ridley and Geoffrey Alderman, and Festival of HE colleagues James Seymour and Patrick Watson. My own office have been sublime, headed by the remarkable Purnima Anhal and including Jenny Carter, Sharon Horwood and Heidi Stopps. Diana Blamires and Emily Reed have been excellent heads of media. The entire book was corrected and re-corrected by Julie Cakebread, a stunning colleague and professional.

Martin Redfern from Northbank has shown why he is the best agent in London, picking up for me so capably from the sadly departed Ed Victor. Biteback have been an excellent publisher, and I must thank in particular James Stephens, Olivia Beattie, who edited the whole book, and Suzanne Sangster, who did the publicity. Jane Sherwood chose the photographs, and Nic Nicholas produced a superb index.

I would like to thank all of those who agreed to be interviewed. The 175 interviews varied between half an hour and four hours. Because many are officials or still serving in government, it would be wrong to mention them by name, apart from those who have agreed to extracts appearing in the text. To those who served in 10 Downing Street, thank you to Gavin Barwell, Keelan Carr, Nikki da Costa, Denzil Davidson, Alex Dawson, Robbie Gibb, John Godfrey, Fiona Hill, Lizzie Loudon,

James Marshall, JoJo Penn, Raoul Ruparel, James Slack, Peter Storr, Tom Swarbrick, Will Tanner, Nick Timothy and Chris Wilkins.

To those in Parliament, both now and formerly, thank you to Steve Baker, Lord Bilimoria, Karen Bradley, Graham Brady, Lord Bridges, Greg Clark, Geoffrey Cox, David Davis, Iain Duncan Smith, Michael Fallon, Liam Fox, Michael Gove, Justine Greening, Ben Gummer, Philip Hammond, Damian Hinds, George Hollingbery, Jeremy Hunt, Seema Kennedy, Andrea Leadsom, Oliver Letwin, Brandon Lewis, David Lidington, Patrick McLoughlin, Nicky Morgan, Lord O'Shaughnessy, George Osborne, Dominic Raab, Amber Rudd, Julian Smith, Keir Starmer and Gavin Williamson.

Thank you too to those in Europe who took the time to help inform the book, most of all Martin Selmayr and Guy Verhofstadt.

Many took immense trouble to help. Nineteen individuals read the entire book, or sections of it, to help ensure accuracy and completeness. Again, I thank them all, even though I cannot mention them by name, except for the academic Professor Vernon Bogdanor, former diplomat Sir Anthony Goodenough, Jonathan Caine, Alex Dawson, Christopher Everett, Will Macfarlane and Joseph Moore. Their wise comments were invaluable.

Having very few published books to guide us, it meant we were even more reliant on outstanding works by, above all, Tim Shipman, as well on the pivotal 2017 general election, by Dennis Kavanagh and Jason Cowley, and by Tim Ross and Tom McTague. Rosa Prince wrote a very thoughtful and insightful study of Theresa May's earlier years.

These were boosted by some very fine reporting and commentaries in the newspapers. We would like to thank David Aaronovitch, Katya Adler, Katy Balls, Adam Boulton, Stephen Bush, Philip Collins, Jason Cowley, Francis Elliott, James Forsyth, Laura Kuenssberg, Anne McElvoy, Fraser Nelson, Matthew Parris, Nick Robinson, Heather Stewart, Rachel Sylvester and many, many more for their fantastic reporting in these turbulent times.

I would like to thank Suzanne Heywood for allowing me to dedicate this book to her late husband, Lord Heywood of Whitehall, whose influences is felt on almost every page, long after his death in late 2018.

Parts of the book were written while staying in Dorset with John and Lou James, on weekends in Budapest, Stratford-upon-Avon, the Peak District and the trenches, and in my spiritual home, Saint-Jean-de-Côle on the Limousin–Périgord border. I would like to thank Herman, Anne and Cate from Agence Immobilière, and all our many friends in the incomparable village.

The six-month crush on this book meant I neglected my responsibilities to the bodies I am associated with and care about, but who nevertheless were uniformly understanding and supportive, including Action for Happiness, the Royal Shakespeare Company, 14–18 NOW, the National Archives Trust, the No. 10 History Project, the Via Sacra/Western Front Way Association, the International Positive Education Network, iDEA and more.

Many people have influenced my thinking over my six books on Prime Ministers. At Oxford, David Butler, Vernon Bogdanor, Copper Le May, Gillian Peele, and Dick Smethurst were my principal inspirations. At the LSE, it was my supervisor John Barnes and colleague George Jones. At the Institute of Contemporary British History, it has been Peter Hennessy, Dennis Kavanagh and Kathleen Burk. My earlier associates or co-authors on previous books have guided me enormously, even if unconsciously: Lewis Baston, Daniel Collings, Peter Snowdon, Stuart Ball and Guy Lodge.

I would like to thank my own children, Jessica, Susie and Adam, who have been such supports and inspirations. It is the first book on a Prime Minister I've written since my wife Joanna died in December 2016. I missed her every day I was researching and writing this book. She was prodigiously bright, superhumanly thoughtful, and my best friend.

BIBLIOGRAPHY

BOOKS

Jon Davis and John Rentoul, *Heroes or Villains? The Blair Government Reconsidered* (Oxford University Press, 2019)

Dennis Kavanagh and Philip Cowley, *The British General Election of 2017* (Palgrave Macmillan, 2018)

Oliver Letwin, *Hearts and Minds: The Battle for the Conservative Party from Thatcher to the Present* (Biteback Publishing, 2017)

Craig Oliver, *Unleashing Demons: The Inside Story of Brexit* (Hodder & Stoughton, 2016)

Rosa Prince, *Theresa May: The Enigmatic Prime Minister* (Biteback Publishing, 2017)

Andrew Rawnsley, *The End of the Party* (Viking, 2010)

Tim Ross and Tom McTague, *Betting the House: The Inside Story of the 2017 Election* (Biteback Publishing, 2017)

Anthony Seldon, *Churchill's Indian Summer: The Conservative Government, 1951–55* (Faber & Faber, 2010)

Anthony Seldon, *Blair Unbound* (Simon & Schuster, 2007)

Anthony Seldon, *John Major: A Political Life* (Weidenfeld & Nicolson, 1997)

Anthony Seldon and Guy Lodge, *Brown at 10* (Biteback Publishing, 2011)

Anthony Seldon and Jonathan Meakin, *The Cabinet Office 1916–2016: The Birth of Modern Government* (Biteback Publishing, 2016)

Anthony Seldon and Peter Snowdon, *Cameron at 10: The Verdict* (William Collins, 2016)

Tim Shipman, *All Out War: The Full Story of Brexit* (William Collins, 2017)

Tim Shipman, *Fall Out: A Year of Political Mayhem* (William Collins, 2016)

ARTICLES AND REPORTS

Peter Foster, 'Fiasco: The inside story of the Brexit talks', *Prospect*, 2 September 2019

Tom McTague, 'How the UK lost the Brexit battle', Politico, 27 March 2019

Matthew Taylor, 'Good Work: The Taylor Review of Modern Working Practices', Gov.UK, 2017

DOCUMENTARIES

The Brexit Storm: Laura Kuenssberg's Inside Story, BBC Two, 20 April 2019

Panorama, 'Britain's Brexit Crisis', BBC One, 18 July 2019

Storyville, 'Brexit: Behind Closed Doors', BBC Four, 8 and 9 May 2019

WORKS BY ANTHONY SELDON

Churchill's Indian Summer: The Conservative Government, 1951–55 (Hodder & Stoughton, 1981)

By Word of Mouth: 'Élite' Oral History (with Joanna Pappworth, Methuen, 1983)

Ruling Performance: British Governments from Attlee to Thatcher (ed., with Peter Hennessy, Basil Blackwell, 1987)

The Thatcher Effect: A Decade of Change (ed., with Dennis Kavanagh, Oxford University Press, 1989)

UK Political Parties Since 1945 (ed., Philip Allan, 1990)

Politics UK (joint author, Philip Allan, 1991)

Conservative Century: The Conservative Party Since 1900 (ed., with Stuart Ball, Oxford University Press, 1994)

The Major Effect (ed., with Dennis Kavanagh, Macmillan, 1994)

The Heath Government 1970–1974: A Reappraisal (ed., with Stuart Ball, Longman, 1996)

The Contemporary History Handbook (ed., with Brian Brivati and Julia Buxton, Manchester University Press, 1996)

The Ideas that Shaped Post-war Britain (ed., with David Marquand, Fontana, 1996)

How Tory Governments Fall: The Tory Party in Power Since 1783 (ed., Fontana, 1996)

John Major: A Political Life (with Lewis Baston, Weidenfeld & Nicolson, 1997)

10 Downing Street: The Illustrated History (HarperCollinsIllustrated, 1999)

The Powers Behind the Prime Minister: The Hidden Influence of Number Ten (with Dennis Kavanagh, HarperCollins, 1999)

Britain Under Thatcher (with Daniel Collings, Longman, 2000)

The Foreign Office: An Illustrated History of the Place and its People (HarperCollinsIllustrated, 2000)

A New Conservative Century? (Centre for Policy Studies, 2001)

The Blair Effect (ed., Little, Brown, 2001)

Public and Private Education: The Divide Must End (Social Market Foundation, 2001)

Partnership not Paternalism (Institute for Public Policy Research, 2002)

Brave New City: Brighton & Hove, Past, Present, Future (with Matthew Nurse, Edward Twohig and Chris Horlock, Pomegranate Press, 2002)

The Conservative Party: An Illustrated History (with Peter Snowdon, Sutton, 2004)

New Labour, Old Labour: The Wilson and Callaghan Governments, 1974–79 (ed., with Kevin Hickson, Routledge, 2004)

Blair (with Chris Ballinger, Daniel Collings and Peter Snowden, Free, 2004)

The Blair Effect 2001–5 (ed., with Dennis Kavanagh, Cambridge University Press, 2005)

Recovering Power: The Conservatives in Opposition since 1867 (ed., with Stuart Ball, Palgrave Macmillan, 2005)

Blair Unbound (with Peter Snowdon and Daniel Collings, Simon & Schuster, 2007)

Blair's Britain 1997–2007 (ed., Cambridge University Press, 2007)

Trust: How We Lost it and How to Get it Back (Biteback Publishing, 2009)

An End to Factory Schools: An Education Manifesto 2010–2020 (Centre for Policy Studies, 2010)

Why Schools, Why Universities? (Cass, 2010)

Brown at 10 (with Guy Lodge, Biteback Publishing, 2011)

Public Schools and the Great War: The Generation Lost (with David Walsh, Pen & Sword Military, 2013)

Schools United: Ending the Divide Between Independent and State (The Social Market Foundation, 2014)

Architecture of Diplomacy: The British Ambassador's Residence in Washington (with Daniel Collings, Flammarion, 2014)

Beyond Happiness: The Trap of Happiness and How to Find Deeper Meaning and Joy (Yellow Kite, 2015)

The Coalition Effect, 2010–2015 (ed., with Mike Finn, Cambridge University Press, 2015)

Cameron at 10: The Inside Story 2010–2015 (with Peter Snowon, William Collins, 2015)

Teaching and Learning at British Universities (Social Market Foundation, 2016)

The Cabinet Office 1916–2016: The Birth of Modern Government (with Jonathan Meakin, Biteback Publishing, 2016)

The Positive and Mindful University (with Alan Martin, Higher Education Policy Institute, 2017)

The Fourth Education Revolution: Will Artificial Intelligence Liberate or Infantilise Humanity (with Oladimeji Abidoye, University of Birmingham Press, 2018)

ENDNOTES

CHAPTER 1: MADE IN THE HOME OFFICE

1   *The Guardian*, 13 July 2016.
2   Interview, John Godfrey.
3   Interview, Fiona Hill.
4   Interview, Nick Timothy.
5   Interview with Theresa May, Eleanor Mills, *Sunday Times*, 27 November 2016.
6   Theresa May, BBC Radio 4, *Desert Island Discs*, 23 November 2014.
7   Rosa Prince, *Sunday Telegraph*, 26 May 2019.
8   Interview, Fiona Hill.
9   Theresa May, BBC Radio 4, *Desert Island Discs*, 23 November 2014.
10   Interview with Theresa May, *Daily Telegraph*, 21 December 2012.
11   Rosa Prince, *Sunday Telegraph*, 26 May 2019.
12   Theresa May, BBC Radio 4, *Desert Island Discs*, 23 November 2014.
13   Rosa Prince, *Sunday Telegraph*, 26 May 2019.
14   Interview, Ed Whiting.
15   Interview, Chris Wilkins.
16   Diabetes.co.uk, 'Theresa May'.
17   Interview, Chris Wilkins.
18   Interview, Chris Wilkins.
19   Interview, Nick Timothy.
20   Anthony Seldon, *Blair Unbound*.
21   Interview, Nick Timothy.
22   Interview, Fiona Hill.
23   Interview, Nick Timothy.
24   Interview, Will Tanner.
25   *New Statesman*, 24 May 2019.
26   Interview, Nick Timothy.
27   *New Statesman*, 24 May 2019.
28   Interview, Chris Wilkins.
29   Interview, Chris Wilkins.
30   Interview, Nick Timothy.
31   Interview, JoJo Penn.
32   Interview, Nick Timothy.
33   Interview, Nick Timothy.
34   Anthony Seldon, *Cameron at 10*.
35   *The Sun*, 1 October 2014.
36   *The Sun*, 1 October 2014.
37   Patrick Sawer, *Sunday Telegraph*, 23 November 2014.

38 *Daily Mail*, 25 November 2014.
39 Telegraph Online, 25 November 2014.
40 Interview, Will Tanner.
41 Interview, Fiona Hill.
42 Interview, George Osborne.
43 Interview, Nick Timothy.
44 Anthony Seldon, *Cameron at 10*.
45 Interview, Nick Timothy.
46 Interview, Craig Oliver.
47 Tim Shipman, *Fall Out: A Year of Political Mayhem*, p. 30.
48 Interview, Nick Timothy.
49 Tim Shipman, *Fall Out*, p. 30.
50 Interview, Nick Timothy.
51 Interview, Nick Timothy.
52 Interview, Nick Timothy.
53 Interview, Will Tanner.
54 Interview, Will Tanner.
55 Interview, Will Tanner.
56 Interview, Fiona Hill.
57 Interview, Nick Timothy.
58 Interview, Nick Timothy.
59 Interview, Fiona Hill.
60 Interview, Will Tanner.
61 Private correspondence.
62 Interview, Will Tanner.
63 Interview, Nick Timothy.
64 Interview, Will Tanner.
65 Interview, Lizzie Loudon.
66 Interview, Will Tanner.
67 Interview, Luke Tryl.
68 Interview, Nick Timothy.
69 Interview, Tim Loughton.
70 Interview, Nick Timothy.
71 Interview, Nick Timothy.
72 Interview, Michael Gove.
73 Interview, Fiona Hill.
74 Interview, Tim Loughton.
75 *The Times*, 9 July 2016.
76 Interview, Tim Loughton.
77 Interview, Rachel Sylvester.
78 Interview, Fiona Hill.
79 Interview, Lizzie Loudon.
80 Interview, Fiona Hill.
81 Interview, Nick Timothy.
82 Interview, Fiona Hill.
83 Interview, Lizzie Loudon.

CHAPTER 2: FORTRESS NO. 10
1 Interview, Nick Timothy.
2 Interview, Will Tanner.
3 Anthony Seldon, *John Major: A Political Life*.
4 Interview, Chris Wilkins.
5 Interview, Lizzie Loudon.
6 Interview, Craig Oliver.

7   Interview, Chris Wilkins.
8   Interview, Nick Timothy.
9   Interview, Nick Timothy.
10   Interview, Nick Timothy.
11   Interview, Fiona Hill.
12   Interview, Fiona Hill.
13   Interview, Ben Gummer.
14   Interview, Nick Timothy.
15   Interview, Will Tanner.
16   Andrew Rawnsley, *The End of the Party*; Anthony Seldon and Guy Lodge, *Brown at 10*.
17   Tim Shipman, *Fall Out*.
18   Interview, Fiona Hill.
19   Interview, Nick Timothy.
20   Anthony Seldon, *The Cabinet Office*.
21   Anthony Seldon and Guy Lodge, *Brown at 10*.
22   Interview, Nick Timothy.
23   Interview, Chris Wilkins.
24   Interview, Fiona Hill.
25   Interview, Fiona Hill.
26   Interview, John Godfrey.
27   Interview, Chris Wilkins.
28   Interview, Chris Wilkins.
29   Interview, JoJo Penn.
30   Interview, Fiona Hill.
31   Interview, Nick Timothy.
32   Interview, Ben Gummer.
33   Andrew Gimson, ConservativeHome, 1 March 2017.
34   Interview, Fiona Hill.
35   Interview, Will Tanner.
36   Interview, Nick Timothy.
37   Interview, JoJo Penn.
38   Interview, JoJo Penn.
39   Interview, Ed Whiting.
40   Interview, Ed Whiting.
41   Interview, Nick Timothy.
42   Heather Stewart, *The Guardian*, 14 July 2016.
43   Anthony Seldon, *Cabinet Committees and Coordination*.
44   Interview, Fiona Hill.
45   *Daily Mirror*, 14 July 2016.
46   Interview, Fiona Hill.
47   Interview, Nick Timothy.
48   Interview, Philip Hammond.
49   Interview, Fiona Hill.
50   Interview, Fiona Hill.
51   Interview, Nick Timothy.
52   Anthony Seldon, *Cameron at 10*.
53   Interview, George Osborne.
54   Interview, George Osborne.
55   *Daily Telegraph*, 13 September 2017.
56   Interview, Fiona Hill.
57   Tim Shipman, *All Out War*, pp. 587–8.
58   Interview, Luke Tryl.
59   Interview, Nick Timothy.
60   BBC News, 14 July 2016.

61 Heather Stewart, *The Guardian*, 14 July 2016.
62 Interview, Nick Timothy.
63 Interview, Gavin Williamson.
64 Interview, Nick Timothy.
65 Interview, Will Tanner.
66 Interview, John Godfrey.
67 Interview, Nick Timothy.
68 Interview, Nick Timothy.
69 Interview, Will Tanner.
70 Jessica Elgot, *The Guardian*, 10 August 2016.
71 Interview, Fiona Hill.
72 BBC News, 5 September 2016.
73 Interview, Gavin Williamson.
74 Anthony Seldon, *Churchill's Indian Summer*.
75 Interview, Ben Gummer.
76 Tim Shipman, *Sunday Times*, 2 October 2016.
77 Interview, Jason Cowley.
78 Interview, Nick Timothy.
79 Nick Timothy, ConservativeHome, 20 October 2015.
80 Interview, Nick Timothy.
81 Interview, Fiona Hill.
82 Laura Kuenssberg, BBC News, 15 September 2016.
83 Interview, Nick Timothy.
84 Interview, Nick Timothy.
85 Interview, Rachel Wolf.
86 Graham Brady, *Daily Telegraph*, 19 July 2016.
87 ITV News, 6 September 2016.
88 Interview, Tom Swarbrick.

CHAPTER 3: A HARD COURSE TO BREXIT, 2016–17
1   Interview, Fiona Hill.
2   Anthony Seldon and Peter Snowdon, *Cameron at 10*.
3   Message, Nick Timothy to author, 4 April 2019.
4   Interview, Fiona Hill.
5   Interview, Will Tanner.
6   Interview, Peter Storr.
7   Interview, Peter Storr.
8   Interview, Fiona Hill.
9   Interview, Ivan Rogers.
10 Interview, Ivan Rogers.
11 Oliver Letwin, *Hearts and Minds: The Battle for the Conservative Party from Thatcher to the Present*, pp. 25–6.
12 Oliver Letwin, *Hearts and Minds*.
13 Interview, Peter Storr.
14 Interview, Denzil Davidson.
15 Interview, Ivan Rogers.
16 Interview, Chris Wilkins.
17 Interview, Ivan Rogers.
18 Interview, Nick Timothy.
19 Interview, Nick Timothy.
20 Interview, Nick Timothy.
21 Interview, Ivan Rogers.
22 Interview, Ivan Rogers.
23 Interview, Ivan Rogers.

24 Interview, Peter Storr.
25 Interview, Chris Wilkins.
26 Interview, Guy Verhofstadt.
27 Interview, James O'Shaughnessy.
28 Interview, Michel Barnier.
29 Interview, Martin Selmayr.
30 Interview, George Osborne.
31 Interview, Ivan Rogers.
32 Interview, Nick Timothy.
33 Interview, Martin Selmayr.
34 Theresa May, resignation speech, 24 May 2019.
35 Interview, Chris Wilkins.
36 Interview, Craig Oliver.
37 *The Times*, 3 March 2015.
38 BBC Radio 4, *Today*, 20 November 2018.
39 Interview, Nick Timothy.
40 Interview, Nick Timothy.
41 Interview, Ivan Rogers.
42 Interview, Peter Storr.
43 Interview, Chris Wilkins.
44 Interview, Will Tanner.
45 Interview, Nick Timothy.
46 Interview, Ivan Rogers.
47 Interview, Nick Timothy.
48 Interview, Nick Timothy.
49 Interview, Chris Wilkins.
50 Interview, Nick Timothy.
51 Interview, Chris Wilkins.
52 *The Guardian*, 12 October 2016.
53 *Washington Post*, 5 October 2016.
54 *The Guardian*, 10 October 2016.
55 Interview, Ivan Rogers.
56 Interview, Nick Timothy.
57 Interview, Peter Storr.
58 Interview, Ivan Rogers.
59 *The Economist*, 7 January 2017.
60 Interview, Fiona Hill.
61 Interview, Ivan Rogers.
62 *Daily Telegraph*, 15 December 2016.
63 Interview, Ivan Rogers.
64 Interview, Chris Wilkins.
65 Interview, Nick Timothy.
66 Interview, Fiona Hill.
67 Interview, Philip Hammond.
68 Interview, Nick Timothy.
69 *The Guardian*, 31 May 2016.
70 *Daily Mail*, 4 November 2016.
71 Interview, Denzil Davidson.
72 Interview, Nick Timothy.
73 Interview, Guy Verhofstadt.
74 Interview, Fiona Hill.
75 Interview, Martin Selmayr.
76 *Frankfurter Allgemeine Zeitung*, 29 April 2017.
77 Interview, Denzil Davidson.

78   Interview, Martin Selmayr.

CHAPTER 4: BUILDING HER BRAND

1   Interview, Fiona Hill.
2   *The Times*, 15 May 1973.
3   Interview, Chris Wilkins.
4   *The Guardian*, 5 October 2016.
5   Interview, Tom Swarbrick.
6   Interview, Fiona Hill.
7   *The Guardian*, 17 November 2016.
8   Interview, Fiona Hill.
9   BBC News, 13 November 2016.
10   'Theresa May's Underwhelming Visit', *The Hindu*, 11 November 2016.
11   Interview, Lord Bilimoria.
12   Interview, Fiona Hill.
13   *The Guardian*, 19 January 2017.
14   Interview, Nick Timothy.
15   *Daily Telegraph*, 10 November 2016.
16   Interview, Nick Timothy.
17   Interview, Fiona Hill.
18   Interview, Fiona Hill.
19   Interview, Chris Wilkins.
20   Interview, Chris Wilkins.
21   Interview, Nick Timothy.
22   *The Times*, 27 January 2017.
23   Interview, Chris Wilkins.
24   Interview, Chris Wilkins.
25   Interview, Fiona Hill.
26   Interview, Chris Wilkins.
27   Interview, Fiona Hill.
28   Interview, Fiona Hill.
29   Interview, Patrick McLoughlin.
30   Interview, Fiona Hill.
31   Interview, Fiona Hill.
32   Interview, Nick Timothy.
33   Interview, Philip Hammond.
34   Interview, Philip Hammond.
35   Interview, Will Tanner.
36   Interview, Will Tanner.
37   Interview, John Godfrey.
38   Interview, Fiona Hill.
39   Interview, Will Tanner.
40   *The Guardian*, 23 November 2016.
41   Interview, Ben Gummer.
42   Interview, Chris Wilkins.
43   Chris Wilkins, 'Long Read: Inside No. 10, July 2016 to July 2017', The UK in a Changing Europe, 5 February 2016.
44   Chris Wilkins, 'Long Read: Inside No. 10, from July 2016 to July 2017', The UK in a Changing Europe, 5 February 2016.
45   Interview, Chris Wilkins.
46   Interview, Will Tanner.
47   *Daily Telegraph*, 3 October 2016.
48   Interview, Will Tanner.
49   May hosted a reception for DrugFAM at No. 10 on 27 November 2017.

50   Interview, Chris Wilkins.
51   Interview, Will Tanner.
52   Interview, Will Tanner.
53   Interview, Chris Wilkins.
54   Tim Shipman, *Fall Out*, p. 149.
55   Interview, Nick Timothy.
56   Interview, Nick Timothy.
57   Interview, Lizzie Loudon.

CHAPTER 5: THE PIVOT: THE 2017 GENERAL ELECTION
1   Jon Stone, *The Independent*, 18 April 2017.
2   Email, Stuart Ball to author, 26 May 2019.
3   Interview, Nick Timothy.
4   Interview, Fiona Hill.
5   Interview, Patrick McLoughlin.
6   Interview, Nick Timothy.
7   Interview, Philip Hammond.
8   Interview, Nick Timothy.
9   Interview, James Slack.
10   *The Guardian*, 29 March 2017.
11   Interview, Nick Timothy.
12   Dennis Kavanagh and Philip Cowley, *The British General Election of 2017*, pp. 58–9.
13   Interview, Lynton Crosby.
14   William Hague, 'The Case for an Early General Election: Theresa May should be free to put her Brexit plan to the British people', *Daily Telegraph*, 6 March 2017.
15   Dennis Kavanagh and Philip Cowley, *The British General Election of 2017*, pp. 56–7.
16   Interview, Fiona Hill.
17   Interview, Chris Wilkins.
18   Interview, Chris Wilkins.
19   Interview, Fiona Hill.
20   Interview, Nick Timothy.
21   Interview, Fiona Hill.
22   Interview, Chris Wilkins.
23   *The Independent*, 7 February 2005.
24   *The Observer*, 2 April 2016.
25   Interview, Chris Wilkins.
26   Interview, Fiona Hill.
27   Interview, Lynton Crosby.
28   *The Guardian*, 19 March 2018.
29   Tim Shipman, *Fall Out*, p. 192.
30   Dennis Kavanagh and Philip Cowley, *The British General Election of 2017*, p. 64.
31   Interview, Gavin Williamson.
32   Interview, Gavin Williamson.
33   Interview, Fiona Hill.
34   Interview, Fiona Hill.
35   Interview, Patrick McLoughlin.
36   Interview, Gavin Williamson.
37   Interview, Lizzie Loudon.
38   Interview, Patrick McLoughlin.
39   Interview, Gavin Williamson.
40   Interview, Tom Swarbrick.
41   Interview, Patrick McLoughlin.
42   Tim Shipman, *Fall Out*, pp. 193–4.
43   Tim Shipman, *Fall Out*, p. 5.

44   Interview, Nick Timothy.
45   Dennis Kavanagh and Philip Cowley, *The British General Election of 2017*, p. 167.
46   Interview, Patrick McLoughlin.
47   Dennis Kavanagh and Philip Cowley, *The British General Election of 2017*, p. 170.
48   Interview, Nick Timothy.
49   Interview, Fiona Hill.
50   Dennis Kavanagh and Philip Cowley, *The British General Election of 2017*, pp. 156–7.
51   Interview, Ben Gummer.
52   Interview, Ben Gummer.
53   Interview, Nick Timothy.
54   Interview, John Godfrey.
55   Interview, Will Tanner.
56   Dennis Kavanagh and Philip Cowley, *The British General Election of 2017*, pp. 185–6.
57   Interview, Fiona Hill.
58   Dennis Kavanagh and Philip Cowley, *The British General Election of 2017*, pp. 186–8.
59   Dennis Kavanagh and Philip Cowley, *The British General Election of 2017*, pp. 189–90.
60   Interview, John Godfrey.
61   Dennis Kavanagh and Philip Cowley, *The British General Election of 2017*, Chapter 8.
62   Interview, Will Tanner.
63   Interview, Chris Wilkins.
64   Interview, Fiona Hill.
65   Interview, Nick Timothy.
66   'Forward, Together', Conservative Party manifesto, May 2017.
67   *The Guardian*, 21 May 2017.
68   Andrew Dilnot, BBC Radio 4, *Today*, 18 May 2017.
69   Interview, Fiona Hill.
70   Dennis Kavanagh and Philip Cowley, *The British General Election of 2017*, p. 195.
71   Dennis Kavanagh and Philip Cowley, *The British General Election of 2017*, p. 196.
72   Interview, Nick Timothy.
73   Dennis Kavanagh and Philip Cowley, *The British General Election of 2017*, pp. 196–7.
74   *Sunday Times*, 21 May 2017.
75   Interview, Tom Swarbrick.
76   Interview, Lynton Crosby.
77   BBC News, 22 May 2017.
78   Interview, Fiona Hill.
79   Interview, Chris Wilkins; Message, Chris Wilkins to author.
80   Dennis Kavanagh and Philip Cowley, *The British General Election of 2017*, pp. 218–21.
81   Interview, Craig Oliver.
82   Dennis Kavanagh and Philip Cowley, *The British General Election of 2017*, p. 203.
83   BBC News, 30 April 2017.
84   Interview, Lynton Crosby.
85   Interview, Lynton Crosby.
86   Interview, Fiona Hill.
87   BBC News, 2 June 2017.
88   Interview, Fiona Hill.
89   Interview, Lynton Crosby.
90   *The Guardian*, 3 May 2017.
91   Interview, Chris Wilkins.
92   Dennis Kavanagh and Philip Cowley, *The British General Election of 2017*, p. 217.
93   *Financial Times*, 1 June 2017.
94   *Daily Telegraph*, 13 May 2017.
95   Dennis Kavanagh and Philip Cowley, *The British General Election of 2017*, p. 180.
96   Interview, Patrick McLoughlin.
97   Email, Stuart Ball to author, 26 May 2019.

98   Interview, Lynton Crosby.
99   Interview, Gavin Williamson.
100 Dennis Kavanagh and Philip Cowley, *The British General Election of 2017*, p. 231.
101 Murphy did, however, receive the text, as it later appeared in Dennis Kavanagh and Philip Cowley's book *The British General Election of 2017*.
102 Interview, Fiona Hill.
103 Interview, Nick Timothy.
104 Dennis Kavanagh and Philip Cowley, *The British General Election of 2017*, p. 244.
105 Interview, Tom Swarbrick.
106 Interview, Fiona Hill.
107 Interview, Fiona Hill.
108 Interview, Philip Hammond.

CHAPTER 6: NOTHING HAS CHANGED
1   Interview, Gavin Williamson.
2   Interview, Gavin Williamson.
3   Interview, David Davis.
4   Interview, David Davis.
5   Interview, Michael Fallon.
6   Interview, David Davis.
7   Tim Shipman, *Fall Out*, p. 433; Interview, Philip Hammond.
8   Interview, Amber Rudd.
9   Interview, Gavin Williamson.
10   Tim Shipman, *Fall Out*, p. 441.
11   Interview, Chris Wilkins.
12   Tim Shipman, *Fall Out*, p. 443.
13   Interview, George Hollingbery.
14   Tim Shipman, *Fall Out*, p. 442.
15   Interview, George Hollingbery.
16   Interview, Michael Fallon.
17   Interview, Gavin Williamson.
18   Interview, Ben Gummer.
19   Interview, Julian Smith.
20   Interview, Gavin Barwell.
21   Interview, John Godfrey.
22   Interview, Will Tanner.
23   Interview, Chris Wilkins.
24   Interview, Robbie Gibb.
25   Interview, David Davis.
26   Interview, Nick Timothy.
27   Notes, George Hollingbery, 12 June 2017.
28   Interview, Michael Gove.
29   *Evening Standard*, 9 June 2017.
30   Interview, George Osborne.
31   Interview, Julian Smith.
32   Interview, David Davis.
33   Interview, Gavin Williamson.
34   Tim Shipman, *Fall Out*, p. 431.

CHAPTER 7: A DEAL WITH THE DUP
1   Interview, Gavin Williamson.
2   Interview, Gavin Williamson.
3   Interview, Gavin Williamson.
4   Interview, Jonathan Caine.

5   Dennis Kavanagh and Philip Cowley, *The British General Election of 2017*, pp. 250–51.
6   Interview, Gavin Williamson.
7   Dennis Kavanagh and Philip Cowley, *The British General Election of 2017*, p. 251.
8   Interview, Gavin Williamson.
9   John Major, BBC Radio 4, *The World at One*, 13 June 2017.
10   *The Guardian*, 10 June 2017.
11   Sky News, 11 June 2017.
12   BBC News, 11 June 2017.
13   Diary, George Hollingbery, 18 June 2017.
14   BBC News, 13 June 2017.
15   *Daily Telegraph*, 17 June 2017.
16   Interview, Gavin Williamson.
17   Dennis Kavanagh and Philip Cowley, *The British General Election of 2017*, pp. 251–2.
18   Interview, Julian Smith.

CHAPTER 8: THE WEEK AFTER: THE 1922 COMMITTEE AND GRENFELL

1   BBC One, *Andrew Marr Show*, 11 June 2017.
2   Interview, Michael Fallon.
3   Interview, Sajid Javid.
4   Interview, Patrick McLoughlin.
5   Notes, George Hollingbery.
6   Interview, Julian Smith.
7   *Daily Mirror*, 12 June 2017.
8   Interview, George Hollingbery.
9   *The Guardian*, 12 June 2017.
10   *The Guardian*, 12 June 2017.
11   BBC News, 13 June 2017.
12   *Evening Standard*, 14 June 2017.
13   LBC Radio, 14 June 2017.
14   *The Independent*, 15 June 2017.
15   *The Guardian*, 15 June 2017.
16   *The Guardian*, 17 June 2017.
17   Sky News, 18 June 2017.
18   BBC News, 17 June 2017.

CHAPTER 9: HARD ROAD TO HELL

1   *The Guardian*, 4 September 2017.
2   *The Guardian*, 12 June 2017.
3   Interview, Lord Bridges.
4   Interview, Oliver Letwin.
5   Queen's Speech, 21 June 2017.
6   Interview, Julian Smith.
7   Interview, David Lidington.
8   Authors' note: this interview was conducted in May 2019, before Theresa May's resignation.
9   Interview, David Lidington.
10   Interview, Denzil Davidson.
11   Interview, Oliver Letwin.
12   Gavin Barwell, Twitter, 12 September 2015.
13   Interview, Martin Selmayr.
14   Interview, Lord Bridges.
15   Interview, Fiona Hill.
16   Interview, Fiona Hill.
17   *Financial Times*, 20 June 2017.
18   *The Guardian*, 19 July 2017.

19   *Financial Times*, 20 June 2017.
20   Interview, Michael Fallon.
21   Interview, Lord Bridges.
22   Interview, David Davis.
23   Interview, Martin Selmayr.

CHAPTER 10: RE-FINDING HER AGENDA

1   *Daily Telegraph*, 21 June 2017.
2   Interview, Gavin Williamson.
3   *The Guardian*, 21 June 2017.
4   Interview, James Marshall.
5   BBC News, 14 September 2017.
6   *The Guardian*, 1 July 2017.
7   *Times Higher Education*, 4 October 2017.
8   *Daily Telegraph*, 15 September 2017.
9   *New Statesman*, 18 September 2017.
10   *The Sun*, 30 September 2017.
11   *The Guardian*, 4 October 2017.
12   Interview, Chris Wilkins.
13   Tim Shipman, *Fall Out*, p. 505.
14   Interview, Seema Kennedy.
15   *Financial Times*, 4 October 2017.
16   *Financial Times*, 4 October 2017; *The Guardian*, 4 October 2017; *The Times*, 4 October 2017.
17   *New Statesman*, 5 October 2017.
18   Interview, Gavin Williamson.
19   Interview, Gavin Williamson.
20   *The Times*, 7 October 2017.
21   *The Independent*, 10 October 2017.
22   Nicholas Soames, Twitter, 6 October 2017.
23   PoliticsHome, 6 October 2017.
24   *The Guardian*, 9 October 2017.
25   Interview, David Lidington.
26   *Sunday Times*, 8 October 2017.

CHAPTER 11: DAWN DASH TO BRUSSELS: THE DOUBLE-EDGED JOINT REPORT

1   Interview, Guy Verhofstadt.
2   Interview, Martin Selmayr.
3   Interview, Robbie Gibb.
4   *The Guardian*, 19 September 2017.
5   *The Guardian*, 22 September 2017.
6   Open Europe, 23 October 2017.
7   Open Europe, 23 October 2017.
8   Interview, David Davis.
9   Interview, David Davis.
10   Interview, Julian Smith.
11   Interview, Robbie Gibb.
12   Interview, Gavin Barwell.
13   Interview, James Slack.
14   Interview, Robbie Gibb.
15   Interview, Liam Fox.
16   Interview, Denzil Davidson.
17   Interview, Julian Smith.
18   Interview, Amber Rudd.

CHAPTER 12: PARADISE LOST: A BOTCHED RESHUFFLE

1   *Sunday Times*, 29 October 2017.
2   *The Observer*, 5 November 2017.
3   *Sunday Times*, 29 October 2017.
4   *The Guardian*, 2 November 2017.
5   *Daily Telegraph*, 31 October 2017.
6   BBC News, 6 November 2017.
7   *The Times*, 6 November 2017.
8   BBC News, 21 December 2017.
9   *The Times*, 15 November 2017.
10 Interview, Alex Dawson.
11 *Daily Telegraph*, 22 November 2017.
12 Interview, Justine Greening.
13 Interview, Alex Dawson.
14 *Sunday Times*, 7 January 2018.
15 Interview, Gavin Barwell.
16 Interview, Justine Greening.
17 Interview, Damian Hinds.
18 Interview, David Lidington.
19 Interview, Brandon Lewis.
20 *Daily Telegraph*, 8 January 2018.
21 *Sunday Times*, 14 January 2018.
22 Interview, Liam Fox.
23 Interview, David Lidington.
24 Interview, Liam Fox.
25 Interview, Karen Bradley.
26 Interview, Emily Maitlis.
27 Interview, Robbie Gibb.
28 Interview, Robbie Gibb.

CHAPTER 13: AUTHORITY REASSERTED: SALISBURY AND SYRIA

1   *Sunday Times*, 31 December 2017.
2   *The Guardian*, 2 February 2018.
3   Interview, James Slack.
4   Interview, Amber Rudd.
5   *The Guardian*, 13 March 2018.
6   *Daily Telegraph*, 22 March 2018.
7   *The Guardian*, 23 March 2018.
8   *New Statesman*, 27 March 2018.
9   The account that follows rests heavily on a particularly brilliant article by Tim Shipman, *Sunday Times*, 15 April 2018.
10 BBC News, 8 April 2018.
11 *The Times*, 11 April 2018.
12 BBC News, 11 April 2018.
13 Anthony Seldon and Peter Snowdon, *Cameron at 10*; Anthony Seldon, *Sunday Times*, 12 August 2018.
14 *Sunday Times*, 15 April 2018.
15 *Sunday Times*, 15 April 2018.
16 *Sunday Times*, 15 April 2018.
17 *Sunday Times*, 15 April 2018.
18 *Sunday Times*, 15 April 2018.
19 *New Statesman*, 16 March 2018.
20 YouGov, 9 April 2018.
21 YouGov, 9 April 2018.

22   YouGov, 14 April 2018.
23   Interview, Damian Hinds.
24   Interview, Alex Dawson.
25   Interview, James Marshall.
26   *Daily Telegraph*, 17 March 2018.
27   Sky News, 27 March 2018.
28   *Daily Telegraph*, 17 June 2018.
29   BBC News, 17 June 2018.
30   Interview, Gavin Barwell.
31   Interview, Amber Rudd.
32   BBC News, 18 April 2018.
33   Interview, Amber Rudd.
34   Interview, Amber Rudd.

CHAPTER 14: CHEQUERS: JOURNEY INTO OBSCURITY
1   Interview, Oliver Letwin.
2   brexitcentral.com, 20 February 2018.
3   BBC News, 20 February 2018.
4   *Daily Telegraph*, 3 March 2018.
5   *Daily Telegraph*, 3 March 2018.
6   BBC News, 28 February 2018.
7   BBC News, 28 February 2018.
8   BBC News, 23 March 2018.
9   Interview, David Davis.
10   Interview, Martin Selmayr.
11   Interview, Guy Verhofstadt.
12   Interview, Gavin Williamson.
13   Interview, David Davis.
14   Interview, David Davis.
15   Robert Peston, Facebook blog, 3 July 2018.
16   Interview, David Davis.
17   Interview, David Davis.
18   Sky News, 5 July 2019.
19   Interview, David Davis.
20   *Sunday Times*, 8 July 2018.
21   *The Guardian*, 6 July 2018.
22   *Financial Times*, 5 July 2018.
23   Politico, 5 July 2018.
24   Interview, Michael Gove.
25   *Sunday Times*, 8 July 2018.
26   BBC News, 5 July 2018.
27   Politico, 5 July 2018.
28   *Daily Telegraph*, 6 July 2018.
29   Interview, Michael Gove.
30   Interview, David Davis.
31   Interview, Gavin Barwell.
32   Interview, Liam Fox.
33   Interview, Michael Gove.
34   *Financial Times*, 6 July 2018.
35   Interview, David Davis.
36   *Sunday Times*, 8 July 2018.
37   Interview, David Davis.
38   Interview, Michael Gove.
39   Interview, David Davis.

40   BBC News, 7 July 2018.
41   Interview, Liam Fox.
42   Interview, David Davis.
43   *Sunday Times*, 8 July 2018.
44   BBC News, 7 July 2018.
45   PoliticsHome, 7 July 2018.
46   *Mail on Sunday*, 8 July 2018.
47   Interview, David Davis.
48   Interview, David Davis.
49   Interview, Robbie Gibb.
50   Interview, David Davis.
51   Interview, Conor Burns.
52   Interview, Michael Gove.
53   Interview, Gavin Barwell.
54   Interview, Gavin Barwell.
55   *The Economist*, 11 July 2018.
56   *The Economist*, 11 July 2018.
57   Interview, Iain Duncan Smith.
58   *Financial Times*, 6 July 2018.
59   *The Spectator*, 14 July 2018.

CHAPTER 15: INTO THE EYE OF THE STORM

1   *Sunday Times*, 15 July 2018.
2   *Sunday Times*, 15 July 2018.
3   *The Times*, 8 June 2018.
4   *The Independent*, 1 July 2018.
5   Interview, Iain Duncan Smith.
6   *The Guardian*, 13 July 2018.
7   *Sunday Times*, 15 July 2018.
8   *The Sun*, 13 July 2018.
9   *The Independent*, 10 November 2017.
10   *The Sun*, 15 July 2018.
11   *The Times*, 16 July 2018.
12   *The Spectator*, 14 July 2018.
13   *Sunday Times*, 15 July 2018.
14   *The Spectator*, 15 July 2018.
15   Sky News, 3 August 2018.
16   Interview, Keelan Carr.
17   *New York Times*, 31 August 2018.
18   *The Independent*, 30 August 2018.
19   Interview, Keelan Carr.
20   Sky News, 18 August 2018.
21   *The Times*, 8 September 2018.
22   *The Times*, 10 September 2018.
23   *Mail on Sunday*, 9 September 2018.
24   *The Guardian*, 10 September 2018.
25   Sky News, 10 September 2018.
26   *Sunday Times*, 9 September 2018.
27   *Daily Telegraph*, 16 September 2018.
28   *The Guardian*, 17 September 2018.
29   *Sunday Times*, 23 September 2018.
30   *Sunday Times*, 30 September 2018.
31   *Sunday Times*, 30 September 2018.
32   *The Independent*, 2 October 2018.

33   *Daily Telegraph*, 2 October 2018.
34   *The Times*, 4 October 2018.
35   Interview, Geoffrey Cox.
36   *Daily Express*, 4 October 2018; *Daily Mail*, 4 October 2018.
37   *Financial Times*, 3 October 2018.
38   *Financial Times*, 25 June 2018.
39   *Evening Standard*, 16 October 2018.
40   *The Spectator*, 4 October 2018.
41   *Sunday Times*, 21 October 2018.
42   *Sunday Times*, 7 October 2018.
43   *Sunday Times*, 21 October 2018.
44   *The Times*, 23 October 2018.
45   *New Statesman*, 22 October 2018.
46   *The Guardian*, 24 October 2018.
47   BBC News, 29 October 2018.
48   BBC News, 29 October 2018.

CHAPTER 16: BREXIT: NO WAY THROUGH
1   Interview, Guy Verhofstadt.
2   *The Guardian*, 8 September 2018.
3   Interview, Dominic Raab.
4   Interview, Dominic Raab.
5   *Die Welt*, 19 September 2018.
6   Nick Robinson, BBC One, *Panorama*, 17 July 2019.
7   *The Guardian*, 20 September 2018.
8   *The Independent*, 21 September 2018.
9   Interview, Dominic Raab.
10   Interview, Robbie Gibb.
11   *Daily Telegraph*, 21 September 2018.
12   *Financial Times*, 24 September 2018.
13   Interview, Graham Brady.
14   *The Guardian*, 9 November 2018.
15   *The Spectator*, 14 October 2018.
16   *The Guardian*, 18 October 2018.
17   Interview, Martin Selmayr.
18   Interview, Nikki da Costa.
19   BBC Four, *Brexit Behind Closed Doors*.
20   Interview, Dominic Raab.
21   Interview, Raoul Ruparel.
22   Interview, Jeremy Hunt.
23   Interview, Nikki da Costa.
24   Interview, Nikki da Costa.
25   Interview, Nikki da Costa.
26   Interview, Dominic Raab.
27   Interview, Geoffrey Cox.
28   Interview, James Brokenshire.
29   Interview, Michael Gove.
30   Interview, Julian Smith.
31   Interview, Dominic Raab.
32   Interview, Karen Bradley.
33   *Evening Standard*, 15 November 2018.
34   Interview, Michael Gove.
35   Interview, Michael Gove.
36   Interview, Michael Gove.

37 *Daily Mail,* 30 November 2018.
38 BBC News, 25 November 2018.
39 *The Guardian,* 25 November 2018.
40 Interview, Julian Smith.
41 *Sunday Times,* 18 November 2018.
42 Interview, Julian Smith.
43 Interview, David Lidington.
44 Interview, Jeremy Hunt.
45 *Sunday Times,* 18 November 2018.
46 Interview, Brandon Lewis.
47 *Sunday Times,* 25 November 2018.
48 *Sunday Times,* 25 November 2018.
49 BBC News, 26 November 2018.
50 BBC News, 1 December 2018.
51 Interview, Geoffrey Cox.
52 *The Guardian,* 6 December 2018.
53 Interview, Jeremy Hunt.
54 *The Guardian,* 10 December 2018.
55 Interview, Julian Smith.
56 *The Guardian,* 10 December 2018.
57 Interview, David Lidington.
58 Interview, Amber Rudd.
59 Interview, Graham Brady.
60 Graham Brady, 'The Inside Story of the No Confidence Vote', *The House,* 17 December 2018; Interview, Graham Brady.
61 Interview, Graham Brady.
62 Interview, Graham Brady.
63 Interview, Keelan Carr.
64 BBC News, 12 December 2018.
65 Interview, Julian Smith.
66 Interview, Iain Duncan Smith.
67 Interview, Amber Rudd.
68 Interview, Seema Kennedy.
69 *The Guardian,* 12 December 2018.
70 *Financial Times,* 12 December 2018.

CHAPTER 17: FIRST ATTEMPT AT PARLIAMENT: MAY'S QUEST FOR A DOMESTIC LEGACY

1   BBC News, 17 December 2018.
2   Interview, David Lidington.
3   *The Spectator,* 14 December 2019.
4   *Sunday Times,* 6 January 2019.
5   Interview, Julian Smith.
6   *The Guardian,* 19 December 2018.
7   Interview, David Lidington.
8   Interview, Karen Bradley.
9   YouGov/Best for Britain, 10–11 January 2019.
10 Interview, David Lidington.
11 *The Times,* 6 January 2019.
12 BBC One, *Panorama,* 17 July 2019.
13 Interview, Martin Selmayr.
14 *Sunday Times,* 16 December 2018.
15 *Sunday Times,* 13 January 2019.
16 *The Guardian,* 16 January 2019.
17 Interview, Geoffrey Cox.

18   *Financial Times*, 15 January 2019.
19   Interview, Michael Gove.
20   BBC News, 16 January 2019.
21   Interview, JoJo Penn.
22   *The Guardian*, 20 September 2017.
23   *The Independent*, 8 March 2018.
24   Interview, James Marshall.
25   Interview, Justine Greening.
26   Interview, Simon Wessely.
27   Interview, JoJo Penn.
28   Interview, Amber Rudd.

CHAPTER 18: THE SECOND ATTEMPT AT PARLIAMENT
1   *Sunday Times*, 20 January 2019.
2   *Sunday Times*, 27 January 2019.
3   *Financial Times*, 17 January 2019.
4   *Sunday Times*, 20 January 2019.
5   *The Sun*, 22 January 2019.
6   Interview, Nicky Morgan.
7   Interview, Nicky Morgan.
8   *Daily Telegraph*, 28 January 2019.
9   Interview, Iain Duncan Smith.
10   Interview, Nicky Morgan.
11   *The Spectator*, 28 January 2019.
12   *Financial Times*, 28 January 2019.
13   *The Guardian*, 29 January 2019.
14   *Sunday Times*, 27 January 2019.
15   *The Guardian*, 29 January 2019.
16   *The Spectator*, 29 January 2019.
17   *The Spectator*, 2 February 2019.
18   *Daily Telegraph*, 30 January 2019.
19   *The Spectator*, 2 February 2019.
20   Interview, Karen Bradley.
21   *The Guardian*, 5 February 2019.
22   Interview, Philip Hammond.
23   Interview, Gavin Barwell; BBC One, *Panorama*, 'Britain's Brexit Crisis', 18 July 2019.
24   BBC News, 6 February 2019.
25   Sky News, 8 February 2019.
26   *The Guardian*, 12 February 2019.
27   *The Guardian*, 12 February 2019.
28   CNN, 15 February 2019.
29   *The Guardian*, 14 February 2019.
30   *Sunday Times*, 17 February 2019.
31   BBC News, 17 February 2019.
32   BBC News, 20 February 2019.
33   BBC News, 20 February 2019.
34   Interview, Julian Smith.
35   *The Guardian*, 24 February 2019.
36   BBC News, 24 February 2019.
37   BBC News, 25 February 2019.
38   *Sunday Times*, 3 March 2019.
39   *Sunday Times*, 3 March 2019.
40   *New Statesman*, 12 February 2019.
41   BBC News, 1 February 2019.

42   BBC News, 4 March 2019.

43   ConservativeHome, 8 March 2019.

44   *The Spectator*, 8 March 2019.

45   Interview, Geoffrey Cox.

46   Interview, Jeremy Hunt.

47   Interview, Geoffrey Cox.

48   Interview, Geoffrey Cox.

49   Bloomberg News, 15 March 2019.

50   Interview, Julian Smith.

51   Interview, Julian Smith.

52   This remark was made three weeks before Johnson reappointed Cox as Attorney General.

53   Interview, Geoffrey Cox.

54   Bloomberg News, 12 March 2019.

55   *The Guardian*, 12 March 2019.

56   Interview, Greg Clark.

57   *Daily Mail*, 23 February 2019.

58   BBC News, 14 March 2019.

59   Interview, Amber Rudd.

60   *The Spectator*, 14 March 2019; *The Guardian*, 14 March 2019.

61   *Sunday Times*, 17 March 2019.

62   *Sunday Times*, 17 March 2019.

63   Interview, Michael Gove.

64   Interview, Jeremy Hunt.

65   Interview, Olly Robbins.

66   Interview, Karen Bradley.

CHAPTER 19: THIRD AND FINAL MEANINGFUL VOTE

1   William Shakespeare, *King Lear*, Act IV, Scene 1.

2   BBC News, 18 March 2019.

3   *The Guardian*, 18 March 2019.

4   PoliticsHome, 9 January 2019.

5   *The Sun*, 19 March 2019; *Daily Express*, 19 March 2019; *Daily Mail*, 19 March 2019.

6   *The Guardian*, 20 March 2019.

7   *Sunday Times*, 24 March 2019.

8   Interview, Robbie Gibb.

9   *The Guardian*, 21 March 2019.

10   Politico, 21 March 2019.

11   *New York Times*, 21 March 2019.

12   Interview, Greg Clark.

13   *Financial Times*, 22 March 2019.

14   *The Guardian*, 22 March 2019.

15   *Financial Times*, 22 March 2019.

16   *The Times*, 23 March 2019.

17   Politico, 23 March 2019.

18   BBC News, 23 March 2019.

19   *Sunday Times*, 24 March 2019.

20   Interview, David Lidington.

21   *Daily Mail*, 24 March 2019.

22   Interview, Steve Baker.

23   Interview, Michael Gove.

24   Interview, David Lidington.

25   Interview, Gavin Barwell.

26   Interview, Steve Baker.

27   Interview, Iain Duncan Smith.

28   *Financial Times*, 25 March 2019.
29   Interview, Gavin Barwell.
30   *Daily Telegraph*, 26 March 2019.
31   *The Guardian*, 27 March 2019.
32   Interview, Iain Duncan Smith.
33   Interview, Graham Brady.
34   Interview, Iain Duncan Smith.
35   *The Independent*, 27 March 2019.
36   Interview, Raoul Ruparel.
37   Interview, James Brokenshire.
38   Interview, Karen Bradley.
39   Interview, David Lidington.
40   *Sunday Times*, 31 March 2019.
41   BBC Radio 4, *Today*, 29 March 2019.
42   Interview, Gavin Barwell.
43   Interview, David Lidington.
44   Interview, Gavin Barwell.
45   Interview, Steve Baker.
46   Interview, Steve Baker.
47   BBC Two, *The Brexit Storm*, 1 April 2019.
48   *Financial Times*, 31 March 2019.

CHAPTER 20: THE LAST THROW OF THE DICE: TALKS WITH LABOUR

1   BBC News, 2 April 2019.
2   *i*, 2 April 2019.
3   BBC News, 2 April 2019.
4   BBC Two, *The Brexit Storm*, 1 April 2019.
5   *The Times*, 2 April 2019.
6   *The Times*, 2 April 2019.
7   Interview, Michael Gove.
8   Interview, Geoffrey Cox.
9   Interview, Jeremy Hunt.
10   *Financial Times*, 2 April 2019.
11   Sky News, 2 April 2019.
12   *Daily Telegraph*, 2 April 2019.
13   *Daily Telegraph*, 3 April 2019.
14   ConservativeHome, 1 April 2019.
15   *Daily Telegraph*, 4 April 2019.
16   *Daily Telegraph*, 3 April 2019.
17   *The Sun*, 4 April 2019.
18   *Financial Times*, 3 April 2019.
19   Interview, Oliver Letwin.
20   *Daily Telegraph*, 9 April 2019.
21   BBC News, 15 April 2019.
22   *Financial Times*, 23 April 2019.
23   *The Guardian*, 17 April 2019.
24   Interview, Graham Brady.
25   Interview, Graham Brady.
26   Interview, Karen Bradley.
27   PoliticsHome, 11 May 2019.
28   *The Times*, 7 May 2019.
29   Interview, Philip Hammond.
30   *Daily Telegraph*, 16 May 2019.
31   *The Guardian*, 16 May 2019.

32   *The Guardian*, 16 May 2019.
33   *Daily Mail*, 17 May 2019.
34   Interview, Michael Gove.
35   Interview, David Lidington.
36   Interview, Amber Rudd.
37   BBC News, 21 May 2019.
38   BBC News, 21 May 2019.
39   Interview, Andrea Leadsom.
40   Interview, Andrea Leadsom.
41   Interview, Liam Fox.
42   Interview, Amber Rudd.
43   Interview, David Lidington.
44   BBC News, 22 May 2019.
45   Interview, Michael Gove.
46   *The Guardian*, 22 May 2019.
47   Interview, David Lidington.
48   Interview, Karen Bradley.
49   Interview, Keelan Carr.
50   Interview, Graham Brady.

EPILOGUE
1   My book *Life After 10* is currently being written.
2   *Financial Times*, 7 June 2019.
3   Interview, Conor Burns.
4   *The Guardian*, 30 May 2019.
5   Politico, 3 June 2019.
6   BBC News, 28 June 2019.
7   BBC News, 28 June 2019.
8   Anthony Seldon, *Blair Unbound*, pp. 564–6.
9   *The Guardian*, 10 July 2019.
10   BBC News, 15 July 2019.
11   *Washington Post*, 17 July 2019.
12   *The Times*, 8 June 2019.
13   *The Times*, 9 July 2019.
14   Interview, Philip Hammond.
15   *Daily Mail*, 11 July 2019; BBC News, 12 July 2019.
16   Sky News, 20 July 2019.

PICTURE CREDITS

INDEX

Theresa May is TM throughout.

1922 Committee
    meetings with TM 237, 284–7, 468, 510,
        549, 611–12
    no-confidence letters 430, 457, 463, 467,
        506–11
    TM resignation 591–2, 615, 620

Abbott, Diane 459
Adams, Nigel 607
Adler, Katya 603
Adonis, Andrew 15
Africa 459–60
AI sector 531
Allen, Heidi 557
Article 50
    author of xvii
    Bill 196, 198
    extensions 522, 554, 570, 579–85, 609–10
    letter 143, 307
    process xiv–xv, xvi, xviii, 124
    triggering 115, 118, 125, 127–30, 141–4, 308
Assad, Bashar al- 393, 394
Attenborough, David 533–4, 536
Attlee, Clement 86, 150
Augar, Philip 60, 321

Badenoch, Kemi 376
Bailey, DS Nick 387, 389
Baker, Steve
    and Brexit Party 611
    and Davis 430
    ERG chair 263, 322, 338, 556, 587–8
    and MV3 593, 596–7
    no-confidence vote 507, 508
    resignation 460, 499

supporting government 525–6
    and TM 461, 500
    and WAB 546–7
Baldwin, Stanley 194, 231
Ball, Stuart 194
Balls, Katy 457, 466
Baltic States 391
BAME community 537, 538
Banks, Arron 37
Bannon, Steve 161–2, 164
Barber, Lionel 379
Barclay, Stephen 497, 505, 563, 566, 591, 609
Barnier, Michel
    'the clock is ticking' 144
    and Committee of Permanent
        Representatives 343–4
    and 'divorce bill' 343
    and negotiations 306, 310, 337, 340, 432
    softens tone 445, 484
    and TM deal 119, 145–7, 475
    UK–EU joint report 410
Barrow, Tim 110, 138, 140, 143, 337, 349, 434, 476
Bartholomew, Sarah 82
Barwell, Gavin
    1922 Committee 285
    advisor 256, 353, 500
    and Cabinet members 366, 374–5, 441, 490,
        620–21, 636
    and Chequers away-day 433
    chief of staff xiv, 254, 257–60, 282, 291, 311
    and da Costa 489–90
    and customs union 541, 543
    driving policy 318, 326
    and Gove 262, 263, 434
    on Heywood 404–5
    Housing Minister 179, 290
    and MPs 583